2004
Sundays Year C
Weekdays Cycle 2

AN ALMANAC OF PARISH LITURGY

SOURCEBOOK

FOR SUNDAYS AND SEASONS

Paul Turner

LTP
LITURGY
TRAINING
PUBLICATIONS

SOURCEBOOK FOR SUNDAYS AND SEASONS 2004: AN ALMANAC OF PARISH LITURGY © 2003 Archdiocese of Chicago: Liturgy Training Publications, 1800 North Hermitage Avenue, Chicago IL 60622-1101; 1-800-933-1800, fax 1-800-933-7094, e-mail orders@ltp.org. All rights reserved. See our website at www.ltp.org.

Printed in the United States of America.

ISBN 1-56854-426-X

SSS04

Artist Julie Lonneman depicts the evangelist Luke with
his traditional symbol—the winged bull—holding sheaves
of wheat, a reminder that the story of the eucharist
is told by Luke through ten meal stories. Traditional images
of the liturgical year complete the scene: the owl calls
to mind Lady Wisdom of Advent; ass and holly evoke
Christmas; the peacock's plumage is a sign of resurrection.
Hovering above, the ever-present Spirit of God: creation,
resurrection, mission, church, all brought together
on Sunday, the first day of the week, the Lord's Day.

CONTENTS

THE PASCHAL TRIDUUM

EASTER

SUMMER AND FALL ORDINARY TIME

RESOURCES

From the Author

Hi, everybody!

I send you this year's *Sourcebook* from my office at St. Munchin Church in Cameron, Missouri—not to be confused with the world's other St. Munchin Catholic Church in Limerick, Ireland. I've communicated with Bishop Donal Murray of Limerick this year, and we think we have the only two St. Munchins on the planet. If you hear of any others, please let one of us know!

As I write this to you I have just finished my first year here as pastor. We have a mission church of several dozen people at St. Aloysius in Maysville. I've been learning a lot about adaptations in the liturgy and liturgical preparation in small town and rural settings. All in all, it's been a pleasant experience for me, and I feel blessed to be part of these communities.

I've also learned a deeper appreciation for the simple things of the liturgy—like the altar cloth.

You see, part of my ministry has been to our local prison. We have a medium-security state institution here, where I celebrate Mass on a weeknight once a week. The correctional facility holds about 2,000 residents. In the ministry we prefer calling them "residents," but each one wears a state-issued badge that reads "offender." Of those, about ten percent are Catholics and about ten percent of those Catholics come for the weekly Mass. The result of that math is that I get to see the cream of the crop, the 20 best "offenders," the most spiritually alive Catholic residents of the facility.

When I enter the prison I sign in at the front desk and proceed to an airlock. I wait for the door to unlock. I enter and make a quick exchange: I turn in one of my two state-issued badges—the one that holds the emergency phone numbers for my next of kin and close associates—and wear the other. When I turn in the first badge, the officer at the desk gives me a body alarm.

The other door of the airlock opens. I walk across the yard to the chapel door. The prison is fairly new, so this is a pleasant walk across the well-manicured landscape. No one expects that I'll actually need to use my body alarm. But if something goes wrong, all I have to do is flip the switch and it emits a piercing scream—even more piercing than the one I will surely be emitting at the time.

Beauty is rare at the prison. We treasure the little spaces of beauty we have, like the flowers I see on my walk to the chapel as my pocketed body alarm bumps against my thigh. The chapel officer lets me in the door. He is always well prepared. He's got the altar moved to the middle of the room and the stackable chairs set up. He helps set out the participation aids, the liturgical books and vessels, as well as the vestments. Many different groups use the chapel—including fundamentalist Christian, Muslim and Wiccan. The furniture gets rearranged depending on who's coming in.

When we have the room prepared, the doors are unlocked so the participants can come in. They sign a register. There's a dress code. They have to wear their full prison grays. They can't come in wearing just a T-shirt. This is a classy joint.

We have an altar cloth. One of the residents had this idea. "Why can't we have an altar cloth?" he asked. The short answer is we've never ordered one. There is a budget, and as with most budgets, it's a good idea to spend what you can. They hadn't spent much lately. So our first thought was to buy a cloth.

Then I reconsidered. We had just done a time and talent survey at St. Munchin, and one member inscribed on the form a talent we had not asked about: sewing. I suggested that I ask her to make a cloth.

So, we took the measurements of the altar, and I called our volunteer to see if she'd accept the task. She agreed to make a cloth for an altar she had never seen, in a room where she had never set foot, for a community of people she would never meet. She lives just outside of town, and she often passes the prison. It has a blue roof. People here call it "the blue-top inn."

She made a beautiful cloth.

After I got it, I realized I had not asked permission from the prison to bring the altar cloth into the chapel. It took a couple of weeks to secure this. The night I brought it in, the officer on duty at the front desk was expecting it. She had gotten the memo. She had read the memo.

She unlocked the first door of the airlock, and I entered, the door slamming behind me with its hollow thud. I exchanged my badge for the body alarm. And she took the cloth. She treated it with absolute reverence. She inspected it to make sure it wasn't concealing a saw. Then she returned it to me and unlocked the other door. I brought the cloth with me across the yard, carrying a thing of beauty along the well-manicured lawn, my body alarm bumping against my thigh.

As the guys assembled that night, I said a prayer from the *Book of Blessings* over the new cloth. Then we unfolded it over the altar—and the community of "offenders" burst into applause.

We take a lot for granted: the freedom to choose where we want to live, which friends we want to see each day and which chapel we call our own. My local prisoners are grateful for a stranger who did them a little favor—and for the altar cloth.

This long book is about little things. Sometimes the details are tedious. But God is in the details.

Paul Turner

From the Editor

■ MANY people move this book from being electronic impulses (the manuscript is sent to LTP via e-mail) to being a book. Jane Kremsreiter designed the 1991 edition. Mary Bowers made modifications to the design, and Ana Aguilar-Islas designed the cover.

As production editor, Carol Mycio has the task of crafting language to house style, checking facts, conforming manuscript to design, and proofing each stage along the way. Lucy Smith is the design artist and Mark Hollopeter is the production artist. Their work turns *Sourcebook* into a thing of beauty.

Bryan Cones

Welcome to 2004!

NORMALLY the first leap year of the new century is the first one in eight years. If you were alive in 1900 you may recall that it was not a leap year. You may have forgotten a lot of other things, but that piece of trivia would certainly be hard to forget. We have leap years every four years, with an exception: The centennial year is not a leap year. But there is an exception to the exception. Every centennial year divisible by 400 is a leap year. So if you were alive in the year 2000 you lived through the first centennial leap year since 1600. And this year, the leap year of 2004, is, well, not all that special.

But there is an exception. Any year we receive from the hand of God is special. With one more day to give God praise, we begin this year of grace hopeful for our church and for our country, hopeful that the hungry may be fed, the sick cured and the gospel proclaimed to the poor in ways that will bring light and life to the world.

Sourcebook for Sundays and Seasons will guide you through this new year of grace. It follows the liturgical calendar of the Roman Catholic Church, while attending to several other calendars as well. Guided by *Sourcebook,* you can negotiate the joys and sorrows of this year as you behold the mystery of Christ unfolding all around you.

SOURCEBOOK 2004: ORGANIZATION

Sourcebook is divided according to the seasons of the liturgical year: Advent, Christmas, Lent and Easter. The Paschal Triduum, the center of the Christian life, also receives its own section. Ordinary Time appears in two parts: winter and summer/fall.

When you open the lectionary or sacramentary, you find Ordinary Time together in one place, but each year it divides into two unequal and somewhat unpredictable parts. *Sourcebook* takes out the guesswork for you and divides Ordinary Time as you will experience it this year. The first part of Ordinary Time ends in these pages as Lent begins, and *Sourcebook* returns you to the proper week of Ordinary Time when the Easter season concludes.

Within each of those sections you will find two further divisions: the season and the calendar. The seasonal overview features several parts.

- *The Meaning:* the basic purpose of the season
- *The Saints:* how to celebrate days devoted to saints this season
- *The Liturgical Books:* how the lectionary, sacramentary and other ritual texts capture the season's meaning
- *The Art and Environment:* ideas for the seasonal appearance of places of worship
- *The Music:* the music that enhances the changing times of year
- *The Parish and Home:* prayer within the domestic church
- *Texts:* suggestions for seasonal adaptations

The calendar section is an almanac. It guides you through each season day by day. You can look up any day of the year and find the basic liturgical information about it, along with a few other ideas.

Sourcebook gives you ideas for each day, but its primary purpose is to help you celebrate Sundays and seasons. For this reason, you will find these four components on each Sunday and solemnity:

- *Orientation:* the background to this particular day
- *Lectionary:* an explanation of the scriptures for the day
- *Sacramentary:* insights into our prayers, ideas for implementing options
- *Other Ideas:* more thoughts to keep in mind

■ BULLETIN INSERTS: Help your people reflect more deeply on the scriptures each week with the bulletin inserts included in *Sourcebook*. Each seasonal chapter concludes with a set you can reproduce for all the Sundays and principal feast days of the year. They use the first readings at Mass as a starting point for meditation.

Inserts may be reproduced within the weekly bulletin, participation aid or other handout given to parishioners at no charge. Be sure the person who prepares the bulletin knows about them! They will touch on the mystery of each Sunday's liturgy, invite further reflection and study of the scriptures, and assist parishioners in becoming more and more literate in the language of the liturgy.

CALENDAR OVERVIEW: NOVEMBER 30, 2003, TO NOVEMBER 27, 2004

■ ADVENT AND CHRISTMAS: The secular world starts marketing Christmas several months in advance, but it kicks into overdrive on Thanks-

giving weekend. We begin Advent of this new liturgical year at the same time.

December 8 will fall on a Monday. In the United States the obligation to participate at Mass remains because Mary is our patron under the title Immaculate Conception. Christmas comes on a Thursday, exactly four weeks after Thanksgiving.

■ WINTER ORDINARY TIME: There are nearly six weeks of Ordinary Time between Christmas and Lent. The final day of the Christmas season falls on January 11 (the feast of the Lord's Baptism), while the first day of Lent is February 25 (Ash Wednesday).

■ LENT, TRIDUUM AND EASTER: The First Sunday of Lent will be "leap day," February 29. Easter falls on April 11, the Sunday following the first full moon of spring. The Triduum begins on Thursday, April 8.

Ascension will fall on Thursday, May 20, or Sunday, May 23, depending on your region. Pentecost concludes the Easter season on May 30, Memorial Day weekend. The school year and the 90 days of Lent and Easter will end together.

■ SUMMERTIME WILL USHER IN ORDINARY TIME. The Sunday before Lent began week seven of Ordinary Time, but we will begin again after Pentecost with the weekdays of the ninth week in Ordinary Time. There is no week eight this year because the church year of 2004 has to end with the thirty-fourth week of Ordinary Time before Advent begins on November 28.

■ FESTIVAL DAYS IN 2004: Independence Day in the United States, July 4, falls on a Sunday this year, but parishes will observe the Fourteenth Sunday in Ordinary Time. The solemnity of the Assumption (August 15), though, will replace the Twentieth Sunday. Halloween comes on Sunday, too, making the solemnity of All Saints a Monday, on which the obligation to participate at Mass in the United States will not apply. The solemnity of Christ the King will precede Thanksgiving on November 21.

LECTIONARY OVERVIEW 2004: YEAR C

Luke's gospel will predominate on the Sundays of this year. We have abundant opportunities to hear from Luke, even during the seasons of Advent, Lent, Christmas and Easter, when other years of the lectionary cycle often turn to other gospels for inspiration. Luke paints a thorough portrait of Christ, and the lectionary enjoys giving us as much of him as it can.

Due to a few solemnities that take precedence over the Sundays of Ordinary Time, we will not hear the raising of the only son of the widow of Nain (Luke 7:11–17, Ordinary Time 10), nor the story of the sinful woman who anoints the feet of Jesus (7:36—8:3, Ordinary Time 11), nor Jesus' somber words that he brings division and not peace (12:49–53, Ordinary Time 20). The break between winter and summer Ordinary Time causes the loss of some aphorisms (6:39–45, Ordinary Time 8) and the cure of the centurion's slave (7:1–10, Ordinary Time 9).

But many of Luke's most popular stories will ring out, including the Good Samaritan (10:25–37, Ordinary Time 15) and the Prodigal Son, which we will hear twice (15:1–32, Lent 4 and Ordinary Time 24). Incredibly, these parables appear only in Luke, and we get to hear them this year.

■ THE AUTHOR OF LUKE'S GOSPEL: The real identity of the writer of the third gospel is unknown. The text itself does not claim to be written by somebody named Luke. The first one to call it "Luke" was Irenaeus at the end of the second century, a hundred years or so after the gospel was written. A lot can happen in a hundred years. Memories fail. Stories warp. Evidence is lost.

Irenaeus probably thought of the Luke mentioned in Colossians 4:14, Philemon 24, and 2 Timothy 4:11. *That* Luke was a companion of Paul. Indeed, it is very likely that the same person wrote both this gospel and Acts of the Apostles. The last part of Acts, which describes the missionary activity of Paul, shifts the narrative into first person plural, using "we" and "us" when describing events. The writer claims to have gone with Paul on mission.

Still, some scholars dispute even that. Acts shows no knowledge of Paul's letters, neither what they contained nor even that he wrote letters at all. Wouldn't a companion of Paul, and a writer, have said something about this?

As a writer, Luke is the greatest of the evangelists. He tells stories with immediacy and immense power. He arranges the book in a coherent way, and he even develops parallels between the gospel and Acts of the Apostles. The arrest and martyrdom of Stephen, for example, shares many similarities with the arrest and crucifixion of Jesus. Jerusalem is a central theme throughout both books: Luke's infancy

narrative brings Jesus to the holy city, and the three temptations end with Jerusalem. Indeed, the whole second half of the gospel places Jesus on a journey toward Jerusalem, and the city hosts a gathering of apostles in Acts. Both in little details and in the overall arrangement, Luke shows his skills as a writer.

Other themes develop throughout the book. The gospel shows the importance of prayer, deference for the poor, the significant role of women in the reign of God, and the power of the Spirit.

Luke probably relied on his own unique material and on Mark's gospel. The finished product resembles Mark and Matthew so much that together the three are called the Synoptic Gospels. But Luke's author crafted the narrative distinctively and stamped it with a unique style.

■ FIRST AND SECOND READINGS: As usual, Sunday's first readings shift from book to book throughout the year. The lectionary skips through the Bible to find passages that fit the theme of the gospel or of the season or feast.

The second readings during Advent, Christmas, Lent, Triduum and Easter are also chosen to fit the themes of the particular season. During Ordinary Time, however, we hear semicontinuous readings from several New Testament books over the period of several Sundays. The number of books is quite large during Year C. We begin, as we do every year, with Paul's first letter to the Corinthians, this time hearing the last few chapters, which include some famous passages about the body of Christ, the virtue of love, and life after death. The other letters this year are Galatians, Colossians, Hebrews, Philemon, 1 Timothy, 2 Timothy and 2 Thessalonians. (A table of the order of the second readings for Sundays in Ordinary Time can be found in the study edition of the Sunday lectionary published by LTP.)

■ *LECTIONARY FOR MASSES WITH CHILDREN:* Again this year you will find comments about the Sunday lectionary for children. In the seasonal overviews you will catch a glimpse of what to expect: which readings and psalms are included, omitted or altered.

SACRAMENTARY OVERVIEW

Although the Sunday lectionary spans a three-year cycle of readings, the sacramentary in use for the United States offers the same options year after year. The presider selects from one of two opening prayers, but otherwise the presidential prayers remain constant. There is greater variety in the prefaces for each weekend.

■ A RICH AND VARIED RESOURCE: The sacramentary also includes texts for the proper and commons of saints, ritual Masses, Masses and prayers for various needs and occasions, votive Masses, and Masses for the dead. Helping you steer your way through the many options within the sacramentary is one of *Sourcebook*'s tasks. Among these, the ones most likely to appear on a Sunday are the ritual Masses, which are related to the celebration of certain sacraments and sacramentals.

If a wedding Mass takes place on a Saturday night in Ordinary Time, for example, the ritual Mass for marriage may replace the presidential prayers of the Sunday.

The local ordinary (usually the bishop of the diocese) may call for an appropriate Mass to be celebrated on a Sunday in Ordinary Time in cases of serious need or pastoral advantage. For example, the bishop could request the "Mass in Time of War or Civil Disturbance," or "For the Election of a Pope or Bishop," if either of these seem opportune. These texts from the lectionary and the sacramentary would replace the Ordinary Time Sunday texts at the bishop's direction.

In any case, most of these prayers can be rewardingly and easily used on weekdays in Ordinary Time.

■ THE CLOUD OF WITNESSES: The Roman martyrology was updated and republished by the Vatican in 2001. It lists about a dozen lesser-known saints for every day of the year. Unless a given day is already an obligatory memorial, feast or solemnity, you have the option of celebrating one of these saints as a memorial, and the parish's patrons should be observed as a local solemnity. The reason these saints are not on the general calendar is to give it some room to breathe and to return the celebration of certain saints to the localities where they have special significance.

Be sparing in exercising the option of these saints' days. If you do so, choose the prayers for the saint from the commons in the back of the sacramentary. Although you may also choose readings from the lectionary commons, the lectionary itself suggests that it's best to leave the weekday course of readings intact, even on saints' days (see the Introduction to the *Lectionary for Mass*, 82–83).

Again you will find in this year's *Sourcebook* expanded references to important days on the calendar of countries in Latin America. Many parishes in the United States include people from these regions, and these references should alert you to these festivals.

You will also find the additional optional memorials from the third edition of the Roman Missal. Many new saints' days have been included in the general calendar.

■ ENTRANCE AND COMMUNION ANTIPHONS AND PSALMODY: *By Flowing Waters: Chant for the Liturgy* (Collegeville, The Liturgical Press, 1999) is the first complete edition in English of the Simple Gradual, one of the church's official songbooks. Of the 680 chants in *By Flowing Waters,* there are 63 entrance antiphons and psalms, and 62 communion antiphons and psalms that provide seasonal music and propers for solemnities and feasts of the church year.

By Flowing Waters also has a complete set of commons for parishes celebrating the solemnities of their dedication and of their patron saint. There is a wealth of information about how to use these chants in the songbook's performance notes—pages 417 to 428—and generous reprint permission for assembly editions—pages 429 to 432.

LITURGY OF THE HOURS OVERVIEW

In addition to the Sunday eucharist, your community will gather for other types of prayer. You may gather for school functions, community events, meetings or at times of social need. You may choose the structure of the Liturgy of the Hours for these events if you wish. This prayer flows from the eucharist and leads the faithful back there.

A full celebration of the Liturgy of the Hours includes an office of readings, morning prayer, daytime prayer, evening prayer and night prayer. Very few parishes offer the full range of this liturgy every day. Some offer morning or evening prayer daily. But a larger number offer some parts of the Liturgy of the Hours at special events throughout the year.

■ FOUNDATIONAL PRAYER: The two hours on which the entire liturgy turns are morning and evening prayer, which share a similar structure. Generally, after an opening versicle, the community sings a hymn. Then one, two or three psalms are sung. A reader proclaims a short passage from scripture, and a responsory follows. All sing a canticle from Luke's gospel—Zechariah's *Benedictus* in the morning, Mary's *Magnificat* in the evening. Then the community offers petitions and the Lord's Prayer. A prayer of the day (for instance, the opening prayer of Mass that day), a blessing and a dismissal conclude the liturgy.

■ REPEATED PRAYER: The Liturgy of the Hours gains its strength from the daily recurrence of a predictable form. Like the rosary, its spirit comes not from variety but from its repetitive, meditative pace. The prayer is so word-heavy that we traditionally sing the psalms to understated melodic lines known as psalm tones. This allows the community to focus on the texts effortlessly. The construction of this liturgy assumes that the community prays some of it every day.

Wherever the Liturgy of the Hours is more occasional, the faithful may find help in more varied musical presentations of the psalms. If you're planning morning or evening prayer for your community, select a good hymn and psalm settings that will invite participation from the faithful. The assigned texts may help you determine what type of music to seek: hymns that celebrate the time of day, the season or occasion, and psalms that do the same.

SACRAMENTS OVERVIEW

The primary celebration of the initiation sacraments each year takes place at the Easter Vigil, when the community celebrates baptism, confirmation and eucharist. That liturgy deserves the fullest attention to detail in its preparation and the fullest measure of participation in its celebration. The initiation of adults occurs in our parishes at the moment we celebrate Christ's rising from the dead. In baptism we enter the mystery of dying and rising. It expresses our commitment to discipleship and gives us a foretaste of the heavenly banquet.

■ THE BAPTISM OF CHILDREN: The Rite of Baptism for Children may be celebrated at a Sunday Mass or on some other occasion. Celebrating baptism at Mass will let the entire community witness the sacrament and participate in its liturgy, and will invite the community's support of the new life in its midst.

Baptisms may be celebrated on any day of the week, but Sunday, the Lord's Day, the day of resurrection, is always the best.

If baptisms take place apart from Mass, plan ways to make them good celebrations with strong participation. Greeters to welcome visitors, musicians to lead singing, prepared readers—these ministers will enhance the community's celebration of the sacrament on a day and occasion when visitors are many.

■ OTHER CELEBRATIONS OF CONFIRMATION AND FIRST COMMUNION: The parish may celebrate the Rite of Confirmation on diverse occasions. The bishop may visit, or he may delegate another priest to preside.

Baptized candidates may celebrate the Rite of Reception into the Full Communion of the Catholic Church at any time during the liturgical year. When they do so, the priest who presides also confirms. Most catechumenate teams still prepare their baptized candidates for the Rite of Reception at the Easter Vigil. But the proper time to receive candidates is not necessarily Easter. It is whenever they are ready.

In case of an emergency, a priest who baptizes may confirm at once, even if the candidate is an infant. But confirmation is best celebrated in the midst of the faithful. The public celebration of confirmation allows the entire community to renew its commitment to prayer and service.

If the candidate for confirmation is already a baptized Catholic, the bishop is the ordinary minister of the rite. So if some of your candidates are adult Catholics who have been away from the faith for a while and were never confirmed, the bishop is the ordinary minister for them. Many bishops will delegate the pastor to confirm in this instance, but permission must be received. One important exception to this rule is danger of death. A priest may confirm any Catholic who is dying. No further permission is needed—no service projects, either.

First communion will be the highlight of the year for many families with young children. The parish may celebrate this sacrament at a regularly scheduled Mass or at a separate occasion. You may observe the principles of the *Directory for Masses with Children,* including adaptations to the presidential prayers, readings and the use of special eucharistic prayers.

■ RECONCILIATION AND HEALING: Our ministry of reconciliation comes most clearly to light in the sacrament of penance. Most parishes schedule confessions once a week. Although Saturday afternoon remains the most popular day and time, other occasions may be chosen. Schedule communal celebrations of reconciliation well in advance. Are these already on the parish calendar? Have you coordinated these with the times set by neighboring parishes?

Our ministry of healing extends also to the sacrament of anointing the sick. Be sure the homebound of your community have opportunities for this sacrament during the year. One or more of the faithful could accompany the priest when he visits the homebound, or he may set a time when family and friends of the parishioner may attend. Many parishes schedule a communal celebration of the sacrament at church or in nursing homes on one or more occasions during the year. Is this sacrament available to those eligible for it in your community?

■ ORDINATION AND PROFESSION: A parish celebration of ordination is rare, but it does happen. Who in the parish is being called to ordination as a deacon or priest? Who is called to profession to religious life? Does your community have a committee promoting ordained ministry and religious life? If you celebrate an ordination, careful planning will highlight its spirit of servant leadership.

■ WEDDINGS: The celebration of marriage should be a happy day for both families involved, and even for the liturgical ministers! Many of us approach weddings with a sense of dread, but as ministers of the good news of Christ, we should approach weddings in a way that supports the joy of the families.

The *Rite of Marriage* situates the wedding within a liturgy, so liturgical principles come into play. In general, the principles that apply to the parish community's Sunday eucharist apply to parish weddings as well. Liturgical guidelines about music, the communion rite and decorations should fit the general liturgical practice of the parish.

■ FUNERALS: Of course, you never have much notice before celebrating a funeral. Decisions have to be made rapidly and efficiently. Some parishes have become beautifully skilled at offering attentive care to the bereaved in their time of grief. It would help to have one or more people on your liturgy team familiar with planning and presiding over a vigil service and a funeral, knowledgeable about scriptures and music, and able to offer consolation and guidance.

It would also help to have cantors help lead the liturgical vigil (wake). Plan these services with good music, observing the rituals in the *Order of Christian Funerals*. A good cantor will help avoid the dreadful practice of piping in recorded music at funeral home services. Have a cantor there or celebrate the service in the church.

Many people assume you must have a rosary for a Catholic wake. The word *rosary* never appears in the *Order of Christian Funerals*, which recommends a scripture service. We cannot reasonably rely on the judgment of those in mourning to plan the liturgy. Parish ministers can give careful direction to assist mourners in preparing the funeral liturgies.

The more and more frequent choice of cremation among the faithful calls for certain changes in funeral customs and attitudes. Is your community prepared for the celebration of the funeral rites with the ashes of the deceased? Does your copy of the *Order of Christian Funerals* include the appendix for cremation?

ANNUAL CELEBRATIONS OVERVIEW

■ PATRONAL/TITULAR DAYS AND DEDICATION ANNIVERSARIES: Your parish will have some unique celebrations each year. You should observe the annual day of the dedication of your church and also your patronal solemnity. Are these marked on the parish calendar? Is there another day of particular importance to your community?

■ DAYS OF PRAYER: In place of rogation days, the church now invites us to set aside special days of prayer. In the United States, the Conference of Bishops suggested that each diocese determine days or periods of prayer for the fruits of the earth, for human rights and equality, for world justice and peace, and penitential observance outside Lent (*Appendix to the General Instruction of the Roman Missal,* 331). Does your diocese have these? Are they noted in your parish calendar for this year?

Your parish may have other traditional observances. Look ahead and see how they fit with the liturgical year. Sometimes a sudden crisis or tragedy within the parish or the wider community demands liturgical prayer. Who in the parish is able to make liturgical decisions as needed when the unexpected happens?

■ DEVOTIONS: Your parish may also have traditional devotional prayers. For example, how is

First Friday observed each month? Do you offer Stations of the Cross during Lent? Is there a group gathering for prayer around the cross in the Taizé tradition? Are there novenas, litanies or processions?

Are there special celebrations in honor of Mary? Is there a celebration in connection with the Assumption on August 15 or with Our Lady of Guadalupe on December 12?

How are the saints honored? Are there occasions for drawing attention to the religious art and statuary that adorn your church? Given the particular mission and charism of your community, are there some saints who should be especially honored there as heroes?

■ BLESSINGS: Sit down once or twice a year to review the parish's schedule of blessings. Coordinate the blessings with the liturgical calendar and with parish need. A blessing is a true liturgy and requires liturgical ministers to do well. Each season *Sourcebook* suggests orders of blessings (primarily chosen from the church's *Book of Blessings*) that can be part of the life of prayer of the local community.

Be familiar with that great little book with the self-explanatory title, *Catholic Household Blessings and Prayers*. Make it available to people and warmly recommend its use in their homes.

About the Art

THE illustrations within *Sourcebook for Sundays and Seasons 2004* are by Corey Wilkinson, an Illinois artist. The art for Sundays and seasons employs zoological images, and art for feast days makes use of botanical ones.

The associations of such natural images with an occasion or season are drawn mostly from Christian folklore. Several associations are mentioned in the 1868 book *Flowers and Festivals* by W. A. Barrett of Saint Paul's Cathedral in London. Thanks to Peter Scagnelli for sending LTP a copy! The following explanations of the art were written by Peter Mazar.

■ SUNDAY—DOVE: On the first day, the Spirit of God brooded over the dark waters. Then God said, "Let there be light," and there was light. The Lord's Day, the day of resurrection, is the day of the giving of the gift of the Holy Spirit.

■ ADVENT—OWL: In traditional art, Lady Wisdom, whom the scriptures describe as God's bride, sometimes is shown with a wise old owl nearby. During Advent we ask Lady Wisdom to "come and show your people the way to salvation."

■ CHRISTMAS—OX AND ASS: The gospels don't mention these animals. The opening chapter of the book of the prophet Isaiah does, however, which says that even the ox and ass know who feeds them. In a like manner we should recognize the Lord in our midst.

■ WINTER ORDINARY TIME—DEER: Psalm 42 has been a favorite for members of the church, especially during the procession toward the baptismal font: "As a deer longs for flowing streams, so my soul longs for you, O God."

■ LENT—SNAKE: Genesis tells us about a talking snake. Adam ate the forbidden fruit, gaining death for himself and his progeny. In a desert Jesus fasted, and through the obedience of Christ we are invited home to God's garden.

■ TRIDUUM—LAMB: John the Baptist called Jesus the lamb of God. The paschal lamb upon God's throne is also our Good Shepherd, who lays down his life for the sheep.

■ EASTERTIME—PEACOCK: Few things are more glorious than a peacock fully fledged. The molting of peacocks and the renewal of their plumage are ancient signs of resurrection.

■ SUMMER AND FALL ORDINARY TIME—LION: Folklore associates the sun with the zodiacal sign of Leo, perhaps because the warmest days in the Northern Hemisphere are during the weeks that the sun passes through this sign, perhaps also because the golden mane of a male lion is imagined to resemble the sun.

■ IMMACULATE CONCEPTION—WHITE PINE: Our ancestors were mystified about how conifers reproduce. Where are the flowers? And yet without flowers conifers produce abundant seeds. For this reason pines became symbols of the Virgin Mary.

■ CHRISTMAS—HOLLY: Christmas has a lot of Easter in it. Holly's prickly foliage has been called "Christ's thorn," and the red berries are compared to his blood. The evergreen foliage is a sign of the life that is stronger than death.

■ HOLY FAMILY—PAPERWHITE NARCISSUS: Winter-blooming flowers are signs of paradox, of the things (in the words of G. K. Chesterton) that "cannot be but that are," of the mystery of the incarnation in which immortality is wrapped within the mortal.

■ MARY, MOTHER OF GOD—ENGLISH IVY: The ivy vine using holly as its support is a sign of the Christian clinging to Christ. Ivy is transfigured in treetops from a flowerless vine into a fruitful and sturdy shrub, and for this reason has become a symbol of Mary, as well as of every Christian made fruitful in baptism.

■ EPIPHANY OF THE LORD—MISTLETOE: Mistletoe magically roots itself in tree branches and so seems suspended between earth and sky. No wonder that it, like the olive borne by Noah's dove, has become an emblem of the reconciliation of heaven and earth!

■ BAPTISM OF THE LORD—OLIVE: According to ancient laws even warfare is not an excuse to chop down an olive. Human societies come and go, olives live for centuries.

■ PRESENTATION OF THE LORD—SNOWDROP: These earliest of flowers are sometimes called "Candlemas bells." Like the day itself, they stir the heart for spring.

■ SAINT JOSEPH—CROCUS: Tradition holds that Joseph died on the final day of winter. On his grave the first flowers of spring erupted.

■ ANNUNCIATION OF THE LORD—MADONNA LILY: This day, Joseph's Day and Eastertide (and a host of other days) are celebrated with lilies, which along with roses, as emblems of purity and ardor, are imagined to fill heaven to the brim.

■ PALM SUNDAY—PUSSY WILLOW: Many northern Europeans call pussy willow "palm" since it's carried in today's procession. All sorts of willows, as water-loving trees, are associated with the elected catechumens preparing for baptism at Easter.

■ HOLY THURSDAY—FORSYTHIA: Even in the north this shrub comes into bloom about now. The crosswise, fragrant flowers, like all members of the olive family, have become emblems of the Christian Passover.

■ GOOD FRIDAY—HAWTHORN: Hundreds of species of plants have been imagined to be the kind used for Jesus' crown of thorns. This is one of the thorniest and most common.

■ HOLY SATURDAY—MYRTLE: According to Middle Eastern folklore, Myrrha mourned the death of her son. In pity the powers of heaven transformed her into the myrtle tree. Her tears became fragrant myrrh, a resin used to embalm the dead.

■ EASTER VIGIL—PASSION FLOWER: Few flowers are as complex in appearance as passion flowers, whose blooms hold five anthers (said to be Christ's five wounds), three stigmas (said to be the three nails), and a corolla of petals (said to resemble the crown of thorns).

■ EASTER SUNDAY—FLOWERING DOGWOOD: *Cornus florida,* a North American native, is imagined as the tree of the wood of the cross. The flowers bear crosswise bracts marked at the tips in bloody brown and centered by the true flowers, which some claim to resemble Jesus' crown of thorns.

■ OCTAVE OF EASTER—DAFFODIL: Is there a merrier flower than a daffodil? It seems to trumpet the Easter words of Christina Rosetti: "Spring bursts today, for all the world's at play."

■ ASCENSION OF THE LORD—LILY-OF-THE-VALLEY: "I am the rose of Sharon and the lily of the valley," says one of the lovers in the Song of Songs. Eastertime, the *al fresco* season, leads us from the fragrant valley up to the mountain of the ascension, from the confines of the upper room out into the streets of the city.

■ PENTECOST—PEONY: A central European title for the peony is "Pentecost rose." The intense fragrance of peonies and roses and other flowers has become a sign of the Holy Spirit in much the same way that sacred chrism is a sign of a God whose presence infuses creation.

■ THE HOLY TRINITY—IRIS: Late spring is when irises bloom in profusion. Many species favor water, and irises that blossom by waterside (sometimes called "flags"), with their three-part flowers, are signs of baptism in the name of the Trinity.

■ BODY AND BLOOD OF CHRIST—WHEAT: Now is the season when wheat ripens across the Great Plains of the United States. This most important harvest gives us "our daily bread."

■ BIRTH OF SAINT JOHN THE BAPTIST—DAISY: The "day's eye" is among the sunniest of flowers. It blooms in June and has become associated with Midsummer Day and the fiery prophet John.

■ SACRED HEART OF JESUS—ROSE: Roses are classic symbols of love and passion. A rose's richness, complexity, fragrance and even its thorns tell us something of love.

■ SAINTS PETER AND PAUL—POPPY AND BACHELOR BUTTON: Along with daisies, these "cornflowers" form a red, white and blue carpet alongside European wheat fields. Red poppies are Peter's flowers, and blue bachelor buttons, of course, are Paul's.

■ TRANSFIGURATION OF THE LORD—SUNFLOWER: Any of the flowers that turn their heads toward the sun as the day passes (the meaning of the word "heliotrope") are symbols of the Christian who follows the Lord, who on this day shone more brightly than the sun.

■ ASSUMPTION OF MARY INTO HEAVEN—GLADIOLUS: The flower's name means "sword." It has an association, thanks to Simeon's prophecy, with this "Mary's month" that includes the festivals of her assumption, birth and sorrows.

■ HOLY CROSS—BASIL: Legends tell of the herb basil, with its crosswise and fragrant foliage, covering Golgotha when Helen discovered the wood of the holy cross.

■ ALL SAINTS—CHRYSANTHEMUM: The Japanese especially use chrysanthemums in profusion during their autumn festivals. Mexican folklore claims that the pungent foliage of these and marigolds stir memories of the dead.

■ ALL SOULS—MUSHROOM: Autumn is a time to hunt for mushrooms—carefully. The deadliness of some species is infamous. Christian lore sees in mushrooms a sign of the mystery of abundant life arising from death.

■ DEDICATION OF THE LATERAN BASILICA—GOURD: Gourds are symbols of the Christian. From one seed can come an endless array of fruit, each crammed with hundreds of seeds. But the vines need support, and we need Christ.

■ CHRIST THE KING—OAK: Oaks have been associated with royalty even as long ago as Roman times, perhaps because they are so long-lived, and perhaps because they take so long to come to maturity.

ADVENT

The Season

The Calendar

The Meaning

If you want God, and long for union with him, yet sometimes wonder what that means or whether it can mean anything at all, you are already walking with the God who comes. If you are at times so weary and involved with the struggle of living that you have no strength even to want him, yet are still dissatisfied that you don't, you are already keeping Advent in your life. If you have ever had an obscure intuition that the truth of things is somehow better, greater, more wonderful than you deserve or desire, that the touch of God in your life stills you by its gentleness, that there is a mercy beyond anything you could ever suspect, you are already drawn into the central mystery of salvation.

—Maria Boulding, *The Coming of God,* Third edition (Conception, Missouri: The Printery House, 2000), p. 1.

ADVENT beckons us into the great spiritual journey in which we come to meet God. We think of it as the time that God comes to us, yet God's coming is long before any of our thoughts, dreams, aches or hopes. Our anticipation of Christmas is like our hope for a deeper union with God, who crossed all barriers to become like us. When we find the One for whom we long, we discover that God was already there, all along.

The liturgies of Advent direct our attention to the two comings of Jesus. He came first in a humble birth at Bethlehem; he will come again in glory at the end of time. While preparing for the annual celebration of Christ's birth, we prepare our hearts for his return.

The season lasts through four Sundays. In four swift weeks we recall the 4,000 slow years that ancient Israel waited for God to fulfill a promise. For young children, the wait for Christmas seems interminable. For thoughtful adults, the wait for deeper faith seems unbearable. We find hope in the eyes of children who intuitively unlock the secret of Advent joy.

■ "THE HOLIDAYS": What will your Christmas card say this year? "Seasons greetings"? "Happy Holidays"? Or will it carry a message of faith? "Christ is born!" "Merry Christmas!" "Peace on earth!" Even your choice of postage stamp bears the potential for evangelization.

When you call a place of business this month, you may hear a voice saying, "Happy holidays!" Businesses seeking to appeal to a large audience will avoid references to the faith-filled term "Christmas" and simply call this season "the holidays." Just as Christianity has its holidays and moral codes, the retail business world has its specific code of behavior for people: shopping.

The sacred and secular frequently jockey for attention, but never is this more true than during Advent. The marketplace knows that faith in Christ is strong, and it powerfully launches a campaign that permits religious expression without advocating it. It advocates worldly commerce, not the divine *commercium* of God becoming human. Those who plan the Sunday liturgy help the faithful keep their focus in the midst of a world that swallows them with sales.

More positively, the sacred and secular worlds happily combine their goals in making this a season for charity. From Thanksgiving until Christmas, people contribute generously to causes that benefit the poor and the needy.

"God so loved the world," the famous passage of John 3:16 begins, "that he gave his only Son, so that everyone who believes in him may not perish but may have eternal life." The first Christmas happened because of love. That love inspires the world to similar acts of selflessness in Advent.

■ ADVENT'S FOCUS: Advent focuses the heart on the mystery of the incarnation. It keeps the love of God ever before our eyes. Even as Advent raises our vision to the promised return of the eternal Son, it creates a place for the human heart to wait in hope and wonder.

Throughout Advent the scriptures and antiphons create a vivid picture of this season's themes. Advent begins with a breathtaking vision of the end of time. It recalls the prophecies of promise to Israel in exile. It holds up John the Baptist, the bridge between the former and the new covenant. And it draws us into the private life of a virgin who enfolds the hopes of endless ages, the hopes of every heart. From the general to the specific, from the heavenly to the homely, Advent sweeps us into its mystery.

The Saints

B Y happy coincidence, many of the saints we meet on our Advent journey support the themes of this season. The days that honor them are of differing importance, but they never draw our attention completely away from Advent.

In the United States and in Latin America the two most important of these days on the Advent calendar are December 8 and 12. Both days honor Mary, the mother of God. The first, a solemnity, remembers her under her title of the Immaculate Conception. The second, a solemnity in Mexico and Guatemala, and a feast in the United States and the rest of Latin America, honors her as Our Lady of Guadalupe. Because Mary is one of the central figures of Advent, these days honoring her blend well with the season's character.

This year both days are during the same week. In the United States the obligation to participate at Mass on certain holy days is suspended when they fall on a Monday or Saturday. But neither the Immaculate Conception nor Christmas Day is included in that legislation. Christmas, obviously, is too important a day to fail to take part in the eucharistic celebration. The Immaculate Conception is also important because Mary is patron of the United States under that title. Consequently, the obligation to participate at Mass on Monday, December 8, stands.

■ OBLIGATORY MEMORIALS: Only two obligatory memorials occur during Advent this year, and one falls on a Saturday—December 13. Lucy, a fourth-century martyr, bears a name that means "light," making her an appropriate saint for Advent. Francis Xavier, the sixteenth-century disciple of Ignatius of Loyola, also appears on the calendar this month (Wednesday, December 3). The other Advent saints whose memorials are obligatory, Ambrose and John of the Cross, fall on Sundays this year (December 7 and 14), so they are not part of this Advent's calendar of saints.

On an obligatory memorial during this first part of Advent, the saint's vestment color and opening prayer take precedence. You may take the other presidential prayers (preface, prayer over the gifts and communion prayer) from the Advent weekday, the saint's day, or the commons in the back of the sacramentary.

The Advent lectionary offers daily readings and they need not be supplanted on an obligatory memorial. However, you could choose from the readings offered by the commons in the back of the lectionary. Guidelines do not advise this (see *Introduction to the Lectionary for Mass*, 82–83), but if you have some good reason, you may do so. What's a good reason? Is your parish named after Lucy? Would the regular Advent readings be inappropriate because of some local issue? Then turn to the commons.

■ THE OPTIONAL MEMORIALS OF ADVENT fall into two groups: those that occur before December 17 and those that occur after. You may ignore optional memorials of either group. After all, you will want Advent to feel like Advent, and these memorials are called optional because, well, they're optional. But if you observe any of them, beware of some differences between the two groups.

An optional memorial observed prior to December 17 follows the guidelines for memorials in Advent. After December 17, we have only one optional memorial this year, John of Kanty (Tuesday, December 23), because Peter Canisius's day (December 21) also falls on a Sunday. If you take the option and celebrate John of Kanty, you may use his own opening prayer instead of the one for Advent, or use it as the conclusion to the general intercessions. But everything else (even violet vesture) comes from the Advent weekday.

In general, a community will benefit from honoring the season rather than the optional memorials. They are optional so that a community dedicated to these saints or their apostolate may celebrate them. The priest "should not

omit the readings assigned for each day in the weekday lectionary too frequently or without sufficient reason, since the Church desires that a richer portion of God's word be provided for the people" (GIRM, 316).

■ VOTIVE MASSES: The liturgical books also supply texts for votive Masses and Masses for various needs and occasions. These texts are used during Advent only in cases of serious need or pastoral advantage. However, they may not be used on any Sunday or on the solemnity of the Immaculate Conception. Only a bishop can direct that they replace the texts for the feast of Our Lady of Guadalupe. The priest who presides for Mass can make the decision on any other day during the season. Ordinarily, though, it's not a good idea. The texts of Advent are well chosen to highlight the significance of this season.

The Lectionary

THROUGHOUT Advent, the readings put us in touch with ancient Israel's wait for the arrival of the messiah. They also awaken our hope for Jesus' return in glory.

The gospels of the four Sundays always follow the same pattern. The first week presents Jesus' vision of the second coming. The second and third week present John the Baptist, and the fourth week tells part of the story leading up to the first Christmas Day. Unlike last year, when the four Sundays gave us material from three evangelists, all four readings this year come from Luke.

Normally, Isaiah dominates the first readings of Advent. But during Year C of the lectionary cycle, Isaiah steps aside so we can hear some glorious prophecies from Jeremiah, Baruch, Zephaniah and Micah. Lest he be completely ignored, Isaiah subtly appears in the canticle that serves as the responsory after the first reading on the Third Sunday of Advent this year. The other responsories are all classic psalms of Advent: 25, 126 and 80.

The second readings this year come from 1 Thessalonians, Philippians and Hebrews. The first three passages exhort the early Christians to prepare for the coming of Christ, and the last reflects on the obedient service of Jesus. In the final week of Advent, all the scriptures turn our attention toward the historical birth of Christ at Bethlehem.

■ THE SUNDAY *LECTIONARY FOR MASSES WITH CHILDREN* contains most of these passages. On Sunday of weeks one and four, though, this lectionary omits the second reading. It also abbreviates several other passages to simplify the liturgy of the word with children. On the whole, however, you have the same passages for children and adults this year.

The weekday lectionary for children has four sets of readings for Advent. The first introduces a gospel not found in the regular lectionary for this season and pairs it with an abbreviated version of the first reading found in the second set. The second set draws both readings from the first Saturday of the season. The first reading for the third set comes from Wednesday of the second week; the accompanying gospel comes from Wednesday of the third week. The final set introduces a new first reading for the season and takes the gospel from December 22.

Children's Masses need not correspond with these dates, but you may want to avoid a duplication of readings for those attending daily Mass.

The Sacramentary

■ INTRODUCTORY RITES: If the visual images are strong, you may not need many words to introduce the Mass. The presence of the Advent wreath and the purple vesture will signal a change to people even without many words of introduction. After the sign of the cross, the presider may simply say, "The Lord be with you," pause after the response to establish eye contact with as many as possible, and then begin the penitential rite.

■ PENITENTIAL RITE: Try opening the penitential rite with a text that reminds people of the season. It could come from the opening song or one of the scriptures. (See Texts, p. 11, for an example.) If you plan to use penitential rite C, be sure to note the sample one for Advent in the sacramentary at C-ii. Option B is briefer, and if your community is unfamiliar with it, this could be a season to put it into the repertoire. Some communities have blessed the wreath in place of the

penitential rite on the first Sunday (but see the *Book of Blessings*).

■ THE GLORY TO GOD is omitted on the Sundays of Advent. This streamlines the entrance rites and drives the liturgy more directly toward the scriptures. When the hymn returns at Christmas, it will lift hearts high with joy.

■ ALL THE PRESIDENTIAL PRAYERS of this season first appeared in older liturgical books. The opening prayers for the first and second Sundays come from the Gelasian Sacramentary (eighth century). The prayer over the gifts and communion prayer for the first Sunday, the opening prayer of the third, and the communion prayer of the fourth all come from the Veronese Sacramentary (sixth century). The others appeared later in the Middle Ages.

The opening prayers are full of allusions to the scriptures and themes of the Advent season. Part of the genius of the Roman rite is its ability to pack a lot of thought into a few phrases of prayer. The International Commission on English in the Liturgy has published a separate set of opening prayers for Advent and for all the liturgical year in a separate volume. Those prayers include rich allusions to the scriptures for each Sunday.

■ THE GENERAL INTERCESSIONS are the texts of the Mass that allow the freest composition. A sample for Advent appears in the sacramentary's first appendix, #3. You will find additional samples in LTP's *Prayers for Sundays and Seasons, Year C.*

■ THE TWO PREFACES for Advent introduce the sacramentary's complete set of over 80 prefaces. These first two entries are intended for each of the two halves of Advent. Begin the first on the first Sunday, and switch to the second on December 17. That one may be used through the morning of Christmas Eve.

The first preface perfectly presents the two main themes of Advent. It recalls the incarnation, when Christ humbled himself to come among us, and it announces that we watch for the day when he will return in glory. The second preface focuses more on the coming commemoration of the birth of Jesus, as the scriptures of this part of the season do. This preface traces the line from the prophets through Mary and John the Baptist—all preparing the way for the coming of Jesus. Both prefaces have antecedents dating back to the fifth century.

■ THE EUCHARISTIC PRAYERS FOR RECONCILIATION may be used with other prefaces that refer to penance and conversion (see *Notitiae* 19 [1983], 270). So if you want to highlight the penitential aspect of this season, you may choose one of these prayers and substitute an Advent preface. Prayer II speaks of "your Son who comes in your name" and pictures the great eschatological banquet "in that new world" at which are gathered "people of every race and language and way of life."

The Book of Blessings

ALTHOUGH this book has innumerable uses throughout the year, most people will find it helpful at the start of the year because the United States edition presents a blessing for an Advent wreath. The blessing does not appear in the sacramentary.

The *Book of Blessings* (BB) recommends blessing the wreath on the first Sunday of the season after the homily (1509). The wreath may also be blessed outside Mass in a celebration of the word of God, or even with a simpler rite of blessing. It is hard to imagine why this would be done because the blessing during Mass activates the symbol on behalf of the entire worshiping community. However, if this year you have another event on the schedule for this day—a workshop, a retreat day or other parish gathering—you could schedule a blessing of the wreath at that time apart from Mass. Turn to the *Book of Blessings,* chapter 47, for assistance.

During this season you might use this book for other blessings as well. For example, on the Fourth Sunday of Advent you could offer a blessing of those awaiting the birth of a child in their families (BB, 215–35). Let them step forward before the general intercessions and conclude the community's prayers with a blessing for parents before childbirth, on the day the gospel tells of Mary's pregnancy. You could also bless engaged couples (195–214) or travelers (617–38). (See p. 11 for a blessing of travelers to use on the Third Sunday of Advent.)

The Rite of Christian Initiation of Adults

IF you have catechumens in your community, they may be dismissed at each Mass during this and every season of the year. Sample dismissals appear at RCIA, 67.

The First Sunday of Advent is not the ideal time to celebrate the Rite of Acceptance into the Order of Catechumens and the Rite of Welcoming the Candidates. Some communities used to do this to parallel the Rite of Election on the First Sunday of Lent. The rites of acceptance and welcoming should be celebrated two or even three times a year (RCIA, 18.3), depending on when the catechumens and candidates are ready for them. This means that some people will be joining a group where others have more experience. But those who need more time in formation can take it. With so much happening during Advent, this may not be the best season to schedule these liturgies, but if the catechumens and candidates are ready, you certainly may.

The Liturgy of the Hours

THE principle hours to honor are always morning and evening prayer. These are the two hinges on which the Liturgy of the Hours turns. If some in your community can gather for prayer apart from the eucharist, these are the most important celebrations.

The format for the hours remains the same through every season of the year, but during Advent some psalms appear that we do not use during the rest of the year. These passages tell about the history of Israel. By introducing them into the liturgy during this season, our prayer can help us meditate on Israel's long wait for the promised messiah.

The specific changes are as follows: Psalm 105 replaces Psalms 131 and 132 on the first Saturday; 106 replaces 136 on the second Saturday; and 78 replaces 55 and 50 on the Friday and Saturday of the fourth week. All the replaced psalms still occur in other spots of the four-week cycle. If you are planning only an occasional celebration of the hours this month, try incorporating one of the psalms that develop the character of the season.

If you use the four-volume set, note that the *General Instruction of the Liturgy of the Hours* appears only in the first volume, the one set aside for Advent and Christmas. Why not add it to your seasonal reading this year?

■ THE "O ANTIPHONS" are a special jewel of the Advent hours. These beautifully crafted texts serve as the antiphons for the *Magnificat* during evening prayer from December 17 through December 23. Each addresses Christ with a different title and begs him to come for salvation.

You are familiar with the content of the antiphons if you have ever sung the popular Advent hymn, "O Come, O Come, Emmanuel." The hymn puts the seventh antiphon first, then jumps back to the first and sings the rest in sequence.

■ THE OFFICE OF READINGS includes some treasures from the early Christian writers. For example, on the Third Sunday of Advent you'll find this from a sermon by Augustine: "John is the voice, but the Lord is *the Word who was in the beginning.* John is the voice that lasts for a time; from the beginning Christ is the Word who lives for ever."

■ NIGHT PRAYER always concludes with an antiphon to Mary. There are four to choose from, but the traditional one for Advent is "Alma redemptoris mater." You can find the beautiful chant original in the *Liber cantualis,* as well as in the *Collegeville Hymnal,* available from The Liturgical Press.

The Rite of Penance

MANY parishes offer a communal rite of reconciliation during the season of Advent. Be sure to schedule yours well in advance, and let people know when it will be. Promote it frequently in the weeks ahead.

The *Rite of Penance* also suggests a different kind of celebration during Advent, a nonsacramental liturgy of penitence. It envisions that the community would gather simply to reflect on their sins and to seek God's forgiveness on an occasion when the sacrament may not be offered. When celebrated by the faithful, children and catechumens—not all of whom are eligible for the sacrament—it will foster a spirit of penance in the community. The celebrations may also be useful in areas where no priest is available for sacramental absolution.

In other areas, such celebrations may be adapted to include the sacrament of reconciliation. In such cases, the rite of penance follows the homily. Readings recommended for Advent (Appendix II, #II) are Malachi 3:1–7a, Psalm 85:2–14, Revelation 21:1–12, and Matthew 3:1–12 or Luke 3:3–17. Other readings may be chosen for a parish celebration of reconciliation in preparation for Christmas.

Be sure to consult the *Rite of Penance* when preparing your communal celebration of reconciliation.

OUTLINE OF THE RITE FOR RECONCILIATION OF SEVERAL PENITENTS WITH INDIVIDUAL CONFESSION AND ABSOLUTION:

Introductory Rites
  Song
  Greeting
  Introduction
  Opening Prayer
Celebration of the Word of God
  First reading
  Responsorial psalm
  Second reading
  Gospel acclamation
  Gospel
  Homily
  Examination of conscience
Rite of Reconciliation
  General confession of sins
  Litany or song
  Lord's Prayer
  Individual confession and absolution
  Proclamation of praise for God's mercy
  Concluding prayer of Thanksgiving
Concluding Rite
  Blessing
  Dismissal

The Pastoral Care of the Sick

THE sick in your community may be anointed at any time during Advent. The sacrament may be celebrated during or outside of Mass and may take place in homes, hospitals or at church.

Some communities have celebrated this sacrament at a Sunday Mass during the Advent season, but this may not be advisable. Those who administer the sacrament during Advent and Lent accentuate its penitential aspect, and indeed, this sacrament does forgive sins. They also guarantee that the sacrament will be available to those who need it at regular intervals during the year. But because these seasons are filled with other themes and needs, it may be best to schedule the rite of anointing at one or two other times of the year on a Sunday in Ordinary Time.

Anointings during Advent have no special form. If you schedule a communal celebration of the sacrament during a Sunday Mass in Advent, you keep the scriptures and presidential prayers of the Sunday. They should not come from the Rite of Anointing within Mass. The same does not need to apply on a weekday. However, if you anoint the sick at a weekday Mass, it is best to keep the Advent scriptures. When celebrating apart from Mass, consider using the rite's scriptures that recall Advent's promise of salvation, like the prophecies of Isaiah.

The Rite of Marriage

IF weddings take place during Advent, they should keep the spirit of the season. The promised joy that bubbles through Advent will itself lend a note of anticipation for the wedding.

If the wedding takes place on a Saturday evening during Mass, the readings and prayers of the Advent Sunday are used. The same applies to the celebration of marriage on any Sunday this season or on Monday, December 8, the solemnity of the Immaculate Conception. The couple or the presider may substitute one reading from the Sunday or holy day with one from the *Rite of Marriage* (#11), but otherwise the scriptures are set. Any Saturday night Mass fulfills the Sunday obligation.

If the wedding does not include a Mass, or if the wedding Mass does not take place on a Saturday night, Sunday or solemnity, the scriptures and prayers from the *Rite of Marriage* may be used in their entirety during the ceremony.

Decorations for the wedding should respect those already in place for Advent. Light the wreath during the ceremony. Let the season of the year assist the ritual celebration.

The Order of Christian Funerals

A funeral may take place on any day during Advent. On ordinary Advent weekdays the funeral Mass may replace the readings and prayers of the day. If a funeral is celebrated on an Advent Sunday or on the solemnity of the Immaculate Conception, the readings and prayers already assigned for that day take precedence. It is possible to have a funeral on a holy day of obligation, but the prayers and readings of the holy day are used. Be careful though: Many Catholic cemeteries close on holy days.

When selecting readings for a funeral on an Advent weekday, consult the daily lectionary texts first. They may offer a note of hope for the mourners. If you choose to replace them, look for ones that keep the spirit of the season. For example, the funeral lectionary contains passages from the book of Isaiah.

In the United States, we usually see white vesture for funerals, but violet may be worn (*Order of Christian Funerals*, 39). That color may not look out of place for an Advent funeral, but most still prefer white vesture.

The Art and Environment

INSIDE and outside the church, decorations can give worshipers a real feel for the season. The contrast between the long period of Ordinary Time and the sudden appearance of Advent environment can summon the faithful to prepare in their hearts a way for Christ.

Advent decorations "should be marked by a moderation that reflects the character of this season" (*Ceremonial of Bishops*, 236). Advent has a penitential feel to it, but more than anything it is a season for holding back, so that the joy of Christmas can unfold. It is like a slow prelude that leads to an exuberant fugue.

Remember to decorate several areas: outside the building, inside where people gather, and the worship space itself. There, be sure to decorate the area where most of the people assemble, not just the sanctuary. Otherwise it looks like the ministers celebrate Advent while everybody else watches them do it.

■ THE VIOLET VESTURE for this season invites comparisons to Lent. Indeed, Advent has origins as a penitential season. Today we focus less on the penitential nature and more on the double focus of anticipation: standing with ancient Israel as the chosen people await their messiah, and standing as contemporary Christians awaiting the messiah's return. Both call for a spirit of penitence, but wrapped around a message of hope.

If you have several sets of violet vestments, designate one of them for Advent. People will subconsciously make the association between that vestment and Advent's call to them for preparation. Some parishes prefer a more blue-hued violet for this season, to distinguish it from the purple of penitence in Lent. You may also choose a similar shade of violet for other appointments in the church—altar frontals, tablecloths and wall hangings. But keep it subdued. You don't have to decorate everything. Save something for Christmas.

The rose-colored candle on the Advent wreath is reserved for the third Sunday. Some people still have not made the connection. The candle signifies that the season is half over. Christmas is coming soon. We may rejoice even in the colors we wear. So the candle wears rose. Presider and deacon also may wear rose vesture, signaling that the full joy of Christmas is drawing near.

■ CHRISTMAS DECORATIONS do not yet belong in church. Stores and streets and homes are filled with lights, poinsettias and evergreen trees, but they do not enter our worship space until Christmas has arrived. Resist the temptation, just as musicians must do with Christmas carols, and save Christmas for Christmas. Give Advent its due.

■ PREPARE AN ADVENT WREATH. For ideas, see the *Book of Blessings* (1510–12), but be sure to visit other churches in your area as time permits. Gather ideas from your neighbors and share some of yours.

Customarily, the wreath is a circle of evergreen branches, and four candles stand upon it. Traditionally three candles are violet and one is rose, but four violet or four white candles may be used instead. Some communities add a fifth candle, the Christ candle. They light this white candle at Christmas.

The size of the wreath varies from place to place; wreaths appropriate for home will appear too small in church. In a public setting, the wreath should be large enough for all to see it. Some suspend it from the ceiling or place it on a stand. This creates a glorious impression and announces loudly the spirit of the season. If the wreath extends into the area where the assembly gathers for prayer, it will draw them into the celebration of the season. But it should not obstruct people's view of the altar, ambo or chair.

Some parishes place the four candles at the corners or walls of the church, wrapping the entire assembly in the embrace of the wreath. The idea is well intentioned, but if the immensity of the wreath causes people to lose the simplicity of its design, you may consider other solutions. Think about one wreath with four candles in a designated area of the church, but arrange groups of four candles in windows all around the church apart from the wreath. The appropriate number of these could be lit as the weeks of the season's progress.

■ STATUES, PAINTINGS AND OTHER IMAGES OF MARY AND JOHN THE BAPTIST or one of the prophets already adorn many churches. This would be an appropriate season to draw attention to the ones in yours. Some parishes erect a Jesse tree with symbols of the ancestors of Jesus, or a "giving tree" of gifts for the needy. (See "The Parish and Home" below.)

The Music

ADVENT comes with a vast array of hymnody from many parts of the Christian world. These traditional songs put the community in touch with the season as well as with all those who have celebrated it in every time and place.

■ HYMNS ABOUT JOHN THE BAPTIST are especially fitting on the second and third Sundays of Advent. Those are the days when the gospel tells some aspect of John's life and ministry. This is true every year during Advent.

■ HYMNS OF THE VIRGIN MARY will be especially appropriate on the feasts of the Immaculate Conception and Guadalupe, as well as on the Fourth Sunday of Advent, when the gospel tells part of the story leading up to the birth of Jesus. Our music books brim with Marian hymnody. "Immaculate Mary" will come to mind, but consider other hymns that especially fit the feast or season: "Behold a Virgin," "Ave Maria," "Magnificat," and the classic Polish anthem, "Serdeczna Matko" or "Stainless the Maiden." A skilled choir ready for a challenge will warm to David Conte's "Ave Maria" (E. C. Schirmer 4729). Worth a look is "Asi andando," by Tomás Pascual (Max Quin) (ca. 1595–1635) arranged for singers and instruments by Christopher Moroney (WLP 12713). This piece tells part of the story of the miracle of Guadalupe and is sung in seventeenth-century Spanish.

By Flowing Waters has a fine English version (#658) of the Advent Marian antiphon "Alma redemptoris mater," as well as a lovely setting (#411–414) of the ancient entrance antiphon "Beata Mater," with Psalm 46, "God is our refuge."

■ GOSPEL ACCLAMATION: Choose an alleluia that will last throughout the season. As always, the verses will change, but the lectionary groups them into those for the first (#192) and second (#201) parts of the season. The first set features

scriptures that announce the coming of the Savior together with non-scriptural proclamations of the same hope. The second group represents the O Antiphons from evening prayer. These seven verses are completely interchangeable, but careful planning will unite them to the *Magnificat* antiphon sung that evening or the previous one.

■ PSALMS: *By Flowing Waters* includes two settings for the Advent entrance and communion antiphons and psalms, as well as responsorial psalms.

■ FOR EUCHARISTIC PRAYER ACCLAMATIONS, choose one set and stay with it throughout Advent and on into Christmas. People will be able to sing these as true acclamations if they stop wondering which one it will be this week. This practice also gives the season an identifiable sound. You might even use the same set each year to help people make more associations between the music and the season. Any of the memorial acclamations may be sung, but the first three announce the theme of Christ's coming better than the last does.

■ TWO LATIN CHANTS FROM THE *LIBER CANTUALIS* are traditional for this season. The tune for *Conditor alme siderum* should be well known; it can be found in most hymnals as "Creator of the Stars of Night" (*Worship, Ritualsong* and *Gather Comprehensive* from GIA Publications; most subscription hymnals contain it as well). *Rorate caeli* is less popular, but it is a good challenge for a choir or assembly to add to its repertoire; it can be found in *The Collegeville Hymnal* as "O Heavens, Send Your Rain upon Us." The chant O Antiphons are lovely pieces for a choir disciplined enough to sing them. Find them in the *Antiphonale monasticum*. Traditionally, a bell may be rung while singing these antiphons at evening prayer.

■ HYMNODY: Traditional hymnody includes: "Wake Awake," "Come, Thou Long Expected Jesus," "On Jordan's Bank" and "Comfort, Comfort, Ye My People." These, of course, are useful for any liturgical gathering during the season.

Take a look at two fine Advent hymns by Steven C. Warner. "Take Comfort, My People" is based on Isaiah 40 (WLP 8653) and "Maranatha! Come, Lord Jesus" is based on 1 Corinthians 16:22 (WLP 7221). Both are arranged for choir, assembly and instruments.

GIA offers a significant collection of *Hymns for the Gospels* (G-5654). The book includes a hymn for every Sunday of the liturgical year, most arranged for four-part harmony. Ken Macek's "I Believe (with all my belief)" (WLP 7390) lends stirring music to everyone's firm Advent hope for the coming of Christ.

An index of music that reflects the scripture passages can be found in good hymnals and other resources from publishers.

■ CHOIR MUSIC: Let your choir shine during this season with music that will prepare hearts for the coming of Christ. J. Michael Thompson's arrangement of the popular hymn "Redeemer of the Nations, Come" (WLP 5793) and Richard DeLong's arrangement of "Come Thou Long-Expected Jesus" (E. C. Schirmer Music Company 4852) are fine compositions. A three-part choir will enjoy Alan J. Hommerding's arrangement of the spiritual "Keep Your Lamps Trimmed and Burning" (WLP 5739).

It is hard to limit recommendations from John L. Bell's inspired collection of music for Advent and Christmas, "God Comes Tomorrow . . ." (GIA G-5485). "Why Don't You Tear Apart the Heavens" carries an appealingly strange tune (G-5500). "Lift Up Your Heads" gives everyone a song based on Psalm 23 (G-5494). "A Voice Proclaims" is an easy, trumpet-like version of Isaiah 40 (G-5499). "Voces angelorum" reflects on the role of angels in the coming birth of Christ (G-5496).

■ YOUTH: The prolific Ed Bolduc has written two songs that should especially please young voices during Advent. "Rain Down" (WLP 7412) and "Look to the One" (WLP 7418) will add energy and punch.

■ CHILDREN: For even younger children, don't overlook the pieces in the *Music for Children Series* from World Library Publications. Dolores Hruby's "Lamps for a Wedding" and Julie Howard's "Two Psalms for Advent and Christmas" are childlike but not childish. These pieces will engage the children with songs that will satisfy more advanced musical tastes in the assembly.

■ A POPULAR ORGAN SOLO for the Advent season is the chorale prelude on "Wachet Auf" by J. S. Bach. A good tenor and accompanist may bless the assembly with a live rendition of the opening movements to G. F. Handel's *Messiah:* "Comfort Ye" and "Every Valley." Try to avoid recorded music for live worship.

Be alert to the needs of musicians. This season demands a lot of them. Make sure they can keep the meaning of these days in their hearts.

The Parish and Home

■ THE GIVING TREE: A giving tree takes some coordination, but it is well worth it. The basic idea is that people buy gifts for the poor and place them under the tree. It's a tree where churchgoers are *giving* gifts, not getting them.

Set up a tree in a public place like the gathering space, vestibule or reception area. Staff members who know the needy can solicit from them a list of gifts that would help. Volunteers write the needed gift on an ornament and place it on the tree, keeping confidential the name of the person it will benefit. Members of the community then take an ornament, purchase the gift, wrap it, and attach the ornament on the outside of the package so the staff and volunteers who distribute the gifts will know who gets what. Households learn the importance of sharing with those in need at a time of year when the satisfaction of gift-giving runs high and our Dickensian attention to the poor is strong.

■ ADVENT WREATH: The wreath in church should encourage people to set one up at home. Let people know how to obtain one. Perhaps a group in the parish could take orders and make them available. Prepare prayer cards for use at home throughout the season. Those who gather at home at the start of the day or for the evening meal may light the candles and join in prayer.

■ SAINT NICHOLAS: There are many delightful stories of Saint Nicholas. Look for him in collections of lives of the saints or on websites. Coming to know this saint will help everyone recover the origins of the Santa Claus legend. Exchange gifts on his feast, December 6. Listen to Benjamin Britten's cantata in his honor.

■ FAMILY ADVENT DAY: The parish could host a day for families early this month, offering educational activities related to the season. Information about Advent's history, scriptures, themes and customs might be welcome, especially by parents who want to hand on Catholic traditions to their children.

You can help parents of young children by sponsoring a Saturday event for children so parents are free to go Christmas shopping. Gather everyone at the beginning or at midday for prayer, sing the hymns of Advent, make wreaths and prayer cards for mealtime rituals. The day could conclude with all joining in a parish celebration of evening prayer.

LTP's could also distribute copies of useful resources. LTP's *Take Me Home* and *Take Me Home, Too* contain activity pages for families for each week of the season. LTP's *Welcome, Yule!* provides a handout for the weeks of Advent and Christmas to be included in bulletins or passed out to families.

■ CALENDARS: LTP's *Year of Grace 2004* is a large poster families will enjoy hanging at home. They can track the entire liturgical year. Clear the refrigerator door! In 2004 the calendar features many celebrated saints.

LTP's calendar *Fling Wide the Doors!* for Advent and Christmas comes with perforated doors and windows that reveal drawings to match the prayer for each day, found in an accompanying booklet. It will delight all ages.

Texts

■ GREETING:

Rejoice, for Christ is coming! The Lord,
    be with you.

From the one who is, who was, and is to come,
    grace and peace be with you.

■ INTRODUCTION TO THE PENITENTIAL RITE:

May the Lord make us increase and abound in
    love for one another and for all at the coming
    of our Lord Jesus Christ. Let us call to mind
    God's mercy for us.

We lift our souls to the Lord. Let us be mindful
    of our sins, that God may teach us the paths
    of salvation.

■ RESPONSE TO THE GENERAL INTERCESSIONS:

Lord, come and save us.

Come, Lord Jesus.

The *Book of Common Worship* for the Presbyterian Church (U.S.A.) and the Cumberland Presbyterian Church recommends this prayer

for Advent (p. 173). It could conclude the general intercessions:

Eternal God
through long generations you prepared a way
for the coming of your Son,
and by your Spirit
you still bring light to illumine our paths.
Renew us in faith and hope
that we may welcome Christ to rule our thoughts
and claim our love,
as Lord of lords and King of kings,
to whom be glory always. Amen.

■ DISMISSAL OF CATECHUMENS:

Sisters and brothers, we pray always with joy in our every prayer for all of you, because of your partnership for the gospel. We are confident of this, that the one who began a good work in you will continue to complete it until the day of Christ Jesus. Go in peace.

■ A BLESSING FOR TRAVELERS ON THE THIRD SUNDAY OF ADVENT (ADAPTED FROM THE *BOOK OF BLESSINGS*): *After the communion prayer, the parish announcements are made as usual. Then the deacon, cantor or presider begins in these or similar words:*

Deacon: We offer a blessing today for all those who will be traveling over the Christmas holidays. Please step forward and face the assembly.

(Pause while those who will be traveling come forward.)

Presider: The Lord be with you.

All: And also with you.

Deacon: Let us extend our hands in blessing over our brothers and sisters.

Presider: (cf. *Book of Blessings,* 631)

All-powerful and merciful God,
you led the children of Israel on dry land,
parting the waters of the sea;
you guided the Magi to your Son by a star.
Help these, our brothers and sisters,
    and give them a safe journey.
Under your protection
    let them reach their destination
and come at last to the eternal haven
    of salvation.
We ask this through Christ our Lord.

All: Amen. (*All lower their hands.*)

Presider: May almighty God bless you all,
the Father, the Son, and the Holy Spirit.

All: Amen.

Deacon: Go in peace.

All: Thanks be to God.

November 2003

Lectionary #3 (Lectionary for Masses with Children [LMC] #3)   violet

✺ **30** **First Sunday of Advent**

ORIENTATION

The taste of turkey drippings will still be in the mouths of many faithful who come to church this weekend. At church they will see sights and hear sounds that announce the beginning of Advent, the beginning of a new church year, a shift in seasons from doing things the ordinary way.

Make sure people see something different outside the church, in the gathering area, near their places in the worship area, and in the sanctuary. Set the Advent wreath where it will be visible. Make arrangements for blessing it at least at the first Mass this weekend.

Make sure people hear something different. The voices of cantors and greeters can show a more businesslike attitude than before. Let people know that the work of the season has begun. The music may bring back memories of Advents past.

LECTIONARY

Preparing for the scene at the little town of Bethlehem is Advent's minor theme. Preparing for the scene at the second coming of Christ is Advent's major theme. The first Sunday of the season always begins with the major one. "People will die of fright" is a verse of scripture people might expect on Halloween, but here it is introducing Advent. Welcome to Luke's gospel. We enter it in hair-raising fashion.

The first readings come from prophets other than Isaiah this year. Yet Jeremiah's prophecy today includes a verse that reminds us of Isaiah 11: "I will raise up for David a just shoot." Jeremiah looks for the day when Jerusalem will be so secure that people will nickname the city "The Lord our justice." How we long for that day.

In response we sing one of Advent's common psalms, Psalm 25. See #174 in the lectionary for the complete list of these. If you are building musical repertoire at your parish, you have the option of singing this psalm every Sunday of the season. This psalm fits Advent for several reasons. It calls God "my *savior*," a title that translates the name "Jesus." The psalmist sings, "I *wait* all the day" for that savior. The psalm celebrates the *covenant* between God and the chosen people, which will reach its fulfillment in the incarnation. And it promises *justice* for the humble, a virtue that will be especially manifest at the second coming of Christ, and which is underlined in today's first reading.

Paul's first letter to the Thessalonians may be the earliest of all the New Testament books. Throughout the letter you can taste the expectation of Jesus' imminent return. There is a direct reference to this expectation in today's second reading. Paul prays that his readers may increase in love and be blameless in holiness "at the coming of our Lord Jesus with all his holy ones." He clearly states Advent's major theme.

SACRAMENTARY

The sacramentary offers a selection of presidential prayers for each Sunday of the year and on many weekdays. They do not follow the three-year cycle of lectionary readings. Look over the two opening prayers and choose one that speaks to your community.

The sacramentary recommends Psalm 24 for the entrance antiphon: "No one who waits for you is ever put to shame." A verse from Psalm 84 is suggested for communion, a provocative image of God showering the earth with gifts and the land yielding fruit. The greatest gift showered upon us, of course, will be the incarnation.

The *Book of Blessings* places the blessing for the Advent wreath after the homily. Some communities move it to the position of the penitential rite instead. They open with the hymn, sign of the cross and greeting, then continue with the wreath blessing and conclude it with the opening prayer for the Mass. See the *Book of Blessings* (chapter 47) for the primary texts.

If the blessing of the wreath follows the homily, Mass opens as usual with the penitential rite. Note that the second option under rite C was written with Advent in mind. The Glory to God is omitted.

Advent Preface I (P1) applies today. It may be used with Eucharistic Prayers I, II or III, or with either of the prayers for reconciliation. Alan Griffiths published another translation of this in his collection of eucharistic prefaces from the Ambrosian Rite (Sunday 1 of Advent), *We Give You Thanks and Praise* (Sheed & Ward, 2000).

The solemn blessing suggested for this day looks for the coming of Christ in glory. Still, it is only one option. Consider substituting a prayer over the people, such as #4, which prays that they may find in God "the fulfillment of their longing."

OTHER IDEAS

Families may have guests this Thanksgiving weekend. You may wish to acknowledge visitors who have joined you for worship.

Begin Volume I of the *Liturgy of the Hours* today.

Mail out a parish Christmas card or letter, giving times for the communal reconciliation service, reconciliation of individual penitents, and the Christmas Mass schedule. Wouldn't it be nifty to have this information on a refrigerator magnet? Include in the Christmas card an examination of conscience and one or more of the new forms of the prayer of the penitent (act of contrition) from the *Rite of Penance* (#45). Promote the same events in the bulletin.

The celebration of evening prayer this weekend and throughout the season can help people pray in the gathering darkness for the coming of the Light.

December

M
O
N
#175 (LMC #172–175)   violet
Advent Weekday

From today through Wednesday next week, the weekday lectionary features a series of readings from Isaiah. We hear these prophecies in a semi-continuous order. This means that if you look them up in Isaiah, you will find them in this order. But we skip over a lot of passages from Isaiah in between the ones that appear in the lectionary. The psalms and the gospels during this period are chosen because they echo a theme from the first reading. The gospel passages during this part of Advent are not semi-continuous. They jump around the synoptics (Matthew, Mark and Luke) because the first reading is setting the pattern.

Because this is Year C, select the customary first reading (Isaiah 2:1–5). Next year this passage will be the first reading for the First Sunday of Advent, and we will substitute the alternate passage for Monday. Isaiah presents a glorious image of all the nations streaming toward the Lord's mountain. There they will experience unity and peace. "They shall beat their swords into plowshares."

The psalm develops the theme of the mountain. It is a processional psalm, sung by pilgrims on their way to the mountain of God, Jerusalem. We Christians sing it in anticipation of our ascent to the new Jerusalem.

The gospel develops the theme of inclusion. In his conversation with a Gentile centurion, Jesus observes that people will come from the east and the west and find a place at the banquet in God's reign. This faith-filled Gentile will have his place with the descendents of the Hebrew patriarchs and matriarchs. As we saw yesterday, Advent opens with the big theme of the second coming of Christ, the promise of redemption for all the faithful.

Use the first Advent preface today (P1). The recommended antiphon for the introductory rites echoes the theme of the readings. It invites the nations to hear God's message and make it known to the ends of the earth.

T
U
E
2
#176 (LMC #172–175)   violet
Advent Weekday

In a passage that inspired the Jesse tree and the list of gifts of the Holy Spirit, Isaiah prophesies that a great leader, filled with the spirit of justice, shall descend from the family of Jesse. Even the Gentiles shall seek him. Psalm 72, favored throughout Advent, echoes the theme of the just ruler. In the gospel, Jesus, filled with the Holy Spirit, tells the disciples that

prophets and kings longed to see and hear what they are witnessing. God is fulfilling the covenant.

■ TODAY IS THE 23RD ANNIVERSARY of the martyrdom of American missionaries to El Salvador: Maura Clarke, Ita Ford, Dorothy Kazel and Jean Donovan. Missionaries in Central America continue to lay down their lives for the sake of the poor. Remember them in prayer and imitate their example of love.

W
E
D
3
#177 (LMC #172–175)   white
Francis Xavier (+ 1552), presbyter, religious, missionary
MEMORIAL

Isaiah envisions a bounteous feast on the Lord's mountain. The prophecy, supported by the ever-popular Psalm 23, foreshadows the heavenly banquet.

Jesus gives depth to this vision by feeding a multitude. Your parish's efforts to supply food for the hungry make this work of Jesus present again. All these passages use banquet metaphors to express Advent's major theme, our anticipation of the return of Jesus, who comes to bring us to a happy, eternal home.

■ TODAY'S SAINT: Francis Xavier, a Spaniard of noble descent, became a disciple of Ignatius of Loyola and a driving force behind the missionary activity of the Jesuits in Asia. His celebration is an obligatory memorial, so the presidential prayers come from the proper of saints, not the Advent weekday. But you could use the Advent prayer or one from the Masses "For the Spread of the Gospel" with a shorter ending ("We ask this through Christ our Lord") to conclude the general intercessions.

THU 4 #178 (LMC #172–175) violet
Advent Weekday

Optional Memorial of John of Damascus (c. + 754), presbyter, monastic, doctor of the church / white ▪ Isaiah's prophecy salutes a city built strong on its firm purpose. Other cities will be trampled by the needy and the poor. The psalmist invites us to take refuge in God, not in people.

Jesus praises those who build their city on the rock of his words. Justice, not might, provides civic strength. These passages shed more light on the kind of world we await this Advent whenever we pray for the coming of God's reign.

▪ TODAY'S SAINT: John of Damascus served as a financial officer before becoming a monk near Jerusalem. His dogmatic theology served as a textbook for the Greek church. He vigorously defended the use of images in worship. His life blended the secular, academic and spiritual worlds, and, because of his work with the Muslim leaders in his area, he might be considered a patron of Muslim-Christian dialogue. The texts of hymns like "The Day of Resurrection" and "Come, You Faithful, Raise the Strain," are based on John's work. You sometimes see his name as John Damascene. It is pronounced "DAM-a-seen," not "DAM-a-sheen." His memorial is optional; unless your community has a special devotion to John of Damascus, celebrate the Advent weekday.

FRI 5 #179 (LMC #172–175) violet
Advent Weekday

Matthew alone records Jesus' cure of two blind people at once. The story perfectly illustrates the fulfillment of Isaiah's prophecy of a miraculous day on which, among other marvels, the eyes of the blind shall see. With new sight we sing Psalm 27, "The Lord is my light and my salvation."

With this prophecy and fulfillment, we see on two levels the kind of messiah that Advent awaits: one who works physical cures and one who provides spiritual sight.

SAT 6 #180 (LMC #172–175) violet
Advent Weekday

Optional Memorial of Nicholas (+ 399), bishop / white ▪ Isaiah's prophecy promises a day when God will hear the people of Zion, give them bread and water, teach them, guide them, fatten their herds, fill their streams, brighten the very light of day and give them no more cause to cry. The psalm praises the goodness of God who rebuilds Jerusalem. Its refrain comes from the same chapter of Isaiah that provides the first reading today. In the gospel, Jesus cures the illnesses of the crowds and sends his disciples to do the same.

▪ TODAY'S SAINT: The saint revered as Santa Claus appears today in the Advent calendar. Nicholas served as bishop of Myra in modern day Turkey and became the subject of innumerable legends and icons. Patron of sailors, scholars, travelers, thieves, virgins and children, his generosity continues to inspire the giving of gifts. According to one story, he rescued three virgins from prostitution by an anonymous gift toward their dowries. Artists sometimes depicted the gift with three bags of coins. It is possible that the three bags were misinterpreted as the heads of three children, giving rise to another legend. That story claims that Nicholas raised from the dead three boys who had been killed and pickled in brine. The three bags live on in iconography today as the symbol for pawnshops. Provide some activities for children today, recalling stories from the life of Nicholas and supplying gifts for the needy.

✷ 7 #6 (LMC #6) violet
Second Sunday of Advent

ORIENTATION

John the Baptist plays the central role today and next Sunday. As an Advent figure, John points not to the birth of Christ but to Christ's ministry and ultimately to Christ's death. Advent prepares us for the coming of Christ in many ways. Light a second candle on the wreath today.

LECTIONARY

Luke gives John the Baptist a solemn entrance in the gospel. He situates John among the great historical figures of his day. Later historians have questioned the gospel's accuracy in aligning these dates, but the point should not be obscured: John, the son of Zechariah, is a historical figure to be reckoned with, on the scale of high priests, tetrarchs, governors and caesars. He preaches a message of repentance for the forgiveness of sins. John is a transitional figure between the old and new covenants, and he calls for a transformation of the soul, as the earth undergoes a transformation of time.

The first reading comes from Baruch; you were maybe expecting Isaiah. After all, the gospel quotes Isaiah 41, and normally the lectionary will not miss the opportunity to present in full a first reading that the gospel cites in brief. This Sunday is different. Throughout the lectionary cycle, all three gospels for the Second Sunday of Advent cite the same passage from Isaiah. We heard the full text as the first reading last year. For variety, we hear other prophecies in the other two years of the cycle, to announce more fully the meaning of Advent.

This year's choice is a stirring clarion from Baruch, a prophet who opens his mouth in the Sunday lectionary only today and at the Easter Vigil. "Up, Jerusalem!" he commands. "Stand upon the heights! See your children gathered from the east and the west." Those who had been led away in exile are returning to the holy city. Our exile, too, will end when God gathers us to our eternal home, the new Jerusalem.

Today's psalm describes the same event, the return of Israel from exile. The singers, remembering the homecoming of the captives to Zion, felt like they were dreaming.

The second reading is the first of two passages from Philippians we will hear on Advent Sundays this year. Its theme is similar to last week's passage from 1 Thessalonians. Paul anticipates the return of Jesus and prays that his readers will conduct themselves in a way that prepares them to be pure and blameless "for the day of Christ."

SACRAMENTARY

Today's opening prayer is based on an Advent prayer from the eighth century. The alternative prayer levels a timely holiday caution against greed. To conclude the general intercessions try one of the opening prayers for June 24. The solemn blessing over the people is brief, but you may use the generic threefold blessing for Advent.

The sacramentary suggests opening the celebration with music based on Isaiah 30: "The Lord will

come to save all nations." The recommended communion refrain quotes today's first reading.

OTHER IDEAS

Call attention to the images of John in your church. Many places of worship have one at least in the baptistry. You need not move the image to highlight it. The focus of Mass should always be the table and the word.

Be sure to announce Monday's holy day of obligation; it may surprise some people who are expecting that the obligation to participate at Mass will not apply.

An Advent penance service this week can build on John's call to repentance.

#689 (LMC #429)   white

M O N 8 The Immaculate Conception of the Blessed Virgin Mary
SOLEMNITY

ORIENTATION

Today we celebrate our belief that Mary, even before she was born, was free from sin from the moment of her conception. People frequently confuse the immaculate conception of Mary with the virginal conception of Jesus. The idea of Mary's complete sinlessness was first expressed in the earliest Christian centuries, and in 1854 Pope Pius IX proclaimed it a dogma. Many new parishes

established about that time adopted this title of Mary. The date of today's celebration was set nine months before the feast of the Birth of Mary (September 8).

The solemnity of the Immaculate Conception is the patronal feast for the United States. Other countries claiming the same patronage include Nicaragua and Panama. Today is observed as a holy day of obligation throughout the United States, even when it falls on a Monday or a Saturday. This also pertains to the diocese of Honolulu, which retains only today and Christmas as days of obligation.

Today is the patronal feast of Paraguay, but under the title Our Lady of Caacupé. Tradition holds that a newly converted Indian escaped after an attack by pagans and carved a wooden statue of Mary, which has been enshrined at Caacupé. This solemnity is observed as a holy day of obligation in all Latin American countries except Costa Rica, the Dominican Republic, Ecuador and Mexico.

LECTIONARY

The Bible is silent about the dogma of the Immaculate Conception itself. The gospel of the annunciation, however, remembers Mary as a person who cooperated with God's plan. Read as prophecy, the Genesis passage anticipates the coming of a woman whose offspring will oppose the serpent of temptation. For this reason, Mary the Immaculate Conception is frequently depicted in iconography standing on a snake.

Paul speaks of our predestination for glory, a mystery made personal in Mary's preservation from sin. The marvels of the God who can accomplish these things are sung in today's psalm.

SACRAMENTARY

The alternative opening prayer asks God to "prepare once again a world" for the Son. Otherwise, no hint of Advent appears in the prayers. The Glory to God and the creed are said or sung. Note the special preface for this solemnity. Eucharistic Prayer III was composed with days like this in mind. Consider using the Advent solemn blessing instead of the optional one that appears in the sacramentary for this day. If you prefer the blessing for the feast, you can find it with inclusive language in the *Book of Blessings,* Appendix II, #20 ("Blessed Virgin Mary").

OTHER IDEAS

Sing the same gospel and eucharistic prayer acclamations throughout the Advent season, including today. They will add cohesion to the season and simplify matters for the assembly. Sing a setting of the Glory to God that you plan to use at Christmas, to help everyone sing it well on that special day.

By Flowing Waters (393–402), from The Liturgical Press, has a complete suite of antiphons and psalms for this solemnity.

Decorate the images of Mary in and around your worship space with flowers and candles. Introduce the liturgy with an explanation of the feast's meaning. Find model general intercessions and concluding collects in LTP's *Prayers for Sundays and Seasons.* Consider intercessory prayers for those awaiting the birth of a child, those yearning for justice, and the development of the charisms of women in church and society.

TUE 9 #182 (LMC #172–175) violet
Advent Weekday

Optional Memorial of Juan Diego (Cuatitlatoatzin) (+ 1548), hermit, visionary/white ▪ The first reading, the consoling opener to 2 Isaiah, was quoted in Sunday's gospel. It looks to a comforting day when exile is ended, as a voice cries out to prepare the way of the Lord. Boisterous Psalm 96 draws its confident refrain from the first reading today: "The Lord our God comes with power." The immense care God offers individuals shines through Jesus' parable of the hundred sheep.

▪ TODAY'S SAINT: Juan Diego (Cuatitlatoatzin) saw the vision of Our Lady of Guadalupe (see December 12) and received her image on his cloak. His Chichimeca name means "talking eagle." His memorial is obligatory in Mexico and optional in Argentina, Bolivia, Chile, Colombia, Costa Rica, Cuba, the Dominican Republic, Ecuador, El Salvador, Guatemala, Honduras, Nicaragua, Panama, Paraguay, Peru, Puerto Rico, Uruguay and Venezuela.

Ecuador lists this date as an obligatory memorial for Blessed Narcisa de Jesús Martillo Morán (+ 1869), who devoted her life to prayer and painful penance.

WED 10 #183 (LMC #172–175) violet
Advent Weekday

Those feeling exhausted already by holiday preparations will find comfort in today's texts. Isaiah says God "does not faint nor grow weary." The Almighty gives strength to the fainting and makes vigor abound for the weak. The gospel answers this theme with Jesus' supportive words, "Come to me, all you who labor and are burdened, and I will give you rest." Today's psalm blesses God, who is slow to anger and abounding in kindness.

Today is the anniversary of the death of the Cistercian monk and spiritual writer Thomas Merton (+ 1968). Consult his writings and audiotapes for spiritual advice that relates even to people outside a monastery's walls.

THU 11 #184 (LMC #172–175) violet
Advent Weekday

Optional Memorial of Damasus I (+ 384), pope/white ▪ Starting today the daily lectionary turns its full attention to John the Baptist. From now through December 16 we have a series of gospels that mention this prophetic figure. Jesus himself introduces John today. This year's semi-continuous readings from Isaiah end today with another passage from the book of consolation, predicting comfort for the afflicted. Psalm 145 takes up the same theme: The Lord is kind and merciful.

For the remainder of the season, the first readings will now follow the gospel's theme, reversing the pattern of the first part of Advent, during which the passages from Isaiah set the theme for the day, and the gospels answered.

▪ TODAY'S SAINT: Damasus was the son of a priest and eventually served the same parish his father administered in Rome. A poet, reformer and pious man, he served the poor and won the esteem of the irascible Saint Jerome, who served as his secretary when Damasus became pope.

FRI 12 #707–712 (LMC #447–451) white
Our Lady of Guadalupe
FEAST

ORIENTATION

Today's feast honors the mother of Jesus as mother also of the Americas. Mary appeared to a local Native American, who then presented himself to the bishop. At first doubtful, the bishop believed in the apparition after Juan Diego returned, his tilma filled with roses from the hills of Tepeyac. When the roses fell to the ground they revealed the image of Mary on the tilma, now enshrined in Mexico City.

On the tilma Mary resembles a *mestiza,* a woman of Native American and European heritage, representing God's affirmation of all American natives. She wears the blue band of expectant Aztec women, and on her womb appears a flower, the Aztec symbol for new life and a new era. She blocks the sun, which the natives had worshiped as a god. Like the church in Advent, she awaits the birth of Christ who will usher in a new era of peace and justice.

Today is the patronal feast of Mexico, where it is a holy day of obligation. Mexico and Guatemala observe today as a solemnity. Today's observance does not appear on the church's universal calendar, but it is kept as a feast in the United States, and also in Argentina, Bolivia, Chile, Colombia, Costa Rica, Cuba, the Dominican Republic, Ecuador, El Salvador, Honduras, Nicaragua, Panama, Paraguay, Peru, Puerto Rico, Uruguay and Venezuela.

LECTIONARY

Any readings from the common of the Virgin Mary may be used today, although in making choices, keep an eye toward the readings heard on December 8 and those to be heard on the Fourth Sunday of the season. Recommended are Zechariah 2:14–17 (707.11) or Revelation 11:19a; 12:1–6a, 10ab (708.2); and Luke 1:26–38 (712.4) or Luke 1:39–47 (712.5). These readings can be found together at lectionary #690A. Two readings will suffice, but you may choose three.

SACRAMENTARY

The Mass calls for the Glory to God, but not the creed. Today's presidential prayers can be found in the 1994 Sacramentary Supplement. Either preface of Mary (P 56 or P 57) may be used. The second echoes Mary's *Magnificat.* A third preface can be found in the sacramentary's Appendix X, #4 for the Mass of Mary, Mother of the Church. A solemn blessing may be taken from those for Advent (#1) or Mary (#15). Another solemn blessing for Advent can be found in the *Collection of Masses of the Blessed Virgin Mary,* at the end of the Order of Mass.

OTHER IDEAS

Today, as a feast, provides another opportunity to sing the Glory to God you will use at Christmas. Your community may provide a bilingual celebration, fiesta or music that will highlight the national origin of the feast. Honor the image of Our Lady of Guadalupe in your church.

S A T 13 #186 (LMC #172–175)   red
Lucy (+ 304), martyr
MEMORIAL

Today's gospel continues the series of references to John the Baptist from Matthew. Jesus connects John with Elijah, one of the greatest prophets. Because the Bible never reports Elijah's death—only that he ascended in a fiery chariot—speculation abounded that he would return, as reported in today's first reading. Psalm 80 calls upon God to save, a frequent Advent theme that will be realized in the birth of a child whose name means "Savior."

■ TODAY'S SAINT: The Sicilian Lucy took a silent vow of virginity early in her life, prayed to Saint Agatha for the healing of her mother's hemorrhage, was arrested during

a persecution of Christians, and martyred. Because her name means "light," her feast appropriately falls during Advent, and Christian art depicts her holding her own eyes. According to one legend her tormentors removed her eyes; according to another the virgin herself gouged them out and presented them to a disappointed suitor.

The opening prayer comes from the proper of saints. You may choose the other presidential prayers from the Advent weekday or the commons of virgins or martyrs. The preface for martyrs (P 66) may be used. Lucy is among the saints listed in the first eucharistic prayer.

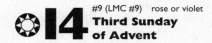

#9 (LMC #9)   rose or violet
Third Sunday of Advent

ORIENTATION

John the Baptist continues his central role as the prophetic figure whose life and ministry points the way to Jesus. The optional rose vestments and rose candle on the wreath announce that the season of waiting is nearing its end. This is one of the Sundays that used to be identified by the first Latin word of its entrance antiphon, and hence the first word of the day's Mass. Some people still call it *Gaudete.*

LECTIONARY

What should we do? is the question that permeates today's gospel. The crowds, soldiers and tax collectors all pepper John the Baptist with the same query. Advent is the season for preparing the food and fun of Christmas, but it is also the season of preparing the heart for Christ.

Keeping the theme of joy for Advent's third Sunday, Zephaniah urges Israel to shout and sing, to be glad and exult. The prophet looks for "that day" when God will be in the midst of the people as a mighty savior. Not only will the people be filled with joy, but God will sing joyfully because of the people.

The indomitable Isaiah makes his only appearance in the Sunday liturgy of the word this Advent by supplying the canticle that responds to today's first reading. Its confident spirit of joy perfectly echoes Zephaniah's prophecy, singing of the mirth that results from the Holy One of Israel's appearance among the people.

Paul's letter to the Philippians returns again this week. By now it will come as no surprise that the theme of this excerpt is "Rejoice!" Paul says the people should have no anxiety at all. The Lord is near—the source of all joy. Paul is referring to the return of Christ in glory, but we also start to sense the joy that the Christmas celebration itself will bring to our homes and community.

SACRAMENTARY

As with all the Sundays of Advent, the Glory to God is omitted. Both versions of the opening prayer highlight the theme of rejoicing. The first has roots in the fifth century. The message of either prayer will convince if the presider's face and voice radiate joy. The liturgy calls for the first Advent preface again today, even though the second says more about John the Baptist. A solemn blessing appears in the sacramentary, identical to the one for the first Sunday. The prayers over the people provide other suitable options, like #5.

OTHER IDEAS

You may open the liturgy with a song that recalls the entrance antiphon from Philippians 4:4–5. "Rejoice in the Lord always; again I say, rejoice! The Lord is near." The text comes from this year's second reading. The recommended communion antiphon comes from Isaiah: "Our God will come to save us." Festive music will help keep the spirit of this Sunday consistent with its prayers.

MON 15 #187 (LMC #172–175)   violet
Advent Weekday

The popular story of the Magi has some background in the lesser-known story of Balaam. In the prophecy we hear today, Balaam envisions a star advancing from Jacob, one that Christians believe later guided the Magi to the coming Savior. You can almost hear an echo of this application in the psalm for the day: "Your ways, O Lord, make known to me." This is one of the common psalms for Advent and may be used throughout the season.

We have already heard the principal texts about John the Baptist, but the lectionary serves up any reference it can find during this period of Advent. Today's comes from a controversy between Jesus and the chief priests and elders. The interpretation of John's baptism becomes a source of dispute. Here, John points the way to Jesus as the Messiah so focused on his mission that he will cause division.

TUE 16 #188 (LMC #172–175)   violet
Advent Weekday

In Matthew's gospel, John the Baptist has long left the stage by the time Jesus tells the chief priests and elders the parable about the two sons who say one

thing and do another. But Jesus summons the memory of John to drive home the point. Some people hear one thing then do something else.

Zephaniah gave us a message of rejoicing this past Sunday, but today's prophecy opens with words of woe to the rebellious and polluted city that has not trusted God. But God promises to rescue a remnant of Israel, a people humble and lowly who take refuge in God. Both readings contrast those who hear God's word but never put it into practice with those who live that message.

The psalm refrain reassures the singers with the message from the first reading: "The Lord hears the cry of the poor." God's care for the lowly is another of Advent's themes. God established the eternal covenant with a lowly people, and fulfilled the covenant by becoming lowly in the incarnation. This message concludes the first part of Advent this year.

WED 17 #193 (LMC #172–175)   violet
Late Advent Weekday

Today begins the final stage of Advent. The octave before Christmas shifts Advent into a proclamation of the historical birth of our Savior. We leave John the Baptist behind after following parts of his story for the past week. Note that the proper lectionary and sacramentary texts are the ones entitled "December 17"—not "Wednesday of the Third Week of Advent." The lectionary directs us to the solemn opening of Matthew's gospel, a text that requires practice and patience, impressive in proclamation more by its overall effect than by its details. It is paired with a prophecy from Genesis that the scepter of governance shall never depart from Judah. Psalm 72 returns, a prayer for the coming of a ruler who is just.

The opening prayer of the day recalls the humanity and divinity of Jesus, a perfect preparation for the gospel. The second Advent preface should now be proclaimed. Alan Griffiths published another translation of this (Weekdays before Christmas 2) in *We Give You Thanks and Praise* (Sheed & Ward, 2000).

THE O ANTIPHONS

These antiphons provide the most strikingly beautiful feature of these days before Christmas. Composed centuries ago for the *Magnificat* at evening prayer, they now also appear as versicles for the gospel acclamation at Mass (although the lectionary fails to distinguish which antiphon is assigned to which day). Each of the antiphons calls for the coming of Christ by addressing him with a different title, and sometimes multiple titles pile up in profusion. The antiphons receive a distant but profound echo on the solemnity of the Ascension, with its antiphon calling for the coming of the Spirit. That Ascension chant follows the same musical formula as the Advent antiphons do.

The antiphons begin this evening with "O Sapientia," "O Wisdom": "teach us to walk in the paths of knowledge." If your community has one or more persons who can sing chant, they will beautify the liturgy by singing this classic antiphon. If you decide to sing a verse of "O Come, O Come Emmanuel" with the alleluia each day, begin today with verse two. Other settings include Marty Haugen's "My Soul in Stillness Waits" (GIA 2652); Michael Joncas's "Let the King of Glory Come"; and the chant adaptation in *Worship: Liturgy of the Hours, Leader's Edition* (GIA Publications).

THU 18 #194 (LMC #172–175) violet
Late Advent Weekday

Matthew's account of the infancy of Jesus continues from yesterday's genealogy. In a story much briefer than Luke's, Matthew tells of the betrothal, annunciation, virginal conception, prophecy, naming and even the birth of Jesus. More verses from Psalm 72 announce the justice of God's reign, a theme explored in the prophecy from Jeremiah. The birth of this child will bring justice to the earth.

■ O Adonai: Adonai, a sacred title for the ineffable name of God, translates most commonly into English as "Lord." When the O Antiphon assigns this title to the coming of Christ, it proclaims the incarnation. The God who redeemed Israel with an outstretched arm comes in human form.

FRI 19 #195 (LMC #172–175) violet
Late Advent Weekday

We turn now to Luke's account of the events leading to the birth of Jesus. His story guides the daily Mass lectionary from today's celebration through the octave of Christmas. It begins with the birth of John the Baptist. The angel announces John's birth in today's passage, showing him to be the forerunner of Christ even in the manner of his birth. The consecration of a child to God from the mother's womb appears also in Psalm 71. In the first reading the angel's annunciation of Samson's birth and spiritual discipline prefigures the annunciation of John.

■ O Radix Iesse: The image of today's O Antiphon is the root of Jesse, prophesied in Isaiah 11, a passage popular in Advent and in celebrations of the sacrament of confirmation.

■ Hannukah: Our Jewish sisters and brothers begin their eight-day celebration of Hanukkah this evening. This festival of lights celebrates fidelity to the covenant in the face of tyranny and forced cultural assimilation. (See 1 and 2 Maccabees.) This year's celebration stretches across several days on the calendar that depend on the theme of light: tomorrow's O Antiphon that greets the rising sun, the winter solstice and Christmas. Include a prayer for our Jewish neighbors, that God's light may shine through their witness to the covenant. See LTP's publication *Teaching Christian Children about Judaism.*

SAT 20 #196 (LMC #172–175) violet
Late Advent Weekday

Luke's poetic account of the annunciation is one of his finest literary creations. The proclamation of the good news of salvation meets the perfect recipient, a servant of God, ready to follow the divine will. Bernard of Clairvaux's homily in today's Liturgy of the Hours perfectly complements the religious spirit surrounding the annunciation to Mary. Isaiah prophesies to Ahaz that a young woman shall bear a son, Emmanuel. The gospel and the liturgy see beyond that ancestral prophecy all the way to the birth of Jesus. Pilgrims on their way to the Jerusalem temple sang what is now called Psalm 24. We sing it today, bidding the Lord to enter the temple, bidding the Word to enter the womb of Mary.

■ O Clavis David: The one who holds the key of David (Isaiah 22:22, Revelation 3:7) opens and closes with absolute authority. Today's O Antiphon salutes the Key of David, the personification of authority, and the one whose judgment we both fear and welcome.

☼21 Fourth Sunday of Advent

#12 (LMC #12)   violet

ORIENTATION

Lighting the last candle on the wreath sets the full symbol ablaze with light, alerting us to the imminent celebration of Christ's coming. For many weeks the secular culture has been celebrating the Christmas season while we have been celebrating Advent. We have heard the prophecies that proclaim the coming of Jesus not just at Bethlehem, but as judge at the end of time. Today for the first time our Advent scriptures tell of the events that led to the birth of Christ.

In the lectionary, the sacramentary and the *Liturgy of the Hours,* the texts for December 21, including the optional memorial of Peter Canisius, yield to those for the Fourth Sunday of Advent. Only the O Antiphon for the day holds.

LECTIONARY

The visitation of Mary and Elizabeth is one of the warmest episodes of the pre-Christmas story. Two women, both impossible candidates for a pregnancy, one too old and the other a virgin, meet. Elizabeth feels her baby jump for joy. We do, too, as we sense the nearness of our salvation.

Incidentally, when Luke tells of the baptism of Jesus in 3:21, he uses the passive voice: "when Jesus also had been baptized." From the other gospels, we know that John performed the baptism. But Luke does not use active voice to say, "John baptized Jesus." As a result, the only explicit reference to the meeting of John and Jesus

in Luke's entire gospel is today's passage, and it happens *in utero.*

Everyone knows that Jesus was born in Bethlehem, but when the gospels present the origins of the adult Jesus they most frequently say he is from Nazareth. One of the main reasons Luke insists that the birth took place in Bethlehem is today's prophecy. Micah announces God's promise that from Bethlehem shall come forth the ruler in Israel.

As the first reading alludes to the coming ruler of Israel, so the psalm today calls upon the shepherd-king of Israel to save the people.

For three weeks we have heard passages from Paul's letters looking forward to the coming of Christ at the end of time. This week the epistle looks back on the coming of the Son of God in human flesh. In a rare reference to the incarnation, the letter to the Hebrews speaks of the coming of Christ into the world to offer himself to God. It explains the reason behind the festival we celebrate this week: the loving desire to do God's will.

■ O ORIENS: Singers of today's O Antiphon in Latin relish the opening phrase, "O Oriens." It has the (musically) biggest "O" of all the antiphons. It applies the image of the rising sun, the East, to the coming of the Savior. On the darkest day of the year, it calls for the sun to shine with redemption.

SACRAMENTARY

Turn back a few pages from yesterday's celebration to find today's. We still omit the Glory to God. Today's opening prayer, which appeared in the missal for the first time after the Council of Trent, also concludes the recitation of a popular devotional prayer, the

Angelus. The alternative recalls how Mary placed her life at the service of God's plan. The second Advent preface (P 2) continues throughout the second part of the season, even though the *Collection of Masses of the Blessed Virgin Mary* includes one for the Visitation (3). The entrance and communion antiphons today present two classic texts for the season, the *Rorate caeli* and the Emmanuel prophecy. A simple prayer over the people is provided after the communion prayer, but the seasonal solemn blessing may also be used. Another solemn blessing for Advent can be found in the *Collection of Masses of the Blessed Virgin Mary,* at the end of the Order of Mass.

Today's entrance antiphon, *Rorate caeli,* comes from Isaiah 45, "Let the clouds rain down the Just One, and the earth bring forth a Savior." Some translations say "justice" for "Just One" and "salvation" for "Savior," but the antiphon personifies these virtues to help us recognize the prophetic anticipation of the Messiah's birth. The suggested communion antiphon comes from Isaiah's prediction of the birth of Emmanuel (7:14).

OTHER IDEAS

You could sing a version of the *Magnificat* today. It is the canticle that Mary sings in the verses immediately following today's account of the Visitation in Luke's gospel.

Be sure everyone receives a printed copy of the liturgical schedule for Christmas, or e-mail it to parishioners today. Invite people to assist with decorations, and provide refreshments or simple gifts for those who do. If you offer evening prayer on Christmas Eve, the office of readings or a vigil preceding midnight or late evening Mass, be sure people know when these events will occur.

MON 22 #198 (LMC #172–175) violet
Late Advent Weekday

By happy coincidence, the gospel assigned for December 21 the weekday is the same as the one assigned for the Fourth Sunday of Advent in Year C, which is December 21 this year. Those who follow the weekday lectionary hear the complete gospel story in sequence. Enjoy the moment. The next time this happens will be Sunday, December 21, 2036. In today's gospel Mary sings the *Magnificat,* a hymn of praise to God for the miracles within and around her.

Many scripture commentators think that the song of Hannah in the first book of Samuel influenced Luke's composition of the *Magnificat.* The story concerns a woman thought to be barren who conceives a child and offers the boy to God's service. The story and the song are captured in today's first reading and responsory.

▪ O REX GENTIUM: Today's O Antiphon calls for the coming of the king of all the nations and the cornerstone that binds together the "mighty arch" of humankind. Even though Jesus kept his focus on Israel throughout his ministry, his apostles took the message to the ends of the earth, to fulfill the prophecy that the Messiah would unite the world's peoples.

TUE 23 #199 (LMC #172–175) violet
Late Advent Weekday

Optional Memorial of John of Kanty (+ 1473), priest / violet ▪ The sequence of events leading up to the birth of Jesus reaches a climax in the birth of John the Baptist. John, who will point the way to Jesus in his ministry and death, is shown preparing us for Jesus also by his birth.

We finally hear from Malachi one of the reasons why Elijah figures into the story of John the Baptist. The prophecy says that God will send Elijah before the day of the Lord comes. John resembles Elijah not just in dress but also as God's messenger. The seasonal psalm calls out for God the Savior, and its refrain comes from Jesus' own words predicting the coming of the Son of Man.

▪ O EMMANUEL: Not surprisingly, the O Antiphons conclude this evening with this great title of Jesus, Emmanuel. It sums up the theme of Matthew's gospel: Jesus appears by this title at the beginning and promises to "be with" his followers at the end. This, the last of antiphons, is better known as the first verse of the popular hymn based on the series.

In Latin, the antiphons form a reverse acrostic. Take the first letter of each of the titles of Jesus, spell them backward, and you get "ero cras," "I will be [there] tomorrow."

▪ TODAY'S SAINT: John studied at the university of Kraków, was ordained a priest and lived a very ascetic life in imitation of the desert monks. Unable to adapt to parish life, he had a successful teaching career in the field of scripture. He died on Christmas Eve.

WED 24 #200 (LMC #172–175) violet
Late Advent Weekday

There is no O Antiphon because this evening will begin the celebration of Christmas. Many parishes with a full evening liturgical schedule do not offer Mass this morning, but those who do will find it a beautiful conclusion to the celebration of Advent.

Luke's account of the events leading up to the birth of Jesus concludes with the prophecy of Zechariah, a hymn known as the *Benedictus,* sung at morning prayer every day of the year. The

text, which rejoices in the salvation arriving "in the house of David," is paired with a prophecy about the permanence of David's "house," a theme echoed in Psalm 89. The gospel acclamation may repeat any of the O Antiphons, but "O Radiant Dawn" or "O Emmanuel" from yesterday are most appropriate.

The opening prayer for this morning is a rare oration addressed directly to Jesus, not through Jesus. It sums up Advent's mighty call, "O Come, O Come."

The Roman martyrology commemorates all the ancestors of Jesus today, those "who pleased God and were found just and died according to faith, receiving no [fulfillment of] promises, but seeking and greeting them from afar." These holy ancestors express our longing to embrace all our human family in the wedding of heaven and earth, consummated in the incarnation and paschal mystery of Jesus, who sanctifies us in love.

NOVEMBER 30, 2003
First Sunday of Advent

Hungry for Justice and Peace
Jeremiah 33:14–16
I will raise up for David a just shoot.

THE scriptures of Advent open this year with an appeal for justice and security. Our society longs for a better life the same way ancient Israel and Judah did. We long for safety within our borders. We long for leaders of blameless conduct. We long for these blessings to last.

During Advent we want to see the fulfillment of God's promises. God promises peace. God promises safety. God promises good leaders. God promises food, drink and strength. During Advent we anticipate the fulfillment of God's main promise: salvation. We await the annual celebration of the birth of Jesus, whose name means "Savior" and whose mission brought redemption.

But we still await something more. We need God's presence in our midst now. We need peace in our lives now. We need leaders in whom we can trust, leaders we can admire, leaders who cooperate with the plan of God. And we need them now.

Through Jeremiah, we hear God's promise for something unique and wonderful: "a just shoot." God promises a strong sprout of new growth nudging up from the earth. This shoot will flower with justice. The earth and rain will fertilize its seed and make it grow from year to year.

This Advent our society yearns for a just shoot, the fulfillment of God's promise.

Written by Paul Turner. © 2003 Archdiocese of Chicago, Liturgy Training Publications; 1-800-933-1800; www.ltp.org.

DECEMBER 7, 2003
Second Sunday of Advent

Restoring the Lost
Baruch 5:1–9
Jerusalem, God will show your splendor.

IF something you loved was ever taken away from you, you know the feelings of loss, invasion, injustice and confusion. "Why would someone take from me the desire of my heart? Why would someone hurt me? How can this happen when I lead a good life? How will I continue in the face of this loss?"

The one who suffered a loss in this passage from Baruch was not a person. It was a city. Jerusalem had lost many of her inhabitants to invaders, many of her treasures to thieves. The entire city was cloaked in mourning and misery.

But Baruch urges the people to stand on the heights and look east. There they will see their scattered children brought together again. Carried away by enemies, they return on thrones.

God promises that the hills will be leveled and the valleys will be filled. Those returning will speed their way on the road home.

Jerusalem suffered immeasurable loss. Those returning had been changed by their experience of exile and redemption. Those at home had been changed by their hurt and their hope.

During Advent, we celebrate God's promise of restoration. If we have suffered a loss, God can make things new again. We might be changed by what we experience. The memory of our ache may never fade, but God can restore trust, hope and confidence for all who have lost what they most loved.

Written by Paul Turner. © 2003 Archdiocese of Chicago, Liturgy Training Publications; 1-800-933-1800; www.ltp.org.

DECEMBER 8, 2003
The Immaculate Conception of Mary

Mary, the New Eve
Genesis 3:9–15, 20
I will put enmity between your offspring and yours.

HAVE you ever seen an image of Mary standing on a snake? Look at statues or paintings around your church or in your home. One of the most popular depictions of Mary, the mother of Jesus, shows her standing on a snake.

You don't have to be an expert on the gospels to know that there is no record of such an episode in Mary's life. Rather, the image depicts the fulfillment of a prophecy from the book of Genesis.

After Adam and Eve sinned, God punished them both, along with the serpent. God predicted that Eve's offspring would strike at the serpent's head and the serpent would strike at the offspring's heel.

Christians see in this passage a prediction of the birth of Jesus. Mary is the new Eve and her son would crush the power of sin, temptation and death. Whenever you see Mary standing on a snake, you know she is the mother of the One who put an end to death and revealed the resurrection.

Is there a snake tempting you? Is there a sin that bothers you? You can find in Mary and Jesus strength and power to resist temptation.

Written by Paul Turner. © 2003 Archdiocese of Chicago, Liturgy Training Publications; 1-800-933-1800; www.ltp.org.

DECEMBER 14, 2003
Third Sunday of Advent

Lessons Learned
Zephaniah 3:14–18a
The Lord will rejoice over you with gladness.

WHEN punished children finally get permission to play, they take new delight in their freedom. They learn the importance of good behavior. They also learn that parents have authority that can be used for punishment or release. If parents have done their job well, children learn that both punishment and release happen because of their parents' love.

When ancient Israel ended up in exile, the people interpreted their loss as punishment for their sins. They had not listened to God. They had not been faithful to the covenant. In their punishment, they learned the importance of good behavior. They also learned that God had authority over them, that God would remain faithful to the covenant, and that their actions have consequences.

Imagine the freedom they felt at these words from Zephaniah: "The Lord has removed the judgment against you." Their time of punishment was over. They could return to their homeland to worship, to work, to reunite with family—and to play. God gave them release.

Children who delight in freedom sometimes miss another truth: Their parents are happy too. When punishment is over and children are free, parents are proud that their children have grown.

God does not take delight in what we experience as punishment. God takes delight in the lessons we learn and in the love we share when we are free.

Written by Paul Turner. © 2003 Archdiocese of Chicago, Liturgy Training Publications; 1-800-933-1800; www.ltp.org.

DECEMBER 21, 2003
Fourth Sunday of Advent

From Out of Nowhere
Micah 5:1–4a
From you shall come forth the ruler of Israel.

VICTORY is always exciting. But when the hero is a complete unknown who comes seemingly out of nowhere and performs as a pro, the victory is much more electrifying. The previously unknown hero thrills in many arenas—in sports, the arts, politics and even religion.

Micah prophesied that God's chosen people would receive a new leader from a town of no reputation, some place called Bethlehem. This village was too small to be listed among the clans of Judah. Even so, God spoke through the prophet that Bethlehem would supply Israel with a ruler able to govern with divine strength. This ruler's greatness would reach the ends of the earth and bring peace.

For Christians, the identity of this ruler is well known: Jesus, who, according to Luke, was born in Bethlehem. Jesus brings excitement to the history of religions because he came from nowhere, from a town that had never accomplished anything great.

But the real significance of Jesus is not his unfamiliar birthplace. It is the extent and result of his reign. He rules the spirits of believers all over the world. He brings peace to those whose hearts are heavy. He brings hope to those who live in obscurity, whose good deeds go unnoticed and whose love goes without reward. The heroism of the just will never escape God's sight.

Written by Paul Turner. © 2003 Archdiocese of Chicago, Liturgy Training Publications; 1-800-933-1800; www.ltp.org.

CHRISTMAS

The Meaning

Part of the poignancy of the scene is that it is unrepeatable. History is like that; thousands of years converged upon that moment, and the little group at Bethlehem will never be found together again. They cannot even have stayed together for long then. The nativity scenes catch them poised in one historic moment, with all the poetry of the particular. It will not come again in history, but it is not lost, for all that. In God no beauty, no truth, no moment of glory can ever be lost. The uncreated beauty that spilled itself into history that night is waiting for us.

—Maria Boulding, *The Coming of God,* Third edition (Conception, Missouri: The Printery House, 2000), p. 54.

EVEN though we celebrate a historical event on Christmas Day, its meaning does not rest in the past. Today is born our Savior. God is born this day in our hearts, to fill us with hope, to dignify the tawdriest corners of our lives, to raise us from anybodies to somebodies.

The Son of God, the eternal Word, became flesh as Jesus the Christ. Our belief and actions bring Christmas to life. Whenever we give a gift of charity, sing of God's goodness, or support the needy, we are the body of Christ, newly born, bringing life and redemption to a wary world.

■ CHRISTMAS CRIES OUT FOR COMMUNITY. We are saddened whenever we hear of someone celebrating Christmas alone. This day is meant to be shared. People travel great distances to be with those they love, and others telephone or send cards to family and friends. This celebration of love, symbolized in the custom of giving gifts, sits within the framework of the incarnation. God's love inspires us to show love for others.

■ A FESTIVAL OF MANY DAYS: The liturgical celebration of Christmas extends for several weeks beyond Christmas Day. The mystery is so deep that the liturgical calendar gives us a series of occasions to enter it again and again.

Epiphany and the Baptism of the Lord celebrate the implications of Christmas Day. It is not enough that God became one like us. This mystery must be shared with the world. This manifestation (epiphany) of Jesus inspires the Magi at Bethlehem and John the Baptist at the Jordan. It shows the global significance of the incarnation. Jesus comes not just for a few people, not just for one race. His arrival announces salvation to all the nations of the world.

■ A FESTIVAL AT THE ONSET OF LENGTHENING DAYS: The date of Christmas coincides with the time of year in the northern hemisphere when the days begin to lengthen. The return of the sun's rays symbolizes the birth of God's Son, shining the light of eternal life upon the entire world. In some works of art, the light seems to shine from the baby Jesus upon the faces of those gathered around. He is the source of light for all who believe.

■ THE DATE OF JESUS' BIRTH IS UNKNOWN. No accurate records tell us the day or even the year of Jesus' birth on the calendar. December 25 was eventually chosen probably because it falls nine months after the solemnity of the Annunciation, a date that had already appeared on the calendar.

March 25 was selected for the Annunciation because it had already been acknowledged as the presumed date of the crucifixion. That date had been calculated as Passover in the year Jesus died.

Among the ancients, some regarded it a sign of greatness if an individual died on the anniversary of the day she or he was born. A slightly different tradition formed that Jesus died on the day he was conceived, giving him status as the divine and perfect human.

So, the theory goes that our ancestors thought Jesus died on March 25 because that was Passover, and that he was conceived on March 25 because he was great enough to die on the day of his conception, and that he was born nine months to the day after he was conceived, December 25. But in the end, we do not know exactly the day on which Jesus was born.

The year of Jesus' birth was determined by Dionysius Exiguus ("Dennis the Short"), a learned scholar engaged by Pope John I to perform this task. Using the best data at hand, Dionysius computed that Jesus was born 753 years after the founding of Rome. For various reasons, scholars believe he fixed the date four to six years too late. The most devastating argument against Dionysius' reckoning concerns Herod the Great. The two stories of the birth of Jesus (from Matthew and Luke) do not agree on many details. Whenever the two do agree, the detail gains importance. One of those points of agreement is that Jesus was born during the reign of Herod the Great. Modern dating of Herod, though, places his death around 4 BCE. That is why it is generally thought that Jesus was born, paradoxically, in the period of time we call "before Christ."

■ CHURCH ATTENDANCE ON CHRISTMAS DAY IS HIGH, largely because it is social expectation. People come for different reasons. Some genuinely want to celebrate their faith. Others want their children to experience Christmas. Still others want to keep peace in the family.

Be prepared to offer hospitality to everyone who comes. This is not the day to gripe about "where are all these people the other 364 days of the year?" Have extra greeters on duty so that everyone who enters the building receives a cheery "Merry Christmas!" Be church. Be joy. Be as welcoming to all as would Jesus, who came to save all.

After Christmas Mass, hand out copies of the parish bulletin and the diocesan newspaper. Include lots of information in the bulletin this day, including the address for the parish website and a list of activities and opportunities for members and visitors, as well as phone numbers for various needs. Have visitor's cards available in places easily accessible. Make sure those who want to leave a message for the parish have a simple way to do so. If your music ministry is preparing a special printed program for Christmas, see that it includes at least the address, phone number and website of the church, so those who want to contact you later can do so easily.

The most important evangelization we give this day is a joyful celebration of Christmas. From presider to greeter to choir, let the face of every liturgical minister glow with the joy of salvation.

The Saints

THE saints and festivals of Christmastime keep the spirit of joy alive throughout this season. The saints of the Christmas season have been called the *comites Christi,* Christ's companions, a privileged retinue gathered around their Savior. The octave of Christmas shares time with them, and the liturgy serves up a peaceful sharing of prayers among the feasts needing recognition at the Liturgy of the Hours and at the eucharist. You may sing the Glory to God many times during this period.

■ OBLIGATORY MEMORIALS OCCUR DURING THE CHRISTMAS SEASON, but, by design, not during the Christmas octave. The opening prayer of a memorial takes precedence over the seasonal prayer. So does its vestment color, but it will not be noticed when it calls for white since white is Christmas' seasonal color. The preface, prayer over the gifts and the communion prayer may be drawn from the Christmas weekday, from the saint's day or from the relevant commons. The scriptures may be taken from the lectionary common, but it is better to observe the sequence of seasonal weekday readings.

■ WHEN AN OPTIONAL MEMORIAL OCCURS ON A WEEKDAY IN THE CHRISTMAS SEASON following the Christmas octave, you may celebrate the Mass of the Christmas weekday or of the saint. You may also choose one from the martyrology. In doing so, you may choose the prayers for the saint from the sacramentary as well as readings from the lectionary commons. But normally you will observe the seasonal day to lend unity to these weeks. Another possibility is to use the opening prayer for the saint's day as the conclusion to the general intercessions.

Some days in the Christmas octave are not designated as feasts or solemnities, but as octave days. If you choose to observe an optional memorial on those days, it is treated as a commemoration like those of the last week of Advent. You may use the opening prayer of the saint in place of the seasonal opening prayer, or else use the saint's prayer as the conclusion of the general intercessions. Otherwise, the prayers and vesture for the octave all take precedence.

■ VOTIVE MASSES and the Masses for various needs and occasions are used sparingly during Christmas. During the weekdays of the octave, only the bishop may direct their usage for serious need or pastoral advantage. On other weekdays, the presider may choose them only for serious reasons.

The Lectionary

THE mystery of salvation becomes clearer to us as we hear the extraordinary collection of passages from the Christmas lectionary. Ask people what Bible passages would be appropriate for the Christmas season, and they will think of the infancy narratives. Matthew and Luke relate the birth of Jesus. Luke records the events of the eighth day remembered on the Christmas octave, and Matthew tells of the visit of the Magi. All four gospels refer to the baptism.

But there is more. The prophecies, sermons and letters of the Christmas lectionary sing out a full-throated proclamation of salvation. As we move through the season, the readings advance to later events in the life of Jesus: the miracles, or epiphanies, which support our belief in the power of the Word made flesh.

■ ON WEEKDAYS, Luke's story dominates the first part of the Christmas season because he tells more than others about the events following Jesus' birth, like the presentation in the temple and the finding of Jesus there. John's first letter, so filled with ideas basic to Christian belief, accompanies these passages. After Epiphany we hear about the manifestation of Jesus in a variety of gospel stories, notably the miracle accounts. The first readings return to the spirit of Advent. Together, the passages from the close of the Christmas season show the fulfillment of Advent's dreams.

■ THE COMMON PSALMS for Christmas and Epiphany are 98 and 72 respectively. Psalm 98 sings of God's salvation, a central theme to the season because the name Jesus means "Savior." Psalm 72, a royal psalm, appeared frequently in Advent. It returns now to celebrate the fulfillment of its prophecy.

■ GOSPEL ACCLAMATION: Versicles for the gospel acclamation are found in lectionary #211 and #218. In general they announce the coming of Christ and his manifestation to the world.

■ THE SUNDAY *LECTIONARY FOR MASSES WITH CHILDREN* makes only a few adaptations. It offers one set of readings for Christmas Day. The first reading and gospel come from the Mass at midnight. The second reading, however, comes from the Mass at dawn. For the Holy Family, the children's lectionary offers only the options for Year A, readings which may be used at the parish Mass all three years of the cycle. For Mary, Mother of God, it omits the second reading, as it does for the Epiphany. For the Baptism of the Lord, it recommends the gospel from Year C every year, which works especially well this year.

The Sacramentary

■ THE ASSEMBLY: People gather at church for a common purpose. Sometimes they behave like a single body of believers. Other times they act like a gathering of individuals. At funerals and weddings, for example, frequent churchgoers often forget when to stand, sit and kneel, and even the words of their prayer. They behave more like individuals at prayer than as a single body. At Christmas, though, you will probably have an assembly that yearns to act as one.

You can help people form this community. They already have a common experience. They have made time to worship together on a day they have been anticipating for weeks. Give them a chance to meet one another. Give them songs to sing. Give them a beautiful experience to share.

On Christmas Day and throughout this period our churches welcome many visitors.

Consider inviting the assembly to stand and greet those around them before the entrance song this season. Ask parishioners to welcome visitors, and encourage people to exchange names and the greetings of the season.

If your space permits it, you could even invite your regulars to introduce their guests, or ask visitors to announce where they come from. On Christmas, this non-invasive question can make visitors feel welcome and give the regulars an opportunity to rejoice in the gathering of faithful far and near.

■ GREETING: For the opening greeting of this season try something that announces the feast: "Christ was born for our salvation. The peace and love of God our Father, which has been revealed in Christ, be with you." Or try, "The grace of the Lord Jesus, who became human for us, be with you."

■ THE PROCLAMATION OF THE BIRTH OF CHRIST may introduce the Christmas Eve Mass. The 1994 *Sacramentary Supplement* for the United States suggests it follow the greeting of the Christmas Mass during the night. In this case, the penitential rite is omitted, and the Glory to God forms a joyous sung response. See "Texts" below.

J. Michael Thompson has composed a simple but effective setting of this text for SATB choir and cantor (WLP 5747). It's a fine piece, even though it carries an inexact title: "The Christmas Martyrology." It's the proclamation of the birth of Christ from the Roman martyrology.

■ PENITENTIAL RITE: Among the sacramentary's options for petitions in the penitential rite, C-iii focuses on the mystery of the incarnation and the role of Mary. The blessing and sprinkling of holy water might effectively replace the penitential rite on the feasts of Epiphany and Baptism of the Lord, or even on all Sundays of the season. As we celebrate the birth of Jesus, we remind ourselves of our rebirth in baptism.

■ THE GLORY TO GOD returns on Christmas and throughout its octave, as well as on Sundays and solemnities of the season. The opening words come directly from the Christmas story. As the angels sang this phrase on the first Christmas Day, it is most fitting to sing the Glory to God throughout the Christmas season.

■ REGARDING PRESIDENTIAL PRAYERS, almost all are based on texts from older missals. One of the oldest is the opening prayer for the Christmas Mass during the day, which appeared at least by the sixth century. The opening prayer and the prayer over the gifts for the Baptism of the Lord, by contrast, are new compositions.

Suggested collects for the season appear in LTP's *Prayers for Sundays and Seasons.* You will also find introductions to the Lord's Prayer, invitations to communion and dismissal texts.

■ THE PROCLAMATION OF THE DATE OF EASTER may be made on the feast of the Epiphany after the homily or after the communion prayer.

■ THE CREED is recited or sung on Sundays and solemnities. Although the Glory to God is sung on weekdays during the Christmas octave, the creed is not recited. On Christmas Day, we genuflect during the words that recall the incarnation. Ordinarily, we bow at this time. We used to genuflect at these words every time we recited the creed, so the bow is a recent moderation.

This particular bow, incidentally, is a profound bow from the waist, not a head bow. This may be a good season to catechize people about this simple gesture.

■ SAMPLE FORMULAS FOR THE GENERAL INTERCESSIONS appear in the sacramentary's first appendix. See #4 for those suggested for the Christmas season.

■ THERE ARE FIVE PREFACES FOR THE CHRISTMAS SEASON. The first three (P 3–P 5) are for Christmas and its octave, as well as the weekdays of the season. The second of these is a new text based on a fifth-century sermon by Pope Leo the Great. Another translation can be found among the Ambrosian prefaces (weekdays between Epiphany and the Baptism of the Lord, Tuesday). See Alan Griffiths, *We Give You Thanks and Praise.* The same collection offers another translation of the Roman Christmas Preface III (seventh day in the Christmas octave). The fourth Roman preface (P 6) is for Epiphany and may be used as an alternative for the first three during the weekdays following January 4 this year. (See the Ambrosian preface for the vigil of the Epiphany for another translation.)

The last Roman preface concludes the Christmas season with the celebration of the Baptism of the Lord. It also appears as the second preface for the same feast in the Ambrosian tradition.

Additional prefaces for this season can be found in the *Collection of Masses of the Blessed Virgin Mary* (4–9).

■ WHEN EUCHARISTIC PRAYER I is used at Christmas and during its octave, look for the special

insert in the text at the phrase that begins, "In union with the whole church." It may be used even on weekdays of the octave. On Epiphany you will find another insert for the same phrase. The sacramentaries of other language groups suggest a seasonal insert for Eucharistic Prayer III as well. If the nature of your celebration calls for using one of the eucharistic prayers for reconciliation, you may use a preface from the season that refers to penance and conversion. If you use Eucharistic Prayer IV, however, you retain its preface.

Christmas will be a good season to use the third eucharistic prayer for Masses with children, which suggests that all sing "Glory to God in the highest" as an acclamation during the prayer. If your community sings the Glory to God during Christmas, you could use the opening notes as the acclamation of this eucharistic prayer.

■ ACCLAMATIONS DURING THE EUCHARISTIC PRAYER may be the same as those used during Advent. Add instruments or harmonies from the choir. Some communities choose a new musical setting for these acclamations during Christmas to set off the season. It is a short season, though, so it may be simpler for assembly and musicians to stay with the Advent set.

■ BLESSINGS for the season include Solemn Blessing #2 for Christmas, #3 for the Beginning of the New Year, and #4 for Epiphany. Among the prayers over the people, #14 especially fits the time of year. Another solemn blessing for the Christmas season can be found in the *Collection of Masses of the Blessed Virgin Mary,* at the end of the Order of Mass.

The Book of Blessings

THE *Book of Blessings* includes prayers for a manger or nativity scene (ch. 48), a Christmas tree (49) and homes (50). You could incorporate blessings over the environment to begin or end the time for decorating the church. Or make these texts available for families to use at home.

Other blessings that fit this season include those over a family (ch. 1-I), a married couple (1-III), children (1-IV) and travelers (9).

The Rite of Christian Initiation of Adults

As usual, catechumens may be dismissed after the liturgy of the word at every Mass. Sample formulas appear at RCIA, 67, and in "Texts" below. Many catechumens enjoy the time after dismissal to reflect on the word with a catechist, but Christmas Day may not provide a good opportunity because of family responsibilities. Consider offering another time when catechumens can reflect on Christmas and its scriptures together. Or try a different form of catechesis this season. Let catechumens spread Christmas cheer by donating time to the needy. Be sure to invite college students who are catechumens. Those who spend the school year away from home can use Christmas break to make a connection with their parish and to continue their catechumenal formation.

One tough topic for catechumens and for all who struggle with living the Catholic way of life is keeping the Christmas season in tune with the liturgical year. It can be news to people that there is such a thing as the Christmas season and that it reaches its crescendo at Epiphany. Better than talking about such things is to provide opportunities to celebrate the season "with heart and soul and voice."

The rites of acceptance and welcoming may be celebrated at any time of year, whenever the candidates are ready. But this season, so filled with solemnities and symbols, may not provide the best opportunity.

The Rite of Baptism for Children

CHILDREN may be baptized almost any day, but the first two Sundays of the new year make good occasions. Just as we celebrate that Jesus was manifest to the nations (Epiphany) and is God's anointed one (Baptism of the Lord), so the newly baptized go forth into the world as ambassadors for Christ, anointed with God's Spirit.

The Liturgy of the Hours

THE historical psalms added to the Advent office of readings continue through the brief Christmas season. Morning and evening prayer during the Christmas octave juggle the season with the feast days from the cycle of saints.

Among the treasures in the office of readings are excerpts from the greatest Christmas homilist of all time, Leo the Great. On Christmas Eve you'll find these words: "In the very act in which we are reverencing the birth of our Savior, we are also celebrating our own new birth. For the birth of Christ is the origin of the Christian people; and the birthday of the head is also the birthday of the body." Look for an opportunity to share a longer passage like this one with your community, either in written or oral form. Open choir practice with it or use it for part of a Christmas gathering of staff.

The Rite of Penance

THE busy time for the sacrament of reconciliation is before Christmas, not after. But some in your community will want to come. You may even have some visitors from Christmas Eve or Christmas Day whose hearts were moved to seek reconciliation. Be sure to include the times for this sacrament in the bulletin for Christmas and on the parish website. If the reconciliation room is hard to find in your church, post signs that direct visitors to it. Are times posted near the door of the church? If the church is locked when visitors arrive, will they know what time to come back for reconciliation?

The Pastoral Care of the Sick

THE sacrament of anointing may be celebrated at any time this season for those in need. With so much else going on this time of year, it may not be the best season to offer the communal celebration. If you do choose to celebrate anointing within the context of Sunday Mass, the texts come from the Mass of the day, not from the Mass of the sacrament.

ignore the season. The church will be filled with signs of Christmas, and the music and texts can complement these.

The Rite of Marriage

As in Advent, the Rite of Marriage may be celebrated, but be mindful of which Mass may be used on what days. If the wedding takes place on the evening before or the day of Christmas, Mary, the Mother of God, Epiphany, or the Baptism of the Lord, the readings and prayers for the Sunday or solemnity take precedence, although one reading may be substituted with one from the Rite of Marriage.

If the wedding does not include Mass, or if the wedding Mass does not take place in conjunction with a solemnity this season, the scriptures and prayers for marriage may be used. The celebration of the Holy Family (December 28 this year) falls into this latter category. A Saturday evening wedding Mass on December 27 may use the Mass of marriage in its entirety.

When decorating for the wedding, be sure to work with the Christmas decorations already in place. Keep a photo album of seasonal decorations. Let the couple see what the church will look like at Christmas when they are preparing details in summer.

The Order of Christian Funerals

A funeral may take place on any day during the Christmas season. If for some extraordinary reason the funeral needs to happen on Christmas Day, the Mass of Christmas must be celebrated. On other days the funeral Mass may replace the readings and prayers of the day, but consider using the scriptures of the day. Some of them may help the family integrate their loss into the promise of this season.

In guiding a bereaved family in making choices for music and readings, you need not

The Art and Environment

THE art and environment crew has its work cut out for it. This year there are a few days between the Fourth Sunday of Advent and Christmas Eve, so there should be time to plan and execute the Christmas beautification of your space.

You will need extra hands. Get the word out early to potential volunteers. Which parishioners do a great job decorating their home at Christmas? Make a few phone calls to invite the help you need. Post appeals in the bulletin and on the website. Be prepared with a list of responsibilities so that when people walk in to help, you know exactly what task to assign.

■ OUTDOOR DECORATIONS will put worshipers in a festive mood before they sing their first carol at church. Do you have trees you can brighten with floodlights or strings of bulbs? Some churches line the walk with luminarias, paper bags weighted with sand holding small candles. If you do so, be careful of fire hazards. Other communities set up banners with a seasonal greeting. Remember, "Merry Christmas" will evangelize better than "Season's Greetings."

■ CANDLES inside the church will announce the coming of the Sun of Justice (Malachi 4:2) and the Light of the World (John 8:12). Arranged in patterns and colors, candles create a visual appeal that can touch the heart of any worshiper.

■ EVERGREENS, by their very title, announce the eternal promise of life. The Christmas tree will profess our belief in eternity and in the power of God. Uprooted from its place of life, the tree comes indoors where all can enjoy its beauty, protected from the elements. It gives up its life for our enjoyment and becomes the place for our gifts, themselves symbols of our self-sacrifice. The tree dies in decorated splendor, giving hope to all mortals who yearn for the salvation of the eternal Christmas. Become aware of civil restrictions regarding evergreens and work with local authorities to observe them while expressing the freedom of religion.

Holly brightens at its best in the winter. Its thorny leaves and red berries have made it a symbol of the passion in the midst of Christmas joy. The poinsettia serves a similar purpose. Wreaths symbolize victory and union, the victory of Christ and the union of the Savior with the church.

■ THE NATIVITY SCENE will attract many visitors, young and old. Some people go from church to church to pray at the local manger. The gathering of the poor, the foreigner, the angel and the animal invite every viewer into the scene. More than any other symbol of Christmas, the nativity scene shows how the different gospel stories of Christmas are fused in the popular imagination. The shepherds appear only in Luke. The Magi arrive only in Matthew. The ox and ass symbolize faith in the opening chapter of Isaiah. Yet they all find happy company under a roof in Bethlehem. Our church doors will open this Christmas to faithful and sinner, rich and poor, dark- and light-skinned.

Be careful about the size and placement of the crèche. If indoors, it should not distract attention from the altar. It belongs in areas of more private prayer, perhaps in a gathering space or a side area of the church. A larger scene may be constructed outside the church, to draw attention to the place and the season. Some churches set the manger out early, but without the infant and with the Magi at a distance from the rest of the scene. They set the infant in the manger on Christmas Eve and move the Magi closer for Epiphany.

■ WHITE VESTURE (or gold or silver) adorns the presiding ministers this season. If you have several sets of white vestments, select one that can be identified each year with this season.

The Music

SING carols. Traditional carols awaken old memories for believers and unbelievers alike, and their familiar words and melody allow the entire assembly to sing with full voice. The powerful message of God's love touches the human heart in extraordinary ways through the simple singing of a Christmas carol.

■ CAROLS: For a church reveling in its universal appeal and diversity of membership, Christmas carols provide a natural opportunity to celebrate our catholicity and the global implications of the incarnation. Learn carols from other countries, and sing some in other languages. The assembly that sings both "Adeste Fideles" and "Stille Nacht" will expand their appreciation of the season.

The useful collection of "Descants for Christmas" by James J. Chepponis makes a worthy addition to your repertoire (WLP 7971). The score is for full choir, descant, guitar and keyboard. But even if God has blessed you with only one coloratura instead of a full choir, or a high schooler learning trumpet, you can add more splendor to the five popular carols in this folio.

The merriest Christmas Mass will absolutely drench worshipers in their favorite Christmas carols. They have abstained from singing these throughout the season of Advent, even though carols have been piped into every supermarket, elevator and waiting room they've entered. Now is their chance. Let the people sing!

■ THE RESPONSORIAL PSALMS for the Christmas season have been set by many composers. Michel Guimont offers a set of descants for his (GIA G-4986A), to add just a touch of delight to a simplified setting. If you are using a lot of loud music for the entrance rites at Christmas, your cantor might enjoy leading something simpler.

■ THE RETURN OF THE GLORY TO GOD to the liturgy expresses the joy of the season as the celebration opens. Use the same setting throughout the season, on all its Sundays and solemnities. You don't have one in your repertoire? Or you'd like to learn a new one? This is the perfect season to learn, because you will have many opportunities to repeat it over a few weeks.

■ CHOIRS WILL FORM FOR CHRISTMAS more easily than for other times of the year. There are terrific opportunities for them to sing a simple four-part arrangement of a traditional carol or a thrilling rendition of the "Hallelujah Chorus" from Handel's *Messiah*.

Publishers continually produce new music for Christmas. You'll be tempted to try some out and will have success adding to the repertoire. See Steven C. Warner's "Watchman, Tell Us of the Night" (WLP 8643), Timothy Dudley-Smith and Steven R. Janco's "Wood Is for the Manger" (WLP 8707), John M. Neale and Richard Proulx's "Here Is Joy for Every Age" (WLP 5784) and

Robert Lau's "Ave, Ave, the Angel Sang" (Wayne Leupold Editions 100023). Proulx has a lovely setting of a traditional Czech carol, "Hearken, Hearken, Mother Dear" (WLP 5785) for the rare choir with too many basses, scored for SATBB, flute and oboe.

John L. Bell's collection for Christmas, "God Comes Tomorrow . . . ," supplies an unending source of great new music (GIA G-5485). "Two African Christmas Carols" bounce with Christmas joy (GIA G-5487). "He Came Down" is adapted from a Cameroon song (GIA G-5497). The text for "It Was to Older Folk" will convince you that Christmas isn't for children at all (GIA G-5492). Rather, it is a celebration of God's love for the elderly. The infectious "Sing a Different Song" will raise hopes and spirits (GIA G-5501). Just get the whole collection.

The prolific David Haas offers several fine pieces as well. "Birthsong" has a lovely text by Brian Wren about the relationship of the new-born Jesus and his mother (GIA G-3455). Shirley Erena Murray wrote the texts for "Child of Joy and Peace" (GIA G-5215) and "Star-Child." Haas captures the different spirit of these texts and sets them convincingly.

■ YOUTH: Some songs popular with youth will also fit the season. These could include "Lord, I Lift Your Name on High" by Rick Founds (WLP *Voices as One,* 60).

■ CHILDREN: Julie Howard's "Two Psalms for Advent and Christmas" (WLP 7129) includes a jolly refrain for Psalm 96. Kids can also shake maracas and beat bongos for this number.

■ MUCH SOLO MUSIC based on Christmas carols has been written for organists. Whether it's "Gesu Bambino" or "Quelle est cette odeur agréable?" people will hum along not knowing why the tune is familiar.

The organist or handball players who prepare a festive postlude for Christmas will reward worshipers with an extra measure of seasonal joy. Check out "Three Festival Carols for Two or Three Trumpets & Organ" by Paul Roberts, available from GIA (G-4716). Any of these three pieces would bring your Christmas Mass to a thrilling close. See also Scott M. Hyslop's arrangement of "Sonata natalis," by Pavel Josef Vejvanovsky for two trumpets and organ (GIA G-5179).

■ INTERESTED IN A SERVICE OF LESSONS AND CAROLS? The United Church of Canada gives a model with excellent ideas in *Celebrate God's Presence* (pp. 105–10).

The Parish and Home

PEOPLE should not need much encouragement to bring the spirit of Christmas to their homes, but it never hurts to promote the obvious. Outdoor lights and seasonal displays can evangelize an entire neighborhood. Indoor customs of the Christmas tree and manger scenes will remind the family of the season and create enthusiasm among children. Sending cards connects people more personally at this time of year.

You can provide households with texts for blessing seasonal religious articles at home and for praising God for the family meal. Have children draw pictures for them. Put some texts and drawings in the bulletin or on the parish website. Table prayer for Christmas Day might be drawn from the *Book of Blessings* (#1038ff, 1048–49), or the simpler version in *Catholic Household Blessings and Prayers* (pp. 50–54).

More ideas for families to celebrate this season can be found in Peter Mazar's *Winter: Celebrating the Season in a Christian Home* (LTP, 1996), as well as in LTP's *Welcome, Yule!*

Texts

■ GREETING:
(Adapted from the sacramentaries of other language groups.)

Christ was born for our salvation. The peace and love of God our Father, which has been revealed in Christ, be with you.

The grace of the Lord Jesus, who became human for us, be with you.

■ INTRODUCTION TO THE PENITENTIAL RITE:

The kindness and generous love of God our Savior appeared not because of any righteous deeds we had done but because of his mercy. Let us call to mind our sins.

■ RESPONSE TO THE GENERAL INTERCESSIONS:

Word made flesh, hear our prayer.

Hear us, Savior of the World.

■ CONCLUDING PRAYER FOR GENERAL INTERCESSIONS: The *Book of Common Worship* for the Presbyterian Church (U.S.A.) and the Cumberland Presbyterian Church recommend this prayer for Christmas (p. 187). It could conclude the general intercessions:

> All glory to you, great God,
> for the gift of your Son,
> whom you sent to save us.
> With singing angels,
> let us praise your name,
> and tell the earth his story,
> that all may believe, rejoice, and bow down,
> acknowledging your love;
> through Jesus Christ our Lord,
> who lives and reigns with you
> in the unity of the Holy Spirit,
> one God, now and forever. Amen.

■ DISMISSAL OF CATECHUMENS:

In times past, God spoke in partial and various ways to our ancestors through the prophets; in these last days, God has spoken to us through the Son. May the Word made flesh resound in your hearts. Go in peace.

December

25
#13–16 (LMC #13)   white

The Nativity of the Lord: Christmas Day
SOLEMNITY

ORIENTATION

The liturgy offers four sets of texts for the Christmas Mass, titled with different times of day. The vigil Mass is intended for use in the evening of December 24 and sets the stage for celebrating the great mystery. The Mass *in nocte* ("during the night") need not take place at midnight. Yes, Jesus spoke of the coming of the bridegroom at midnight, but it's not like they wore watches in those days. Mass at dawn remembers the arrival of the shepherds to greet the newborn king. Mass during the day celebrates a deeper reflection on the Christmas mystery.

The faithful may participate fully and share communion at more than one Mass, but no parish is obliged to celebrate all four. In fact, the scriptures for any Mass may be proclaimed at any time. The general outline of the four Masses, however, is helpful for planning the community's prayer for Christmas Day.

Today is a holy day of obligation in the United States (including the diocese of Honolulu, which has reduced the number of holy days) and throughout Latin America.

LECTIONARY

The lectionary offers a completely distinctive set of readings for each of the four Masses of Christmas. The first set really has a vigil in mind. That is, it presumes the faithful will be back to celebrate Christmas Mass the next day. The other three sets of readings, even though they have recommended designations, may be proclaimed at any Mass on Christmas Day, judging from pastoral need. The most "Christmasy" of all the readings are those for midnight ("during the night"), with dawn running a close second. The gospels of the genealogy (vigil) and the prologue to John's gospel (day) fail to resonate as well with the worshiper who participates in only one Mass at Christmas.

■ VIGIL: Matthew's genealogy has to be the most boring passage in the lectionary, but in the hands of a skilled homilist it can come to life. Raymond Brown treats the genealogy in eye-opening detail in *The Birth of the Messiah* (New York: Doubleday, 1993). The passage from Isaiah draws on the metaphors of the dawn and a marriage. The light of Christ will break forth like the dawn, and God will espouse Israel, even as the Word becomes flesh. Acts offers us part of Paul's preaching in which he proclaims that Jesus has descended from David. Psalm 89, a royal hymn about David, relates more to the readings that follow it than to the one before. Together, these scriptures, collected with dusk in mind, announce a new dawn: the coming of Christ through the line of David.

■ MIDNIGHT: Luke's marvelous account of the birth of Jesus proclaims the heart of today's mystery. Not only does it tell the story of the birth, but it also involves the census, the shepherds and the multitude of angels. It's the famous story most people yearn to hear when they come to Mass at Christmas. Paired with it is the short passage from Titus, which urges the people to act temperately as they await the appearance of Jesus in glory. This brief but significant passage says that the meaning of Christmas goes beyond Bethlehem to the anticipation of our redemption at the second coming of Christ. The prophecy from Isaiah, proclaimed in the middle of the night, announces that the people who walked in darkness have seen a great light. That light, we believe, is Jesus. Psalm 96, a hymn exulting the coming of the judgment of God, takes its refrain from the gospel.

The first reading and the gospel in the children's lectionary come from the Mass at midnight.

■ DAWN: The lectionary continues the story from Luke's gospel, focusing now completely on the shepherds, who go, presumably at dawn, to see the child born during the night. The letter to Titus explains why God our Savior has appeared, and Isaiah announces in joy that the Savior comes. Psalm 97 proclaims the kingship of God, and the dawning of light for the righteous. These passages all celebrate the coming of our Savior and the honor due to him.

The second reading in the children's lectionary comes from this Mass.

■ DAY: Theologically the deepest of the Christmas readings, John's prologue announces the mystery in language we hear often, "The Word became flesh." Isaiah proclaims that all the ends of the earth will behold God's salvation, indicating the full extent of the mission of the body of Christ. Psalm 98 takes up the same theme. The three psalms recommended for Christmas Day (96,

97 and 98) all sing praise to God. The letter to the Hebrews speaks of the coming of the Son, the refulgence of God's glory, and looks already to his ascension to the right hand of God. These scriptures focus on the mysterious incarnation and the glorification of the Son.

SACRAMENTARY

Complete texts for four Masses appear here. They bear the same titles as the Masses in the lectionary, but in this case the prayers are more carefully constructed to fit the time of day. You would not read the prayers for the Mass at dawn while celebrating Mass at the vigil.

All the Masses call for a genuflection during the creed at the words of the incarnation. If the deacon or priest or cantor introduces the creed with an invitation to genuflect, the assembly will be more likely to do so together. For example, "As we recite our creed today, let us genuflect together during the words that recall the incarnation." Why not take a longer pause? Let everyone kneel to meditate a moment on the birth of Christ, as they perhaps do during the Passion on Good Friday, in awe over the death of Christ. Just be sure someone is ready to start up again with the words "for our sake," or you may end up with an uncomfortable pause while people try to regain the flow of the creed!

If you use Eucharistic Prayer I at any of these Masses, you insert the special form of the prayer that begins "In union with the whole church . . ."

■ VIGIL: As in the lectionary, the vigil is intended for those celebrating a late afternoon or evening Mass on December 24 but planning to return for Christmas

Mass the next day. If the community gathering in your church on Christmas Eve is really celebrating Christmas, it makes more sense to use the prayers for midnight. Both opening prayers for the vigil Mass suggest that we are still waiting for the birth of the Son, not actually celebrating it. Any Christmas preface may be used, but the second may better fit the readings that tell of David's lineage. If you prefer to conclude the Mass with a more solemn or pertinent blessing, see solemn blessing #2 for Christmas.

Israel's exodus from Egypt inspired the antiphon recommended for the introductory rites. At that time, God promised Israel that they would behold the glory of the Lord "in the morning." The communion antiphon recalls an Advent prophecy of Isaiah, that all would see the salvation of God. When you hear "salvation" in a text like this, think "Savior." The liturgical tradition personifies the Christmas virtues of judgment and salvation, and imagines them incarnate in Christ.

■ MIDNIGHT: Even though the Mass is called "Midnight," it need not begin at that hour. Some communities start the Mass earlier, still in the dark of night, for the convenience and safety of the assembly. You may begin this liturgy with a vigil of psalms, silence, readings and prayers. It gives the choir an opportunity to share the wealth of music for the feast, and invites members of the assembly to enter into the spirit of the day, even if they got there early just to find a good seat.

The *Liturgy of the Hours* offers a suggested celebration of the office of vigils (Vol. I, p. 399 and p. 1622ff). It could happen this way:

Entrance procession: After the people have gathered in a semi-dark church, members of the community process in with the candles from the Advent wreath.

The ministers follow. They might light candles held by the assembly. A setting of the invitatory psalm (95, 24, 67 or 100 for example) could accompany the procession. More candles may be lit at the altar.

Greeting: V. Light and peace in Jesus Christ our Lord. R. Thanks be to God.

Office of Readings: The *Liturgy of the Hours* recommends "What Child Is This?" for the hymn, followed by a selection of psalms. The readings themselves include a classic Christmas passage by Leo the Great.

The Office of Vigils: One or more canticles may be sung, as indicated (vol. I, p. 1622ff), then the gospel of the resurrection may be proclaimed. Since this is Year C, most fitting would be Luke's version (24:1–12). Then follows the gospel of the Christmas vigil, Matthew 1:1–25 or just 1:18–25.

The Proclamation of the Birth of Christ: This announcement may be chanted. The text and music can be found on page 50, as well as in the 1994 *Sacramentary Supplement.* Acolytes with lighted candles might lead a procession. A deacon, cantor or reader may lead the proclamation from the ambo. All stand, but all kneel for the words "having passed since his conception, was born in Bethlehem of Judea of the Virgin Mary." Then all rise for the final sentence. Make sure the ministers know this so they can cue everyone else by their posture.

Mass: Mass begins with the Glory to God.

Some communities, not wanting to observe the entire vigil outlined above, may select some of its elements, or replace some with alternative scriptures and favorite carols.

If there is no celebration of the office of vigils, Mass begins in the usual way. Carols may be sung as preludes. The Proclamation of the Birth of Christ may follow the greeting.

Both opening prayers assume that this Mass takes place in the dark of night. Surprisingly, it is the alternative opening prayer for the Mass at dawn that makes the Christmas liturgy's only allusion to a passage from the book of Wisdom about God's Word leaping down from heaven "in the silent watches of the night." In Wisdom, the story concerns the exodus, but at Christmas, that line feeds the tradition of having Mass at midnight, the traditional time for the birth of Christ.

Two antiphons are offered for the introductory rites. One comes from the second psalm, a text that seems natural for Christmas, but that the New Testament frequently applies to the resurrection: "You are my Son; this day I have begotten you." The version from *By Flowing Waters,* 19, is especially effective with handbells. The alternative antiphon is nonscriptural, but acclaims the spirit and meaning of the celebration. The communion antiphon comes from the gospel of the Mass during the day and proclaims the central doctrine of Christmas: The Word of God became flesh.

From the Latin, the opening line of the solemn blessing, "When he came to us as man," is more literally translated, "By his incarnation." Similarly, in the third part, "When the Word became man" renders the same Latin expression, literally, "becoming flesh."

■ DAWN: The prayers that open the liturgy celebrate the coming of light into the world. The prayer over the people that appears in the sacramentary may be replaced by the solemn Christmas blessing, #2.

The opening antiphon blends passages from Isaiah and Luke, to announce the shining of God's divine light this day. Another text associated with Advent appears in the communion antiphon, to announce that the Savior, the one we have awaited, has come.

If the early Mass at your parish lamentably includes no music, this is the day to repent and change your ways. Haul out a couple of familiar carols and acclamations. Every scrooge will happily sing on Christmas Day.

■ DAY: The opening prayer for this Mass is the oldest of the set. The Latin text praises God for creating "the dignity of human substance" or "being." The prayer over the gifts recalls the great gift of peace.

The entrance antiphon echoes a prophecy heard at midnight Mass. The communion antiphon repeats the refrain from the responsorial psalm. The citations appear to be different because the lectionary follows the Hebrew numbering of the psalms and the sacramentary observes the vulgate numbering.

OTHER IDEAS

Publicizing the Mass times is essential, and the parish office will still receive innumerable phone calls. When recording the message, wish everyone a Merry Christmas and tell the Mass schedule first, or give the caller a mailbox number to press. People are calling for Mass times. They don't need to hear a long list of extensions.

Use the website, the Christmas card, the bulletin, signs in front of the building—whatever means you have to make the times public.

If you know some Masses will be overcrowded, for example on the vigil of Christmas, consider not publicizing those on the telephone recorder or the website, but through the parish bulletin instead. This might encourage the visitors to come at a time when you have more room and more opportunity to greet them.

If you publish a participation aid for Christmas, include the parish phone number and website for easy access, and don't be shy about publishing upcoming events to which visitors will be welcome.

You may want to celebrate evening prayer as a community. If so, the best time would probably be before the first vigil Mass. But reserve your strength. You'll need it for the full schedule of Masses and visitors.

If you use incense only rarely, this is the day to get it out. If you use it regularly, reserve a special fragrance for today's celebrations.

Given the importance of today's gospel, the procession cries out for candles and incense. The deacon or priest may chant the good news. See *Chants for the Readings* (Joseph T. Kush, GIA G-2114) and *Liturgical Music for the Priest and Deacon* (Columba Kelly, St. Meinrad's Archabbey, St. Meinrad, Indiana).

At the end of Mass carefully choose a few additional parish announcements so visitors hear about opportunities to return to the community.

Leave the church open today, if possible. Announce it at Mass and invite people to return with visitors to show off the local worship space and to spend some time in prayer.

If some people wish to return to the church for vespers, you may offer evening prayer to conclude the day's activities.

#696 (LMC #437, 458–460)
red
F R I **26 Stephen, first martyr**
FEAST

The joy of Christmas gives way to the shock of martyrdom. Stephen, known as the protomartyr, "the first witness," reveals the price paid by those who place their faith in the newborn king. The first reading recounts the story of Stephen's martyrdom, an event foreshadowed in the gospel where

Jesus predicts that his followers will suffer persecution. A quotation from the psalm for the day appears on the lips of Stephen at his death, as it did on the lips of Jesus at the crucifixion. The children's lectionary offers a different option for the gospel.

The readings for Mass today and tomorrow are in the back of the lectionary with the saints, but the presidential prayers are in the front of the sacramentary with the seasons.

Today is "Boxing Day" in the United Kingdom and in Canada, a day for sharing gifts of charity. The custom reflects Stephen the deacon's care for needy members of the church.

Sing the Glory to God today, reprising the one from Christmas Day. If you're using Eucharistic Prayer I, which includes the name of today's saint, see the special insert for the octave of Christmas. Sing Christmas carols at Mass this week. Even those who rarely sing will welcome the invitation to join lustily in the music of the season.

S A T **27** #697 (LMC #452–454 and 438)
white
John, apostle, evangelist
FEAST

On the feast of John we begin the semi-continuous reading of the first letter that bears his name. The opening words resemble the beginning of the fourth gospel, also attributed to John. "The disciple whom Jesus loved" experiences a defining moment in today's gospel, becoming a witness to the resurrection. We hear the story of Easter in the context of Christmas. It honors the memory of the beloved disciple while unfolding the whole mystery of salvation in Christ.

Scholars insist that the John of the gospels, the beloved disciple, the evangelist, the author of three New Testament letters, and the seer of the book of Revelation may not be the same person, but church tradition has conflated them into one, all recognized as the saint of this day. Today's psalm is seasonal, expounding nothing further about John, but singing of the joy of Christ's coming at Christmas. The versicle for the gospel acclamation is the opening of the classic hymn *Te Deum*. Its most familiar adaptation in English is "Holy God, We Praise Thy Name." The chant is in the *Liber cantualis*.

Sing the Glory to God today in honor of the feast. Eucharistic Prayer I includes an insert for the Christmas octave as well as the name of today's saint.

This year's celebration of Hanukkah, the Jewish Feast of Lights, ends tonight.

☀28 #17 (LMC #14)   white
The Holy Family of Jesus, Mary and Joseph
FEAST

ORIENTATION

This feast, with roots in the seventeenth century, was added to the universal calendar in 1921 to build up devotion in family life. It upholds Jesus, Mary and Joseph as the ideal family. We now celebrate this feast on the Sunday within the octave of Christmas. It used to fall during Epiphany's octave, but now it follows more faithfully the sequence of seasonal events. This feast comes at a time when our thoughts turn to the creation of the holy family at the birth of Jesus, as well as the gathering of our families and loved ones this season of the year.

LECTIONARY

The arrangement of readings is hopelessly complex. The first set of readings may be used in all years—A, B and C. It includes a first reading from Sirach and a psalm. The second reading from Colossians has a longer and shorter form, marked A and B in some editions of the lectionary, which do not refer to the year of the cycle. Then the lectionary offers a selection of three gospels, marked A, B and C, which *do* refer to the year of the cycle.

The confusion does not end there. After this complete set of readings you will find optional first and second readings and responsorial psalms for years B and C of the cycle. So, for this year (Year C), there is a complete liturgy of the word: a first reading, psalm, second reading, alleluia verse and gospel.

This means that you have choices. You may choose the first two readings from either Year A or Year C. The gospel should come from Year C. You will get the most variety over the three-year cycle if you take the first two readings and the psalm for Year C this year.

The first reading of Year C comes from 1 Samuel. It tells of the birth of Samuel, and how his mother Hannah dedicated him to God. Hannah's story appeared in the Advent lectionary this past Monday. She was thought to be barren, yet conceived a son and presented him to God. Her family foreshadows the story of the holy family. In the latter case, Mary, the mother of Jesus, was a virgin, not barren, yet conceived a son by the miraculous intervention of God. There are many beautiful stories today of women who long for a child, yet only conceive after adopting another. In fact, the birth of every child happens by the miraculous intervention of God.

The psalm proclaims the loveliness of God's dwelling place. It is chosen because Hannah brings Samuel to the temple of God at Shiloh and leaves him there. As we sing the psalm, we imagine it being sung by the infant Samuel, who will find happiness living in the house of God. It also foreshadows the gospel account of Jesus finding himself quite at home in the temple.

The second reading of Year C comes from 1 John. It develops the metaphor of "children of God" as a title for the entire Christian community. It broadens the notion of holy families beyond the domestic unit into the village and beyond.

Luke's gospel returns frequently to the theme of Jerusalem, and today's excerpt is a good example. The story of Jesus' childhood ends with him at the temple in Jerusalem, astounding the teachers there. The story proclaims the wisdom of Christ even in his childhood, but it will resonate with many parents who struggle to fulfill their responsibilities as good guardians of their children.

You may decide to use the first two readings from Year A. The passage from Sirach extols the honor due to parents. The Canadian lectionary translated the last few verses in the plural, demonstrating that the child owes care not just to the father but to both parents. Psalm 128, one of the options in the wedding lectionary, praises God for the blessings of

family. The letter to the Colossians invites the Christian community to put on its virtues like clothing, and bind them all with love. The shorter version of this passage eliminates the concluding verses, which are troublesome: "Wives, be subordinate to your husbands" is a command that may be dangerously misunderstood in abusive relationships. It would be better to take the shorter version of this passage.

SACRAMENTARY

The presidential prayers today all mention the holy family, making it hard for anyone to miss the theme of the feast. No special preface is provided, though. Choose from the three prefaces for Christmas, but you may want to look at the *Collection of Masses of the Blessed Virgin Mary* for one called Our Lady of Nazareth (P 8). The special insert for the octave of Christmas may be used with Eucharistic Prayer I. Alternate blessings include the one for the Christmas season (solemn blessing #2) and prayers over the people #2 or #9.

The suggested chants for entrance and communion present a prophetic passage from Baruch and a fulfillment from Luke: God establishing a home among the people. The prayer for the holy name of Mary in Appendix X of the sacramentary (#5) might conclude the general intercessions today.

OTHER IDEAS

The *Book of Blessings* offers a full array of blessings for families, and *Catholic Household Blessings and Prayers* includes one for "a Family or Household" (206–10). Religious articles received as Christmas gifts could be included as part of the final blessing for Mass, or

afterward in a gathering at the manger. See the *Book of Blessings* (ch. 44) for the shorter rite.

The day's themes are captured in two choices for the entrance antiphon in *By Flowing Waters,* 28 or 29, with the "family psalm," Psalm 128.

#202   white

MON 29 Fifth Day in the Octave of Christmas

Both readings come from the front part of the lectionary now. You'll find them after the weekday Advent readings. The first few days of the Christmas octave were also feast days, so those readings came from the back, among those for December's saints.

You will discover that the sequence of first readings begun last week with Saint John continue this week. All are taken from the letters of John. Today John urges his readers to act in a way that demonstrates that God's love lives in them. In words that blend well with the season, he says the darkness is over and the real light has begun to shine. We sing the opening verses of Psalm 96, one of the songs of praise that fits the Christmas season.

In the gospel we hear of the presentation of Jesus in the temple. Simeon receives him in his arms, a symbol of ancient Israel that longed for the day when the messiah would come. Now, Simeon prays, God may let him rest in peace. His canticle is recommended for night prayer in the *Liturgy of the Hours.* At the end of every day, we give thanks for all the wonders we have witnessed and assure God that it is all right to let us go in peace.

During the Christmas octave, we sing the Glory to God each day. If you use Eucharistic Prayer I, you may include the special insertion for this week.

TUE **30** #203 white
Sixth Day in the Octave of Christmas

The first letter of John addresses listeners of every age group, urging them to forsake the enticements of this world. We sing several more verses of Psalm 96, a seasonal hymn of praise.

The gospel concludes the story of Jesus' infancy with the second part of Luke's account of the presentation in the temple. Today, Anna the prophetess thanks God and tells everyone about Jesus. She is a model of prayer and evangelization.

Sing the Glory to God. You may use the insert for the Christmas octave in Eucharistic Prayer I.

WED **31** #204 white
Seventh Day in the Octave of Christmas

Optional Memorial of Sylvester I (+ 335), pope/white ▪ Today's gospel presents the prologue of John. One of the alternate passages for Mass on Christmas Day, it appears here in a more subdued setting for peaceful reflection, apart from the hectic demands of Christmas Day. The first reading recalls division within the early church amid a somber proclamation of the coming of the antichrist in the final hour, an ominous text for a New Year's Eve. We finish singing the remaining verses of seasonal Psalm 96.

Still within the octave of Christmas, the liturgy calls for the Glory to God and the optional insert to Eucharistic Prayer I.

▪ TODAY'S SAINT: One of the longest reigning popes in the history of the church, Sylvester served during a time of great councils, including Nicea, which clarified our belief in the divinity of Christ.

January

THU **1** #18 (LMC #15) white
Octave of Christmas Mary, the Mother of God
SOLEMNITY

ORIENTATION

We celebrate many events today. The octave of Christmas brings our weeklong celebration to a close. The secular calendar celebrates New Year's Day. Many Eastern calendars emphasize the circumcision of Jesus, an event the gospel notes on the eighth day of his birth. Some churches of the Reformation honor the naming of Jesus, an event the gospels place on the same day. Pope Paul VI designated this as a day of prayer for world peace. Many of the faithful will participate at Mass simply as a good way to start the new year.

This is a holy day of obligation in the United States (except in the diocese of Honolulu) and throughout Latin America, except in Chile, Paraguay and Uruguay.

LECTIONARY

The gospel explains the original cause of this celebration. Luke records the circumcision and naming of Jesus on the octave day of his birth. The same text mentions Mary, whom we honor today as "Theotokos," mother of God, reflecting in her heart on the birth of Jesus.

The lectionary adds a blessing from the book of Numbers for those who invoke the name of God, and a passage from Galatians. Paul's letters tell us nothing about the life of Mary, but in this one passage he alludes to God's son, "born of a woman." He never reveals her name, but the lectionary adopts this lonely reference from Paul on this and other days in honor of Mary. Psalm 67 echoes the theme of blessing from the first reading.

SACRAMENTARY

All the presidential prayers express the theme of Mary's motherhood. The liturgy calls for the first preface of the Blessed Virgin Mary (P 56), but notice the one for Mary, the Mother of the Church, in Appendix X of the sacramentary, and Mother of the Savior in the *Collection of Masses of the Blessed Virgin Mary* (P 5). All the eucharistic prayers refer to Mary by today's title, Mother of God. This could be a good day to reflect on its paradoxical meaning. (How can God have a mother? Only through the incarnation.) On this last day of the octave, the special insert for Eucharistic Prayer I may still be used. The sacramentary suggests a prayer over the people, but the solemn blessing for the new year (#3) would also be appropriate. See the solemn blessing for the Christmas season at the end of the Order of Mass in the *Collection of Masses of the Blessed Virgin Mary.*

The communion antiphon, "Jesus Christ is the same yesterday, today, and for ever," seems to have the new year in mind. The entrance antiphon combines a prophecy from Isaiah with a fulfillment in Luke. The alternative text comes from the works of Sedulius, a fifth-century Roman who authored a poetic version of the gospels.

OTHER IDEAS

You might conclude the general intercessions with the collect for the Mass of "Beginning of the Civil Year" (Various Needs and Occasions, #24), from texts that otherwise cannot be used today.

Music for today may continue with the singing of Christmas carols. Good choices include "What Child Is This?" and "Of the Father's Love Begotten." Christopher Walker's stately gospel version of "At the Name of Jesus" from the collection of the same name is available from Oregon Catholic Press. Fitting for the day is the *Te Deum,* most popularly sung as "Holy God, We Praise Thy Name." The original chant is in the *Liber cantualis.*

Among the prayers of thanksgiving after Mass in the sacramentary's first appendix is one to the Virgin Mary, acknowledging her as Mother.

NEW YEAR'S EVE

Some parishes merge a New Year's Eve party with liturgical celebration. Many members will appreciate a safe and sober family event. A party could follow the evening eucharist, or lead up to a midnight prayer of vigils or eucharist.

A celebration of vigils inspired by the *Liturgy of the Hours* (vol. I, p. 479ff, and Appendix I, p. 1622ff) could happen as follows:

Entrance procession: While the church is in semidarkness, ministers may light the candles of the altar and assembly while a version of the invitatory (Psalm 95, 24, 67 or 100) is sung.

Greeting: V. Light and peace in Jesus Christ our Lord. R. Thanks be to God.

Office of Readings: The *Liturgy of the Hours* suggests "Virgin-Born, We Bow Before Thee" for the hymn, followed by a selection of psalms. The readings include a passage from a letter of Saint Athanasius, concerning Mary's role in the incarnation.

Office of Vigils: One or more canticles may be sung, as indicated (vol. I, p. 1622ff). Then the gospel of the resurrection may be proclaimed. You may repeat Luke's version (24:1–12) if you used it at Christmas vigils, or perhaps use John's (20:1–8). Then follows the recommended gospel (John 20:19–31). The Office of Vigils says that text may be substituted by another gospel from the feast, "which is not read at Mass this year," but those do not exist. Tonight, John's prologue, from the Mass during the day on Christmas Day, seems perfect: "In the beginning . . ."

Mass: If Mass follows, omit the *Te Deum* and begin with the Glory to God.

If you do not want to observe the entire vigil outlined above, select some of its elements, or replace some with alternative scriptures and Christmas carols.

The *Book of Common Worship* for the Presbyterian Church (U.S.A.) and the Cumberland Presbyterian Church recommend this prayer for peace, composed by Brother Roger of Taizé (p. 795). It could conclude the general intercessions:

> Lord Christ,
> at times we are like strangers
>   on this earth,
> taken aback by all the violence,
>   the harsh oppositions.
> Like a gentle breeze, you breathe
>   upon us the Spirit of peace.
> transfigure the deserts
>   of our doubts,
> and so prepare us to be bearers
>   of reconciliation
> wherever you place us,
> until the day when a hope of peace
> dawns in our world. Amen.

#205   white

Basil the Great (+ 379) and Gregory Nazianzen (+ 389), bishops, monastics, doctors of the church

F R I **2**

MEMORIAL

The first letter of John urges the readers to be faithful to the teachings they have received, to the promise of eternal life, and not to fall subject to false teaching. Psalm 98 is seasonal, repeating the text from Christmas Day. The gospel verses follow those we heard on December 31. This week's continuous reading from the first chapter of John tells the events accompanying the appearance of Jesus. Today, John the Baptist announces his coming. Incidentally, the fourth gospel never calls this prophetic figure "the Baptist." He is simply John.

■ TODAY'S SAINTS: Basil and Gregory, both great theologians of the Eastern tradition, were also best of friends from school days in Athens. Basil's monastic rule serves as the ideal for monastic life in the East. An anaphora attributed to Basil is a direct ancestor to Eucharistic Prayer IV. Gregory's remains lie in Saint Peter's in Rome. His tribute to Basil is in today's Office of Readings.

#206   white

S A T **3**

Christmas Weekday

Optional Memorial of the Most Holy Name of Jesus / white ■ More verses of the seasonal Christmas psalm (98) follow today's passage from the first letter of John, which proclaims that we are children of God. In the gospel, John the prophet introduces Jesus as the "Lamb of God who takes away the sin of the world." Today's passage from the fourth gospel also presents its description of the Lord's baptism, which is almost an afterthought by comparison with the stories in the other gospels;

John's account never even says explicitly who baptized Jesus. These scriptures reveal more about the child born in Bethlehem and the implications of his birth for believers.

■ TODAY'S OPTIONAL MEMORIAL, removed from the calendar after the Second Vatican Council, was restored in the third edition of the Roman Missal. Devotion to the Holy Name earned a date on the liturgical calendar rather late in history, 1721. At that time the Holy Name was to be observed on the Sunday between January 2 and 5, or on January 2 if no Sunday intervened. The Litany of the Holy Name can be found in *Catholic Household Blessings and Prayers* (pp. 335–39.) Paul Inwood's "Litany to Jesus Christ" (GIA G-5535) was inspired by this text.

#20 (LMC #16)   white
4 The Epiphany of the Lord
SOLEMNITY

ORIENTATION

At first, the antiphon for this morning's Canticle of Zechariah sounds hopelessly confused: "Today the Bridegroom claims his bride the Church, since Christ has washed her sins away in Jordan's waters; the Magi hasten with their gifts to the royal wedding; and the wedding guests rejoice, for Christ has changed water into wine, alleluia."

But it is easier to interpret in the light of the antiphon from Mary's canticle at tonight's evening prayer: "Three mysteries mark this holy day: today the star leads the Magi to the infant Christ; today water is changed into wine for the wedding feast; today Christ wills to be baptized by John in the river Jordan to bring us salvation."

These antiphons unveil the church's tradition that there were three major epiphanies of Christ: the visit of the Magi, the baptism in the Jordan and the miracle at Cana. In all three events, Jesus is made manifest as the Messiah.

Prior to 1969 the connection was easy to make every year, because the gospel for the Sunday after the Baptism of the Lord was that of the wedding at Cana. In the revision of the calendar, this now happens only in Year C, so this is the only year when we hear all three gospels about the traditional manifestations of Jesus. We will be celebrating the Second Sunday in Ordinary Time when the full meaning of these antiphons sinks in.

Epiphany means "manifestation," referring to the appearance of Jesus. The significance of this day is not just the arrival of the Magi, but the coming of Gentiles to adore the newborn King of the Jews. The event recognizes Jesus' rule over the entire world. Today celebrates his epiphany, manifestation or revelation to the nations as Son of God.

Many traditions about the Magi have evolved. The influence of Psalm 72 on the seasonal liturgy led to the belief that they were kings. An alternate translation calls them astrologers. The blessing today calls them wise men. The Bible says there were three gifts, but never says how many Magi brought them. Nonetheless, tradition claims there were three and even ascribed to them the names of Melchior, Balthasar and Caspar. In iconography, one is often depicted with dark skin. Their remains are said to be contained in an elaborate reliquary in the cathedral of Cologne, Germany.

Although most of the rest of the Christian world celebrates Epiphany on January 6, Catholics in countries where the day is not a holy day transfer the celebration to the nearest Sunday. This allows everyone to celebrate this festival in a Sunday gathering.

LECTIONARY

Use the readings for the Epiphany of the Lord. Texts for the Second Sunday after Christmas are for countries that celebrate the Epiphany liturgy Tuesday.

Matthew alone tells the story of the Magi. It contrasts the innocent newborn king with the deceitful Herod, while it recalls prophecies about the Messiah's birth. The refrain for Psalm 72 announces the theme of Jesus' universal kingship, even as it foretells the arrival of kings who will pay homage to God's own just king. Because of this psalm, the Magi often appear in iconography wearing crowns. Isaiah prophesies the arrival of caravans of camels bearing gold and frankincense to praise the Lord. But the short passage from the letter to the Ephesians states the main theme of this day most clearly: The Gentiles are coheirs and co-partners in the promise through Christ Jesus.

SACRAMENTARY

The Proclamation of the Date of Easter may follow the homily or communion prayer. The text and music are on page 52 and in the 1994 *Sacramentary Supplement*. Adjust the dates as follows: the Triduum celebrated between the eighth and the eleventh of April, Ash Wednesday on the twenty-fifth of February, Ascension on the twentieth (Thursday) or twenty-third (Sunday) of May, Pentecost on the thirtieth of May, and the First Sunday of Advent on the twenty-eighth of November.

The opening prayer recalls the revelation of Jesus to the Gentile nations. The prayer over the gifts refers directly to the gifts of the Magi. The communion prayer asks that we might recognize Christ in the eucharist, presumably as the Magi recognized him by the light of the star.

The preface is proper for the day (P 6) and refers to the revelation of Christ by the star's light. The preface for "Mary and the Epiphany of the Lord" from the *Collection of Masses of the Blessed Virgin Mary* (P 6) develops the same themes. If you use Eucharistic Prayer I, you may insert the special form of the prayer "In union with the whole Church." Eucharistic Prayer for Reconciliation II concludes with an Epiphany theme: "Gather people of every race, language and way of life to share in the one eternal banquet with Jesus Christ the Lord."

The solemn blessing is eloquent, but you may substitute another text, like prayer over the people #3 or #7.

The communion antiphon comes directly from the gospel, and the antiphon for the introductory rites recalls two prophecies fulfilled on this day.

OTHER IDEAS

The *Ceremonial of Bishops* suggests that there be a "suitable and increased display of lights" (#240). An ancient title for this day is "festival of lights." Additional candles and candle bearers for the entrance procession can set this feast ablaze in light from its beginning.

Be sure to sing all the verses of "We Three Kings," and enjoy the elaborate catechesis of the text.

The priest or deacon may sing the gospel to a simple tone, to highlight the importance of its message and this day.

Make a special presentation of gifts. In place of gold, funds for the poor; in place of frankincense, letters to legislators on behalf of the needy; in place of myrrh, gifts for the homebound and dying. Use your imagination, or rely on local traditions. This idea is also based on the *Ceremonial of Bishops*, 240.

You could bless chalk at the conclusion of the Mass, in imitation of Eastern traditions. Prepare small pieces of chalk in envelopes that bear the inscriptions:

20 +C +M +B 04

The number of the new year is split at the beginning and end. The initials C, M and B represent Caspar, Melchior and Balthasar, and the three crosses stand for "saint." The letters also abbreviate the prayer "Christus mansionem benedicat," "May Christ bless the house." As part of the blessings at the conclusion of Mass, include a text like this:

> May God, who provided a safe dwelling for the eternal Word, bless this chalk, the homes of the faithful, and the people who live there, through Christ our Lord.

Then give one piece of chalk to representatives of every household as people leave. They may take it home, gather around the inside of the front door, and use the chalk to inscribe the numbers and letters on the lintel while saying, "May Christ bless the house." Throughout the year those who come and go through that door will enjoy the blessing of Christ.

Coincidentally, the month of January takes its name from the Roman god Janus, the guardian of thresholds. This ritual casts a Christian interpretation over the threshold we cross at the beginning of the calendar year.

Another blessing for homes on Epiphany is in the *Book of Blessings* (ch. 50). See the shorter rite at #1617ff. Yet another is in *Catholic Household Blessings and Prayers*, pp. 126–29.

You may conclude the celebration of Epiphany with vespers or a concert by the parish choir. They may present again the music they have practiced for so long. Candlelight, incense and carols for everyone will create a festive gathering. Add a parish supper or open house. Show appreciation to all who worked to make Advent and Christmas a time of beautiful, glorious prayer. If you offer this event on Saturday night, you may celebrate the office of vigils, as outlined in the *Liturgy of the Hours*. See Christmas and Mary, the Mother of God, above for ideas.

Today's celebration suppresses the memorial of Elizabeth Ann Seton (+ 1821), the first American citizen to be canonized a saint. Her efforts to establish Catholic schools achieved enormous success. You may remember her and Catholic education in today's general intercessions.

#212 white

M O N 5 **John Neumann (+ 1860), bishop, religious, missionary, educator**
MEMORIAL

Readings for today are located in the lectionary under the title "Monday after Epiphany or January 7." That means these readings should be proclaimed the day after Epiphany, whenever it is celebrated in your country. In the United States, do not use the readings marked "January 5" today. You can use those in the year 2008 when January 6 falls on a Sunday.

The gospels this week take us through the four evangelists to show the coherence of evidence concerning Jesus' divinity as Messiah. In today's passage from Matthew, Jesus succeeds the ministry of John the Baptist, fulfills a prophecy about the rising of a great light, announces the theme of his preaching, and cures great crowds in demonstration of his power and mission. Continuing the first letter of John, today's first reading asserts the union of belief and love in the life of the Christian. Psalm 2, from a collection of royal poetry, states the Epiphany themes of the reign over all nations and the manifestation of Jesus as ruler.

Today's presidential prayers are from the saint of the day, not the season.

■ TODAY'S SAINT: John Neumann, a Redemptorist priest from Bohemia, served as bishop of Philadelphia from 1852 to 1860. A promoter of national parishes and the Forty Hours devotion, he also fostered the development of Catholic schools.

#213 white

T U E 6 **Christmas Weekday**

Optional Memorial of Blessed André Bessette (+ 1937), religious / white ▪ In performing the miracle of the loaves, Jesus establishes himself as the promised one and just ruler who provides for the hungers of his people. The first reading says that God loved us first and calls us to love in turn. This season especially encourages believers to share their love for all. Psalm 72, which appeared in Advent to prophesy the coming of the just king, reappears after Epiphany in fulfillment.

In the sacramentary the opening prayer and suggested antiphons restate the revelation of Christ among us. Use any Christmas or Epiphany preface.

This week's presidential prayers are in the sacramentary under the title "after Epiphany to the Baptism of the Lord." The opening prayer and suggested antiphons especially highlight the Epiphany theme. Use any Christmas preface or the one for Epiphany. Reviewing the Christmas prefaces this week enables us to pray them with Epiphany vision.

■ TODAY'S SAINT: André Bessette, Canadian by birth, lived a while in the United States before joining the Brothers of the Holy Cross. He spent most of his ministry in or near Montreal, where he lived a life of humility and service.

Puerto Rico, the Dominican Republic and Uruguay observe Epiphany today as a holy day of obligation.

#214 white

W E D 7 **Christmas Weekday**

Optional Memorial of Raymond of Peñafort (+ 1275), presbyter, religious / white ▪ Jesus walks on the water, an event the lectionary presents as a manifestation of his divinity. Gospels this week are showing "epiphanies" of who Jesus is. More verses of yesterday's psalm express the same mystery. John invites us into the mystery of God's love but also into acknowledging that Jesus is the Son of God, a proclamation that appears strongly here.

The opening prayer sustains the theme of the light of the nations.

■ TODAY'S SAINT: Raymond balanced careers of preacher, canonist and confessor to Pope Gregory IX. His treatment of canon law became foundational in the development of the church's discipline. He died at age 100.

#215 white

T H U 8 **Christmas Weekday**

Moving into Luke's gospel, we hear Jesus reveal himself as God's anointed one, as he reads a passage from Isaiah in the synagogue. The psalm of the past two days, acclaiming God's just king, continues. The first letter of John develops the expectations on the one who believes in God. If you love God, you must love your neighbor.

The antiphons for today are two classic passages from John's gospel, proclaiming the Word made flesh and God's promise of eternal life. The opening prayer again elaborates the theme of light.

#216 white

F R I 9 **Christmas Weekday**

To proclaim Jesus' fulfillment of messianic prophecies, the lectionary chooses a miraculous cure of a leper from Luke. There is nothing distinctive about the cure of this leper compared with that of others in the gospels, except that this one otherwise appears nowhere in the lectionary. Today's psalm of praise again captures the theme of the season more than the specific themes of the readings. In the first reading we hear of the testimony of life in the Son of God.

The opening prayer makes a direct reference to Epiphany's star, and the antiphons repeat the themes of the season.

■ TODAY GUATEMALA observes an optional memorial of the Spanish priest and martyr, Eulogius of Córdoba (+ 859), listed in the martyrology on March 11.

SAT 10 #217 white Christmas Weekday

Finally entering John's gospel, the week's readings about the manifestations of Jesus as Messiah conclude with a statement from John the Baptist, setting the stage for tomorrow's feast. This passage makes the claim that Jesus performed baptisms, a practice that the same evangelist elsewhere denies (4:1–3). The readings from the first letter of John conclude today with the affirmation that the Son of God has come and given the faithful the ability to recognize the One who is true. Another psalm of praise joyfully concludes the Christmas weekdays.

The antiphons recall the divinity of Jesus and the sharing of his riches with the faithful. The opening prayer blends the themes of incarnation and new creation.

■ IN PERU, today is a memorial of Blessed Anne of the Angels of Monteagudo (+ 1686), a Dominican who suffered physical ailments and spiritual trials.

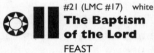

#21 (LMC #17) white
The Baptism of the Lord
FEAST

ORIENTATION

The baptism of the Lord is another epiphany, a manifestation of Jesus' identity to the public. Last week, Gentile Magi recognized him. Today, God proclaims him the beloved Son before the witnesses to the baptism. This feast concludes the Christmas season. The lectionary subtitles today the First Sunday in Ordinary Time. Vesture, however, is white.

The baptism of Jesus became difficult to explain early in Christian history. If baptism represents the forgiveness of sin, and if Jesus is sinless, why should he be baptized? You can see some growing embarrassment with the baptism as the gospels unfold. The synoptic gospels all present it rather plainly, and even the Acts of the Apostles refers to the event. But John's version, which appeared in the weekday lectionary on January 3, gives a more oblique account of the event. The baptism could not be ignored, and it seems that everyone tried to make sense of it.

On the simplest level, the baptism functions as the beginning of Jesus' public career and a manifestation of his true identity. That identity comes not from the washing of sins but from the booming

voice of the Father: "You are my beloved Son."

LECTIONARY

You have a choice of readings this weekend. The lectionary assigns Luke's account of the baptism as the gospel for Year C. But you may take the other readings from Year A or from Year C. You will hear the widest variety of readings over the three-year cycle by choosing all the Year C readings this year. But you may choose from Year A, with the exception of the gospel. That will be Luke.

Luke's account tells the story in two parts. We hear an announcement from John the Baptist that he is not the Christ. Then a voice comes from heaven announcing that Jesus is the beloved Son. The baptism itself is reported as a past event: "After Jesus had been baptized and was praying . . ." Luke downplays the baptism and highlights the theophany, the divine manifestation.

Luke's account may reveal some discomfort in the apostolic church over Jesus' baptism. The point of the event, and of today's feast, is not so much that Jesus was baptized, but that he is manifest as God's Son. Luke's peculiar description of the baptism does not say explicitly that John baptized Jesus. That information is clearest in Mark's account. As explained above in the commentary on the Fourth Sunday of Advent (December 21), the only explicit "meeting" between John and Jesus in Luke's gospel happens before they were born, at the visitation of Mary and Elizabeth.

The first reading for the Year C option comes from Isaiah. We often associate this prophecy with the season of Advent, because the gospels cite it when introducing

John the Baptist. It still makes a good complement for today. John the Baptist, one of the main Advent figures, is also an important Epiphany figure. He represents the culmination of the old covenant and the proclamation of the new. The Advent lectionary chooses other prophets for the first reading in Year C, so it is a relief to hear Advent's great prophet, Isaiah, close the Christmas season.

The psalm includes many Epiphany themes. It acclaims God "robed in light as with a cloak," dwelling "upon the waters," and sending forth the Spirit to renew the face of the earth.

The second reading for Year C is a combination of the two passages from Titus that appeared as the second readings for Christmas midnight Mass and the Mass at dawn. We may hear them again today to close the Christmas season. Its phrases ring with the sound of Epiphany: "The grace of God has appeared, saving all," and "the kindness and generous love of God our Savior [has] appeared." This appearance of God is especially evident in the baptism of Jesus.

You may choose the first and second readings from Year A instead. Peter's speech in the house of Cornelius recalls the baptism as the time when God anointed Jesus with the Holy Spirit and with power. The frequency with which this story appears in the New Testament gives testimony to its historicity. We hear from Isaiah the passage to which the voice of God in the gospel alludes. Psalm 29 is chosen because of its reference to the voice of the Lord thundering over the waters, an image made real in the gospel.

SACRAMENTARY

The entrance antiphon refers to Matthew's account of the baptism, and the communion antiphon mentions the testimony of John.

In place of the penitential rite today, consider using the rite of sprinkling with holy water. You may take this option on any Sunday, but today it will especially unite the themes of baptism and body of Christ.

There are three options for the opening prayer today. The first, a new composition, expresses the significance of the feast most clearly and remains free of the non-inclusive language that mars the alternative opening prayer. The extra prayer recalls strongly the image of the incarnation and may help conclude the season with a reflection on the meaning of Christmas. The preface (P 7) marvelously blends the themes of the baptisms of Christ and of the faithful, as well as the images from today's scriptures concerning the dove, the anointing and the gospel of salvation for the poor. The recommended prayer over the people provides a good blessing, but other choices could be made, like solemn blessing #2, #3 or #4.

OTHER IDEAS

Keeping the Christmas decorations in place till today may make people wonder if you have been postponing the task, but it is appropriate. You may catechize about the Christmas season's continuation through today.

By Flowing Waters (38–46) has a complete suite of antiphons and psalms for Epiphany and the Baptism of the Lord. At the sprinkling rite, you can sing "Springs of Water" from the Easter Vigil, with verses from 199 (see the performance note on p. 420).

Sing the Glory to God today, the same version you have used throughout this season. It will bring the celebration to a joyful conclusion. You may also sing Christmas carols, since it is still the season of Jesus' birth. Conclude also the singing of the acclamations you have used throughout the seasons of Advent and Christmas.

You may want to conclude the Christmas season with evening prayer tonight, a prayer of thanksgiving for the mystery revealed in a manger.

DECEMBER 25, 2003
The Nativity of the Lord

Salvation's Eyewitnesses
Isaiah 52:7–10
All the ends of the earth will behold the salvation of our God.

WHENEVER you *see* something great, you can feel the excitement. *Hearing about* something great just isn't the same. Travelers give vivid accounts of their journeys, the people they've met, the places they've seen and the events they've experienced. If something exciting happens on your street, you'll want to see it for yourself. Then you can feel the excitement.

Christmas is a celebration for the eyewitnesses of salvation. We have not just heard about it; we have experienced it. We know the fulfillment of God's promises, the presence of Christ and the hope of believers. We have experienced the wonder of God in our families, our friends, our church and our community. God is redeeming people.

Isaiah says that when those announcing good news about God come to the mountain of Jerusalem, they are beautiful to behold from head to toe. Even their feet are beautiful. "They see directly, before their eyes, the Lord restoring Zion." These eyewitnesses bring back to the city the exciting reports of God's work. It is not enough for us to hear about it. We look, see and experience firsthand the marvels God has done.

This Christmas we reflect on God's action in our lives. We experience the birth of salvation within us. We know from our own experience that God saves us. When we share that good news, we are beautiful. Even our feet are beautiful.

DECEMBER 28, 2003
The Holy Family of Jesus, Mary and Joseph

Offering What We Have Received
1 Samuel 1:20–22, 24–28
Samuel, as long as he lives, shall be dedicated to God.

IF you took a toddler to church and left the child there for the pastor to raise, you might be accused of negligence. But when we hear about Hannah performing a similar action in the first book of Samuel, we are to emulate the holiness of her family.

Hannah had gone childless throughout her life; in distress she prayed for a child in the temple at Shiloh and promised she would dedicate her son to God's service. Eli, the Hebrew priest at the temple, first mistook Hannah for a drunkard. But then he also prayed that God would grant her request. God answered Hannah's prayer, and Hannah made good on her promise. She brought a bull, some flour, some wine—as well as her son, Samuel—and gave them all to Eli. (See 1 Samuel, ch. 1, for the whole story.) She later bore five more children. Samuel eventually succeeded Eli as priest of the temple.

Although Hannah's specific actions would seem strange today, the general intent of her spiritual life remains an admirable model. Hannah asked God for a particular petition. When God granted her heart's desire, Hannah returned thanks to God by sacrificing what God had given her.

All our families strive to be holy, and every family can learn the basics of a friendship with God. If you want something, ask. If you receive it, give thanks.

JANUARY 1, 2004
The Blessed Virgin Mary, the Mother of God

Blessings of Protection, Grace and Peace
Numbers 6:22–27
They shall invoke my name upon the Israelites, and I will bless them.

WE begin the new year with hope. It is filled with possibility. Our calendars look empty, but they will soon be filled with activities and events. Some are already planned, while others will surprise us. We realize that this year will bring its measure of sorrow, but we trust it to bring its measure of joy.

Let this day and this year be a blessing!

Today we hear the words of blessing spoken by God to Moses. "The LORD bless you and keep you." They are words of protection. "The LORD be gracious to you." They are words of favor. "The LORD give you peace!" They are words that wish the finest blessing, the gift of peace.

This new year, with all its promise, gives us the possibility of blessing. Perhaps you have withheld blessing from someone you know. Perhaps you especially need God's gift of peace. Perhaps you fear the absence of God's protection. Let this blessing calm your heart. Let it inspire you to breathe God's gift of peace to all you meet this day and this new year.

Let the blessing of God, first spoken to Moses and echoing throughout the ages, enter your home and warm your hearth.

JANUARY 4, 2004
The Epiphany of the Lord

Camels Bearing Hope
Isaiah 60:1–6
The glory of the Lord shines upon you.

ABOUT those camels, we're not too sure about them. Yes, every nativity scene shows the Magi seated on stately dromedaries, or leading their beasts of burden by bit and rein. But, quite honestly, the story of the Magi never tells us how they got there. They could have traveled on foot, in chariot, by camel, on horseback, even on an elephant—we just don't know.

The reason we keep putting them on camels in our art is because of Isaiah's prophecy. He predicted that caravans of camels would fill Jerusalem, and that people from the East would come bearing gold and frankincense. "Rise up in splendor, Jerusalem!" he proclaims. "Your light has come."

In Matthew's story, the Magi realize that Jerusalem's light has come. They follow the star and bring their gifts of gold and frankincense—myrrh, too. By telling about these gifts, Matthew turns our attention back to Isaiah. Reading that prophecy, we realize that the light Isaiah mentioned is the Light of the World, Jesus Christ.

When we see the Magi seated on camels, we are remembering Isaiah. When we remember Isaiah, we remember the light that came to shatter the darkness of our world. Those camels carry hope.

JANUARY 11, 2004

JANUARY 11, 2004
The Baptism of the Lord

God's Grandeur
Isaiah 40:1–5, 9–11
The glory of the Lord shall be revealed and all people shall see it.

WHENEVER we glimpse the glory of God we experience briefly the happiness for which we hope. We can see that glory in the icy sparkle of a winter's day, in the birth of a child, in the excellence of athletes or in the beauty of the arts. The glory of God can be revealed in many ways, and it always brings joy.

We can only glimpse God's glory because its fullness remains hidden. As wonderful as this world is, the promised world of eternal life will be far greater. That hidden world opens to us in slits of time, in meteoric glints of space. We see God's glory in small signs, but they suffice to alert us to the grandeur of heaven.

Isaiah prophesied that the glory of God would be revealed in the reshaping of land and the witness of people. Deserts and wastelands would become paved paths, and all people would see it together. Exiles would return and God would appear with power.

The desert of Israel's longing became eternally transformed in the splash of Jordan's waters. There the glory of God was revealed as never before, at the baptism of Jesus.

As the Christmas season draws to its close, we reflect back on its joy. In the shimmering glow of a celebration that pushes back the enveloping darkness of nature's winter, we glimpse the glory of God.

THE PROCLAMATION OF THE BIRTH OF CHRIST

Introduction

1. The *Roman Martyrology* for Christmas Day contains a formal announcement of the birth of Christ in the style of a proclamation. It begins with creation and relates the birth of the Lord to the major events and personages of sacred and secular history. The particular events contained in the proclamation help to situate the birth of Jesus in the context of salvation history.

2. *The Proclamation of the Birth of Christ* may be sung or proclaimed after the greeting and introduction of the Christmas Midnight Mass. The Gloria and opening prayer immediately follow the proclamation.

3. The proclamation may also be sung or proclaimed at the Liturgy of the Hours. If it is used at morning or evening prayer, it follows the introduction of the hour and precedes the hymn. When it is proclaimed during the Office of Readings, it precedes the *Te Deum*.

4. According to circumstances, the proclamation may be sung or recited at the ambo by a deacon, cantor, or reader.

5. After the greeting of the Mass, the celebrant or another minister may briefly introduce the Mass and *The Proclamation of the Birth of Christ* which follows, using these or similar words.

Throughout the season of Advent, the Church has reflected on God's promises, so often spoken by the prophets, to send a savior to the people of Israel who would be Emmanuel, that is, God with us. In the fullness of time those promises were fulfilled. With hearts full of joy let us listen to the proclamation of our Savior's birth.

6. The deacon (or other minister) then proclaims the birth of our Lord Jesus Christ:

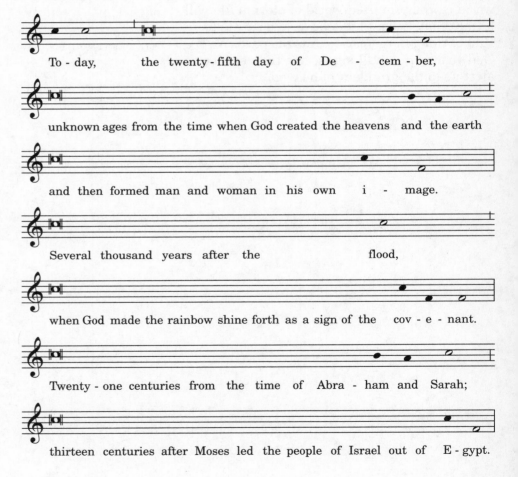

To - day, the twenty - fifth day of De — cem - ber,

unknown ages from the time when God created the heavens and the earth

and then formed man and woman in his own i - mage.

Several thousand years after the flood,

when God made the rainbow shine forth as a sign of the cov - e - nant.

Twenty - one centuries from the time of Abra - ham and Sarah;

thirteen centuries after Moses led the people of Israel out of E - gypt.

Eleven hundred years from the time of Ruth and the judges;

one thousand years from the anointing of David as king;

in the sixty-fifth week according to the prophecy of Dan - iel.

In the one hundred and ninety - fourth O - lympiad;

the seven hundred and fifty-second year from the foundation of the city of Rome.

The forty - second year of the reign of Octavian Augustus;

the whole world be - ing at peace, Jesus Christ, eternal God and

Son of the eternal Father, desiring to sanctify the world

by his most merciful coming, being conceived by the Ho - ly Spirit,

and nine months having passed since his conception,

was born in Bethlehem of Judea of the Virgin Ma - ry.

Today is the nativity of our Lord Je - sus Christ according to the flesh.

THE PROCLAMATION OF THE DATE OF EASTER ON EPIPHANY

Introduction

1. *The Proclamation of the Date of Easter on Epiphany* dates from a time when calendars were not readily available. It was necessary to make known the date of Easter in advance, since many celebrations of the liturgical year depend on its date. The number of Sundays that follow Epiphany, the date of Ash Wednesday, and the number of Sundays that follow Pentecost are all computed in relation to Easter.

2. Although calendars now give the date of Easter and the other feasts in the liturgical year for many years in advance, the Epiphany proclamation still has value. It is a reminder of the centrality of the resurrection of the Lord in the liturgical year and the importance of the great mysteries of faith which are celebrated each year.

3. The proclamation may be sung or proclaimed at the ambo by a deacon, cantor, or reader either after the gospel or after the prayer after communion.

4. Each year the proper dates for Holy Thursday, Easter, Ash Wednesday, Ascension, Pentecost, and the First Sunday of Advent must be inserted into the text. These dates are found in the table which is included with the introductory documents of the *Sacramentary*. The form to be used for announcing each date is: the *date* of *month*, e.g., "the seventh of April."

5. On the solemnity of the Epiphany, after the homily or after the prayer after communion, the deacon or, in his absence, another minister announces the date of Easter and the other feasts of the liturgical year according to the following text.

Dear broth-ers and sis-ters, the glory of the Lord has shone up-on us, and shall ever be manifest among us, until the day of his re-turn. Through the rhythms of times and sea-sons let us celebrate the mys-ter-ies of sal-va-tion. Let us recall the year's cul-mi-na-tion, the Easter Tri-du-um of the Lord: his last supper, his cruci-fix-ion, his burial, and his rising, celebrated be-tween the eve-ning of the eighth of April and the eve-ning of the eleventh of April. Each Eas-ter as on each Sun-day the Holy Church makes present the great and sav-ing deed

by which Christ has for ev-er con-quered sin___ and death.

From Eas - ter are reckoned all the days we keep ho - ly.

Ash Wednesday, the beginning of Lent, will occur on the twenty-fifth of February.

The As-cension of the Lord will be commemorated on the twentieth of May.
[twenty-third] [May]

Pente - cost, the joyful conclusion of the sea-son of Easter,

will be celebrated on the thirtieth of May.

And this year the First Sunday of Advent will be on the twenty-eighth of No-vember.

Like-wise the pilgrim Church proclaims the passover of Christ

in the feasts of the holy Mother of God, in the feasts of the A-pos-tles and Saints,

and in the commemoration of the faith-ful de-part - ed. To Je-sus Christ,

who was, who is, and who is to come, Lord of time and history,

be endless praise, for ev-er and ev - er. A - men.___

Alternate Amen

A - men.___ A - men.___ A - men.

WINTER ORDINARY TIME

The Meaning

However artificial the conditions of modern living, however out of touch people may be with the earth and its cycles of growth and decay, it makes for sanity and wholeness if we can still respond through our bodies to the elemental experiences from which our forebears learned wisdom. Winter means darkness, cold and apparent barrenness; or, more precisely, a sensory experience of certain contrasts: darkness and light, frozenness and thaw, sterility and fruitfulness. . . .

Midwinter darkness must have been a vast, powerful, mysterious reality for generations with no electricity or gas and very little oil. The forests were thicker and more extensive than today, and there were no lighted buildings or motorways to provide islands or strips of luminosity: only a huge engulfing superstitious terror; the winter was a time to dread, when food would be short, some members of the tribe might die, and everyone would be cold and hungry.

—Maria Boulding, *The Coming of God,*
Third edition (Conception, Missouri:
The Printery House, 2000), pp. 27–28.

ORDINARY Time appears each year in two periods of unequal length. It fills the short space between the Advent/Christmas cycle and the Lent/Triduum/Easter cycle, and the long space that follows the Easter season and runs to the end of the year. The precise dates and length of this time are based almost entirely on the date of Easter. The later Easter falls, the longer the first part of Ordinary Time.

This time is "ordinary" not in the sense that it is "plain" or "unusual," but because it is "counted"; it keeps pace with the order of time. Perhaps a better name would be "ordinal time."

■ ORDINARY TIME BEGINS with the Baptism of the Lord. The lectionary explains that the Baptism, which closes the Christmas cycle, is the First Sunday of Ordinary Time. As John the Baptist bridges the Old and New Testaments with his prophetic testimony, so the Baptism of the Lord bridges two seasons. It is a further manifestation of Jesus in a season marked by epiphanies. It is the beginning of the public ministry of Jesus, which we will follow in sequential gospel readings throughout both parts of Ordinary Time.

■ THIS YEAR WINTER ORDINARY TIME IS OF AVERAGE LENGTH. Between 1998 and 2009, the season ends precisely on February 24 three times.

■ THE CARNIVAL SEASON BEGINS at Epiphany and reaches its crescendo on the night before Ash Wednesday. We call that day Mardi Gras, or "Fat Tuesday." Parades and parties increase in the days before Lent as people make festival before making fast. Although the liturgical texts do not support a pre-Lenten season resembling the joy of Easter, the secular world has introduced the custom among those bracing themselves for the rigors of Lent.

■ FEBRUARY IS BLACK HISTORY MONTH. Intercessions, homilies and music from the African American tradition will help the community recognize this observance.

The Saints

DURING Ordinary Time, the celebration of the saints may progress unfettered by seasonal restrictions.

■ DAYS RANKED AS "FEAST" receive full attention and replace the other days of Ordinary Time. However, two feast days fall on Sunday this year. We will celebrate neither the Conversion of Paul on January 25 nor the Chair of Peter on February 22, unless your community has Peter or Paul as patron under these titles. The only feast we celebrate on a weekday this winter is the Presentation of the Lord, February 2. Its opening ritual for the lighting and blessing of candles always calls for careful preparation.

Last year when February 2 fell on a Sunday it took precedence over Ordinary Time because the Presentation is a feast of the Lord. Feasts of the Lord take precedence over Ordinary Time Sundays. Other feasts, like those of the apostles, do not.

■ WHEN AN OBLIGATORY MEMORIAL COMES UP (and there are many of these ranging from the virgin and foundress Scholastica, February 10, to the bishop and martyr Polycarp, February 23), use its vestment color and presidential prayers, including the preface. If the saint comes without a complete set of proper prayers, turn to the relevant common of martyrs, pastors, doctors, virgins or holy men and women.

On memorials the scriptures should generally continue the semi-continuous readings of Ordinary Time, but you may take them from the lectionary common appropriate for the saint. Many of the saints' days have recommended readings in the proper of saints, but these, too, are optional.

■ WHEN AN OPTIONAL MEMORIAL OCCURS ON A WEEKDAY (and there are many of these also, ranging from the bishop and martyr Blase, February 3, to Our Lady of Lourdes, February 11), your community may elect to celebrate the Ordinary Time Mass or the Mass of the saint. You may also choose from the list of many lesser-known saints in the martyrology. You may then choose the prayers for the saint from the sacramentary as well as readings from the lectionary commons. But ordinarily, follow the readings of the Ordinary Time weekday. That allows those who participate in daily Mass to hear the semi-continuous course of readings, to unite themselves with those at home whose daily prayer incorporates the lectionary, and to observe the recommendation of the lectionary.

When a Saturday in Ordinary Time calls for the weekday liturgy, a Mass from the *Collection of Masses of the Blessed Virgin Mary* or from the commons may be used. During this period, however, only two Saturdays are free of obligatory observances: February 7 and 21.

■ Special concerns, devotions and civic events: The lectionary and sacramentary also supply the texts of Masses for various needs and occasions. These texts may be used throughout Ordinary Time. On Ordinary Time weekdays and optional memorials, you may freely but sparingly choose from these Masses (GIRM, 327). On obligatory memorials during this period, the presider may choose a Mass for various needs and occasions only for serious need or pastoral advantage. For example, if the community fears the threat of a serious winter storm, the presider may choose the prayers from the appropriate Mass (#37), even on Agatha's day, February 5. Only your bishop may authorize the same Mass for a Sunday in Ordinary Time.

Included during these weeks each year is the national holiday in remembrance of the life and work of Martin Luther King Jr. Two events span a series of days during this period as well: the Week of Prayer for Church Unity and Catholic Schools Week call for some kind of liturgical recognition. You may find inspiration in the Masses and Prayers for Various Needs and Occasions: #13, For Unity of Christians; #14, For the Spread of the Gospel; #18, For Those Who Serve in Public Office; #21, For the Progress of Peoples; or #22, For Peace and Justice. Schedule times of prayer to recognize these events on the parish calendar.

The Lectionary

THE gospel for the Second Sunday of Ordinary Time comes from John in all three years of the cycle. After that weekend, though, the year's featured evangelist settles in. The lectionary draws primarily from chapters 4 to 6 of Luke's gospel during these weeks, detailing the Galilean ministry of Jesus.

Every Winter Ordinary Time opens with second readings from the first letter of Paul to the Corinthians. During Year C, we hear the final chapters of this important epistle. This year, all the second readings in Winter Ordinary Time come from this same book. The body of Christ, the hymn to love and the doctrine of the

resurrection—all themes that appear in popular excerpts this year—will delight the readers and hearers of God's word.

The first readings for this set of Sundays come primarily from the prophets. They are chosen, of course, because each carries a theme that foreshadows an event or saying in the gospel.

Each Sunday comes with its own responsorial psalm, but your community may build its musical repertoire by selecting one from the common psalms for Ordinary Time. They may be used on any Sunday throughout the season. These psalms (19, 27, 34, 63, 95, 100, 103 and 145) explore the greatness of God, the wonders of God's word, and the thirsty spirit yearning for divine union.

■ The Sunday *Lectionary for Masses with Children* follows the same course of readings, with minor variations. The shorter form of readings is preferred. Sometimes a verse is added or subtracted, but substantially all the texts are the same. The second reading is omitted entirely only on the Seventh Sunday. The psalm on the Sixth Sunday changes from 1 to 40. The refrain that day comes from Psalm 40 in the main lectionary, and the children's lectionary shifts the verses to match it.

The Sacramentary

■ Sample formulas for the general intercessions appear in the sacramentary's first appendix. (See #1–2 and 9–10 for those suggested for Ordinary Time.)

Ordinary Time is a good time to evaluate some of the things we do ordinarily. Consider, for example, the communion rite. The communion rite includes the Lord's Prayer and its doxology, the sign of peace, the breaking of the bread, the private preparation of the priest, communion, the communion song, the period of silence or song of praise, and the prayer after communion.

■ The Lord's Prayer is one of the treasures of our faith. We formally hand it on to the elect during the Fifth Week of Lent each year. It also forms the backbone of the fourth part of the *Catechism of the Catholic Church.*

Many communities sing the prayer each Sunday. This laudable practice adds elegance to the prayer and sets the tone for the entire communion rite. The words of the Lord's Prayer are so special that a musical setting can elevate them far beyond normal speech. All communities should at least know the chant version found in Appendix III of the sacramentary. Oddly, the chant in the middle of the sacramentary is not as well known. Other musical settings are quite fine, especially those by Christopher Walker and Steve Warner (WLP 7204).

What to do with one's hands? The most ancient gesture for prayer is to raise one's hands toward heaven. The priest adopts this posture whenever he prays the Lord's Prayer, as he does with the presidential prayers in general. In some communities the faithful join the priest in this gesture, so all pray in the same way. Because of its potential for uniting the entire community in the same gesture and its ability to join today's assembly with those of the early church, this gesture may be the best option.

Other communities, however, join hands. This gives the faithful a sense of bonding together in a text prayed in the first person plural. After all, it's not "My Father, give me today my daily bread and forgive me my trespasses."

Still others fold their hands. These hands, so busy and versatile, rest folded quietly in reverence to help center the spirit during prayer.

Different gestures can be found within the same community. What do your people do? Why do they do it?

■ THE SIGN OF PEACE allows the community to express its unity before sharing it in the sacrament of the eucharist. The now-traditional handshake makes it look like we are greeting people next to us for the first time. That may be true, but that is not the purpose of the sign of peace. It is a rite by which the members of the assembly offer some sign of their unity and mutual love for each other. The time to shake hands and introduce oneself is *before* Mass. This is the time for peace.

Some communities take a long time for this ritual. People leave their places and circulate through the room to let the love of the Spirit spill out and overflow. Others are more reserved. Still others do not offer the sign of peace at all. It still remains an option in the liturgy, but to omit it may raise suspicions that the community has no unity of mutual love to share.

The sign of peace is not the time for the choir to check page numbers, for the presider to correct the servers, for making appointments or offering birthday greetings. It is the time to share peace.

■ THE BREAKING OF THE BREAD was so significant in the apostolic church that it became the title for what we call eucharist or Mass.

The ritual has a practical purpose. It divides the consecrated bread and wine so that many people can share the sacred species.

It has a symbolic purpose. It binds us as one because we share of the one bread and the one cup.

It has a mystical purpose. As the body of Christ is broken and the blood of Christ is poured, we experience again the sacrifice Jesus made for sinners. The breaking of bread is an action of love.

In many communities this doesn't take much time at all because the presider uses a 3¼" host that he divides into three with a couple of quick snaps. Many presiders drop a small portion in the cup and then consume the other two. This completely obliterates the purpose of breaking the bread. When the assembly eats from pre-formed hosts, they eat bread that was broken months before Mass takes place. When they eat the hosts from the tabernacle, they are even further removed from the sign of the one bread and one cup.

In other communities the presider consecrates larger hosts or loaves of bread that can be broken at this time. Everyone receives part of something. The breaking of the bread will take some time, and the assembly can better meditate upon its many meanings.

Although this ritual is named after the bread, the consecrated wine is poured at this time as well. A pitcher or flagon may rest on the altar throughout the liturgy of the eucharist, together with one cup. At this time, other cups are brought to the altar and the blood of Christ is poured. This keeps the altar uncluttered throughout the eucharistic prayer and allows people to visualize the cup of salvation.

During the breaking of the bread the Lamb of God is sung. It makes more sense to sing this if the breaking takes more than two snaps and if the pitcher is poured into multiple cups.

■ THE PRIVATE PREPARATION OF THE PRIEST is one of several prayers the presider says quietly or "inaudibly," as the sacramentary puts it. Two options are given. The text is meant to help the presider remain at prayer all the time, even when not speaking aloud. At Mass the priest leads the community in prayer with invitations like "Let us pray." He should be immersed in the action of prayer, centered on God, throughout the liturgy.

These prayers should not be prayed aloud, although sometimes they are, with the assembly answering "Amen." This strangely adds another collect to the liturgy, one not intended by the rite. The *General Instruction of the Roman Missal* (#56f) notes that the people should also be preparing to receive communion "by silent prayer." Presiders should avoid saying or doing things at the public liturgy that are private by nature; at the same time, this is a prayer that pertains to his role and his heart.

■ COMMUNION FOLLOWS. For the communion rite to have its full meaning, it is important that the faithful share from the bread and wine consecrated at the Mass they attend. Trips to the tabernacle should be rare. Many parishes commonly send one communion minister to the tabernacle to retrieve hosts consecrated at previous Masses. Such a policy is contrary to the spirit of the liturgy and obstructs the conveyance of the meaning of communion. Set out enough bread and wine before Mass, as you would prepare enough food for your family for dinner.

Communion under both forms is the fuller and more complete sign of the eucharist. Jesus said, "This is my body; take and eat." He did not say, "This is my blood, but you can pass if you like." Many Catholics have the deplorable habit of not receiving under both forms, and many parishes do not even offer the cup. Stranger still is the funeral or wedding where the family or the couple have determined ahead of time whether or not the assembly will be offered the cup. Why even ask such a question? A parish policy could make the cup available at *every* Mass.

The rubrics of the Mass in the missal of Paul VI never invited the assembly to kneel after the Lamb of God. But globally the practice became quite common. Members of the assembly still commonly kneel after the Lamb of God, stand to join the communion procession, and then kneel after returning to their place. None of that kneeling was envisioned in the reforms of the Second Vatican Council, although it is permitted in the revised *General Instruction of the Roman Missal*. Nonetheless, in the language of liturgy, standing is the main posture for prayer. The sharing of communion is an action of the body, not just of individuals. It calls for a common posture of praise and unity.

Having several communion stations should help the flow of the rite. In some parishes, communion takes a long time because of an inadequate number of stations. No one should feel rushed, but communion is an action that should happen within a fairly short period of time so that the sense of unity—not individuality—is maintained.

■ SINGING THE COMMUNION SONG will improve if the assembly stands for the rite. Communion is the most appropriate time for singing, because the song blends the voices of the community in ecstatic praise of God who loves us enough to become part of us. Usually a song with a refrain works best, so people need not be encumbered by books when processing and sharing communion.

■ THE PERIOD OF THANKSGIVING that follows communion may invite people to silence or song. If the members of the community have stood for the communion rite, they are seated after all have shared communion and after the song is complete. Then they may sit together, as a body, for the period of thanksgiving. In many parishes, the closing of the tabernacle door cues people to sit, a ritual that exists nowhere in the rubrics. The signal that communion is over is the end of communing and the end of song, not the reposition of leftover hosts.

In some parishes, this silence is broken by announcements. This totally misconstrues the purpose of the period. It is a time for all to turn their attention to God, not to the presider or cantor.

If a song is sung, it would be appropriate to stand for it. The singing will be more robust and purposeful.

■ THE PRAYER AFTER COMMUNION closes the communion rite. It takes place at the chair, not at the altar. A server should hold the book and be in place even before the presider says, "Let us pray." If a period of silence has just happened, the presider need not introduce another one here. But the presider should be praying. Anytime we recite the words of a prayer, our hearts should be completely centered on God.

The Book of Blessings

A community that has been blessed by God will want to offer blessings in turn. These include those for a mother before and after childbirth (ch. 1-VIII), parents after a miscarriage (1-IX), parents and an adopted child (1-X), birthdays (1-XI), the sick (2), pilgrims (8) and travelers (9). There are also blessings for a new school (14), a new library (15), a parish hall or catechetical center (16), a gymnasium or athletic field (20), means of transportation (21), technical installations and equipment (23), tools (24), fields and flocks (26), seeds at planting time (27), an athletic event (29) and meals (30).

These blessings may be incorporated into the community's Sunday worship or take place on some other special occasion.

The Rite of Christian Initiation of Adults

■ FOR THOSE LOOKING TOWARD BAPTISM THIS EASTER, Winter Ordinary Time becomes a crucial period. During these weeks the community should be making its final assessment, discerning who is called to the sacraments this spring. This discernment should precede the Rite of Election, which usually coincides with the First Sunday of Lent. All ministers, including the entire community, "should, after considering the matter carefully, arrive at a judgment about the catechumens' state of formation and progress" (RCIA, 121). You might consider a special evening of prayer to help those who are making this deliberation.

For a book that develops ideas for the liturgy as well as the music for the rites, see OCP's "Christ We Proclaim" (11293), edited by Christopher Walker. This remarkable collection offers a thorough presentation of the rites of initiation, complete with practical suggestions for adaptation and celebration. It contains some music for all the rites and makes suggestions for other music easily found in other collections.

■ OTHER LITURGIES OF THE CATECHUMENATE may take place in full force during this time. The Rite of Acceptance into the Order of Catechumens may be celebrated two or three times a year (RCIA, 18-3). Schedule it for some Sunday this season if you have inquirers this year. Most likely, these will not be baptized this Easter, but will remain catechumens through this year until next, in order to complete their formation (*National Statutes for the Catechumenate*, 6).

■ YOU MAY ALSO CONDUCT CELEBRATIONS OF THE WORD OF GOD (RCIA, 81–89). These may include minor exorcisms (#90–94), blessings of the catechumens (#95–97), or even an anointing with the oil of catechumens (#98–103). If the community does not often witness the use of the oil of catechumens, this provides a good opportunity for catechesis and celebration. If the supply is low, the local priest may bless more, a ritual that could also take place in the presence of the community. (While a priest may bless the oil of the sick and the oil of catechumens, only a bishop consecrates chrism. If you run out of chrism, get more from the bishop.)

The Liturgy of the Hours

TURN to Volume III of the four-volume set for this season's Liturgy of the Hours. New users will find this the perfect season of the year to become acquainted with the format. The feasts and seasons of the year require many ribbons just to keep the flow of the liturgy, but the Ordinary Time prayer is arranged rather neatly. You could introduce morning and evening prayer at different occasions of this season to celebrate any of its special events. Follow the liturgy in the book, or adapt it with a sung celebration in the parish involving cantors, musicians and ministers.

Don't forget about the beautiful collection of religious poetry in Appendix IV. These compositions by Augustine, Dante, Saint Theresa and John Donne, among others, will enrich your people. Provide a text as a live meditative reading or as a printed poem in the bulletin or on the website.

The Rite of Penance

THE way pastoral practice has unfolded, this is usually "off-season" for reconciliation. Advent and Lent become primary times for the celebration of this sacrament. Still, sin knows no season, and opportunities for reconciliation will challenge the community toward its continuous spiritual development.

Make sure the regular celebration of individual confession of sins and absolution is well advertised. Use the bulletin, the signage at the church and the website. If you plan a communal reconciliation service, expect it to be poorly attended. Most Catholics will wait for Lent, but some will take advantage of the opportunity to make amends with God and the community.

If you are affiliated with a Catholic school, this may be a good season to celebrate the sacrament communally. It will spare the confessors who have a busy season coming up in March and April. When celebrating the sacrament with children, try to keep the service brief. Do several short communal services in a row for small groups of children, rather than one large one that keeps all the children waiting. With several confessors, you can celebrate for each group of children in about a half an hour.

■ FEW CONFESSIONS actually observe the outline for the reconciliation of individual penitents as explained in the 1975 *Rite of Penance*. This may be a good season to catechize people. Most penitents start with "Bless me, Father, for I have sinned. It has been (number) of (weeks, months, years) since my last confession. These are my sins." But the rite has another outline in mind.

The priest welcomes the penitent warmly (*Rite of Penance*, 41). The penitent makes the sign of the cross, and the priest invites the penitent to trust in God (#42). The priest may read a passage of scripture (#43). *Then* the penitent confesses the sins (#44).

Many Catholics celebrate reconciliation infrequently, and it may be hard for them to establish a new pattern. But a parish could make an effort to include scripture in the celebration of reconciliation—through preaching, adult education and the preparation of children.

The Pastoral Care of the Sick

IF you have not celebrated this sacrament communally at Mass, this would be a good season to do so. Those beleaguered by winter weather, yet freed from the demands of Christmas and Lent, might appreciate an opportunity to celebrate the anointing of the sick. The introduction to this rite (#1–4) opens with a beautiful meditation on human sickness and its meaning in the mystery of salvation. It deserves much reflection to help people distinguish between sickness and sin. Illness is not a punishment from God. But it can be an opportunity for grace. Care should be taken that the faithful understand who is eligible for the anointing (#8–15). The illness should be serious.

The Rite of Marriage

THROUGHOUT Winter Ordinary Time, there is little restriction on the celebration of the Rite of Marriage at Mass. If the wedding takes place on a Saturday night or Sunday, the wedding Mass may be used with its prayers and scriptures. Any Saturday evening wedding Mass fulfills a Sunday obligation.

This could be a good season to evaluate the parish wedding celebration. How do the entrance rites flow for the wedding? Do couples ever take advantage of the description of the procession in the *Rite of Marriage* (19), which indicates that they come in together? There is no rubric for a father giving away a daughter. There is an option for both parents to be part of the procession.

How is the sanctuary configured? Can the bride and groom be seen by the faithful when they give their consent? If the presider stands between them and the assembly, all should see their faces. Can the bride and groom be heard by the faithful? Attach a wireless microphone to the groom's lapel so all will hear the words of both bride and groom.

The Order of Christian Funerals

WINTER funerals may require some accommodations. If the assembly arrives wearing coats, is there a visible place to hang them up? If snow covers the ground, will assistance be needed at the cemetery?

Evaluate the celebration of funerals at your parish. How is the vigil conducted? The *Order of Christian Funerals* gives the outline for a beautiful scripture service. Is it observed, or does your community expect someone to lead a rosary at the wake? Who leads this service? It need not be a priest. If lay ministers lead it, have they received training and evaluation? Where does the wake service take place? It may be celebrated at the church, where the faithful are accustomed to gather, where hymnals are present, sanctuary furniture is in place, musical instruments are always prepared, and the spirit of prayer already abounds. Is there a secure place to keep the body of the deceased overnight at church? Are there volunteers who will truly keep vigil?

Many people find it easier to attend the vigil service rather than the funeral Mass the next day because of their work schedules. Has your community made the vigil a real liturgy? Are ministers of music available? Readers? Greeters?

The Art and Environment

THE look of the church should reflect the simplicity of Ordinary Time but not the barrenness of Lent. Transitional environment will help people make the shift out of the Christmas season, lulling them into the commonplace before the austerity of Lent. Use the winter plant life of your region. If possible, duplicate the shade and fabric of the vesture in appointments for the church. Be sure to give attention to the place of the assembly. Simple decorations where the assembly enters and gathers are just as important as those that adorn the sanctuary.

The Music

■ EUCHARISTIC ACCLAMATIONS: Choose a set of acclamations for the eucharistic prayer. Use them throughout this season. This could be a good time to learn a new set of acclamations. If the assembly has been singing a familiar set throughout the Christmas season, they may be ready for something new. It will also help mark the change in season.

■ YOU MIGHT ALSO EXPAND THE ASSEMBLY'S REPERTOIRE in a different way. For example, the people might learn a setting of the general intercessions or of the Our Father. Steven C. Warner's "The Lord's Prayer" (WLP 7204) could become a weekly staple in your parish, singable and prayerful.

Take a look through the indexes of your hymnal and participation aids. Use this period to become more familiar with the way you can reference scripture passages and the themes that emerge from them. Does your repertoire of hymnody need expansion to include songs of discipleship, service, mission or social concern?

Collections of hymns are available from a variety of publishers, and not many of these selections appear in popular participation aids. You will find it worthwhile to spend time with books like these: *Worship & Praise Songbook,* a collection of folk and contemporary music available from Augsburg Fortress, 1999; *Voices: Native American Hymns and Worship Resources,* a remarkable resource for hymns and prayers that speak to the heart, available from Discipleship Resources in Nashville, Tennessee; *Swift Currents and Still Waters* by John A. Dalles, which includes 65 hymn texts you can use with tunes in the book or to tunes your community knows (GIA G-5366); *Awake Our Hearts to Praise!* by Herman G. Stuempfle, another collection of hymn, song and carol texts that can be sung to a variety of tunes (GIA G-5302); and Randall Sensmeier's *Teach Our Hearts to Sing Your Praise* (GIA G-5632), which offers more hymn tunes, songs and carols. All these resources will offer your community fresh texts to sing and new tunes to learn. No one should be overburdened with too much new material, but you may find just the text you'd like for a special occasion.

You can add new life to old hymns by adding choir and instruments. See "Spirit Divine, Attend Our Prayer," arranged by Robert W. Schaefer for assembly, choir, percussion and brass (WLP 8704); "Sent Forth by God's Blessing, by Omer Westendorf and John Schiavone (WLP 8517); "We Are Your People," a text that fits the tune of "For All the Saints," arranged by Steven R. Janco (WLP 8623); "Concertato on Ellacombe," better known as "Go Make of All Disciples"; and "The Day of Resurrection," by Charles Thatcher (WLP 8656); and a "Concertato on Hymn to Joy," an arrangement of Beethoven's most popular hymn by Paul M. French (WLP 8698). See also "Jesus Christ, Bread of Life," by Steve Schaubel for a setting of the Largo from Dvořák's New World Symphony (WLP 5230).

Broaden the ethnic appeal of your repertoire with James V. Marchionda and Mark Rachelski's setting of "Just a Closer Walk with Thee" (WLP 8576) and Steven R. Janco's fine and fun arrangement of "Is There Anybody Here Who Loves My Jesus?" (WLP 8609). Henry Mollicone's "Hear Me, Redeemer" (Schirmer 4511) borrows a similar style. There is no end to the reflective, useful music from Taizé (GIA). In Spanish, it is hard to top "Nada te turbe," a confident hymn of trust, based on words by Saint Theresa of Avila.

■ PSALMODY: Settings of the psalms appear in almost every participation aid, but you may want to give attention to some fine octavos.

When it comes to responsorial psalmody, a very simple chant-like setting may be the very tonic to draw more attention to words than to music. See the very simple, practical and spiritual "Six Psalms for Sundays and Seasons," by Thomas M. Cosley (WLP 6208). Paul Lisicky's "You Are My Guide" (WLP 6204) accomplishes the same result.

If you want something a little more interesting, try Alan J. Hommerding's "Psalms in Canon" (WLP 6235), which enables choirs to sing in parts just by learning one melody. Michael Hay's "We Will Rest in You" (WLP 6246) is as effective a setting of Psalm 134 as you will find, and Paul Inwood's "Search Me, O God" (WLP 6217) is a moving rendition of Psalm 139. "How Happy Are They," by James J. Chepponis is a serviceable setting of Psalm 84.

If you want something even more jazzy, look for Paul A. Tate's "Glorify the Lord with Me!"

based on Psalm 111 (WLP 7487). "Show Us Your Way, Lord," by Ed Bolduc (WLP 7358) is syncopated enough for youth but relaxed enough for more settled tastes. "You Are My Rock," by Michael T. Pierce (WLP 6229) sounds like a spiritual. Paul A. Tate's "In You, Lord, I Have Found My Peace" (WLP 7395) interprets Psalm 31 with an ostinato for the assembly. Nicholas Palmer sets Psalm 116 to a bluesy accompaniment, "I Will Walk Before the Lord" (WLP 6256).

Psalm settings in Spanish and English include Julie Howard's "Here I Am, God" (WLP 7128), Pedro Rubalcava's "Alaben Todos" (WLP 12678) and Peter M. Kolar's "El Señor Es Compasivo" (WLP 12670).

■ CHOIR: Your parish choir may use this season to expand its repertoire. The classical literature is endless, but some recent reprints by composers of historical importance make this music even more available to you. Look for "Dixit Maria ad angelum" (WLP 5791) by Hans Leo Hassler (1564–1612); "I Will Not Leave You Comfortless" (Schirmer 1676) by William Byrd (1543–1623); "Hallelujah, Amen" (Schirmer 304) by George Frideric Handel (1685–1759); and "How Lovely Is Thy Dwelling-Place" (Schirmer 1713) by Johannes Brahms (1833–1897).

Richard Proulx has edited an entire collection of motets under the title "Catholic Latin Classics" (GIA, G-5776). The serious choir will want to have several of these in its repertoire.

From the contemporary literature for choir, consider "I Believe in the Lord," by William A. Wollman (WLP 8617), a beautiful hymn of trust; "God, Be Merciful unto Us," by David Seitz, a setting of Psalm 67 that is mostly in unison, unaccompanied; "Canticle of Daniel," by Jeffrey Honoré (WLP 8690), a difficult setting of a useful text; and an arrangement of the popular song, "The Gift to Be Simple," by Robert W. Schaefer (WLP 8687). The youth will enjoy "Give Us Your Peace" by Michael Mahler (GIA), a quiet, but insistent appeal to "let all the fighting cease."

Let your children's choir explore pieces like "Children of the Lord," by James V. Marchionda (WLP 7848) and the delightful "Two Copper Coins," by Dolores M. Hruby (WLP 7119).

■ ORGANIST: GIA is publishing an impressive series of compositions for organ solo. J. Christopher Pardini's "Toccata on 'Amazing Grace'" (G-5523) is a show-stopping postlude that is easier than it looks. Raymond H. Herbek's arrangements of "Four Schubert Classics for Organ" include "Ave Maria" and "Serenade" (GIA G-5385). Harold Owen offers "Twenty-Five Organ Harmonizations" that can be played to wake up a verse of some classic hymn tunes like "Nicaea" and "Ellacombe" (GIA G-5384).

■ HANDBELLS: GIA has published a wide range of music for handbells, as more Catholic parishes indulge this musical form that other Christian communities embraced long ago. There are dozens of titles, all of them well written and not difficult to perform. For a single collection, see "Hymns for Handbells," arranged by Philip L. Roberts (GIA G-5770), although it only scratches the surface.

The Parish and Home

ENCOURAGE reflection on the Sunday scriptures at home by providing people with references to them or to resources where they can be found. The United States Conference of Catholic Bishops' website is useful. See also LTP's *At Home with the Word* and *Palabra de Dios.*

Your religious education ministry could sponsor a table of resources making scripture study and commentaries available. Consider offering additional information about Luke's gospel, as we work through its early chapters.

■ RECOMMEND USE OF *CATHOLIC HOUSEHOLD BLESSINGS AND PRAYERS* for a wide variety of home celebrations. These include blessings for waking, washing and dressing; going out from home each day, at noon and coming home. Table prayers for Sundays can also be found.

LTP's *Blessings and Prayers* can be used for teaching children to pray.

The more ambitious may want instructions for praying the Liturgy of the Hours at home. You could provide catechetical sessions for those who are interested in the one volume edition.

■ THE FEAST OF THE PRESENTATION OF THE LORD, February 2, comes during this season. Encourage people to bring candles from home for the blessing. They may light them for family prayer throughout the year.

Texts

■ GREETING:
(Adapted from the sacramentaries of other language groups.)
Grace and peace in the holy assembly of God's church be with you.
The grace of our Lord Jesus Christ, the love of God, and the communion of the Holy Spirit be with you always.

■ INTRODUCTION TO THE PENITENTIAL RITE:
Brothers and sisters, before we hear the Word of God and celebrate the sacrifice of Christ, we should prepare ourselves and ask God for the forgiveness of our sins.
Let us prepare for the celebration of the eucharist by recalling that we are sinners.

■ RESPONSE TO THE GENERAL INTERCESSIONS:
The *Order of Christian Funerals* uses a formula with which many Catholics are unfamiliar. You could acquaint people with it by using it for the Sundays of Ordinary Time. Each petition concludes with "Lord, in your mercy." All respond, "Hear our prayer."

■ DISMISSAL OF CATECHUMENS:
Catechumens, God has filled the church with many spiritual gifts. Go forth now to develop your gifts through conversation, prayer and service. Go in peace.

■ EUCHARISTIC PRAYER: A Spanish sacramentary includes inserts for Sundays in two eucharistic prayers. In Prayer II, after the words "Lord, remember your church throughout the world," the presider adds, "and gathered here on Sunday, the day on which Christ conquered death and made us partakers of his immortal life." The same expression appears in Prayer III after the words "the entire people your Son has gained for you."

The German sacramentary has a similar practice. On Sundays, in Eucharistic Prayer II, following the words "You are holy indeed, the fountain of all holiness," the presider adds these words: "We come before your presence and celebrate in communion with the whole church the first day of the week as the day on which Christ rose from the dead. Through him, whom you have raised up to your right hand, we pray." The same sentence occurs in Eucharistic Prayer III on Sundays, after the words "a perfect offering may be made to the glory of your name."

January

MON 12
#305 (LMC #193–227) green
Weekday (First Week in Ordinary Time)

The readings for Ordinary Time weekdays appear in the lectionary right after those of the Easter season.

The gospels of Ordinary Time weekdays present semi-continuous readings of the synoptics in the order in which scholars believe they were written. We start with Mark, progress to Matthew and conclude the year with Luke. Mark's comparatively terse account presents a Jesus more rough-hewn than the other gospels describe. Mark's narrative moves swiftly, and his Jesus is the kind of character about whom we want to know more.

We start this gospel today not at its beginning but after the opening episodes of John the Baptist's proclamation, the baptism of Jesus and the test in the desert. We begin with the Galilean ministry of Jesus, as he summarizes his entire message and calls his first disciples.

The first readings for the next several weeks take us through an important period in Israel's history. The books of Samuel and Kings tell the story behind the prophetic and royal figures who animated the life of the chosen people during the years leading up to their exile. Traditionally these books make up part of what was called the "former prophets," and some scholars treated them as a unit of four books of Kings.

The story begins today with the rivalry of Hannah and Peninnah, the barren and fertile wives of El-kanah. Elkanah's plaintive question to the depressed Hannah— "Am I not more to you than ten sons"—implies the cheerless response, "Well, no." The emptiness that hangs over this story conceals the joy that will accompany a miraculous birth but foreshadows the void awaiting Israel as the books proceed.

The optimistic tone of Psalm 116 knows something the reader does not, that Hannah's prayers will be answered.

The sacramentary offers a set of presidential prayers for the first week in Ordinary Time, following those for the Easter season. You may choose any other Ordinary Time prayers you wish. Consider also the text "For the Spread of the Gospel" (Various Needs and Occasions #14). The entrance antiphon draws on images from the book of Revelation. The communion antiphons present Jesus as the source of life.

TUE 13
#306 (LMC #193–227) green
Weekday

Optional Memorial of Hilary (+ 367), bishop and doctor of the church / white ▪ The yearned-for happy conclusion to yesterday's first reading appears today. Hannah conceives and gives birth to her first child, Samuel. In place of a psalm, we respond with the words of Hannah, a canticle that inspired Luke's rendering of Mary's *Magnificat*.

Early in his ministry, Jesus exorcises an unclean spirit from a man in the synagogue. From the beginning of Jesus' ministry, Mark shows us the real enemy of the Son of God: the forces of evil. Jesus, who is all-good, stands in contrast to the unclean spirit.

Among the sacramentary texts, consider those for the Mass in Thanksgiving (Various Needs and Occasions #39A).

▪ TODAY'S SAINT: Hilary was born in Poitiers, nearly contemporary with a baptismal font that still exists in the city. He defended the church against Arians and suffered exile under Constantine. The lectionary's proper of saints recommends alternate readings that stress faith, priesthood and preaching. Readings of the weekday are generally recommended.

WED 14
#307 (LMC #193–227) green
Weekday

Jesus continues his ministry of healing, giving new life to those suffering from physical infirmity as well as those possessed. Mark establishes Jesus' authority over various forces of nature at the beginning of the narrative.

Samuel proves to be the perfect servant of the Lord. He answers the call in the temple, a theme of readiness echoed by Psalm 40. Today's first reading is a popular one among those seeking a direction from God in their lives.

The Mass for Priestly Vocations (Various Needs and Occasions #9) might be appropriate today.

THU 15
#308 (LMC #193–227) green
Weekday

Yet another miracle story is reported in today's gospel. A leper kneels to request a cure. Characteristic of the Jesus of Mark's gospel, the healer tells the leper to keep the cure secret.

In a blow to Israel the Philistines defeat the Israelite army and carry off the ark of the covenant. In this dramatic shift from yesterday's passage, the reading concludes in sadness. In Psalm 44, the community asks God for mercy.

Consider the sacramentary's prayers for the sick (#32).

The people of Guatemala celebrate their patronal feast today,

Jesus Christ of Esquipulas (Santísimo Jesucristo Señor Nuestro de Esquipulas).

FRI 16 #309 (LMC #193–227) green
Weekday

Reacting to Israel's sorry political situation, representatives ask the now-aged Samuel for a king as other nations have. Samuel basically says, "You'll be sorry." God alone is ruler over Israel. The royal psalm chosen for today includes several verses confessing that God is the splendor of Israel's strength.

After a few days, Jesus returns to Capernaum to preach. When believers present a paralyzed man to him for a cure, his first thoughts are to cure the sinful soul.

See the sacramentary's Mass prayers for those who serve in public office (#18).

SAT 17 #310 (LMC #193–227) green
Anthony (+ 356), monastic founder
MEMORIAL

To placate the people, Samuel anoints Saul as king over Israel in obedience to God's choice. Another royal psalm celebrates the strength God gives the king.

God's often incomprehensible choice appears in the gospel as well, as people question the pedigree of Christ's followers.

■ TODAY'S SAINT: Heralded as the founder of monasticism, Anthony gave away his possessions, fled to the desert, and attracted a band of followers. Use the texts in the sacramentary for today's memorial. The preface for Virgins and Religious (P 68) suits the day well. The lectionary's proper of saints recommends readings that reflect on the spiritual life, but the readings of the day are generally preferred.

18 #66 (LMC #61) green
Second Sunday in Ordinary Time

ORIENTATION

Although we have been celebrating Ordinary Time on weekdays, this is the first green-vestment Sunday. Simpler church decorations and green vesture will signal the gathered assembly that the ordinary days of winter have arrived. But something special is needed to keep these days from being cheerless, something more than leftover poinsettias.

The framers of liturgical texts chose to keep Epiphany in the forefront this Sunday: The gospel tells the manifestation of Jesus to his first followers. The antiphon for the introductory rites acknowledges that all the earth should give God worship and praise.

Today begins the week of prayer for Christian Unity. Under the old calendar, the octave began on this day with the celebration of the Chair of Peter, but the feast is now celebrated on February 22. The octave still concludes with a feast of the conversion of Saint Paul (although it will not be celebrated this year, since January 25 falls on a Sunday). On weekdays you may choose texts from the Mass for the Unity of Christians in the sacramentary (Various Needs and Occasions #13A, B and C, and preface P 76) and even the lectionary. Include this prayer for Christian unity among the intercessions. Use the first version of the Eucharistic Prayer for Various Needs and Occasions with this Mass if you wish, "The Church on the Way to Unity." *By Flowing Waters* (p. 292) has a complete suite of antiphons and psalms for the Votive Mass for the Unity of Christians.

LECTIONARY

Today's gospel used to be proclaimed every year on the Sunday after the Baptism of the Lord. Today it occurs only in Year C of the cycle. The story of the wedding at Cana in Galilee comes near the beginning of John's gospel, so it has some chronological appeal this early in Ordinary Time. But its real purpose is to continue the theme of manifestation, begun on the Epiphany and continued with the Baptism of the Lord. All of these events manifested Jesus to people. As we begin our Winter Ordinary Time, we meet Christ in his glory and power. Everything we do is in response to that manifestation of our Savior.

The first reading is a late passage from Isaiah that explores the theme of marriage. In reestablishing the covenant, God promises to call Zion "My Delight" and "Espoused." God rejoices in Israel as a husband rejoices in the bride. After hearing this first reading, the layers of meaning in the gospel become more complex. The miracle in the gospel is not just another hat trick to draw attention to Jesus. It is a sign that takes place at a wedding to indicate the love that God holds for the chosen people.

The psalm clearly has an Epiphany theme in mind. Its refrain exhorts us to proclaim God's marvelous deeds "to all the nations."

The second reading begins this year's semi-continuous passage from Paul's first letter to the Corinthians. No one will remember this, but we resume this letter where we left off last March. Each year of the lectionary cycle turns to this letter for the second readings that open Ordinary Time. In today's passage, Paul explains the many spiritual gifts that God puts at the service of the church. Although the gifts are many, there is one Spirit producing them and distributing them individually.

SACRAMENTARY

The alternative opening prayer includes the theme of God's watchful care. The prayer over the gifts cites 1 Corinthians 11:26—not today's lectionary passage, but from the same New Testament book that serves as the second reading this season. The entrance antiphon's universal theme fits with the continued celebration of Epiphany and with the week of prayer for Christian unity. Although the first communion antiphon comes from one of the most popular psalms, the rendering of the second phrase, "[The Lord has] given wine in plenty for me to drink," will cause those dealing with alcoholism to shudder. Any of the prefaces for Sundays in Ordinary Time may be used (P 29–36), and one of these presents the mission of Jesus (P 32). But notice P 76 for Christian unity, which refers to today's second reading. Or, if your community has not heard Eucharistic Prayer IV in a while, you may revive it today with its unchangeable preface. For the final blessing, Solemn Blessing #14 for Ordinary Time offers a generic possibility. But consider a simple prayer over the people, like #11. Both refer to heavenly gifts.

Another idea is to choose a solemn blessing from those listed for Ordinary Time at the end of the Order of Mass in the *Collection of Masses of the Blessed Virgin Mary.* Mary plays a role in today's gospel, so one of these might make a good closing to the celebration. Avoid the second, though, which assumes today is a memorial of Our Lady.

OTHER IDEAS

Since this long weekend honors Dr. Martin Luther King, you may include petitions for racial harmony and the further development of the nation's moral conscience.

MON 19 #311 (LMC #193–227) green
Weekday

U.S. civil observance: Martin Luther King Jr. ▪ The gospel assigned for this day resumes the early ministry of Jesus from Mark's gospel. Jesus finds himself in controversy over the behavior of his disciples, makes a pronouncement that distances himself from rote application of the law, and offers two sayings about cloth and wineskins to drive home the point.

Saul, God's chosen king, proves disappointing in his behavior. For his disobedience, Saul loses the favor of God. Instead of a royal psalm, we pray one that expresses God's disappointment in the hypocrisy of the sinner.

We remember Dr. Martin Luther King, a martyr for the causes of civil rights. Educational and worship materials in English, Spanish and Vietnamese are available from the National Catholic Conference for Interracial Justice, 202-529-6480. LTP offers one resource for commemorating Dr. King: "Amazing Days: Martin Luther King's Birthday," a handout with quotations, prayers and commentaries that can be used as a bulletin insert.

All the prayers for Mass may be replaced with a set recalling the work of Dr. King; for example, "For the Nation" (#17), "For the Progress of Peoples" (#21) or "For Peace and Justice" (#22). Even the scriptures may be taken from an appropriate celebration in the lectionary, like the Mass for Peace and Justice.

Remember to pray for church unity.

TUE 20 #312 (LMC #193–227) green
Weekday

Optional Memorial of Fabian (+ 250), pope and martyr/red ▪ *Optional Memorial of Sebastian (+ c. 250), martyr/red* ▪ The history of the kings of Israel continues as Samuel anoints David as Solomon's successor. David, the prototype of Jesus' royal reign, also appears in the royal psalm that responds to the reading. Although this reading is buried in an Ordinary Time weekday, it is one of the pivotal moments in Israel's history.

In the gospel passage, controversy with religious leaders continues as Jesus supports the morality of his disciples' behavior, which was attacked as contrary to the law.

▪ TODAY'S OPTIONAL MEMORIALS are for martyrs who suffered under the persecution of Diocletian. Fabian was chosen pope when a bird landed on him. Little is known of Sebastian, but he is a popular subject in the history of Christian art because his persecutors shot him with arrows. Both are buried in Roman catacombs. The lectionary's proper of saints recommends readings for Fabian that allude to his papal leadership. Those for Sebastian pertain to his martyrdom. The usual weekday readings are recommended, though.

The church unity octave continues today.

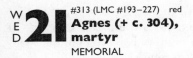

WED 21 Agnes (+ c. 304), martyr
#313 (LMC #193–227) red
MEMORIAL

Jesus again meets opposition, this time for curing on the Sabbath. Already the Pharisees and Herodians develop a plot to stop his ministry.

Young David establishes his authority in Israel by slaying the giant Philistine Goliath with a slingshot. The psalm chosen for this text includes a very bad pun in the refrain, "Blessed be the Lord, my Rock!"—exclamation point and all.

■ TODAY'S SAINT: Agnes died in the persecution of Diocletian at the age of 13. Sentenced to a house of prostitution for being a Christian, she maintained her virginity and her sanctity until her death. The acts of her martyrdom, dating from the fifth century, are unreliable. Today in Rome lambs are sheared at the Church of St. Agnes outside its walls. The wool is used to make the *pallium,* the special collar worn during liturgy by archbishops throughout the world. The Latin word for lamb, *agnus,* resembles the saint's name.

The opening prayer comes from the proper of saints. Draw the other texts from the many available options. If you used martyrs' prayers yesterday, consider those for virgins today. Agnes is among the saints listed in the first eucharistic prayer. The lectionary's proper of saints recommends readings about innocence and commitment. The psalm mixes the metaphor of shepherd and lamb. The readings of the weekday are preferred.

■ THE DOMINICAN REPUBLIC celebrates its patronal feast today, Our Lady of the Altagracia, or "full of grace." It is a holy day of obligation there. An image of Mary bearing this title was venerated in Santo Domingo as early as 1502. The painting was probably made in fifteenth-century Spain, but tradition holds a different story about a young girl who saw the image in a dream and begged her father for a copy. He was unable to locate one, but a mysterious old man with a white beard produced one from a satchel and then disappeared. Mary wears what became the national colors of the Dominican Republic.

THU 22 Weekday
#314 (LMC #193–227) green

Special Day of Prayer / violet ▪ Optional Memorial of Vincent (+ 304), deacon, martyr / red ▪ Unhappy with David's popularity, Saul plots to kill the new hero. Jonathan, Saul's son and David's friend, reports the news to David. A psalm of trust follows.

The darkness of controversy gives way to a bright day at the lake, as Mark's gospel begins a new section. Jesus preaches and cures great numbers of people.

You may use the sacramentary texts from the Mass for the Unity of Christians during this week of prayer.

■ TODAY'S SAINT: Vincent suffered under the persecution of Diocletian, as did Agnes, Fabian and Sebastian. Deacon to Bishop Valerius of Saragossa (in modern Spain), his name appears in sermons by Augustine. The lectionary's proper of saints recommends readings about persecution and martyrdom, but the readings of the weekday are generally preferred.

Today is also the anniversary of the Supreme Court's decision legalizing abortion in the United States. The American bishops have set aside today as a special day of prayer for human rights and equality, justice and peace. The Mass for Peace and Justice (#22) is celebrated today with violet vesture signifying penitence.

Chile, the country of her birth, and Argentina, the country of her death, have an optional memorial today for Blessed Laura Vicuña (+ 1904), a child who labored to earn tuition, suffered refusal to join a religious order, and was beaten by her mother's lover. At 13, she is the youngest person not a martyr to have been beatified.

FRI 23 Weekday
#315 (LMC #193–227) green

While the king of Israel relieves himself in a cave, David cuts off the end of the royal mantle. He uses it as proof that he could have killed Saul if he had wished. Saul weeps at David's generosity and accepts the future of David's kingship.

In Mark's gospel, Jesus appoints a group of companions known as "the Twelve." He gives them authority to preach and to expel demons. Throughout the New Testament, the names of the Twelve suffer some minor variation, but they always begin with Peter and include James, John and Andrew in the first group of four. The fifth is always Philip. Judas is always last.

This is the last day this week to use the sacramentary's prayers for Christian unity.

■ IN GUATEMALA, today is the optional memorial of the Spanish saint Ildephonse (+ 667), pupil of Isidore of Seville and bishop of Toledo.

SAT 24 Francis de Sales (+ 1622), bishop, religious founder, doctor of the church
#316 (LMC #193–227) white
MEMORIAL

Jesus has faced controversy with several groups of his enemies. It is surprising to modern readers to learn of the controversy he had with his family. Mark says that Jesus' relatives tried to seize him because they thought he was out of his mind.

David learns of the deaths of Saul and Jonathan. His grieving is one of the most soulful laments in the Bible. The psalm addresses God as the shepherd of Israel and appeals for salvation in a time of tears.

■ TODAY'S SAINT: A devout bishop and strong defender of the faith, Francis de Sales preached tirelessly, ministered to the needy, and wrote about spirituality. He died with the name of Jesus on his lips. Prayers come from the proper of saints, and recall Francis's compassion, gentleness and love. The lectionary's proper of saints recommends readings about preaching and love, but the readings of the weekday are recommended.

■ IN ARGENTINA today is the optional memorial of Mary, Queen of Peace.

☀25 #69 (LMC #64)   green
Third Sunday in Ordinary Time

ORIENTATION

Luke, the featured evangelist of Year C, makes his Ordinary Time appearance today in a remarkable piece of good news and good editing.

The week of prayer for the unity of Christians concludes today. Originally spanning the days between the celebrations of the Chair of Peter and the Conversion of Paul, the week sat under the patronage of the apostles most responsible for the spread of the Christian faith. The feast of the Conversion of Paul is suppressed

this year because today is Sunday. But if this is your church's patronal feast it takes precedence.

LECTIONARY

As we begin Luke's gospel, we hear the opening four verses of the entire book. Then the lectionary's editors have us pole vault over to chapter four, but with good reason. In the opening verses of the gospel we hear Luke's intent: to write down an orderly sequence of events so his patron may realize the certainty of the teachings. It sounds like Luke thinks he can do a better job than others have done, and his work is masterful. By leaping to the fourth chapter, we omit the story of the birth of Jesus, the genealogy, the arrival of John the Baptist and the temptation in the desert. Those texts are read aloud in the appropriate seasons of the year. But in the fourth chapter, Jesus enters the scene "in the power of the Spirit," goes to Nazareth, walks into the synagogue on the Sabbath, and reads some lines from Isaiah. While all eyes are upon him in hushed wonderment, he announces, "Today this Scripture passage is fulfilled in your hearing." Today's gospel introduces Luke the writer and Jesus his subject.

The first reading tells about another open book. In this case, Ezra reads the text of a recently discovered holy book—possibly Deuteronomy—to call the people back to God's law. The leaders announce, "Today is holy to the Lord your God." The reading of scripture sanctifies the day, the community and the event. It lets the voice of God speak to willing ears.

The psalm gives praise for God's word. It comes with a refrain from John's gospel, where Peter confesses his belief in the words of Jesus.

In his first letter to the Corinthians, Paul mines the image of the human body to help his readers grasp the concept of the body of Christ. The opening chapter of his book complained against the divisions in Corinth. In this passage he makes another vivid appeal for unity. It is a perfect text for the close of this octave of prayer for Christian unity.

SACRAMENTARY

A general chorus of praise appears as the entrance antiphon. The alternate communion antiphon makes a good choice for the day Jesus assumes his ministry: "I am the light of the world." The opening prayer implies that the power of God should impel us toward efforts of making peace. Any preface from Ordinary Time may be used, but P 30 dwells on the mission of Jesus.

Eucharistic Prayer IV with its own unchangeable preface unfolds a full picture of Jesus' life and ministry. Among the prayers over the people, #6 asks for a complete change of heart.

OTHER IDEAS

If you repeat the same musical acclamations throughout this period of Ordinary Time, you will help people grasp the unity of the season. You could also build your parish's repertoire with a new Glory to God to highlight its absence when Lent arrives. Many communities, though, recite the Glory to God during Ordinary Time. It gives the assembly an opportunity to speak a common text of praise.

#520 and #317 (LMC #248 and 193–227) white

MON 26 Timothy and Titus, bishops
MEMORIAL

The first reading comes from the proper of the saints in the lectionary, because both Timothy and Titus are biblical figures. Either passage makes a good choice, and a psalm like the one that follows these options or one from the common of pastors would work better than the one assigned for the weekday today.

For the gospel, you may choose one from the common of pastors or from the proper of saints (where Luke 10:1–9 about discipleship appears). The gospel assigned for the day entertains questions about the origins of Jesus' power. He rebukes the accusation that he colludes with Satan.

Many scripture scholars doubt the authenticity of Paul's authorship of the letters to Timothy and Titus, but both men appear in other passages of the New Testament as companions of the saint, and tradition holds that they served the early church as bishops. Today's celebration extends the message of yesterday's feast.

The opening prayer comes from the proper of saints. The other prayers come from those for bishops from the common of pastors (#3 or 4), but #9 presents other good texts.

#318 (LMC #193–227) green

TUE 27 Weekday

Optional Memorial of Angela Merici (+ 1540), virgin and religious founder / white ▪ Questions about Jesus' origins appear again today. This time, he restates who are his true relatives: those who do the will of God.

David expands the symbols of his kingship by bringing the ark of the covenant to his city. We respond with a processional psalm, one of the songs of pilgrims on the road to Zion.

See the sacramentary's prayers for the commons of the dedication of a church (2B).

■ TODAY'S SAINT: Desiring to provide better education for children, Angela Merici organized a group of young women to live in poverty, chastity and obedience, but in their own homes rather than as a convent. The Ursulines became a formally approved religious congregation a few years after Angela's death. The lectionary's proper of saints suggests readings about service and youth, but the readings of the weekday are recommended.

#319 (LMC #193–227) white

WED 28 Thomas Aquinas (+ 1274), presbyter, religious, doctor of the church
MEMORIAL

Among David's plans for the new city is a house for God, a temple. Nathan the prophet tells David that God is not impressed. Instead, God will build the house, providing a permanent lineage from the king. The same prophecy appears in the verses of the royal psalm.

Mark's collection of parables begins the same way as the one in Matthew, with the sower. Jesus, who has already revealed his power to cure, now demonstrates his skill at making parables. Jesus interprets the meaning for his followers.

■ TODAY'S SAINT: Italian by birth, Dominican by vocation, Thomas Aquinas became a philosopher of unparalleled importance for the church. Reputed to be a terrible student as a child, he became an undisputed intellectual giant. Catholic Schools Week generally includes his feast. You may find hymns by Thomas in your participation aid. Thomas's prayers of preparation for Mass and of thanksgiving after Mass are in the first appendix of the sacramentary.

The opening prayer for the Mass comes from the proper of saints. Among the options for the other prayers, those from the common of doctors of the church (#2) are especially fine today. The lectionary's proper of saints suggests readings about wisdom and teachers, but the readings of the weekday are recommended.

#320 (LMC #193–227) green

THU 29 Weekday

In prayer, David understands the great gift God has given him. Not only has he received prosperity in his own day, now God also promises prosperity for future generations. The covenant with David is recalled in today's psalm.

Mark has collected several brief sayings demonstrating Jesus' wisdom and has packed them in a few brief verses. In the midst of the parables, these "mini-parables" are easily remembered words to live by.

Variation A of the Eucharistic Prayer for Masses for Various Needs and Occasions remembers the covenant God kept throughout all generations.

#321 (LMC #193–227) green

FRI 30

David's sin is set at the time of year when kings go off to war. Illicit sexual relations lead to the murder of Bathsheba's husband, Uriah. Anticipating God's judgment on the affair, the lectionary offers a penitential psalm in response.

Returning to parables, Jesus, the master teacher, labors to explain the reign of God with lively, everyday images.

The grave tone of the first reading, appearing on a Friday, suggests the use of the first eucharistic prayer for reconciliation.

#322 (LMC #193–227)   white

SAT 31 John Bosco (+ 1888), presbyter, religious founder, educator
MEMORIAL

A few of the miracle stories of Jesus demonstrate his power over natural forces. Today's gospel is an example. It challenges the Gentile belief that the gods who governed nature held the most powerful sway.

"You are the man!" is a compliment in colloquial American English. But when Nathan shouts these words at King David, they indict him for his sin. Nathan leads David to the realization of his sin by telling the tale of a poor man's ewe. The psalm associated with David's remorse follows.

■ TODAY'S SAINT: John Bosco founded the Salesian Society of Saint Francis de Sales and the Daughters of Mary, Help of Christians. He cared for children by founding a kind of "boys' town," and also a center for girls, training them for life in the church and the world.

The opening prayer is found in the proper of saints. You may draw the others from those for teachers among the common of holy men and women (#10). The lectionary's proper of saints suggests readings about praise and children, but the readings of the weekday are recommended.

February

 #72 (LMC #67)   green

Fourth Sunday in Ordinary Time

ORIENTATION

By now things should start feeling normal in the lectionary. After last week's introduction to Jesus' ministry, we enter the story of his ministry, following a semi-continuous reading of Luke.

LECTIONARY

The opening verses of today's gospel recap the conclusion to last week's reading. We can still sense the glow of approval when a question shatters the tranquil atmosphere: "Isn't this the son of Joseph?" Immediately, Jesus meets controversy. He aggravates matters by comparing his listeners to the faithless covenantal community over whom God's favor passed to alight upon the Gentiles. In only a few verses, Jesus goes from *wunderkind* to *bête noir*. The crowd even makes an attempt on his life—this is his first day on the job!

Preceding this dramatic gospel is the call of Jeremiah the prophet. Jeremiah served almost as reluctantly as Jonah. Jeremiah learns from the time of his prophetic call that he will face enemies who will fight but not prevail over him. His will not be an easy ministry. Through the psalmist, we sing of God as refuge and hope. As God told Jeremiah, "Before I formed you in the womb I knew you," so the psalmist sings to God, "On you I depend from birth; from my mother's womb you are my strength."

This passage from Paul's first letter to the Corinthians is one of the most famous and beloved passages in the Bible. Whether Paul wrote it or imported it, he included this hymn to love as an exhortation to the Corinthian community. But almost every engaged couple reads it as a description of their love for each other.

SACRAMENTARY

The first option for the opening prayer asks for God's help to love, a theme that fits today's second reading. The antiphon for the introductory rite and the first antiphon for the communion rite both call upon God's help, making them good texts for today's first reading and gospel.

Eucharistic Prayer IV continues to be a good choice for outlining the ministry of Jesus, but the third preface for marriage (P 74) sounds strongly the theme of love.

OTHER IDEAS

Tomorrow we celebrate the Presentation of the Lord. The Mass begins with a blessing of candles. Invite people to bring from home any candles they would like blessed to accompany their prayer. Put the word out in the bulletin, the announcements at Mass, the telephone answering machine and the website. Procure extra candles today for those who do not have the means or the memory to bring their own.

M
O 2 #524 (LMC #252)   white
N
**The Presentation
of the Lord**
FEAST

ORIENTATION

Forty days after the birth of a child, the people of Israel presented the newborn at the temple in Jerusalem. The gospels say that the parents of Jesus obeyed this law. In doing so, they revealed him as the fulfillment of the law.

Forty days after our celebration of the birth of Jesus the church remembers his presentation at the temple. Today's feast used to close the Christmas cycle. Although that season now ends with the Baptism of the Lord, today's feast is still calculated from Christmas Day. Formerly called the Purification of Our Lady and regarded as a Marian feast, the day is now honored as a feast of Christ.

Today is also the patronal feast of Bolivia, Our Lady of Copacabana. The title honors a wooden statue of Mary carved in the form of an Inca princess by the Indian Francisco Tito Yupanqui. The statue is venerated in Copacabana, on an isthmus on Lake Titicaca in the Andes.

LECTIONARY

The readings are found under Solemnities and Feasts of the Lord and the Saints. Luke's account of the event is selected for the gospel. The long form completes the story with the prophetess Anna.

Malachi prophesies that God will send a messenger, bringing the divine presence into the temple. The surprise here is that the fiery messenger comes under the guise of an infant.

The psalm we sang last week to remember the arrival of the ark of the covenant in Zion appears again today, as we remember the arrival of Jesus in Zion's holy temple.

The reading from the letter to the Hebrews states that Jesus' acceptance of humanity enabled him to redeem humanity. This feast celebrates that saving incarnation.

If you are using the *Lectionary for Masses with Children* today, you will need the volume of readings for weekdays. The Year C volume does not include today's readings.

SACRAMENTARY

This Mass begins in an unusual fashion, and it is important to be prepared beforehand. The members of the assembly need candles, like those for the Easter Vigil, as they gather outside the church. They may supply their own, or you may provide them. The presider will need holy water and a sprinkler. Prepare incense if you like.

The blessing follows one of two forms. Given the nature of the feast, it would be preferable to use the first, the procession of all the faithful. If those arriving early for Mass have already taken their seats in the church, invite them outside the main doors for the opening ritual. The opportunity to hold lighted candles for the entrance rite will please many a churchgoer and strengthen the celebratory nature of the feast. Catholic spirituality has strong roots in rituals like this. Today you can engage people anew in the traditions of the faith.

When all are in place, the candles are lighted. Unlike the Easter Vigil, it is not necessary that these be lit from a single source. The symbol is the candles, not the fire.

A short refrain may be sung, either the one proposed in the sacramentary or another using the theme of light. The presider makes the sign of the cross, greets the people, introduces the feast and blesses the candles, sprinkling them with holy water.

The procession enters the church at the invitation of the presider (or deacon). The censer, the cross between two candles (two glorious candles, preferably), and the book of the gospels lead the way. The presider follows, and the rest of the assembly of the faithful then enters with song.

When all have taken their places, the Glory to God is sung, perhaps using the one from Christmas, as a faint reminder of the solemnity we recall today. Since any hymn may be sung in the procession, some communities use the Glory to God as the processional song, to avoid singing two substantial pieces of music in immediate succession. The opening prayer for the Mass follows the Glory to God.

There is no instruction for extinguishing the candles. It may be impractical for all to keep them lit throughout the Mass. All will probably extinguish their candles as they are seated for the liturgy of the word, but they could be lighted for the gospel or even the eucharistic prayer. The rest of Mass continues in the usual way.

The sacramentary includes a text for the entrance antiphon,

but it is not clear when this might be sung. It perhaps works best as an alternate suggestion for other music in the introductory rites. The presidential prayers eloquently express the significance of the feast, as does the proper preface (P 49).

The German sacramentary provides inserts to the eucharistic prayers for this day. For example, in Prayer III, after the words "a perfect offering may be made to the glory of your name," the prayer continues, "And so we come into your presence, and in union with the whole church we celebrate that day when your only-begotten Son was presented in the temple. Through him, the Light of your Light, we bring you these gifts. We ask you to make them holy. . . ."

MUSIC

The Latin chants for this day are among the most beautiful in the repertoire. The community might enjoy hearing or singing *Lumen ad revelationem gentium* as the processional hymn or even as the gathering refrain. Find it in the *Liber cantualis*. Another good choice would be a sung version of the Canticle of Simeon, the *Nunc dimittis*, which comes from today's gospel. It appears in the *Liturgy of the Hours* every night for night prayer. Check the hymn index under temple, Mary, church and Christ for more suggestions. *By Flowing Waters* (302–315) has a complete suite of processional chants, antiphons, psalms and the sung Canticle of Simeon.

OTHER IDEAS

A Hispanic custom gaining in popularity throughout North American parishes is the "presentation of the Christ Child": people bring with them to church the figure of the infant Jesus from their home nativity scenes. The figures are wrapped in lace and held up at Mass for a blessing this day.

The presider may wear the vestments from the Christmas season. This is a favorite day each year for celebrating a school liturgy. Creative pastors, teachers and parish liturgical ministers will bring something of the celebration into the school year, will invite students to participate today, will join with the religious education program in preparing a celebration that unites the parish. LTP's *School Year, Church Year* and *Preparing Liturgy for Children and Children for Liturgy* offer ideas for keeping this feast in the parish school and among students in religious education programs.

If your community offers the blessing of throats on St. Blase's Day, make the announcement today and prepare the candles for tomorrow.

TUE **3** #324 (LMC #193–227)   green
Weekday

Optional Memorial of Blase (+ c. 316?), bishop and martyr / red ▪ *Optional Memorial of St. Ansgar (+ 865), bishop / white* ▪ Mark interweaves two miracle stories, the healing of a woman's hemorrhage and the raising of the daughter of Jairus from death to life. The second of these, the most dramatic miracle thus far in Mark, seems to require two proofs of the cure: the girl walks and eats.

Absalom meets an untimely and uncommon death. David, who had reason to rejoice at the death of an enemy, weeps instead in mournful lamentation for the loss of his son. A psalm of lamentation follows.

For the blessing of throats today, prepare candles ahead of time. Traditionally, two crossed candles are tied with a red bow. Prepare also cards with the text of the blessing for those who need one for reference.

It is best if the ministers memorize the text of the prayer. Priests and deacons who find memorization difficult may place the printed text in the hand that holds the candles (practice this!) so their other hand is free to make the blessing.

The blessing of throats generally takes longer than communion does. If you have more throat ministers than communion ministers, the assembly will not need to wait long for the ceremony to conclude. Lay ministers blessing throats may invoke the saint with the proper text, but they should not conclude it with the sign of the cross.

After the intercessions, ministers go to their stations. The faithful process forward. Place the crossed candles onto the neck of each and pray the blessing. Alternatively, the blessing may be given once over the entire assembly.

▪ TODAY'S SAINTS: Blase (also spelled Blaise, and pronounced like *blaze* and not *blasé*) is said to have been a bishop in Armenia, but little can be known for sure. Legend holds he suffered a brutal martyrdom under Diocletian, having his flesh ripped open by metal wool combs, then was decapitated. There is a legend that from his cave lit by candles he removed a fish bone from the throat of a boy. This story has made him patron for those with sore throats, and a blessing may be given to the faithful today in his honor.

Blase is also the patron of woolcombers. He is patron of Paraguay, where today's celebration ranks as a feast. The lectionary's proper of saints suggests readings about suffering and evangelization.

Ansgar was born in Amiens, became a monk at Corbie, developed a talent for preaching, then went on mission to Denmark, where he is remembered as the patron. He not only preached the gospel, he lived it. He washed the feet of the poor and waited on them at table.

The prayer that concludes each psalm in the *Liturgy of the Hours* was his idea. The lectionary's proper of saints suggests readings about mission, but the readings of the weekday are recommended.

Today is also the patronal feast for Honduras, Our Lady of Suyapa. Indian laborers sleeping by the roadside on a Saturday night in February 1747 discovered a small statue of Mary buried in the dirt. They built a small church for it, and it has been a popular pilgrimage site ever since.

WED 4 #325 (LMC #193–227) red
Weekday

In spite of the miracles he worked and the wisdom he preached, many of Jesus' own people still reject him. Mark concludes this section of his gospel with a reminder that Jesus faced controversy throughout his life, even among his own people.

David sins again, this time by counting the people of Israel, contrary to God's will. He chooses a punishment that will afflict himself and his family, not the rest of the people. A psalm of repentance follows.

The sacramentary includes a Mass for forgiveness of sins (#40).

Most of the church will celebrate the memorial of Agatha tomorrow, but it is transferred to this date in Mexico, where the feast of Philip of Jesus will take precedence.

THU 5 #326 (LMC #193–227) red
Agatha (+ c. 251), martyr
MEMORIAL

Beginning a new section of the gospel dealing with discipleship, Mark tells how Jesus sent the Twelve out on mission to preach repentance and to cure the sick. Our practice of anointing the sick is partly inspired by the testimony of this passage.

With David's death, the reign passes to his son Solomon. The responsory comes from the parallel account in the first book of Chronicles. The text is David's final hymn of praise to God before his death and the anointing of Solomon.

■ TODAY'S SAINT: Agatha, one of the earliest Christian martyrs, died during the persecution of Decius. Her tortures included the removal of her breasts (according to a sixth-century legend), and so she is now a patron of women with diseases of the breast. Her name is remembered among the women martyrs of Eucharistic Prayer I.

The opening prayer for Mass comes from the proper of saints. Options exist for the other prayers, but consider the Common of Martyrs (#7). The lectionary's proper of saints suggests readings about weakness, suffering and loss, but the readings of the weekday are recommended.

■ IN MEXICO AND VENEZUELA, today is the feast of Philip (de las Casas) of Jesus (+ 1597), protomartyr of Mexico. The day is an optional memorial in Honduras. Philip, the oldest of 11 children, was born in Mexico of newlywed parents who had emigrated from Spain. As a youth, he learned to work with silver, and at age 20 he traveled to Manila, where he decided to join the Franciscans. Seeking ordination to the priesthood, he boarded a ship from the Philippines back to Mexico, but the boat ran ashore at Japan, where the persecution of Christians was in force. Philip was crucified on this date together with 25 other Christians, including Paul Miki, on a hill outside Nagasaki.

#327 (LMC #193–227) red
FRI 6 **Paul Miki (+ 1597), martyr; and his companions, martyrs**
MEMORIAL

Before leaving behind the story of David, the lectionary turns to the book of Sirach for a text that praises the life and service of this important figure in salvation history. The passage comes from a section of the book that has collected fond remembrances of other significant individuals from the Old Testament from Enoch to Josiah. The psalm praises God who gave victories to the anointed King David.

By placing the story of John the Baptist's death after the story of the mission of the Twelve, Mark foreshadows the crucifixion of Jesus and the suffering of those who followed him. The account of John's martyrdom is especially poignant.

■ TODAY'S SAINT: Caught in the midst of political machinations and fear of national conquest, Paul Miki and his companions, including some altar servers, were crucified at Nagasaki. Celebrating this obligatory memorial of martyrs from Japan reminds Catholics from other places of the global witness to the faith.

The opening prayer comes from the proper of saints. Choose the other presidential prayers from the common martyrs. There are five groups of texts for days that honor a plurality of martyrs. Use any you wish, but note that the communion prayer of the first set makes a reference to the cross. The lectionary's proper of saints suggests readings about crucifixion, suffering and mission, but the readings of the weekday are recommended.

■ IN BOLIVIA, today is the memorial of Philip of Jesus, Paul Miki and companions. The country combines yesterday's Mexican feast with today's universal memorial.

S A T 7 #328 (LMC #193–227)   green
Weekday

Optional Memorial of the Blessed Virgin Mary / white ▪ Having sent the Twelve in the passage we heard on Thursday, Jesus receives them back from their mission. He invites them to spend some time away, but a large crowd interrupts the plan. Service continues.

Continuing the history of the kings of Israel, we begin the story of Solomon, found in the first book of Kings. Solomon asks God for wisdom; God grants wisdom and much more. Some verses from the longest psalm (Psalm 119) follow, every line praising the wisdom of God in some way.

Prayers for charity (#41) might be useful today. If you take the optional memorial of the Blessed Virgin, see the texts for Seat of Wisdom (#24) in the *Collection of Masses of the Blessed Virgin Mary.*

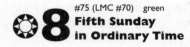

8 #75 (LMC #70)   green
Fifth Sunday in Ordinary Time

ORIENTATION

Even though Christmas was not so long ago, it is already time to start making plans for Lent. The assembly will enjoy this hiatus of Ordinary Time, but musicians and church decorators may want to meet to gather ideas for the start of the Forty Days later this month.

The second Sunday in February is World Marriage Day. Offer prayers and thanksgivings for the married couples in the community.

LECTIONARY

Luke's beautiful account of the call of Simon paints a vivid portrait of the disciple who will become the leader of the Twelve. Frustrated at not catching fish, Simon comes up with a classic excuse not to follow Jesus' advice: "We tried that before." In the end, Simon asks Jesus to leave, "for I am a sinful man." But Jesus calls him, James and John into the wondrous ministry of fishing for people.

Last week we heard the call of Jeremiah. This week we hear the call of Isaiah. Where Jeremiah was reluctant, Isaiah is eager. "Here I am," he calls, "send me!" One of the defining characteristics of disciples of Jesus is that they responded to a personal call, just as the prophets did.

Psalm 138 follows because of its reference to angels, that appear in the gauzy vision of Isaiah.

We finally reach the fifteenth chapter of Paul's first letter to the Corinthians. Each year Ordinary Time begins with several weeks of excerpts from this same letter. Now in Year C we reach the climactic chapter. After several weeks of very familiar texts, we enter one of the most important sections of the letter, Paul's treatment of the resurrection. He hands on his faith in the resurrection, much as he handed on his knowledge of the eucharist. He speaks of the resurrection appearances of Jesus to individuals, to groups, and to himself, the least of the apostles. In Paul's view, Jesus appeared to a variety of witnesses to make it easier for more people to believe in the resurrection.

SACRAMENTARY

The first of the communion antiphons praises the kindness God shows people. The first opening prayer says all our hope is in God.

Among the prefaces for Ordinary Time, Ordinary Time III (P 31) remembers that God came to our rescue. The first preface for funerals (P 77) says, "In him, who rose from the dead, our hope of resurrection dawned." The second solemn blessing for Ordinary Time (#11) prays for the peace of God that is beyond all understanding.

OTHER IDEAS

Invite people to bring last year's palm branches to church over the next few weekends. They may be burned for this year's ashes.

M O N 9 #329 (LMC #193–227)   green
Weekday

Construction of the temple of David's dreams fell to Solomon. Under his watch the ark of the covenant moved from its place in the city of Zion to the newly constructed temple in Jerusalem. The memory of the event is recalled in today's psalm.

Mark provides a summary statement of Jesus' ministry with his disciples. People came primarily to benefit from his power to heal.

The first version of the Eucharistic Prayer for Various Needs and Occasions expresses eloquent prayers for the church.

▪ IN ECUADOR, today is the feast of San Miguel Febres Cordero (+ 1910), a Christian Brother, and of his martyred companions. Miguel is remembered as an educator, scholar and grammarian. The day is an optional memorial in Venezuela.

T U E 10 #330 (LMC #193–227)   white
Scholastica (+ 547), virgin, religious founder
MEMORIAL

Solomon, stretching his hands toward heaven, offers a prayer before the altar in the magnificent new temple. The psalm sings of the temple's loveliness.

Jesus confronts the Pharisees on ritual purification and hypocrisy. Instead of being warm and comforting, Jesus has harsh words for the religious leaders of his day.

■ TODAY'S SAINT: Scholastica, the sister of Benedict, joined him in dedicating her life to prayer and work, and is the patron of Benedictine nuns. All the information about her comes from the *Dialogues* of Gregory the Great. In a famous story, Benedict refused to extend his visit with Scholastica one evening, in spite of her entreaty. So she prayed and God sent a storm that required her brother to remain. They enjoyed spiritual conversation, a pastime too rarely pursued in a high-speed world.

The opening prayer comes from the proper of saints. Choose the other presidential prayers from the common of virgins. There are four sets from which to choose. But avoid the fourth, which is for days that honor more than one virgin. The lectionary's proper of saints suggests readings about love, praise and hospitality, but the readings of the weekday are recommended.

W E D **11** #331 (LMC #193–227) green
Weekday

Optional Memorial of Our Lady of Lourdes/white ▪ The queen of Sheba, still a symbol of power and wealth, makes her entrance in the story of Solomon. In spite of her material prosperity, she still admires Solomon's wisdom and the expanse of his court. A psalm about wisdom fittingly follows this reading.

After his jeremiad against the Pharisees, Jesus explains more to his disciples. Impurity has more to do with right intention than with compulsive action.

■ TODAY'S MEMORIAL: On this date in 1858 is recorded the first of a series of apparitions of Our Lady to Bernadette Soubirous at Lourdes. Clothed in white, she identified herself as the Immaculate Conception. The popular shrine has been a place of pilgrimage and miraculous healing. The lectionary's proper of saints suggests a reading about healing and a story about Mary, but the readings of the weekday are recommended.

Consider offering the sacrament of the anointing of the sick at the daily Mass.

T H U **12** #332 (LMC #193–227) green
Weekday

Solomon's fidelity did not last. The writer blames Solomon's wives for turning the king's heart away from God. One of the historical psalms tells of the faithlessness of God's chosen people.

In parts of Mark's account, Jesus appears more rattled than we customarily think of him. After dealing with the religious leaders in passages earlier this week, Jesus now meets a Syro-Phoenician woman who asks him to cure her daughter. He refuses because she is a Gentile, but he finally relents at her clever persistence.

The first eucharistic prayer for Masses of reconciliation might make a good choice today.

F R I **13** #333 (LMC #193–227) green
Weekday

The twelve tribes will be divided, the prophet Ahijah tells Solomon's son Jeroboam. The unity of Israel under its king is beginning to unravel. God laments through the psalm, "My people heard not my voice."

Jesus cures a deaf man with a speech impediment. Aspects of this cure make it a model of ini-

tiatory discipleship: The man is brought by believers, who ask Jesus to lay a hand on him. He prays that the man will be opened, and the man then speaks plainly. Through testimony and prayer, people will be opened to catechesis and discipleship.

The second eucharistic prayer for Masses for reconciliation acknowledges that in God, "nations seek the way of peace together."

S A T **14** #334 (LMC #193–227) white
Cyril (+ 869), religious, missionary; and Methodius (+ c. 884), bishop, missionary
MEMORIAL

Jeroboam completely forsakes the God of his ancestors and creates two golden calves, placing them at opposite ends of the kingdom, Dan and Bethel. The writer says the house of Jeroboam would be cut off from the heart because of this sin. The psalm recalls an earlier and better-known story of the making of a calf at Horeb, to serve as a false god. This is not a pretty story, but it ends our survey of Old Testament history on a note that might inspire some repentance before Lent.

Mark tells of the miracle of the loaves. Four thousand people eat from seven loaves and a few fish. Jesus' actions (taking, thanking, breaking and giving) foreshadow the eucharist.

■ TODAY'S SAINTS: Cyril and Methodius are patrons of Europe. Missionaries to Bulgaria, Moravia and Dalmatia, these two brothers tirelessly served the church. They translated the scriptures into Slavic, developing its "Cyrillic" alphabet. Formerly optional, this day is now an obligatory memorial. The lectionary's proper of saints suggests readings about evangelization and service, but the readings of the weekday are recommended.

Most people, of course, assume we celebrate Saint Valentine today. But the information on that Roman martyr is not reliable enough to win him a spot in the universal church calendar. Vestment color should be white today. Wrap chocolates in red.

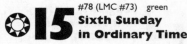

#78 (LMC #73)   green

15 Sixth Sunday in Ordinary Time

ORIENTATION

Preparations for Lent should be well underway, even though the community is celebrating a very ordinary Ordinary Time Sunday. We hear more from chapter 15 of Paul's first letter to the Corinthians and more of Jesus' Galilean ministry.

LECTIONARY

Where Matthew writes about a sermon "on the mount," Luke writes a similar account of a sermon Jesus gives "on a stretch of level ground." As in Matthew, Luke remembers Jesus opening this speech with a set of Beatitudes. There is an important difference, though. Matthew reports eight, Luke only four. Luke goes on to include four woes for those who do not accept the word of Christ. This is one of the passages that make many biblical scholars believe that Matthew and Luke both worked from a collection of sayings of Jesus that Mark did not have, and that now has been lost. That document, often called "Q" (from the German word *quelle* meaning "source"), probably influenced the way both Matthew

and Luke reported this event in the life of Jesus.

From the prophecy of Jeremiah we find a text that offers a curse and a blessing, just as we have in the gospel. Those who trust in the Lord are like a tree planted beside waters. The same image appears in the psalm, which, like these two readings, separates the blessed from the wicked.

Paul preaches the centrality of the resurrection. If Christ has not been raised, our faith is in vain. But Christ has been raised from the dead, as the witnesses listed in last week's reading concur.

SACRAMENTARY

The first opening prayer says God promised to remain with those who do what is just and right. The promise of eternal life appears in the second antiphon for the communion rite. Eucharistic Prayer IV recalls Jesus preaching good news to the poor.

The first solemn blessing for Ordinary Time (#10) is a classic text of blessing that might fit well with today's gospel.

OTHER IDEAS

Remind people of coming programs that will help them prepare for Lent and Easter. Encourage them to bring old palm branches from home if you are burning them to make ashes for Ash Wednesday.

#335 (LMC #193–227)   green

MON 16 Weekday

A sigh rises from the depths of Jesus' spirit as the Pharisees demand some heavenly sign from him. He refuses, exasperated at their lack of faith, and leaves town.

The weekday lectionary now presents a series of New Testament letters called "catholic" epistles because they are addressed

to a general audience. They are all rather brief, but because of the date of Ash Wednesday this year, the only one we will hear from is James. The book runs a series of topics, all rather interesting, though not well connected to one another. The authorship is disputed, and the traditional assignation of the book to James the brother of the Lord is unlikely.

Having just surveyed a segment of Old Testament history that concludes with the splitting of the twelve tribes, we hear the sorrowful opening of this letter, addressed "to the twelve tribes in the dispersion." James's audience has suffered trials, and he urges them to keep their faith strong. Today's excerpt from Psalm 119 cites verses about clinging to God's statutes in spite of affliction.

In the fourth version of the Eucharistic Prayer for Masses for Various Needs and Occasions, we hear that Jesus proclaimed to the world that God cares for us as a parent cares for children.

#336 (LMC #193–227)   green

TUE 17 Weekday

Optional Memorial of the Seven Founders of the Order of Servites (+ thirteenth century) religious / white ▪ God does not tempt people, James argues. When things go wrong, people still tend to blame God or wonder if God is punishing them. James says that is not the time to break from God but rather a time to hold on. In the psalm we sing of God's mercy that sustains us when our feet slip.

Jesus chooses the wrong metaphor to explain to his disciples how exasperated he is with the Pharisees. Be on guard against their yeast, he says. Since the disciples were short on food they missed the point altogether. Jesus finds that neither friend nor foe fully understands him.

If you pray for those who suffer famine (#28), remember, too, those who suffer from spiritual hunger.

■ TODAY'S SAINTS: Internal feuding and immoral behavior plagued their society. But the seven young men who joined the Confraternity of the Blessed Virgin devoted themselves to spiritual renewal, recruited new members and evangelized by their prayer and penance. The seven were Buonfiglio Monaldi, Alexis Falconieri, Benedict dell'Antela, Bartholomew degli Amidei, Ricovero Uguccione, Geraldino Sostegni and John Buonagiunta. It is easier to remember them as the "seven founders." The lectionary's proper of saints suggests readings about the just life and following Christ, but the readings of the weekday are recommended.

WED 18 #337 (LMC #193–227) green
Weekday

"Be doers of the word and not hearers only," James says. Too many people say the right thing but do nothing about it. This reading begins an examination of conscience a week before Lent. A psalm about the just person follows the reading.

Only Mark reports this instance of Jesus curing the blind by stages. Jesus touches the eyes of a blind beggar with spittle, imposes hands, and then the man sees people but they look like walking trees. Jesus tries a second time and the man sees perfectly. This story threatens to make Jesus appear ineffective in his first attempt. The other gospels, probably written after Mark, do not include it in their depictions of the Son of God.

Eucharistic Prayer IV summarizes the ministry of Jesus.

THU 19 #338 (LMC #193–227) green
Weekday

"If you show partiality, you commit sin." James minces no words. Too many people were showing preference to the rich and avoiding the poor. In the psalm we remember that God hears the cry of the poor. Time spent with the poor is time spent with God.

Mark's gospel reaches its turning point with Peter's affirmation that Jesus is the Messiah. This episode takes place in the northern reaches of Palestine—Caesarea Philippi—and from there, as Jesus alludes, the story moves to Jerusalem. Peter, having received good marks for identifying the Messiah, fails when it comes to interpreting his affirmation. Jesus calls him "Satan."

The fourth version of the Eucharistic Prayer for Masses for Various Needs and Occasions says Jesus was moved with compassion "for the poor and the powerless."

FRI 20 #339 (LMC #193–227) green
Weekday

Faith without works is dead, James says. If you say you believe something, show it in your actions. Be especially attentive to the hungry. Another psalm about the just person answers this reading.

Just after predicting his passion to his disciples, Jesus summons the crowd to tell them what discipleship will cost: Take up a cross, he says, and follow. Life with Jesus is not all loaves and fish. It will include suffering.

Prayers from the Triumph of the Cross (September 14) may drive home the point.

SAT 21 #340 (LMC #193–227) green
Weekday

Optional Memorial of Peter Damian (+ 1072), bishop, monastic, doctor of the church / white ▪ *Optional Memorial of the Blessed Virgin Mary / white* ▪ "The tongue is a small member and yet has great pretensions." James's essay on the human tongue is a graphic, poetic affirmation of how the tongue can lead to perfection or destruction. It can help, like the bit in a horse's mouth or the rudder of a ship. It can hurt like a fire or poison. The psalmist laments that people lie about their neighbors and speak with "smooth lips."

At the transfiguration, Jesus takes Peter, James and John to a high mountain where the disciples see Elijah and Moses conversing with their Rabbi. A discussion about Elijah ensues, a sign that Jesus is an eschatological figure.

■ TODAY'S SAINT: Peter Damian, a Benedictine abbot, bishop and doctor of the church, worked with the great reformer Pope Gregory VII. The lectionary's proper of saints suggests readings about ministry and union with God, but the readings of the weekday are recommended.

If you celebrate the optional memorial of the Blessed Virgin, see the texts for Mother of Good Counsel (#33) in the *Collection of Masses of the Blessed Virgin Mary.*

☀22 #81 (LMC #76)   green
Seventh Sunday in Ordinary Time

ORIENTATION

This is the last Sunday before the beginning of Lent. Our series of readings from 1 Corinthians finally draws to its close, and we abruptly interrupt Luke's story of Jesus' ministry.

LECTIONARY

Luke continues to report Jesus' sermon on the plain. Today we hear a series of brief sayings about loving one's neighbor. Jesus gives one of the hardest commands in the gospels to uphold: "Love your enemies." When countries are at war, these are difficult words to swallow.

Saul has been pursuing David, and David has a golden opportunity to do away with his enemy. But David respects Saul as God's anointed king and will not authorize any harm. David prefigures Jesus' gospel command to love the enemy. As encouragement, we sing of God's love and mercy in the psalm.

Paul compares Christ to Adam in this final passage from the three-year cycle of readings from 1 Corinthians. In life we bear the image of the earthly Adam, but in eternity, we shall also bear the image of the heavenly one. Paul's faith in the goodness of resurrection is firm.

SACRAMENTARY

The second eucharistic prayer for Masses for reconciliation says that in God "enemies begin to speak to one another" and "those who were estranged join hands in friendship."

The communion prayer asks help in living the example of love we celebrate in the eucharist. Prayer over the people #23 asks for true love for one another.

OTHER IDEAS

Announce the Ash Wednesday schedule. Include helps in the bulletin this week for those who want to make a good Lent. Remind people of the laws of fast and abstinence for this Wednesday and Friday.

M O N 23 #341 (LMC #193–227)   red
Polycarp (+ c. 155), bishop and martyr
MEMORIAL

James next attacks those who claim to have wisdom but have bitter jealousy and selfish ambition in their hearts. If you cultivate peace, you will reap righteousness. Today's psalm sings in joy of the true wisdom that comes from God's law.

Mark's gospel enters its second half. Today's passage comes after both Peter's confession that Jesus is the Messiah and the transfiguration of Jesus. These events form the centerpiece of Mark that answers the foundational question of the gospel, "Who is Jesus?" Throughout the second half, Jesus works his way toward Jerusalem and the cross.

Today Jesus cures a possessed child. The father states both his belief and his dependence on Jesus to sustain it. The pair of stories—the transfiguration and the cure of the possessed boy—is depicted in Raphael's famous painting of the transfiguration.

■ TODAY'S SAINT: Polycarp, bishop of Smyrna, was killed by the sword in his mid-80s during a persecution led by the pagans of his town. It is thought that he received his training directly from the apostles and disciples of Jesus. A traditional legend holds that he was a disciple of John the Evangelist. Irenaeus of Lyons (June 28) knew Polycarp in his youth. Ignatius of Antioch (October 17) addressed one of his seven letters to today's saint. The lectionary's proper of saints suggests readings from John, but the readings of the weekday are recommended.

T U E 24 #342 (LMC #193–227)   green
Weekday

James believes that wars and conflicts arise from passions, and that passions keep us from praying properly. "To be a lover of the world means enmity with God." The psalm also invites us to throw our cares on God, who will not permit the just to be disturbed.

Following the transfiguration and the cure of the possessed child, Jesus again warns the disciples about his approaching fate. They don't get it and instead talk tastelessly about which of them is the most important. Jesus uses a child to teach a lesson.

Eucharistic Prayer II's own preface affirms the humility of Christ who took on flesh and opened his arms on the cross.

Today the weekday scriptures of winter's Ordinary Time end before this year's Lent. James warns his readers about materialism. Jesus predicts his passion. The ground is prepared for the seed.

JANUARY 18, 2004
Second Sunday in Ordinary Time

God's Beloved, God's Delight
Isaiah 62:1–5
The bridegroom rejoices in his bride.

How do you describe your relationship to God? Do you consider God a father? Do you think primarily of Jesus when you pray? Is God a friend? A judge? Some people feel like God is their authority figure. Others imagine they have a very close friendship with God.

But people rarely think of God as their spouse. God thinks differently. In the prophecy of Isaiah, we hear that God's relationship to us is like groom to bride. God's love for us is so intense, God's delight in us is so complete, that the only metaphor the prophet can find is that of a newly married couple. Who would dare speak of the relationship between God and humanity this way? Well, God would.

Our experience of God changes. As we grow, we come to understand God better through the events of our lives. Some of those events challenge our perceptions of God. Others affirm those images.

Everyone goes through a spiritual desert from time to time. We feel like God is far away or imagine that God has forsaken us and left us desolate. Such feelings are normal.

But God never abandons us. Sometimes we simply cannot feel the warmth of God's love. Isaiah says God calls us "My delight" and "Espoused." If you have ever felt compassion toward someone who felt alone, you know how God feels toward us.

Written by Paul Turner. © 2003 Archdiocese of Chicago, Liturgy Training Publications; 1-800-933-1800; www.ltp.org.

JANUARY 25, 2004
Third Sunday in Ordinary Time

Family History
Nehemiah 8:2–4a, 5–6, 8–10
They read from the book of the law, and they understood what was read.

Whenever you open up an old family photo album, you may be struck with the power of ancestry, realizing that you come from a people who share many things with you.

When you look at old photos, you may want to learn more. Who were these people? Where did they live? How did they live? What part of me have I inherited from them? If you can converse with older members of your family, you can ask these questions directly. But for others, only the photos exist to tell the tales.

In the Old Testament, Ezra the priest came before the assembly of people and brought out for them an old book that had been lost. It was too early in history, of course, for a photo album.

But he now possessed a record of the holy words revealed by God to their ancestors. Now that the book had been discovered, its contents were proclaimed to the people.

They listened attentively. These were the words that shaped the lives of their ancestors. As they heard them, they learned what was important to the people who gave them life.

The Bible has been revered by many of our ancestors. It contains a record of the stories they told and the values they held. When you take that old book off the shelf at your home, the word of God, you can meet the people who gave you life.

Written by Paul Turner. © 2003 Archdiocese of Chicago, Liturgy Training Publications; 1-800-933-1800; www.ltp.org.

FEBRUARY 1, 2004
Fourth Sunday in Ordinary Time

God's Gifts
Jeremiah 1:4–5, 17–29
Before I formed you in the womb I knew you.

WHEN you discover what you are good at, you cannot let go. You may have a gift for parenting, teaching, listening or playing a hand of bridge—or a round of golf. Once in a while we find out something else about the gifts God gave us. We may not know why we have them, but events may call us to use our gifts in a way that reveals God's will.

You may have given advice that somebody needed. You may have helped a child overcome an obstacle. You may have lifted someone's spirits. You may have saved someone's life. You did all this because you had a gift, and when the moment arrived, you used the gift God gave you.

"Before I formed you in the womb I knew you." God's words to Jeremiah ring deep within our souls. Think about this: God knew you before you were born. God had you in mind before you were conceived. God designed gifts for you from the very beginning. God had a plan.

We are born without knowledge of God's plan. We aren't sure how we fit. We may never know. God may be using us in ways beyond our awareness. The gifts we have are not ours. They belong to God.

When we use God's gifts, they bring us satisfaction. We cannot let go of what God meant us to be and do. God knows us better than we know ourselves.

Written by Paul Turner. © 2003 Archdiocese of Chicago, Liturgy Training Publications; 1-800-933-1800; www.ltp.org.

FEBRUARY 8, 2004
Fifth Sunday in Ordinary Time

Childlike Enthusiasm
Isaiah 6:1–2a, 3–8
Here I am! Send me!

STAND in front of a group of kids and say these words: "I need a volunteer." Every hand will go up.

Stand in front of adults and the results will be different. We hesitate to reply. We need a personal invitation. We need to know it won't waste our time. We need to know someone respects our gifts as well as our responsibilities. Maybe, just maybe, we will volunteer.

We are usually glad when we do.

In the year King Uzziah died, Isaiah received a call from God. Isaiah saw a vision of seraphim calling out to one another of God's holiness in a dwelling filled with smoke. Isaiah thought himself unworthy to be there until one of the angels touched his mouth with a burning ember. Cleansed from sin, Isaiah responded like a young child ready to volunteer: "Here I am! Send me!"

Sometimes we don't volunteer because we feel unworthy. We are painfully aware of our sin. But once we have the vision, once we perceive God's presence, once we experience God's mercy, we do respond to God's call. We have to.

In the end, there is no volunteering among Christians. There is only ministry, the natural response to the life of grace.

Written by Paul Turner. © 2003 Archdiocese of Chicago, Liturgy Training Publications; 1-800-933-1800; www.ltp.org.

FEBRUARY 15, 2004
Sixth Sunday in Ordinary Time

Trusting God's Ways
Jeremiah 17:5–8
Blessed is the one who trusts in the Lord.

WE want things to go our way. There are things we want. There are situations in which we hope to prevail. Sometimes we can arrange to make that happen. Sometimes other people suffer for it. Sometimes they benefit because our vision is actually quite good.

But sometimes our way is not God's way. We may not agree with God's way. We may think God is making a mistake. We may think our ideas are better and that God should listen to us.

But God has a plan. It is a mysterious plan. It is a plan incomprehensible to humans. And sometimes God's plan is not our plan.

"Cursed is the one who trusts in human beings, who seeks strength in flesh," God says through the prophet Jeremiah. Trust in anything that is not divine, and you will be a barren bush in the desert, standing in a lava waste, salt and empty earth. It won't be pretty.

But if we trust in God, we are blessed. We are like trees planted beside waters with roots stretching to the stream. Our leaves will stay green, and we will bear fruit even in drought.

But it may mean giving up the things we want and accepting what God wants.

FEBRUARY 22, 2004
Seventh Sunday in Ordinary Time

Life's Sanctity
1 Samuel 26:2, 7–9, 12–13, 22–23
Though the LORD delivered you into my grasp, I would not harm you.

THE position of the Catholic church against capital punishment has caused soul searching among many of the faithful, especially in the United States, where the culture promotes punishment for wrongdoing and vengeance against aggressors. Many have found it difficult to reconcile the position of the Catholic church with their own.

For many, the most convincing arguments against capital punishment are not those that the church puts forward. Some people say there should not be capital punishment because judges and juries make mistakes. Additional evidence might come to light. Others say there should be no capital punishment because it is expensive to keep prisoners on Death Row for long periods of time while costly litigation continues without ceasing.

But the Catholic church believes in the sanctity of human life. Even a prisoner on Death Row, because he or she is human, deserves the respect owed to any human being as a child of God.

In the first book of Samuel, David had the opportunity to kill his enemy, King Saul, and assume the throne. He discovered Saul asleep, his spear nearby, and all the soldiers slumbering. All David had to do was pick up the spear and thrust it into the king.

But he could not do it. "Who can lay hands on the LORD's anointed and remain unpunished?" he wondered. David slew plenty of other enemies, but in one brief moment he glimpsed the truth about human life: It belongs to God.

LENT

The Season

The Calendar

The Meaning

God's forgiveness, healing and mercy are much more than an amnesty for us. We do not go back to the primal innocence but through to something better. The garden of the beginning is replaced by the city of Revelation.

—Maria Boulding, *The Coming of God,* Third edition (Conception, Missouri: The Printery House, 2000), p. 163.

LENT is the season of penance for the faithful and for the purification and enlightenment of the elect. In both cases it prepares the community for its celebration of Easter, the most important feast of the church year.

All are encouraged to make Lent a season of self-denial and spiritual preparation. Ash Wednesday, the day the season begins, is a day of obligatory fast and abstinence. The fast reappears after Lent on Friday and Saturday of the Triduum. Abstinence from meat is practiced on all the Fridays of the season, as well as on Good Friday. Many Catholic-based organizations sponsor a Friday night fish fry so people can socialize while observing the spirit of the season. Although each individual seeks a personal path of penance, the community's collective involvement makes this a very social season.

■ DURING THIS SEASON the parish community prays and supports the elect in their preparation for baptism. The faithful give witness to the belief of the church, while the elect inspire the faithful with the intensity of their final preparation.

Parish organizations will probably want to keep meeting during Lent, but you might be able to combine their gatherings with occasions for worship, catechesis or service.

The Saints

TWO solemnities, Saint Joseph and the Annunciation, will occur during Lent this year. They completely replace the liturgy of the day, and the vesture will be festive white those days. Both days call for the Glory to God, even though it is omitted on Sundays of the season. The gospel acclamation, though, remains lenten throughout. The creed will be recited on both solemnities, as well, as we continue to do on the Sundays of this season and throughout the year.

■ NO OBLIGATORY MEMORIALS appear during the next six weeks: Perpetua and Felicity are replaced by the Second Sunday of Lent. John Baptist de la Salle is replaced by Wednesday of Holy Week.

■ WHAT ARE THE LENTEN RULES FOR CELEBRATING A SAINT'S DAY? If you choose to celebrate an optional memorial during this season, you may choose the opening prayer for the saint from the sacramentary as a replacement for the opening prayer of the lenten weekday. Or you may use the saint's prayer to conclude the general intercessions. In any case the vesture remains lenten violet and all the other orations and readings remain those of the lenten weekday. That's how important the lenten course of weekday texts are to the life of the church.

■ VOTIVE MASSES and the Masses for various needs and occasions are prohibited on the Sundays of Lent.

The Lectionary

■ THE SUNDAY LECTIONARY DURING LENT follows the same structure each year. The gospels on the first two Sundays tell of the temptation of Jesus in the desert and the Transfiguration respectively. We hear these stories as told by the evangelist who dominates the gospels of the year in the lectionary cycle, Luke this year (C). The gospels of weeks three, four and five offer stories of repentance and renewal.

During Year A the gospels for these middle weeks bear special significance for the elect who are completing their preparation for baptism: the woman at the well, the man born blind, and the raising of Lazarus. Consequently, these may be used in any community any year. They make the most sense if you have elect preparing for baptism, since they celebrate scrutinies on those Sundays.

■ THE FRAMERS OF THE CATECHUMENATE restored the scrutinies to these Sundays with gospel texts that probably accompanied them in the early church. Their idea was not just to restore an ancient practice, but to show a progression of sin over which Jesus had power: individual sin, social sin, and the effects of sin in human death. The first readings trace significant events in salvation history, and the second readings refer to a theme that arises from one of the other two each Sunday.

Even though the Year A readings may be used effectively this year whether or not you have elect in your community, the gospels for Year C are particularly beautiful. This year you may hear two parables from Luke's gospel: the barren fig tree and the parable of the Prodigal Son, as well as John's account of the woman caught in adultery.

■ RESPONSORIAL PSALMS FOR THE SEASON are 51, 91 and 130. These may be used for any seasonal Mass. The first is a classic psalm of repentance. The last carries a similar theme. Psalm 91 includes a text that Jesus cites in his temptation, according to Matthew and Luke.

■ ON WEEKDAYS the scriptures develop various themes of Lent throughout the first half of the season. But during the second half we hear a semi-continuous reading of John's gospel. The lectionary chooses those passages that lead up to the death of Jesus. The first readings for the second half of Lent are chosen to match the gospel's theme each day.

■ THE SUNDAY *LECTIONARY FOR MASSES WITH CHILDREN* makes several abridgements during Lent. The first reading is omitted on the second and fourth Sundays. The psalms on those Sundays are changed to make a better response to the "second" reading, which in the children's lectionary is the first. The second reading is omitted on the first, third and sixth (Palm) Sundays. Only the fifth Sunday presents the entire suite of readings.

If the parish is celebrating a scrutiny, consider letting the children hear the readings from Year A for third, fourth and fifth weeks of Lent.

The Sacramentary

■ Use a simple greeting to open the Mass. Fast from words.

■ Among the options for penitential rite form c, iv and v are especially good for Lent. Form A makes a good choice for this season, because it allows the community to confess its sins together.

Some communities kneel for the penitential rite during Lent. One of the roles of the deacon is to indicate a change of posture with the traditional phrases, "Let us kneel" and "Let us stand."

Although the sprinkling rite is permitted on Sundays throughout the year, you may wish to avoid it during Lent. If you sprinkle on Sundays of the Easter season, the symbol of water will speak more clearly.

Does your community know a sung setting of the penitential rite? This would be a good season to sing it. Use a setting of "Lord, have mercy" or invite people to sing one of the traditional chants of the traditional Greek "Kyrie eleison." These may be incorporated into form C.

■ The Glory to God is omitted on the Sundays of Lent. It will be sung, however, for the two solemnities, Saint Joseph on March 19 and the Annunciation on March 25.

■ Gospel acclamation: Characteristic of this season is the change in the text for the gospel acclamation. In a spirit of penitence, the liturgy "abstains" from the alleluia. We replace it with texts like "Praise to you, Lord Jesus Christ, king of endless glory." Or else we observe silence. If the gospel acclamation is not sung, it may be omitted.

Because *alleluia* means "praise God," the substitute acclamation is a kind of English translation of the Hebrew, which seems strange. Still, this alteration of the usual pattern in greeting

the gospel remarkably creates a sense of the season, because the alleluia remains "buried" even on Sundays and solemnities until Easter.

■ Sample formulas for the general intercessions appear in the sacramentary's first appendix. See #5 and #6 for those suggested for Lent.

■ The sacramentary offers a variety of seasonal prefaces (P 8 to P 19), a broader selection than was formerly available. Together they catechize the faithful about the demands of the season while lifting our praise to God.

The Ambrosian rite has several prefaces that parallel those in the Roman. Translations by Alan Griffiths appear in *We Give You Thanks and Praise*. (P 8 resembles Wednesday 5 of Lent; P 9 resembles Sunday 2 (2); P 10 resembles Thursday 1; P 14 resembles Sunday 2 (1); P 17 resembles Wednesday of Holy Week; P 18 resembles Tuesday of Holy Week; P 19 resembles Palm Sunday.)

■ Eucharistic Prayers for Reconciliation I and II are both appropriate for this time of repentance. The first one seems to suggest Lent when it prays, "Now is the time for your people to turn back to you and to be renewed in Christ your Son, a time of grace and reconciliation." You may replace the prefaces of these prayers with a seasonal one during Lent.

■ Inserts in the eucharistic prayer: Under the ritual Masses for Christian initiation, the one for the scrutinies (#2) adds the names of the godparents for the elect to the text of Eucharistic Prayer I. The *Rite of Christian Initiation of Adults* says the godparents and the elect are remembered in the eucharistic prayer (156), and it does not limit this to Eucharistic Prayer I. The sacramentary provides no text for the other eucharistic prayers. If using Eucharistic Prayer II, invert the order of the phrases. After "In memory of his death and resurrection, we offer you, Father, this life-giving bread, this saving cup," add the phrase, "We offer them especially for the men and women you call to share your life through the living waters of baptism." Similarly, before the phrase, "Lord, remember your Church throughout the world," it would be fitting to hear, "Remember, Lord, these godparents who will present your chosen men and women for baptism," and then the list of their names.

■ For the solemn blessing on Sundays, the sacramentary on the first and third Sundays suggests the one that the collection of solemn blessings envisions for the passion, at the end of Lent (#5). Because other blessings may replace this one, better choices can be found in the prayers over the people, #6, #16 or #24. A solemn blessing for the season appears in the *Book of Blessings,* Appendix II, the fifth option at #2047. Near the end of Lent, the solemn blessing for the passion will prepare people for the Triduum. So will prayer over the people #17. Another solemn blessing for Lent can be found in the *Collection of Masses of the Blessed Virgin Mary,* at the end of the order of Mass.

The prayer over the people, with its bow of the head, was once the traditional form of blessing during Lent. It is permitted and encouraged to use the three-part solemn blessing during Lent, and to use the prayer over the people throughout the year.

■ DISMISSAL: The Roman rite never calls for a recessional hymn at the end of Mass, and yet this has become a much-observed custom. In the past, some instrumentalists took the opportunity to end the service with organ music, a custom still observed in some parts of the world, which makes the dismissal more of a dismissal. "Go in peace" really means "Go," not "Wait a minute while we sing another song." During Lent, you could end the Mass in silence for a feeling of austerity.

The Book of Blessings

YOU may wish to offer some other blessings during the season, to draw attention to some aspects of parish and community life. You may bless organizations concerned with public need (ch. 7), or bless pilgrims (8), seeds (27), meals (30), ashes (52) or a Saint Joseph's table (53). The solemn blessing for Lent at #2047 may also be used for other liturgical events.

The Rite of Christian Initiation of Adults

DURING this season of purification and enlightenment, the rites for the elect come frequently and intensely. The liturgy provides no less than eight ceremonies for them, which can be augmented by many more. In some traditions of the early church, those preparing for baptism took part in daily exorcisms and anointings during the weeks before their initiation. The number of rites we offer during Lent highlights the importance of the interior transformation guided by the Holy Spirit.

■ THE RITE OF SENDING is the first of the series. It should precede the Rite of Election, normally celebrated on the First Sunday of Lent. The date for the Rite of Election varies from one diocese to the next. Therefore, some communities may anticipate the Rite of Sending even before Lent begins.

In many dioceses, the signing of the Book of the Elect takes place at this parish celebration. In other dioceses, the signing takes place at the cathedral as part of the Rite of Election. If catechumens sign the Book of the Elect during the Rite of Sending at your parish, they should not be confused into thinking that the signature constitutes their election. Rather, it is the proclamation by the bishop during the Rite of Election that achieves this status for them.

Because the giving of the name is a pre-baptismal ritual, it pertains to the unbaptized catechumens to do so, not the baptized candidates for the Rite of Reception into the Full Communion of the Catholic Church. Because they are baptized, their names are already numbered among God's chosen people. Writing down the names and submitting them to the bishop is a practical and symbolic means of preparing for baptism.

■ THE RITE OF ELECTION takes place at the cathedral church, ideally on the First Sunday of Lent, either as a service of the word, or during the liturgy of the word of a Mass. The ritual text envisions that the service takes place at the bishop's Mass for the First Sunday of Lent, but dioceses commonly avoid celebrating this rite at a Mass, primarily because the dismissal of the elect poses practical problems. Do they go into a catechetical session? Where? How? Who leads it? Or do they just go home while the faithful remain for the liturgy of the eucharist?

In the early church, all the rites took place at the cathedral, including baptism. Since the elect may come from a large number of parishes spread over a large area, the modern liturgy assigns only one rite for celebration at the cathedral, election. Ideally, all those preparing for baptism should celebrate this rite, and it is imperative that their godparents be present for it. It is the godparents who make the all-important testimony on behalf of those who desire baptism.

If for some reason a catechumen is unable to attend the Rite of Election at the cathedral, the pastor should request delegation from the bishop to conduct the rite in the parish church on a subsequent occasion as soon as reasonably possible. Being named among the elect is an important step toward baptism. Very few pastors seek this delegation, and very few bishops are probably aware that they should give it. But if a catechumen to be baptized at Easter must miss the diocesan rite of election for any reason, the parish should take steps to conduct the rite so that the catechumen may be numbered among the diocesan elect.

■ THREE SCRUTINIES for the elect take place on the Sundays of Lent. These are offered on the third, fourth and fifth Sundays for those who are preparing for baptism.

Given the nature of the texts for this service, it is not appropriate to pray them over those who are already baptized. The purpose of the scrutinies is to drive away from the elect whatever might keep them from baptism, and to strengthen what is good within them.

Throughout the American edition of the *Rite of Christian Initiation of Adults,* the baptized and unbaptized may be invited to celebrate stages together in combined rites. However, there are no combined rites for scrutinies. The Canadian edition has no combined rites at all.

When celebrating the scrutinies at a parish Mass, note the change in the order of service. Petitions for the elect may be combined with the general intercessions, and all these may precede the creed. Or the general intercessions and the creed may be omitted. Probably the ones who most need to know this are the ushers, because it changes their cue for when to start the collection.

■ THE PRESENTATIONS OF THE CREED AND THE LORD'S PRAYER should take place apart from the Sunday Mass, during the third and fifth weeks of Lent. They may even be anticipated at another time of year, but historically they took place in the weeks preceding baptism.

You might consider having these presentations as part of an evening lenten Mass or Stations of the Cross or evening prayer, or in conjunction with another event at the parish—an adult education night, for example. In that way members of the faithful may be present for these rituals.

It is especially important that the faithful are present and understand their role at the presentation of the creed. After all, they are the ones making the presentation. In the liturgy, the presentation of these texts is made orally, not in calligraphy on parchment.

Permission is given to offer the presentations at other times of the year. The framers of the catechumenate realized that Lent would be top-heavy with rituals for the elect. For this reason, catechumens may receive the creed and Lord's Prayer some other time—during Ordinary Time, for example. Permission is also given to celebrate the presentation of the Lord's Prayer on Holy Saturday morning as part of the preparation rites. This fits a chronology from the writings of Saint Augustine. If the fifth week of Lent is crowded at your parish with other activities, you may consider this option, moving the presentation to Holy Saturday morning. However, the most traditional occasions for these presentations remains a weekday during the third and fifth weeks of Lent, at a time when the faithful may gather.

■ IF THERE ARE CANDIDATES FOR THE RITE OF RECEPTION INTO FULL COMMUNION, they may celebrate a penitential rite on the Second Sunday of Lent, a ceremony resembling a scrutiny, but with texts that honor their baptism. Those who have never professed the Nicene Creed may receive the presentation of the creed as well.

Remember, though, that the Rite of Reception may take place any time of year, and there are good arguments for conducting the ceremony apart from the Easter Vigil. This practice better connects the Easter Vigil to baptism, permits those already baptized (though not yet in full communion) to come to the table when they are ready to do so, and lightens up a ceremony that will already be quite long.

■ Throughout this period, blessings and minor exorcisms may continue to be offered for the elect during their catechetical sessions.

A parish may also have unbaptized inquirers or catechumens who will not be expecting baptism this Easter because their preparation thus far has been too short. The other rites and stages of the catechumenate still pertain to them. In other words, you may have inquirers, catechumens and elect all in the parish at the same time. Not every catechumen becomes one of the elect during this season.

■ Infant baptism: Many parishes refrain from baptizing children during the season of Lent. The *Circular Letter concerning the Preparation and Celebration of the Easter Feasts (Circular Letter)* says, "It is not fitting that Baptisms and Confirmation be celebrated [during Holy Week]" (#27). But it would help heighten the anticipation for baptism if infant baptisms could be deferred from Lent to the Easter season. There are exceptions, of course, and in an emergency baptism should be administered without delay.

The Liturgy of the Hours

THE same psalm changes that occurred in Advent and Christmas return for Lent and Easter. Psalm 105 replaces Psalms 131 and 132 on the first Saturday; 106 replaces 136 on the second Saturday; and 78 replaces 55 and 50 on the Friday and Saturday of the fourth week.

On Sundays, Evening Prayer II replaces the New Testament canticle from Revelation with one from the first letter of Peter. This canticle, a meditation on the sufferings of Christ, otherwise appears in the evening prayer psalter only in the common of martyrs.

Some beautiful texts appear in the office of readings. Note especially the one by Gregory of Nazianzen on Saturday of the third week of Lent. There he encourages the faithful to take care of Christ in the poor. "Let us then show [the Lord of all] mercy in the persons of the poor and those who today are lying on the ground, so that when we come to leave this world they may receive us into everlasting dwelling places." If your parish is looking for some kind of prayer to add during the season, consider a Sunday night

vespers or morning prayer on a day there is no early Mass.

The Rite of Penance

LENT is a beautiful season to celebrate the sacrament of reconciliation. The prayers and practices of this season help us call to mind our sins and God's forgiveness. As we grow in awareness of our faults, we can bring them to God in a spirit of repentance, open to growth in grace, awaiting the full expression of mercy and love.

Many parishes offer a communal celebration of reconciliation so the faithful can bring their lenten penance to a sacramental moment. If several parishes are all planning a communal service, publish announcements about them together in the bulletin and on the website. Start all the services at a common time.

■ If children in Catholic schools or religious education programs are to celebrate the sacrament, offer communal services for them early in the season to avoid scheduling confessors for too much work at the end. For children, a series of short services is better than one long one. Although many adults have patiently tolerated what might be called "communal waiting services," children have a shorter attention span.

■ Individual reconciliation should also be available. Publish the times in a prominent space in the bulletin, and encourage all to include the sacrament in their lenten renewal. Publish also the times the sacrament is available at neighboring parishes. Advertise all opportunities well so the parish knows when reconciliation will be offered.

■ Non-sacramental penitential services for Lent can be found in Appendix II of the *Rite of Penance*. They may be used with any group wanting to express sorrow and pray for forgiveness. They also offer readings and prayers that could be incorporated into a communal sacramental celebration. The first suggests sprinkling with holy water as an act of repentance, but without proper catechesis it will seem like an anticipation of Easter. The second suggests adoration of the cross or Stations of the Cross to conclude the service. Because the veneration of the cross is a highlight of the Good Friday liturgy, it may seem odd to anticipate it. Stations, however, might make a fitting conclusion to the celebration.

Seen another way, a penitential service might make a good prelude to stations. The custom of Friday stations is observed throughout the Catholic world, although there is no universal liturgical rite for the prayer. Many publishers make quality materials available. LTP publishes three different individual sets of texts for the assembly—*Traditional Jerusalem Stations, Scriptural Stations Used in Rome,* and *With the Women of the Gospels*—and a leader's book with all three services.

The Pastoral Care of the Sick

THE sacrament of the sick may be given at any time during this season, but because of the large number of other liturgical prayers vying for attention, it may be best to celebrate communal anointing of the sick during another season of the church year.

The penitential services in the *Rite of Penance* include an example of one for the sick. This option offers a time of prayer with the sick when the sacraments are not administered.

The Rite of Marriage

MARRIAGES may take place during Lent. The parish priest is asked to advise the couple to take into consideration the special nature of the season (*Rite of Marriage,* 11, and *Ceremonial of Bishops,* 604).

If the wedding takes place during a Saturday evening Mass, the readings and prayers for the Sunday in Lent take precedence. The couple is free to select only one alternative scripture passage for the wedding Mass during Lent.

If the wedding does not include a Mass, or if the wedding Mass does not take place on a Saturday evening or Sunday, the scriptures and prayers for marriage may be used.

No other special texts or scriptures apply to weddings during Lent. The gospel acclamation should be one of those offered for Lent, not the alleluia.

When decorating for the wedding, the couple should honor the seasonal appearance of the church. It will contribute to the ecclesial context in which the wedding takes place.

The Order of Christian Funerals

FUNERALS may take place on any day of Lent. On weekdays, consult the daily lectionary. Sometimes the daily readings of Lent seem suitable for a funeral Mass. But the funeral lectionary may be used. If a funeral needs to take place on a Sunday in Lent, the Sunday Mass is used with its prayers and scriptures.

Purple vesture is permitted for funerals throughout the year. Although most parishes celebrate the Mass in white, the color of Lent may also be used.

The Art and Environment

THE spare use of materials in this season will inspire the spare use of food, drink and extraneous activity. A sober environment fits the season of Lent.

■ CONSIDER THE OUTSIDE AS WELL. There may be something you can remove during the season, to restore it later. Less is more.

■ DROUGHT: Some communities empty the holy water stoups or the baptismal font during the season. The practice has some grassroots support, but it does not appear in the liturgical books. We sign ourselves with water upon entering the church as a reminder of baptism, but it can also function as an act of ritual cleansing in harmony with the spirit of the season and the nature of the eucharist.

The Easter candle continues to reside near the font, but perhaps in a less prominent place. It will look rather stubby by now.

■ IF CATECHUMENS SIGNED THE BOOK OF THE ELECT at your parish, you may display it someplace where the faithful can observe it. Names and faces of the elect should be on bulletin boards, if not in the weekly bulletin and on the website during Lent. Have kids cut out crosses and print a different name of one of the elect on each one. Stuff them in the bulletin so they can end up on refrigerators at home, to remind each household to pray for at least one of the elect by name.

■ THE COLOR FOR VESTURE IS VIOLET. If you have a set more purple than the bluish tint used during Advent, use it to distinguish these seasons. The Fourth Sunday permits the use of rose vestments. The final Sunday of Lent takes red vesture. The two solemnities, Saint Joseph and the Annunciation, call for white. Otherwise, go purple.

The Music

A rich heritage of music for Lent has evolved in every age.

■ CHANT: Some of the Latin chants are especially lovely. Your community could sing "Attende, Domine" and "Parce, Domine" (found in the *Liber cantualis*), "Vexilla Regis," "Pange, lingua," and all will hold up well with repeated use during the season. Consider using a set of chant acclamations for the eucharistic prayer. Has your community learned the one in English in the sacramentary?

Entrance and communion antiphons and psalms, as well as the responsorial psalms and other chants between the readings, appear in *By Flowing Waters*. These can be especially effective at daily Mass when only a cantor is available to lead the singing. This collection of unaccompanied song for assemblies, cantors and choirs includes settings for the penitential rite (606, 611 and 612), eucharistic acclamations (578–81), a threefold Great Amen (583) and the fraction rite (605, 610, 615, 616, 621 and 622).

■ HYMNS: The classic hymns for Lent include "Lord, Who Throughout These Forty Days" and "This Is Our Accepted Time." Your community could really belt out "Lift High the Cross" using William Ferris's arrangement for choir, descant, trumpets and organ (WLP 8688). Michael Ward has a fine arrangement of the traditional spiritual "Near the Cross" (WLP 8526).

Delores Dufner's collection of hymn texts, "Sing a New Church," is a treasure (OCP 9922). For the season of Lent she offers a one-verse hymn to follow the proclamation of each Sunday's gospel.

■ YOUTH: The entire community may also learn songs meaningful to teens and expressive of the season, like Rich Mullins's "Awesome God" (WLP, *Voices as One,* 7) or Bob Hurd's "Be with Me" (OCP, *Spirit and Song*). Henry Mollicone's "Hear Me, Redeemer" (Woodland Hills Music Press 4511) is in a gospel style. Ed Bolduc's "If Today You Hear the Voice of God" (WLP 7352) has a relaxed, rocky design. Tony Alonso perfectly set Shirley Erena Murray's disturbing text "I Am Standing Waiting" (GIA G-5612). It is sure to send people into lenten self-scrutiny.

■ PSALMODY: Richard Proulx's "Six Choral Introits for the Church Year" (WLP 5783) includes a beautiful one for Lent, text from Joel, tune based on the haunting *tonus peregrinus*. William Ferris has a simple setting of Psalm 91, "Be with Me, Lord," (WLP 6221). Christopher Walker's "O Lord, Heal Us" works for Lent and Passiontide (OCP 10799). Robert Schaefer's choral setting of Psalm 51, "Be Merciful, O Lord," is in English and Spanish (WLP 6241).

Other noteworthy settings of lenten psalms include Psalm 137: "Let My Tongue Be Silenced," by Mike Hay (WLP 6224) and "Beside the Streams of Babylon," by Paul Lisicky; Psalm 91: "God Has Put the Angels in Charge of You," by Kathy Powell (WLP 6234); and Psalm 51: "Psalm for Mercy," by Stephen Pishner (GIA G-4707), based on the hymn "Wondrous Love."

■ THE SCRUTINIES AND PRESENTATIONS will also require music. Be sure to plan for involvement of musicians and assembly in these events. J. Michael Thompson's piece for unison choir, "God, Give Us Grace These Lenten Days," blends the themes of Noah's ark and baptismal rebirth (WLP 5777). Jerry Galipeau's "Three Litanies for the Scrutinies" (WLP 5235) will help you incorporate local petitions into a sung framework.

And do not overlook the oddly named "RCIA Suite" by Omer Westendorf and Robert E. Kreutz (WLP 8551), the same team that brought us "Gift of Finest Wheat" and a host of other singable, creditable compositions. The suite alternates instrumental and choral music. The texts are remarkably poetic. (Whoever thought you could sing the word *catechumen*?) And the choral writing is superb. Use the entire suite as part of a lenten prayer service, or use bits of it throughout the season for Sunday worship.

Christopher Walker edited OCP's collection of music for the rites of Christian initiation, "Christ We Proclaim" (11293), which is filled with suggestions for the liturgy and music, like Bernadette Farrell's "Restless Is the Heart" and Walker's much-needed litany and prayer of exorcism. Who could resist singing Farrell's "Christ, Be Our Light" for the second scrutiny?

■ THE AVOIDANCE OF INSTRUMENTAL MUSIC IN LENT, a longstanding tradition, causes its own penance for a community who would love to hear J. S. Bach's chorale preludes like "O Mensch, bewein' dein' Sünde groß" or one of the many versions of the Passion Chorale "O Sacred Head" for organ, like "Herzlich tut mich verlangen" by Johannes Brahms.

Other compositions are Harold Owen's "Three Meditations for Organ on Lenten Hymns," available from GIA (G-5414). These are well-composed, useful pieces based on tunes that many assemblies know.

The Parish and Home

THE parish will do all families a service by providing texts for prayer at home. Lent is a season when families may build a spirit of communal prayer. Provide mealtime prayer cards and suggestions for decorating the table. You will find several good suggestions in *Catholic Household Blessings and Prayers,* like the Ash Wednesday blessing of the season and a place for prayer (beginning on p. 132), the blessings of Lenten disciplines (p. 137 and following), and the Passion Sunday placing of branches in the home (beginning on p. 140).

LTP's two-volume *A Lent Sourcebook* (1990) is an outstanding resource of texts useful for prayer and meditation. *What Am I Doing for Lent This Year?* (2000) will help individuals and communities think about the spiritual growth they wish to attain and make a practical plan for the season.

Start planning the Easter Sunday bulletin. You may have to submit the copy early in Holy Week to get it back while the office is still open. Brainstorm about the information you want visitors to know. What's coming up after Easter that they could return for? What opportunities for community life should they know about?

Texts

■ GREETING: Sacramentaries from other language groups suggest greetings like this:

The grace of the Lord Jesus, who suffered for us, be with you.

■ INTRODUCTION TO THE PENITENTIAL RITE:

My sisters and brothers, let us repent and believe in the gospel.

■ RESPONSE TO THE GENERAL INTERCESSIONS:

Lord, have mercy.

Be merciful, Lord, and hear our prayer.

The *Book of Common Worship* for the Presbyterian Church (U.S.A.) and the Cumberland Presbyterian Church recommends this prayer for Lent (p. 237), which could conclude the general intercessions or be incorporated in some other seasonal prayer:

Holy God,
your Word, Jesus Christ,
     spoke peace to a sinful world
and brought humanity the gift of reconciliation
by the suffering and death he endured.
Teach those who bear his name
to follow the example he gave us.
May our faith, hope, and charity
turn hatred to love, conflict to peace,
and death to eternal life;
through Christ our Lord. Amen. [217]

■ DISMISSAL OF CATECHUMENS AND ELECT:

We do not live on bread alone, but on every word that comes forth from the mouth of God. Catechumens and elect, feast yourselves on God's word until you come again to feast at this table. Go in peace.

February

ORIENTATION

"Come and admit you are wrong" is hardly an invitation the typical American loves to hear. But the power of Ash Wednesday calls believers to their place of worship in droves to confess their sin and even to wear a public sign of their repentance.

The blessing and imposition of ashes opens this season of sorrow and mercy. Ash Wednesday has been observed throughout the universal church for over 900 years. It invites the baptized faithful into a spirit of repentance. Even those who do not frequent the Mass come to express their sorrow and to receive the symbol of repentance.

This is a day of fast and abstinence. The faithful may eat one meal, but the other meals should not equal another full meal. There should be no snacking. We abstain from meat today, which includes poultry and amphibians, but not seafood. Still, the idea is to eat simply, not lavishly.

Other services may be offered in addition to Mass—the Liturgy of the Hours, for example, or even a word service that includes the giving of ashes. See the *Book of Blessings* for a complete order of service (ch. 52). Some parishes offer a simple fasting evening meal following Mass or evening prayer, to accommodate those coming from work. Ashes are distributed only as part of communal prayer. Those who wear ashes this day signify their acceptance of penance and their participation in community.

LECTIONARY

The gospel outlines three divisions of penitential disciplines: prayer, fasting and almsgiving. Through the prophet Joel, God invites the people to turn from sin with fasting. Paul tells the Corinthians that now is the time of their salvation. The psalm invites us all into a confession of our sins before God. Overall, the readings proclaim the existence of sin, the need for repentance, and the means to execute it. They should inspire a 40-day response.

SACRAMENTARY

Ashes are made from the previous year's palm branches. There is no liturgical ceremony that accompanies their burning. This can be done simply, well in advance of the liturgy. Perhaps one household in the community could prepare the ashes each year. Parishioners who don't know what to do with leftover palm branches will appreciate the opportunity to bring them to church for this purpose.

Set the ashes someplace visible before the service begins. If necessary, provide cards for the ministers with the text they will recite. Washing bowls, pitchers of water, and slices of lemon will help ministers clean up after the distribution of ashes. (See notes on this day in G. Thomas Ryan's *The Sacristy Manual,* available from LTP, pp. 194–5.)

Mass begins with a hymn or song based on the entrance antiphon acclaiming God's mercy. A simple refrain, chanted a capella, may be effective, or a hymn that establishes the theme of the 40 days. The presider makes the sign of the cross, greets the people, and then immediately offers the opening prayer. There is no penitential rite and no Glory to God today. The giving of ashes—even

though it follows the homily—replaces the penitential rite.

At the blessing and giving of ashes, no introduction is offered, but one could be devised based on a text in the *Book of Blessings* (#1663) either at this point or after the greeting before the opening prayer. Following the homily, the presider invites all to silent prayer and then blesses the people or the ashes (depending on which version of the prayer you use), sprinkling the ashes with holy water.

The presider and other ministers then rub ashes onto the foreheads of all who come forward, reciting one of the texts provided. (One need not be a priest or deacon to distribute ashes.) A song of repentance is sung. Psalm 50 is recommended. (That is the alternate numbering for the psalm marked 51 in the lectionary, the same one used for the responsory at this Mass.) After the ministers wash their hands, the general intercessions are prayed.

The preface recommended for Ash Wednesday (P 11) is entitled "The Reward of Fasting," but actually treats the "observance of Lent," not just fasting.

The liturgy today makes no allusion to the catechumens who will become elect. Ash Wednesday developed at a time in our history when catechumens were few and the church needed to begin this season with a penitential service for all the faithful. The catechumens, of course, make their entry into the season with the Rite of Election this coming Sunday.

OTHER IDEAS

Choose music with an easily memorized refrain for the distribution of ashes. As with the communion procession, it is cumbersome for people to process with a hymnal in hand. Good options include "My Soul Is Longing for Your Peace" and "Grant to Us, O Lord" by Lucien Deiss (WLP), and "Give Us, Lord, a New Heart," by Bernadette Farrell (OCP 710). For liturgies celebrated with children, consult *Preparing Liturgy for Children and Children for Liturgy,* p. 81.

Since the sixth century the text from the book of Wisdom has been sung as the entrance song for Ash Wednesday; it may be found in *By Flowing Waters* (50–51). All 19 verses of Psalm 51 are available for singing during the distribution of ashes at 55–56.

Among the prayers of thanksgiving after Mass in the sacramentary's first appendix is the universal prayer attributed to Pope Clement XI. It may make a good prayer for Lent.

T H U 26 #220 (LMC #176–184)   violet
Lenten Weekday

The first reading sets out that we can choose either life or death. Moses enjoins the people to choose life by following God. The same two ways appear in the psalm. We will reject the way of evil and accept the way of God in the renewal of our baptismal promises this Easter Vigil. The lectionary is already preparing us for the liturgy after the end of Lent. Meanwhile, during this time of renewal, we will be called to observe more closely the path we are choosing. Already in the gospel the shadow of the cross falls across this season. We who follow Christ will take up his cross.

The third preface for Lent (P 10) uses the theme of self-denial.

■ IN URUGUAY THE VOTIVE MASS OF THE VIRGIN MARY, MOTHER OF RECONCILIATION, is encouraged during Lent. (See the texts in the *Collection of Masses of the Blessed Virgin Mary,* #14.)

F R I 27 #221 (LMC #176–184)   violet
Lenten Weekday

We abstain from meat today. The opening prayer seems to allude to this lenten custom.

In the gospel Jesus speaks of the need to fast when the bridegroom is taken away. In the first reading, Isaiah explains the full implications of a fast—a discipline not just concerning food, but an entire way of life. The penitential Psalm 51 returns. The first preface for Lent (P 8) relates charity to prayer.

S A T 28 #222 (LMC #176–184)   violet
Lenten Weekday

Jesus invites a sinner into discipleship, giving hope to all. Isaiah gives advice for the authentic practice of belief. The psalm expresses a sinner's aspiration to overcome evil and do good.

The suggested communion antiphon quotes from Matthew's version of today's gospel. The second preface for Lent (P 9) expresses the goals of this season of repentance. You may use it with the first eucharistic prayer for Masses of reconciliation.

✸ 29 #24 (LMC #20)   violet
First Sunday of Lent

ORIENTATION

Although Lent started several days ago, this will be the first day many in the community become aware of it. It is also the day when the elect begin their period of purification and enlightenment, after celebrating the Rite of Election.

The time frame within which one must fulfill Easter duty begins today. It hardly seems necessary to remind people, but they are expected to share communion at least once between today and Trinity Sunday.

Today is Leap Day. The next time it will fall on the First Sunday of Lent will be in 2088—in case you were wondering.

LECTIONARY

The gospel each year tells of the temptation of Jesus in the desert. His 40 days there give us the length of Lent. In fact, some people reckon the 40 days of Lent beginning today and ending on Holy Thursday.

Luke's version of the temptation is a beautifully crafted account, based on Mark, expanded by the "Q" source he probably shared with Matthew, and refined in Luke's own inimitable style. Luke notes that Jesus was filled with the Holy Spirit, whose activity in the later church Luke will reveal in Acts of the Apostles.

The most obvious difference between Matthew and Luke's versions of the temptations is the sequence of the tests two and three. In Luke's account, the final test takes place on the parapet of the temple in Jerusalem. One theory is that this was the original sequence because it ends the series more dramatically. Another theory is that Luke switched the two temptations in order to have the series end in Jerusalem. Jerusalem plays an important role in Luke's writing, and he may have wanted to draw attention to the city by placing its involvement last, rather than buried in the middle.

Today's psalm is the full text of the passage Jesus excerpts in his response to the third temptation. Both Jesus and the devil quote scripture at each other. We quote it along with them. This is a rare instance where the responsorial psalm relates to the gospel, not at all to the first reading. But because of the custom of the Roman lectionary, we sing the psalm after the first reading as usual.

Throughout the season, the first readings will trace principal events in salvation history. The series begins today with Deuteronomy. Moses invites the people to make a confession of their faith in God who led their ancestors into Egypt, out of slavery, and then into a land flowing with milk and honey. They offer God thanks with the first fruits of the soil that God gave them. This anamnesis, or "remembering," observes the same function as many of our prayers that recall the great deeds of God. We hear this reading on the day set aside for the Rite of Election, when the church admits a group of catechumens into the body known as the elect, or the chosen people. They are the new chosen people, whom God is leading from the slavery of sin into the freedom of the body of Christ.

The second reading is chosen because of its relationship to the first. Paul encourages the Romans to make a confession of faith, just as Moses asked the chosen people to confess theirs. For Paul, the confession is simple, yet profound: Jesus is Lord. Jesus possesses the same identity that God revealed to Moses in the burning bush.

SACRAMENTARY

The Glory to God is omitted. The suggested texts for the entrance and communion antiphons rely on today's gospel. The preface for the first Sunday (P 12) recalls the temptation, but other choices may be made. Given the theme of sinful humanity in the other scriptures today, one of the eucharistic

prayers for reconciliation would also make a good choice. You may use either of them with the lenten preface if you wish. For the final blessing a good choice might be prayer over the people #24.

OTHER IDEAS

The *Circular Letter* (#23) recommends a penitential procession to open the Mass for the First Sunday of Lent. The *Ceremonial of Bishops* (#261) suggests a procession for all the lenten Sundays wherever the bishop presides. The community gathers someplace outside the church and a procession forms. The presider may wear a violet cope. During the procession the Litany of the Saints is sung. Upon entering the church, all take their places, the presider reverences the altar and then goes to the chair. The opening prayer for Mass follows immediately. If the Kyrie was not incorporated into the litany, it may precede the opening prayer.

By Flowing Waters includes a solemn form of the Litany of the Saints (663–675) for this Sunday (see Performance Note on pp. 419 and 426–427). See also Richard Proulx's "Litany for the Season of Lent" (WLP 5228), based on texts from the *Book of Common Prayer*. It's not a litany of the saints, but a litany worth considering at the beginning of Lent.

Psalm 91 (62 and 63 of *By Flowing Waters*) has been traditionally the psalm of the First Sunday of Lent. In 64, the rapid return of the refrain, "Because I have sinned against you," after every verse of the psalm illustrates the disastrous effects of our sinfulness on all of our relationships.

If your community has not yet celebrated the Rite of Sending for the Rite of Election, you may do so today. It should take place, of course, before the Rite of Election.

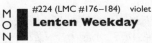

March

M O N **1** #224 (LMC #176–184)   violet
Lenten Weekday

The demands of Christian charity are no more eloquently explained than in Jesus' image for the last judgment in Matthew 25. Everyone knows what the final exam will be. Whatever we do for the least of our brothers and sisters we do for Jesus.

Proper treatment of neighbors is also the theme of today's passage from Leviticus. Because it is drawn from the Torah, we sing a psalm in praise of God's law. The refrain comes from Jesus' own description of his discourse on the bread of life. His words are spirit and life.

The suggested communion antiphon today comes from the gospel.

The fourth preface for Lent (P 11) explains the rewards of a faithful lenten observance.

T U E **2** #225 (LMC #176–184)   violet
Lenten Weekday

Prayer, one of the topics of the gospel from Ash Wednesday, returns in today's gospel. In fact, this is the passage excised from the gospel that day, in which Jesus teaches the Lord's Prayer. This passage will return during the community's celebration of the presentation of the Lord's Prayer to the elect during the fifth week of Lent. Is that event on the parish calendar?

The first reading explains the effectiveness of God's word, implying the effectiveness of the Lord's Prayer. The psalm recalls that the Lord will hear the cry of the just.

The second preface for Lent (P 9) invites us to purify our hearts.

W E D 3 — #226 (LMC #176–184) violet
Lenten Weekday

Optional Memorial of Katharine Drexel (+ 1955), virgin, religious / violet • Hearing the Jonah story today makes us think of it as a foreshadowing of Jesus' burial and resurrection. But the lectionary has something else in mind. Jesus says the point of the story of Jonah is the conversion of the people. That is its lenten message today. Psalm 51 returns to round out the theme of repentance.

The first eucharistic prayer for reconciliation makes a good choice today.

■ TODAY'S SAINT: Born in Philadelphia to an affluent family, Katharine became devoted to society's poor and to American Indians. She founded the Sisters of the Blessed Sacrament and pursued the ministry of evangelization. After a heart attack in 1935 she spent her last 20 years of life in prayerful retirement.

T H U 4 — #227 (LMC #176–184) violet
Lenten Weekday

Optional Memorial of Casimir (+ 1482) / violet • Another text on the benefit of prayer couples nicely with Tuesday's scriptures. Jesus invites us to ask God for what we want. Queen Esther prays for guidance before she appears before the king to plea for the freedom of her people. The psalm gives thanks for prayers answered. This story is remembered in the Jewish feast of Purim, which will be celebrated this coming Sunday this year.

The first preface for Lent (P 8) acknowledges our spirit of reverence for God.

■ TODAY'S SAINT: Casimir, son of the king of Poland, led an austere, celibate life. His religious devotion meant more to him than the national crown of Hungary. The season of Lent makes a fitting setting for the remembrance of his asceticism.

F R I 5 — #228 (LMC #176–184) violet
Lenten Weekday

The message of reconciliation sounds out clear this Friday in Jesus' plea for those who cannot get along. Make peace on your way to the altar, he says. And whenever possible, settle disputes outside of court.

Ezekiel encourages a similar conversion of heart. The wicked who turn from their sins will find forgiveness. We pray for forgiveness with one of the greatest psalms of human sorrow and divine mercy.

The second eucharistic prayer for reconciliation says, "Your spirit changes our hearts: enemies begin to speak to one another."

S A T 6 — #229 (LMC #176–184) violet
Lenten Weekday

Jesus' command to love enemies is a measure of Christian perfection. This season calls us to charity as part of its discipline. Moses reminds the people of the importance of observing God's commands, and the first verses of Psalm 119 meditate on the same.

Service to neighbor is highlighted in the first preface for Lent (P 8).

✷ 7 — #27 (LMC #23) violet
Second Sunday of Lent

ORIENTATION

Today, as on every Second Sunday of Lent, we hear the story of the transfiguration of Jesus, a glimpse of what is to be. With the apostles we climb the mountain of Lent to behold Jesus at the summit in glory. If there are baptized candidates for the Rite of Reception at Easter, they may celebrate a penitential rite at Mass today (RCIA, 459). But remember. their reception may take place any time of year. If your baptized candidates will be received apart from the Easter Vigil, you may omit this optional rite.

LECTIONARY

Luke's version of the transfiguration of Jesus draws the reader's attention to one unusual word: *exodus*. In the vision, Moses and Elijah appear in glory and speak with Jesus about his exodus in Jerusalem. With one word, Luke opens up a vast and important interpretation of this event and of Jesus' death and resurrection. The topic of conversation at the transfiguration is the passion we will commemorate at the conclusion of Lent. The passing of Jesus from death to life is likened to the exodus, the crossing of the chosen people into their promised land.

The first reading on the Second Sunday of Lent each year tells some part of the story of Abraham. This year we hear God establish the covenant with him. Count the stars, God invites the patriarch, if you can: So numerous shall your descendents be. God also promises land to Abraham and his descendants. God promises blood and soil—endless life symbolized by many descendents and a land that will last forever. All God asks for in return is relationship. "I am your God," the voice says. The psalmist believes that the bounty of the Lord will be revealed in the land of the living. If we wait for God, we will not be disappointed in the divine promise.

The second reading comes in longer and shorter forms. Both versions contain the key phrase for this weekend: "[Jesus] will change our lowly body to conform with his glorified body." This verse affirms the power Jesus holds as God, as well as his desire to use it for the benefit of believers. All this is expressed while addressing the change a body undergoes on the road to glory. This reading prepares us to hear the transfiguration of Jesus in the gospel.

SACRAMENTARY

Begin simply in the spirit of the season. Perhaps you will sing the penitential rite. The Glory to God is omitted. Both versions of the opening prayer build on the theme of light. The preface recommended for today (P 13) is a good choice, but others suit the season just as well. A prayer over the people is suggested, but consider also #7.

OTHER IDEAS

The Rite of Reception for baptized candidates may take place any time of year. It need not happen at the Easter Vigil. The timing pertains more to the candidates' readiness than to a season of the year. Even if they are received into the full communion of the church at Easter, the penitential rite offered today is optional. However, if your community chooses to celebrate it, it may serve as a prelude to the scrutinies over the next few Sundays. You might invite the other members of the assembly to extend their hands over the candidates during the presider's imposition of hands. The deacon or a representative from the Christian initiation team might impose hands as well. The liturgy encourages catechists to take a strong liturgical role (RCIA, 16).

Today is Purim, the Jewish Feast of Lots. The celebration commemorates God's deliverance of Israel through the courage of Esther and the wisdom of Mordecai.

MON 8 #230 (LMC #176–184) violet
Lenten Weekday

Optional Memorial of John of God (+ 1550), religious founder / violet ▪ Among the charitable attitudes Jesus commends to his followers is nonjudgmental pardon. In the first reading Daniel confesses the sins of the people to God, speaking himself the words of a communal expression of sorrow. The psalm asks God not to treat us as our sins deserve.

The second eucharistic prayer for reconciliation fits the themes today.

▪ TODAY'S SAINT: Portuguese by birth, shepherd and warrior by profession, John changed jobs at the age of 40 and devoted his life to caring for the sick.

TUE 9 #231 (LMC #176–184) violet
Lenten Weekday

Optional Memorial of Frances of Rome (+ 1440), married woman, religious founder / violet ▪ Jesus condemns hypocrisy and invites people into authentic religious observance. The psalm asks in a similar vein, Why do people profess the covenant with their mouth but cast God's words behind them?

The passage from Isaiah is a little more generic in its call to renewal, but in the context of the other readings, it also challenges formalism—those who merely go through the actions of worship without any heart.

In this spirit of repentance, the first eucharistic prayer for reconciliation would work well today.

▪ TODAY'S SAINT: Frances of Rome married at a young age and led a life of fervent piety. She founded a congregation of sisters who adapted the Rule of Benedict and later joined the community herself after the death of her husband. Her former residence in Rome is open to pilgrims on her feast day.

WED 10 #232 (LMC #176–184) violet
Lenten Weekday

The shadow of the cross returns as Jesus predicts his own passion. Completely oblivious to its implications, Zebedee's family asks for favors. The first reading recalls the prophet Jeremiah's persecution, a precursor to the suffering of Christ. Even the psalmist hears the frightening whispers of the crowd from every side, plotting to kill.

The fourth preface for Lent (P 11) acknowledges our faults and God's call to grow in holiness.

THU 11 #233 (LMC #176–184) violet
Lenten Weekday

The parable of Lazarus and the rich man forms a graphic illustration of the importance of sharing one's gifts with the needy. Jeremiah suggests that those who trust in God will demonstrate that in peaceful, steadfast behavior. The psalm repeats the theme of the tree that receives life because it is planted beside the water of God's word.

The third preface for Lent (P 10) fits these themes.

F R I 12 #234 (LMC #176–184)   violet
Lenten Weekday

The readings give us another somber Friday in Lent. Jesus' parable of the wicked tenants reads like an omen of his own suffering and death. Yet, as the first reading shows, we have seen it all before in the story of Joseph, sold for 20 pieces of silver. That story is retold in the psalm. The Joseph story's happy ending is hidden from view as we are made to face the horror of sinful human behavior in need of redemption.

The first eucharistic prayer for reconciliation will put this in perspective.

S A T 13 #235 (LMC #176–184)   violet
Lenten Weekday

"A man had two sons." So begins one of the most famous stories in the history of the world. The Prodigal Son is a masterful tale woven by Jesus, artfully recounted by Luke. It moves the reader to repentance. Paired with this is Micah's beautiful reflection on the mercy of God, who casts our sins under the sea.

The communion antiphon today quotes the gospel. The second eucharistic prayer for reconciliation will fit this liturgy.

#30 or 28 (LMC #26 or 24)
violet
14 Third Sunday of Lent

ORIENTATION

This Sunday and the next two form a unit especially in communities where members of the elect are preparing for baptism. On all three Sundays we have the option of proclaiming the scriptures from Year A. Although this option is not restricted to communities with elect, it makes most sense to exercise it when you celebrate the scrutinies. You may use the Year A readings only at scrutiny Masses, or you may replace all the Year C readings at all Masses with those from Year A. You may even use the Year C readings at a scrutiny Mass, but they will not fit as well with the theme of their prayers.

LECTIONARY

■ YEAR A READINGS: The gospel of the woman at the well forms the centerpiece of the scriptures this weekend and gives shape to this part of Lent. She does not approach Jesus; Jesus approaches her. He has living water. She asks for some. He reveals his knowledge of her. She becomes a believer. She also becomes an apostle, proclaiming that Jesus is the Messiah. For all these reasons, she becomes a kind of patron for the elect, whom God has approached, who have asked for the living water of baptism, who are expressing their belief, and who must become apostles of the Good News.

The first reading continues the series summarizing salvation history. Each year the first reading on the Third Sunday of Lent gives us a story of Moses. In Year A it recalls Israel's thirst in the desert, and God's gift of water from the rock. The psalm sings critically of the same event, when Israel tested God at Massah and Meribah, even though the people had seen God's work.

The second reading reinforces the theme of Christ dying for sinners.

■ YEAR C READINGS: Repentance and reconciliation are recurrent themes in Luke's gospel, so his book continues to supply the material for the gospels in Year C on almost all the Sundays of Lent. Today we hear Jesus' warning that people will perish badly if they do not repent. His parable of the fig tree, though, sounds a note of toleration. God will give us a chance to produce fruit. For the faithful, Lent is our fertilizer.

The first reading for this Sunday in Year C tells of Moses and the burning bush. This passage reveals the name of God as well as the divine mission. God chooses Moses to act as liberator. In return, God asks for relationship, a covenant with the children of Abraham forever. Christians believe we have inherited the covenant as the new chosen people, commissioned by God to liberate all those held under the bondage of sin, oppression and despair. The psalm that follows this reading celebrates the covenant between the chosen people and a God who is kind, merciful and slow to anger.

Moses appears again in the second reading, a passage from 1 Corinthians. Paul draws parallels between the exodus from Egypt and the Christian life. He calls the exodus a baptism and notes that the chosen people shared a special spiritual food and drink. He also says the rock in the desert was Christ.

Paul relies on a belief that the rock followed Israel around in the desert. This belief evolved from a problem in the scriptures: The story of God giving Israel water from the rock appears twice in the story of the exodus, each time at a different location. Many scholars today assume that the same story was recounted two different ways, but early liturgists reached a different conclusion: The rock followed Israel. Paul says the rock— their source of nourishment and their companion on the journey— was Christ. The typology of this passage helps us place our lenten penance in the context of Israel's journey from slavery to freedom.

SACRAMENTARY

The prayers for the Third Sunday of Lent appear where you expect to find them, but if you are celebrating the scrutinies at one or more Masses this weekend, you may also use the prayers under Ritual Masses: Christian Initiation, The Scrutinies (2). The text frequently refers to the "chosen ones," a translation for the same Latin word that is rendered "elect" in the *Rite of Christian Initiation of Adults*. The eucharistic prayer may include a remembrance of the elect and a mention of the names of their godparents. Print out the names of each group so the presider can include them at the appropriate place in the prayer. If there are no elect in your community, use the prayers for the Third Sunday of Lent. Two communion antiphons are suggested, depending on which gospel is proclaimed.

The preface for today is proper (P 14), but its references to the gospel of Year A make it a better choice if you are celebrating scrutinies. Otherwise consider the first lenten preface (P 8). The suggested solemn blessing perhaps too soon anticipates the passion. prayer over the people #6 offers a better text.

OTHER IDEAS

Plan out how people should be arranged for the scrutiny (RCIA, 150–56). Visibility and audibility are important. One option is to have the elect in the sanctuary but facing the assembly, with the priest in the center aisle facing them. Another is to place the elect and their godparents throughout

the church so the faithful can see at least one of them up close. Churches with antiphonal seating can line up the elect on both sides of the altar and assembly.

The rite never explains how the elect get there. Perhaps the deacon or catechist could read their names and invite them forward. Or perhaps the godparents are rehearsed to escort the elect forward at this time without a verbal cue.

The presider invites first the assembly and then the elect to silent prayer. The elect bow their heads or kneel. Then they stand again. Some presiders have them kneel or prostrate throughout, but physical demands should not get in the way of the prayer.

Two options for intercessions exist. The first offers prayers for the elect, their families, the assembled community and the whole world. The second uses imagery from the gospel. If you wish, the general intercessions may also be invoked at this time. You may include intercessions that name the struggles the elect experience in their own lives, in society or in the church.

These intercessions conclude with the exorcism. There are two options for the text, both in trinitarian form. The presider says the first part, hands joined, to God. He imposes hands on the elect in a gesture calling on the Holy Spirit. He prays to Jesus Christ with hands outstretched over the elect. All these prayers ask for the banishment of whatever keeps them from accepting Christ, and for the gift of the Spirit to strengthen their resolve.

In some communities the deacon, the director of the catechumenate, the godparent, a catechist or other members of the faithful join the imposition or extension of hands.

A song may be sung, and then the elect may be dismissed. If

there are catechumens preparing for initiation the following year, they are not included in the scrutiny prayers, but they may be dismissed at this time.

There are three ways of handling the creed and the general intercessions. If the general intercessions were added to the scrutiny invocations, you may recite the creed after the dismissal of the elect and catechumens, and then begin the preparation of the altar and gifts. If you choose this first option, alert the ushers that the collection will follow the creed, not the intercessions today. In the second option, if general intercessions were not included in the scrutiny invocations, they may follow the dismissal and creed as usual. In the third option, the creed and the intercessions may both be omitted. If you pick one way of doing it and repeat it for the three weeks, it will be easier for ministers and assembly to enter into the spirit of the prayer.

Be sure to rehearse the scrutiny. It is best if the presider, catechist, godparents, servers, musicians and others involved in the rite meet at the church at least a day before the scrutiny to review cues so all can flow smoothly. If you can manage it, do not include the elect in the rehearsal. Let the scrutiny happen to them. If their godparents know what is going on, that should be enough.

The lectionary offers an optional Mass for the third week of Lent, with texts borrowed from the Year A readings of today. In the rare event that scrutinies take place apart from Sunday, these texts may be used. Or if you have not heard these texts on Sunday, you may use them at another Mass this week. For example, if you have an evening Mass on one weeknight during Lent, you may choose the readings from the optional Mass.

The presentation of the creed takes place sometime this week, not on Sunday. You may wish to choose an evening when several other members of the community will be on site. If committees are meeting, or if there is an adult education session some weeknight, schedule the presentation of the creed so that these groups may participate also. It does not take long, but it will involve the faithful in the all-important task of handing on their belief.

MON 15 #237 (LMC #176–184) violet
Lenten Weekday

Today's passage from Luke records a little-remembered attempt on Jesus' life. He very nearly died by being tossed from a cliff. One of the stories that lies behind the uproar is told in today's first reading, the healing of Naaman the Syrian in the waters of the Jordan. The psalmist expresses thirst for the streams of the living God. The passages appear today because they tell the severe consequences of the prophetic ministry and prepare us for the more effective attempt on Jesus' life that we recall at the end of this season.

The second preface for Lent (P 9) stresses the discipline that nurtures a prophetic stance. Although it is a bit early to use a preface for the passion, the gospel text makes a case for using P 18, with its phrase "the days of [Jesus'] life-giving death and glorious resurrection are approaching."

TUE 16 #238 (LMC #176–184) violet
Lenten Weekday

The practice of forgiveness sets the theme for today's gospel. If the disciplines of Lent are having their effect upon the faithful, they will heed Jesus' plea to practice in charity the forgiveness they receive from God.

Daniel prays for forgiveness in the first reading. The presider recites part of this passage every day at Mass as a private prayer just before the washing of the hands. The psalm reiterates Daniel's prayer for a contrite heart. Even the communion antiphon recalls the theme of the blameless life.

The first eucharistic prayer for reconciliation will foster the desire for a forgiving heart.

WED 17 #239 (LMC #176–184) violet
Lenten Weekday

Optional Memorial of Patrick (+ 461), bishop, missionary / violet ▪ In other passages, Jesus seems to take the law into his own hands, but today he insists he has come not to abolish the law but to fulfill it. Devotion to the law also appears as the theme of the first reading, and the gift of God's law to Israel is praised in the psalm. Within the context of Lent, we know that the first law is charity, and that obedience to the law establishes a pattern of discipline that keeps us focused on a lenten renewal of heart.

The fourth preface for Lent (P 11) stresses the importance of observing Lent.

▪ TODAY'S SAINT: Patrick came from Great Britain and suffered a period of slavery in Ireland. After a dramatic escape, he became a priest, then a bishop, returned to Ireland and preached the gospel there. If the parish gathers today in his honor, your choir might want to sing his Lorica, "Christ Be Near at Either Hand" (WLP 7200), arranged by Gerard Gillen and Steven C. Warner. Note that the vestment color for today is purple, even if celebrating Patrick.

THU 18 #240 (LMC #176–184) violet
Lenten Weekday

Optional Memorial of Cyril of Jerusalem (+ 386), bishop, doctor of the church / violet ▪ In casting out a devil, Jesus distances himself from those who claim he received this power from Satan. The passage alerts us to a growing enemy faction swelling around Jesus during his ministry. God's disappointment in the people's response to the covenant becomes obvious in the passage from Jeremiah. The psalm invites people to return to God. The readings foreshadow the passion even as they invite us to recommit ourselves to Christ.

The third preface for Lent (P 10) remembers the disciplines that sustain our resolve, and you might use Eucharistic Prayer I, the Roman Canon.

▪ TODAY'S SAINT: Cyril served as bishop in Jerusalem about the time Egeria made her pilgrimage there. Together their testimonies reveal a great deal about the fourth-century Holy Week liturgy of the church in Jerusalem. He participated in the council of Constantinople, which finalized the creed we use each Sunday. This would make an ideal day to celebrate the presentation of the creed to the elect.

FRI **19** #543 (LMC #272)   white
**Joseph, Husband
of the Virgin Mary**
SOLEMNITY

ORIENTATION

We interrupt Lent for this special celebration. Foster father of Jesus, patron of the universal church, Joseph enjoys widespread devotion among the faithful. Although his influence has been enormous, the New Testament records not a single word that issued from Joseph's mouth.

Joseph is also patron of Costa Rica.

LECTIONARY

Two choices appear for the gospel today. In the first, a puzzled Joseph learns of the pregnancy of his betrothed and receives advice from an angel. In the second, he searches for the child he lost in Jerusalem. Both stories show very real examples of a man trying to do his part while dealing with the struggles of family life.

The first reading and the psalm that follows it concern the lineage of David, out of which Joseph will come. The second reading pushes the lineage back all the way to Abraham, and we also find in Abraham an example of the faithful father realized later in Joseph.

SACRAMENTARY

Today's solemnity calls for the Glory to God and the creed. A preface for the day is provided (P 62). Eucharistic Prayer I includes Joseph's name. Pope John XXIII authorized that addition, the last change to the Roman Canon before the opening of the Second Vatican Council.

The gospel acclamation of Lent continues. Hymnody to Joseph is rare but useful. Check the indices of your hymnals.

The suggested antiphons today recall the faithfulness of Joseph's service.

OTHER IDEAS

For the white vesture, you may want to use a set from the Christmas season, recalling Joseph's role in the story of the incarnation.

Your community may host a Saint Joseph's Table. The Italian tradition combines a meal for the faithful with donations for the poor. The *Book of Blessings* includes an "Order for the Blessing of St. Joseph's Table" (ch. 53). Abstinence does not apply this Friday in Lent because of Joseph's solemnity.

See *Catholic Household Blessings and Prayers* for domestic prayer (p. 165) and a litany (p. 36).

SAT **20** #242 (LMC #176–184)   violet
Lenten Weekday

In a parable, Jesus recommends humility in prayer. Israel, guilty of the formalism of insincere prayer, hears Hosea say that love is a higher call than empty ritual sacrifice. That request from Hosea becomes the refrain to today's psalm, a song from a penitent who promises to offer not a sacrifice, but a contrite spirit.

The third preface for Lent (P 10) says we should conquer our pride. The communion antiphon comes from today's gospel.

#33 or 31 (LMC #29 or 27)
rose or violet
**21 Fourth Sunday
of Lent**

ORIENTATION

Today is the second of three Sundays reserved for scrutinies during Lent. The halfway point of Lent, this Sunday permits wearing rose vestments. Once again, you have a choice of following the readings of Year A or Year C. If you have elect for the scrutinies, the Year A readings will be more appropriate, but you are free to choose either set.

LECTIONARY

■ YEAR A READINGS: The gospels include several stories of Jesus healing the blind. They all carry an undertone of movement from the darkness of unbelief to the light of faith. None of the stories reads as eloquently as John's masterful telling. Along the way, Jesus corrects assumptions about the relationship between sin and health, while pointing out the problems of religious blindness in his contemporary society. The story became a natural to accompany prayer for the elect on their journey of purification and enlightenment toward Easter.

The metaphor of light appears also in the second reading, where the writer of the letter exhorts the readers with baptismal images to act like Christians: "You were once darkness, but now you are light in the Lord."

The first reading continues the story of salvation history leading up to the meaning of Jesus' coming. We hear the choice and anointing of David as king of Israel, a prototype of Jesus, the anointed one of God. Psalm 23, often chosen for its shepherd theme, appears today because of the royal phrase, "You anoint my head with oil."

■ YEAR C READINGS: For the faithful Christian, no story seems to embody the spirit of Lent as well as the prodigal son. This extraordinary tale of youthful foolishness and parental love inspires sinners to repent and to fall into God's loving embrace. Many preachers resist giving up this gospel if scrutinies are celebrated. However, the same text will reappear on the Twenty-fourth Sunday in Ordinary Time this year (September 12).

Furthermore, while the story of the prodigal son captures the spirit of Lent for the faithful, the story of the man born blind better captures the spirit of Lent for the elect. The task of Lent is to blend these two levels of conversion: The unbaptized are coming to faith for the first time, a journey symbolized in the man born blind; and the faithful come to renewed repentance after sin, a journey symbolized in the prodigal son.

The second reading presents a similar theme of reconciliation. The world has been reconciled to God through Christ, and God has entrusted this ministry of reconciliation to us. Being reconciled is hard enough, but this passage challenges us to be agents of reconciliation for others as well.

The first reading continues its sweeping survey of salvation history. Today we hear a story of Passover from the book of Joshua. The Israelites have entered the promised land and celebrate the feast there for the first time. They

no longer need manna, for now they eat the produce of the land of Canaan. More than a historical account, this reading sets the prototype for the Christian belief in salvation. Upon our entry into the promised land of heaven, we shall no longer need the food and drink of our earthly journey, but we will celebrate the ultimate Passover forever, nourished by the food of eternal life.

SACRAMENTARY

If the second scrutiny is celebrated today, use the prayers from the back of the sacramentary, Ritual Masses: Christian Initiation, The Scrutinies (2). Otherwise, the prayers for the Fourth Sunday of Lent take precedence. The proper preface refers to the man born blind (P 15), but if you have no scrutinies and are using scriptures from Year C, consider Lent II (P 9), with its themes of renewal and passage to a new life. For the prayer over the people, consider #13.

OTHER IDEAS

Celebrate today's scrutiny the same way as last week's. (See the Third Sunday of Lent, p. 96.) It is an unusual form of prayer, and the assembly will enter its ritual more easily if it follows a predictable rhythm for three weeks. You'll help musicians, godparents and other ministers as well if they know that they need not learn a new routine from week to week.

You may use the readings for the optional weekday Mass any time this week. It offers the selections from Sunday in Year A. If you have a special gathering this week, you might consider these texts.

MON 22 #244 (LMC #176–184) violet
Lenten Weekday

Today begins a semi-continuous reading of John's gospel. The selections are chosen because they reveal the events that lead up to the passion. With one exception (Wednesday of Holy Week), John supplies the text for the daily Mass gospel from now until Good Friday. The setting for today's miracle is Galilee, prompting an ominous reminder from the evangelist that a prophet receives no esteem in the home country.

The passage from Isaiah promises the new heavens and earth that will come from God's creating hand. Even as Jesus demonstrates power over illness, we reaffirm our belief in his power over death. The psalm praises God who rescues the singer from among those going down to the netherworld.

The first preface for Lent (P 8) invites us into the joy of the paschal mystery.

TUE 23 #245 (LMC #176–184) violet
Lenten Weekday

Optional Memorial of Toribio de Mogrovejo (+ 1606), bishop / violet
■ Jesus cures a paralytic who is found near waters. The waters foreshadow baptism, the cure hints at Jesus' power to give eternal life, and the fact that Jesus heals on the Sabbath provokes the enemies of Jesus to persecute him further, directing our attention toward the cross.

Ezekiel's vision of water from the temple suggests the life coming from the eternal temple by means of the water of baptism. The stream that gladdens the city of God reappears in the psalm.

The entrance antiphon invites all to the waters of God, and the communion antiphon mentions the "waters of peace."

The fourth preface for Lent (P 11) remembers the offer of everlasting life.

■ TODAY'S SAINT: A Spaniard by birth, Toribio became bishop of Lima, Peru, where he worked tirelessly for 25 years. He learned the local *patois,* and baptized and confirmed close to a million people! The lectionary's proper of saints suggests readings about service and evangelization, but the readings of the weekday are recommended.

The churches of Bolivia, Ecuador, Colombia and Honduras celebrate today's saint with an obligatory memorial.

Uruguay celebrates a votive mass of the Virgin Mary, Mother of Reconciliation, today. See #14 in the *Collection of Masses of the Blessed Virgin Mary.*

WED 24
#246 (LMC #176–184)   violet
Lenten Weekday

The opening of today's gospel explains that the reason people were more determined to kill Jesus was that he spoke of God as his own father. The first reading, a passage that feels more at home during Advent, foretells the salvation promised to those in darkness, hunger and thirst. In spite of the gathering gloom, the psalmist proclaims in confidence, "The Lord is kind and merciful."

Eucharistic Prayer for Reconciliation II urges peace for those who are at odds.

Today is the twenty-fourth anniversary of the martyrdom of Oscar Romero, archbishop of San Salvador, whose defense of the poor cost him his life. He is openly revered at his tomb there in the cathedral.

THU 25
#545 (LMC #274)   white
The Annunciation of the Lord
SOLEMNITY

ORIENTATION

More a feast of the Lord than a feast of Our Lady, the Annunciation recalls the appearance of the angel Gabriel to Mary, who announces the immediate coming of the Messiah. Mary agrees to God's will and sets into motion the events of our salvation.

LECTIONARY

Luke alone records the event we celebrate today, and it is his gospel we hear. (Matthew reports an angel's annunciation to Joseph instead.) Even though it is Matthew, not Luke, who draws a parallel to a passage from Isaiah, that prophecy appears as today's first reading. Psalm 40, "Here am I, Lord; I come to do your will," and the selection from the letter to the Hebrews, perfectly capture Mary's disposition.

SACRAMENTARY

Lines from the first two readings appear as suggested opening and communion antiphons today. All the presidential prayers reflect on the mystery of the incarnation. There is a preface for the feast (P 44).

The white vestments today might be those of Christmas.

Sing the Glory to God. During the creed, all are to genuflect at the words describing the incarnation. You may cue the faithful immediately before this begins with a statement like, "In our church's tradition, we genuflect during the creed today after the words 'born of the Virgin Mary'." You could extend the genuflection into a full change of posture, allowing people to kneel and pause for a while in humble recollection of the good news of our salvation, just as they kneel and pause at the news of the death of Christ during the Passion of Holy Week.

The solemn blessing for Advent (#1) or for the Blessed Virgin Mary (#15) might conclude the celebration.

OTHER IDEAS

Celebrate evening prayer today as a way of extending the feast and showing its difference from the season of Lent. The annunciation is one of the most popular images of religious art. If you have such a representation in your church, call attention to it today, or open a book of art reproductions to display one by Leonardo da Vinci or Fra Angelico.

The German sacramentary includes a special insert for Eucharistic Prayer I: "In union with the whole church we celebrate that day when Mary received your eternal Son through the Holy Spirit. We praise her above all the saints, for she is the glorious ever-Virgin mother of Our Lord and God Jesus Christ."

The chant "Ave maris stella" is a beautiful hymn for today. Find it in the *Liber cantualis.*

F R I **26** #248 (LMC #176–184)   violet
Lenten Weekday

An attempt is made to arrest Jesus, but his hour has not yet come. His enemies still do not understand him. A plot against the righteous takes hold in the first reading. The wicked do not discern the reward offered to the innocent. The verses from Psalm 34 are chosen for their affirmation of God's protection over the trials of the just.

In a spirit of contrition, the first eucharistic prayer for reconciliation makes a good choice on this Friday in Lent.

S A T **27** #249 (LMC #176–184)   violet
Lenten Weekday

The enemies of Jesus seem reluctant to make their move. His teaching makes them nervous. While plotting to arrest him, they have to discuss whether or not he is the Messiah. Jeremiah, another innocent victim, trusted God like a lamb led to slaughter and prayed to witness God's vindication over the wicked. The psalmist prays in confidence of the shelter God provides to the innocent.

The third preface for Lent (P 10) states the importance of mastering our own sinfulness.

28 #36 or 34 (LMC # 32 or 30)   violet
Fifth Sunday of Lent

ORIENTATION

Today is the last of the scrutiny Sundays. If you have had no scrutinies, you will probably take the readings from Year C.

Some remnants of calling these final two weeks of Lent "Passiontide" persist (the shift in the prefaces for example), but today's celebration fits more with the previous Sunday's than with the next one.

LECTIONARY

■ YEAR A READINGS: The last and greatest sign of Jesus' ministry in John's gospel is also the last and greatest sign of the season of Lent: the raising of Lazarus. Jesus demonstrates in no uncertain terms his power over death. He seems to delay his arrival precisely to show the extent of God's power. For the elect, who are making their final preparation for the full commitment of their lives to Christ, this passage reveals the potency of this period of purification and enlightenment. Christ wants to bring them from death to life.

Year A's series of passages from salvation history concludes with a proclamation from the prophets, especially fitting today with its theme of death and life. Ezekiel announces God's promise to open graves and have people rise from them. A great psalm of longing follows the reading today: "Out of the depths I cried to you, O Lord."

The theme reappears in the second reading in a different form. Paul writes the Romans about the "death" of the body in sin, and the "life" that comes from the Spirit.

■ YEAR C READINGS: Only on this Sunday of Lent does the lectionary abandon Luke and turn to John, a favorite evangelist of the season. We hear from John the account of Jesus forgiving the woman caught in adultery. Once again, this Sunday's gospel pertains more to the way the faithful experience Lent—as a period of penance, accepted in a spirit of

contrition for our sins. The ultimate embarrassment of the religious leaders prompts all of us to recognize our sins, while the magnanimous act of Jesus inspires us to forgive others.

The series of first readings concludes today with a prophecy. As Isaiah recalls the marvelous deeds of God in past, he announces that God is doing something new. A road appears in the desert and rivers spring in the wasteland. As Easter draws near, this passage sounds like a prophecy of baptism. The psalm for today celebrates the return of Israel from exile, the context for the first reading. Together, the reading and the psalm advance the story of salvation history to the period of Israel's exile and restoration, a prototype of the Christian's "exile" in this life and of our ultimate full restoration in Christ at the end of time.

In the second reading Paul accepts suffering as a means to attain the resurrection from the dead. The Christian can forsake all things because of the greater good, the prize God offers us in Christ Jesus.

SACRAMENTARY

If the third scrutiny takes place today, that Mass uses the prayers under Ritual Masses: Christian Initiation, The Scrutinies (2). Otherwise, use the prayers from the Fifth Sunday of Lent.

The preface (P 16) is proper for today if you use the Year A readings, a proclamation based on the raising of Lazarus. If you have no scrutinies at Mass, consider the third lenten preface (P 10) with its theme of self-denial. The text for the communion antiphon comes from the gospel. The prayer over the people recommended for today is a good one, but so is #16. There is a solemn blessing for Lent in the *Collection of Masses of the Blessed Virgin Mary.* Find it at the end of the order of Mass.

OTHER IDEAS

You may use the texts for the optional weekday Mass for any special eucharist on a weekday this week. During the coming week, celebrate the presentation of the Lord's Prayer with the elect.

MON 29 #251 (LMC #176–184)   violet
Lenten Weekday

Choose the alternative gospel today. Normally we hear the story of the woman caught in the act of adultery. However, this is Year C, and we just heard that story yesterday. Instead, read the subsequent verses in which Jesus announces that he is the light of the world. Jesus asserts his divinity with this "I am" statement and with his declaration concerning the validity of his testimony. The reading concludes with the portentous reminder that his hour has not yet come. Soon, though, it will.

Susanna, falsely accused of adultery, is freed from her punishment. Those who "walk through the dark valley," as the psalmist phrases it, have no fear. This passage offers an image of the rescue of the innocent, one of the themes of Jesus' own death and resurrection.

The recommended entrance antiphon stresses the same theme of rescue from enemies. The first communion antiphon is marked erroneously for Year C. It applies to other years when the correlating gospel is read.

The first preface for the passion (P 17) sets the tone.

TUE 30 #252 (LMC #176–184)   violet
Lenten Weekday

Jesus commit suicide? The thought would never cross our minds, but the Pharisees wonder about it in today's gospel. The gulf widens between Jesus and his enemies. Their origins, their future, their morality and their identity are as far apart as belief and unbelief.

The book of Numbers tells the story of the attack of saraph serpents in the desert and the cure worked through the bronze serpent mounted on a pole. The gospels see in this story a foreshadowing of the healing Jesus works through his suffering on the cross. The psalm is a cry for help from a people in distress.

The fourth lenten preface (P 11) prays for growth in holiness.

WED 31 #253 (LMC #176–184)   violet
Lenten Weekday

Continuing with the passages from John's gospel that fit this season, the lectionary offers another incidence of controversy with Jesus. This time the topic concerns the legitimacy of the descendants of Abraham and the sincerity of one's devotion to God. We hear another passage from Daniel, this time the story of the three young men in the fiery furnace, who retain their devotion to their own God in face of persecution. Their song in the furnace serves as today's responsory.

Rescue from enemies is the theme of the entrance antiphon. The first passion preface is in use this week (P 17), but the first eucharistic prayer for reconciliation also makes a good choice.

April

THU 1 #254 (LMC #176–184)   violet
Lenten Weekday

Another attempt is made on Jesus' life, as his enemies pick up rocks to stone him. This time, he seems to equate himself with the eternal God of Abraham. God's covenant with Abraham is told in the first reading, and the psalm remembers this eternal covenant.

The covenant is the theme of the entrance antiphon. You may use the first passion preface (P 17) today.

FRI 2 #255 (LMC #176–184)   violet
Lenten Weekday

Optional Memorial of Francis de Paola (+ 1507), hermit / violet ▪ Another attempt at stoning Jesus opens today's gospel. His enemies say he blasphemed when he claimed to be God's Son. Enemies surround Jeremiah and the psalmist as well. On the last Friday of Lent, the cross seems closer than ever.

▪ TODAY'S SAINT: Francis came from Paola in Italy, lived the life of a hermit, and invited others into the same spiritual life. His congregation was later called the Order of Minims. He died in Tours, France. His advice to his confreres sounds very lenten: "Death is certain. Life is short and vanishes like smoke."

▪ FRIDAY OF THE FIFTH WEEK OF LENT is observed as the feast of Our Lady of Sorrows in El Salvador, and as an optional memorial in Argentina and Peru.

In Venezuela, today is the feast of Blessed Mary of Saint Joseph (+ 1967), recognized as the founder of the Augustine Recollects of the Heart of Jesus.

S A T **3** #256 (LMC #176–184)   violet
Lenten Weekday

The Sanhedrin concludes that the whole world will believe in Jesus because of his signs. Caiaphas makes the unwitting prediction that it is good to have one person die for the sake of the people. The plan to kill Jesus takes shape, and the people ask a question that will be answered royally with tomorrow's liturgy: "Is he likely to come to Jerusalem for Passover?"

Ezekiel's prophecy of the gathering of all the nations resonates with the one uttered by Caiaphas. The gathering of scattered Israel also appears in today's responsory from Jeremiah.

You may use the first passion preface (P 17).

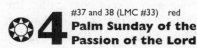 #37 and 38 (LMC #33)   red
Palm Sunday of the Passion of the Lord

ORIENTATION

Today's gospel commemorates Jesus' entry into Jerusalem for Passover and for his own passion. Palm branches recall the day of his entry, and the proclamation of the passion recalls the day of his death. We read the passion today partly to hear another evangelist's version before John's on Friday, and partly to accommodate those of the faithful who will be unable to attend the celebration of the Lord's Passion on Good Friday this year.

Prepare for the day with an ample supply of palm branches. Let people have sizable branches of a generous quantity. Arrange a space outside the church with a suitable place for the proclamation of the gospel, plenty of holy water and a sprinkler that sprays far and wide, and sufficient equipment for good amplification of the voices of the ministers. Prepare banners for the procession. Walk the processional path ahead of time, looking for trouble spots. Will banners and cross fit through tight spaces and under low ceilings? Will the head of the procession be visible? Are there places where part of the procession can be delayed, where people can trip, get confused or take shortcuts?

LECTIONARY

During the blessing of palms, the gospel for Year C comes from Luke. Jesus seems in complete control of the events that will unfold. He even knows how the owners of a colt will react when his disciples fetch it for him.

The proclamation of the Lord's Passion is the heart of today's scriptures. This year we hear Luke's version, beloved for its inclusion of Simon the Cyrenian, the weeping daughters of Jerusalem and the good thief. The passion opens without the greeting ("The Lord be with you") and without the crosses. No incense is used, and no candles are carried to the ambo. The passion may be sung or proclaimed with different voices: Christ, narrator, the crowd and others. Some divide the narrative into a few larger sections, each proclaimed by a different speaker. Time for silent reflection, sung acclamations or sacred songs could set the tone.

The psalm for today is one quoted by Jesus on the cross. For singing, consider Richard Proulx's setting (WLP 6225). Jonathan Rothman's rendition of the same psalm (GIA G-5234) perfectly captures the plaintive spirit of the text in a kind of slow blues.

The first reading comes from one of Isaiah's suffering servant songs, and the second reading is a classic hymn from Philippians, singing of the debasement and exaltation of Christ.

The versicle to the gospel acclamation is another gem from the chant repertoire, "Christus factus est." In addition to the chant, there are many choral motets based on the text, like the one by Bruckner.

A brief homily may be given. Gabe Huck gives a fine model in *The Three Days* (LTP, 1992 [revised edition], Appendix: part three).

Note that a brief homily may also be given after the gospel for the blessing of palms. Although most celebrations include only one homily after the passion, the liturgy allows two. The liturgy also permits that the homily be given after the first gospel, with no homily after the passion. This affords the homilist a more contained text for reflection. But if the palm ceremony takes place outdoors, people will be standing through the homily and their attention will waver.

SACRAMENTARY

The commemoration of the Lord's entrance into Jerusalem takes place at every Mass today in one of three forms of declining solemnity. The first form includes the procession and it is envisioned for the principal Mass today. The faithful assemble in a secondary church, chapel or other suitable place, but apart from the church to which the procession moves. All carry palms. The presider may wear a red cope or chasuble, the deacon, a red dalmatic. If you have a set of red vestments that works for Pentecost and confirmations, keep it in the closet today and use another one for martyrs and the cross. The liturgy opens with the singing of "Hosanna to the Son of David." The original Latin chant is not difficult, but see Richard Proulx's English adaptation in *Worship*. See also Proulx's choral setting, "Fanfare for Palm Sunday" (GIA G-2829) and John Angotti's spirited "Sing Hosanna to Our King" (WLP 7432). Ann Celeen Dohms has written a singable, straightforward setting for choir, "Hosanna for Palm Sunday" (WLP 5718). Four procession antiphons and psalms are in *By Flowing Waters*, including a fine, new English version of the ninth-century hymn, "Gloria, laus, et honor," based on Matthew 21:1–3, 8–11. The Latin chant is in the *Liber cantualis*.

The presider makes the sign of the cross, then greets the people and gives them a catechetical summary on the concluding season of Lent. This instruction may highlight some of the efforts made by the whole parish community throughout the season, while pointing them toward the coming celebration of the death and resurrection of the Messiah. The deacon may also give this summary.

Choose between the two prayers offered over the palms. One blesses the branches; the other acknowledges that we use them to honor Christ. The second prayer makes more sense if an earlier Mass included a blessing over all the branches used this weekend. If the people hold their branches aloft for this prayer, they will appear more united in faith, prayer and purpose. A minister could announce just before the prayer of blessing, "Let us raise our branches." The branches are sprinkled with holy water.

Before the gospel of the palms is proclaimed, incense may be used. If a deacon is proclaiming the gospel, he asks for a blessing from the presider. Afterward, a homily may be given, but it may also be omitted here.

The invitation to enter the church sounds like a direction from the deacon, but in his absence the celebrant or another suitable minister may give it.

Incense leads the way, then the minister carrying a decorated cross between two candle-bearers, then the priest and faithful follow. Meanwhile, all sing "All Glory, Laud, and Honor" or another appropriate song. "The King of Glory" is another popular choice, based on the entrance antiphon of the day. Space singers out throughout the procession to keep the music strong, but be forgiving. It probably will not go as well as you hope it will. This is one of the most difficult environments for singing in the entire liturgical year. A portable audio system may help. If the presider has been wearing a cope, he switches to a chasuble before the opening prayer.

The second form is called the solemn entrance, and pertains to situations where the faithful cannot gather outside due to constraints like lack of space. If the community must resort to the second form, it should ask when the time will come to make appropriate renovations or constructions so that the procession may occur. In the solemn form, the ministers group themselves outside the sanctuary, but in view of most of the faithful.

In the third form, the simple entrance, the entire opening rite takes place in the sanctuary.

For general intercessions, see examples in the back of the sacramentary for Holy Week.

The preface for today explains the meaning of the celebration (P 19). The suggested solemn blessing is a fitting conclusion to the celebration.

An alternative blessing is in the *Collection of Masses of the Blessed Virgin Mary*. The solemn blessing for "Lent" there includes themes more pertinent to Holy Week. If your parish is named for Mary or has a devotion to Mary, you might prefer this solemn blessing, found at the end of the order of Mass.

OTHER IDEAS

Cancel other activities in the parish this week. Let nothing keep people from attending the services throughout the Triduum. That may mean giving up several evenings, so encourage people to free their other evenings this week to make attendance at the community's prayer a priority.

The processional cross may be decorated with palms or otherwise festooned. See *The Sacristy Manual*, pp. 203–4, for more advice.

Catholic Household Blessings and Prayers provides prayers for placing of branches in the home on Palm Sunday (p. 140) and prayers of the Triduum (p. 143).

Give the community the reminders it needs: If members of the assembly will be invited to have their feet washed on Holy Thursday, they should dress accordingly. If you will collect food for the hungry that evening, remind people about it today. Announce that Friday is a day of fast and abstinence, and that we encourage a fast on Saturday in solidarity with those to be baptized.

Provide a good holy week resource for people this week. Consider LTP's *What Am I Doing for Triduum This Year?*

MON 5 #257 (LMC #176–184)   violet
Monday of Holy Week

The gospel reports an event six days before the Passover, the anointing of Jesus, who has his own burial on his mind. The first reading begins the series of the four songs of the suffering servant, and the psalm repeats one of its themes. God promises to make the servant a light for the nations, and we sing the psalm as Christians who identify that suffering servant with Jesus, the Lord, who is light and salvation.

See the suggested general intercessions for Holy Week in the sacramentary's first appendix (#7). The second passion preface (P 18) is used.

The 1994 *Sacramentary Supplement* includes a parish rite for the reception of the holy oils blessed at the chrism Mass. It suggests the Holy Thursday Mass as a time when this might take place, but allows other occasions. Given the complexity of the Holy Thursday Mass, you might consider receiving the oils at another celebration this week. A weekday Mass like today's would be one appropriate option—assuming, of course, that the chrism Mass has taken place and that the parish is in possession of the oils. If you have singers available, you could sing Alan Griffiths and Paul Inwood's "Procession of the Oils" (WLP 5779), written with the chrism Mass in mind, but effective in a parish on an occasion like this.

The first seder of Passover this year will be celebrated tonight in Jewish homes.

TUE 6 #258 (LMC #176–184)   violet
Tuesday of Holy Week

The second song of the suffering servant assigns ministry not just to Israel but to the Gentiles as well. The psalm sings of God's salvation. The series of passages from John's gospel climaxes today at the Last Supper, where Jesus predicts one disciple's betrayal and another's denial.

The second passion preface (P 18) is good, but you may also consider using it with the first eucharistic prayer for reconciliation.

Tonight our Jewish brothers and sisters celebrate the first day of Passover.

WED 7 #259 (LMC #176–184)   violet
Wednesday of Holy Week

On a day formerly called "Spy Wednesday," we hear Jesus identify Judas as his betrayer and predict his condemnation. The third song of the suffering servant becomes today's first reading, a text of brave endurance. The psalm takes the same attitude: "For your sake I bear insult."

The opening prayer summarizes the meaning of Lent and Passiontide. Conclude the season with the second passion preface (P 18). The communion antiphon summarizes the meaning of Jesus' ministry.

Instructions for tomorrow's Mass of the Lord's Supper indicate that the tabernacle should be empty for the beginning of the liturgy. Communion ministers or the faithful may consume tabernacle breads today, reserving only a few in a pyx for emergencies.

THU 8 Chrism Mass #260   white
Liturgy of the Hours   violet
Holy Thursday morning and afternoon

There is no morning Mass today, except for the gravest pastoral necessity and with permission of the diocesan bishop. The faithful gather this evening for the principal Mass of the Lord's Supper and the opening of the Triduum.

If a funeral is celebrated today, observe the form "without Mass" in the *Order of Christian Funerals*. Most grieving Christian families already understand the special nature of this day and may erroneously assume that no funeral may happen. They may welcome the simpler service that keeps an observance of the church's calendar while it honors the loss of a faithful Christian. They may also wish to return to the church for the opening of the Triduum.

If you have a community accustomed to gathering for a morning Mass, celebrate morning prayer with them today. You could augment it with a proclamation of the passages from the office of readings: the letter to the Hebrews on the high priesthood of Jesus and the homily of Melito of Sardis. These texts are lengthy and difficult. If you use them, be sure the reader prepares well to convey their meaning.

Communion may be brought to the sick today if necessary, but this should happen after the evening celebration of the Mass of the Lord's Supper, not during the day. The idea is to bring communion to the sick from the community's eucharist, not from the tabernacle.

If your parish school is still in session, gather the children for morning prayer and encourage their attendance at the Triduum.

Whether the chrism Mass happens today or earlier, promote attendance from your community at this diocesan event. The chrism consecrated at this Mass will be used for the Easter Vigil baptisms. Many others in the community will be anointed with it at infant baptisms and confirmation. Still more will benefit from the oil of catechumens and the oil of the sick at community prayer this year.

FEBRUARY 25, 2004
Ash Wednesday

Sin's Heavy Weight
Joel 2:12–18
Rend your hearts, not your garments.

FAST from food. Repent from your sins.

On Ash Wednesday we stand as sinners before God. We reflect on the misdeeds of our past and on the ill habits of our present. Our frail spirits wrestle with sin, even as our frail bodies fight off death. We accept ashes as a reminder of our mortality. We fast from food as a sign of our sorrow.

Our sins weigh us down, but it could be worse. We could have a plague of locusts darkening the sky over the place where we live. That happened once before. The prophet Joel addressed a people who were losing everything because they could not stop an advancing army of locusts. They believed God was punishing them for their sins, so they fasted as a sign of their repentance.

In our lives, sin does not bring locusts, but it brings other sorrows. Sin brings estrangement from the people we love, guilt when we lift our eyes to heaven, loss to a world starved for charity.

Can you imagine yourself living your life a better way? In the quiet of your heart, do you know what sin is darkening your sky? Are you willing to name it, specifically?

Accept ashes. Fast from food. Repent.

FEBRUARY 29, 2004
First Sunday of Lent

Offering the Fruits of Our Labor
Deuteronomy 26:4–10
The people brought gifts to God's altar.

VERY few people pay their taxes willingly. We try to find ways around paying income tax. We give to charities not because we feel good about supporting their cause but because we benefit from lower taxes. Some people give only to save.

Imagine a different kind of society. Imagine a place where people knew their taxes provided good roads, good schools, a fire department and a recycling service. Imagine people believing so strongly in these goals that they gladly paid their taxes and even contributed additional funds. Imagine that as they paid taxes each year, each person made a statement renewing citizenship, professing a belief in the community's goals and reverence for its past. In such a society, individuals would care more for the community than for themselves.

In the Old Testament, Moses instructed the people to perform this kind of action. They prepared a basket of their first fruits and brought it to their religious leader. There they made a statement of faith, beginning with, "My father was a wandering Aramean." They recounted the history of God's interventions in the lives of their ancestors. They acknowledged their dependence on the faith of their parents and on the goodness of God. Consequently, they brought their gift in gratitude.

Did everyone really do what Moses asked? If they were like us, probably not. But just imagine—imagine if we did this as a society—or as a church.

MARCH 7, 2004
Second Sunday of Lent

God's Gifts and Our Desires
Genesis 15:5–12, 17–18
God made a covenant with Abraham.

FOR may of us there are two desires that lie deep within our souls: descendants and property. Some people are blessed with plenty of each. Others have very little to show, even for a life lived well.

Some people receive descendants and property in different ways. They have students, disciples or friends who admire them and strive to be like them. Or they have access to the land that others own. One need not have blood descendants and deeds of property to make life worthwhile. But it is what many people want.

It is what Abram wanted. He was an old man, childless. He lived in Ur of the Chaldeans, in modern-day Iraq. God made him a promise. God promised him the two desires that lay deep within his soul: descendants and property. "Count the stars, if you can. Just so shall your descendants be," God said. And then, "To your descendants I give this land, from the Wadi of Egypt to the Great River." It was an amazingly generous gift. It could only come from God. It was beyond what someone could even hope for.

Because these desires are so strong, people react strongly when something goes wrong with them. If a child turns out different from what one hoped, or if property is vandalized, damaged or lost, people feel a huge sense of betrayal and despair.

Remember that God knows the desires of our hearts, and God wants to fulfill them with the descendants and property that will unfold the divine plan.

MARCH 14, 2004
Third Sunday of Lent

God Answers
Exodus 3:1–8a, 13–15
"I am" sent me to you.

WE all want to have our prayers answered. We think that would make life easier. But sometimes God answers prayers in ways we don't expect, making life more challenging.

Young Moses was minding his own business, tending the flock of his father-in-law, when God decided it was time to answer some prayers. For years the chosen people had been held in Egypt as slaves. They longed to return to their own land, the land that God had given them. They prayed for release.

God answered their prayers by appearing to Moses in a flaming bush that was not consumed. God asked Moses to lead the people out of slavery into freedom.

This was probably not the answer Moses had in mind. Moses would have been content to let someone else lead the people to freedom. He wanted an end to slavery as much as anyone else, but he never envisioned that he would lead the exodus. God was answering his prayers, but in a way that caused anxiety for Moses.

When we want something done, God hears from us. When God wants something done, we hear from God. It may come as a surprise, but God may have us in mind to answer someone else's prayer.

MARCH 21, 2004
Fourth Sunday of Lent

Simple Blessings
Joshua 5:9a, 10–12
The people of God entered the promised land and there kept the Passover.

UNLEAVENED cakes and parched grain doesn't sound like much of a menu, but it was a banquet for the Israelites of long ago.

Freed from slavery in Egypt, they made the long trek through the desert to reach the promised land. They trudged a long, tiring and dangerous journey. Moses, their leader, had died. Now Joshua, his successor, had brought them to their homeland again.

It was Passover, the festival commemorating their departure from Egypt. So the people celebrated the feast with food from their new home: unleavened cakes and parched grain. They no longer ate the food of Egypt. They no longer ate the manna from the desert. Now, camped on a plain in Gilgal, they ate the food of their new home, the food of freedom.

You appreciate things more if you have had to go without them. Food tastes better if you are hungry. Employment is more satisfying if you were unemployed. Shelter feels safer if you have been without a home. God's presence feels stronger when you rediscover prayer.

It may not seem like much—unleavened cakes and parched grain, but for the Israelites it was a banquet. They may not seem like much, these little blessings God gives us, but for those who experience God's mercy, they are heaven.

MARCH 28, 2004
Fifth Sunday of Lent

Flowing Waters
Isaiah 43:16–21
See, I am doing something new.

IF you turn on the faucet at home you get running water. Drinking water is close at hand, ready to use and abundant, even if the water source is a distance away. The faucet is a sign of God's promise.

But it wasn't always that way. People could not live far from a water source. Desert areas went uninhabited and uncharted because no one could stay there very long without ample drinking water.

Through Isaiah, God promises a day when water will flow in the desert. As proof of God's power, Isaiah invites the people to recall the marvels God has done in the past. During the exodus, as the Israelites fled Egypt, they went through the sea dry-shod, but the waters closed in on the pursuing chariots, horses and army of Pharaoah.

God marvelously preserved the Israelites in the past, and God promises to marvelously preserve them again. God is doing something new. It springs forth in the sight of believers.

As Easter draws near, we think about the water God keeps close at hand—not just the water of the faucet but the water of the church's font. There water flows freely for those who seek Christ. God has prepared a way in the deserts of the human heart for water to flow, to give life and to transform.

This Lent we reflect on the desert of our sin, but also on the signs of God's presence. "In the desert I make a way," God says, "in the wasteland, rivers."

APRIL 4, 2004
Palm Sunday of the Lord's Passion

Isaiah 50:4–7
"My face I did not shield from buffets and spitting."

THE speaker of today's first reading is a victim. He speaks, but people beat him, pull out the hairs of his beard, slap and spit at him. Why? He suffers all this because he has spoken God's word. Every morning God speaks to him and enables him to speak to others. This word gets him into trouble.

But the speaker does not quit. Nor does he curse God who gives these pointed words. This "suffering servant" remains firm, committed to the word God gives him, even in the face of resistance.

Although Isaiah wrote about the difficulties faced by faithful Israel in the midst of enemies, Christians see in these lines the example of Jesus. He received God's word, spoke it with eloquence, and suffered at the hands of his enemies.

Do your words ever get you into trouble? Does it happen even when you say the right thing? If so, you stand in a long line of those who suffer because they are servants of God.

The victim on the cross hangs in full view in our churches. Christians can face the agony of suffering as it befell Jesus—and as it comes to us—because we know there is something more.

THE PASCHAL TRIDUUM

The Season

The Meaning

The resurrection is the other face of [Jesus'] obedient surrender. It is not simply the reversal of what went before, though in certain respects it is that; it is the full revelation of what went before, the open manifestation of the glory of the love between Father and Son. The resurrection is the Father's acceptance of the Son's gift, and the penetration by the Spirit of their mutual love into every fiber of Jesus' body and mind, into every dimension of the personhood which had become the means of expressing love. We think more readily of his risen body, but his mind is glorified too. He has heard the Father's word with his whole being. Son though he was all along, he learned obedience and grew to perfect, achieved freedom by the things he suffered. He

*is Son now to the utmost depths of his
human psyche.*

—Maria Boulding, *The Coming of God,*
Third edition (Conception, Missouri:
The Printery House, 2000), p. 76.

TRIDUUM means "three days." The days from
Holy Thursday until Easter Sunday are
unique so we call them "the three days," and
everyone should know what we mean.

Throughout his ministry, Jesus predicted
his passion by referring to the "third day." Today
we enter that sacred time outside of time in
which we spend these days with Christ, to serve,
to suffer, to die and to rise.

On these days the elect reach the climax of
their initiation. The faithful bring their lenten
retreat to its fulfillment.

■ HOLY SPRING: The date of Easter is calculated
according to the turning of the cosmos. First we
wait for spring in the northern hemisphere,
Jerusalem's hemisphere. Then we wait for the
first full moon. Then we wait for the first day of
the week. That is when we celebrate the rising
of Christ from the dead, the rising of the elect
to new life in baptism, the rising of the faithful
to renewed commitment to Easter faith and joy.

During these days the entire parish goes on
retreat. Invite all families, staff, youth and the
homebound to spend these days in a spirit of
prayer and reflection. "On Good Friday and, if
possible, also on Holy Saturday until the Easter
Vigil, the Easter fast is observed everywhere"
(*General Norms for the Liturgical Year and the
Calendar,* 20). Those who fast on Good Friday
should continue the fast as much as possible
until the beginning of the Vigil.

To help everyone celebrate these days as
fully as possible, provide copies of LTP's *What
Am I Doing for Triduum This Year?*

The Saints

THE Triduum replaces absolutely every other
celebration on the liturgical calendar. It
holds the highest rank on the table of liturgical
days. The only change on the general liturgical
calendar this year is the suppression of the
memorial of Stanislaus. On the local calendar,

however, if your community celebrates a
patronal solemnity for any saint listed in the
martyrology for April 8 to 11 (for example,
Maximus of Alexandria, Demetrius, Liborius,
Hugh, Fulbert or Boniface Zukowski among
others), it transfers to the nearest available day
on the calendar. This year, because of the solemnities of the Easter octave, the first available
day will be April 19.

In general, parishes with patronal days
that are routinely impeded by festivals may
consider locating on the calendar another regular, annual and more useful day to celebrate the
patron. The general Roman calendar made use
of this principle in transferring out of Lent or
Advent certain saint's days. For instance, in the
calendar reform of 1969, Pope Gregory the
Great's memorial was moved from March 12 to
September 3. The apostle Thomas's feast was
transferred from December 21 to July 3.

■ ABOUT THE RANKING OF THE TRIDUUM: Notice
in the *General Norms for the Liturgical Year
and Calendar* that the Triduum transcends all
other days, beyond "feast" or "solemnity," beyond
even holy day of obligation. The liturgical spirit
sees within the Paschal Triduum a festival that
gives meaning and life to all festivals, that contains within itself the mystery of all other days
and seasons.

Make a concerted effort in the parish to
cancel all other activities. The liturgies for the
Three Days should be the top priority on everyone's calendar this week.

The Lectionary

NOTHING proclaims the significance of these
days like the gospels assigned for their
celebration. The washing of the feet, the passion
and the ecstatic proclamation of the resurrection
announce the meaning of our gathering and draw
us into worship.

■ CHOOSE READERS WHO CAN PROCLAIM THESE
TEXTS WELL. Give them ample time to practice.
Rehearse the readings in church, with the microphone on—even if people usually just rehearse
at home. It will remind the readers how important their proclamation is these days and give
the liturgy more focus. The first two readings on

Holy Thursday are narrative and therefore easy on the ears in proclamation. The first two readings on Good Friday require more skill to convey the message. The epistle for the Easter Vigil should be a centerpiece. Perhaps choose a reader from the Christian initiation team, whose very presence will help people connect this passage to the baptisms that follow.

The seven Old Testament readings for the Easter Vigil also require readers of great skill. They may need help interpreting how their reading fits into the overall picture of the Vigil. Use a different reader for each if you can. And avoid cutting down on the number of readings. Although permission is granted for fewer readings for this celebration, altogether they create a sense of vigil more than any other part of the service. The liturgy's preference is that all nine readings be proclaimed on this night.

■ THE SUNDAY *LECTIONARY FOR MASSES WITH CHILDREN* includes no texts for the principal liturgies of the Triduum, and rightly so. Invite children to participate in the parish liturgies on those days.

For Easter Sunday, the children's lectionary offers all the texts for the Mass of Easter Day, even the alternatives for the second reading.

The Sacramentary

■ THE SACRAMENTARY'S INTRODUCTION TO THE TRIDUUM develops the spirit of these days and answers some questions we often forget. A companion document, the 1988 *Circular Letter Concerning the Preparation and Celebration of the Easter Feasts (Circular Letter)* also is very useful. Priceless in interpreting these is Paul Niemann's helpful work, *The Lent, Triduum, and Easter Answer Book* (Resource Publications, 1998).

■ CHRISTIAN INITIATION: For the Easter Vigil, be sure to use the *Rite of Christian Initiation of Adults*. Its description of Part III, the liturgy of baptism, replaces what is in the sacramentary. There are a few changes now if you have both elect to be baptized and baptized candidates to be received into the full communion of the Catholic church. The sequence of the Rite of Reception and the renewal of the community's baptismal promises shifted since the sacramen-

tary was first published. Keep the *Rite of Christian Initiation of Adults* on hand for Part III of the vigil.

■ MUSIC: Ample musical notation appears in the sacramentary for these days. They remind us of the importance of singing many parts of the rites. The *Circular Letter* frequently encourages singing the chants of the Triduum.

The Book of Blessings

BLESSINGS may be given at any time, but during the Three Days our full attention is fixed on the primary liturgical celebrations. This is not the best time to explore the *Book of Blessing* for additions to the liturgy. Nonetheless, it does include a good blessing for homes during the Easter season (ch. 50) and of food for the first meal of Easter (54).

The Rite of Christian Initiation of Adults

TWO celebrations requiring your attention are the preparation rites on Holy Saturday morning and the sacraments of initiation at the Easter Vigil. If there are infants to be baptized at the Vigil, you may wish to invite the parents to bring them to the preparation rites Saturday morning.

If you have a community that gathers each morning for Mass, why not schedule the preparation rites at that time and invite them to participate? All, of course, should make every effort to attend the Vigil.

■ DISMISSAL: There are two schools of thought about dismissals during the Holy Thursday Mass of the Lord's Supper and the celebration of the Passion on Good Friday. Because Thursday's gathering is for a Mass and because we dismiss catechumens and elect from any Mass, many believe that they should also be dismissed from this celebration after the liturgy of the word. Others suggest the elect and catechumens should remain. They argue that there are no dismissals for the *faithful* at the conclusion of the Holy Thursday and Good Friday liturgies, and that the spirit of the Triduum just about demands that the entire church assemble as one.

The Liturgy of the Hours

A natural time to celebrate the hours at church is when the community is already in the habit of coming for a daily Mass. Holy Thursday and Good Friday both provide excellent opportunities for the celebration of morning prayer in the parish.

Those who participate in the evening Mass of the Lord's Supper do not celebrate evening prayer from the *Liturgy of the Hours,* even in private. The same applies to those who celebrate the Lord's Passion on Good Friday. Holy Saturday is the only Saturday of the liturgical year with its own evening prayer. All the other Saturday evening prayers are really the first vespers for Sunday. But there is no Evening Prayer I for Easter Sunday. Those who participate in the Easter Vigil do not celebrate the office of readings for Easter Sunday.

The psalms and scripture citations from the *Liturgy of the Hours* may be commended to the faithful as sources of meditation during the Three Days.

The Rite of Penance

THE opening rubric for Good Friday states, "According to the Church's ancient tradition, the sacraments are not celebrated today or tomorrow." The *Circular Letter* modified this statement: ". . . except for the sacraments of Penance and Anointing of the Sick" (see #61 and #75).

Nonetheless, the celebration of reconciliation fits more with the spirit of the season of Lent than with that of the Triduum. Schedule penance services prior to the Triduum and encourage people to make this sacrament part of their preparation for Holy Week.

The Pastoral Care of the Sick

THE rubrics for Holy Thursday state that holy communion "may be brought to the sick at any hour of the day." But the *Circular Letter* says it is more appropriate to bring communion to the sick "directly from the altar" of the evening Mass (#53). In this way, their communion with the faithful at the one celebration of Holy Thursday is clearer. On Good Friday, communion may be brought to the sick at any time. Others do not share communion apart from the celebration of the Lord's Passion—not even at Stations of the Cross. On Holy Saturday, communion outside the Vigil may only be given as viaticum for the dying.

The sacrament of anointing of the sick may be celebrated during the Triduum, but other times of the year are much more appropriate. Of course, if someone is in need of this sacrament, it may be given on any day.

The Rite of Marriage

MARRIAGE is among the sacraments not to be celebrated on Good Friday and Holy Saturday. The *Circular Letter* "strictly" forbids it (#61 and #75).

This becomes an issue especially if marriage convalidations need to happen for the elect, candidates for full communion or the faithful. If any of these are in a marriage that the Catholic church does not recognize, and if no canonical impediments apply, they may seek to have their marriage convalidated. This means celebrating the Rite of Marriage in the Catholic church, normally before a priest or deacon with at least two witnesses. Convalidation frees Catholics in irregular marriages to fully participate in the celebration of the sacraments again—notably, to receive communion.

Such convalidations should not be put off until the last moment. They may be celebrated as soon as possible for the benefit of the faithful. The Catholic partner in such marriages may then begin sharing communion right away, not waiting for Easter. If for some reason the Rite of Marriage needs to be celebrated during this time, it could take place outside of Mass during the day on Holy Thursday, or even during the Mass on Easter Sunday, but neither of these solutions frames the sacrament deservingly.

The Order of Christian Funerals

A funeral may take place on Holy Thursday, Good Friday or Holy Saturday, but not a funeral Mass. The funeral service without Mass can be found in the *Order of Christian Funerals* (#179). The *Circular Letter* says that a Good Friday funeral should be celebrated without singing, music or the tolling of bells (#61), a strange rubric that tolerates the singing of psalms at morning prayer on Good Friday but not for the death of a faithful Christian.

The Art and Environment

THE environment should be unique for each day, yet should not overwhelm those who make the changes. See *To Crown the Year* (pp. 74–119) and *The Sacristy Manual* (pp. 207–19) for ideas and checklists.

■ VESTURE: Launder the servers' vesture. Prepare the chasubles and dalmatics, as well as a humeral veil for Holy Thursday. The red vesture for Good Friday should appear to be celebrating martyrs, not Pentecost. Save the best white vesture for the Easter Vigil.

Prepare white garments for neophytes. Many communities that practice immersion also prepare non-white, opaque-when-wet, alb-like vesture to clothe the elect before entering the font and during their baptism. Some vest cantors and lectors to lend solemnity to these days.

■ PREPARE THE FLOWERS. Have them ready for the Vigil. If plants and flowers are to be delivered, arrange a time when the church will be open.

■ DOUBLE-CHECK THE LIGHTING AND SOUND. Replace bulbs and realign spotlights. Correct the sound system. Do all the microphones work, including the wireless ones? Are the batteries fresh? Are there loose wires causing static? How about the speakers? Wouldn't this be a good time to make sure things work?

■ SPRING CLEANING: Clean up the grounds and the church. Spruce up every place people will see, and even places that no one ever sees. Make these days look special. Besides, cleaning the church symbolizes the cleaning of one's soul. It makes a good spiritual exercise for the conclusion of Lent and the beginning of Triduum.

■ SET OUT THE VESSELS: the censer, the boat, containers for oil, cups and plates for communion, pitchers and bowls for washing feet. Clean and polish them as well. Iron the altar materials.

Clean the font for baptisms by immersion. Replace the water. Some communities arrange a temporary font to accommodate immersions in a visible place within the church. Praiseworthy as this is, a more permanent solution should be sought as part of the parish's long-range plans.

Prepare the place for the Easter fire. Make ready the paschal candle and the smaller ones for the assembly.

■ SET THE ENVIRONMENT FOR THE CHAPEL OF RESERVATION. To give purpose to the procession and to establish a place conducive to meditation and prayer, prepare a room apart from the church if possible, rather than a side altar within the church. Clear the path of the procession. Walk it and watch for problem areas.

The Music

CANTORS and choirs will be busy these days. Their support for the Triduum is essential to the sense of celebration. The presider should also rehearse those parts of the services that he may sing, including the eucharistic prayer on Thursday, Saturday and Sunday.

"Christ Our Light" is a complete booklet of music for the Triduum, available from World Library Publications. This intelligent presentation of the music and liturgy of the Three Days gives plenty of options for the principal liturgies as well as secondary ones like Stations of the Cross. If you like the music, this resource will save you the effort of publishing something yourselves each year.

Less successful overall, but still worth a look, is Dan Schutte's "Glory in the Cross: Music for the Easter Triduum" (OCP 11480). For the washing of feet, "Where Love Is Found (*Ubi caritas*)" includes verses from 1 Corinthians 13, Paul's hymn to love. For the veneration of the cross, "Behold the Wood" is over 25 years old, and it has the marks of a classic. Music for the solemn intercessions of Good Friday, "We Beseech You, O Lord," deftly weaves spoken word with instrumental accompaniment and a response from the assembly that includes the "Kyrie eleison" from the "Missa XI Orbis factor."

"Christ We Proclaim" contains music for the initiation rites at the Easter Vigil, as well as music for all the other rites of Christian initiation. Edited by Christopher Walker, this remarkable collection is available from OCP (11293).

Chants worthy of the repertoire include "Ubi caritas" and "Pange lingua" for Holy Thursday (both in the *Liber cantualis*), the opening acclamation for the Easter Vigil ("Christ our light"), the Exsultet, baptismal acclamations, and the Easter sequence, "Victi-mae Paschali laudes."

Let the choir work up a barnstormer like Handel's "Hallelujah, Amen" from *Judas Maccabaeus* (Schirmer 304).

The Parish and Home

THE faithful should keep the spirit of these days as much as possible at home. They lead a quieter, simpler life on Friday and Saturday, and rejoice with one another on Sunday. All should keep the paschal fast between the Mass of the Lord's Supper and the Easter Vigil, joining with the elect in prayer as they prepare for baptism. Most people do not realize the church suggests this fast on Saturday, calling them to solidarity with the elect.

A sample prayer for the home is *We Watch and Pray during the Paschal Triduum* (LTP, 1995). This easy-to-follow card allows families, groups or individuals to pray in common at home or at church.

Some parishes encourage families to make or decorate their own Easter candles. These are brought to church during the Vigil, then brought home (lit!) and relit during prayer throughout the Fifty Days of Easter. Many Greek Orthodox families do this; Roman Catholics can, too. If you have a gas stove at home, and if you can get a candle all the way home from the Vigil in safety, why not light the pilot with the blessed Easter fire? The light of Christ will bless every meal you prepare this year.

Texts

■ GREETING: Sacramentaries of other language groups suggest:

The Lord of glory and the Giver of every grace be with you.

■ INTRODUCTION TO THE PENITENTIAL RITE:

Let us call to mind our sins and call upon the Lord's mercy.

■ RESPONSE TO THE GENERAL INTERCESSIONS:

Christ our Savior, hear our prayer.

■ DISMISSAL OF CATECHUMENS:

The Lord Jesus gave us an example of service in the midst of suffering. Go in peace, and remember the example of our Savior.

April

#39   white

8 Holy Thursday Evening: The Lord's Supper

ORIENTATION

This evening's celebration opens the Triduum with the Mass of the Lord's Supper. It commemorates the institution of the eucharist and the priesthood, as well as Jesus' command of love and service. It should be the only parish Mass today.

■ ALL MINISTERS FULFILL THEIR MINISTRIES: Priests concelebrate, deacons and lay ministers assist. Some may bear the holy oils from the chrism Mass in procession. Eucharistic ministers may bring communion to the homebound at the close of the liturgy. For the washing of the feet, the seating, pitchers, bowls and towels could be prepared ahead of time and kept in full view as part of the environment for the night.

In anticipation of tonight's celebration, check this list:

- Get holy oils.
- Prepare pitchers, bowls and towels.
- Prepare sufficient bread for tonight and tomorrow's communion.
- Prepare sufficient wine for tonight's communion.
- Prepare baskets or other receptacles for gifts for the poor.

- Prepare white altar paraments and vestments.
- Prepare humeral veil.
- Prepare place of reservation with tabernacle and candles.
- Empty tabernacle, leave doors open and extinguish vigil candle.
- Tell those responsible for bells during the Glory to God: servers or choir members for small bells indoors, maintenance personnel or ushers for tower bells.
- Train servers for processions and incense.
- Arrange for stripping altar and church after Mass.

LECTIONARY

■ THE FIRST READING presents the story of the first Passover, a celebration of the freedom of God's chosen people. At the time of Passover, Jesus gathered his disciples for a meal, the Last Supper, which shaped the structure, content and themes of the Christian eucharist. Elements of prayer and the preparation of unleavened bread and wine signify a link between the first freeing of God's chosen people and the liberation of Christians from sin and death.

■ THE SECOND READING is our earliest record of the Last Supper. The letters of Paul predate the composition of the gospels. Paul passes on to the church at Corinth what he has learned about the meal on the night before Jesus died. Already in the first generation of Christians, Paul can speak of a tradition concerning the eucharist.

■ PSALM: Another verse from the same letter serves as the refrain to the responsorial psalm, which expresses thanks to God by lifting up a cup of salvation. In some ways, the psalm anticipates the second reading more than it reflects back on the first. See Marcy

Weckler's "Our Blessing Cup" (WLP 6201) and Paul M. French's "Two Psalms for Holy Week" (WLP 6228).

■ GOSPEL: John's account of the Last Supper features the washing of the feet. His treatment of the eucharist occurs much earlier, in the sixth chapter of the gospel. In John's gospel Jesus speaks of the eucharist only in that discourse early in his ministry. John's gospel does not record Jesus sharing the eucharist at the Last Supper. But it does tell of his washing feet. In hearing this gospel tonight, we reflect on the implications of the eucharist, which calls the faithful into service. Recent well-intentioned efforts to introduce signs of adoration into the communion rite of Mass threaten to overlook the important consequences of service embedded in the privilege of sharing the bread of life. The highlight of Mass is not adoration, but communion, and communion implies service.

The homily segues from John's gospel to the washing of the feet.

SACRAMENTARY

■ THE ENTRANCE ANTIPHON for this evening celebrates the cross, not the eucharist. Consider a piece like Michael Ward's arrangement of "Near the Cross" (WLP 8526). The sacramentary antiphon, "We should glory in the cross of our Lord Jesus Christ," is set to a stirring chant in By Flowing Waters, 118. It widens our attention to the entire Triduum, rather than on tonight's celebration only.

Ring the bells during the Glory to God. Choir members may perform this service indoors. An usher, greeter or other volunteer could handle the tower bells.

■ THE WASHING OF THE FEET is optional, but try to include it. Jesus' words are quite strong about foot washing ("You should do what I have done"). The full meaning of tonight's celebration so hinges on this gesture that the parish really should observe it.

This gesture of humility and service expresses the responsibilities of those who share the eucharist. Resist suggestions to replace this gesture with one more culturally expressive. Deplorably, washing hands or shining shoes have been proposed. Peter's defiant response shows that Jesus' action was not culturally attractive from the beginning. The sign expresses profound drama when presiders, the leaders of prayer, fall to their knees to serve others in the community.

In the sacramentary, no words introduce the washing of the feet, nor do they seem necessary. The presider's removal of the chasuble will signal strongly that the washing is about to begin. The singing may begin, and the participants, cued ahead of time, may move to their places.

The sacramentary does not specify how many people should have their feet washed. Some communities invite the assembly to participate. They establish several stations. Each station might have one or two chairs where people may sit to remove shoes and socks, another chair for people to sit for the washing of their feet, an ample bowl, towels and warm water in a pitcher. Where priests and deacons are in short supply, some communities have other staff or parish leaders assist at the various stations.

The symbol is that the leader of the community gives an example of humble service and inspires others to do the same. Some people think that those who have their feet washed should literally wash the feet of others right away. Although this spreads the example

of service throughout the church, it differs from what Jesus probably had in mind. He washed the disciples' feet and invited them to do the same, but John does not say that they literally began washing one another's feet. More likely they were moved by this example and offered humble service to the church in a thousand ways.

If at all possible, the presider or pastor should wash feet. It gives the wrong signal if the pastor sits down and watches while volunteers or staff members wash feet. We should see an example of service rather than supervision.

Music for the washing of the feet may include Steve Janco's "Whenever You Serve Me" (WLP 6210) and "A New Commandment" (WLP 5773) with verses in Polish and Spanish; Taizé's "Mandatum novum" (GIA G-2433); Michael Ward's "A New Commandment" (WLP 7579); Steve Warner's "The Garment of Love" (WLP 7211); Chrysogonus Waddell's "Jesus Took a Towel" (*Worship* #432); Christopher Walker's "Faith, Hope, and Love" (OCP 7149); and the Ghanaian "Jesu, Jesu" (*Worship* #431).

The dismissal of catechumens and elect may follow the washing of the feet. But if you need volunteers to have their feet washed, do not turn first to the elect. This is not an initiation ceremony. It is a ceremony for the whole church.

■ INTERCESSIONS: Petitions from today's evening prayer in the *Liturgy of the Hours* could be adapted for the general intercessions of the eucharist.

■ GATHERING GIFTS: "At the beginning of the liturgy of the eucharist, there may be a procession of the faithful with gifts for the poor." The *Circular Letter* says that the gifts for the poor may especially include "those collected during Lent as a fruit of penance" (#52). Canned goods for a food

pantry, rice bowls for Catholic Relief Services, or other gifts are appropriate today. The faithful may bring them forward from their pews, or a few may bring up a selection of gifts.

In this single instance, the sacramentary suggests a text to be sung during the procession of the gifts: "Ubi caritas." Many parishes customarily sing something during the preparation of the altar and gifts, but this is the only time the liturgy actually recommends a particular text for the song. The refrain of the original Latin chant from the *Liber cantualis* is not difficult and could become part of the parish's repertoire. Other versions include Taizé's (*Worship* #604) and "Where Charity and Love Prevail" (*Gather* #443); one by Mark Hill (WLP 8593); and an English translation in *By Flowing Waters* (123).

■ THE EUCHARIST: Use the first preface of the Holy Eucharist (P 47). Eucharistic Prayer I has three inserts proper for tonight's Mass. Other eucharistic prayers may be used. Singing the prayer would be very appropriate tonight. Try Richard Proulx's "Corpus Christi Mass" for unaccompanied choir, cantor and congregation, based on "Adoro te."

The suggested communion antiphon draws its text from today's second reading. Settings of Psalm 34 also make a good selection because of the verse "Taste and see that the Lord is good." See also Robert Hutmacher's "Love Is His Word" (*Worship* #599); Richard Proulx's arrangement (WLP 8677); Alan Hommerding's "Litany for the Holy Eucharist" (WLP, *We Celebrate,* 29) and Lucien Deiss's "Song of My Love" (WLP 2561).

If communion ministers bring communion to the sick, they could process out together after the faithful have shared the eucharist. They could return to the church

later for adoration. The rest of the eucharistic bread should be collected in one vessel on the altar. Use a second only if necessary.

After a period of silence, the prayer after communion is sung or said. That prayer concludes the spoken texts of the liturgy. There is no greeting, no blessing and no dismissal.

■ PROCESSION: After this prayer the presider puts incense in the thurible, kneels and incenses the Blessed Sacrament on the altar. After receiving the humeral veil, he then picks up the vessel containing the body of Christ and covers it with the veil.

Cross, candles and incense lead the procession through the church to the place of reposition. Other ministers and the assembly of the faithful follow. All sing "Pange, lingua" or another suitable song. Repeat the first four verses of "Pange, lingua" if necessary. See Frank Quinn's fine translation in *By Flowing Waters* (#126 and #648).

At the place of reposition, the presider sets the vessel down before the empty tabernacle. He adds incense to the thurible, kneels, incenses the Blessed Sacrament, and all sing "Tantum ergo." The tabernacle door is then closed, perhaps by the deacon.

The *Circular Letter* notes that a monstrance is not to be used (#55). Adoration will take place before the closed tabernacle, not before the exposed eucharist.

There is no dismissal of the faithful. They may remain or go home and return as they wish. They continue their prayer and fasting before the next moment within the liturgy of the Paschal Triduum.

■ EUCHARISTIC ADORATION: The altar is stripped in silence and without ceremony. Crosses should be removed or covered in red or purple cloth. The *Circular Letter*

asks that no candles burn before images of saints (#57).

The materials used during the washing of the feet will require some extra housekeeping.

From the transfer of the eucharist to midnight, all should be encouraged to continue in prayer before the Blessed Sacrament. The *Circular Letter* (#56) calls for John chapters 13 to 17 to be read as part of this prayer time. Different groups in the parish may assemble at a given time to offer vocal prayer and song.

Many parishes conclude the period of adoration by singing night prayer from the *Liturgy of the Hours* just before midnight. In place of the usual responsory, "Into your hands," the church uses "Christ became obedient" throughout the hours of the Triduum, adding a phrase each day.

OTHER IDEAS

On Good Friday, and if possible on Holy Saturday, we abstain from meat and observe the paschal fast. In order to observe the fast, the faithful should have time to eat before tonight's liturgy. You may encourage them to finish their supper with the Lord's Supper. In a traditional Jewish seder, participants drink four cups of wine. We do not know for certain, but it is possible that if Jesus followed this protocol, he served the best wine, his own blood, last.

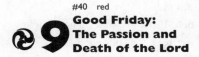

#40 red

9 Good Friday: The Passion and Death of the Lord

ORIENTATION

Good Friday is a celebration of Jesus' passion, the suffering and death by crucifixion. Because this event won salvation for sinners, the day is called "Good," and the liturgy reflects on love as much as loss. For the faithful, today's commemoration drives home the full weight of our sin, even as it lifts us up by the incomparable measure of God's love. For the elect, today's drama awakens them to the demands of discipleship, while it prepares them to receive God's love in the promise of eternal life by the waters of baptism.

■ THREE O'CLOCK IN THE AFTERNOON: The sacramentary recommends that today's celebration begin at 3:00 PM. This places the prayer closer to the traditional hour of Jesus' death, and may actually make it more accessible to many parishioners. Some will prefer daylight hours. Many communities plan all three Triduum celebrations in the evening, but some staff and parishioners may like the idea of spending Friday night at home. Those who take off work to attend an afternoon service give witness to the importance of the Triduum.

■ TODAY'S LITURGY IS IN THREE MAIN PARTS: the liturgy of the word, featuring John's account of the passion, the veneration of the cross and holy communion.

■ IN ANTICIPATION OF THE CELEBRATION, check the following list:

- Practice singing intercessions.
- Arrange microphones for the passion.
- Prepare the cross.
- Prepare candles and incense (with matches).
- Set altar cloth and corporal nearby.
- Arrange for collection for the Holy Land.
- Prepare red vesture.
- Prepare a private place for reservation of any remaining consecrated bread.
- Prepare a central place for the cross to remain.

LECTIONARY

■ THE PASSION ACCORDING TO JOHN is the centerpiece of the liturgy of the word. Proclaim it as you did Matthew's passion on Palm Sunday. Use multiple readers and musical acclamations after the principal sections, as recommended by the Canadian lectionary. A refrain like "Be Near Me Lord, When I Am in Trouble," or even a verse of "Were You There?" make good choices.

■ OTHER SCRIPTURES: The first reading comes from the suffering servant songs of Isaiah. It concludes the series begun on Monday, Tuesday and Wednesday of Holy Week. The refrain of the psalm, actually coming from Luke's gospel, is itself a quote from the psalm: Jesus' last words on the cross. The passage from Hebrews recalls the suffering of Christ, through which he became the source of eternal life.

SACRAMENTARY

■ THE CELEBRATION BEGINS IN SILENCE. As much as possible, limit the greeting in the gathering space before Mass. This is not a day for rehearsing music with ministers and the assembly. Keep the mood somber as people enter. If the song leader avoids announcements before the service it will contribute to the spirit of quiet in the church.

The priest and deacon wear red chasuble and dalmatic. This is the only occasion on which a chasuble is worn apart from the Mass. It signifies the unity of this liturgy with yesterday's eucharist and the one tomorrow.

No entrance rite is described— no cross, no candles, no song, no solo instruments. The rubrics say the ministers "go to the altar." They could actually take their places in their chairs 10 or 15 minutes before the liturgy begins. Then they could "go to the altar" and reverence it with a kiss to signal the beginning of communal prayer.

■ PROSTRATION: The priest and deacon prostrate or kneel. Prostration, the more dramatic posture, will signal the seriousness of today's prayer. "This act of prostration, which is proper to the rite of the day, should be strictly observed, for it signifies both . . . abasement . . . and also the grief and sorrow of the church" (*Circular Letter,* 65).

The assembly stands for the entrance (according to the *Circular Letter* again) and thereafter kneels in silent prayer. If space permits, other ministers and even the assembly could choose to prostrate themselves.

The silence should be long enough for the power of this gesture to sink in and for this silence to evolve into prayer. When the priest goes to the chair with the ministers, the assembly will rise. For the opening prayer, the presider does not introduce it with a greeting, nor does he say, "Let us pray." Prayer has already begun. He extends his hands as usual and is seated afterward.

■ THE RESPONSORIAL PSALM will be the assembly's first song of the celebration. Paul M. French has a setting in his "Two Psalms for Holy Week" (WLP 6228). See also the effective rendering in *By Flowing Waters* (127). The gospel acclamation should also be sung as usual.

■ IF YOU CHOOSE TO SING THE PASSION, see the setting available from GIA (G-1795). Or you may divide the parts among several speakers.

A single reader with oratorical skill can also effectively proclaim the passion. In some communities several readers take turns in succession, each proclaiming a block of the text. A musical refrain by the assembly may separate the sections.

In any case, use no incense, no candles, no greeting and no signs of the cross. The reading begins simply with "The Passion of our Lord Jesus Christ according to John."

If several readers or singers are involved, let them practice movement, not just words. Have them come together, bow to the altar and go to their stations before beginning the passion. After the proclamation, they may come together and bow to the altar again before going to their places.

Customarily, the assembly kneels in silence for a while after the verse announcing Jesus' death. Do say, "The gospel of the Lord" at the end, but do not kiss the book (*Ceremonial of Bishops,* 319).

■ A BRIEF HOMILY MAY BE GIVEN. The theme need not stray at all from the focus of today's celebration: the love of God for us, in spite of our sin. After the homily, allow a time for silent meditation (*Circular Letter,* 66; *Ceremonial of Bishops,* 319).

■ SHOULD THE ELECT AND CATE-CHUMENS BE DISMISSED? Some say yes, because the intercessions are prayers "of the faithful." Others argue that they may remain because one of the prayers is for those to be baptized. Your local community may decide.

■ THE GENERAL INTERCESSIONS TAKE ON A SOLEMN FORM. The deacon or another minister announces the intention from the ambo and the priest prays accordingly from the chair or the altar. Certainly the chair makes a better choice.

The faithful may kneel or stand throughout the prayers, but the traditional changes in posture add to the solemnity of the prayer: Stand for the intention, kneel in silence, stand for the prayer. The deacon may give these instructions, but people will catch on without repetitious directives.

As an alternative, the assembly may sing an acclamation after the intention is announced and before the prayer. Consider a Kyrie, "Oye nos, mi Dios," or another imploring refrain. The bishop may suggest additional intentions for your diocese. Is there a special need toward which your region should devote attention?

■ FOR THE VENERATION, USE ONE CROSS. This could be the main cross in the church if it can be made accessible. A processional or another devotional cross may also serve. The *Circular Letter* advises, "Let a cross be used that is of appropriate size and beauty" (#68).

Choose one of the two forms for showing the cross. The first envisions a procession of a veiled cross, flanked by candles, into the sanctuary. Three times the priest unveils part of the cross, sings "This is the wood of the cross," raises it, and all kneel in silence. (Either the deacon or the printed program may have to direct this posture.) The second envisions the procession of an unveiled cross

through the church. Again, all kneel after each refrain.

For veneration, make sure the cross is accessible to the elderly and those who use a wheelchair. Some have ministers hold it. Others place it on the ground or against a prop—but not against the altar or some other religious object. See *To Crown the Year* (pp. 98–103) for ideas.

Processions may come from several directions. Ushers may assist. When people approach, a genuflection toward the cross is most appropriate, but another sign of reverence may be given. Many kiss the cross. The *Ceremonial of Bishops* (#322) has the presider remove his shoes, like Moses before the burning bush. If the presider and other ministers lead the way, the faithful will probably follow.

During the veneration, sing "We Worship You" from the sacramentary, or settings by Howard Hughes, David Isele and Michael Joncas in *Praise God in Song* (GIA G-2270). Prepare several pieces, because the veneration may take time. Try "Pange, lingua"; "Crucem tuam" from Taizé (GIA G-3719); "Adoramus te Domine I" from the same community (*Gather* 221); "Jesus, remember me" (*Gather* 167); and Owen Alstott's "Wood of the Cross" (OCP 8826). Steven C. Warner's "Crux fidelis" (WLP 7230) is another fine choice. Richard Felciano's four-part arrangement of "Were You There?" is available from Schirmer (4061).

Music for the reproaches is found in the sacramentary, but their text sounds anti-Jewish to many people. A revision of the verses appears in the United Methodist *Book of Worship*.

■ THE COMMUNION RITE TAKES PLACE SIMPLY. Ministers could

reverently cover the altar with a cloth and corporal. The sacramentary may be placed there if needed, but a good presider should be able to lead this part of the service from memory. Candles may accompany the consecrated bread to the altar, but again, keep it simple. Have the candles placed near the altar or on it.

The candles might be those used in the veneration. The servers who carried the candles in procession might stand by the cross throughout the period of veneration, facing each other. As veneration concludes, they might go with their candles with the minister who brings the Blessed Sacrament to the altar.

The presider leads the community in the Lord's Prayer and the invitation to communion. No sign of peace is given (*Circular Letter,* 70), probably because of the scandal of the kiss of Judas.

The sacramentary says a communion song "may" be sung. The *Circular Letter* suggests Psalm 21 for communion (probably the Latin numbering that equals Psalm 22, the responsorial psalm for Palm Sunday). Or repeat the song from last night. David Haas's "Now We Remain" (*Gather* 498) is also appropriate. But you might consider an entirely different option: no song at all. Sharing communion with no music will bring this service to a closing as stark as its opening.

Communion is under one form for this communion service. This is not a celebration of the eucharist.

■ AFTER COMMUNION, the remaining Blessed Sacrament is carried without ceremony by an assisting minister to a suitable place outside the main worship space. This is a place of convenience, not really a place for adoration. A period of silence is observed, and then the presider leads the prayer after communion.

The service concludes with the prayer over the people. The presider does not introduce it with the greeting, but simply extends hands over the people for the prayer. No dismissal is given.

Four candles are to be set by the cross (*Circular Letter,* 71), which will remain in place for those who wish to continue praying. Perhaps the assisting ministers could put these candles in place after the prayer over the people and before the presider leaves.

Then all the ministers may come together and genuflect toward the cross before departing reverently in silence (*Ceremonial of Bishops,* 331).

OTHER IDEAS

Whenever anyone enters or leaves the church, or passes in front of the cross between now and the Vigil, the proper reverence is not a bow to the altar, not a genuflection to the tabernacle, but a genuflection to the cross. This is the only time in the church's liturgy that we genuflect to anything besides the Blessed Sacrament (*Ceremonial of Bishops,* 69). There is no Mass today, and the instrument of the passion becomes the center of our devotion.

■ TENEBRAE: The morning of Good Friday could include a combined celebration of the office of readings and morning prayer. The practice is recommended by the *Ceremonial of Bishops* (#296), the *Liturgy of the Hours* (#210) and the *Circular Letter* (#40, 62). The latter recalls that this combined office used to be called *Tenebrae,* the Latin word for "darkness."

Prior to the mid-twentieth century reforms of the Roman rite, many places of worship lit a 15-post candelabrum before the service and extinguished one candle

after each of the psalms of the service, until one was left, recalling the abandonment of Jesus by his friends and the encroaching threat of death—an antithesis to the coming fire rite that will open the Easter Vigil, in which a growing light will spread to dispel darkness.

That single shining candle at Tenebrae, signifying the light of Christ, was placed briefly behind the altar, while sounds of chaos rattled the darkness. People might have banged their hymnals against the pews, for example.

Although the liturgical documents recommend the praying of the office of readings and morning prayer on these days, they do not mention the restoration of the allegorical practices associated with the evening Tenebrae.

To combine the hours, consult *Liturgy of the Hours* (#99). Basically, start with the office of readings but use the hymn from morning prayer. Omit the final prayer of readings and the opening versicle of morning prayer, and cut to the psalms of that office, proceeding to its conclusion. The extensive prayer allows for a diversity of ministers and a variety of musical interpretations of the psalms.

Be sure children are invited to attend the principal liturgy.

■ IF YOU OFFER STATIONS OF THE CROSS TODAY, they should not in any way detract from the principal celebration of the Lord's Passion (*Circular Letter,* 72).

■ NIGHT PRAYER could be offered at the end of the day, perhaps following a fasting meal.

10 Holy Saturday morning and afternoon

ORIENTATION

Holy Saturday commemorates the day Jesus lay in the tomb. There is no Mass during the day. Communion may be given only as viaticum. Reconciliation and anointing of the sick may be celebrated today. However, Lent would have been a better time for reconciliation, and if the anointing can reasonably be deferred a few days it can be celebrated in the glow of Easter.

During the day today we continue the paschal fast. The elect should be fasting today in preparation for their baptism, and the faithful join them in solidarity of spirit. This recommendation dates back to about the year 100, where it appeared in the *Didache,* or *The Teaching of the Twelve Apostles.* We continue in a prayerful spirit. The climax of the Triduum, the Easter Vigil, begins when darkness arrives. The Easter Vigil launches us into the Easter season and it should not be confused with Holy Saturday itself.

■ PROPER RITES FOR THESE HOURS: The community may gather in the morning for morning prayer or with the elect for the preparatory rites (RCIA, 185–205). A combined office of readings and morning prayer may take place as it did on Good Friday. Although the community may gather for prayer at midday or evening, many will use this time to make preparations for the Easter Vigil.

The combined office of readings and morning prayer will give the faithful the opportunity to hear the patristic homily assigned for today. It depicts Christ's triumphant entrance into Sheol, his meeting with our first parents, and the beginning of the great victory procession by which the souls of the just are liberated by the conquering savior, King Jesus. In place of the responsory, the Triduum antiphon from Philippians is chanted in its fullness.

■ NO VESTMENT COLOR IS SPECIFIED FOR HOLY SATURDAY. White may be the best choice, especially if the preparation rites are celebrated. They begin the ceremony of baptism.

■ PREPARATORY RITES BEFORE BAPTISM: If there are elect to be baptized at tonight's Vigil, be sure to conduct the preparatory rites early in the day. They form an important prelude to baptism. During Lent, the elect received the creed from the faithful and, having meditated on it, commit it to memory. Today they recite the creed, returning it back to the faithful, demonstrating their readiness for the questions they will hear tonight: "Do you renounce?" "Do you believe?"

If the Lord's Prayer has not yet been presented, that ceremony may take place at this time. Augustine gave testimony to this practice. But in the normal course of events, the presentation of the Lord's Prayer takes place during the fifth week of Lent.

If you exercise the option to present the Lord's Prayer today as part of the preparation rites, the gospel for that rite is probably the best one to use. The Ephphetha and the return of the creed each recommend gospels also, but hearing three gospels in the same ceremony this morning would be too much. The presentation of the Lord's Prayer happens in the actual proclamation of the gospel, so that text should probably take precedence over the others.

If infants will be baptized at the Vigil, the *Rite of Baptism for Children* (#28) calls for preparatory rites for them as well. This should involve receiving them at the door, exorcism and anointing. Adults, however, will not be anointed today. The elect had opportunities for anointing while they were catechumens.

A service combining the reception of infants with preparation of the elect is possible, uniting in one assembly the prayers and expectations of the elect, the parents, the sponsors and the catechists. The format could go as follows, with possible rites listed in RCIA (#185.2), and readings at #179–180, 194, 198:

- *Gathering hymn,* with entire assembly at the entrance. An appropriate text is found on page 170 of the *Triduum Sourcebook.*
- *Reception of infants (Rite of Baptism for Children* [RBC], 35–41)
- *Procession* of all to seating near ambo; refrain or hymn sung by all
- *Reading* related to preparatory rites (presentation of the Lord's Prayer [RCIA, 180], if this did not happen during the fifth week of Lent)
- *Homily*
- *Preparation rites* for infants: exorcism (RBC, 49), anointing with oil of catechumens (RBC, 50)
- One or more of the preparation rites for adults and children of catechetical age: Ephphetha (RCIA, 199) or recitation of the creed (#195)
- *Prayers of blessing* (RCIA, 204)
- *Dismissal* (RCIA, 205)

Note that in the *Rite of Christian Initiation of Adults,* the Ephphetha appears after the recitation of the creed, but if both are included in the preparation rites, the Ephphetha comes first.

■ SOME COMMUNITIES INVITE CHILDREN TODAY TO COLOR EGGS, hear and dramatize the scriptures from the Vigil and to assist in preparing the worship space. Their participation in the preparation rites will be important, especially if there are children of catechetical age in this year's group.

■ EVENING PRAYER may be celebrated by the community, on its own or in conjunction with the preparation rites. This is the only Saturday of the liturgical year with its own evening prayer. Because the Vigil is to take place at night, some communities may actually start it in the early hours of Sunday morning. Especially in those cases, a Saturday evening prayer will be welcome. "Be Still, My Soul" (Finlandia) makes a beautiful hymn for the occasion.

10-11

#41   white
The Easter Vigil

ORIENTATION

The Easter Vigil is the most important eucharist of the year. It celebrates our faith in the resurrection, the cornerstone of our belief. Ranking highest among the celebrations of the liturgical year, it should rank highest in the spiritual life of the faithful.

■ THE FOUR PARTS OF THE EASTER VIGIL move us through a gradual unfolding of its mystery. The fire rite immediately shatters the gathering darkness. The liturgy of the word opens up the path of God's plan throughout salvation history. The liturgy of baptism draws the elect into the promise of eternal life and renews the baptismal belief of the faithful. The liturgy of the eucharist brings the celebration to its climax as we experience the presence of the risen Christ in the community.

LECTIONARY

■ READINGS: Nine scripture readings are offered for tonight's celebration. You may reduce the number of Old Testament readings, but the exodus story (Exodus 14:15—15:1) must always be included. The permission to reduce the readings is given "if necessary." The sense of the liturgy is that ordinarily the readings will all be proclaimed. If this is not yet your custom, consider expanding the Vigil's word service this year.

■ LENGTH: One of the symbols of the Easter Vigil is its length. We take time for community prayer around this mystery of resurrection because nothing else matters more. Hearing the nine readings will be a challenge for communities unaccustomed to it, but they do convey more fully the mystery of God's plan of salvation, while they give the sense of what a vigil is.

■ CHILDREN: The introduction to the *Lectionary for Masses with Children* forbids a separate liturgy of the word for children (#30) due to the importance of the community celebrating one Easter Vigil. But to help children through the length of the Vigil, some communities dismiss them during the scriptures to perform other activities and to reflect on the meaning of the celebration. They could, for example, rejoin the assembly for the proclamation of the gospel, in keeping with the permission to reduce the number of readings for children on Sundays and holy days (*Directory for Masses with Children,* 42).

■ THEMATICS: The scriptures work together to blend the themes of creation, covenant, baptism and resurrection.

Water appears as a theme in the first reading (the story of creation), as well as in the prophecies of Isaiah and Ezekiel in readings five and seven. The responsorial psalms with these texts repeat the water and creation imagery. They foreshadow the covenant of baptism.

Rescue is the theme of readings two and three, where God liberates Isaac and then all of Israel. The responsorial psalms with these and the fourth reading repeat the idea. Tonight we celebrate Jesus' resurrection and our own rescue from death.

God's covenant becomes evident in readings four and six. The covenant, filled with wisdom (Baruch) and everlasting in its strength (Isaiah), reaches its fulfillment in Jesus. Again, the responsorial psalms echo these themes.

The epistle, which formerly followed the baptismal liturgy at the Vigil, plainly explains the connection between the baptism of the faithful and the resurrection of Jesus. The psalm that follows returns to the theme of rescue: The rejected stone has become the cornerstone.

The gospel announces the good news of resurrection, the message we have longed to hear. Luke's version reintroduces the women who had come from Galilee with Jesus. Luke avoids the term "disciples" for these women, but that may have been a linguistic problem: There is no feminine form for that word. They walk and talk like disciples, unquestionably. They see the stone rolled away and the empty tomb. They are puzzled until two men in dazzling garments announce the good news: "He is not here, but he has been raised."

The women then announce these words to the eleven and to others. They are the first evangelists. Luke gives us their names: Mary Magdalene, Joanna and Mary, the mother of James. Their testimony is not completely accepted, however. Peter, symbol of leadership and discipleship, goes to the tomb, sees and believes. By corroborating the testimony of the women, Peter confirms the mission of Christ to the lowly, the outcast, the rich and the poor.

Use Gail Ramshaw's *Words around the Fire* (LTP, 1990) for additional reflections on these scriptures. See Rory Cooney's "Genesis Reading for the Great Vigil" (GIA G-5018C) for an idea for the first reading. A complete set of utterly simple chant settings of the responsorial psalms—capable of being sung in the dark, without printed music for the assembly—is found in *By Flowing Waters* (131–141).

SACRAMENTARY

■ DARKNESS: The entire Vigil takes place at night. The lateness of the hour and the length of the Vigil cause inconvenience for some of the faithful. It is hoped, however, that the Vigil is the kind of experience for which people willingly inconvenience themselves. On some special occasions you give up sleep for entertainment, shopping, family and friends. Tonight we give up sleep for faith.

Some communities start the Vigil in the early hours of Sunday morning. This is completely permissible. It makes Saturday a real day in the tomb with Jesus, a full day extending Friday's fast and heightening the anticipation for baptism and resurrection. It rouses the faithful from slumber in the early hours of Easter Day and plunges them into an extended celebration that reaches its joy in the eucharist at dawn.

Celebrating the Vigil early Sunday morning is worth considering, but think too about the needs of the ministers you will have on duty for the parish Masses as the day continues.

PART ONE IS THE SERVICE OF LIGHT.

■ BONFIRE: A blazing fire may greet the faithful as they arrive. The *Circular Letter* says this fire should be of some size, so that it actually dispels darkness and lights up the night (#82). It is best to prepare the fire outdoors. It is a bonfire, not a fondue. The place need not be far from the church, but outside it. If you have the space, prepare the fire outdoors. If you do not have the space, make a five- or ten-year plan for obtaining it.

Put the fire in the hands of people who know what they are doing. A scout troop often makes the best guardian for this symbol. Most are skilled in the safe preparation of a campfire and can douse the flame and restore the earth in such a way that you will never know they were there. Good fire-builders know how to do this in a downpour.

Fire may be prepared on asphalt or on a lawn if a thick tarp with ten inches of sand is put down. A livestock trough may also serve, with sand or cinder blocks beneath for insulation.

For safety, dried hardwood is better than pine or other softwoods. Be sure to consult with local fire marshals for whatever permissions might be required. Many municipalities have regulations about fires, even on private property. Officials generally respect religious customs. Be prepared with extinguishers in case the fire becomes too large, blankets to put out stray sparks, and hoses. Have a volunteer crew keep a careful eye on the blaze.

■ THE CHURCH SHOULD REMAIN IN DARKNESS. You need not lock the doors to keep people from entering, but you might obstruct them in some way. At the very least, have greeters on duty early enough to steer the assembly away from pews and toward the fire.

■ A LARGE NEW PASCHAL CANDLE OF WAX IS MANDATORY (*Circular Letter,* 82)—large enough, the letter continues, to evoke the truth that Christ is the light of the world.

No artificial candles may be used, and no second-use candles from previous years. Easter candles are available from a number of producers. The handcrafted quality of the Marklin Candle Company's products is noteworthy (http://www.liturgy2000.com).

Some communities rely on a local artisan to decorate the blank candle they purchase. Although the candle traditionally comes with a cross, the numbers of the year and the alpha and omega, the presider may carve these images into the wax during the preparation of the candle. If the candle comes with these symbols already in place, it lessens the argument for exercising the option of the ritual preparation of the candle during the service of light.

■ PREPARE CANDLES FOR THE ASSEMBLY. Candles inside cupped plastic shields give better protection from the flames than those with circular cardboard wheels.

■ BEGINNING: The faithful gather in the dark. Before the liturgy begins, a greeter might invite members of your community to introduce their guests to the assembly, and ask visitors to say where they come from.

The ministers may assemble early together with the community or may make an entrance. Try to begin on time. It will be a long night.

The sign of the cross opens the Vigil (*Ceremonial of Bishops,* 339), and then the presider greets the people. He then may improvise an introduction for the celebration. He blesses the fire, which has been burning before his arrival.

The *Ceremonial of Bishops* says the bishop and deacon light the candle (#340), but the sacramentary does not specify which minister performs this function. A member of the community might do this. The censer is also lit from the new fire (#340), but this will delay the effect of incense for several minutes. Another solution is to put charcoal in the fire ahead of time. After the blessing, use tongs to place the burning charcoal in the censer.

Deacon and assembly alternate the dialogue, "Christ our light." Another acclamation may be used, but the tradition behind this one is strong. Candles should be lit when the deacon reaches the church door, but this rubric makes more sense if it refers to the candles of the principal ministers. In a larger assembly, the lighting of candles might begin after the first intonation. Have several ministers prepared to begin. The faithful will take it from there.

Lights in the church come on after the third intonation, but many communities turn them on after singing the Easter Proclamation, so that the light of the blessed fire, not artificial light, illumines the church for the first part of this great night.

■ The Easter Proclamation (Exsultet) is now available in several musical forms. The chant in the sacramentary is closest to the original idea, but it takes a skilled cantor, unafraid of setting a brisk pace and letting the joy of the season radiate from eyes, mouth and the whole face. See Robert Batastini's adaptation (GIA G-2351) and Christopher Walker's setting (St. Thomas More, OCP 7175). J. Michael Thompson's arrangement is available from WLP (#5716) and Everett Frese's comes from Pastoral Press. See also the much-abbreviated text and still powerful music of "This Is the Night" by Jeffrey Schneider (WLP 5721).

In the Middle Ages the deacon in many communities sang the Exsultet from a scroll decorated with upside-down images illustrating the text. As he sang the proclamation, the scroll fell in increasing lengths over the top of the ambo, and the images would become visible right side up to those nearby. No publisher offers such a scroll today, but it would make a great addition for the opening of the Vigil.

If the presider ends up singing the Easter Proclamation from the ambo and walks back to the chair afterward, you might need some instrumental filler. Check out the flute solo based on the Exsultet chant in "Meditations for Unaccompanied Flute" by Richard Proulx (GIA G-5335).

■ Pace: All in all, keep the service of light moving. Many Easter Vigils get off to a sluggish start because ministers are unaware of cues. Make sure everyone knows who is responsible for what. What is the cue for starting the sign of the cross? For moving the procession? For starting the Easter Proclamation? Make sure the musicians and altar ministers

are prepared and let the whole service of light flow with deliberate purpose. It should set the tone for the joy of this night. If it looks confusing or amateurish from the start, you have set the wrong tone for what follows.

If you left the electrical lights of the church off from the start of the fire through the singing of the Exsultet, now is a good time to turn them on.

The sacramentary does not say what to do with the assembly's candles, but the *Ceremonial of Bishops* says they are extinguished after the Easter Proclamation. If the presider and ministers visibly blow out their candles after the proclamation without saying a word, the assembly may follow suit. If not, the deacon could give this instruction: "You may extinguish your candles and be seated."

If children are dismissed to a catechetical session before the gospel, that could happen here.

PART TWO IS THE LITURGY OF THE WORD.

The sequence of readings, silences, psalms and prayers sets a meditative pace for the true vigil part of the Vigil.

■ Regarding the number of readings, the *Circular Letter* says that wherever possible, "all the readings should be read in order that the character of the Easter Vigil, which demands that it be somewhat prolonged, be respected" (#85). Some communities pride themselves on Vigils under 90 minutes, or on an interpretive mixture of readings that shortens the liturgy of the word. They undermine the purpose of the Vigil.

■ To introduce the readings, the presider may give an instruction to the faithful. If you have

printed programs, you may also help people by printing a summary sentence of what the reading is about, or why it was chosen for tonight's celebration. Such catechetical devices help the faithful ease into the prayerful spirit required for tonight's liturgy of the word.

The spirit is formal and yet relaxed. We are here tonight because there is nowhere else we would rather be.

Allow some moments of silence after each reading. Allow the change of posture for the prayers. All this will establish a rhythm and help the assembly enter into the spirit of the readings.

■ Musicians should choose the responsorial psalms carefully. People should sense their cohesion as if they are a series of movements. Think of the psalms as a suite, as a single multi-movement musical composition with moments of excitement and moments of calm.

Many communities link the third reading directly to its responsory, which comes from the next verses of Exodus. Near the end of the reading, it says, "Then Moses and the Israelites sang this song to the Lord." There's another line of text, but it copies what will follow in the responsory. Advise the reader to omit the final line of the reading and the phrase, "The word of the Lord," and let the musicians jump in with the responsory when the reading itself gives the cue.

■ Glory to God: After the prayer of the last Old Testament reading, the Glory to God rings out. As the Glory to God begins, servers light the altar candles, ring bells inside and outside the building, and turn on any lights still slumbering. Some favorites include Peter Jones (OCP), Richard Proulx "Gloria for Eastertime" based on *O filii et filiae* (GIA G-3086 or choral version G-3087), and "Gloria of the Bells" by C. Alexander Peloquin (*Worship* #258).

You may also decorate the worship space at this point. (See *To Crown the Year,* pp. 111–12). A procession of flowers and other items is the most orderly way to do this. Ask volunteers, perhaps a committee or organization in the parish, to rehearse this on Holy Saturday after the flowers are delivered. Assign clusters of volunteers to zones of the space. After the rehearsal bring the materials to a side room or rear pew. During the psalm before the Glory to God, have these helpers quietly go to the materials, pick them up and stand ready. As the Glory to God begins, they then go in procession to place the decorations as rehearsed.

■ THE OPENING PRAYER FOR THE MASS FOLLOWS. We've had plenty of prayers already, but this one parallels the typical opening prayer for the beginning of Mass.

Back in the old days, baptisms happened after the Old Testament readings and before the Glory to God. Then, after baptism, came the New Testament readings.

Now all the readings ensue in nearly uninterrupted sequence, and the liturgy of baptism follows the homily, when we usually celebrate other sacraments (for example, marriage and confirmation). Still, as a leftover from the older rites, the Glory to God appears in the midst of the liturgy of the word.

It's the Easter Vigil. A few things will be different.

■ GOOD NEWS: After the glorious epistle that compares baptism to resurrection, all rise for the gospel acclamation.

Actually, the *Ceremonial of Bishops* allows for something else to happen. After this reading, one of the deacons or the reader goes to the bishop and says, "Most Reverend Father, I bring you a message of great joy, the message of Alleluia." Then all stand and the bishop intones the alleluia. (It's hokey, but you gotta love it!)

Imagine this. A member of the catechumenate team has read the epistle. Then, she or he goes to the presider and says, "Father N., I bring you a message of great joy, and the message is *(pause for dramatic effect)* Alleluia." Then a fanfare erupts from the instruments and the choir bellows out the word we have not sung for almost seven weeks. All rise and we sing three magnificent verses of acclamation.

Here's another way to do it. The one who delivers the message is the cantor, standing at the cantor stand. At the last word of the message, the cantor intones the alleluia, and all repeat—three times. If not the traditional chant, use Christopher Walker's "Celtic Alleluia" (OCP 7106), (and please pronounce it "Keltic" in rehearsal—Christopher says so), with handbells if possible; "Easter Alleluia" (*Gather* #307), based on "O filii et filiae," verse by Marty Haugen; Richard Proulx's "Alleluia and Psalm for Easter" (GIA G-1965), specifically written for this night, with familiar threefold Mode VI Alleluia (congregation, choir, cantor, organ and handbells) and Donald Regan's "Fanfare and Alleluia" (WLP 7959).

If the presider sings the traditional Easter alleluia, he raises the pitch each time (*Circular Letter,* 87). For the gospel, use incense, but no candles. The Easter candle should suffice. Sing the introduction and conclusion. Sing the gospel! Sample tones can be found in the *Graduale Romanum.*

A homily, "no matter how brief" (*Circular Letter,* 87), is given.

PART THREE IS THE LITURGY OF BAPTISM.

Turn to the *Rite of Christian Initiation of Adults* (218–43) for this service, unless you have no one to be baptized. In that case, refer to the sacramentary.

In the *Rite of Christian Initiation of Adults* there are versions of the ritual order for the reception of baptized Christians (279–498) and for the combination of the sacraments of initiation and the Rite of Reception (566–594).

■ RESERVING EASTER FOR BAPTISM: The Rite of Reception of the Already Baptized into the Full Communion of the Catholic church may take place at any time of year, and there are arguments for celebrating it when the candidates for reception are ready, not necessarily in conjunction with Easter. There is no connection between the Rite of Reception and any day in the liturgical year. If the Easter Vigil is reserved for the unbaptized celebrating the rites of initiation, the full significance of baptism will shine more clearly.

■ THE CELEBRATION OF BAPTISM BEGINS WITH THE PRESENTATION OF THE CANDIDATES. If the font is in view of the assembly, the participants for this rite will move there. If not, you may assemble a temporary font in the sanctuary. After Easter, you may also have discussions about a more permanent solution to the architectural needs for a baptistry visible to the assembly in your church.

Someone calls the names of the elect. The deacon or someone from the catechumenate team may do this. Be sure this person knows how to pronounce everyone's names. Godparents present the elect, and parents present infants for baptism.

■ LITANY OF THE SAINTS: The presider invites all to prayer, and the litany of the saints is begun. This litany may accompany the procession to the font (RCIA, 219B).

You may add names to the litany. Include the patrons of the parish, the diocese and of the elect if these are not already on the list.

The litany groups the saints by category. It opens with saints from the Bible (up to Stephen), then early Roman martyrs (up to Agnes), the four great church fathers, and a group that influenced the course of church history, ending with doctors Catherine and Teresa. In general, the list is chronological. It will take a little work, but if you want to add some saints, figure out where they belong in the sequence and insert them accordingly.

Sing the litany. The traditional chant is worth having in the community's repertoire (WLP, *We Celebrate,* 102). Other settings include ones by John Becker (OCP), David Haas (GIA, *Who Calls You by Name,* Vol. I), Matthew Nagi (*We Celebrate,* Vol. 2, cycle A) and Paul Page (*We Celebrate,* Vol. 1, #165).

Paul Ford has provided three petitions as the climax of the Litany of the Saints (*By Flowing Waters,* 143): "Give new life to these chosen ones by the grace of baptism: Lord, hear our prayer. Give new life to these chosen ones by the grace of baptism [pause] and pour out your Holy Spirit: Lord, hear our prayer. Give new life to these chosen ones by the grace of baptism [pause], pour out your Spirit [pause], and feed them with your body and blood: Lord, hear our prayer."

■ THE BLESSING OF THE WATER TAKES PLACE AT THE FONT. Arrange the ministers so the candle can be plunged into the water. The presider may chant the blessing. Notation appears in the blessing (RCIA, 222A). See *By Flowing Waters* (144) for another version. David Haas incorporates a familiar refrain for the assembly, the alleluia from *O filii et filiae* (GIA, *Who Calls You by Name,* Vol. II).

The assembly sings an acclamation at the end. A chant appears in the ritual text, but David Haas concludes his setting of the blessing with another option. Other versions are by Thomas Savory (GIA G-2549), Donald Fellows (GIA G-3639), Mike Hay (WLP, *We Celebrate,* 103) and Richard Proulx (GIA G-3097).

■ THE ELECT NOW RENOUNCE SIN AND PROFESS THEIR FAITH. Throughout Lent the elect have experienced purification and enlightenment. They have received and recited the creed. Now they answer personally the questions of faith. Parents and godparents answer for infants.

The renunciation of sin may be made as a group (#224), but each professes faith individually. This is no time for efficiency.

■ BAPTISM IN THE CATHOLIC CHURCH IS BY IMMERSION OR POURING. The options are always listed in that order. The *General Introduction to Christian Initiation* says, "As the rite for baptizing, either immersion, which is more suitable as a symbol of participation in the death and resurrection of Christ, or pouring may lawfully be used" (#22). The National Statutes for the Catechumenate in the United States say, "Baptism by immersion is the fuller and more expressive sign of the sacrament and, therefore, is preferred" (#17).

If the parish does not have a font, you may set up something for temporary use, but plans should be underway for a font suitable to celebrate the sacrament with adults and children.

Some parishes clothe the elect in a non-white, loose-fitting, opaque-when-wet garment that they can wear over whatever clothing they don't mind getting wet. If the font is of such size that the presider also enters it, he removes his chasuble, shoes and socks. His stole and alb and the clothing they conceal will get wet. If he wears a wireless microphone, prudence suggests that he remove it before stepping into the water.

■ AFTER EACH BAPTISM the assembly may sing an acclamation. Any alleluia works well, but consider these also: Lisa Stafford, "Acclamation for Baptism" (WLP 5229); "You Have Put on Christ," by Chrysogonus Waddell (WLP 7249), by Howard Hughes (GIA G-2283) or by Gary Daigle (GIA G-5021); Arthur Hutchings, "Rejoice, You Newly Baptized" (*ICEL Resource Collection,* GIA G-2514); Marty Haugen, "Song Over the Waters" (*Gather* #409); Lynn Trapp, "Rite of Christian Initiation of Adults" (Morning Star MSM-80-907A); or John Olivier, "You Have Put on Christ" (*People's Mass Book*).

You may use this acclamation at other baptisms throughout the year.

■ THE UNHAPPILY NAMED "EXPLANATORY RITES" COME NEXT. Anoint infants on the crown of the head (*Rite of Baptism for Children,* 62) but not the adults. Clothing with the white garment is optional, surprisingly. Ideally, infants would be clothed with the baptismal garment at this time, not before the baptism. Most families bring their infants to baptism already clothed in the white garment they should be receiving afterwards. (Watch how the Greek Orthodox baptize babies; Roman Catholics can do likewise.)

If adults and children of catechetical age have been immersed and go to a separate room to dry off and change clothes, they receive their garments from the godparent and then put them on. If godparents present the white garment in the privacy of the changing room, give them the text to say as they make the presentation (#229). Some communities do not give a white garment and allow the newly baptized to wear their Easter finest.

The presider invites godparents to light candles from the Easter candle, and they present it to the newly baptized. Any candle will suffice. Some companies sell special ones. Some parishes provide decorated candles. The Marklin Company makes smaller versions of its paschal candles for this rite (www.liturgy2000.com).

■ CONFIRMATION follows immediately if there are no candidates for the Rite of Reception. The link between baptism and confirmation and the mission of the Son and the outpouring of the Spirit (RCIA, 215) is better ritualized when the Rite of Reception does not interrupt the flow of the rites of initiation.

A song may begin the confirmation. Try "Veni, Sancte Spiritus" or "Confitemini Domino," both ostinatos from Taizé, or Christopher Walker's "Veni, Sancte Spiritus" (St. Thomas More/OCP 7116), or even "Come, Holy Ghost." But if the neophytes are dripping wet, you may want to omit this song and get started with confirmation.

The priest who baptizes has the faculty to confirm all adults and children of catechetical age whom he baptizes, and he must exercise this faculty for their benefit (canon 883/2 and 885/2). He does not have the faculty to confirm infants. Many people are surprised that a presider would confirm a child younger than the diocesan age for confirmation. The *Code of Canon Law* is very strict on this point. It gives the faculty directly to the presider assigned to the parish. The faculty does not come from the bishop. The presider "must

use it" for the benefit of the newly baptized, regardless of the relationship of their age to the diocesan age of confirmation. Some parents, priests and bishops prefer to defer the confirmation of baptized children of catechetical age, but they have no authority to do so. Let the sacrament benefit the child.

The presider introduces the rite and invites all to pray in silence. The next section is called "laying on of hands," but it describes an extension of hands. Still, if hand-laying is possible, it offers a better symbol. The presider may sing or recite the prayer for confirmation.

Use a generous amount of chrism on the neophyte's head, and be sure to smear the forehead in the sign of the cross. If you do not, you ritualize the anointing on the crown of the head that accompanies infant baptism, not confirmation on the forehead. The priest says, "Peace be with you," but no rubric is given for a gesture. An embrace would certainly be appropriate.

If the neophytes have been immersed let them leave the church now to change clothes.

■ RENEWAL OF BAPTISMAL PROMISES: All relight their candles with fire from the Easter candle or from those of the neophytes. Have ministers prepared to assist.

The faithful then renew their baptismal promises and are sprinkled with baptismal water. The presider should ask the questions in a strong voice, inviting a strong response. This ceremony signifies the climax of the assembly's period of renewal. Throughout Lent they have prepared themselves to recommit themselves to Christ. Now, at this moment, renewing their baptismal promises, they do just that.

For further effect, add Christopher Walker's convincing musical refrain, "We believe" (from "Christ We Proclaim," OCP 11293). The

English text is more convincing than the Spanish translation, but OCP should be applauded for its commitment to Spanish-language music.

In some communities, instead of being sprinkled, the faithful come to the font to sign themselves with water as they generally do upon entering the church. If the presider entered the font for baptism by immersion, he could change clothes now while the faithful come to the water.

A song may accompany the rite. Try Richard Hillert's "Lord Jesus, from your Wounded Side" (*Worship* #271) and Michael Joncas's adaptation of "O Healing River" (*Gather* #408).

If sprinkling, be sure everyone feels the water. Ministers should walk through all the aisles to sprinkle everyone. Branches from evergreen bushes or trees make excellent sprinkling implements. Tie several together to form a generous surface. Tape the stems at the bottom to form a handle and to keep sap off ministers' hands. Colorful ribbons may be added. An assistant carrying the bowl of water might accompany each person who sprinkles.

During the sprinkling, other ministers could replenish any holy water fonts in the church.

■ RITE OF RECEPTION: If there are candidates for the Rite of Reception as well as elect to be baptized, follow the rites in the *Rite of Christian Initiation of Adults* (#580–91). Do not follow the sacramentary, which was published earlier and observed a different sequence of ceremonies.

After the explanatory rites, the presider invites all to renew their baptismal promises. This places the candidates for reception on equal footing with the rest of the community. All share the same baptism and all renew their promises together. Sprinkling or signing with water comes next, as a ritual expression of the verbal renewal that just happened.

If in this combined rite the presider needs to change clothes after entering the font for immersions, he may do so at this time while the music for the water rite continues.

The Rite of Reception takes place in the sanctuary. The celebrant names the candidates in his opening remarks, but a member of the Christian initiation team could announce the names first, to introduce the group to the assembly. If there is a procession to the sanctuary, you may sing a song. Arrange the candidates so the assembly can see their faces. Sponsors, perhaps, stand behind them and the presider stands before, back to the assembly.

The candidates make their profession of faith by reciting the sentence of belief (RCIA, 585). It is best if they have this memorized, and if there is a group of them, they may recite the text together. Cue one of them, though, to take the lead, so they are not all waiting for someone to start.

For the act of reception, the presider speaks to each person individually. The rubric says he lays his right hand on the head of any who will not be confirmed, but it is difficult to imagine who they might be. The priest has the faculty to confirm all those he receives in this rite and is obliged to exercise the faculty. The exceptions would be people who were validly confirmed in a schismatic church, like an Orthodox congregation, but they are not to be received in a formal ceremony like this. Those who were confirmed in mainline Protestant churches or other similar ecclesial communities in the West will celebrate confirmation with their reception. Although we regard confirmation in the Eastern Orthodox traditions equivalent to that in the Roman

Catholic tradition, we do not extend the same equivalency to the confirmation of churches in the West. The hand on the shoulder is a kind of reconciling gesture, and should be avoided. If some human contact feels right, the presider might try grasping the hands of the one being received.

If at all possible, the presider should memorize the text for the act of reception (#586). This will enable him to look the candidate in the eye while saying the words. The words are few, but their meaning is huge.

Confirmation follows. If there are neophytes, they return at this point. If logistically possible, confirm the whole group near the font; if not, use the sanctuary.

The Rite of Reception apart from the Easter Vigil adds a sign of welcome by the presider (RCIA, 495) and the assembly (#497). The kiss of peace in the communion rite then may be omitted, but that will seem odd. Although the texts for the Easter Vigil do not suggest the sign of welcome, it would make a fitting gesture, a hand or embrace of Christian peace. Consider inviting all those who wish to step away from the seats, up to the front, and welcome the newest members of the eucharistic community.

■ THE NEOPHYTES JOIN THE COMMUNITY FOR THE GENERAL INTERCESSIONS. If they have been dismissed throughout their period of formation, this is their first time joining the prayers we call "of the faithful." Use all the languages of the community in the petitions.

PART FOUR IS THE LITURGY OF THE EUCHARIST.

The neophytes bring up the bread and wine for the eucharistic meal in which they will share for the first time. Sing a familiar Easter hymn to unite the voices of the

assembly and to give everyone a sense of purpose as you enter the final and most familiar part of tonight's service.

■ INSERTS: If possible, the presider should sing the eucharistic prayer. When using the preface for Easter I (P 21), use the text "on this Easter night." The Ritual Mass for Christian Initiation: Baptism (3) provides inserts for four eucharistic prayers.

If you use Eucharistic Prayer I, there are additional inserts for "In union" and "Father, accept." The first alludes to this Easter night, the second, to the newly baptized. But if there were baptisms tonight, take the text for "Father, accept" from the Ritual Mass for Christian Initiation: Baptism (3) as well, because it includes an additional line.

■ ACCLAMATIONS: You might start the new set of eucharistic acclamations for the Easter season. These will be used throughout the 50 Days. If you choose "Dying you destroyed our death" as the memorial acclamation, you will find it matches well with the first Easter preface (P 21), whenever it is used throughout the season.

■ COMMUNION: Before saying, "This is the Lamb of God," the presider may briefly remind the neophytes of the preeminence of the eucharist, which is the climax of their initiation and the center of the whole Christian life (RCIA, 243). Prepare a text expressing the community's joy and welcome, while affirming the centrality of our belief in and celebration of the eucharist.

Use recently baked bread and a good wine.

Music for the communion procession might include Tom Parker's "Praise the Lord, My Soul" (GIA, *Gather* #393 or G-2395); a setting of Psalm 34 with the refrain "Taste and see the goodness of the Lord" (suggested by the *Circular Letter*, 91); Paul Hillenbrand's "Eucharistic Litany" (WLP 520); "I Received the Living God" (*Worship* #735 and GIA G-3071) by Richard Proulx or the concertato version by Ellen Doerrfeld-Coman (WLP 7215); Taizé's "Eat This Bread" (GIA G-2840); or Michael Joncas's "Take and Eat" (GIA).

If there is a breakfast or reception for the neophytes and all who shared the Vigil, a blessing of the food may be given after communion (*Book of Blessings,* ch. 54).

■ THE SOLEMN BLESSING suggested for this Mass does not appear in the sacramentary where you expect it, probably because of space and not with the intent of omitting it. You may find it easily by turning the page to the Mass for Easter Sunday. It also appears later in the sacramentary as the sixth in the set of solemn blessings.

■ TONIGHT'S DISMISSAL calls for the double alleluia. Sing the traditional chant melody, a signature acclamation of Easter.

Your choir and brass ensemble can raise the rafters with Wallace Nolin's "Fanfare for Easter Morn" (WLP 2330), based on familiar Easter hymns. See also "Descants for Easter" by Michael Joncas (WLP 8513) and "Festival Hymns for Organ, Brass and Timpani," Set VI—General, by John Ferguson (GIA G-5260).

OTHER IDEAS

Work to make the entire celebration a parish event. Perhaps involve different committees in some of the preparation and celebrations. Provide written materials in advance so that everyone knows the importance of the Vigil. Keep the names of the elect and candidates for reception before the community, and find ways to introduce them at parish events.

■ MAKE EASTER WATER AVAILABLE for people to take home tonight and tomorrow. Easter eggs and fresh flowers may be given to all as they leave or during breakfast. The eggs may have been colored by children from the community or by young Catholic candidates for confirmation.

The breakfast or reception after the eucharist follows a tradition revered among many ethnic groups.

#42; afternoon or evening
#46   white
Easter Sunday
SOLEMNITY

ORIENTATION

The resurrection of Jesus from the dead demonstrates God's ultimate power over all other forces, including death. By his resurrection, Jesus opens the door of eternity to all believers. The mystery of redemption, first intimated at the incarnation, reaches its purpose in the resurrection. Belief in the resurrection is the cornerstone of Christian faith.

Today concludes the celebration of the Triduum and begins the great 50 Days. After 40 days of fast, we have 50 days of feast.

Some who celebrated the Vigil or who plan to participate at the eucharist later today may wish to offer morning prayer together, or to join with other Christian churches in a sunrise service.

People who have taxes on their minds this week might appreciate a petition in the general intercessions for the prudent usage of our country's tax dollars.

LECTIONARY

The Easter gospel is John's account of the resurrection, but you may also choose Luke's from the Vigil. For a Mass this afternoon or evening, you may even choose Luke's account of the journey to Emmaus. These passages mark the events of Easter Day—the resurrection in the early morning, an apparition in the late afternoon.

Today's psalm is a seasonal acclamation of joy proclaiming this day as the day the Lord has made, or on which God has acted. The psalm moves the celebration of Easter away from a mere historical remembrance to one of present participation. The mystery of God's promise is proclaimed in the adage about the rejected stone.

There are two choices for the second reading. The passage from Colossians announces the effect of Jesus' resurrection on the believer and the expectations of the believer's behavior. From 1 Corinthians we hear a comparison between the celebrations of the resurrection and of Passover.

The Easter sequence is sung today. We have only a few such texts in the liturgy. A sequence is a hymn that follows the second reading and precedes the gospel for certain special occasions. Musical versions can also be found under its Latin title, "Victimae Paschali laudes." The original chant is in the *Liber cantualis*. World Library's *Psalms and Ritual Music* includes several simple, effective settings. Settings include ones by Peter Scagnelli (*Worship*

#837), by Richard Proulx (GIA G-3088) and by Ann Colleen Dohns (WLP 5718), which includes congregational refrains. The hymn uses Passover imagery to proclaim the news of resurrection.

The lectionary presents only one option for the first reading, a catechetical sermon that Peter gives in the house of Cornelius. In that talk, Peter proclaims the core of Christian belief, and the message of resurrection resounds loud and clear. Peter says the prophets testified that Jesus would rise, and that believers are now called to testify by preaching.

Together, these passages proclaim the nucleus of the gospel, the resurrection of Jesus, as well as its implications for the behavior of believers and their future glory.

SACRAMENTARY

Incense would lend solemnity to this celebration. The solemnity of the Easter Mass should be clear.

■ IN PLACE OF AN INTRODUCTION TO THE MASS, the presider might lengthen the greeting and say, "Alleluia! The Lord is truly risen! His grace and peace be with you all."

Even if you plan to celebrate the rite of sprinkling in place of the penitential rite throughout the Easter season, wait a week to begin. The sprinkling today occurs in conjunction with the renewal of baptismal promises after the homily.

■ BOTH OPENING PRAYERS acclaim the meaning of today's solemnity while invoking divine aid in the renewal of our lives.

■ PLAN THE GOSPEL PROCESSION with a solemnity that befits the day. Bring incense and include ministers in the procession.

■ THE HOMILY may proclaim hope because of resurrection. It is not the time to intimidate once-a-year churchgoers. John Chrysostom said, "Come, you all: Enter into the joy of your Lord. You the first and you the last, receive alike your reward. You rich and you poor, dance together. You strong and you weak, celebrate the day. You who have kept the fast, and you who have not kept the fast, rejoice today." (See LTP's *Triduum Sourcebook,* 335).

■ RENEWAL OF BAPTISMAL PROMISES: In the United States, the creed is replaced with the renewal of baptismal promises. This gives everyone the opportunity to state their belief as answers to questions, in repetition of one of the key moments of the Easter Vigil. A variation on the renewal suitable for home use appears in *Catholic Household Blessings and Prayers* (p. 372).

Sprinkle with holy water as at the Vigil. Assisting ministers may carry buckets or bowls filled with water from the font to accompany those who sprinkle. Fill the bowls from the font so that the association is clear. Use evergreen branches or the traditional aspergilla. Walk all around the church and sprinkle lavishly. Be sure everyone feels the water of rebirth. All sing "Vidi aquam" or another song of baptismal character. A rousing alleluia would also cheer the heart at this time.

■ EUCHARIST: The first Easter preface should include the phrase "on this Easter day" (P 21). When Eucharistic Prayer I is used, you may include the special Easter forms of "In union" and "Father, accept." If there are infant baptisms at Mass on Easter Sunday, you may use the inserts to the eucharistic prayers found in the Ritual Mass for Christian Initiation: Baptism (3).

The suggested entrance and communion antiphons draw on several scripture texts that refer to the resurrection or use the image of rising.

■ THE DISMISSAL today includes a double alleluia. The chant deserves to be in the repertoire of every assembly.

You'll probably want to conclude the service with a hymn everyone knows, but if you want to add something simple but jazzy to the repertoire, check out the "Dismissal Amen" by Denise Pyles (WLP 5238). It could be used almost any time of year, but the bouncy hallelujahs make it a good choice for Easter.

BLESSING EASTER FOOD

The blessing of food links the Easter eucharistic table to the family table. Families may bring baskets of food including children's Easter baskets to any Mass, even the Vigil.

Set up tables and ask ushers to direct people to place their baskets there, especially at the Vigil when people arrive as darkness gathers. Alternatively, household members may keep baskets with them in their places and raise them up for the blessing prayer and sprinkling (although a crowded church makes this difficult).

According to the *Book of Blessings* (ch. 54), the Order of the Blessing of Food for the First Meal of Easter could take place after the prayer after communion. Sprinkle the baskets with water from the font.

OTHER IDEAS

■ HOSPITALITY: Give a spring flower to all as they leave Mass today. Easter eggs are a traditional gift with sacred significance. Offer coffee and hot cross buns after Mass, so everyone can socialize and rejoice in their faith. If your tendency is to abandon the weekly after-worship coffee-and-doughnuts today due to the demands of home and family, reconsider. Despite the large numbers of worshipers, this is an important occasion for hospitality. An Easter egg hunt can be held for children after Mass or in the afternoon before evening prayer.

The community may also gather for midday prayer and an Easter meal. The blessing of the first Easter meal may take place on this occasion. Or you can provide texts for people to bless the first Easter meal at home.

■ THE PARISH BULLETIN: Be sure plenty of information is available in this week's bulletin. Visitors may want to know when they might return to share in the community's life. The schedule for getting copy to the printer no doubt was unusual this past week, and the people who ordinarily provide copy were busy with other duties. That means that the Easter Sunday bulletin, to be done well, probably required attention weeks ago. Add that duty to next year's lenten calendar.

PASCHAL VESPERS

Evening prayer to conclude the Triduum is recommended in the *Circular Letter* (#98), the *Ceremonial of Bishops* (#371) and the *General Instruction of the Liturgy of the Hours* (#213). It reconvenes the community and the neophytes to prolong the prayer of Easter joy.

■ A PRINCIPAL PASCHAL LITURGY: As the disciples met and touched the risen Lord and received their commission, so the church gathers this evening in the peace of the risen Christ to usher out the Triduum and to begin living within the 50 Days, the foretaste of

paradise. Thanks to its history, some people regard paschal vespers, along with the Mass of the Lord's Supper, the celebration of the Lord's Passion and the Easter Vigil, as a principal liturgy of the Triduum. Like these liturgies, evening prayer on Easter Sunday is an occasion for once-a-year rites.

Afterward be sure to have Easter treats to share. Also traditional afterward (and through the week) at sunset time is an "Emmaus Walk," a walk through the neighborhood in search of spring—and of Christ's presence in the world.

■ THIS LITURGY MAY BE STATIONAL: Components may be celebrated in different locations ("stations") in the church complex.

According to tradition the paschal candle remains burning without interruption throughout Easter Sunday, from the Vigil until this evening. It burns as people gather for evening prayer.

Here is a suggested order of service (psalms, hymns and other music may be drawn from the parish's repertory):

- *gathering*: Assembly gathers near the paschal candle.
- *service of light*: V. Christ our light. R. Thanks be to God. Assembly's candles and all church candles are lit from the paschal candle.
- *hymn*: "At the Lamb's high feast" (The ancient melody for *Ad coenam Agni providi/Ad regias Agni dapes* is worth the effort to learn, although the metrical version set to the carol SONNE DER GERECHTIGKEIT [*Worship* #460] is grand.)
- *thanksgiving for light,* sung by cantor or presider: For Easter texts, see GIA's *Praise God in Song* or *Worship: Liturgy of the Hours* (leader's edition). The assembly's candles may be extinguished as the lights needed for psalmody are turned on.
- *psalmody*: Sunday, Evening Prayer II, Week I. The psalms should be sung.

- *canticle* from Revelation or Psalm 114: During the canticle or psalm a congregational alleluia is repeated as cantors sing verses, and the assembly processes to the font, led by incense-bearer, minister with paschal candle, and presider. Take the route used last night. Depending on the size and location of the baptistry, all remain there until after the baptismal commemoration or until the end of the service.
- *reading*: Luke 24:13–35 (*Lectionary for Mass,* 46) or Luke 24:35–48 (#47)
- *patristic selection* from the Easter octave texts in the *Liturgy of the Hours,* or a brief homily on symbols of Easter, or silent prayer and reflection
- *sung responsory* as at morning prayer: "This is the day"
- *thanksgiving over the water* (adapt RCIA, 222 D or E, or from C of the rite of sprinkling in the sacramentary)
- *signing*: All approach the font to sign themselves or each other while singing the antiphon, as at the blessing of water at the Vigil.
- *canticle of Mary*: sung with proper antiphon while all are honored with incense. Procession to the altar may take place during the canticle.
- *intercessions* from *Liturgy of the Hours*
- *Lord's Prayer*
- *concluding prayer* of Easter Sunday
- *solemn blessing*
- *dismissal*: Easter tone with double alleluia
- *closing hymn*: "Come, ye faithful, raise the strain" (*Worship* #456) or "The day of resurrection" (*Hymnal 1982* #210) Or, although this would be proper to night prayer, close with the Marian antiphon for the Easter season, "Regina caeli."

APRIL 8, 2004
Holy Thursday of the Supper of the Lord

Remembering Our Story
Exodus 12:1–8, 11–14
It is the Passover of the Lord.

THE story of Passover is ugly. God's chosen people had been reduced to slavery in Egypt under Pharaoh's intolerable leadership. A series of plagues failed to soften Pharaoh's heart. A final, ghastly plague threatened to kill the firstborn sons of Egypt. The Israelites slaughtered lambs, ate the flesh and sprinkled the blood on their doorposts. God's avenging angel committed the threatened homicides but passed over the homes of the Israelites. They won their freedom, but it wasn't pretty.

As we enter the Triduum, the sacred Three Days, we remember this terrible story. Only a word of liberation could quiet the wails of sorrow. We hear this account again with all its horror and all its hope.

The church invites us into these three days unafraid of what terror we may know. We have suffered pain. We have grieved loss. We have known despair. We have tried to forgive. The dreadfulness of our stories do not matter. We gather together as a community to remember and pray.

There are moments in life we would rather forget—moments of sin, moments of suffering. But there is a safe time to remember. That time is this holy night.

Written by Paul Turner. © 2003 Archdiocese of Chicago, Liturgy Training Publications; 1-800-933-1800; www.ltp.org.

APRIL 9, 2004
Good Friday of the Lord's Passion

God's Chosen Hero
Isaiah 52:13—53:12
My servant shall be raised high and greatly exalted.

HEROES risk their own lives to save others. Some heroes live to hear accolades. Others die in the struggle. The one who risks her or his life for another can bring healing beyond measure.

Who has done this for you? Who raised you in the weakness of your infancy? Who taught you in a spirit of service? Who kept you from getting into trouble? Who fought for the safety of your land? Who saved your life when you were in danger? Who has redeemed you?

Isaiah recognizes a servant of God known for heroism. God laid the guilt of the people upon this servant, and the servant suffered chastisement for their sake. Christians see in Isaiah's testimony a description of Jesus: "Because he surrendered himself to death, he shall take away the sins of many."

On Good Friday we remember the wondrous love of God, whose Son suffered death so that we might have life. Jesus stands tall among the models of heroism. His death brought healing beyond measure.

Whenever you accept responsibility, whenever you admit blame, whenever you risk your popularity or your very life, you love like a hero.

Written by Paul Turner. © 2003 Archdiocese of Chicago, Liturgy Training Publications; 1-800-933-1800; www.ltp.org.

APRIL 10, 2004
The Vigil in the Holy Night of Easter

Christ's Redeeming Sacrifice
Genesis 22:1–18
I know now how devoted you are to God.

ON the happiest night of the year we hear one of the most shocking stories of the year. God asked Abraham to kill his son. Abraham had waited a hundred years for the birth of his first child. Now, God asked him to kill his son, "Isaac, your only one, whom you love."

Today this story seems horrible. Certainly God would never ask someone to pull a knife on a child. Our church stands for the protection of children, not for their destruction. The story seems contrary to all that we believe—even though it has a happy ending.

The reason we remember this story at the Easter Vigil is because it shares some similarities with the story of Jesus' death and resurrection. Jesus was also an only son, the one whom God loved. Jesus also was selected for sacrifice. Although no heavenly messenger stopped the crucifixion the way one stopped the slaying of Isaac, Jesus was rescued from death in a different way. He went through death, not around it. He escaped on the other side of death into eternal life.

We remember this story not because it shows how God asks difficult things. We remember this story because it shows how God redeems.

This is the happiest night of the year, but you may be carrying sorrows to your prayer. Rejoice! God rules over life and death! Jesus is risen! Alleluia!

APRIL 11, 2004
Easter Sunday of the Resurrection of the Lord

All Is New
Acts 10:34a, 37–43
God raised Jesus on the third day.

WHAT'S new?" That's what we ask when we want to hear a story. Stories celebrate the great moments of life. When you hear one, it fills you with delight. When you tell one, you fulfill an inner desire to share what has shaped your life anew.

After Jesus rose from the dead, the disciples did not wait for people to ask, "What's new?" They proudly proclaimed it: "God raised Jesus on the third day and granted that he be visible to us witnesses." Now, that's new!

If you have kept a good Lent, you know very well what is new with you. *You* are what is new! You have faced your sin, admitted your fault, and accepted your dependence upon God's help. You have prayed and fasted with the community. You have loved your neighbor. Because you have emptied a place inside yourself, you created a space for God's Spirit to enter. Christ is risen indeed, and he has appeared to you! You are now a witness of all that God can do.

This Easter Day, tell your story. Tell your faith. Let joy radiate from your face and loosen your tongue! Jesus lives!

EASTER

The Meaning

The risen body of Christ is the seed of the new creation planted within the old chaos. Christ the man is related to the whole cosmos, as is every other human being, by an immensely complicated web of genetic, chemical, physiological, intellectual and cultural ties. But this part of the cosmos, the part which is Christ's manhood, is risen and glorified. The shock waves go through the whole; every part is affected. His risen body is like a radioactive substance lodged in the heart of the universe.

—Maria Boulding, *The Coming of God,* Third edition (Conception, Missouri: The Printery House, 2000), pp. 158–59.

Christ is risen! Alleluia!

The resurrection of Jesus affects everything in the cosmos. All creation is renewed, and humanity is once again made whole. Death has no more power over us. The hope and promise of that message is the central belief of Christianity. It takes 50 days to celebrate the resurrection of

Jesus and its implications for humanity. One week is not enough. A week of weeks is not enough. It takes seven times seven days, plus one. A fullness of time observes the fullness of Easter.

■ THROUGHOUT THIS SEASON THE CHURCH REJOICES WITH THOSE BAPTIZED AT EASTER. They bring new life, new awareness, deeper prayer and renewed service to the community. Their period of postbaptismal formation is called mystagogy.

■ THE EASTER SEASON GENERALLY COINCIDES WITH THE NORTHERN HEMISPHERE'S SPRING. Easter Day comes every year on the Sunday following the first full moon of spring. We enter a natural season of new life and rebirth. As nature flowers around us, Christians enter its spirit.

The season will conclude with Pentecost, the fiftieth day. The feast of Pentecost already existed in the Jewish calendar. The coming of the Holy Spirit on that day allowed Christians to compare the two Pentecosts. On the first, God gave the covenant to Moses amid lightning and thunder. On the second, God gave the Spirit to the disciples amid wind and tongues of fire. Some writers in the early church referred to the whole season of Easter as "Pentecost"—the Fifty Days.

The Saints

■ THE SOLEMNITIES OF EASTER, ASCENSION AND PENTECOST ANCHOR THE SEASON. But in the weeks ahead we will have ample opportunity to celebrate all the more. The octave of Easter itself ranks as a week of solemnities.

The date of the Ascension varies throughout the United States and the world. In some regions it falls on a Thursday, the fortieth day of Easter, in keeping with the tradition from Acts of the Apostles. This year, that will be May 20. In other areas it is transferred to replace the Seventh Sunday of Easter, so that more of the faithful may celebrate the feast. This year, that will be May 30, when the United States celebrates Memorial Day weekend.

■ BOTH FEASTS OF SAINTS during this Easter season recall apostles. Philip and James have their feast together (May 3), and Matthias follows the next week (May 14). Mark normally appears on April 25, but his celebration is suppressed for the second year in a row—last year due to the Easter octave, this year because it falls on Sunday. If Mark is patron of your community, you may transfer his celebration to the following day.

■ WHEN AN OBLIGATORY MEMORIAL OCCURS DURING EASTER, its vestment color and presidential prayers take precedence over the Easter weekday. This year Catherine of Siena (April 29) and Philip Neri (May 26) fall into this category. Both celebrations call for white vesture, so there is no change in liturgical color on their days. The preface may be taken from the Easter weekday or from the relevant common of pastors, virgins or holy men and women. The scriptures could be taken from the lectionary common appropriate for the saint, but most communities will laudably observe the Easter lectionary, as the guidelines advise. (See *Introduction to the Lectionary for Mass,* 82–83.)

■ SEVERAL OPTIONAL MEMORIALS occur on Easter weekdays this year. Your community may elect to celebrate the Mass of the Easter weekday or of the saint whose memorial is optional.

If you wish to remember the saint of the day without eclipsing the season of Easter, consider using the saint's opening prayer as the conclusion to the general intercessions.

■ OTHER CELEBRATIONS: The liturgical books also supply texts for votive Masses and for Masses for various needs and occasions. These texts may be used during Easter only for some real need or pastoral advantage.

The Lectionary

THE Easter lectionary hugs the New Testament tight, even on Sundays. We close the Old Testament for these 50 days. The only exceptions are the daily responsorial psalm and the readings at the Pentecost vigil. In the lectionary the psalms bring the scriptures into the living, praying community that hears them. They bring us into the eternal dialogue between God and the covenanted people, mediated by the divine Word.

■ DURING THE OCTAVE OF EASTER, the gospels consistently announce the resurrection through stories of the appearances of the risen Jesus. Easter Day and its octave celebrate the resurrection in history as well as the resurrected Christ present in our midst.

■ THE WEEKDAY LECTIONARY otherwise features the semi-continuous reading of Acts of the Apostles and selections from John's gospel that open wider the mystery of the resurrection. During the final part of the season, the week or more between Ascension and Pentecost, the readings continue their pattern, but the weekday psalms all sing of God's sovereignty, an Ascension theme.

■ THE GOSPELS FOR THE SUNDAYS OF EASTER EACH YEAR follow a predictable pattern. Easter Sunday, of course, features the gospel of the resurrection, and the following Sunday tells of the events "eight days later."

The third Sunday reveals some aspect of the community's mission, while the fourth draws on the tenth chapter of John, which develops the image of the Good Shepherd. The fifth, sixth and seventh Sundays all take gospel passages from the final discourse and prayer of Jesus from John's account of the Last Supper.

In communities where the Seventh Sunday of Easter is suppressed and Ascension is celebrated, the gospel relates Jesus' farewell.

■ THE FIRST AND SECOND READINGS: In the three-year cycle for the Easter season, all first readings come from Acts of the Apostles and the second readings feature one other New Testament book, Revelation, this year.

Several New Testament books are attributed to John: the gospel, three letters and Revelation. More likely they come from the authors of a Johannine school. The meaning of Revelation is hotly debated among Christians of every stripe. Catholic scripture scholars commonly see it as an exhortation to first-century Christians undergoing persecution. The message is delivered in coded language that has evoked valid and not-so-valid interpretations in every generation of the faith.

■ THE SUNDAY *LECTIONARY FOR MASSES WITH CHILDREN* makes one notable difference from the full lectionary. It omits the reading from Revelation on the second, third, fourth and seventh Sundays of Easter. The passages on the fifth and sixth are the upbeat visions of the new Jerusalem, easier for children to grasp and less likely to cause nightmares than the rest of the Bible's last book.

Three readings are provided for Easter, Ascension and Pentecost. However, the children's book draws from Year A for the second reading of Ascension as well as the second reading and gospel of Pentecost. On these solemnities you may choose the Year A readings from the main lectionary any year, but the options for Year C are not included in the Sunday *Lectionary for Masses with Children*.

As usual, many of the longer readings are abbreviated. The Pentecost vigil readings are entirely omitted.

The Sacramentary

■ NOTICE THE ATTENTION GIVEN TO THE OCTAVE OF EASTER. The gospels tell of the resurrection appearances. The Easter sequence may be sung every day. In addition, each day is treated as a solemnity of the Lord (*General Norms for the Liturgical Year and Calendar,* 24), and it ranks even above other solemnities. Each day calls for the Glory to God. Ordinarily, solemnities also call for the creed (*General Instruction of the Roman Missal,* 43), and the octave of Easter used to require it each day, but the present sacramentary has dropped the creed from these days without explanation.

Throughout the Easter octave the first preface of Easter (P 21) may be used with the expression "on this Easter day," because every day of the octave is one with the paschal festival. The inserts to Eucharistic Prayer I may also be included. This is especially fitting if the newly baptized join the community for the daily eucharist. This custom, much encouraged in the history of the catechumenate, is urged nowhere in the *Rite of Christian Initiation of Adults.* But Mass texts like these still presume that neophytes are present for the eucharist every day for a week.

During the octave the double alleluia is added to the dismissal dialogue. If your community has not yet learned the traditional chant, this week provides an opportunity for instruction.

The octave celebrates time outside of time, a week eight days in length, a celebration that earthly time cannot measure. (Even John Lennon and Paul McCartney recognized that some love was so powerful it had to be given eight days a week.) Because of the historical interest in celebrating this week with neophytes and the way the sacramentary texts support the former custom, you might schedule one or more evening Masses this week. Let the neophytes meet more members of the community. Swap stories. Show a video of the vigil. And do mystagogy: Talk about the symbols of that holy night, about what they expressed and about what the neophytes experienced.

■ THE BLESSING AND SPRINKLING OF HOLY WATER MAY REPLACE THE PENITENTIAL RITE ON ANY SUNDAY. The Easter season provides an excellent opportunity for this option. Many communities sprinkle the assembly throughout the season, to highlight the symbol of baptismal water. The rite even provides a special blessing for the Easter season (C). Note the option for blessing salt to be added to the water. The prayer quotes an episode in the life of Elisha (2 Kings 2:19–22), a story that unfortunately appears nowhere in the lectionary.

If you choose to use Penitential Rite C at any time in the season, options v, vi and vii rely on Easter themes.

■ A SAMPLE FORMULA FOR THE GENERAL INTERCESSIONS can be found in the sacramentary's first appendix. Prayers for the Easter season are at #8.

■ BESIDES P 21, OTHER EASTER PREFACES (P 22–25) may be used throughout the season. Although these additional prefaces were not found in the Roman Missal immediately before the Second Vatican Council, they all have antecedents in the liturgy prior to the eighth century.

For Ambrosian rite prefaces, see Alan Griffiths's translations in *We Give You Thanks and Praise* (Roman P 22 resembles the one for Easter Friday, P 23 for Saturday 3 of Easter, P 27 for Wednesday 7 of Easter).

■ IN ADDITION TO THE INSERTS FOR THE EASTER OCTAVE, Eucharistic Prayer I provides texts for Ascension and Pentecost.

■ THE SOLEMN BLESSING for the Easter season is the seventh in the sacramentary's collection. It appears on the page, strangely, only for the even-numbered Sundays of the Easter season. Various prayers over the people appear on the other Sundays. But you may use the solemn blessing throughout the season.

At weekday Masses early in the season, consider prayers over the people #3, 14 and 18. Later, try #20, 23 and 24.

Another solemn blessing for the Easter season can be found in the *Collection of Masses of the Blessed Virgin Mary* at the end of the order of Mass.

The Book of Blessings

SOME seasonal blessings should be noted. Homes may be blessed during the Easter season (ch. 50), and the first meal of Easter has its own blessing (54), as previously indicated. The blessing of homes could be difficult to organize, but it could also draw the community together. All pastoral ministers could be involved because the church provides forms for blessings offered by lay ministers; or make brief orders of blessings available for families to use.

■ MOTHER'S DAY will fall on the Fifth Sunday of Easter this year, and its blessing might conclude the general intercessions or replace the solemn blessing that day.

See also the blessings for mothers before and after childbirth (1, VIII), students and teachers (5), a new building site (10), fields and flocks (26), seeds at planting time (27), a new baptistry or font (31), holy water (41), religious articles (44), rosaries (45) and scapulars (46). For other materials contact the National Catholic Rural Life Conference, 4625 SW Beaver Drive, Des Moines IA 50310; www.ncrlc.com.

The Rite of Christian Initiation of Adults

■ EASTER IS THE SEASON FOR MYSTAGOGY OF THE NEOPHYTES. The *Rite of Christian Initiation of Adults* gives precious little information about this (#244–51). Primarily, the newly baptized are to continue formation through their experience of the sacraments (#245). Postbaptismal catechesis is to involve the faithful as well (#246).

The homily and general intercessions "should take into account the presence and needs of the neophytes" (#248). Homilies that unfold the primary mysteries of faith, creation, resurrection, baptism, eucharist and community will foster good mystagogy. For help in preparing mystagogic homilies, see Craig Satterlee's excellent book, *Ambrose of Milan's Method of Mystagogical Preaching* (Collegeville: The Liturgical Press, 2002).

Other Sacraments of Initiation

■ CONFIRMATION: Easter may be the season in which confirmation is celebrated for Catholics baptized as infants. The sacrament may be offered any day of the year, but some bishops and diocesan worship offices prefer to schedule them during Easter as much as possible.

Celebrations should stress the gift of the Holy Spirit, not the achievement of candidates. Provide a generous amount of chrism to encourage a liberal anointing. Arrange the ministers in a way that the assembly of the faithful can see the faces of the candidates.

Avoid the use of stoles on those being confirmed. Stoles are vesture reserved for priests and deacons.

■ FIRST COMMUNIONS ALSO MAY TAKE PLACE DURING THE EASTER SEASON. There is no universal rite of first communion, nor any recommended time of year for its celebration. Whenever the children are ready, they may join the community at the holy table. Some parishes celebrate a special first communion Mass, apart from the regular schedule. Others incorporate the first communions—perhaps in smaller groups—into the regular Sunday celebration to honor the individual readiness of the children and to allow the whole community to rejoice with the children. In this way, first communions may appear at Sunday Mass just as catechumenate rites, baptisms and special blessings do. They keep the whole community together for important events.

A reference to first communion for children can be found in volume IV of the lectionary (#769). This is the first time such a reference appears in any official liturgical book in the history of the Roman Catholic Church. The heading for first communion follows the readings for confirmation, according to the tradition that communion is the climax of Christian initiation. The lectionary does not say much: Readings may be taken in whole or in part from the Mass of the day, the Mass of Christian Initiation or the votive Mass of the Holy Eucharist. But this brief rubric makes liturgical history.

The Liturgy of the Hours

PARISHES are encouraged to make at least morning and evening prayer available year round. If you honored this practice during the season of Lent, it may continue throughout Easter. Some communities open evening prayer by lighting the Easter candle and repeating the Vigil's dialogue, "Light of Christ," "Thanks be to God." A special evening prayer for Pentecost will close the day and the season with appropriate festivity.

Changes in the psalms for the office of readings, begun during Lent, continue throughout Easter. An alleluia is added to the end of many antiphons throughout the season.

Among the fine passages in the office of readings for Easter, see the excerpt from Augustine's discourse on the psalms, where he explains the Easter alleluia. You can find it on Saturday of the Fifth Week of Easter. "[W]e keep the first season [Lent] with fasting and prayer; but now the fast is over and we devote the present season to praise. Such is the meaning of the *Alleluia* we sing."

During the octave of Easter and on the day of Pentecost, the double alleluia concludes the dismissal dialogue, as at Mass. For examples of notation, see the first and third examples in the sacramentary under Easter Vigil (#56). The Episcopal church keeps this double alleluia in all dismissals during the 50 Days.

To conclude night prayer throughout the season, you may sing any of the Marian antiphons. But the most traditional one for the Easter season is the "Regina caeli" from the *Liber cantualis*.

The Rite of Penance

BECAUSE of Lent's strong penitential character, few parishes emphasize the sacrament of reconciliation during the Easter season. Still, it is important for the community to know when the celebration happens. Some may have experienced new birth and spiritual insight as a result of this holy time of year. They may appreciate another opportunity for a communal celebration.

The newly baptized need not be rushed into the celebration of the sacrament because baptism has cleansed them from sin. But they may want to seek the opportunity to celebrate this sacrament sometime during this season, to further their experience of the Catholic way of life.

If you have a communal celebration of this sacrament during the Easter season, it would keep the spirit of the lectionary to draw the readings from the New Testament.

The Pastoral Care of the Sick

ONCE again, there is no season especially appropriate for this sacrament, but a communal celebration could happen during Easter. The chrism Mass has provided a fresh stock of oil for the community, and it could be offered to the sick as a way of entering into the hope of Easter. Whenever celebrating this sacrament, or even in visiting the sick, prayer should include scripture. In keeping with the spirit of the lectionary, texts from the New Testament are more appropriate throughout the Easter season.

The Rite of Marriage

IF a wedding takes place during the Mass of any solemnity (including the morning or early afternoon of Easter Saturday, April 17), or on any Saturday evening of this season, the readings and prayers for the day take precedence.

Only one reading may come from the Mass of marriage. Throughout this season, the couple is not free to select completely alternative scripture passages for the wedding Mass unless it takes place on a weekday of lesser rank or before evening on any Saturday except April 17. The nuptial blessing, of course, is included no matter which Mass is celebrated.

If the wedding does not include a Mass, or if the wedding Mass does not take place on a solemnity, a Saturday evening or a Sunday, the scriptures and prayers for marriage may be used. When choosing scripture texts, keep in mind the lectionary's preference to draw all the readings from the New Testament.

The Order of Christian Funerals

BOTH the *Order of Christian Funerals* and the sacramentary provide texts for a funeral during the Easter season. The sacramentary collects them under Masses for the Dead, Funeral Masses: During the Easter Season (C). The Order of Christian Funerals offers an opening prayer for a funeral Mass (#164 D). The communion prayer during the Easter season from the sacramentary can also be found at #410 C, and will avoid the presider's need to switch books hastily at the end of the funeral Mass.

Even though the weekdays of the octave of Easter are treated as solemnities, the church does permit the substitution of the scriptures and prayers assigned for these days with those for a funeral Mass. Still, you may suggest that the bereaved family and friends hear the scriptures of the day, because they will eloquently proclaim the resurrection. You might conclude the rite of committal with a double alleluia during the Easter octave. If a funeral takes place at a Mass on a Sunday of the Easter season or on Ascension, however, the Mass of the day is celebrated and the funeral rites are included.

The Art and Environment

■ GIVE ATTENTION TO THE OUTDOORS. Let people driving by know that Easter is underway. Bunting and banners, maypoles and streamers, spring-time garlands and wreaths are all possible.

■ FOR INSIDE DECORATIONS, consult *The Sacristy Manual* (p. 220) and *To Crown the Year* (pp. 122–52).

■ THE EASTER CANDLE deserves a commanding place near the ambo throughout the season. It returns to the font after evening prayer of Pentecost. Tall and stately, it should acclaim that Christ is the light of the world. Be sure it is lit for absolutely every service that takes place during the 50 Days. Decorate the stand for the season.

■ WHEREVER THE FONT IS LOCATED, draw attention to it with flowers, lighting or some other means. If you used a temporary font to make Easter baptisms visible to the assembly, you may keep it for the 50 Days, as long as its impermanence and construction does not distract from celebration. It is better to make plans for a permanent, visible font.

An old custom invites neophytes to attend the eucharist during the octave of Easter, dressed in their white garments. They and their godparents may have a special place reserved throughout the season, perhaps near the font, the ambo or the candle. Decorate that area accordingly (RCIA, 248).

■ FLOWERS ARE "DISCOURAGED IN LENT, DEMANDED BY EASTER" (*To Crown the Year*, 149–52). If you blanket the church with lilies on Easter Sunday, have something in reserve to make it through the 50 Days. Wilting flowers do not proclaim Easter promise. Peter Mazar, author of *To Crown the Year*, suggests backyard flowers—forsythia, flowering plum, and apple and pear blossoms. Create a mood of festivity and anticipation.

Your procession cross could also be festooned during the Easter season. As it enters the liturgical space, it will announce the excitement of Easter.

If you use incense only on occasion, the Easter season is about as good an occasion as you will find.

■ AS MAY BEGINS, YOU MAY DECORATE THE IMAGE OF MARY. If your community is planning a crowning of Mary this month, consult the Order of Crowning an Image of the Blessed Virgin Mary. Rather than adding a litany or a decade of the rosary to the eucharist, plan a prayer service to honor Our Lady, including hymns and readings from scripture. For good texts, see the common of the Blessed Virgin Mary in the sacramentary, lectionary and *Liturgy of the Hours*, as well as the *Collection of Masses of the Blessed Virgin Mary*. Beware of moving a statue front and center for the month if it would compete with the altar, ambo and Easter candle. It is better to decorate the image where it usually stands.

The Music

ONE word should predominate: Alleluia! Choose hymns and songs that let it resound throughout the 50 Days.

Instrumentalists who have abstained from preludes and postludes during the previous season can offer their assemblies many delights throughout Easter. Organists can play stately trumpet voluntaries. The literature is expansive, but don't overlook choral preludes by J. S. Bach and Flor Peters, or the flashy toccatas by Widor and Vierne. Easter is the season to let the organ thrill its listeners.

■ THE SPRINKLING WITH HOLY WATER provides a good instance for the assembly's song. "Vidi aquam" from the *Liber cantualis* is a Gregorian chant written for the occasion. See also Howard Hughes's "You Have Put on Christ" (GIA G-2283), David Hurd's "Vidi aquam" (GIA G-2512) and Michael Ward's "I Saw Water Flowing" (WLP 8548).

■ GLORY TO GOD: Easter is another good season for singing the Glory to God. If your community does not sing this hymn year round, now is the time to build the repertoire. Use the version from the Vigil throughout the season. Consult the musical selections in your worship aid.

■ THE COMMON PSALMS for the season of Easter are 118 and 66. Check the scripture index of your community's hymnal for suggestions. See settings of Psalm 118 by Michael Joncas in volume one of *Psalms for the Cantor* (WLP), by Richard Proulx (GIA G-1964), by Christopher Willcock in *Psalms for Feasts and Seasons* (Liturgical Press), by Christopher Walker and by Scott Soper (OCP), by Hal H. Hopson in *10 Psalms* (Hope, HH 3930) and by Bob Hurd (OCP 9458).

The refrain to all the responsorial psalms for the Sundays and weekdays in Easter may also be "Alleluia." *By Flowing Waters* contains 46 such "Alleluia" psalms, set to just six melodies for ease of memorization (160, 161, 169 and 170).

■ THE EASTER SEQUENCE can be sung in its original chant, or in some English adaptations. See the suggestions above at Easter Sunday. The sequence is obligatory on Easter Sunday and optional on all the other days of the Easter octave.

■ THE GOSPEL ACCLAMATION should stand out throughout the season. The refrain of "O filii et filiae" is a perfect choice. See John Schiavone's version for Easter, Ascension and Pentecost (GIA G-1262). Robert Hutmacher has a "Gospel Processional" (GIA G-2450), J. Biery has a "Gospel Fanfare for Easter morning" (GIA G-2719) and Jeremy Young has verses for each Sunday of Easter (GIA G-3175).

■ FOR THE EUCHARISTIC ACCLAMATIONS, choose festival settings with parts for brass and percussion, like Richard Proulx's "Festival Eucharist" (*Worship* #306–8 or GIA G-1960), Paul Inwood's "Coventry Acclamations" (OCP 7117), Christopher Walker's "Festival Mass" (OCP 7154) and Carrol T. Andrews's simpler "Easter Carol Mass" (GIA G-1398).

In the Episcopal church, in place of the "Lamb of God" may be sung, "Alleluia. Christ our Passover is sacrificed for us; therefore let us keep the feast. Alleluia."

■ COMMUNION SONGS for the season may include Suzanne Toolan's "I am the Bread of Life" (see Rory Cooney's arrangement, GIA G-5016) and Richard Hillert's "Worthy Is Christ." Taizé offers "Surrexit Christus" and "Christus Resurrexit" (*Music from Taizé,* volume II, GIA G-2788). Bob Hurd (*Gather* #605) and Michael Ward (WLP 7950) offer pieces called "In the Breaking of the Bread."

■ EASTER HYMNODY could include "The Strife Is O'er," "Hail Thee, Festival Day," "Come, Ye Faithful, Raise the Strain," "At the Lamb's High Feast," "Now the Green Blade Rises" (note Hal H. Hopson's setting, GIA G-3443), "This Joyful Eastertide" and "That Easter Day with Joy Was Bright." Michael Joncas wrote a set of descants for six popular Easter hymns (WLP 8513). See also Brian Wren and Carl Johengen's fine hymn, "At the Table of the World" (WLP 2612).

Let the parish choir work up a motet like "One Fold, One Shepherd" for two-part choir, by Russell Woolen (WLP 660), or the piece by Hans Leo Hassler, "Quia vidisti me, Thoma," for four-part choir (WLP 5778), especially fitting for the Second Sunday of Easter. César Franck's "Panis angelicus" is available from GIA as a solo. It is published in three different keys, depending on the vocal range of your soloist (G-5243, G-5244 and G-5245).

Your youth choir could lead everyone in a rousing rendition of John Angotti's "He Is Risen" (WLP 7362). *With One Voice* (Augsburg/ Fortress, 1995) has "There in God's Garden," "Come Away to the Skies, My Beloved, Arise," "Christ Is Risen! Shout Hosanna!" and "Alleluia! Jesus Is Risen!" Ed Bolduc's setting of Psalm 16, "Show Us Your Way, Lord" (WLP 7358), is worth learning. Tony Alonso sets the right tone with "Alleluia, Christ Is Risen" (GIA G-5607). "Your Sacrifice," by Thomas Lucas, for SATB choir, guitar and keyboard is a soul-stirring hymn of communion from the African American tradition of music. It works well for Easter or any time of year (WLP 1210).

The children's choir may enjoy "We Receive Power" (WLP 7113) or "Jesus, Bread of Life" (WLP 7855), by James V. Marchionda.

The United Church of Christ's *New Century Hymnal* has "Because You Live, O Christ, the Garden of the World Has Come to Flower," "These Things Did Thomas Count as Real" and "At the Font We Start Our Journey, in the Easter Faith Baptized." Hal H. Hopson has a bouncy setting of the Caribbean song "Halle, Halle, Halle" (MA 503, Hope Publishing Company). John Angotti's "On a Journey Together" might call to mind the story of Emmaus (WLP 7482). Jerry Galipeau's "On the Wings of Change" will stir up Easter faith (WLP 5209).

GIA's *Hymnal for the Hours* has "Sing of One Who Walks beside Us" and *Worship* offers "Daylight Fades."

Music for Mary will be requested during the month of May. Let choirs sing a chant "Ave Maria" from the *Liber cantualis,* "Ave Maria" by David Conte (Schirmer 4729), "Ave, Maria" by

Lisa L. Stafford (WLP 8695) and "O Mary of Graces" as arranged by William Ferris, with a text by Alan J. Hommerding. Steven C. Warner arranged the same tune, "O Mary of Promise" (WLP 7265).

Soloists may wish to haul out Franz Schubert's "Ave Maria," available from GIA in three different keys (G-5687, G-5688 and G-5689), but purists will insist on the last of these options, in B-flat, the way Schubert wrote it. Richard Proulx arranged the Bach-Gounod "Ave Maria" for SATB voices and harp or piano with string quintet and organ (GIA G-5416FS).

Remember, though, the season is Easter, not "May." It is not necessary to sing a Marian hymn every Sunday, but an occasional use of the repertoire—on Mothers' Day, for example—is most appropriate.

For instrumental music, consider Scott M. Hyslop's arrangement of "Sonata paschalis" by Pavel Josef Vejvanovsky for two violins and organ (GIA G-5154).

The Parish and Home

SEE *Catholic Household Blessings and Prayers* for a blessing at table (p. 84), of the home (153), of children before confirmation (230) or first communion (231), for Mother's Day (197), as well as prayers for fields and gardens (166) and a prayer to complete the Easter season on the solemnity of Pentecost (157). See also the prayers for the Holy Eucharist (359), in honor of Mary, Mother of God (362), and baptismal promises and creeds (371).

LTP's *Take Me Home* and *Take Me Home, Too,* both contain activity pages for families for each week of the season.

Texts

■ GREETING: The sacramentaries of other language groups suggest:

The grace of the Lord Jesus, who was raised for us, be with you.

■ INTRODUCTION TO THE PENITENTIAL RITE:

Christ our hope is risen! Let us call to mind our sins.

■ RESPONSE TO THE GENERAL INTERCESSIONS:

Risen Savior, hear our prayer.

Hear us, Christ our Light.

■ DISMISSAL OF CATECHUMENS:

The One who sat on the throne said, "Behold, I make all things new." My brothers and sisters, go in peace that you may share fully one day in the new life of Christ.

The *Book of Common Worship* for the Presbyterian Church (U.S.A.) and the Cumberland Presbyterian Church recommended this prayer for Easter (p. 317). It could conclude the general intercessions:

O God,
you gave your only Son
to suffer death on the cross for our redemption,
and by his glorious resurrection
you delivered us from the power of death.
Grant us so to die daily to sin,
that we may evermore live with him
    in the joy of his resurrection
through Jesus Christ our Lord,
who lives and reigns with you and the Holy Spirit,
one God, now and forever. Amen.

April

#261 (LMC #185–192)   white
MON 12 Easter Monday
SOLEMNITY

Today begins the semi-continuous reading of Acts of the Apostles, the book that contributes the first reading virtually every day of the Easter season. The story opens today in the second chapter, on Pentecost Day, as Peter delivers a sermon about a Christian's central belief. He preaches about Psalm 16, which becomes today's responsory, and which followed the second reading of the Easter Vigil.

The gospel today begins a week-long march through the accounts of the resurrection appearances. They all agree on some points and disagree on other details. The events were so important and so different from anything else in history that the stories have been handed down to us in their unreconciled exuberance. We start in Matthew with Jesus' appearance to the women at the tomb and the gossip spread by the bribed guards.

Today's liturgy calls for the Glory to God. The sequence is optional, but by using it you will set the octave apart from other days in noble joy. The creed is not said, probably to avoid its overuse during the week. Use the first Easter preface (P 21) with the phrase "on this Easter day." If you use Eucharistic Prayer I, include the special forms of "In union" and "Father, accept." The solemn blessing for Easter (#6) would be appropriate. Conclude the dismissal with a double alleluia. A community gathered for daily Mass this week should be able to build a musical repertoire of many of these elements, including the sequence and the solemn Easter dismissal.

In the opening prayer, note the reference to the neophytes, new members giving the church constant growth.

#262 (LMC #185–192)   white
TUE 13 Easter Tuesday
SOLEMNITY

Peter concludes his Pentecost sermon and the people ask how they should respond. Peter invites them to reform their lives, and three thousand step up for baptism. The psalm says that the earth is full of God's goodness, a belief evident to the early church from the numbers of those accepting Jesus. It is evident to us whenever the newly baptized join us for the eucharist.

John's gospel recounts Jesus' appearance to Mary Magdalene. She, the apostle to the apostles, brings the good news.

Sing the Glory to God and the sequence. Omit the creed. Use the inserts for the first Easter preface and Eucharistic Prayer I. Give the solemn Easter blessing (#6). Dismiss with the double alleluia.

In the communion prayer today we pray for the newly baptized.

#263 (LMC #185–192)   white
WED 14 Easter Wednesday
SOLEMNITY

Peter and John cure a disabled man by the beautiful gate of the temple. They have already proclaimed the power of Jesus Christ. Now they demonstrate the power of his name, active still in the community. The psalm opens with the command to "invoke the name" of the Lord.

One of the most beloved stories of Easter is the resurrection appearance to the disciples on the road to Emmaus. Its two parts—discussion of scripture and breaking of bread—foreshadow the way the Christian community will celebrate its eucharist.

The suggested communion antiphon comes from today's gospel.

The Glory to God is obligatory. The sequence is optional. The creed is omitted. Use the inserts for the first Easter preface and Eucharistic Prayer I if that prayer is your choice today. Give the solemn

Easter blessing (#6) if you like. Dismiss with the double alleluia.

#264 (LMC #185–192)   white
THU 15 Easter Thursday
SOLEMNITY

In the glow of the miraculous cure, Peter preaches another sermon, this time building upon the guilt of his hearers to accept Jesus as the one whom the prophets foretold. The name of God is praised again in today's psalm.

We hear Luke's sequel to the Emmaus story. While the disciples tell the others what they witnessed, Jesus appears and opens their minds to the scriptures.

Today's opening prayer and prayer over the gifts refer again to the newly baptized.

The Glory to God is sung. Try singing the optional sequence today and throughout the week. Use the insert for the first Easter preface and those in Eucharistic Prayer I if those are your choices today. The solemn Easter blessing (#6) would be appropriate. The dismissal dialogue includes the double alleluia.

People who have taxes on their minds today might appreciate a petition in the general intercessions for the prudent use of our country's tax dollars.

#265 (LMC #185–192)   white
FRI 16 Easter Friday
SOLEMNITY

Peter and John are put in jail after their sermon. (Today's preachers hope their listeners don't get the same idea.) In spite of efforts to silence the word of God, five thousand put their faith in Jesus. Even on trial, Peter finds a way to preach, using a text from Psalm 118, which serves as today's responsory.

Jesus appears to the disciples again, this time by the Sea of Tiberias, where he fills them with joy and cooks them some fish.

The octave continues. Sing the Glory to God. Include the sequence if you like. When singing the first Easter preface, remember this is still "Easter day" not "Easter season." If you are using Eucharistic Prayer I you may include its inserts, one of which presumes that the newly baptized are present. You may use the solemn Easter blessing (#6) again. Dismiss with the double alleluia.

The suggested communion antiphon comes from today's gospel. The communion prayer is offered for those "saved" in Christ, the newly baptized.

SAT 17 #266 (LMC #185–192) white
Easter Saturday
SOLEMNITY

The court recognizes that Peter and John receive their power not from education but from their experience of Jesus. They are asked to remain silent, but they will continue to proclaim what they have heard and seen. The responsory takes additional verses from yesterday's psalm of deliverance.

All week long the lectionary has presented the resurrection appearances in a kind of reconstructed chronological order. We conclude the series today with "the longer ending" of Mark's gospel. Mark's original probably ended with verse 8. Scholars believe that today's passage, a pastiche of several other stories we have heard this week, was added later to give the gospel a more coherent close.

Sing the Glory to God. You may also sing the sequence. Use the inserts for the preface and eucharistic prayer (I) and invoke the solemn Easter blessing (#6), if you like. Dismiss with the double alleluia.

The opening prayer remembers the newly baptized. You could conclude the general intercessions today with a prayer from the Mass titled, "Holy Mary, Fountain of Light and Life," from the *Collection of Masses of the Blessed Virgin Mary* (#16). It would blend the themes of Mary on Saturday and baptism.

If there is a wedding Mass this morning or early afternoon, it should use the readings of today's solemnity. One reading may be substituted from the lectionary for Masses of marriage.

☀ 18 #45 (LMC #39) white
Second Sunday of Easter
Octave of Easter
SOLEMNITY

ORIENTATION

Today's celebration concludes the octave of Easter. Not only does it serve as the eighth day, but it also includes a gospel that refers to an event on the first octave day of the resurrection. This day used to be called *Dominica in albis,* because the neophytes arrived wearing their albs, the white garments of their baptism.

Although today is also called "Divine Mercy Sunday," the texts of the votive Mass for divine mercy may not be used in place of the prayers for the Second Sunday of Easter.

LECTIONARY

Today's gospel appears in all three years of the lectionary cycle.

It reports an appearance of Jesus on the day of the resurrection and his reappearance a week later. Thomas, absent from the first, present for the second, makes a profound statement of Easter faith: "My Lord and my God."

The first reading begins our Sunday series of texts from Acts of the Apostles. We hear about the honeymoon era. "Many signs and wonders were done among the people at the hands of the apostles." Great numbers of believers were added due to the preaching and action of the first disciples. In communities that celebrated baptism at the Easter Vigil, this memory of the expansion of believers to the apostolic church will cheer the heart. It will challenge all communities to greater evangelization.

Today's psalm is seasonal and appears each year in the lectionary for this Sunday. It sings of the stone rejected by the builders that has become the cornerstone, an image the apostolic church immediately applied to Jesus. We may sing alleluia as its refrain.

Today's second reading begins the semi-continuous proclamation of the book of Revelation. You may need to remind the reader that the title of this book is in the singular, not "revelations." The entire book records a mystical vision by John of Patmos, who is given a word of encouragement from God for all who suffer persecution for their faith. The book is more historical record than prophecy of a cataclysmic future. In today's passage, John sees "one like a son of man" dressed in glory and surrounded by seven gold lamp stands. This one, who was dead and now is alive forever and ever, holds the keys to death and the netherworld. John's vision offers hope for all who believe in Christ, that not even death will keep them from experiencing glory.

SACRAMENTARY

Today concludes the octave of Easter and the liturgy still reflects the excitement of Easter Day.

This is a good season for the blessing and sprinkling of holy water to replace the penitential rite. You may start the custom today and continue throughout the season until Pentecost.

Sing the Glory to God. You may sing the optional sequence as well on this last day of the octave. When using the first Easter preface (P 21), remember this is still "Easter day" because of the octave, not yet "Easter season." Especially if neophytes are present, you may wish to use Eucharistic Prayer I with its inserts. Conclude the Mass with a double alleluia at the dismissal dialogue.

All the presidential prayers today allude to baptism, and the prayer over the gifts includes an optional phrase if the newly baptized are present for the Mass. The solemn blessing for Easter appears conveniently on the page today.

OTHER IDEAS

The *Rite of Christian Initiation of Adults* (#248) suggests that the neophytes be seated with their godparents. You might have a special place for them beginning today. Many historical references urged them to wear their white garments through today. You could invite them to wear something white, or at least their Easter best once again.

A four-part choir could sing Hans Leo Hassler's "Quia vidisti me, Thoma" (WLP 5778), with its text based on today's gospel.

Today is Yom Hashoah, the remembrance of six million Jews who lost their lives in the Holocaust. May such evil never happen again.

MON 19 #267 (LMC #185–192) white
Easter Weekday

The first Christians readily perceived that even the tragic events they experienced were still in the mind and plan of God. Reflecting on the arrest, mistreatment and release of Peter and John, they remembered the words of the second psalm, and recognized that the Holy Spirit was already thinking of them when inspiring the psalmist of long ago. That psalm, about the foolishness of national powers waging war against God's people, appears as today's psalm.

Today we begin a semi-continuous reading of passages from John's gospel, as we experienced during the second half of Lent. At that time, we heard the parts of the story that led up to the passion. Now we hear the parts that unfold the implications of Jesus' resurrection. We open with Jesus' conversation with Nicodemus, a Pharisee who comes at night, perhaps in embarrassment about his illicit interest in this new rabbi, perhaps as a Johannine sign of his movement from the darkness of unbelief to the light of faith. Jesus speaks mystically about baptism, a theme close to the church's heart in these days that follow Easter's octave.

Any Easter preface will do, but the second (P 22) refers to "children of the light."

TUE 20 #268 (LMC #185–192) white
Easter Weekday

We resume the story from Acts of the Apostles with a passage about a remarkable testimony of generosity by one of the new believers. The psalm is seasonal, depicting the majesty of God. Christians sing this psalm imagining the risen Jesus where the psalmist sings of "the Lord."

Today's gospel picks up the conversation between Jesus and Nicodemus. The topics include being born again, the heavenly dwelling place of the Son of Man and the eternal life promised to believers.

In Ecuador, today is the feast of the Most Holy Sorrowful Virgin of the College. On this date in 1906 in the Jesuit school of Saint Gabriel, pupils and teachers saw a picture of Our Lady of Sorrows open and shut its eyes. Miracles have been attributed to Mary under this title.

WED 21 #269 (LMC #185–192) white
Easter Weekday

Optional Memorial of Anselm (+ 1109), bishop and doctor of the church / white ▪ Peter is among the apostles jailed in today's reading. His freedom through angelic intervention is the subject of a fresco by Raphael in the Vatican. The psalm recalls that the angel of the Lord delivers the faithful.

John 3:16, perhaps the most famous of all scripture quotes, opens today's gospel. Jesus explains to Nicodemus the mission of the Son, the light who entered the world.

Among the prefaces, the second Easter preface (P 22) makes a good choice for its images of light and the opening of gates.

■ TODAY'S SAINT: Anselm was born in Italy but became a monk at Bec in Normandy. He succeeded his friend Lanfranc as the archbishop of Canterbury in England, but waged a lifelong struggle with kings over church rights. His famous treatise on the incarnation, *Cur Deus homo,* is one of the reasons he is considered the father of scholasticism. Rome's Pontifical Institute of Liturgy is named after this Benedictine.

■ TODAY IS REGARDED AS THE BIRTHDAY OF ROME. On this day in 753 BCE, legend has it, the city was founded by Romulus and Remus, twins raised by a she-wolf on the Capitoline hill.

THU 22 #270 (LMC #185–192) white
Easter Weekday

The Sanhedrin reminds the arrested apostles that they are forbidden to preach, and Peter simply preaches back to them. We continue singing additional verses from yesterday's psalm, which recalls how God sides with the poor and confronts those who do evil.

Jesus concludes his conversation with Nicodemus by pairing the revelation of God with the expectation of the believer's acceptance of its truth.

FRI 23 #271 (LMC #185–192) white
Easter Weekday

Optional Memorial of George (+ c. 303), martyr/red ▪ *Optional Memorial of Adalbert (+ 997), bishop, martyr/red* ▪ Once again, the apostles escape punishment after an arrest. The Sanhedrin believes that if the movement is not from God, it will die out on its own. The psalm captures the reason for the apostles' spirit: "The Lord is my life's refuge. Of whom should I be afraid?"

We turn now to chapter 6 of John, the famous discourse on the bread of life. We hear the prelude today, the miracle of the loaves.

▪ TODAY'S SAINTS: Legend has it that George was a knight summoned to rescue a city in Libya from a dragon who required a human sacrifice each day. The princess he allegedly rescued led the leashed lizard back into the city, inspiring everyone to be baptized before George slew it. All that is known for sure is that George suffered martyrdom in Lydda sometime before Constantine. His cross appears on the union jack, and he is the patron of Boy Scouts.

Adalbert, the apostle to the Prussians, was a Bohemian prince who became the first native bishop of Prague. Discouraged by the

ineffectiveness of his work, he retired to a monastery near Rome, but Pope John XV sent him back ten years later. He left again to preach among the Hungarians, Poles and Prussians, only to be martyred by a pagan priest. His name was added to the general calendar as an optional memorial under Pope John Paul II.

SAT 24 #272 (LMC #185–192) white
Easter Weekday

Optional Memorial of Fidelis of Sigmaringen (+ 1622), priest and martyr/red ▪ Deacons were created for the early church in order to settle an ethnic dispute over the proper feeding of widows. The controversy and its resolution show the human and divine elements of the struggling community. The psalm, acknowledging God's love for the just, echoes the means of discerning the candidates for the diaconate.

The eerie apparition of Jesus walking upon the water follows the miraculous sharing of the loaves and prepares the reader for the difficult divine teaching about to be revealed in the great discourse on the bread of life.

The fourth Easter preface (P 24) sings of the new age dawning in Christ and of the healing of broken humanity.

▪ TODAY'S SAINT: Fidelis was preaching on the text, "one Lord, one faith, one baptism," when someone from the crowd shot at him. He was trying to renew the faith of the Swiss during the Catholic reformation. He escaped injury and fled town only to be killed by a band of armed men. A lawyer, Capuchin and priest known for his holiness of life, he was honored by the Society for the Propagation of the Faith as its protomartyr.

In Argentina, Saturday of the second week of Easter is the

memorial of Our Lady of the Valley. According to the tradition, Franciscan missionaries at Catamarca in northern Argentina hid a statue of Mary in a cave when Indians attacked them. The statue, found at the end of the sixteenth century, has been enshrined at the site.

☀25 #48 (LMC #42) white
Third Sunday of Easter

ORIENTATION

Each year the scriptures for the Third Sunday of Easter offer us an example of Peter's preaching from Acts and a postresurrection appearance by Jesus that involves a meal. For mystagogic purposes, the texts prompt the preacher to proclaim the divinity of Jesus and the mystery of the eucharist.

The octave of Easter ended last Sunday, so the liturgy does not include the optional sequence during the liturgy of the word or the double alleluia in the dismissal.

LECTIONARY

Today's gospel tells of the resurrection appearance of Jesus to the disciples at the Sea of Tiberias, and the longer version includes the threefold questioning of Peter's love. The excitement of the resurrection is palpable as they see Jesus on the shore. At his command, they haul in so many fish they cannot manage the net.

There are many interpretations about the number of fish—153. Some argue it was the number of known varieties of fish in Jesus' day, thus representing a catch of the whole world. Augustine took a more fanciful interpretation: 153 is the sum of all the numbers from 1 through 17. Seventeen is ten plus seven, representing two sacred numbers in Christian tradition.

In the longer version of the gospel, Peter, who denied Jesus three times, now professes his love three times, and when Jesus says, "Follow me," we know it means through the cross to resurrection.

The apostles are arrested for violating an order not to preach. They use the opportunity to preach some more, and when they are dismissed they rejoice that they are found worthy of suffering. Few people look on suffering so positively.

The psalm develops the theme of rescue. The psalmist was rescued from danger, as the apostles were, and—most dramatically—as Jesus was from the jaws of death.

In today's passage from Revelation, John sees a great throng surrounding the throne and calling out praise of the Lamb that was slain. All fall down and worship. The vision acclaims the slain and risen Christ as the one deserving our praise.

SACRAMENTARY

A communion antiphon for this year, drawn from the gospel, is proposed.

Repeat the sprinkling rite if you are replacing the penitential rite with it this season.

The prayer over the people suggested for today offers nothing special. You may use the solemn blessing of the Easter season (#7), or a different prayer over the people, like #18.

Easter prefaces I, III and V (P 21, 23 and P 25) refer to Christ as the Lamb, as does today's second reading.

OTHER IDEAS

If first communions are being celebrated in your community on a weekday around this time, be sure to consult the fourth volume of the lectionary for suggested scripture readings (#769).

MON 26 #273 (LMC #185–192)   white
Easter Weekday

Acts shifts now to the story of Stephen. False witnesses accuse this innocent deacon of wrongdoing. In his trial, he goes through the same suffering Jesus experienced. The psalmist takes comfort in God, "though princes sit plotting against me." Jesus, developing the image of bread, criticizes the false hunger that drives people to search for him.

The sacrifice of the cross, echoed in Stephen's arrest, appears in the fifth preface for Easter (P 25).

In Guatemala, today is the optional memorial of Isidore the bishop (+ 636), April 4 on most other calendars.

TUE 27 #274 (LMC #185–192)   white
Easter Weekday

The martyrdom of Stephen imitates the martyrdom of Jesus, down to the story's quotation from the psalm that serves as today's responsory. Jesus compares himself to the manna that came down from heaven. He is the bread of life that will nourish the believer on the journey of faith. At this point of the discourse, the image of bread has not yet reached its full eucharistic intent. It more clearly signifies spiritual nourishment in these early verses.

The first preface for Easter (P 21) recalls the mission of Jesus' forgiveness, a trait that Stephen embodied as well.

■ IN ARGENTINA AND PERU, today is the feast of Toribio de Mogrovejo, bishop and patron of the Latin American episcopacy. His optional memorial is observed on the universal church calendar on March 23, a date held as an obligatory memorial in some countries. Today's date, though, is an obligatory memorial for Toribio in Chile, Venezuela and the Dominican Republic.

WED 28 #275 (LMC #185–192)   white
Easter Weekday

Optional Memorial of Peter Chanel (+ 1841), priest and martyr / red ▪ *Optional Memorial of Louis Mary de Montfort (+ 1716), priest / white* ▪ Acts of the Apostles opened with a gleaming description of church community life. But the arrest of the apostles foreshadowed future gloom. Now a persecution of the church has broken out. The martyrdom of Stephen was only the beginning. But as in those earlier cases, the persecutors only sow the seeds of evangelization. They scattered the believers, who kept right on preaching the word. The psalm, fittingly, invites "all the earth" to cry out with joy.

Jesus pursues the image of bread more deeply, this time showing its saving properties. Those who believe in him as the living bread will have eternal life.

The third Easter preface (P 23) proclaims Christ as priest, advocate, victim and Lamb, the one who offers salvation in the midst of suffering.

■ TODAY'S SAINTS: Born in eastern France, Peter Chanel became a priest and then joined the Society of Mary, the Marists. He accompanied the founder of the congregation to Rome to apply for approval of its rule. He then fulfilled a lifelong dream and became a missionary. Efforts at evangelization were difficult on the island of Futuna in the South Pacific, and the king eventually turned on Peter, having a gang attack his catechumens and club the Marist to death.

Louis Mary Grignion de Montfort served France as a priest and was especially devoted to the poor. He organized a group of physically disabled women into a congregation and wrote over the door of their community room the word *wisdom*. He founded the Montfort Missionaries (the Company of Mary) and the Daughters of Divine Wisdom. In his devotion to Mary, he called himself "all yours," in Latin *Totus tuus*. John Paul II adopted this as the motto for his coat of arms. The inclusion of this saint on the universal calendar happened during the reign of this same pope.

#276 (LMC #185–192)   white

T H U 29 Catherine of Siena (+ 1380), virgin, doctor of the church
MEMORIAL

As the mission turns toward the Gentiles, one of the deacons, Philip, is involved in a remarkable story of conversion and baptism. Today's story has parallels to Emmaus, involving a journey, a discussion of scripture, baptism (in place of eucharist) and the mysterious disappearance of the protagonist. The psalm verses continue where yesterday's left off, calling on "all peoples" to bless God.

Jesus compares himself to the Wisdom of God. Those who believe in him share in the bread of life.

The second preface for Easter (P 22) remembers that Christ has made us children of the light, as the Ethiopian experiences in today's episode from Acts.

■ TODAY'S SAINT: Catherine cared for victims of pestilence, and as a third-order Dominican she converted many people by her powerful preaching. She convinced Pope Gregory XI to leave Avignon and move the papal palace back to Rome. Her efforts to quiet the

cardinals responsible for the mounting schism proved ineffective, but she is still regarded as one of the greatest minds of her age. Her visage adorns a dramatic statue at the end of Rome's Via della Conciliazione, staring up toward St. Peter's Basilica, as if commanding the popes in their Avignon exile to go home.

Take the presidential prayers from April 29 in the back of the sacramentary. You may use the preface of virgins and religious (P 68).

#277 (LMC #185–192)   white

F R I 30 Easter Weekday

Optional emorial of Pius V (+ 1572), pope, religious/white ■ Saul, whose ominous presence appeared at the end of Tuesday's reading, reappears today, the personification of the church's persecution. His three days of blindness signify his gradual coming to faith under the catechetical and healing ministry of Ananias. He becomes Paul, the apostle to the Gentiles, and today's responsory could well serve as his personal anthem.

In clear, deliberate and measured statements, Jesus tells his listeners that they must eat and drink the flesh and blood of the Son of Man. The bread of life discourse is reaching its natural conclusion, the identification of Jesus as the eucharistic bread of life.

The healing of Saul might find an echo in the fourth Easter preface IV (P 24), the end of sin's long reign, the restoration of humanity.

■ TODAY'S SAINT: The pontificate of Pius V gave the church a more widespread devotion to the rosary after the battle of Lepanto and a revised Roman Missal, the fruit of the Council of Trent. With minor changes the 1570 missal remained in force until 1969. The lectionary's proper of saints suggests readings about papal service,

but the readings of the weekday are recommended.

May

#278 (LMC #185–192)   white

S A T 1 Easter Weekday

Optional Memorial of Joseph the Worker/white ■ All of a sudden, Luke tells us the church was at peace throughout Judea, Galilee and Samaria. In the midst of persecution, or perhaps because of it, the disciples have found peace in their belief. Peter continues to work miracles, and the number of believers increases. The mission to the Gentiles meets unparalleled success. The psalm recalls God's love for the faithful, even in death, and the thanksgiving offered by believers in their time of deliverance.

The sixth chapter of John ends on a somber note, as Jesus realizes that the core of his teaching has been rejected by some of his hearers. He wonders if even the Twelve will now desert him. Peter says there is nowhere else to go, for they have found the words of eternal life in Jesus.

The eucharistic references in Easter Preface V (P 25) make it a good choice for today.

■ TODAY'S MEMORIAL: After communists and others began to celebrate May Day for workers, Pope Pius XII instituted a memorial of Joseph the Worker on the same day. If you choose to take the memorial, you will find recommended scriptures at #559. All the texts focus on human labor and divine creation. The gospel refers to Jesus as the son of the carpenter.

This is an obligatory memorial in Panama.

O2 #51 (LMC #45) white
Fourth Sunday of Easter

ORIENTATION

The gospel for the Fourth Sunday of Easter comes from the tenth chapter of John in each year of the lectionary cycle, giving today its common designation, "Good Shepherd Sunday." In that chapter, Jesus develops the image of shepherd. Today, by extension, is also the World Day of Prayer for Vocations.

LECTIONARY

This year's gospel passage dwells on the relationship between the shepherd and the sheep. The sheep hear Jesus' voice and follow him, and he offers them eternal life. No enemy can harm this relationship because Jesus and the Father are one.

The psalm today relates more to the gospel than to the first reading. Its refrain, "We are his people, the sheep of his flock," fits with the Good Shepherd.

The story of the early church takes a dramatic turn in the first reading. The apostles take their mission from the unreceptive Jews to the hungry Gentiles. The persecution of the apostles in one place leads to the spread of the gospel in another.

Although we hear generous excerpts from the book of Revelation throughout the Easter season, most of them detail John's vision of God in the heavenly court. The beasts, the destruction of the earth and other frightening scenes yield to the more central part of the book's message: the salvation Christ offers the believer. In today's

passage, a great throng stands before the throne and the Lamb. Some of them are martyrs who have washed their robes in the blood of the Lamb. God will wipe away every tear from their eyes.

SACRAMENTARY

Both opening prayers today take the image of the shepherd. Easter Preface II (P 22) might make a good choice today instead of mixing metaphors and calling Christ the Lamb (see prefaces I, III and V). The solemn blessing for the Easter season appears at the end of today's liturgy. If the month of May prompts a desire for texts and devotions referring to Jesus' mother Mary, see another solemn blessing for the Easter season at the end of the order of Mass in the *Collection of Masses of the Blessed Virgin Mary*.

If you wish, continue the blessing and sprinkling of holy water in place of the penitential rite today and throughout the Sundays of Easter.

The insert for funerals in Eucharistic Prayer III quotes today's second reading.

OTHER IDEAS

Include vocations in the general intercessions today. If your parish has a vocation committee you may honor them with blessing and approval for their work.

A two-part choir could sing Russell Woollen's "One Fold, One Shepherd" (WLP 660).

Although we are still in the season called "Easter," many people subconsciously enter a season called "May." The month of May brings devotion to Mary, graduations, first communions, weddings, ordinations and anniversaries to families, parishes and communities. Keep the spirit of Easter alive.

"Regina caeli," "Be Joyful, Mary" and "Ye Watchers and Ye Holy Ones" all blend Mary's role with the celebration of resurrection.

MON 3 #561 (LMC #290) red
Philip and James, apostles
FEAST

The name *James* appears frequently throughout the New Testament, and it is difficult to tell if the references are to two, three, four or more persons. In the liturgy, we identify today's James as the son of Alphaeus (not the son of Zebedee), also called "the less" (not "the greater," whose feast is July 25). In many traditions he is also the James called "the brother of the Lord," the presumed author of the letter of James in the New Testament. There was only one Philip, the one who appears throughout the gospels. He is not to be confused with Philip the deacon, who appears in Acts. Tradition says these two are buried together in the Church of the Holy Apostles in Rome. The composer Frescobaldi is buried in the same church.

Today's first reading identifies James as the one to whom Jesus appeared after the resurrection. We hear from Philip's naïve request, "Lord, show us the Father," and Jesus' beautiful (exasperated?) response, "Whoever has seen me has seen the Father."

Psalm 19 frequently accompanies a feast of the apostles. Their ministry tells the message of the glory of God to the ends of the earth.

Sing the Glory to God today. The presidential prayers are found under May 3 in the back of the sacramentary. Either preface for the apostles is fitting (P 64 or 65). The names of today's saints appear in Eucharistic Prayer I. The solemn blessings include one for apostles (#17).

■ IN CHILE, HONDURAS, COLOMBIA, EL SALVADOR, GUATEMALA AND VENEZUELA, this is the feast of the Exaltation of the Holy Cross, observed in the universal calendar on September 14. In Mexico today's feast is simply called "Holy Cross," and in Peru it is the feast of the "Veneration of the Holy Cross." In the old calendar, May 3 recognized the finding of the holy cross, and September 14 honored the exaltation, a date that fits with the dedication of the Constantinian basilicas over the sites of the crucifixion and resurrection. After the Second Vatican Council, the universal calendar eliminated the May 3 date in favor of the fall celebration, which has an older history. In some monastic traditions, the monks wore their winter garb in choir "from cross to cross," exchanging it on this date for lighter, springtime attire.

TUE 4

#280 (LMC #185–192)   white
Easter Weekday

Sadly, the lectionary skips chapter 10 of Acts, the great story of the conversion of Cornelius. We cut instead to a story of internal misunderstanding among the early leaders of the church. When the Christians in Jerusalem heard there were Christians in Antioch, they sent Barnabas to check it out. He went to Tarsus to bring Saul to Antioch, and personally vouched for his good behavior. At Antioch, the followers of Christ were called Christians for the first time. The psalm develops the theme of the universal mission of the church and the centrality of Jerusalem.

Jesus continues the shepherd theme. The sheep listening to his voice will know he is the Messiah.

The second preface for Easter (P 22) proclaims the promise of everlasting life for those who have become children of the light.

■ THE COUNTRIES OF Colombia, Peru, Guatemala, Venezuela and Mexico transfer to this date yesterday's feast of the apostles Philip and James.

WED 5

#281 (LMC #185–192)   white
Easter Weekday

As the gospel continues to spread, the community in Jerusalem lays hands on Barnabas and Saul to set them apart as preachers. Fasting and prayer accompany their work. The missionary journeys of Paul have begun. Another psalm of universality complements the reading.

Moving ahead to the twelfth chapter of John, we hear Jesus say he has come to the world as its light, and those who believe will be preserved from the dark.

Again, the second Easter preface's reference to children of the light makes it a good choice (P 22).

THU 6

#282 (LMC #185–192)   white
Easter Weekday

Paul's missionary journey takes him from Perga in Pamphilia to Antioch in Pisidia. There he is invited to speak at the synagogue. Adjusting his script to a Jewish audience, Paul recounts the marvels God accomplished for their ancestors before announcing Jesus, the saving descendant of David. At one point he boosts his argument with a reference to Psalm 89, which then serves as today's responsory.

Our excerpts from John's gospel place us now at the Last Supper, where we will remain for the next few weeks. Having washed the feet of his disciples, Jesus instructs them about service, divine election, scriptural fulfillment, divinity, discipleship and rejection.

The sacrifice of Christ is remembered in the fifth Easter preface (P 25).

FRI 7

#283 (LMC #185–192)   white
Easter Weekday

We continue hearing from Paul's sermon in the synagogue in Antioch in Pisidia. He preaches the core of the Christian message, this time using Psalm 2 as a foundational text. The psalm appears as today's responsory.

Today we begin hearing the farewell discourse Jesus delivered at the Last Supper. Having already celebrated the death and resurrection of Jesus in the Triduum, we look backward now while we have the time to absorb in small doses the last words of Jesus to his disciples. Thanks to Thomas's somewhat stupid question, we hear a marvelous proclamation from Jesus: "I am the way, the truth and the life."

Penitential Rite C-vii borrows from today's gospel text. The third preface for Easter (P 23) mentions Jesus' sacrificial role as priest.

SAT 8

#284 (LMC #185–192)   white
Easter Weekday

First the persecution of Christians caused the spread of the gospel to the Gentiles. Now the mission to the Gentiles causes persecution. Paul and Barnabas shake the dust from their feet and rejoice still in their ministry. The gospel, as the psalm implies, goes to "all the ends of the earth."

Yesterday a question from Thomas provoked a memorable response from Jesus. Today a command by Philip produces the same. "Show us the Father" shows us the ignorance of the disciples, but Jesus seizes the opportunity to express his unity with the Father. Today's gospel is the same text we heard on Monday of this week, Philip's feast.

The fifth Easter preface (P 25) expresses the sacrificial role of Jesus.

■ TODAY IS THE PATRONAL FEAST OF ARGENTINA, Our Lady of Luján. Tradition holds that a Portuguese landowner in Córdoba ordered a statue of the Immaculate Conception from a friend in Buenos Aires in 1630. The friend sent two terracotta images. The oxen transporting the images stopped after two days of travel until one statue was removed. A local landowner built a shrine for that statue in his own house at Luján.

#54 (LMC #48)   white
9 Fifth Sunday of Easter

ORIENTATION

During the second half of the Easter season the gospels are all drawn from the farewell discourse of Jesus in John's gospel. They place us back at the Last Supper, but allow us to meditate unhurriedly on these dense texts.

Today is Mother's Day. Prepare for extra visitors and remember all mothers, living and dead.

LECTIONARY

Even though this is the last year of the cycle, today's gospel is the opening of the farewell discourse from John's gospel. This discourse is the well from which the lectionary draws during the final weeks of Easter. Judas leaves, and Jesus tells the apostles about his glory and the new commandment: Love one another. In a few short verses, Jesus spells out the bottom line of discipleship, its expectations and promise.

The mission to the Gentiles is an unparalleled success. Today's first reading tells of the progress the apostles make in Lystra, Iconium, Antioch, Pisidia, Pamphylia, Perga and Attalia. Everywhere God was opening the door of faith to the Gentiles. In the psalm we pray that creation will make known the might of God to all the earth. The apostles work in concert with creation for the sake of evangelization.

Swiftly the second reading moves us to the final chapters of the book of Revelation, where John sees a new heaven and a new earth, as well as the holy city, a new Jerusalem, coming down out of heaven from God. The first-century Christians, persecuted in an earthly city of terror, will take their place forever in a heavenly city of glory.

SACRAMENTARY

The suggested opening antiphon is a verse from Psalm 97 (98) that also inspired the alternative opening prayer for today.

Continue the rite of blessing and sprinkling of holy water if you wish. Easter Preface IV (P 24) speaks of renewal and restoration.

In place of the prayer over the people suggested for today, look at the solemn blessing for the Easter season (#7) or prayer over the people #20. To acknowledge mothers, see the prayer over the people in the *Book of Blessings* (ch. 55). See also the solemn blessing for the Easter season at the end of the order of Mass in the *Collection of Masses of the Blessed Virgin Mary*.

OTHER IDEAS

If the community is gathering for any other prayer during the next few weeks, consider using a text from John's account of Jesus' farewell discourse. It will keep the spirit of the liturgy.

Sample general intercessions for Mother's Day are in the *Book of Blessings* (ch. 55).

M O N 10 #285 (LMC #185–192)   white
Easter Weekday

Optional Memorial of Blessed Damien Joseph de Veuster of Moloka'i (+ 1889), presbyter, religious, missionary/white ▪ On mission, the apostles shift through events with dizzying swiftness. A plot to stone Paul and Barnabas materializes. They flee and cure a disabled man. The people declare that the apostles are gods. The apostles preach the truth of their mission, but it falls on deaf ears. Psalm 115 turns the believer's attention from worship of false idols to worship of the true God.

Jude asks why Jesus limits his revelation. Jesus says he and the Father will dwell with any true believer, and that they should expect the Holy Spirit to instruct and remind them.

The third Easter preface (P 23) calls Christ the advocate who always pleads our cause.

■ TODAY'S SAINT: Father Damien, a Belgian priest, went to the Sandwich (Hawaiian) Islands as a missionary, where he served the leper colony and improved and tended the physical and spiritual needs of the community. His memorial is optional throughout the world on April 15, but it is observed on this day in the United States. It was on May 10 that Damien traveled from Maui to the settlement of Kalawao on the island of Moloka'i to become the first resident priest to serve the lepers in 1873. The diocese of Honolulu and Damien's own Congregation of the Sacred Hearts of Jesus and Mary were already observing today's date before April 15 was appointed for observance.

■ IN GUATEMALA TODAY is the memorial of John of Avila (+ 1569), priest, writer, mystic and friend of Ignatius of Loyola.

T U E **11** #286 (LMC #185–192) white
Easter Weekday

Not even stoning stops Paul from his mission to preach. He and Barnabas chart a successful journey, proclaiming the gospel with honor. As the psalm says, the works of God tell of glorious divine might.

Jesus gives the disciples his farewell gift of peace, a virtue they will need considering the persecution that lies ahead.

The first Easter preface (P 21) consoles those persecuted with its words about the suffering Christ: "by dying he destroyed our death."

W E D **12** #287 (LMC #185–192) white
Easter Weekday

Optional Memorial of Nereus and Achielleus (+ 2nd c.), martyrs/red ▪ Optional Memorial of Pancras (+ c. 304), martyr/red ▪ The church in Antioch disagreed with the church in Judea about the conversion of Gentiles. The Judeans said Gentiles had to become Jews before becoming Christians. This created "much controversy" with Paul and Barnabas. They return to Jerusalem to discuss the matter as a universal church community. In response, we sing one of the Jerusalem pilgrimage psalms.

Jesus explores the metaphor of the vine and the vine grower. In those images lie the unity, growth and development of the church.

The relationship of Jesus to the church appears as a theme in the second preface for the Easter season (P 22).

▪ TODAY'S SAINTS: Romans Nereus and Achilleus were soldiers who converted to Christianity, renounced warfare and then suffered martyrdom for their faith. Their tomb is in the catacombs of St. Domitilla.

Little is known of Pancras except that he was revered as a martyr from early in church history. Gregory the Great dedicated a monastery to him, which may explain why his emissary Augustine dedicated a church in Canterbury to the same martyr. A popular legend says Pancras was 14 when he died under the persecution of Diocletian.

T H U **13** #288 (LMC #185–192) white
Easter Weekday

Optional Memorial of Our Lady of Fatima/white ▪ The resolution of the dispute over Gentile converts favors the position held by Paul and Barnabas. The dialogue is a marvelous example of early church leadership: Both sides explain their positions and James announces the conclusion. A psalm of praise follows the reading. The nations, that is, the Gentiles, sing that God is their ruler.

Love, obedience and joy intertwine as Jesus instructs his disciples to keep the commandments, live in love and find their joy.

The fourth Easter preface (P 24) speaks of the new age that has dawned.

▪ TODAY'S MEMORIAL appeared on the universal calendar in the third edition of the Roman Missal (2002). It commemorates the day in 1917 that three children saw Mary appear at Fatima, Portugal. She revealed herself as the Immaculate Conception. A would-be assassin shot Pope John Paul II on this date in 1981, and the pope credited his deliverance to Our Lady of Fatima and placed the bullet in the crown of her statue in Portugal.

F R I **14** #564 (LMC #293, 455) red
Matthias, apostle
FEAST

After the death of Judas the apostles decided to replace him. The

story is recounted in today's first reading. A line from Psalm 113 praises God who raises a lowly servant to a seat among leaders. The gospel recalls Jesus' words to his disciples at the Last Supper that it was not they who chose him, but he who chose them. This text coincidentally combines the gospels normally heard on Thursday and Friday of the Fifth Week of Easter. Every word of yesterday's gospel, then, is repeated today, and the second half of today's gospel is the one we normally hear when this is a weekday and not a feast.

Sing the Glory to God. Find the presidential prayers under May 14 in the back of the sacramentary. Either preface of the apostles is fitting, but the first (P 64) emphasizes that the eternal shepherd never leaves the flock untended. Matthias appears in the first eucharistic prayer. Use the solemn blessing for the apostles (#17) if you like.

S A T **15** #290 (LMC #185–192) white
Easter Weekday

Optional Memorial of Isidore the Farmer (+ 1130) and his wife Maria, married couple/white ▪ The circumcision of Timothy seems to negate the conclusion of the meeting in Jerusalem about Gentile converts, but it may be that Paul was making a prudent pastoral decision. His travels continue, and the gospel spreads even farther. The psalm summons all the earth to cry to God with joy.

Jesus predicts the persecution of his followers. Small comfort, but the world hated him before it hated them.

The fourth Easter preface (P 24) holds out hope for a world suffering the reign of sin.

▪ TODAY'S SAINT: Isidore is included on the calendar of the United States as an optional memorial.

Many communities also remember Isidore's wife, Maria, today, if only because Maria and Isidore (Ysidro) are an instance of a married couple, very rarely included in the calendar of saints, whom the church has recognized for their sanctity. Born in Madrid, Isidore worked on a farm. It is said he saw visions of heaven and that angels assisted his work in the field. His wife survived him by a few years. She is called "Maria de la Cabeza" because her head is sometimes carried in procession in times of drought.

Isidore is honored today with a feast in Costa Rica, an obligatory memorial in Guatemala and Venezuela, and with an optional memorial in Argentina and Mexico.

☀️**16** #57 (LMC #51)
Sixth Sunday of Easter

ORIENTATION

The Easter season extends a full 50 days, but secular society has packed away its bunnies and eggs a long time ago. Our celebration continues. Easter decorations should still adorn the outside and inside of church. Easter vesture and paraments remind people of the season. Mystagogy continues for the newly baptized and for the entire community.

Many families celebrate special events this time of year. They do so in the joy of the good news of resurrection.

LECTIONARY

If you will celebrate Ascension next Sunday instead of next Thursday, you have an option this weekend:

You may choose the gospel and second reading from the Seventh Sunday of Easter. If you do, see below for comments on the texts. If you have been featuring homilies or songs based on the series of readings from Revelation, consider exercising this option for the second reading. Your community can then hear the peaceful, evocative conclusion to this stunning book. The gospel is a toss-up. The one for the sixth Sunday contains Jesus' promise of the Holy Spirit, but the one for the seventh is his high priestly prayer for the unity of the followers. You can make a case either way.

The first reading may not be substituted because the one for the Seventh Sunday this year makes an allusion to Christ already being ascended.

In the gospel for the Sixth Sunday of Easter, we find ourselves once again at table with Jesus at the Last Supper. Jesus expects love from his followers. They can expect the Holy Spirit, the Advocate, from him. His farewell gift is peace—though not as the world gives it, he ominously adds.

In the book of Revelation, John records a breathtaking vision of the holy city Jerusalem coming down out of heaven from God. It gleams like jewels. Its 12 gates, carrying the names of the tribes of Israel, are open to the world. Its foundations are the apostles of the Lamb. The city needs no temple, for it has the Lord God Almighty and the Lamb. We celebrate sacraments in earthly temples, but the day will come when sacraments shall cease because the reality we will experience is what our sacraments have been signifying all along.

In the Acts of the Apostles, the conversion of Gentiles among the believers brought a new set of questions. How would these people be integrated into the new

chosen people? The most pressing question affected the Gentile men: Was circumcision required? The leaders gather together and report the decision as one made by the Holy Spirit and by them, not to place on the Gentiles any burden beyond what was necessary. This beautiful story sets a model for how the church resolves questions arising from new circumstances in every age.

Mystagogy today may highlight the role of the Holy Spirit, the decision-making responsibilities of church ministers, sacraments and the gift of peace.

SACRAMENTARY

Continue the blessing and sprinkling of holy water at the beginning of today's liturgy if you have been using this option throughout the Easter season. Sing the Easter Glory to God and the set of eucharistic acclamations. The solemn blessing for the Easter season appears handily on the page today with the day's prayers. Easter Preface III (P 23) refers to Jesus as the advocate, or paraclete, who pleads the cause of believers.

OTHER IDEAS

You could bless cars today (Book of Blessings, ch. 21) for those planning trips this summer.

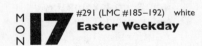 #291 (LMC #185–192) white
Easter Weekday

The Acts of the Apostles reports today the story of Lydia's conversion. This lovely episode reveals her as a person already leading a spiritual life, present at a place of prayer, and ready for the Holy Spirit to open her heart. After Lydia and her household are baptized, she prevails upon the apostles to stay—an invitation for mystagogy and community. She serves as a model for catechumens, who enter the way of faith and conversion "as the Holy Spirit opens their hearts" (RCIA, 1). The psalm says the faithful delight in God, and God delights in them.

Jesus predicts the arrival of the Paraclete, the Spirit of truth, who will give the disciples courage when they are persecuted. The memory of Jesus' words grants perseverance.

The third Easter preface (P 23) refers to Jesus as the advocate.

■ ROGATION DAYS began as early as fifth-century France for protection against earthquakes. The church formerly designated the three days before Ascension Thursday as special days of prayer for protection and a fruitful harvest. They included a procession and the litany of the saints. Today bishops' conferences around the world replace these days with special days of prayer for the needs of all people, "especially for the productivity of the earth and for human labor," and to give God public thanks (*General Norms for the Liturgical Year and Calendar*, 45). In the United States, each diocese chooses its own dates and intentions. Consult your diocesan office for your special days of prayer, and choose a votive Mass for various needs and occasions that suits the celebration.

T U E 18 #292 (LMC #185–192) white
Easter Weekday

Optional Memorial of John I (+ 526), pope, martyr / red ▪ Another household conversion is reported in today's first reading. This time, though, the convert is not a person already practicing a spiritual life like Lydia, but a jailer fearful of the power unleashed by an earthquake. A psalm of salvation follows the reading, affirming the rescue of the apostles and also of the jailer's soul.

The Advocate, Jesus says, will prove the world wrong about sin, justice and condemnation. Jesus' conflict with "the world" will reach its resolution under the influence of the Holy Spirit.

The fourth Easter preface (P 24) honors Christ conquering the reign of sin.

■ TODAY'S SAINT: John I died of hunger while imprisoned in Ravenna under orders of the Arian leader Theodoric the Goth. Some theorize that he was "John the Deacon" whose letter to Senarius of Ravenna contains many details of the sixth-century Roman baptismal rite.

W E D 19 #293 (LMC #185–192) white
Easter Weekday

Paul evangelizes Athens, where he brings his message to the pagan community gathered on the Areopagus, a hillock overlooking the Parthenon. The psalm affirms that God is Lord of heaven and earth.

The Spirit of truth, Jesus says, will announce to the disciples the things to come. In the coming time of darkness the disciples will take comfort from the truth it can never obscure.

You might return to the first Easter preface (P 21), which proclaims our central belief in salvation.

T H U 20 #294 (LMC #185–192) white
Easter Weekday

Some communities in the United States celebrate Ascension today, but others celebrate this coming Sunday, May 23, in which case May 20 is observed as an Easter weekday. All of Latin America transfers the solemnity to the following Sunday. Adapt the following notes to your local calendar.

Optional Memorial of Bernardine of Siena (+ 1444), presbyter, religious, missionary / white ▪ Paul begins his ministry in Corinth. He works as tentmaker and evangelist. His ministry to the Jewish community soured so badly he turned back to evangelize Gentiles. The psalm, overlooking Paul's outburst, placidly sings of God revealing salvation to all the nations.

The disciples remain unable to understand Jesus' sayings. He predicts his departure and the grief it will cause, but also the joy that will result.

The fifth Easter preface (P 25) sings of Jesus' departure by means of the cross. Presidential prayers for this weekday are under Thursday of the sixth week of Easter.

■ TODAY'S SAINT: Bernardine entered the Fathers of the Strict Observance of the Order of St. Francis. His holiness gained him widespread respect, and because of his humility he kept refusing honors and appointments. Nothing gave him more satisfaction than preaching, for which he is best known.

T H U 20 #58 (LMC #54) white
The Ascension of the Lord
SOLEMNITY

ORIENTATION

Not even the New Testament is consistent in dating Christ's Ascension as an event in time, so the variance in dates around the world today need not cause scandal. Although we typically think this day commemorates an event 40 days after Easter, that chronology exists only in Acts of the Apostles. In Luke's gospel, the Ascension appears to have taken place much earlier, even on Easter Day. The original ending to Mark's gospel did not include the Ascension at all, and it can only be inferred from Matthew's conclusion.

The meaning of the celebration is that Jesus has gone to glory with the Father, outside time and space. He intercedes for us and has sent us another Advocate, the Holy Spirit, who pleads our cause. Meanwhile, we await Jesus' return in glory.

LECTIONARY

The readings for all three years of the cycle carry the same lectionary number (#58), but they are subgrouped under A, B and C, with different gospels for each year. For the second reading, you may choose either the one designated for Year C (Hebrews 9:24–28; 10:19–23) or that for Year A (Ephesians 1:17–23).

The first reading is the same every year, the biblical account of the Ascension. Notice what Acts of the Apostles says, that Jesus appeared to instruct the disciples over the course of 40 days. On one of these appearances, presumably (but not conclusively) the final one, Jesus ascended to heaven, being lifted up before the eyes of witnesses in a cloud that took him from sight. This ascension to his royal throne seems foreshadowed in today's psalm refrain, which also remains constant throughout the three-year cycle.

The gospel records the same event by the same author of Acts, but without the reference to teaching or to 40 days. Jesus reminds

the disciples that his life and death is the fulfillment of prophecy and announces that they are witnesses of these things. He sends the Father's promise to help them. He is taken up to heaven, the disciples do him homage, and they return to Jerusalem praising God in the temple. In his departure, Jesus commissions the disciples to carry on his work and equips them with what they need.

This year's second reading affirms that Christ entered a sanctuary not made by hands but into heaven itself. There he intercedes before God on our behalf. Year A's second reading from Ephesians, which you may choose instead, speaks of Jesus raised from the dead and sitting at the right hand of God in heaven. All things are at the feet of Christ, who is head of the church and fills the universe.

SACRAMENTARY

The suggested opening antiphon is taken from today's first reading. Have a festive opening procession—decorate the cross, use candles and incense. Repeat the blessing and sprinkling of holy water. If you have not been singing the Glory to God throughout Easter, revive the music again today.

If you use the preface of the Ascension (P 26), use the bracketed word [Today.] If you choose the first eucharistic prayer, there is a special insert for the feast at "In union." The solemn blessing for the Ascension appears on the page with the Mass prayers.

OTHER IDEAS

If your celebration of the Ascension has replaced the Seventh Sunday of Easter, you may wish to rescue the alternative opening

prayer from that Sunday for its eloquent reflection on God, time and beauty. It might fittingly conclude the general intercessions.

The Easter candle remains burning until Pentecost evening.

Choose a good hymn for the feast like "Hail the Day That Sees Him Rise" (LLANFAIR) or "A Hymn of Glory Let Us Sing" (LASST UNS ERFREUEN). *By Flowing Waters* (175–83) has a complete suite of processional antiphons and psalms, including an inclusive language version of the ancient entrance antiphon.

If you sang the O Antiphons during the last part of Advent this year, you might chant the *Magnificat* antiphon for second vespers, "O rex gloriæ." It follows the same musical and textual pattern. Find it in the *Antiphonale monasticum.*

21 FRI
#295 (LMC #185–192)   white
Easter Weekday

Optional Memorial of Christopher Magallanes, presbyter, and companions, martyrs/red (+ 1915–37) ▪ Paul stays in Corinth a year and a half, long enough apparently for conversions to happen, but long enough also to make new enemies. Gallio refuses to hear a case against Paul because it is not a civil crime. A revolt breaks out against the synagogue official Sosthenes. If this is the same Sosthenes who co-authored the letters to the Corinthians, he converted to Christ as well.

Psalm 47 is seasonal and assumes you have already celebrated the Ascension. The psalmist sings of God mounting a royal throne as the church remembers Christ ascending to his royal throne. If your celebration of the Ascension has yet to take place, this psalm will sound a little out of sorts.

Jesus continues his warnings about persecutions. He compares the sorrow to that of a woman in painful labor. Joy will come, but at a price.

Choose the opening prayer based on the day you celebrate the Ascension. If you have not yet celebrated the Ascension, Easter preface III (P 23) is a good choice, as it acknowledges Jesus as priest. If you celebrated the solemnity yesterday, either Ascension preface (P 26 or 27) may be used. The second (P 27) succinctly summarizes Jesus' role in heaven.

▪ TODAY'S SAINTS: The 22 priests and 3 laymen remembered today suffered during the persecution of the church in Mexico associated with the Cristero uprising between 1926 and 1929. Christopher Magallanes (+ 1927), the parish priest at his home town of Totalice, established catechetical centers and schools, built a dam and created land reform. Arrested as a supporter of the uprising, though committed to nonviolence, he was shot to death by the government while declaring his innocence.

SAT **22** #296 (LMC #185–192)   white
Easter Weekday

Optional Memorial of Rita of Cascia, married woman, mother, widow, religious / white (+ before 1457) ▪ As Paul continues his travels, Apollos surfaces as an influential teacher. Priscilla and Aquila, however, take him aside to correct a few points. If this is the same Apollos in the first letter to the Corinthians, his ministry unfortunately added to the polarization of the community. The seasonal psalm for Ascension, begun yesterday, continues with more verses after this reading.

Jesus encourages the disciples to ask the Father for things in his name. We follow this advice every time we conclude a presidential prayer at Mass in the name of Christ our Lord.

Choose the opening prayer based on the day you celebrate the Ascension.

The third Easter preface (P 23), highlighting Jesus' role as advocate, is appropriate today unless you have already celebrated Ascension. If you choose the first Ascension preface (P 26), omit the word *Today.*

▪ TODAY'S SAINT: Rita's violent and unfaithful husband was murdered. She entered a convent, where her piety and asceticism gave her mystical experiences. She received the wound of the crown of thorns on her forehead. Canonized in 1900, her memorial was added to the universal calendar in the third edition of the Roman Missal (2002).

☀23 #61 (LMC #57)   white
Seventh Sunday of Easter

Some communities celebrate Ascension on Thursday, May 20, but others celebrate today, May 23. Notes for the solemnity of the Ascension are found on page 156. Adapt these notes to your local calendar.

ORIENTATION

This liminal celebration places us between the departure of Jesus in his ascension and the arrival of the Spirit at Pentecost. We gather with the disciples in the upper room of prayerful anticipation during the nine days that formed an original novena for the church.

LECTIONARY

Today's first reading records the death of the deacon Stephen. Chronologically, the story of the Acts of the Apostles has advanced far beyond this point in our series of readings on Sundays. But Stephen's death is chosen for this date because of his vision. He sees "the Son of Man standing at the right hand of God." He sees the ascended Christ. That vision gives Stephen—and us—hope in the face of death. The psalm is a seasonal psalm of Ascension, acclaiming Christ as king, the most high over all the earth.

In the gospel we sit with Jesus once again at the Last Supper. This time, he no longer addresses his words to the disciples but raises his eyes and prays for them. He prays for those at table and for those who will believe because of them. He prays for unity among his followers and for unity between them and the Father. This comforting prayer reminded the original readers of John that Jesus cared for them. He cares for us, too.

In the final passage from the book of Revelation John hears the voice of Jesus saying, "I am coming soon." This expansive book ends with the mutual yearning for unity between Christ and the believer.

Themes for mystagogy this week include the promise of eternal life contained in the eucharistic banquet and the community of believers.

SACRAMENTARY

The opening prayer sets the tone for today's celebration of anticipation. The alternative is an unusually eloquent text relating time to truth and beauty.

You may choose from seven prefaces, but those for the Ascension (P 26 and 27) will keep the community in the Spirit of the feast.

If you used the first on Thursday, you might use the second today.

The first eucharistic prayer says Jesus raised his eyes before he took the bread and the cup. The synoptics make no such statement. Neither does Paul. Jesus raised his eyes before the miracle of the loaves. And in John's gospel, which does not recount the institution of the eucharist at the Last Supper, Jesus raises his eyes at that meal before offering the prayer we hear excerpted today.

The solemn blessing for the Ascension (#8) makes a good choice for today. Prayer over the people #24 might also fit.

OTHER IDEAS

The first preface of the Holy Spirit (P 54) formerly served as the Ascension preface and refers to that feast as well as Pentecost.

M O N 24 #297 (LMC #185–192) white
Easter Weekday

Paul baptizes and imposes hands on a group of disciples in Ephesus. The story implies that Apollos had delivered an incomplete catechesis and baptism. Psalm 68 is another text for the season of Ascension. It opens with the evocative expression, "God arises."

The disciples enthusiastically proclaim their faith in Jesus, but he warns them about the suffering he will endure, which will cause them to ask questions about finding peace.

You may choose from any of seven prefaces, but one of those for the Ascension (P 26 or 27) will keep the spirit of the season.

■ IN VENEZUELA today is the memorial of Mary the Helper. This is an optional memorial in Argentina and Costa Rica under the title "Mary, Help of Christians." Pius VII, having been exiled by Napoleon, established the

day to commemorate the anniversary of his safe return to Rome. The Salesians especially kept the devotion alive, together with their sister organization, the Daughters of Mary, Help of Christians. See the *Collection of Masses of the Blessed Virgin Mary,* 42.

T U E 25 #298 (LMC #185–192) white
Easter Weekday

Optional Memorial of Bede the Venerable (+ 735), presbyter, monastic, doctor of the church / white ▪ *Optional Memorial of Gregory VII (+ 1085), pope, monastic / white* ▪ *Optional Memorial of Mary Magdalene de' Pazzi (+ 1607), virgin, religious / white* ▪ Paul addresses the elders of Ephesus like a man who knows his days are numbered. He presses on toward Jerusalem, aware that a tragic end could await him there. He reiterates his commitment to the gospel, at whatever cost. We sing more verses from yesterday's responsory, a seasonal psalm for the Ascension.

Having finished his instructions to the disciples at the Last Supper, Jesus now turns his gaze toward heaven and begins his final, high priestly prayer to God the Father, on behalf of those he called and loved. He asks the Father to glorify the divine name in the events that will follow.

You may choose one of the Ascension prefaces.

■ TODAY'S SAINTS: The field of optional memorials is especially congested today.

Bede is best known as an Anglo-Saxon historian. He also wrote commentaries on scripture, grammatical works and a treatise on physical science. He began the custom of dating events from the birth of Christ, a date computed by Dionysius Exiguus in the sixth century.

Hildebrand took the name Gregory VII and became one of the most influential reformers in the history of the papacy. He established the supremacy of the papacy within the church and of the church over the state.

Mary Magadelene de' Pazzi was a Carmelite nun from Florence known for her prayer and penance for the reform of the church and the conversion of all people.

■ NOTE TWO LATIN AMERICAN CELEBRATIONS for today. Bolivia has an optional memorial of the virgin Mariana de Jesús, celebrated by more of Latin America tomorrow. Mexico celebrates the optional memorial of Christopher Magallanes and companions, martyrs (+ 1915–37) today instead of on May 21.

W E D 26 #299 (LMC #185–192) white
Philip Neri (+ 1595), priest, founder
MEMORIAL

Paul's tearful departure from Ephesus provokes a lovely farewell address. This is one of a few clear references in the Bible where a community knelt for common prayer. The context was not eucharistic. More verses from the Ascension Psalm 68 follow: "God's power is in the skies."

Jesus now prays to the Father for the well-being of his disciples. He does not ask God to take them out of the world, but to protect them in the world where they live and work.

Prayers are found under May 26, and you may choose the preface for pastors (P 67) if you wish.

■ TODAY'S SAINT: Perhaps the most joyful of saints, Philip attracted friends and admirers in his own day, including Ignatius of Loyola and Francis Xavier, and even later generations marveled at his winning personality. He developed a prayer room around which he founded the Oratorian community. The musical form known as the oratorio began as part of their apostolate in Rome.

Mariana de Jesús (+ 1645) is remembered today with a feast day in Ecuador and a memorial in Colombia and Venezuela. Also known as Saint Mary Ann of Quito, or Mariana Paredes y Flores, she was born in 1618 of a Spanish family in Quito when it was part of Peru. She lived in solitude under Jesuit direction at the home of her brother-in-law, surviving on the barest of needs and receiving spiritual favors.

■ TODAY AND TOMORROW are set aside for the Jewish celebration of Shavuot, the Feast of Weeks. The festival celebrates the giving of the Torah on Mount Sinai. The Christian celebration of Pentecost has this feast in the background. See the second option for the first reading of the vigil of Pentecost.

T H U 27
#300 (LMC #185–192)   white
Easter Weekday

Optional Memorial of Augustine of Canterbury (+ 604), bishop, monastic, missionary/white ▪ Paul is on trial before the Sanhedrin, a group he polarizes by proclaiming his Pharisaic belief in the resurrection. In a vision, Paul realizes he must go to Rome. Psalm 16, a text the lectionary associates with the resurrection (see the second reading of the Easter Vigil), follows this story.

Jesus widens his prayer. He prays not only for the disciples before him, but also for those who will come later, even us. This concludes the lectionary's presentation of Jesus' discourse and prayer at the Last Supper.

Choose from the wide options of seasonal prefaces. Those for Ascension may be preferable.

■ TODAY'S SAINT: A Benedictine monk from Rome, Augustine was the first bishop of Canterbury. Part of this missionary's life is recalled in the historical work of Bede. The lectionary's proper of saints suggests readings about mission and service, but the readings of the weekday are recommended.

F R I 28
#301 (LMC #185–192)   white
Easter Weekday

Under arrest, Paul appeals his case so that it can go to a civil court and not be dismissed as a religious matter. His strategy gives him the opportunity to broaden his audience for the proclamation of the gospel. Another seasonal psalm for Ascension follows: The Lord has set his throne in heaven.

In a farewell conversation with Peter, Jesus asks three questions about love to the disciple who denied him three times. Predicting Peter's death, Jesus gives a command layered with suffering and promise: "Follow me."

The same choices for the preface reappear. Choose from those for Easter or for Ascension.

■ IN COLOMBIA the memorial of Philip Neri is transferred to this date because of its celebration of Mariana de Jesús on May 26.

S A T 29
#302 (LMC #185–192)   white
Easter Weekday

The lectionary texts for Saturday morning differ from those of the Pentecost vigil, assigned for later in the day today.

The first reading concludes the series from Acts of the Apostles. It follows Paul all the way to Rome, where he continues to preach from the capital city of the world. Acts ends here. It is not a biography of Paul, but a biography of the church, a story that has reached its climax by putting the proclamation of the gospel on the highest earthly pedestal, Rome.

Psalm 11 includes another seasonal reference to God on the heavenly throne.

Our series from John's gospel also concludes today, as Jesus and Peter discuss the beloved disciple. This figure, apparently an image of the believer who reads the gospel, continues to live in the world and bear witness to these events.

✱ 30
#62–63 (LMC #58)   red
Pentecost
SOLEMNITY

ORIENTATION

Pentecost celebrates the coming of the Holy Spirit upon the church, as Jesus had promised. The frightened disciples, gathered in their upper room, experience the presence of the Spirit in such a profound way that it drives them out into the world to proclaim and preach the gospel with a courage they did not have before.

Pentecost derives its name from the Feast of Weeks, a Jewish festival of the early harvest celebrated seven weeks (50 days) after Passover (Exodus 23:16), on which the first fruits were offered in gratitude to God. It eventually became associated with the giving of the Torah on Mount Sinai. *Pentecost* was the Greek word for the same festival; the word *Pentecost* means "fiftieth." Early Christians reinterpreted the Jewish festival as a commemoration of the coming of the Spirit; in Acts

(2:1–11) the Spirit descends "when the time for Pentecost was fulfilled." In early Christianity, "Pentecost" came to refer to the whole 50 days of Easter.

This Memorial Day weekend will bring some visitors to church and will cause some regulars to be absent. Be prepared to welcome the stranger.

LECTIONARY

An extensive and complex series of readings is arranged for this solemnity. The vigil Mass offers a selection of four Old Testament readings, one of which is to precede the second reading and the gospel. Another complete set of readings is proclaimed on Pentecost Day, together with a sequence.

■ PENTECOST VIGIL: The *Circular Letter* (#107) recommends "the prolonged celebration of Mass in the form of a Vigil, whose character is . . . of urgent prayer, after the example of the Apostles and disciples." You could, then, choose more than one of the Old Testament passages and extend the celebration of the evening Mass. The pool of readings for the vigil is the same every year of the cycle.

■ OLD TESTAMENT OPTIONS FOR THE VIGIL: The Pentecost vigil marks the first time since the Easter Vigil that the first reading comes from the Old Testament. Each of the choices has special significance:

• From Genesis we hear the story of the Tower of Babel. It explains how human sin caused the development of many human languages. On Pentecost, God's grace allows people who speak many languages to understand the same preacher. The gospel translates well into the common human experience of struggling to understand another's language. It also speaks to all humanity, no matter their language or ethnicity.

• From Exodus we hear the story of Moses receiving the sacred law from God on Mt. Sinai. According to 19:1, the event took place on the third new moon, causing later interpreters to speculate that it coincided with Pentecost, the fiftieth day. The tongues of fire appear on the disciples in a mighty wind, reminiscent of the theophany on Sinai.

• Another image of wind, of God's breath, can be found in the prophecy of Ezekiel. Note how the dry bones are without "spirit," until later in the passage when "the spirit" enters the bones, and in the final lines God promises the gift of "my spirit."

• Joel prophesies that God will pour out the divine spirit upon the chosen people. This important passage appears nowhere else in the lectionary. Peter quotes it at length in his sermon on Pentecost day.

■ VIGIL PSALMODY: The psalm inviting God's spirit to renew the earth, Psalm 104, follows the first reading, no matter which one is selected. The verses vary slightly, but this is the same psalm that followed the first reading of the Easter Vigil.

Settings are offered by C. Alexander Peloquin (GIA G-1662), Robert Edward Smith (GIA G-2122), Paul Lisicky (*Gather* #90), Angelo della Pica (*Psalms for the Cantor,* vol. V), Vern Pat Nelson (WLP 2616), Dan Tucker (WLP 7994), and bilingual settings by Charlotte Struckhoff ("Renueve la Tierra Madre") and Lorenzo Florián ("Ven, O Espiritu").

If you observe an extended vigil, use Psalm 104 after the last reading. In other places, the lectionary recommends Psalm 33 to follow the Babel story from Genesis, Psalm 100 to follow the Sinai account from Exodus, and Psalm 130 to follow the dry bones of Ezekiel.

■ OTHER VIGIL READINGS: In the gospel we hear one occasion when Jesus promised the Spirit. John's comment, "There was no Spirit yet," makes it a serviceable passage for the Pentecost vigil.

Paul's letter to the Romans, though, reassures the community about the Spirit's ability to assist their prayer. A passage like this would have consoled the group of disciples huddled in fear, not knowing how to pray.

Although the above scriptures "may be used" for the vigil, those assigned for Pentecost Sunday carry no such restriction.

The vigil readings are rich and worth hearing on any Saturday evening liturgy, even a wedding Mass, but they would not be used on Sunday. You could, though, proclaim the Sunday readings at a Saturday vigil Mass if that simplifies the preaching and preparation of music, and if you thought the assembly (who will not return on Sunday morning) would benefit from hearing the passages that most directly proclaim the event. Still, it would be a shame to lose those great vigil readings!

■ THE PENTECOST PASSAGE EVERYONE THINKS OF FIRST is Sunday's first reading from Acts. It shows up here in all three years of the cycle. Another example of Luke's masterful writing style, this text allows the hearer to see the fire and feel the wind. Be sure the reader practices the names of the nationalities and places. The overall effect should not be one of stumbling, but of the far-flung, sure-footed effect of the gospel.

The psalmist sings of the life-giving spirit. With it we are created; without it we die. All three years of the cycle call for the same psalm.

■ THE GOSPEL OF PENTECOST DAY WILL SURPRISE PEOPLE. Even though we think of the gift of the Spirit on the fiftieth day in Luke's account from Acts, John's description of the gift of the Spirit occurs on the very day of the resurrection. He offers no account of a later Pentecost. So, according to John, the gift of the Spirit came with the resurrection, primarily for the forgiveness of sins. To remember that event is to embrace a different kind of Pentecost.

■ IN YEAR C THE LECTIONARY PERMITS AN ALTERNATE GOSPEL. The passage from John 14 returns us to the farewell discourse of Jesus. At the Last Supper he promised the disciples he would ask the Father for another Advocate who will teach them everything and remind them of all that he told them.

In 1 Corinthians, Paul explains how the gifts of the Spirit disperse throughout the community. Pentecost is a continuing, creative event.

The Year C lectionary permits an alternative for the second reading. Paul contrasts spirit and flesh for the Romans. If the Spirit who raised Christ from the dead lives also in them, God will raise them to new life. The Spirit also bears witness that we are children of God. This passage shows the benefits the Spirit bestows upon the community of believers.

■ THE SEQUENCE invites the Spirit to come upon the gathered assembly to recreate, heal and forgive. The original chant, "Veni sancte Spiritus" (*Liber cantualis* or *Worship* #857), could be used, or the version from Taizé with the same title. Ann Colleen Dohn's version has responses for the assembly (WLP 5718). See also Richard Wojcik's "O Holy Spirit, by Whose Breath" (*Worship* #475); and Ralph Wright's translation in GIA's *Hymnal for the Hours,* which may be sung to a tune like PUER NOBIS. Note also Deanna Light and Paul Tate's *Come, Holy Spirit* (WLP 7485). Dennis Fitzpatrick and Roger Nachtwey's fine translation of the golden sequence is found in *By Flowing Waters,* 188.

SACRAMENTARY

Texts are offered for the vigil Mass and also the Mass during the day. The suggested communion antiphon for the vigil Mass comes from its gospel.

Choose resplendent red vesture for deacon and priest. The vesture should evoke Pentecost, not martyrdom. Start the procession with incense, cross and candles. Use the sprinkling rite to conclude the Easter season. Sing the Glory to God.

The opening prayers for the vigil Mass all assume we are still awaiting the celebration of the coming of the Spirit, even as they pray for that Spirit to come upon the community today. The opening prayers for the Mass during the day assume that we are now celebrating the Pentecost event.

For both Masses the preface of Pentecost is used (P 28) and if you pray the first eucharistic prayer, you may use the special insert for "In union." Sing the acclamations in use throughout the Easter season, perhaps with additional instruments or harmony.

The prayer over the people at the vigil Mass offers a simple close, but you could turn the page and use the solemn blessing printed there for Pentecost Sunday. The solemn blessing for the Easter season at the end of the order of Mass in the *Collection of Masses of the Blessed Virgin Mary* also makes a good choice today.

Easter's double alleluia returns for the dismissal dialogue.

OTHER IDEAS

After evening prayer, move the Easter candle from its place near the ambo to the baptismal font. It has been lit throughout the 50 Days. Now it will burn for baptisms and funerals.

The newly baptized may want to sit together and dress for the occasion.

A strong tradition in church history made this an alternate day for baptisms. Why not celebrate infant baptism at today's Mass?

Decorate the space in a way that suggests the first fruits of the harvest. See *To Crown the Year* (pp. 145–48).

A staple in the musical repertoire should be the chant "Veni, creator" from the *Liber cantualis.* Hal H. Hopson wrote a dramatic reading of Acts 2:1–17 for singers, readers, handbells and organ (GIA G-3442).

Encourage people at home to have a special family dinner with a decorated table. See *Catholic Household Blessings and Prayers* for texts for Pentecost (p. 157) and the Easter season (p. 84).

You may conclude the community's Easter celebration with Evening Prayer II. It closes with the double alleluia dismissal, signifying the end to the 50 Days. Move the Easter candle to the font afterward.

APRIL 18, 2004
Second Sunday of Easter

Christ's Offer of Life and Healing
Acts 5:12–16
They were all cured.

IF you kept a good Lent this year, you have experienced death and rebirth in your spiritual life. If you celebrated the sacrament of reconciliation before Easter this year, you have acknowledged your sin and experienced forgiveness. You have been healed.

One of the first signs of the resurrection was healing. After Jesus rose from the dead, his apostles inherited many of his gifts. They preached powerful sermons. They forgave sins. They healed the sick. People placed the sick on the streets so that Peter's shadow would fall on them as he walked by. Faith was strong, God's Spirit, even stronger.

Now that this year's Easter has come, the healing power of God's Holy Spirit will be at work within you. At the Easter Vigil you renewed your baptismal promises. You recommitted yourself to Christ. Now in the Easter season, Christ will recommit himself to you. You bask for 50 days in the glow of glory.

Perhaps you have experienced doubt. Perhaps you wondered if you can become a new you. On Ash Wednesday you admitted the sickness of your sin and sought the medicine of Lent. Perhaps now you wonder if the new you will stick. Or will you relapse?

The full grace of this season is yours to receive. The risen Christ stands in glory above the tomb. He offers new life and healing.

Written by Paul Turner. © 2003 Archdiocese of Chicago, Liturgy Training Publications; 1-800-933-1800; www.ltp.org.

APRIL 25, 2004
Third Sunday of Easter

Living a Different Law
Acts 5:27–32, 40b–41
They rejoiced that they had been found worthy to suffer dishonor of the sake of the name.

DURING the 1960s many Americans pressed for civil rights through civil disobedience. They broke the laws they thought were unjust to force the creation of new laws. As a result, greater freedoms came for all Americans.

When Peter and John preached the good news of the resurrection, they were arrested and stood trial before the Sanhedrin. They had disobeyed the law. The rulers had asked them not to talk about Jesus, but they "filled Jerusalem" with their teaching.

In reply, Peter and John did a very clever thing. They preached about Jesus to the Sanhedrin. "God exalted Jesus as leader and savior to grant forgiveness of sins," they said. They disobeyed the law again, right in the face of the legislators.

The religious freedom that exists in most countries of the world came at a dear price. Believers spoke out in the face of oppression. Many of them suffered imprisonment. Some of them died. But their cause has endured. One of the most basic human rights is to speak about what one believes.

There may be times when your faith prompts you to speak up. You may put yourself at risk by doing so. You may be criticized. You may even be arrested. But you will have the happiness that comes from beliefs so strong they cannot be kept quiet.

Written by Paul Turner. © 2003 Archdiocese of Chicago, Liturgy Training Publications; 1-800-933-1800; www.ltp.org.

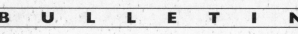

MAY 2, 2004
Fourth Sunday of Easter

God's Unstoppable Spirit
Acts 13:14, 43–52
We now turn to the Gentiles.

No one can stop the Holy Spirit. The Spirit will flow and inspire, filling the earth beyond all borders. No one can stop God's word.

Some tried anyway. The enemies of Paul and Barnabas tried to stop them from preaching, trying to contain the message of the gospel. It didn't work.

Paul and Barnabas, traveling on a missionary journey, spoke at a synagogue at Antioch in Pisidia. Many Jews and worshipers who were converts to Judaism listened. By the following week the crowds were so large that the Jewish leaders of the city tried to stop the apostles from preaching. Paul and Barnabas simply preached to a wider audience. They no longer preached to Jews alone. Now they were preaching to Gentiles.

As Christianity continued to spread, the Jewish leaders started a persecution against Paul and Barnabas, and expelled them from their territory. They did the only thing they could do. They went to another city. And they preached the gospel there.

If the Holy Spirit has a message, that message will be proclaimed. And if the message is within us, we will speak it. Not everyone is prepared to hear the message. Not everyone will receive its point. But the Spirit will speak.

When someone tries to keep you from saying what you know is important, the Spirit may be looking for a wider audience.

MAY 9, 2004
Fifth Sunday of Easter

Words of Encouragement
Acts 14:21–27
Paul and Barnabas strengthened the spirits of the disciples.

EVERYONE needs a little encouragement now and then. When you get hired, get asked or get chosen for some special work, you feel excited about the new responsibility. In time, though, the work becomes challenging. You doubt your ability to continue. The vision of success fades.

It's possible that everything is all right. When enthusiasm wears down and hard work steps up, it's normal to wonder about success. In this situation, perhaps all someone needs is a little encouragement.

At one point in their missionary journey, Paul and Barnabas retraced their steps. They went back to Lystra, Iconium and Antioch. They met again with the disciples they had formed,

and they exhorted the new believers to remain firm in their faith. Hardships are not just normal. Hardships are necessary, they say.

To help out, Paul and Barnabas appointed elders for each community. They also gathered the community to pray and fast at the time these elders were appointed. With organization, prayer and sacrifice Paul and Barnabas strengthened the disciples.

If you have helped someone in the past, this may be a good time to offer additional encouragement. Ask how it is going. Provide direction if you can. Pray. Fast. Give encouragement to those whose strength may be weakening. It is necessary to undergo hardships to enter the reign of God.

MAY 16, 2004
Sixth Sunday of Easter

Resolving Conflicts
Acts 15:1–2, 22–29

It is the decision of the Holy Spirit and of us not to place on you any burden beyond these necessities.

THERE were two main issues that threw the apostolic church into its first internal crisis: legislation and authority.

When preaching to non-Jews, Paul and Barnabas had been preaching that it was not necessary to become Jews in order to become Christians. Not all Christians agreed, however. The questions were simple. Did Paul and Barnabas know the legislation correctly? Did they have any authority to preach it? After all, neither of them was one of the Twelve, and Paul had persecuted Christians before becoming one.

The apostles and elders met in Jerusalem to consider the questions. It was the first time that leaders of the church gathered together to resolve an important issue. Today some people call this "the Council of Jerusalem."

The gathering reached these conclusions: Yes, one could become a Christian without first becoming a Jew. And yes, Paul and Barnabas had the authority to speak for the church. But, just in case the believers in Antioch didn't believe this to be the decision of those gathered in Jerusalem, the Jerusalem church sent along a couple extra representatives to reassure them.

Issues of legislation and authority continue to vex the church. Sometimes people wonder if pastors and bishops have the authority to make rules. Sometimes they question if the rules are in keeping with the spirit of the church. Such questions are as old as the church. They can usually be resolved in charity and with reassurance.

Written by Paul Turner. © 2003 Archdiocese of Chicago, Liturgy Training Publications; 1-800-933-1800; www.ltp.org.

MAY 20 OR 23, 2004
The Ascension of the Lord

Sustained by the Spirit
Acts 1:1–11

Jesus was lifted up, and a cloud took him from their sight.

WE have many ways of saying goodbye: "So long"; "See you later": "Take care."

Goodbyes are softened with the promise of another meeting: "Till we meet again." The time between the goodbye and the reunion is filled with joyful hope and anxious waiting.

Surely the disciples wondered if they had the tools they needed to survive after Jesus' departure. Jesus had been their leader, visionary, Messiah and friend. Without him, life would lose its center.

Jesus' goodbye came with two promises. He promised the Holy Spirit would guide the disciples in his absence, and he promised that he would come again. That left the disciples in an in-between kind of time. After the goodbye, they waited for his coming again.

In fact, that's where we are too. We are "in between" the visits of Jesus, a time of hope and anxiety. We often wonder if we have the tools we need to survive. We need vision and companionship on life's long road.

We have at our disposal the first promise of Jesus, the gift of the Holy Spirit. That Spirit will guide us through times of loneliness, into good decisions, amid the sorrows of sad goodbyes. The Spirit is our center.

Written by Paul Turner. © 2003 Archdiocese of Chicago, Liturgy Training Publications; 1-800-933-1800; www.ltp.org.

MAY 23, 2004
Seventh Sunday of Easter

Hope in Transition
Acts 7:55–60
I see the Son of Man standing at the right hand of God.

TIMES of transition bring happiness as well as anxiety. We celebrate the past, and we look to the future. In the middle we stand at a threshold, not knowing what the future will bring and hoping the past has prepared us well.

Between Ascension Thursday and Pentecost Sunday the church stands at a time of transition. We remember the nine days the disciples marked between Christ's departure and the coming of the Holy Spirit. Surely they felt blessed to have shared the greatest adventure in the history of humanity. But they certainly also felt anxious about what lay ahead. What would it be? Would they be ready? Had Jesus prepared them? How would they know what to do?

Stephen the deacon had preached the gospel faithfully, but his enemies threw rocks at him. Dying, filled with the Holy Spirit, Stephen looked up to heaven and saw the Son of Man standing at the right hand of God.

This vision is the reason we hear about Stephen's death today. We have just celebrated the Ascension of Jesus to the right hand of God. Now we hear that Stephen the dying martyr sees Jesus in heaven, as he had promised.

We transition from one job to another, from school to summer, from work to vacation, from doubt to faith. Whenever we do, we leave something behind and grasp something new. Today we see a vision of hope. Whatever our future brings, Christ will be there.

MAY 30, 2004
Pentecost Sunday

The Power of the Spirit
Acts 2:1–11
They were all filled with the Holy Spirit.

WHAT could change fear into confidence? What power is strong enough to put fears to rest and bring confidence to life?

Our fears come from many sources. Failure, loneliness, and rejection can all make us afraid to try anything.

Confidence often comes from outside, especially when we cannot find it ourselves. Someone else notices a talent in us that we've overlooked. A friend helps us laugh at ourselves. Or by sheer gift, we receive a new power, a new opportunity that makes all the difference in the world.

What changed the disciples' fear into confidence? Something mighty must have happened. The same group that fled at the arrest and crucifixion of Jesus, the same people who cowered

in an upper room after his Ascension—these people started proclaiming the message of salvation to large crowds in every language. How did it happen?

There is only one answer. The Holy Spirit made it happen. The Spirit, promised by Jesus, came in wind and fire to lift up the disciples and bolster their confidence.

No matter where your fear comes from, the Holy Spirit may find you and change your life forever. Will you cooperate? Are you ready to share the gifts of the Spirit?

SUMMER AND FALL ORDINARY TIME

The Season

The Meaning

We have dire need of peace. Superpowers with weapons of unimaginable destructiveness are only the outward manifestation of threatening chaos, because the forces which destroy peace are within our own hearts, and we can wreck our civilization unaided by giving them free play. They are greed and grabbing, ruthless consumerism where there should be reverence and stewardship, the habit of preferring our own short-term advantages to the common good for which society exists, a cleverness untempered by wisdom, a spiritual blindness and ubiquitous fear. We need a peace that will heal the divisions within us and exorcize the fear which looks to violence as the only way to maintain ourselves against the threats from without. Fear of death not only hangs over individuals; people are afraid there may be no peace for the generations to come.

—Maria Boulding, *The Coming of God,*
Third edition (Conception, Missouri:
The Printery House, 2000), pp. 184–85.

ORDINARY Time sounds like nothing special. After 90 days of seasonal liturgies for Lent and Easter, the resumption of Ordinary Time comes as a welcome break. It begins this year when the United States celebrates Memorial Day weekend. The Easter and school calendars come to an end together while the Ordinary Time and summer calendars begin.

Ordinary Time, though, means something ordered, not just ordinary. This long stretch of time between the Easter and Advent seasons marches silently along, drawing no attention to itself, but quietly marking the hum of the cosmos, spinning under God's powerfully creative arms. Day by day this season celebrates the wonder of time and the hope of salvation.

Ordinary Time gives us a chance to practice the virtues that order our lives and create space for peace in the world.

■ WE RESUME ORDINARY TIME AT ITS NINTH WEEK. We interrupted the seventh week to make room for Lent and Easter. The eighth week is not celebrated this year. We almost always lose some of Ordinary Time because the year has to end with the thirty-fourth week. In the second half of this season, then, we anchor the weeks where they will end and figure out what week should follow Pentecost by counting backward. This year's casualty is week eight.

The solemnity of the Assumption (August 15) will fall on a Sunday this year. It will take the place of the Twentieth Sunday in Ordinary Time. Not many will complain about losing the gospel assigned for that day this year. It contains Jesus' difficult statement that he has come not to establish peace on the earth, but rather, division.

The Saints

DURING Ordinary Time, we freely celebrate the cycle of saints' days without the extra context of a primary season of the church year.

■ SOLEMNITIES include holy days of obligation like All Saints (November 1), as well as the Most Sacred Heart of Jesus (June 17), the Nativity of John the Baptist (June 24) and Peter and Paul (June 29). All Souls Day (November 2) is not properly called a solemnity, but it ranks with them.

If the patronal day of your city, state, parish church or religious community falls during this period, it also ranks as a solemnity. If it falls on Sunday, it takes precedence over the Ordinary Time Sunday liturgy.

■ FEASTS during this period this year include several apostles, such as Thomas (July 3) and Simon and Jude (October 28). Other feasts recall the Birth of Mary (September 8) and the Transfiguration of the Lord (August 6). Two feasts celebrate events from the history of the church, the Exaltation of the Holy Cross (September 14) and the Dedication of the Lateran Basilica (November 9). Other saints of note also merit feasts, like the archangels (September 29) and Luke (October 18).

■ OBLIGATORY MEMORIALS APPEAR IN EVERY MONTH OF THE SEASON. Each comes with its own vestment color and presidential prayers, including a preface. If the saint has no complete set of proper prayers, turn to the relevant common of martyrs, pastors, doctors, virgins or holy men and women. Memorials of biblical figures such as Mary Magdalene, Martha and Barnabas, as well as the memorials of Our Lady of Sorrows and of the Guardian Angels, have proper gospels that must replace the weekday gospel.

It is best not to change the scriptures from the semi-continuous readings of Ordinary Time, but you may take them from the lectionary common appropriate for the saint if for some reason it seems better that day.

■ OPTIONAL MEMORIALS APPEAR EVERY MONTH AS WELL. Your community may celebrate the Ordinary Time Mass or the saint whose memorial is optional. If you celebrate the optional saint, use the prayers from the sacramentary. You may also select readings from the lectionary commons, but it is better to follow the readings in the Ordinary Time sequence. When a Saturday in Ordinary Time calls for the weekday liturgy, a Mass in honor of the Blessed Virgin Mary may be used. Prayers and readings may be taken from the Common of the Blessed Virgin Mary or from the *Collection of Masses of the Blessed Virgin Mary*.

■ OTHER OCCASIONS: The lectionary and sacramentary also supply texts for votive Masses and Masses for various needs and occasions. These texts may be used on any Ordinary Time weekday that is not a feast or solemnity.

Several events will occur during this season, including civic holidays and back-to-school celebrations. You will find a rich collection of prayers and scripture readings in the liturgical books under headings like "For the Church" and "For Civil Needs."

The Lectionary

EASTER has ended, but the first two Sundays that follow each year keep up a spirit of celebration: The Most Holy Trinity and the Most Holy Body and Blood of Christ.

When Ordinary Time begins its Sunday sojourn on June 20, we resume at week twelve. We reenter Luke's gospel at the climax of the first half of his book: Peter's confession that Jesus is the Christ of God. Mark's version of this same episode was omitted from last year's Sunday's readings, so it will be good to hear it so prominently this year. On the following Thirteenth Sunday in Ordinary Time, Luke begins to take us on a journey with Jesus to Jerusalem. The journey motif accents the gospel for the rest of Ordinary Time.

The second readings this year come from seven different books, the greatest number to fill a single stretch of Ordinary Time in the three-year cycle. The idea is to hear a series of readings from the same book, but no book continues its series this year beyond four weeks. We start with some excerpts from Paul's letter to the Galatians, and then continue with passages from Colossians. At the end of last year, we heard from the letter to the Hebrews. Because of the length of that letter, its final chapters are reserved for Ordinary Time this summer. The shortest of all New Testament letters, Paul to Philemon, will be heard on Labor Day weekend this year. Then we hear two of the pastoral letters, 1 and 2 Timothy. We conclude the year and the three-year cycle of second readings with one of the earliest books of the New Testament, Paul's second letter to the Thessalonians.

The responsorial psalms may also be drawn from the common psalms for Ordinary Time. These psalms (19, 27, 34, 63, 95, 100, 103 and 145) express different aspects of our belief and provide the community the opportunity to build its musical repertoire.

■ THE SUNDAY LECTIONARY FOR MASSES WITH CHILDREN offers a selection of scriptures for all these Sundays and other major observances.

Many of the readings are abbreviated, as expected. All three readings and the psalm remain virtually unchanged on Sundays 13, 15, 16, 20, 27, 28, 30, 31, 32 and 33 of Ordinary Time. The closer we get to the end of the year, the more the Lectionary for Masses with Children tends to include all the readings.

The second reading is omitted only on Sundays 14, 17, 22 and 23 of Ordinary Time. The first reading is omitted on Sundays 12, 18, 19, 21, 24, 26 and 29. In every instance where the first reading from the full lectionary is omitted, the second reading of the full lectionary becomes the first reading of the children's lectionary. And in every case during Ordinary Time this year, the psalm in the Lectionary for Masses with Children has been changed to fit the theme of the new first reading. This gives better coherence to the scriptures and highlights the importance of the psalm.

There are a couple of further adaptations. On the Twenty-fifth Sunday in Ordinary Time the lectionary for children retains the same gospel, but assigns a new first reading and psalm. Both the reading assigned for the day (1 Timothy 2:1–8) and the one replacing it for children (Romans 12:9–12) address the theme of prayer. Perhaps the Romans reading was thought easier for children to understand.

The other adaptation occurs on Christ the King. The Lectionary for Masses with Children retains all three readings from the full lectionary, but changes the psalm to 47. Perhaps its invitation to clap hands makes it more child-friendly than Psalm 122. But 122 is the psalm that begins and ends the three-year cycle. It appears also on the First Sunday of Advent, Year A, helping to make an inclusion around the lectionary.

The Sacramentary

■ SAMPLE FORMULAS FOR THE GENERAL INTERCESSIONS appear in the sacramentary's first appendix. See #1–2 and 9–10 for those suggested for Ordinary Time.

■ ORDINARY TIME CAN PROVIDE AN OPPORTUNITY TO EVALUATE SOME OF THE THINGS WE ORDINARILY DO. Consider, for example, the concluding rites.

The concluding rites begin with announcements. The announcements should follow the communion prayer, not precede it. Many parishes place the announcements before the communion prayer to accommodate people while they are seated. But the purpose of that time is to render silent thanks to God for the mystery of the eucharist. That silence should not be broken by announcements. The communion prayer concludes the communion rite. The silence prepares us for the prayer.

After the prayer, though, come the announcements. Yes, the people will be standing. Ordinarily, the announcements should be brief and will not inconvenience the assembly.

When preparing announcements, here are some principles to keep in mind:

- *The announcer:* Ordinarily, the cantor or commentator makes the announcements. In some communities, a series of people from different aspects of parish life give reports and invitations. In others, the priest takes on this role. Most important is that the announcements be proclaimed in a way that people can understand them. The priest's role at the Mass is to lead people in prayer, so the exchange of information at this part of the Mass is not properly part of his role. However, when he does make announcements, his role lends more weight to them. This may have beneficial or deleterious effects. Think through what makes most sense for your community.

- *The place:* Announcements should be made from the cantor stand, not from the ambo. If the presider or deacon makes the announcements, he may do so from his chair.

- *Common good:* Include items that pertain to the common good of the people. Announce the things you really want everyone to know about, either because their attendance is invited or because knowledge of the event is important to them.

- *This week:* Ordinarily, announce events that take place this week, not in two weeks, not next month. There are exceptions, but spoken announcements should be quick reminders of events happening before this assembly will meet again.

- *Dates, times and places:* Ordinarily, do announce the date (Monday night, Thursday afternoon) but not necessarily the exact time and place. People cannot remember much spoken information, especially at the end of the eucharist. Times and places should appear in the bulletin and on the website where people can refer to them. If the pastoral council meets Wednesday night at 7:00 PM in the Dorothy Day room, put all that in the bulletin, but announce only that the pastoral council meets Wednesday night.

- *Phone numbers:* Never announce phone numbers—no exceptions. No one will remember them. They clutter the announcements.

- *Number of words:* If your announcements tend to go on too long, limit the words. You can do this by limiting the lines of type on the printed page or by actually counting the announced words. Keep the total words under 200, or even under 150 if you can. That means crossing out extraneous information, or just announcing headlines instead of details. Some exceptional communities want a lot of announcements and a lot of details. They may have them, but most would rather not.

- *Last minute requests:* Just because someone missed the deadline for the bulletin, tardiness gives no license for a spoken announcement. Help people meet deadlines by setting up some standards for what goes into spoken announcements and what stays out.

- *Exceptions:* Sometimes you may need to have a longer announcement. For example, the social justice committee may want to update the entire assembly about their efforts to support upcoming legislation. Consider this: After the communion prayer, the deacon or presider invites everyone to be seated for the announcements. The presider invites the speaker from the committee to come forward, thus demonstrating his support. The speaker limits comments to five minutes. Afterward, the remaining announcements are given while everyone remains seated. Then all stand. In most communities, you may follow this procedure several times a year, but probably not every week.

The greeting follows the announcements. The presider says, "The Lord be with you," and all respond. This greeting introduces the blessing and dismissal.

The deacon or presider then may give the invitation, "Bow your heads and pray for God's blessing." If you are using a solemn blessing, you have probably discovered that people do not have a clear cue for answering "Amen" to each of the three petitions. For a while, it might help if they hear the direction, "Bow your heads, pray for God's blessing and answer Amen to the prayers." Or the presider may sing the threefold blessing, and all will sing Amen from the musical cue.

The deacon gives the dismissal. If there is no deacon, the presider does so. You could occasionally sing the dismissal dialogue to a simple chant.

The closing hymn never appears in the rubrics for Mass. It is a custom widely observed throughout the Catholic world, but the liturgy does not mention it. The procession out is less grand than the procession in. Incense and the book of the gospels may be carried coming in, but they are not carried out. The rubrics imply that the recessional happens immediately after the dismissal. In some communities, the instrumentalists play music while the ministers and the assembly leave. A good organist will have an unending repertoire to fill this need.

The advantage of having instrumental music at the end of the eucharist is that the words of the dismissal take on more authority. The community is sent forth into the world—and they go! A closing song gives a strong ending to the Mass as it does for musical comedies and operas. But closing music may send the assembly out more directly to love and serve the Lord.

The Book of Blessings

PLAN ahead to offer blessings for certain groups in the parish. Occasions for blessings might include wedding anniversaries (ch. 1-IIIA), Father's Day (56), birthdays (1-XI), thanksgiving after harvest (28) and athletic events (29). Blessings for people might include engaged couples (ch. 1-VI), catechists (4-I), and students and teachers (5). Things to be blessed could include cars (21), boats and fishing gear (22), tools (24) and Thanksgiving Day food (58).

These blessings may be incorporated into Mass, or you could provide texts for people to pray at home.

The Rite of Christian Initiation of Adults

WHENEVER someone expresses interest in church membership we should be ready to respond. Too many parishes say, "Classes begin in September," and they lose opportunities for evangelizing. Promote welcome to the church at various times of the year by having the Rite of Acceptance into the Order of Catechumens and the Rite of Welcoming Baptized Adults for Confirmation and/or Eucharist more than once. The unbaptized who become catechumens through the Rite of Acceptance establish an important relationship with the church supported by our liturgical and canonical documents. There is no relationship between the liturgical calendar and the Rite of Acceptance. It should be celebrated when one or more inquirers are ready to become catechumens.

Plan the dates for the Rite of Acceptance when nothing else is scheduled. If it comes at the same Mass when there is a second collection, a presentation of awards or a commissioning of ministers, you will take advantage of the assembly's good will.

The baptism of adults should be reserved to the Easter Vigil, except in the most exceptional circumstances. On the other hand, the Rite of Reception into the Full Communion of the Catholic Church can be celebrated at any time of year. If baptized candidates desire communion in the Catholic church, we may receive them when they are ready. Such celebrations may take place several times a year.

When people realize that the preparation for sacraments has some fluidity, they are more likely to follow the promptings of the Spirit. They may be more receptive to our efforts for evangelization.

■ GROUPS OF CATECHUMENS may have celebrations of the word of God throughout this period of Ordinary Time. This is the period when they may be anointed with the oil of catechumens. The anointing may be given on one or more occasions, either in a word service, or as part of the liturgy of the word at a eucharist. This ritual may take place at Sunday Mass, for example.

■ MYSTAGOGY SESSIONS may continue throughout Ordinary Time as well. The American bishops have recommended such gatherings monthly during the first year following baptism (*National Statutes,* 24). Attendance is usually quite low, but we may promote these events at Sunday Mass. Attempts should be made to give pastoral care to neophytes who are experiencing the fullness of the eucharist throughout the liturgical year for the first time.

■ THE PRESENTATIONS OF THE CREED AND THE LORD'S PRAYER may take place outside the season of Lent. This option may help parishes who find the liturgies of Lent overly burdensome, or whose catechumens seem ready for them and would benefit by having the Creed and Lord's Prayer now as part of their formation. In the history of the catechumenate, however, these rites always came shortly before baptism.

The second form of the sacrament, a communal celebration with individual confession and absolution, frequently appears on a parish's Advent and Lent schedule of activities. But it may happen at any time of year. Although attendance may be smaller during summer or fall, you could offer the sacrament communally for those who would like this opportunity. It could be combined with an evening's retreat for the parish, a school service, or even during the regularly scheduled time for private confessions, to invite those who come individually to acknowledge the communal nature of sin and forgiveness.

The third form of the rite, with the general confession and general absolution of sins, is used only rarely, in extraordinary circumstances after the diocesan bishop has determined that a grave necessity exists for its celebration.

The Liturgy of the Hours

VOLUMES III and IV of the *Liturgy of the Hours* will be used throughout summer and fall. For those unfamiliar with this form of prayer, Ordinary Time is a good time to begin. The editing of the books is simpler during this time than in the other seasons of the year, and those using the one- or four-volume set discover that the prayer requires fewer ribbons and flipping of pages these days.

If a daily Mass is not taking place on one or more days a week or a month, try celebrating morning, midday or evening prayer instead of a communion service to introduce people to this liturgy.

The Rite of Penance

MOST parishes will continue offering the first form of the Rite of Penance every week, usually on Saturday. However, private confession and absolution may be celebrated any day of the week, and if the priest's schedule permits it, you could try offering reconciliation on a weekday evening or Saturday morning.

The Pastoral Care of the Sick

THE sacrament of the anointing of the sick may take place any time of year for the benefit of the faithful. Ordinary Time is a good period to give this sacrament attention, when no other seasons are vying for attention. Choose one or two weekends this summer or fall when the sacrament may be offered at a communal celebration. Or schedule it at a daily Mass for those who might benefit from it.

It is important that the faithful receive catechesis on viaticum. Many times they may confuse "Last Rites" with viaticum and anointing of the sick. Any lay minister may give viaticum, or "last communion," if a priest is unavailable. Prayers for the dying and prayers for the dead may be led by any lay minister. A priest can offer the anointing of the sick with its prayers for healing apart from emergency situations. Help the faithful understand when it is important for a sick relative or friend to receive the pastoral care of the church.

The Rite of Marriage

Marriage may be offered any time of year, many day of the week, but Saturday weddings are still popular in the culture. If the couple comes from two different faith backgrounds, be sure to consider the option of marriage without Mass. Especially if the guests are unfamiliar with the Catholic Mass, the wedding that takes place during a word service puts the members of the assembly on more equal footing. At Mass, the communion rite becomes an important sign of the couple's unity, but if one partner is not Catholic, the symbols of unity begin to break down.

The readings and prayers of the wedding Mass may replace those of an Ordinary Time Sunday Mass if the wedding takes place on a Saturday evening. However, on solemnities, the Mass of the day should be used, and you may substitute one of the readings from the wedding lectionary (*Rite of Marriage,* 11). The Mass prayers for a wedding on those days should come from the feast, not from the *Rite of Marriage*.

But if the wedding takes place on those dates without Mass, the wedding lectionary and the prayers from the *Rite of Marriage* are used.

The Rites of Ordination and Profession

Few parishes will be responsible for the ordination rites of a diocese or the rites of profession within a religious community, but if yours has one this year it will be a time of celebration and renewal for the whole community. In preparing the liturgy, remember that an ordination is not a coronation. The humble, circumspect life of service that the candidates enter should be evident also from the liturgy.

If your parish has no candidates for the diaconate or priesthood or for religious life, this would be a good season to ask why. Does the parish have a vocations committee? Are you suggesting to men and women that they consider the religious life? Could the parish schedule an annual event, perhaps a Mass for religious vocations, to which you invite seminarians or religious to speak?

The Order of Christian Funerals

During the summer months, when many in the community are on vacation, it may be difficult to offer full liturgical ministries for funerals, but it is good to make an effort. Volunteers may be available in your community to support a funeral choir, the ministry of greeter, altar servers and cooks for a post-funeral dinner. The development of these ministries will make the funeral a good celebration for the departed Christian, and it will bring much consolation to a family at a time when they need the support of faith.

Evaluate the wake service, too. The *Order of Christian Funerals* calls for a word service. Celebrating this service at church has some advantages. The church is set up with furnishings and participation aids for a liturgy, and will be more conducive to common prayer than many funeral chapels.

The wake service is called a vigil in the *Order of Christian Funerals*. The official text does not include a rosary, nor does it suggest that it be substituted with a rosary. When people gather on the night before the funeral, the church invites them to prayer that includes scripture. The scripture service is more inviting to all Christians and more faithfully proclaims the mystery of the resurrection than the rosary does.

When the wake service is announced in the newspaper, what title does it carry? Its proper name is vigil.

If the deceased is to be buried in the earth, the funeral rite strongly recommends that the faithful be present for this action. It may take the cooperation of cemetery officials, funeral homes, parish staff and families, but the gathering of the faithful around the actual moment of burial can provide a strong statement of unity and faith in the resurrection. The interment takes place near the beginning of the service at the cemetery, and more prayers are then offered by the faithful who stand, strong in faith, above the grave.

Catholics may choose cremation, and the cremated remains may be brought to the church for the funeral Mass. Ashes should be interred in the ground or in a columbarium where mourners and admirers may come for future generations to remember the deceased. The Catholic church does not support the practice of spreading ashes in the air, over water or on the ground.

The Art and Environment

THE verdure of summer and fall should make its appearance in our worship spaces as well. Be sure to decorate throughout the church, not just the sanctuary. The gathering area and the nave deserve attention so as to facilitate the participation of all the members of the assembly in their liturgy.

■ SHIFTS IN THE LITURGICAL ENVIRONMENT may subtly accompany the shifts of nature. As the community makes a mental adjustment from summer's relaxation to fall's energy, the environment of the liturgical space might change to reflect the different flowers and plants of late summer and early fall. Even the vessels may change: Clay pots and planters of early summer might yield to glass vases as summer progresses, just as metal vases and then woven baskets and a cornucopia could come on the scene as autumn approaches.

■ VESTURE SHOULD APPEAR UNOBTRUSIVE AND NEUTRAL. The very frequency of green garments during the next six months will dull our senses to the fabric. If the vesture tries to do too much, it will lose the sense of ordinariness and threaten the effect of more dramatic vesture for other feasts and seasons. What does your green vesture look like? Is it time for something new?

The Music

CHOOSE a set of music for the eucharistic acclamations for summer, and replace it with another set sometime in fall, perhaps over Labor Day weekend when many people make the mental shift from summer calendar to school calendar.

Two very different settings are worth a look: "Jubilation Mass, by James Chepponis (GIA G-5045EP) and "Mass of Rejoicing, by John Angotti (WLP 7366). You won't believe how much difference there is between "jubilation" and "rejoicing." The "Jubilation Mass" is actually a very simple, chant-like setting that succeeds because it does not try to do too much. The sung eucharistic prayer, for example, works because it is understated. The "Mass of Rejoicing," however, demands a lot of energy. It is perfectly suited for youth groups ready to belt out a rhythmic celebration of our faith.

If you would like to add some music to the repertoire, you have a long period in which this can be accomplished. The following are worth consideration:

- "Enter with a Song," by Paul Inwood, a challenge at first with its unexpected rhythms, but delivering excitement at the celebration's beginning
- "Speak Now, O Lord," by Joe Mattingly (WLP 5204), a soul-stirring prayer of openness to God's word
- "On the Wings of Change," by Jerry Galipeau (WLP 5209), a trumpet-like statement of faith in the resurrection
- "Christ Be Near at Either Hand," by Steven C. Warner (WLP 7200), an effective setting of the Lorica of St. Patrick
- "Gather Your People," by Robert Schaefer (WLP 8691), a setting of Psalm 95 that sets the tone for an important celebration by nicely accompanying a lengthy procession
- "Come to the Living Stone," by Karen Schneider-Kirner and Steven C. Warner (WLP 7243), a rhythmic invitation to prayer
- "Where Armies Scourge the Countryside," by Herman G. Stuempfle, Jr., and Perry Nielson (WLP 8641), a fitting setting for a beautiful text praying for peace
- "Love Is His Word," by Calvin Hampton, arranged by Richard Proulx (WLP 8677), a lovely setting of a hymn that already was lovely
- "Open Wide the Doors to Christ," arr. by Peter M. Kolar (WLP 8683), a quickly learned hymn that assemblies will enjoy
- "Take Courage," by Ruth Duck and Steven R. Janco (WLP 8702), a hymn text that meets a sentiment we all need sooner or later, in a musical setting that fits perfectly
- "Go, Be Justice," by Martin Willett and Kevin Keil (WLP 8710), a challenge to the assembly to put faith into action
- "Wisdom, My Road," by Leslie Palmer Barnhart, based on a text from Ecclesiasticus adapted by

Steven C. Warner (WLP 7263), a lovely prayer for wisdom

- "Draw Near," by Steven R. Janco, based on John M. Neale's translation of a seventh-century hymn (WLP 8567), part of a growing body of communion hymns that finally invites the faithful to share under both forms

A youth choir could build its repertoire, too, either as a summer activity for those attending different schools, or as an opportunity in the fall when education resumes.

- "Gathered as One," by Paul A. Tate (WLP 7452), a lightly syncopated hymn of unity
- "Journey for Home," by Ed Bolduc (WLP 7437), a pleading song of the spiritual life
- "Sing Alleluia!" by John Angotti (WLP 7431), a simple tune that becomes a driving statement of faith
- "God's Holy Mystery," by Paul A. Tate (WLP 7488), a communion song of faith based on the sixth chapter of John's gospel, especially useful late this summer
- "Lay Down That Spirit," by Joe Mattingly (WLP 3674), an energetic song of plea and praise
- Several pieces worth considering by Tony Alonso: "We Stand in Wonder of Creation" (GIA G-5611), with a title that says it all; "Grant Us Peace, Lord" (GIA G-5610), a gentle prayer; "Fresh as the Morning" (GIA G-5602), with words by Shirley Erena Murray, bouncing with energetic joy
- "Strength for the Journey," by Michael John Poirier (WLP 8122), a pulsating song of gentle assurance, with just the right syncopation in the refrain

For children between the ages 8 to 12, see "Great Stories & Songs" (GIA G-5781). GIA has made available a collection compiled in New Zealand. The book is filled with activities for kids and includes songs to help form young Christians.

A similar age group will respond well to *Singing Our Faith,* a hymnal for children (GIA G-5550). The collection of songs is available with accompaniment books and a catechist's manual providing an overview to the *Directory for Masses with Children.*

Lynn M. Trapp has set to music "Eucharistic Prayer II for Masses with Children"—one of the prayers that demands to be sung (WLP 7131).

You may also want to expand your knowledge of music that suits particular needs, like the following:

- "Mass of Redemption," by Steven R. Janco (WLP 3110), another fine setting of texts for the Mass that will hold up even with much repetition
- "Glory to God," by Steven R. Janco (WLP 8559), an easily sung setting for assembly with cantor or choir

- "Light Serene of Holy Glory," by Chrysogonus Waddell (WLP 7271), sets the classic evening text "Phos hilaron"
- "Vespers: A Service of Evening Prayer," by Carla J. Giomo (GIA G-5252), a complete setting of music for evening prayer
- "Magnificat," by Alan J. Hommerding" (WLP 5208), written with a choir in mind, but immediately singable by the assembly at evening prayer
- "Canticle of Zechariah," by Carl P. Daw, Jr., and Steven R. Janco (WLP 8708), a carefully composed text, tune and accompaniment of this song for morning prayer
- "The Guardian's Farewell," by David Haas (GIA G-5658), an achingly moving setting of a powerful text for funerals
- "Song of Farewell," by Mary Beth Wittry (WLP 5225), a song you could introduce on Sundays in the fall, so people can sing it throughout the year at funerals
- "Song of Farewell," by Michael Perza (WLP 5239), beautifully interpreting the text, very effective by a soloist at a funeral, but also by an assembly
- "May Angels Lead You into Paradise," by Richard Proulx (WLP 5227), for those looking for a setting of the *In paradisum* that closes the funeral Mass. (Even Michael Joncas wishes you would find something more fitting for this part of the rite than "On Eagle's Wings.")
- "As We Forgive," by James V. Marchionda (WLP 7117), a song for children about reconciliation.

You may also wish to examine some other resources for hymns. Too many collections abound to name them all, but the following are worth a look:

- *African American Heritage Hymnal* (GIA G-5400)
- *Hymns, Psalms, and Spiritual Songs* (Louisville: Westminster/John Knox Press, 1990)
- *Libro de Liturgia y Cántico* (Minneapolis: Augsburg Fortress, 1998)
- *Flor y Canto, segunda edición* (OCP 10652)
- *This Far by Faith: An African American Resource for Worship* (Minneapolis: Augsburg Fortress, 1999)
- *Unidos en Cristo / United in Christ* (OCP)
- *The United Methodist Hymnal: Book of United Methodist Worship* (Nashville: The United Methodist Publishing House, 1989)
- *Voices United: The Hymn and Worship Book of the United Church of Canada* (Ontario: The United Church Publishing House, 1996)

Pianists should be aware of *Fourteen American Spirituals & Hymns,* by Ann Buys (GIA G-5322).

The Parish and Home

DURING summer people may have more leisure for quiet time with God and even family prayer in common. Provide resources for summer reading and prayer. *I Will Lie Down This Night* and *I Will Arise This Day* by Melissa Musick Nussbaum are lovely introductions to prayer at evening and morning. For those who wish to do more, *Proclaim Praise!* is a fine, simple introduction to praying morning and evening prayer at home. All are available from LTP.

Families may enjoy having copies of LTP's *Table Prayer Card for Summer* and *Table Prayer Card for Autumn and Winter* (1995), an inexpensive purchase available in bulk.

Texts

■ GREETING: Sacramentaries of other language groups includes this greeting:

> The Lord of glory and the giver of every grace be with you.

A greeting based on the opening of the letter to the Colossians is:

> May grace and peace from God our Father be with you.

■ INTRODUCTION TO THE PENITENTIAL RITE: Try an introduction inspired by the second letter to the Thessalonians:

> May the Lord direct our hearts to the love of God and to the endurance of Christ. Let us call to mind God's mercy for our sins.

■ RESPONSE TO THE GENERAL INTERCESSIONS:

> Have mercy on your people, Lord.

> God of glory, hear our prayer.

■ DISMISSAL OF CATECHUMENS:

> The Lord will rescue us from every evil threat and will bring us safe to his heavenly kingdom. To God be glory forever and ever. Go in peace.

May

31 MON
#572 (LMC #302) white
The Visitation of the Virgin Mary to Elizabeth
FEAST

Civic Holiday in the U.S.A.: Memorial Day ▪ In the Middle Ages, the story of the visitation used to be proclaimed on July 2, to commemorate the deposition of Mary's robe at a church in Constantinople. In 1389, at the urgings of the Franciscans, a feast of the Visitation became assigned to the universal church on that day. In today's calendar the feast has been moved forward, where it creates a sequence of events from the Annunciation (March 25) to the Visitation (May 31) to the Birth of John the Baptist (June 24).

Choose one of the options for the first reading, Zephaniah's cry of joy foreshadowing the child's womb-enclosed leap of joy, or Paul's admonition to hospitality from Romans. The canticle from Isaiah prophesies that the Holy One is in the midst of Zion, an image of the expectant mother of God. The gospel narrates the story of the feast.

Prayers for the feast are under May 31 in the sacramentary. Sing the Glory to God. The second preface of Mary (P 57) is based on today's gospel text, the *Magnificat*.

In the *Collection of Masses of the Blessed Virgin Mary* you will find a set of solemn blessings for Ordinary Time at the end of the order of Mass. The first option calls Jesus "the blessed fruit of Mary's womb."

▪ IN ARGENTINA the Monday after Pentecost celebrates Mary, Mother of the Church, a title bestowed by Pope Paul VI at the end of the third session of the Second Vatican Council. See the *Collection of Masses of the Blessed Virgin Mary* (#25–27). See also the votive Mass in Appendix X of the sacramen-

tary. This year, this remembrance coincides with the Visitation.

▪ TODAY IS MEMORIAL DAY IN THE UNITED STATES. Some celebrations may take place at the cemetery. The *Book of Blessings* (ch. 57), provides an order for visiting a cemetery today. So does *Catholic Household Blessings and Prayers* (pp. 178, 280). At Mass, consider pausing during the eucharistic prayer and allow members of the assembly to mention aloud the names of the dead for whom they wish to pray.

June

1 TUE
#354 (LMC #193–227) red
Justin, martyr (+ 165) (Ninth Week in Ordinary Time)
MEMORIAL

As we return to Ordinary Time weekdays, the first readings are drawn from the second letter of Peter, one of the seven "general" or "catholic" epistles of the New Testament. These epistles, grouped as non-Pauline books, are addressed to a general audience and not to a specific church. Today's passage is actually the last of the weekday lectionary's series of excerpts from these epistles. However, because of the timing of Lent and Easter this year, the series began before Lent with passages from James, took a lengthy hiatus, and ends today.

One reason the second letter of Peter is dated near the end of the first century is because of its concern over the delay in the coming of God's day. Today's passage tries to calm the fears of those growing impatient. The psalmist reminds us that a thousand years in God's sight are like yesterday.

During this stretch of Ordinary Time we will hear the end of Mark's gospel and then a series of passages from Matthew and Luke.

The weekdays present these gospels in what most scholars concur is their order of composition.

We resume the story today in the second half of Mark's gospel, as Jesus is making his way toward Jerusalem and the cross. We meet him in the midst of controversy, no surprise to any student of the life of Jesus. The Herodians and Pharisees attempt to catch Jesus in his speech, provoking his famous dictum, "Give to Caesar." The plot against the Savior grows stronger.

▪ TODAY'S SAINT: Justin defended the faith in his *Apologies* and *Dialogue*, but his earnestness gained him enemies, and he suffered martyrdom in one of the early persecutions of Christians in Rome. He is frequently quoted in the *Catechism of the Catholic Church*, notably with a description of the early eucharist (#1345). His loyalty and devotion to the liturgy are remembered in the presidential prayers for his day. The lectionary's proper of saints suggests readings about faith, deliverance and evangelization, but the readings of the weekday are recommended.

2 WED
#355 (LMC #193–227) green
Weekday

Optional Memorial of Marcellinus and Peter (+ 304), martyrs / red ▪ The Sadducees make sport of Jesus' belief in the resurrection. He rebukes them with words, but in the days before his death, he will soon rebuke them with his mighty deed.

The second letter of Timothy is one of the pastoral epistles. Paul's authorship is doubtful, but the letter gives us a good glimpse into ecclesial life and ministry in the first century. Today Paul calls upon Timothy to be faithful to the Spirit he received through the imposition of hands, and to serve the gospel with faithfulness. The trust in God that characterizes this letter appears also in the spirit of today's psalm.

The sacramentary includes prayers for a Mass of the Holy Spirit.

■ TODAY'S SAINTS: Marcellinus was a priest in Rome, and Peter is said to have been an exorcist. They were among the Christians martyred under Diocletian, but little is known of them. As early Roman martyrs, their names appear in the first eucharistic prayer. The lectionary's proper of saints suggests readings about suffering and hatred, but the readings of the weekday are recommended.

THU 3 — #298 (LMC #193–227) red
Charles Lwanga catechist, martyr; and his companions, martyrs (+ 1885–1887)
MEMORIAL

Though near his death, Jesus is still able to preach a sublime summary of his message: the two great commandments. In a way, it serves as the final testimony of his life.

Even though the writer of the letter is in chains, the word of God runs free. That message will be stronger when the reader of the letter lives by it. The psalmist invites us to pray in cooperation with the divine plan, "Teach me your ways, O Lord."

■ TODAY'S SAINT: The faith spread throughout Africa in the nineteenth century, but it also met persecution. Charles Lwanga, a catechist and youth leader, was martyred with a group of Catholic and Anglican friends. Paul VI canonized these martyrs in 1964 in Uganda, and invited the Anglican archbishop to be present. That archbishop, Janai Luwum, later suffered martyrdom under Idi Amin.

The prayers for today are under June 3. The preface is that of martyrs (P 66). The lectionary's proper

of saints suggests readings about martyrdom and holiness, but the readings of the weekday are recommended.

■ IN ALL THE DIOCESES OF LATIN AMERICA, the Thursday before Trinity Sunday is the feast of Jesus Christ, High and Eternal Priest. In Colombia the feast is celebrated on the Thursday after Pentecost, but that is the same day.

■ BLESSED JOHN XXIII, POPE: "In my window," wrote Angelo Roncalli in his diary, "a little light must always shine, so that anyone may knock and enter and find a friend." That light shone one day over St. Peter's Square and the whole world found a friend in "Good Pope John." Today is the forty-first anniversary of the death of Pope John XXIII, who was beatified in the jubilee year of 2000. His vision for the church opened windows and began a long period of transformation.

FRI 4 — #357 (LMC #193–227) green
Weekday

Is Jesus the Messiah? The scribes claim no, that the Messiah was the son of David. But Jesus says David referred to the Messiah as Lord, a designation not appropriate to one's own son. As Jesus' death draws near, he draws very close to asserting his own divinity.

The writer of 2 Timothy praises Timothy for observing the author's teaching and conduct. In the face of persecution, he must remain faithful. Timothy has not only followed the author, he has also followed the scriptures. Today's passage concludes with a famous verse about the divine inspiration of all sacred scripture. In response, we sing verses from a psalm that praises God's word and law.

The fourth eucharistic prayer traces the life of Jesus and his messianic deeds.

SAT 5 — #358 (LMC #193–227) red
Boniface (+ 754), bishop, monastic, martyr
MEMORIAL

The series of readings from Mark's gospel concludes today as Jesus praises the poor widow who gives all she owns to the temple treasury. He himself is about to do the same as he offers his life on the cross. He expects his disciples to give everything for the sake of the gospel.

The readings from the second letter to Timothy also conclude today. The author urges Timothy to preach the word whether convenient or inconvenient. Anticipating his own martyrdom, he says, "I have fought the good fight. I have finished the race. I have kept the faith." The psalmist looks back over life and sings of God, "who has taught me from my youth."

■ TODAY'S SAINT: Born in England, accepted into a monastery, Boniface eventually found his vocation in preaching to those who had not yet heard the gospel in what is today Germany. He resigned as abbot but accepted a post as bishop of Mainz. He was martyred while traveling to administer confirmation.

The opening prayer comes from June 5 in the sacramentary. Options exist for the other presidential prayers. Those for missionaries have not recently been in use. The preface for pastors (P 67) could also be used in place of the one for martyrs that appeared earlier this week. The lectionary's proper of saints suggests readings about preaching and leadership in the face of opposition, but the readings of the weekday are recommended.

■ THE SATURDAY FOLLOWING PENTECOST used to be a traditional day for the ordination of priests. You might remember vocations, seminarians and priests in the general intercessions today.

6 The Holy Trinity
#166 (LMC #160)
SOLEMNITY

ORIENTATION

It's hard to imagine anyone disagreeing with the idea of a feast for the Trinity, but proposals for creating this festival met severe opposition in the Middle Ages. Pope John XXII finally declared it a feast for the universal church in 1334, while the papacy had its residence in Avignon, away from Rome, but near places where Trinity Sunday was already observed. The feast celebrates our belief in Father, Son and Spirit, one God in three divine persons.

LECTIONARY

Today's gospel comes from John's account of Jesus' farewell discourse. He promises the Spirit of truth, who will take what belongs to Jesus and declare it to his followers. "Everything that the Father has is mine," Jesus says. We see the close link between the majesty of the Father, the mission of the Son and the work of the Holy Spirit.

The second reading is a beautiful passage from Romans. Paul reassures the community that the love of God has been poured out into their hearts through the Holy Spirit. Again, the passage is

chosen because it shows the unified yet diverse work of the individual members of the Trinity.

In the first reading, the wisdom of God speaks. God poured wisdom onto the world from the beginning as an agent of creation. Even though Jesus was born in time and sent the Holy Spirit after his death, the Trinity was present from the beginning of time, evidenced by the pre-existent wisdom of God. When we read Proverbs through Christian eyes, we behold with awe the eternal work of the Trinity. A psalm of creation follows this reading.

These texts are located in the lectionary after the Sundays of Ordinary Time. They are sometimes difficult to find, so allow extra time to set the place.

SACRAMENTARY

Prayers for today are located after the Sundays of Ordinary Time. Be sure the place is marked before the eucharist begins.

The alternative opening prayer boldly addresses all three members of the Trinity. The formula is unique in the sacramentary. There is a preface for Trinity Sunday (P 43).

OTHER IDEAS

Even though the celebratory tone of Easter continues, the church year has entered Ordinary Time. This will not be immediately evident to the gathered Sunday assembly, as it should be on weekdays. But it would be appropriate to simplify the environment of the worship space to set this Sunday off from last. You may wish to change the eucharistic prayer acclamations this week as well. If you used the sprinkling rite during the Easter season, go back to the penitential rite today.

If your community still observes the Catholic practice of limiting hymns to two verses, be sure not to omit a verse to the Holy Spirit on Trinity Sunday.

William Tortolano has arranged John Taverner's "In nomine, gloria tibi trinitas" for string quartet or brass quartet with optional voices (GIA G-5271). It isn't clear from the introductory notes just how the arranger envisions all this fitting together, but it is lovely music however you do it.

M O N 7 Weekday (Tenth Week in Ordinary Time)
#359 (LMC #193–227)   green

Having concluded the series of readings from Mark last week, we now begin to hear from Matthew. Matthew probably used Mark to compose his gospel, while drawing on a collection of sayings of Jesus that Luke also knew, as well as his own sources.

Many people find it helpful to think of Matthew's story as a collection of five discourses by Jesus, framed by narrative accounts of his life. We do not begin reading from Matthew at the beginning of the gospel, where we find the story of Jesus' birth, an account more fitting in December than in June. Instead, we start at the first discourse, the famous Sermon on the Mount, which begins with the well-known Beatitudes. Jesus' care for the poor in spirit stands as a manifesto for his ministry.

Selections from Matthew will serve as the gospel for daily Mass from now through the end of August.

Today's first reading begins a series from the historical and prophetic books of the Old Testament. They tell the story of the prophets, leading up to Israel's exile. This series will continue until the last week of August. We open today with the prophet Elijah, powerful in word, ascetic in practice.

With the psalmist he could pray that his help came only from God.

Eucharistic Prayer IV gives a summary of Jesus' ministry, making it a possible choice for the day we begin to hear Matthew's gospel.

TUE 8 #360 (LMC #193–227)   green
Weekday

Stepping into the Sermon on the Mount, we hear Jesus' famous comparison of disciples to salt and light. Both elements can be unproductive, but put to proper use they symbolize the ways Christians glorify the Father.

In a time of famine, the Lord sends Elijah to a poor widow, whom Elijah asks for bread. She obliges the prophet, and in return for her kindness she receives a miraculously unending supply of flour and oil. The psalm says God answers the call of those in need and puts gladness into their hearts more than when grain and wine abound.

Under the category of useless trivia, note the refrains for the psalm for this day in years one and two of the lectionary. This year we sing from Psalm 4, "Lord, let your face shine on us." Next year, on the same Tuesday of week ten, we sing from Psalm 119, "Lord, let your face shine on me." Plural one year, singular the next. Go figure.

WED 9 #361 (LMC #193–227)   green
Weekday

Optional Memorial of Ephrem, deacon, poet and doctor of the church (+ 373), white ▪ Today's gospel continues the Sermon on the Mount from Matthew. Jesus expresses that his role is to fulfill the law and the prophets.

Elijah challenges the people to make their allegiance either to God or to Baal. He holds a contest of the gods to see which is more powerful. The psalmist promises

not to pour out blood libations to other gods.

The third preface for weekdays (P 39) with its appeal to the obedience of all creation, might make a good choice today.

▪ TODAY'S SAINT: Ephrem is the only Syrian honored as a doctor of the church. His evocative poetry also earned him the title "Harp of the Holy Spirit." A theological journal published in India today is named after him. The lectionary's proper of saints suggests readings about the importance of love and putting faith into action, but the readings of the weekday are recommended.

THU 10 #362 (LMC #193–227)   green
Weekday

Jesus urges his hearers to get along. When bringing a gift to the altar, if you remember a conflict with a brother or sister, first make peace and then offer the gift.

At Elijah's prayer, rain returns. He then outruns Ahab to Jezreel. Both incidents show God's mighty power, and the psalmist praises God for the gift of rain.

The second eucharistic prayer for Masses of reconciliation says, "enemies begin to speak to one another."

▪ IN BOLIVIA, CUBA, the Dominican Republic, El Salvador, Mexico, Nicaragua, Puerto Rico and Venezuela, today is the solemnity of the Body and Blood of the Lord (see this coming Sunday), a holy day of obligation in those places.

FRI 11 #580, 363 (LMC #310, 193–227)   white
Barnabas, apostle
MEMORIAL

You may take the gospel from the weekday in sequence—Jesus' position on lust, adultery and divorce. Or you may draw it from June 11 (#580)—Jesus' missionary command to the disciples. The

first reading, though, comes from June 11, the passage from Acts of the Apostles regarding Barnabas' ministry in Antioch.

Barnabas is an apostle like Paul, not one of "the Twelve." He is remembered with a memorial rather than a feast on the liturgical calendar. This is one apostle whose celebration does not call for singing the Glory to God. Use a preface for apostles, perhaps the first (P 64). Barnabas is mentioned in Eucharistic Prayer I.

SAT 12 #364 (LMC #193–227)   green
Weekday

Optional Memorial of the Blessed Virgin Mary/white ▪ Jesus continues his advice on interpersonal behavior and asks his listeners not to take false oaths.

Elisha becomes the attendant of Elijah, but first he must turn away from his former way of life. The psalmist pledges allegiance to God, who provides refuge.

From the *Collection of Masses of the Blessed Virgin Mary* see the texts for Holy Mary, the New Eve (#20), with its opening prayer that we may reject the old ways of sin.

▪ IN ECUADOR, today is the memorial of Blessed Mercedes de Jesús Molina (+ 1883), a local woman who founded a religious community for the care of poor and orphan girls.

#169 (LMC #163) white

13 The Body and Blood of Christ
SOLEMNITY

ORIENTATION

In 1208 Juliana of Retinnes, an Augustinian nun from Belgium, saw a vision of a lunar disk surrounded by rays of dazzling white light. One side of the disk appeared dark, and in her vision she heard God tell her the darkness represented no feast on the calendar to honor the Blessed Sacrament. When her friend James Pantaléon became Pope Urban IV, he extended the feast of Corpus Christi to the universal church.

The origin of the feast shows the influence of an age when the faithful never shared the blood of Christ at communion, rarely shared even the body of Christ due to penitential practices, but adored the real presence of Christ in the reserved eucharistic host as their vicarious participation in divine life. Today's calendar combines this medieval feast with the formerly and strangely separate feast of the Blood of Christ into a single celebration.

LECTIONARY

The texts are found just after Trinity Sunday, in the section of the lectionary following the Sundays in Ordinary Time.

The same Pope Urban IV asked Thomas Aquinas to compose several hymns for the new celebration. One of them, "Lauda Sion," still appears in the lectionary as an optional sequence after the second reading.

The second reading for today is traditional for this occasion, but it appears only in Year C of the cycle. Paul was the first writer in the New Testament to record the sharing of the body and blood of Christ at the Last Supper. The gospels were all composed later than this letter.

To prepare us for this reading, the lectionary offers us the verses about Melchizedek from Genesis. This king of Salem (meaning "king of peace") brings out bread and wine for an offering. He appears without parents and his death is not recorded. He is king and priest. He is a symbol of Jesus, priest and king, the eternal God, who offers bread and wine as a servant of peace. The psalm today mentions Melchizedek as a symbol of eternal priesthood.

Today's gospel is Luke's version of the miracle of the loaves. All four gospels recount this event, and they all use the same four eucharistic verbs to describe Jesus' actions: He took, blessed, broke and gave the loaves and fish to the crowds. This miracle of largesse foreshadows the benevolence God shows us in the eucharist.

SACRAMENTARY

Texts for today are found after the Sundays of Ordinary Time, and immediately following Trinity Sunday. To avoid embarrassing minutes of an anxious search, be sure to mark the place before Mass begins.

The suggested communion antiphon comes from the traditional gospel for this solemnity, which is heard in Year A. The presidential

prayers all reflect on the gift of the eucharist. Of the prefaces for Holy Eucharist, the second (P 48) explores the meaning of the eucharist more fully. Eucharistic Prayer I mentions the sacrifice of Melchizedek. It is also a good day to sing the eucharistic prayer.

A solemn blessing for Ordinary Time (#12, for example) could conclude the celebration if there is no eucharistic procession.

The sacramentary's first appendix includes a priest's statement of intention as a preparation for celebrating Mass.

OTHER IDEAS

Music for today's feast is extensive. Look for organ solos based on "Lauda Sion" and "Sacris solemniis." Jean Langlais has one on the latter text in his Livre Oecuménique, playable on the simplest of instruments with almost no demands for pedal technique.

Classic Latin hymns include "Pange lingua," "Tantum ergo," "Adoro te" and "O salutaris hostia." The sequence, "Lauda Sion," is in the *Liber cantualis*. Steve Schaubel's "Jesus Christ, Bread of Life" blends "Adoro te" with the Largo from Dvorák's Symphony No. 9 (From the New World).

Choirs may know Mozart's "Ave verum corpus," but the chant from the *Liber cantualis* also deserves a place in the repertoire.

If your community wants to learn a setting of the Lord's Prayer, try Steven C. Warner's (WLP 7204).

Communion under both forms should be standard practice in the parish by now. If not, this is a good Sunday to begin. After all, this is the solemnity of the body *and* of the blood of Christ.

Holy Communion and Worship of the Eucharist outside Mass (101–8) recommends a procession

to conclude today's Mass or to follow a period of adoration. After the communion prayer of the Mass, a procession may form from the church to another place of worship, where benediction concludes the service. Along the way, the priest may use the monstrance to bless people at various stations. See also the *Ceremonial of Bishops* (387–94) for notes on the procession.

M
O
N
14
#365 (LMC #193–227)   green
**Weekday
(Eleventh Week
in Ordinary Time)**

The Sermon on the Mount continues with Jesus' advice to turn the other cheek. These simple instructions for a charitable life are difficult to observe.

Elijah will become involved in the story that begins today, but at first he stands in the wings while the terrible saga of Naboth, Ahab and Jezebel unfolds. There is no "good news" in the part of the story we hear today, only greed and murder. The murdered Naboth's name hauntingly occurs five times in the final verses of the passage. The psalmist remembers that God hates all evildoers.

The first eucharistic prayer for reconciliation makes a good choice today.

T
U
E
15
#366 (LMC #193–227)   green
Weekday

Jesus' advice to be charitable reaches its climax today: "Love your enemies." This goes farther than the vengeance and tolerance proposed by other parts of the Bible and moves the Christian into a new sphere of forgiveness.

Elijah confronts Ahab with the grim news that his sin will carry severe punishment. But Ahab repents, and God postpones punishment to the next generation.

Consider the second eucharistic prayer for reconciliation.

W
E
D
16
#367 (LMC #193–227)   green
Weekday

Jesus suggests certain actions for his followers to perform—prayer and fasting—but more importantly he suggests the spirit with which to observe them.

"Swing Low, Sweet Chariot" has the image of today's first reading in mind. Elijah is taken up to heaven in a chariot of fire, a symbol of how any believer will come to meet God. The mantle of Elijah passes now to Elisha. The psalm gives comfort to all who hope in the Lord.

The fourth weekday preface (P 40) takes a humble attitude toward prayer.

T
H
U
17
#368 (LMC #193–227)   green
Weekday

We call one prayer "the Lord's" because Jesus taught it to us. Shortly before the baptism of adults, we present the elect with this prayer. They receive it the way we hear it today, as a reading in the gospel. Jesus speaks through his word directly to the ears of believers today. The only part of the prayer he thought needed extra commentary was that line about forgiveness.

The book of Sirach also describes the ascent of Elijah, so it supplies today's first reading. It brings to a close the first part of our series of readings devoted to the history of Israel by honoring this first great prophet. Psalm 97 recalls the ways God uses nature to appear in glory, causing a good man like Elijah to rejoice in the Lord.

Again, the fourth weekday preface (P 40) takes an appropriate stance on the benefits of prayer.

F
R
I
18
#172 (LMC #166)   white
**The Sacred Heart
of Jesus**
SOLEMNITY

ORIENTATION

A latecomer to the liturgical calendar, the solemnity of the Sacred Heart celebrates not an event but the love of God manifested in the heart of Jesus. Devotion to the Sacred Heart grew throughout the late Middle Ages and reached its climax with the visions of Saint Margaret Mary Alacoque. The feast first appeared in the universal church calendar in 1856. It occurs each year on the third Friday after Pentecost. In the United States, it is more easily reckoned as the Friday following the solemnity of the Body and Blood of Christ.

LECTIONARY

Texts are found right after those for the solemnity of the Body and Blood of Christ, in the brief section of solemnities of the Lord that follows the Sundays in Ordinary Time. Be sure to locate the texts for Year C and mark the place ahead of time.

We hear the parable of the sheep owner who leaves 99 behind to search for the lost one. The loving heart of Christ rejoices when a single sinner repents. The psalm echoes this theme, the shepherd who refreshes the singer's soul.

The first reading also continues the theme of shepherding for this solemnity of the heart of Christ. God promises to look after the flock and to seek out those lost and gone astray.

Perhaps sinners best understand the love of God, for when they repent they experience irrevocable acceptance. Paul says God proves this kind of love in Christ's dying for us while we were still sinners. Together these readings probe the mystery of Christ's love especially within the frame of sin and forgiveness.

SACRAMENTARY

Texts are found among the solemnities of the Lord, following the Sundays in Ordinary Time.

Choose from three opening prayers. The first explains the meaning of the day most directly. The preface is proper (P 45). Eucharistic Prayer III makes a good choice on solemnities.

OTHER IDEAS

Draw attention to images of the Sacred Heart in your worship space through a placement of flowers or special lighting.

Many traditional hymns to the Sacred Heart have been omitted from today's hymnals because of their overly sentimental piety. But hymns like "Love Divine, All Loves Excelling" and "I Heard the Voice of Jesus Say" express the thought of the day very well.

A litany of the Sacred Heart can be found in *Catholic Household Blessings and Prayers* (p. 339) and could be used as a devotional element for the faithful today. It could even replace the general intercessions.

#370, 573 (LMC #193–227, 303)

SAT 19 white
The Immaculate Heart of Mary
MEMORIAL

This day entered the liturgy as a corollary to the Sacred Heart of Jesus but takes a lesser liturgical rank. Only during the reign of Pope John Paul II was it elevated from an optional to an obligatory memorial. It is the last celebration of the liturgical year with a date computed from Easter.

The gospel can be found in the back of the lectionary, between May 31 and June 1. It tells of Mary pondering the childhood of Jesus "in her heart."

There is no proper first reading. The suggested one comes from the common of the Blessed Virgin Mary and is recommended probably because it makes a fitting prelude to the *Magnificat,* the suggested responsory. Both imply that Mary's heart is full of joy.

Still, you may choose any first reading from the common of the Blessed Virgin Mary if you wish, and even a different responsory. Alternatively, you could turn back to the reading of the weekday (#370), for the unsavory murder of Zechariah between the sanctuary and the altar. Jesus refers to this event in his tirade against the scribes and Pharisees (Matthew 23:35). The perpetrators of this murder meet their own punishment, and the psalm recalls God's eternal covenant, but all this remains far from the spirit of the memorial today.

The presidential prayers are found in the sacramentary between May 31 and June 1. The preface for Mary, Mother of the Church (Appendix X of the sacramentary), says, "Mary received your word in the purity of her heart."

■ TODAY IS A SOLEMNITY IN ECUADOR, where Mary is patron under this title.

#96 (LMC #91) green

20 Twelfth Sunday in Ordinary Time

ORIENTATION

Today the Sunday celebration makes a clear return to Ordinary Time. After the Lent and Easter seasons we have celebrated the traditional two solemnities that extend a spirit of joy. Although we have had two weeks of daily Ordinary Time, the return of green vestments this Sunday will let people know we are back to business as usual as "liturgical summer" officially begins.

We remember the fathers of the local community on this day set aside in their honor.

LECTIONARY

Luke's gospel divides into two parts and today's passage concludes the first half. Peter's confession that Jesus is the Christ of God brings the first part of Jesus' ministry to its climax. Mark's version of this passage, so pivotal in the synoptic gospels, was suppressed last year, so it has been two years since the Sunday assembly has heard this important story. Recognizing Jesus as the Messiah is a gift from God, but it also brings the consequence of a cross of suffering.

After Jesus died on the cross, John's gospel says a soldier pierced his side with a spear, and blood and water came out (19:37). The evangelist says this fulfilled the prophecy in today's first reading, "They shall look on him whom they have pierced." This oblique reference to the cross prepares us to hear the gospel, even as it promises God's chosen ones a spirit of grace and petition, and a fountain of purification.

Today's psalm comes from the parched throat of one thirsting for God. It fits the image of Israel longing for deliverance, Jesus on the cross, and the faithful Christian who suffers in the midst of faith.

Paul's letter to the Galatians offers us the second reading for several weeks. We join the letter midstream because the preceding Sundays of Ordinary Time were suppressed this year. In the first generation of Christianity, the Jewish followers of Christ became separated from others in Judaism, and the community opened its mission to Gentile converts as well. The letter to the Galatians offers some of the earliest evidence for these trends. In today's excerpt, Paul explains that members of this mixed community of Christians are equals. There is neither Jew nor Greek, slave nor free, male nor female. All are one in Christ Jesus.

SACRAMENTARY

Texts for today are found back with the Sundays of Ordinary Time, a place in the book we have not used for several months. Be sure to mark the place before Mass begins.

If you have not used Eucharistic Prayer IV on Sundays because of seasonal prefaces the last few months, you might return to it today.

OTHER IDEAS

The *Book of Blessings* includes a prayer for Fathers' Day (ch. 56). See also *Catholic Household Blessings and Prayers* (p. 198).

M O N 21 #371 (LMC #193–227) white
Aloysius Gonzaga (+ 1591), religious
MEMORIAL

One reason the Sermon on the Mount is so popular is the practicality of its advice. Today Jesus urges the disciples not to pass judgment on others without overcoming their own weaknesses first.

In the first reading we hear the terrible story of the deportation of Israel by the Assyrians. All the tribes were conquered except Judah. The author explains this devastation as the result of ancient Israel's infidelity. God's chosen people venerated other gods and ignored the warnings of the prophets. Rare is the nation today that explains its misfortunes as a result of its own sins. The psalm laments God's rejection.

■ TODAY'S SAINT: Aloysius joined the Society of Jesus and was praised for his simplicity and piety. During a plague he cared for the sick in the hospital. These efforts brought on the illness that claimed his life at the age of 23.

The sacramentary offers a complete set of prayers for the day, including an opening prayer that borders on praising a lack of self-esteem. The first preface for holy men and women (P 69) seems appropriate. The lectionary's proper of saints suggests readings about faith and love of neighbor, but the readings of the weekday are recommended—unless, for example, your church is named for Saint Aloysius.

Canadian Native people celebrate First Nations Day today.

T U E 22 #372 (LMC #193–227) green
Weekday

Optional Memorial of Paulinus of Nola (+ 431), bishop/white ▪ Optional Memorial of John Fisher (+ 1534), bishop, martyr, and Thomas More (+ 1535), married man,

martyr/red ▪ Continuing with the Sermon on the Mount, Jesus proposes several aphorisms about treating other people and seeking salvation.

Isaiah makes an appearance in the second book of Kings, as we continue our history of Israel. Hezekiah, having received a threat from Sennacherib, prays to God for deliverance. Isaiah tells him God will indeed preserve a remnant of Israel. God's protection of Zion is remembered in the psalm.

Presidential prayers from Masses for various needs and occasions include one for the nation (#17) and the progress of peoples (#21). You may also use the second form of the eucharistic prayer for various needs and occasions.

■ TODAY'S SAINTS: Paulinus met some of the most outstanding saints of his time, accepted baptism, and was ordained at the insistence of the people. He and his wife gave their wealth to the poor and settled at Nola, where he became bishop. His poetry ranks among the finest in the history of Christendom. The lectionary's proper of saints suggests passages about poverty for those who take the option of this memorial.

John Fisher and Thomas More both became influential in the English courts and suffered martyrdom during the reign of Henry VIII. When John was locked in the tower of London, Pope Paul III made him a cardinal. Thomas, a husband and father, an author and ultimately Lord Chancellor, also refused the king's autonomy and suffered arrest and martyrdom. The lectionary's proper of saints suggests readings about suffering and division, but the readings of the weekday are recommended.

W E D 23 #373 (LMC #193–227) green
Weekday

You know people by their deeds, Jesus says. This simple advice helps his followers to avoid false prophets who attempt to win them away.

A written form of the covenant is discovered and the king has it read in a solemn assembly to the people. Some scholars believe it was a part of the book of Deuteronomy. We respond with the psalmist in submission to the decrees of God.

The Mass for the spread of the gospel (#14) might be appropriate with the second version of the eucharistic prayer for Masses of various needs and occasions, "God Guides the Church on the Way of Salvation."

T H U **24** #586/587 (LMC #316) white
Birth of John the Baptist
SOLEMNITY

ORIENTATION

Six months before the birth of Jesus we celebrate the birth of John the Baptist. Together with the preceding feasts of the Annunciation and the Visitation, this celebration is a very long-range preparation for Christmas, a solemnity far from everyone's minds at midsummer.

In some countries this is a holy day of obligation. The liturgy includes texts for a vigil as well as for a Mass of the day. Some ethnic groups have bonfires or cookouts and fireworks to honor the one who said he must decrease so that Christ may increase. Early

Christians of the northern hemisphere saw in the summer solstice a natural response to that saying: The sun begins its decrease so that Christ may be born at its time of increase.

LECTIONARY

Luke tells of an annunciation of John's conception, and he also gives an account of John's birth. Both stories foreshadow the annunciation and birth of Jesus. The first is the gospel for the vigil Mass; the other is the gospel for Mass during the day.

The vigil includes a famous passage from Jeremiah, about having a vocation from when he was formed in the womb. The psalm uses the same image of the mother's womb to express the completeness of God's call and support. In the spirit of vigil anticipation, the second reading tells of the role of the prophets who searched for salvation. The prophets prepared the way for the birth of Jesus, but they also formed a line completed by John, who is the last of the prophets pointing the way toward Jesus.

In the Mass during the day, another passage speaks of a call from the mother's womb, this time from Isaiah. The responsory praises God for fearfully and wonderfully making the psalmist. For the second reading we hear an excerpt from a sermon of Paul, which clarifies the role of John as the herald of the coming of Jesus.

SACRAMENTARY

The suggested entrance and communion antiphons for both Masses are inspired by Luke's account of John's conception and birth.

Sing or recite the Glory to God and the creed. There is a preface

of John the Baptist (P 61) for today. The solemn blessing for advent (#1) points toward Christ as John did. John's name appears in Eucharistic Prayer I.

OTHER IDEAS

Use vestments from the Christmas season if you want to make the connection to that cycle of feasts. If incense is used, you may bring out the Christmas scent. The *Benedictus* also comes from Luke's account of John's birth. It makes a good text for singing today.

Musicians may enjoy looking at the chant hymn for vespers, "Ut quaeant laxis." The first note of each phrase forms the scale, and the Latin syllable that you sing on each of those notes spells out Ut-re-mi-fa-sol. This is the hymn that gave us the notes of the scale. Somewhere along the line they decided that "Do" was easier to sing than "Ut," and they added "Si" to finish the scale (the abbreviation for *Sancte Ioannes,* or Saint John), which later shifted to "Ti" for ease of singing. You can find the complete hymn in the *Liber hymnarius.*

The German sacramentary proposes an insert to Eucharistic Prayer III: "In union with the whole church we celebrate that day on which John, the forerunner of Christ, was born to prepare the way for him, the redeemer of the world. We remember your saints and praise above all Mary, the glorious, ever-virgin Mother of our Lord and God, Jesus Christ."

F R I **25** #375 (LMC #193–227) green
Weekday

After the Sermon on the Mount, Matthew relates a series of miracle stories. Today, Jesus cures a leper.

Nebuchadnezzar, king of Babylon, advances against Jerusalem for a second deportation (587 BCE).

He slew King Zedekiah's sons before his eyes, then blinded him and had the city burned. A psalm of empty desolation follows the sorrowful account.

The sacramentary includes prayers for those unjustly deprived of liberty.

■ THE FRIDAY FOLLOWING THE THIRD SUNDAY after Pentecost is a solemnity in Ecuador, the Commemoration of the Consecration to the Sacred Heart of the Most Holy Virgin Mary, patron of Ecuador.

S A T **26** #376 (LMC #193–227) green
Weekday

One of the themes of Matthew's gospel is the healing ministry of Jesus and today's episode explains why. In healing the centurion's boy, Jesus shows that redemption is open to Gentiles as well as Jews.

The book of Lamentations contains songs of woe composed during Israel's exile. The first readings have recently traced the downfall of God's chosen people. Today the full sorrow of the situation is poured out in grief. The psalm similarly lifts a cry to God for help.

The sacramentary includes prayers for refugees and exiles.

27 #99 (LMC #94) green
Thirteenth Sunday in Ordinary Time

ORIENTATION

The Year C gospels in Ordinary Time are almost all taken from Saint Luke. Throughout the year, though, we have had little opportunity to hear Luke's story in sequence, due to the important interruptions of the seasons. Today we start hearing the second half of Luke's gospel, the long journey of Jesus toward Jerusalem. We will hear many familiar stories along the way, and the cross, looming at the destination ahead, casts its shadow on the path.

■ BOLIVIA AND PARAGUAY celebrate the solemnity of Peter and Paul today, transferred from June 29 to the nearest Sunday.

LECTIONARY

The gospel opens solemnly. The time has come for Jesus to be taken up. He goes to Jerusalem "resolutely," aware that his time has come. At several intervals in the chapters ahead Luke reminds us that Jesus is on his way to the city of his ultimate fate. Luke 9:51 is the pivotal verse of this gospel. In the first story of the journey, a Samaritan village rejects Jesus, and James and John offer to call down fire from heaven to consume it. Jesus simply journeys on and expects his disciples to do the same.

The first reading contains the story of the discipleship of Elisha to Elijah. Elisha returns home to slaughter his oxen and burn up the plowing equipment. In the gospel, though, Jesus expects a response to his call without delay. The psalmist puts complete trust in God, who will show the path to life. It is the song of a disciple.

Paul, aware of the divisions within the communities of Galatia, reminds people of their freedom and equality, and of their responsibility to love. Especially to those converts from Judaism who felt yoked to the old law, Paul preaches the gospel of the Spirit. That Spirit will unite Jew and Gentile alike.

SACRAMENTARY

The fourth preface for Sundays in Ordinary Time (P 32) tells of the suffering and death of Jesus, the goal of his journey to Jerusalem. The preface for Religious Profession (P 75) acknowledges those who leave all things for the sake of God.

OTHER IDEAS

If it is not the custom in your parish for the members of the assembly to greet one another before the opening song, you might consider this option at least during the weeks of summer. It gives people a chance to welcome visitors and to say hello to those with whom they regularly pray.

M O N **28** #377 (LMC #193–227) red
Irenaeus (+ 202), bishop, martyr
MEMORIAL

The miracle stories of Matthew are interrupted briefly with this interlude on discipleship. Jesus reminds those who would follow him about how much it costs to do so.

Having heard last week the historical incidents leading up to the Babylonian captivity of the southern kingdom, we turn now to a series of prophets from the same period. Amos is the earliest of the prophets whose words were handed on in writing (750 BCE). He came from the northern Kingdom of Israel, where he prophesied that the north would soon fall (as it did in 722 BCE). In today's passage Amos charges Israel with trampling on the needs of the poor. Several accusatory verses from Psalm 50 follow.

■ TODAY'S SAINT: Irenaeus was a disciple of Polycarp, himself a disciple of John the Apostle, making today's gospel a happy coincidence.

Irenaeus studied in Rome and became bishop of Lyons. His theological works, including *Against the Heresies,* are among the most important of the second century.

The sacramentary offers a complete set of presidential prayers for his memorial. You may use the preface for martyrs (P 66). The lectionary's proper of saints suggests readings about leadership and union with Christ, but the readings of the weekday are recommended.

T U E
29
#590/591 (LMC #319)   red
Peter and Paul, apostles
SOLEMNITY

ORIENTATION

Tradition holds that on this day Peter and Paul embraced before marching off to their deaths—Peter on the Vatican hill, Paul outside the city of Rome. They suffered at the hands of Nero, who persecuted Christians to distract the population from the great fire of Rome (64–67). Together these two apostles represent the early evangelization of Jews and Gentiles. In some countries, including Peru, today is a holy day of obligation.

LECTIONARY

The scriptures of the vigil and of the Mass during the day offer passages significant to the ministry of these two great apostles. Stories of Peter include his first miracle (vigil, first reading), his imprisonment (day, first reading), his confession of faith (day, gospel) and his final conversation with Jesus (vigil, gospel). Stories of Paul include his autobiographical comments (vigil, second reading) and prediction of his death (day, second reading). The psalm for the vigil appears frequently with celebrations of the apostles: "Their message goes out." The psalm for the Mass during the day supports the theme of angelic protection in response to the angel's role in delivering Peter from prison.

The *Lectionary for Masses with Children* omits the texts for the vigil Mass.

SACRAMENTARY

Separate presidential prayers are given for the vigil and the Mass during the day. The Masses call for the Glory to God and the creed. Both suggest the preface of Peter and Paul (P 63). This pair of saints is mentioned in Eucharistic Prayer I. A solemn blessing appears at the end of the Mass during the day.

OTHER IDEAS

The hymn "By All Your Saints Still Striving" has a verse for Peter and Paul. "Two Noble Saints," in *Worship* (#699) and "O Light of Lights," in *Hymnal for the Hours* are translations of traditional hymns for this feast.

W E D
30
#379 (LMC #193–227)   green
Weekday

Optional Memorial of the First Martyrs of the Holy Roman Church (+ 64–68) / red ▪ One of the strangest miracles in the gospels captures our imagination today. Jesus meets two possessed men at the Gadarene boundary. They call him Son of God then beg him to expel them into a herd of swine. Jesus performs the miracle, and the swine commit mass suicide. When the people hear about it, they ask Jesus to leave. Not all miracles of Jesus compelled people to become disciples.

"Let justice surge like water," God says through the prophet Amos. If the people want to overcome their misfortunes, they should turn away from shallow public prayer and recommit themselves to living a moral life. The psalm contains a similar prophetic utterance: "To the upright I will show the saving power of God."

The second eucharistic prayer for Masses of reconciliation might make a good choice today.

▪ TODAY'S SAINTS: Peter and Paul were only the best known of many who died under Nero's maltreatment. Today we remember the others who gave their lives in this first of many persecutions. Though nameless, their suffering of torture and death spilled blood that bore the fruit of a stronger faith throughout the Roman world. An alternative gospel appears in the lectionary's proper of saints, a passage in which Jesus predicts the harassment of his followers. The first reading from Romans reflects on triumph over suffering. But the regular weekday readings are recommended.

July

1 #380 (LMC #193–227)   green
Weekday

Optional Memorial of Blessed Junípero Serra (+ 1784), presbyter, religious, missionary/white ▪ Jesus cures a paralytic, but first he forgives the man's sins. The miracle of forgiveness provokes outrage instead of admiration.

Amos faces conflict between the priest's command ("Do not prophesy") and God's command ("Prophesy"). Faithful to his calling, he obeys God. The psalm sings in praise of God's law.

The sacramentary includes a Mass for the forgiveness of sins (#40).

▪ TODAY'S SAINT: Junípero Serra was a Spanish missionary to Mexico and California. He founded several missions, including San Diego and San Juan Capistrano. The mission at Carmel claims his tomb. His beatification caused some controversy because of reports of the ill treatment of Indians in the missions. Remember Native Americans and the work of missionaries today. The opening prayer for this optional memorial is in the 1994 *Sacramentary Supplement*. The Roman martyrology honors this saint on August 28, but the observance is transferred to today in the United States because of the obligatory memorial of Augustine.

▪ TODAY IS CANADA DAY. Canadians may use A Supplement to the Sacramentary (National Liturgical Office, 1991) for special Mass texts.

FRI **2** #381 (LMC #193–227)   green
Weekday

Matthew interrupts the miracle stories again to include a story about discipleship. We hear the call of Matthew, the putative author of the gospel.

Amos rails against a people more concerned about profit than worship. Excerpts from Psalm 119 draw our attention toward the observance of God's decrees.

The sacramentary includes prayers for priestly vocations (9).

SAT **3** #593 (LMC #452–454, 322)   red
Thomas, apostle
FEAST

Although there are more exemplary stories about the apostle Thomas, he is forever remembered as the doubter, as the choice for today's gospel reinforces. Still, even in this episode of doubt, Thomas makes the most sublime proclamation of faith when he finally sees Jesus: "My Lord and my God."

Paul's letter to the Ephesians includes a generic reference to the apostles as the foundation of God's building. The psalmist encourages a spirit of apostleship with a refrain from the end of Mark's gospel: "Go out to all the world and tell the Good News."

The presidential prayers for Thomas are at July 3 in the sacramentary. Sing the Glory to God today. The second preface for apostles (P 65) makes an allusion to the first reading. The apostle is mentioned in Eucharistic Prayer I. There is a solemn blessing for feasts of the apostles (#17).

▪ THOMAS IS ESPECIALLY BELOVED by Christians from India, who regard him as their own apostle. Legend has it that he personally brought the gospel to that country. A group of Saint Thomas Christians survives in India today.

4 #102 (LMC #97)   green
Fourteenth Sunday in Ordinary Time

ORIENTATION

The United States celebrates Independence Day today, but the liturgy remains that of the Ordinary Time Sunday. We do not use the sacramentary's Appendix X, #6, with its Mass for this occasion, nor the optional readings for peace and justice, nor the presidential prayers for July 4. Today is the Fourteenth Sunday in Ordinary Time as far as the liturgical texts are concerned.

Nicaragua, however, moves the solemnity of Peter and Paul to the Sunday following June 29, making today a celebration of those apostles in that country.

In Mexico, the faithful remember Our Lady of the Refuge today. The Conference or Pious Union of Our Lady of Refuge is an archsodality in Mexico. A picture of the Virgin Mary, Refuge of Sinners, moves from house to house for prayer. Members renounce drinking alcohol and practicing prostitution.

LECTIONARY

Today's gospel comes in longer and shorter forms. In the shorter form, Jesus sends 72 disciples out in pairs with a message of peace. In the longer form he educates them how to respond when they are rejected, but the mission meets great success.

Today's prophecy from Isaiah foretells an age when Jerusalem will enjoy enormous prosperity. In this case, the prophecy seems to be fulfilled in the work of the 72, not just in the work of Jesus. The psalm takes up a similar theme, inviting all the earth to rejoice in the marvels God has worked for the land.

The second reading concludes the short series from Galatians. Paul boasts only in the cross of Christ, through which he and the world experience mutual crucifixion—mutual service, mutual suffering and mutual redemption. Circumcision, a Jewish initiation rite not practiced by the Gentiles, grants no one special status in the new creation proclaimed by Christians.

SACRAMENTARY

The alternative opening prayer mentions the sufferings of Christ, which correspond to Paul's words in the second reading today.

Prayer over the people #17 also refers to the suffering of Jesus.

OTHER IDEAS

This Sunday will probably bring extra visitors to parish churches in the United States. Be sure the greeters are on hand to welcome all who visit today. You may offer a blessing for travelers (*Book of Blessings*, ch. 9).

You might conclude the general intercessions with an adaptation of the prayer composed by Archbishop John Carroll for the inauguration of George Washington, as found in the *Book of Blessings* (ch. 69). Another prayer is in *Catholic Household Blessings and Prayers* (p. 199).

You may sing traditional and appropriate patriotic hymns today, like "America the Beautiful." Other songs can be found in hymn indexes under "justice and peace" and "citizenship."

MON 5 #383 (LMC #193–227) green
Weekday

Optional Memorial of Anthony Mary Zaccaria (+ 1539), presbyter, religious founder / white ▪ Returning to the miracle series from Matthew, we hear one of the rare instances where Jesus raises someone from death to life, a foreshadowing of his own resurrection.

First readings this week come from the prophet Hosea. It is generally accepted that he prophesied in the northern Kingdom of Israel shortly after Amos, up to about the time of that kingdom's fall (722 BCE). Today we hear how his marriage became a symbol of God's promise to restore the punished partner. The psalmist proclaims the mercy of God.

The second eucharistic prayer for reconciliation acknowledges that God brought us back when we had wandered far.

▪ TODAY'S SAINT: Anthony Mary Zaccaria gave up his medical practice to become a priest. To seek collaboration between clergy and laity he founded the Barnabites. He also promoted the frequent reception of communion. The lectionary's proper of saints suggests readings about the spiritual life and childlike simplicity, but the readings of the weekday are recommended.

TUE 6 #384 (LMC #193–227) green
Weekday

Optional Memorial of Maria Goretti (+ 1902), virgin, martyr / red ▪ Matthew presents the last of the series of miracles in this section of the gospel with a general statement of Jesus' care for the needy.

In a passage that gave the title to the play *Inherit the Wind,* Hosea promises empty rewards for those who labor in empty causes. A psalm proclaiming one God and no false gods follows the reading.

The third weekday preface (P 39) speaks of God's right to receive the obedience of all creation.

▪ TODAY'S SAINT: At the age of 12, Maria Goretti chose death by stabbing, rather than subject herself to rape. She then pardoned the man who attacked her. She is a model of innocence, chastity, love and forgiveness. The lectionary's proper of saints suggests readings about purity and martyrdom, but the readings of the weekday are recommended.

▪ IN BOLIVIA, today is the optional memorial of Blessed Ignacia Nazaria March, or Nazaria of Saint Teresa March Mesa (+ 1943). Born in Spain, she immigrated to Mexico with her family and brought the gospel to the poor in various Latin American nations. She founded the Institute of the Crucified Missionaries of the Church.

WED 7 #385 (LMC #193–227) green
Weekday

Matthew turns his attention to the call, instruction and mission of the disciples. Today we hear the names of the Twelve, whom, in this passage, Matthew calls "apostles." More than the other gospels, Matthew develops the story of the followers of Christ by identifying the apostles with the Twelve.

Hosea compares Israel to a mutant fruitful vine. The people only build more altars to false gods. Warning the northern Kingdom of evils to come, the prophet implores the people to sow justice and reap piety. Psalm 105 summarizes the history of the chosen people. The opening verses today recall God's judgment over the generations of Israel.

The importance of praising God is one of the themes of the fourth weekday preface (P 40).

THU **8** #386 (LMC #193–227)   green
Weekday

Jesus begins his discourse to the disciples with his slogan, "The reign of God is at hand." He summarizes their work in a useful phrase: "What you received as a gift, give as a gift."

In a passage mined by Matthew to explain the flight of the Holy Family into Egypt, and one that images God as a young mother, Hosea presents God beckoning Moses from Egypt and raising up the chosen people in love. The psalmist asks God to take care of the planted vine of Israel.

In the fourth preface for weekdays of Ordinary Time (P 40) we pray, "our desire to thank you is itself your gift."

FRI **9** #387 (LMC #193–227)   white
Weekday

Optional Memorial of Augustine Zhao Rong, presbyter (+ 1815), and companions, martyrs / red • Jesus warns the disciples that they will face persecution. These words were important to the community for which Matthew wrote the gospel. They, too, faced betrayal and hatred.

We close our series of readings from Hosea with a beautifully eloquent invitation to return to God to seek forgiveness. In response we sing one of the great penitential psalms.

The first eucharistic prayer for reconciliation says, "Now is the time to turn back to you."

■ TODAY'S SAINTS: The Chinese martyrs were added to the universal calendar with the third edition of the Roman Missal. The complete list of names remembered today is quite extensive, and includes bishops, priests, Franciscans, Dominicans, Jesuits, a PIME missionary, Parisian Missionaries, Salesians, Vicentians, Franciscan

missionary sisters of Mary, seminarians, religious, catechists and—the largest group—laity. They died during the persecutions of Christians.

■ TODAY IS THE PATRONAL FEAST OF COLOMBIA, Our Lady of the Rosary of Chiquinquirá. The shrine holds a painting by Alfonso de Narváez, which was miraculously repaired in 1586 while Maria Ramos prayed before it.

In Argentina this is the memorial of Our Lady of Itatí. Tradition holds that Fray Luis de Bolaños founded a shrine at Itatí in 1615, but Indians destroyed it and removed his statue. Some days later Indian children found the statue and the locals built a new sanctuary for the wooden image.

SAT **10** #388 (LMC #193–227)   green
Weekday

Optional Memorial of the Blessed Virgin Mary / white • Again warning of persecution, Jesus offers support to the disciples who will face intimidation from human forces. He means well when he tells the disciples they are worth more than sparrows, but one would hope for a better metaphor.

Next week begins a semi-continuous reading from the prophecy of Isaiah. The call of Isaiah appears in chapter 6, out of sequence, and it serves as a prelude to the series in today's first reading. All the texts will be taken from "First Isaiah," the opening collection of materials dating from the first years of the southern Kingdom's captivity. Isaiah, whose wife was a prophetess and whose book is the longest of all the prophetic literature, lived and preached in Jerusalem. Pre-Christian manuscripts of this book are among the most important finds among the Dead Sea Scrolls. The prophetic call establishes the holiness of God and the eagerness of the prophet. Psalm

93 echoes the magnificence of the divine vision.

The sacramentary includes votive Masses for the Holy Trinity (#1) and the Holy Name (#4), but see the texts for "Mary, Temple of the Lord" in the *Collection of Masses of the Blessed Virgin Mary* (#23).

■ **11** #105 (LMC #100)   green
Fifteenth Sunday in Ordinary Time

ORIENTATION

In the middle of summer, while people often think of travel, we hear the story of the Good Samaritan. It occurs only in Luke's gospel. Jesus himself is on a journey toward Jerusalem as he tells this story.

On the second Sunday of July the people of Venezuela celebrate the feast of the Consecration of the Venezuelan Republic to the Blessed Sacrament.

LECTIONARY

The parable of the Good Samaritan is so popular that it gave us an expression in English for a person who helps a stranger. A scholar of the law prompts this parable by pressing Jesus for information on how to inherit eternal life. Was this scholar a wealthy man who inherited his fortune and assumed that the fortune of eternal life was also inherited? Jesus patiently explains to him the need for showing charity.

Today's first reading recalls the first part of the conversation between Jesus and the scholar of the law. Jesus stresses the importance of keeping the commandments. In Deuteronomy, Moses encourages the people to keep the commandments and statutes with all their heart and soul.

The original lectionary of the Second Vatican Council offered one option for the psalm today, Psalm 69. But the revised lectionary now offers two possibilities, including Psalm 19. The first option fits the parable of the Good Samaritan with its verses about affliction, pain and saving help. The second better fits the theme of the first reading and the opening of the gospel. Either may be chosen. Optional psalms are rare in the lectionary apart from the Easter Vigil.

Today begins a series of passages from the letter to the Colossians. Not all scholars accept the authorship of Paul for this letter because it shows a more developed reflection on Christology and the church. Some false teaching in the community at Colossae prompted the composition of the letter. We hear from the opening chapter today a glorious hymn to Jesus Christ, the image of the invisible God, in whom all things were created.

SACRAMENTARY

Given that Samaritans were regarded as enemies by the readers of Luke's gospel, one of the eucharistic prayers for reconciliation might be appropriate today.

OTHER IDEAS

The memorial of Benedict is suppressed today. His followers were highly instrumental in fostering a spirituality of the liturgy. You might remember Benedictine monks and nuns in your intercessions.

MON 12 #389 (LMC #193–227)   green
Weekday

Jesus concludes his second discourse with bad news and good news. The disciples can expect serious divisions, even in their own families. This probably reflects the situation of the community for whom Matthew wrote the gospel. But he also promises rewards for those who receive the disciples well. Note the phrase that introduces the ending of today's passage: "when Jesus had finished instructing." That is Matthew's cue to the reader that a discourse has come to an end.

The prophecy of Isaiah begins in earnest today. God sounds exasperated through Isaiah's mouth. People have been offering sacrifices, but their lives are filled with misdeeds. Isaiah admonishes the people to make justice their primary aim. Psalm 50, which takes the same attitude toward religious formalism, follows.

The sacramentary includes prayers for the family (#43).

■ CAMILLUS DE LELLIS appears on the American calendar on July 18, and on the universal calendar on July 14, but his optional memorial is transferred to this date in Bolivia.

TUE 13 #390 (LMC #193–227)   green
Weekday

Optional Memorial of Henry (+ 1024), married man, emperor/ white ▪ In the narrative that precedes the third discourse, Jesus meets opposition. Today he lashes out against the towns that have failed to reform in spite of his miracles.

Jerusalem falls under the threat of siege by Aram and Israel. Isaiah urges the king of Judah to remain firm in faith, and Jerusalem will

remain firm as well. A psalm acclaiming God's protection of Jerusalem follows.

The second eucharistic prayer for reconciliation might make a good companion to the first reading.

■ TODAY'S SAINT: Henry II, Duke of Bavaria and husband of Saint Cunegunda, served as emperor, assisted the poor, encouraged reforms in the church and became patron of Finland. The lectionary's proper of saints suggests readings about righteous behavior and the foundation which is Christ, but the readings of the weekday are recommended.

■ IN CHILE AND VENEZUELA, the optional memorial of the teenage virgin Teresa de Jesús de los Andes (+ 1920) is observed today.

WED 14 #391 (LMC #193–227)   white
Blessed Katéri Tekakwitha, the Lily of the Mohawks (+ 1680), virgin
MEMORIAL

In a passage that sounds more like John than Matthew, Jesus expresses the union of the Father and Son by means of their knowledge of one another.

God's word lashes out against Assyria through the mouth of Isaiah. Assyria has thought too proudly of itself and has tried to separate its actions from God's plan. Isaiah prophesies leanness and fire. The psalmist hears the fears of those who say God has forgotten them, but stays firm in the belief that God will not abandon the chosen people.

■ TODAY'S SAINT: Blessed Katéri led many in the United States and Canada to embrace the faith. Her austere life came to an untimely end at the age of 24. Remember the contribution of Native Americans to the spiritual life of the church today.

Francis Solano (+ 1610) is remembered today in Peru with a feast, in Bolivia with a memorial and in Venezuela with an optional memorial. This Spanish Franciscan priest worked tirelessly as a missionary in Peru and other parts of Latin America.

15 THU #392 (LMC #193–227) white
Bonaventure (+ 1274), bishop, religious, doctor of the church
MEMORIAL

A favorite passage among the followers of Jesus, today's gospel gives us the comforting words we often imagine Jesus saying to us. "Come to me. Take my yoke. I am humble of heart. Your souls will find rest."

Confident prayer comes from Isaiah today, a twist from the dire predictions of evil that have filled the week. The psalmist looks for the day when God will rebuild Zion.

■ TODAY'S SAINT: Bonaventure, "the Seraphic doctor," authored many treatises in his life as a Franciscan. He also served as Cardinal of Albano. He died the same year as Thomas Aquinas, causing the church to lose two immensely influential theologians at the same time.

The sacramentary gives an opening prayer for today's memorial. The other presidential prayers may be taken from doctors of the church. You may take the preface of pastors (P 67). The lectionary's proper of saints suggests readings about knowledge and service, but the readings of the weekday are recommended.

16 FRI #393 (LMC #193–227) green
Weekday

Optional Memorial of Our Lady of Mount Carmel/white ▪ Jesus meets opposition from the Pharisees who object to his disciples' disregard for the Sabbath. He uses

the occasion to say he is Lord of the Sabbath.

Isaiah tells Hezekiah, king of Judah, his days are numbered. Hezekiah prays for life and God grants his prayer. Isaiah applies a poultice of figs to Hezekiah's boil, and the sun retraces its course in the sky as a sign that Hezekiah's prayer has been heard. A canticle attributed to Hezekiah on this occasion serves as today's responsory. This concludes the series of readings from Isaiah.

The sacramentary includes a set of prayers for the dying (#33).

■ TODAY'S MEMORIAL: Today is the patronal feast of the Carmelite Order and of the Third Order laity who live the Carmelite spirituality in their secular vocations. That spirituality finds inspiration in the prophet Elijah, who saw from Carmel a cloud in the distance that would bring rain after a drought. That rain-bearing cloud became an image of the savior-bearing Mary. The *Collection of Masses of the Blessed Virgin Mary* has an expanded proper for this commemoration at #32, "Mary, Mother and Teacher in the Spirit." (The Carmelite order, in common with the Byzantine rite and the Roman martyrology, remembers the prophet Elijah on July 20.) The lectionary's proper of saints suggests readings about Mary as daughter of Zion and the one who does God's will, but the readings of the weekday are recommended.

Today is the patronal feast of Chile. It is a solemnity in Chile and in Bolivia, where Mary is also a patron under this title. This is a feast in Venezuela and an obligatory memorial in Argentina, Guatemala, Colombia, Mexico and Costa Rica.

17 SAT #394 (LMC #193–227) green
Weekday

Optional Memorial of the Blessed Virgin Mary/white ▪ The Pharisees plot against Jesus, and Matthew cites a suffering servant song from Isaiah to show Jesus' messianic heritage.

Micah is an exact contemporary of Isaiah. He predicts God's punishment because of the sins of the people, especially those in power. Restoration and peace will follow a period of defeat and exile. The series of readings begins today as Micah tells those lying on comfortable couches plotting the demise of others that God has plans for them, too. The psalmist, recognizing how the wicked take advantage of the poor, appeals to God for intervention.

The sacramentary's Mass for peace and justice (#22) picks up on Micah's theme.

From the *Collection of Masses of the Blessed Virgin Mary,* consider "Mother of Fairest Love" (#36).

✹ 18 #108 (LMC #103) green
Sixteenth Sunday in Ordinary Time

ORIENTATION

Readings today come from the same sources as those from last week. The gospel is from the same chapter as the Good Samaritan. The letter to the Colossians continues, and the first reading comes from the Pentateuch.

LECTIONARY

Having just spoken about hospitality in the parable of the Good

Samaritan last week, Jesus experiences it firsthand as he visits Martha and Mary. This passage is frequently interpreted as a model of the active and contemplative spiritual lives. In the midst of our active lives, the importance of time for contemplation cannot be overemphasized. We all need the challenge to sit once in a while at the feet of Jesus.

Another story of hospitality appears in today's first reading. Abraham and Sarah provide refreshment for three visitors, who promise that the hosting couple will have a son next year. This comes as a surprise to the 90-year old Sarah, but the 100-year-old Abraham has been assured by God that he will still father a child. The scriptures uphold Abraham as a person of great justice, and the psalm today praises such individuals.

In the letter to the Colossians we are told that God's hidden mystery—the Word, Jesus Christ—has been made manifest even to the Gentiles.

SACRAMENTARY

The seventh preface for Sundays in Ordinary Time (P 35) echoes a theme from Colossians, God sending the Son into the world as its redeemer. The fourth solemn blessing for Ordinary Time (#13) prays for peace and freedom from anxiety, traits similar to those Jesus finds in his attentive friend Mary.

OTHER IDEAS

Keep the pace of summer light and easy. Be sure greeters at the door know to watch for visitors. Have musicians plan some music that everyone can sing. Encourage ministers to find substitutes for the weekends they will be away.

If summer is taking its toll on the plants in the church's environment, you may want to refresh them.

MON 19 #395 (LMC #193–227)   green
Weekday

Jesus criticizes the scribes and Pharisees who look for signs. They are missing the sign of his teaching. Even today, people prefer to look for miracles rather than reflect on the miraculous word of God.

Today's passage from Micah closes with a powerful summary of what God asks of us: to do right, love goodness and walk humbly with God.

The fourth version of the eucharistic prayer for Masses for various needs and occasions asks that the church be a living witness to truth and freedom, to justice and peace.

TUE 20 #396 (LMC #193–227)   green
Weekday

Optional Memorial of Apollinaris (+ 2nd c.), bishop and martyr/red ▪ The controversy around Jesus continues as he rejects the members of his family in favor of those who do the will of his Father.

Micah, aware of the sins and sufferings of the people, calls upon God who had mercy on them in Egypt to exercise clemency even now. The psalmist also seeks God's favor. This closes the sequence of readings from Micah.

The first eucharistic prayer for reconciliation addresses the God of love and mercy who is always ready to forgive.

▪ TODAY'S SAINT: Little is known of Apollinaris except that he died as a martyr in the early church and was buried in Ravenna. Later tradition held that he was a disciple of Peter from Antioch and became the first bishop of Ravenna.

Two churches in that city bear his name and boast at having some of the most spectacular mosaics in the world. This optional memorial was added to the universal calendar in the third edition of the Roman Missal.

WED 21 #397 (LMC #193–227)   green
Weekday

Optional Memorial of Lawrence of Brindisi (+ 1619), priest and doctor of the church/white ▪ Our semi-continuous reading of Matthew on weekdays enters the third discourse of Jesus. Of the five discourses, this one includes the parables, beginning with the story of the sower.

Today opens another of the great prophetic books, Jeremiah, from which we will hear for about two weeks. He began prophesying in Judea and Jerusalem as a very young man about 627–26 BCE and continued his turbulent ministry for 40 years, until the fall of Jerusalem (587 BCE). Today we hear the call of Jeremiah, the reluctant prophet. God promises to put words in his young mouth. The responsory sings of the psalmist's personal trust in God.

The sacramentary's prayers for the laity (#12) ask for the Spirit of Christ on those whom God calls to live in the midst of the world and its concerns.

▪ TODAY'S SAINT: Lawrence joined the Capuchins at age 16 and quickly revealed an ability for theology, philosophy and languages. He brought the gospel to Jewish converts and led an army against invading Turks. He died in Portugal as Minister General of his community while advocating on behalf of the people of Naples to their sovereign, King Philip III of Spain. The lectionary's proper of saints suggests readings about service and evangelization, but the readings of the weekday are recommended.

THU 22 Mary Magdalene, apostle to the apostles
#398, 603 (LMC #470–472, 333) white
MEMORIAL

Mary Magdalene was a faithful disciple of Jesus and the first to receive the news of the resurrection. She brought the good news to the apostles, making her the "apostle to the apostles." She has been erroneously identified with the sinful woman of Luke's gospel.

The gospel is proper for the day because Mary Magdalene is a biblical figure. The first readings proposed for her memorial are optional. You may choose the Song of Solomon, a passage in which a lover seeks the beloved, as on the day of resurrection Mary Magdalene went in search of the one she loved. The passage from 2 Corinthians says that although Christ was once known in the flesh, now he is known in the new creation. It is a fitting passage for the Magdalene, who knew Christ in the flesh and saw him in the resurrection.

You may take the first reading from the weekday instead (#398). God laments that the chosen people who shared divine intimacy have now forsaken the one who loved them. "They have dug themselves broken cisterns." But this does not fit neatly with today's memorial, even though the psalm redirects our attention to the true fountain of life.

The recommended psalm for July 22 foreshadows Mary's loving search for the body of Jesus.

Presidential prayers for the day are under July 22. The male apostles are generally recognized with a feast instead of a memorial. Barnabas, not one of the Twelve, is an exception. The Glory to God is sung on feasts of the apostles, and a preface like P 65 is used on those days.

FRI 23 Weekday
#399 (LMC #193–227) green

Optional Memorial of Bridget of Sweden (+ 1373), married woman, religious founder / white ▪ Jesus explains in detail the parable of the sower. Only this parable carries such a lengthy, allegorical interpretation. It sets the table for the remaining parables of the collection.

Through Jeremiah God threatens to overthrow the leadership of Israel and appoint more wise and prudent shepherds. The responsory, from a later passage of Jeremiah, compares God's care of Israel to a shepherd over a flock.

▪ TODAY'S SAINT: Bridget and her husband, Ulfo, lived a devout life and raised eight children, the last of whom, Catherine, is also a saint. After her husband's death, Bridget founded the motherhouse for the community that came to be known as the Brigittines. She is a patron of Sweden. The lectionary's proper of saints suggests readings about union with Christ, but the readings of the weekday are recommended.

SAT 24 Weekday
#400 (LMC #193–227) green

Optional Memorial of Sharbel Makhluf (+ 1898), presbyter / white ▪ Jesus proposes the parable of the weeds and the wheat, a lesson of God's temporary tolerance of wickedness.

Jeremiah stands at the threshold of the temple and warns people not to put too much trust in its endurance. Their deceitful ways are separating themselves from God's patience. The psalmist insists, almost oblivious to Jeremiah's message, how lovely God's dwelling place is.

Francis Solano, who appears on other calendars on July 14, is remembered in Argentina today with a memorial.

▪ TODAY'S SAINT: Sharbel (Joseph) Makhluf served as a Maronite priest. He led the simple life of a hermit, fasting and praying day and night. His memorial was added to the universal calendar in the third edition of the Roman Missal.

☀25 Seventeenth Sunday in Ordinary Time
#111 (LMC #106) green

ORIENTATION

Midway through Luke, midway through Colossians, midway through summer and midway through Ordinary Time we gather today in praise of the God who answers our prayers. Users of the four-volume *Liturgy of the Hours* begin their last week with Volume III today.

LECTIONARY

Jesus reveals the benevolence of God in his parable about prayer. "Ask and you will receive," he reassures the disciples. He also teaches them how to pray. Luke's version of the Lord's Prayer is shorter than Matthew's, and many scholars believe that Luke's came first. It is easier to explain why Matthew would add a few lines than to explain why Luke would leave them out. Only these two gospels include the Lord's Prayer, making some scholars conclude that it is found in a more original source, the so-called "Q document," a collection of sayings of Jesus found only in these two gospels, but in none of the others.

Today's first reading is a beautiful depiction of Abraham at prayer, bargaining with God. The story is so filled with humanity that we can imagine ourselves working at God's mercy in much the same way. Abraham's bold prayer continually praises God's kindness and emphasizes his own unworthiness. It is a classic text of petition. In the psalm, we offer thanks to the God who answers prayers.

The letter to the Colossians compares baptism to death and rising. Sin brings spiritual death, but Christ brings life and forgiveness. Jesus accomplished this wonder through his death on the cross.

SACRAMENTARY

Preface VII for Sundays in Ordinary Time (P 35) praises God for the forgiving mission of the Son, while weekday preface IV (P 40) prays in the spirit of Abraham, "You have no need of our praise, yet our desire to thank you is itself your gift."

Prayer over the people #3 asks that we might know and cherish the gifts we have received.

OTHER IDEAS

Do not forget those who may be suffering from the summer's heat. Help the community be aware of the homeless, the elderly and those too poor to provide cool shelter for themselves.

MON 26
#401 (LMC #193–227) white
Anne and Joachim, parents of the Virgin Mary
MEMORIAL

Jesus continues his survey of parables with short images of the reign of God based on the mustard seed and yeast. In both instances, something small becomes quite large. His central teaching, that God's reign is at hand, inspires even us latter-day disciples to spread the good news.

Anything can reveal a message from God, even dirty laundry. Jeremiah wears soiled loincloth, buries it, and recovers the rotted garment, only so God can show what will happen to Judah. A canticle from Deuteronomy recalls the obstinacy of God's chosen people.

■ TODAY'S SAINTS: The actual names of Mary's parents are lost. A tradition from the apocryphal gospels gives them the names of Joachim and Anne. Presidential prayers are under July 26. You may choose the first preface for holy men and women (P 69).

The lectionary's readings for today's memorial (#606) are optional because Joachim and Anne are not mentioned in the Bible. The passages praise ancestors and prophets who longed to see the fulfillment of their dreams.

In the *Collection of Masses of the Blessed Virgin Mary* you will find optional solemn blessings for Ordinary Time at the end of the order of Mass. The final choice praises God, who "chose to remedy the fall of our first parents."

TUE 27
#402 (LMC #193–227) green
Weekday

Alone with the disciples after the discourse, Jesus explains the parable of the weeds, proclaimed at Mass this past Saturday.

The impending desolation of Judah provokes loud lamentation from the prophet, who wonders if God has forgotten the covenant: "We recognize that we have sinned against you." The psalm also asks for delivery from oppressors and forgiveness from sin.

The first eucharistic prayer for reconciliation says, "Time and time again we broke your covenant, but you did not abandon us."

WED 28
#403 (LMC #193–227) green
Weekday

Jesus tells a parable about the value of the kingdom of God. It is worth more than everything else, more than buried treasure, more than fine pearls.

Jeremiah's suffering causes him to curse his own birth. In bitterness he asks God to explain why he suffers pain when he only did as God commanded. The psalmist, too, prays for deliverance from enemies.

The first version of the eucharistic prayer for Masses for various needs and occasions prays that God's people "may stand forth in a world torn by strife and discord as a sign of oneness and peace."

■ PERU CELEBRATES the feast of Our Lady of Peace today. Benedict XV added the title "queen of peace" to the Litany of Loreto in 1917. See the Collection of Masses of the Blessed Virgin Mary (#45).

THU 29
#404, 607 (LMC #470–472, 337) white
Martha, disciple of the Lord
MEMORIAL

Today's gospel should be taken from those provided for the saint, not the weekday, because Martha is a biblical figure. The first option remembers Martha's belief in the resurrection on the occasion of her brother Lazarus' death. The second, recalling Martha's focus on household tasks, provokes Jesus' statement praising her sister Mary's attention to his teaching.

A suggested first reading on the love of God is also provided for the saint's day, together with a psalm of praise about God's goodness, but you may choose a different combination from the common of Holy Men and Women. You may also choose the first reading about clay from the weekday. Jeremiah goes to the local potter's and learns that Israel is to God like clay is to the hands of a potter. The people are not masters of their own destiny. The psalmist says blessedness comes not from trust in rulers but from hope in God.

The sacramentary's prayers for Martha recall her hospitality, which may alleviate some of the hurt she felt when Jesus seemed to disregard it. The second preface for holy men and women (P 70) would be appropriate.

FRI 30
#405 (LMC #193–227)   green
Weekday

Optional Memorial of Peter Chrysologus (+ 450), bishop, doctor of the church / white ▪ Before Matthew presents the fourth discourse of Jesus, he gives a narrative section of his deeds. Today Jesus meets skepticism in his own hometown.

For Jeremiah a hopeful beginning takes a tragic turn. God asks him to speak in the temple court to the assembled people and invite their repentance. He does so, but they turn on him, saying, "You must be put to death." Jeremiah, the reluctant prophet, continues to meet opposition when he does what God wants him to do. The psalmist, too, bears insults for God only to become an outcast in the family.

The sacramentary includes prayers for persecuted Christians (#15).

▪ TODAY'S SAINT: Peter Chrysologus ("golden-mouth") served as archbishop of Ravenna, practiced personal piety and rooted out heresy from his community. His sobriquet refers to his ability to preach simple, practical, gospel-based sermons. The lectionary's proper of saints suggests readings about preaching and the virtuous life, but the readings of the weekday are recommended.

▪ MEXICO HAS AN OPTIONAL MEMORIAL today for Blessed María de Jesús Sacramentado (+ 1959), founder of the Daughters of the Sacred Heart of Jesus.

SAT 31
#406 (LMC #193–227)   white
Ignatius of Loyola (+ 1556), presbyter, religious founder
MEMORIAL

Jesus learns of the death of John the Baptist. The hideous details are revealed in today's gospel. According to some commentators, Jesus began his spiritual life as a disciple of John, and John's death drove him into his public ministry.

Give Jeremiah credit. Yesterday we heard the people threatening to kill him because of his dour message. Today we hear he will not back down. His fidelity to God's word, unfriendly as it was, won him protection. We recite more verses from yesterday's psalm, a prayer from someone sinking in mire, who proclaims to the lowly that God hears the poor.

▪ TODAY'S SAINT: The founder of the Jesuits, Ignatius was a soldier who authored the *Spiritual Exercises* and founded the Roman college. Among his followers are those silenced for their creative beliefs (for example, Teilhard de Chardin) and martyred for preaching the just word (for example, the Martyrs of El Salvador).

The presidential prayers for Ignatius are at July 31 in the sacramentary. You may use the preface for virgins and religious (P 68). The sacramentary's first appendix includes Ignatius's prayer of self-dedication to Jesus Christ. It is found without attribution among the prayers of thanksgiving after Mass. The lectionary's proper of saints suggests readings about the glory of God (the Jesuits' motto) and the renunciation of possessions, but the readings of the weekday are recommended.

August

#114 (LMC #109)   green
Eighteenth Sunday in Ordinary Time

ORIENTATION

Those using the four-volume set of the *Liturgy of the Hours* switch to the last volume today. We begin the second half of Ordinary Time.

LECTIONARY

Jesus warns against greed, a theme prominent in Luke's gospel. He tells the parable of a man so prosperous that he builds new barns to house his abundant grain, although he is unaware that he will soon lose his life. Luke's Jesus is frustrated with the greedy designs of the human heart.

From the book of Ecclesiastes we hear an ancient echo of Jesus' disparaging attitude toward materialism. All things are vanity, says Qoheleth.

The responsory today does indeed include verses from Psalm 90 as the lectionary says, but the refrain is actually Psalm 95:8. The verses are appropriate to today's first reading, a meditation on the swiftness of human life and a prayer that we might number our days aright.

We conclude our brief series of readings from Colossians today with a beautiful appeal to the spiritual life. The baptized, who were raised with Christ, should seek the things that are above.

SACRAMENTARY

The fourth version of the eucharistic prayer for various needs and occasions says, "Open our eyes to the needs of all." Prayer over the people #20 asks that God will bestow the riches of grace upon the people.

OTHER IDEAS

As summer enters its final month, take a look at the environment of the church. Do plants need to be refreshed? Before the busy fall gets here, is this a good time to clean vessels and vestments?

M O N 2 #407 (LMC #193–227) green
Weekday

Optional Memorial of Eusebius of Vercelli (+ 371), bishop/white ▪ *Optional Memorial of Peter Julian Eymard (+ 1868), presbyter, religious founder/white* ▪ Use the gospel assigned for today. During Year A this gospel is replaced because it repeats the one from Sunday, but that does not apply this year. Today we hear Matthew's account of the feeding of the five thousand, "not counting women and children." Matthew notes that Jesus looked up to pray the blessing. The first eucharistic prayer says Jesus looked up when he prayed at the Last Supper. The gospels never affirm that he did that. But Matthew says he raised his eyes at the miracle of the loaves. Eucharistic Prayer I thus alludes subtly to today's gospel.

Today's prophecy comes late in Jeremiah's career. He finds himself in a shouting match with Hananiah, a false prophet who prophesies the fall of Nebuchadnezzar, king of Babylon, and the restoration of the exiles. Jeremiah reproves this pseudo-good news and restates his own message of woe. Hananiah breaks the yoke Jeremiah carries to symbolize his version of the message, and Jeremiah prophesies Hananiah's demise. The psalmist seeks only God's ways.

▪ TODAY'S SAINTS: Sardinian by birth, Eusebius went to Rome as an infant and eventually Pope Sylvester made him a lector. As bishop of Vercelli he lived with his clergy, blending the clerical and the monastic lives and inspiring the canons regular of the West. Exiled for his defense of Athanasius and opposition to the Arians, he returned by the kindness of Constantine and died in peace. The lectionary's proper of saints suggests readings about faith and holiness, but the readings of the weekday are recommended.

Peter Julian Eymard founded the Congregation of the Blessed Sacrament and the Servants of the Blessed Sacrament, an order of sisters devoted to perpetual adoration. He influenced the establishment of world eucharistic congresses. The lectionary's proper of saints suggests readings about communion and union with Christ, but the readings of the weekday are recommended.

▪ TODAY IS THE PATRONAL FEAST OF COSTA RICA under the title Our Lady of the Angels. It is an optional memorial in Guatemala. The date appears on the Franciscan calendar to honor the title of the beloved Portiuncula shrine where Francis of Assisi died. Tradition says that on this date in 1636 a Costa Rican Indian found a stone statue of Mary, but when he tried to move it, it returned to its original site. Believers constructed a shrine there.

T U E 3 #408 (LMC #193–227) green
Weekday

Use the first option for the gospel today. The second is provided for Year A when the weekday and Sunday lectionaries overlap. Jesus walks on the water and invites Peter to do the same. The miracles continue: He heals the afflicted, many of whom simply touch the fringe of his cloak. Matthew presents a Jesus in complete control over natural elements, while acknowledging the human limits of faith.

Jeremiah prophesies sorrow and gladness. The sins of the people have brought pain without relief. But God promises to restore the tents of Jacob and to have pity on Israel. "You shall be my people, and I will be your God."

The second eucharistic prayer for Masses of reconciliation might be appropriate today.

W E D 4 #409 (LMC #193–227) white
John Mary Vianney (+ 1859), presbyter
MEMORIAL

Jesus tries to stay to his mission to the lost sheep of the house of Israel, but a persistent Canaanite woman convinces him to have a heart for her daughter.

Finally we hear words of comfort from Jeremiah. "With age-old love I have loved you." God will deliver a remnant of Israel. The canticle continues the same passage in responsory.

▪ TODAY'S SAINT: Better known as the Curé of Ars, Jean-Baptist Marie Vianney is the patron saint of diocesan priests. He served humbly the small community of Ars in southeastern France, and became well known for his pious spirituality, religious asceticism and pastoral care as a confessor. The architect who built the church in his honor in Ars also constructed the one in La Louvesc to honor the saint that John Mary Vianney admired, John Francis Regis.

The sacramentary gives the opening prayer for the saint. You may take the other prayers from the common of pastors and the preface for pastors (P 67) as well. The lectionary's proper of saints suggests readings about leadership and compassion, but the readings of the weekday are recommended.

THU 5 #410 (LMC #193–227) green
Weekday

Optional Memorial of the Dedication of the Basilica of St. Mary Major in Rome (c. 431)/white ▪ Matthew's gospel reaches a turning point as Jesus asks the disciples who people say he is. Peter answers correctly and profoundly that he is the Messiah, the Christ, the Son of the living God. In Matthew's account of this event, Jesus goes on to entrust the keys of the kingdom of heaven to Peter. Matthew often clarifies Peter's high-ranking role among the disciples. As in the other gospels, Jesus at this point reveals to his followers the fate that awaits him in Jerusalem. They need formation in understanding just who the Messiah is and what he does. It isn't pretty.

We conclude our series of readings from Jeremiah with a wonderfully comforting message of God's new covenant, this one written on the human heart. These verses are quoted extensively in the letter to the Hebrews (8:8–12).

The sacramentary includes prayers for Peter's successor (the pope) in its Masses for various needs and occasions (#2B).

▪ TODAY'S MEMORIAL: Pope Liberius learned where St. Mary Major should be built when snow fell in the summer of 352 on Rome's Coelian Hill. After the Council of Ephesus declared Mary "*Theotokos*" or "God-bearer" in 431, Pope Sixtus III enlarged

and consecrated St. Mary Major as the first basilica dedicated to the Mother of God in the West. Beneath the altar are the supposed relics of Bethlehem's crib. The lectionary's proper of saints suggests readings about the new Jerusalem and the blessedness of Mary, but the readings of the weekday are recommended.

FRI 6 #614 (LMC #344) white
The Transfiguration of the Lord
FEAST

We remember today the revelation of Jesus' glory to the disciples. Use Luke's account of the event in accord with the custom of Year C. The second letter of Peter remembers the event and purports to give eyewitness testimony. The passage is meant to convince people of Christian teachings and of the church's authority. Daniel's vision of the Son of Man on the clouds of heaven before the Ancient One reads like a prelude to the event we celebrate today. The psalmist, too, proclaims God king upon the clouds.

The sacramentary's prayers for August 6 are all inspired by the scriptural account. Sing the Glory to God. The transfiguration has its own preface (P 50). The first solemn blessing for Ordinary Time (#10) is the blessing of Aaron, a prayer that God's face may shine upon the believer.

On this date in 1890 the electric chair was used for the first time in the United States. On this date in 1945 the United States dropped the atom bomb on Hiroshima. Offer prayers for respect for human life.

Today is the patronal and titular feast of El Salvador.

SAT 7 #411 (LMC #193–227) green
Weekday

Optional Memorial of Sixtus II (+ 258), pope, martyr; and his companions, martyrs/red ▪ *Optional Memorial of Cajetan (+ 1547), presbyter, religious founder/white* ▪ *Optional Memorial of the Blessed Virgin Mary/white* ▪ Jesus cures a child with a serious mental disability after his disciples tried and failed. He seizes the occasion to speak about the importance of faith in overcoming all obstacles.

The prophet Habakkuk makes only two appearances in the entire lectionary. His only weekday appearance is today. He will return for the first reading on Sunday two months from now. He was probably a contemporary of Jeremiah and complained about the moral depravity of the people that led to their conquest by Babylon. The prophet wonders why God gazes on the faithless in silence, and hears the comforting news that "the vision still has its time." The psalm prays confidently that God does not forsake those who seek help.

▪ TODAY'S SAINTS: Sixtus II reconciled the churches of North Africa and Rome. After one year as pope, he and several deacons were arrested while celebrating the eucharist in the catacombs during the persecution of Valerian, who had them beheaded. Sixtus's archdeacon, Lawrence, escaped notice, but not for long. Sixtus is mentioned in Eucharistic Prayer I. The lectionary's proper of saints suggests readings about the death of the just and the specter of martyrdom.

Cajetan founded the Theatines in an attempt to live like the apostles of old. A prayerful, hardworking priest, he cared for the sick and the poor. The lectionary's proper of saints suggests readings about fear of the Lord and simplicity of life, but the readings of the weekday are recommended.

Remembering Jesus' ability to heal, you could include prayers for the sick today (various needs and occasions, 32). If you choose the optional memorial of Mary, consider "Mary, Health of the Sick" (*Collection of Masses of the Blessed Virgin Mary,* 44).

8 #112 (LMC #111)   green
Nineteenth Sunday in Ordinary Time

ORIENTATION

In summer's last weeks many groups will start having meetings to prepare for activities this fall. Some college students may be returning to school already. Provide opportunities for family members and friends to meet and greet.

LECTIONARY

In the shorter form of today's gospel Jesus warns the disciples to be prepared, for the Son of Man will come at an hour they do not expect. The image of the thief coming at an unknown hour repeats so frequently in the New Testament that it must have frightened the first generation of Christians. The longer form of the gospel opens with an admonition to sell belongings and give to the poor. It closes with the parable of the servant whose master delays returning. The servant will either misbehave or remain faithful in a long absence. After Jesus' death, the disciples were like that servant. Some of them misbehaved, but others remained faithful to the gospel.

From the book of Wisdom we hear the story of Passover, a night for which Israel had waited a long time. Those who were faithful in their waiting witnessed the salvation of the just and the destruction of their foes. The psalm praises God who delivers the just from death and famine.

The letter to the Hebrews is so long and so important that its excerpts sprawl throughout two years of the Sunday cycle. This year we hear from the concluding chapters. Today's reading recalls Abraham's faith as he sojourned from his own country, not knowing where he was to go. This reading also comes in longer and shorter forms today.

SACRAMENTARY

The fourth preface for Christian Death (P 80) speaks of God's power and providence, bringing us to birth and ruling our lives. You might consider using the solemn blessings for the dead (#20).

OTHER IDEAS

If students are returning to college this week, collect e-mail addresses, and be sure they know how to access the parish website for updates from home.

9 #413 (LMC #193–227)   green
Weekday

Optional Memorial of Teresa Benedicta of the Cross (+ 1942), religious, martyr / red ▪ The narrative section of Matthew's book four closes with another prediction of the passion and a story of taxes that shows the state's growing distrust of Jesus.

Ezekiel was taken to Babylon in captivity in 597 BCE and prophesied there for about twenty-five years, awaiting the final fall of Jerusalem about eleven years later. He spoke of the sovereignty of God and the divine plan in history. In today's passage, Ezekiel receives his call to be a prophet, while in Babylon he beholds an image of the divine form and recognizes it as God's glory. In response we sing of that glory with the psalmist.

The fourth weekday preface in Ordinary Time (P 40) admits the untouchable greatness of God.

▪ TODAY'S SAINT: Teresa Benedicta is also known by her birth name, Edith Stein. Born into a Jewish family, Edith pursued atheism during her extensive study of philosophy in search of truth. After reading the autobiography of Theresa of Avila, she put her faith in Christ and was baptized in a Catholic ceremony. She joined the Carmelites and took her religious name. As Adolph Hitler came to power, Christians of Jewish descent residing in the Netherlands were sent to Poland. Teresa died in the gas chamber at Auschwitz.

▪ IN URUGUAY today is the memorial of Blessed Mother Francisca Rubatto (+ 1904). This Italian woman founded the Institute of the Capuchin Sisters of Mother Rubatto. She traveled to South America and set up missions in Montevideo, Uruguay and Argentina. She assisted a group of Capuchin friars establish a mission in Brazil, but within two years after she left them the whole community was martyred. Francisca herself died peacefully after years of service to the gospel.

T
U
E
10 #618 (LMC #456–460) red
**Lawrence (+ 258),
deacon, martyr**
FEAST

One of the most influential martyrs of the early church, this deacon is the subject of countless works of art and the patron of more churches in Rome than any other saint except Mary. He merits a feast on the liturgical calendar, an honor generally reserved for apostles. Lawrence is remembered for his extraordinary charity to the poor and hungry, as well as his bravery when roasted to death on a grill, just a few days after the martyrdom of the pope he served.

The lectionary gives special readings for today. Jesus says the seed must die to produce fruit, and welcomes disciples to follow him. We understand those words to predict martyrdom. The first reading remembers Lawrence's charitable practice. Paul says God loves a cheerful giver. The psalm echoes this aspect of Lawrence's life: the just give lavishly to the poor.

The sacramentary has presidential prayers for Lawrence. Sing the Glory to God. You may use the preface for martyrs (P 66).

W
E
D
11 #415 (LMC #193–227) white
**Clare of Assisi
(+ 1253), virgin,
religious founder**
MEMORIAL

Even the church needs skills in conflict resolution. Jesus urges the disciples to work things out as best as they can with the offenders, and reject them only as a last resort. He promises to be present whenever people gather in his name.

Ezekiel sees God calling on a scribe to mark the foreheads of those who bemoan the atrocities in Jerusalem. He orders the rest to be struck down. He imagines the glory of God returning to the temple after this time of purification. God's glory, the psalmist says, is higher than the heavens.

■ TODAY'S SAINT: Clare followed the example of Frances and founded a religious community for those desiring a life of poverty. Barefoot, simple and devout, she led the group of sisters at San Damiano. In a vision she could see Christmas midnight Mass although she was in a different building. She is the patron saint of television.

The opening prayer for the day is in the proper of saints. It stresses Clare's love of poverty. The other presidential prayers might be taken from the commons of holy men and women (for religious, 8). The lectionary's proper of saints suggests readings about union with Christ and discipleship, but the readings of the weekday are recommended.

T
H
U
12 #416 (LMC #193–227) green
Weekday

Many times Jesus stresses the importance of forgiving. The parable illustrates a different point, the importance of forgiving individual offenses, even if they are enormous.

Ezekiel prophesies more trouble for the people. God asks the prophet to bring out his luggage as if he is going to exile, as a sign to the people of what lies ahead. The psalmist also warns us not to forget the works of the Lord.

One of the eucharistic prayers for reconciliation would fit the themes of the scripture verses today.

F
R
I
13 #416 (LMC #193–227) green
Weekday

Optional Memorial of Pontian (+ 235), pope, martyr; and Hippolytus (+ 235), presbyter, martyr/red
■ Matthew begins the final narrative section of his gospel before the last discourse and then the passion. Jesus takes up the prickly topic of marriage and divorce. Matthew reports a stern position, though one with an exception.

As an interlude in the fierce prophecies of Ezekiel, words of comfort come from God. God promises to reestablish the covenant, and the lectionary presents the same theme in a responsory from Isaiah.

The first preface for marriage calls it "an unbreakable bond of love and peace" (P 72).

■ TODAY'S SAINTS: After becoming pope, Pontian was arrested and sent to work in the mines of Sardinia under the persecution of Maximinus, who hated Christians because his opponent Alexander Severus favored them. It appears that Pontian abdicated the throne of Peter while in exile, and Anterus succeeded him as pope.

Hippolytus is remembered as a great theologian who took offense at Pope Calixtus for his too generous mercy. Hippolytus appointed himself bishop and anti-pope but also ended up in the mines of Sardinia with Pontian. The two suffered martyrs' deaths. The lectionary's proper of saints suggests readings about suffering and persecution, but the readings of the weekday are recommended.

It is doubtful that this Hippolytus authored *The Apostolic Tradition,* as many believe, but it might still be a good day to use Eucharistic Prayer II, which was inspired by that document.

S
A
T
14 #418 (LMC #193–227) red
**Maximilian Mary
Kolbe (+ 1941),
presbyter, religious
founder, martyr**
MEMORIAL

In another instance of showing his care for children, Jesus permits them to come close over the objections of the disciples, because the kingdom of God belongs to them.

God speaks through Ezekiel that people will be judged on their own behavior, not on that of their ancestors. Today many parents turn the proverb around. They think if the children eat green grapes, the parents' teeth are set on edge. The psalmist offers in sacrifice a contrite spirit, aware of personal sin.

■ TODAY'S SAINT: Maximilian Kolbe, a Franciscan, was among those imprisoned at Auschwitz during World War II. Founder of the Militia of Mary Immaculate, he gave up his life so that a fellow prisoner, a father of children, could live.

Presidential prayers are under August 14 in the sacramentary. The preface for martyrs could be used (P 66). The lectionary's proper of saints suggests readings about sacrifice and laying down one's life for another, but the readings of the weekday are recommended.

#621/622 (LMC #447–450, 352)
white

⚙15 The Assumption of the Virgin Mary into Heaven
SOLEMNITY

ORIENTATION

Today the church celebrates Mary's welcome to heaven. As we believe that Jesus was the first to rise from the dead, so we believe he has also received his mother first into eternity. Eastern traditions called this event the "Dormition"

or "sleeping" of Mary, indicating that she did not die but was taken to heaven as if asleep. Pope Pius XII declared the bodily assumption of Mary into heaven as a dogma of the church in 1950.

There are two Masses for the solemnity; one for the vigil and another for the day.

Mary is a patron of Guatemala, Panama and Paraguay under this title.

The Twentieth Sunday in Ordinary Time is suppressed this year.

LECTIONARY

There is no biblical account of Mary's death, so the lectionary turns to other episodes in Mary's life. The gospel for the vigil reports Jesus hearing someone bless "the womb that carried you and the breasts at which you nursed." The gospel for the Mass during the day is Mary's visit to Elizabeth. She hears her kinswoman tell her, "Blessed is the fruit of your womb."

Both second readings come from the fifteenth chapter of 2 Corinthians, where Paul treats the theme of the resurrection.

The first readings draw on Marian iconography. At the vigil, we hear of the placement of the ark of the covenant with the holy tent, an image of Mary, the "ark" of divine presence, entering the holy temple of heaven. A psalm about the ark answers in responsory. In Revelation, John sees a woman clothed with the sun, the moon and the stars. Because her child does battle with the dragon, the woman has become an image of Mary in heaven. From the book of Psalms we sing a wedding song in which the queen takes her place on a royal throne—again, an image of Mary's entrance into heaven, where she rules as queen.

SACRAMENTARY

The texts for both Masses proclaim the meaning of the day's celebration, as does the proper preface (P 59). Sing the Glory to God and use the creed today. There is a solemn blessing for the Blessed Virgin Mary (#15).

OTHER IDEAS

The German sacramentary proposes an insert to Eucharistic Prayer III: "In union with the whole church we celebrate that day on which the virgin mother of God was taken up to heaven. We praise her before all the saints, the glorious ever-virgin mother of our Lord and God, Jesus Christ."

Display an icon of the assumption for veneration.

By Flowing Waters (355–63) includes the incomparable responsorial psalm and antiphon, "Come, my beloved, receive your crown," from the Song of Songs, and a unique alleluia psalm. In the ideal this responsorial psalm is sung from the ambo by at least four psalmists: The women of the schola sing verses 2, 4, 6 and 10—as did the bridesmaids in the Song of Songs. Male and female psalmists may represent the groom and bride on the verses.

■ HARVEST BLESSING: Some countries link this celebration to the blessing of the earth's harvest, or else the blessing of earth, sea and sky. See *Book of Blessings* (ch. 26 or 28) and *Catholic Household Blessings and Prayers* (pp. 170–73).

#419 (LMC #193–227)   green

M O N 16 Weekday (Twentieth Week in Ordinary Time)

Optional Memorial of Stephen of Hungary (+ 1038), married man/white ▪ "Keep the commandments," Jesus tells a would-be disciple. He then recites the ten commandments—some of them anyway—and not in the correct order. (A grade school teacher today would expect more accuracy from a pupil.) To do more than these commandments, Jesus says, sell what you have and give the money to the poor.

Ezekiel's wife dies and God asks him not to mourn in the traditional way as a prophecy to Israel that they have not sufficiently mourned their own sin. A bitter canticle follows, from Deuteronomy.

The sacramentary includes a Mass for forgiveness of sins (#40).

■ TODAY'S SAINT: Stephen served as king of Hungary, yet earned a reputation for his charity to the needy. In 2000 the Orthodox church also recognized him as a saint. This marks the first time that the church in both East and West has agreed about a canonization since the eleventh-century schism. The lectionary's proper of saints suggests readings about loving God and sharing with the needy, but the readings of the weekday are recommended.

■ MEXICO HAS AN OPTIONAL MEMORIAL for Blessed Bartholomew Laurel (+ 1627), martyr. Bartholomew was born in Mexico City, joined the Franciscans and served in the Philippines before meeting his martyrdom in Japan.

Argentina observes an optional memorial for Saint Rock (+ 1378) today. This medieval saint is often invoked in times of pestilence because of stories that he miraculously cured others and was sustained in his own illness by a dog that brought him bread in the woods.

TUE 17 #420 (LMC #193–227)   green
Weekday

Following up yesterday's command to the wealthy young man, Jesus says how difficult it is for the rich to enter heaven. He expects total commitment from followers.

Ezekiel prophecies gloom for the prince of Tyre, who holds himself up as a god. The canticle from Deuteronomy reminds us that there is one God who governs life and death.

A Mass for peace and justice (#22A) appears among those for various needs and occasions.

WED 18 #421 (LMC #193–227)   green
Weekday

Optional Memorial of Jane Frances de Chantal (+ 1641), religious / white ▪ One of the most difficult parables heard in a capitalist society, today's reading establishes the superiority of generosity over fairness.

Through Ezekiel, God rails against the problem of bad leadership. Shepherds have been satisfying themselves but not tending for the flock. In a judgment leveled against the leaders, God promises personally to look after the sheep. The psalmist takes comfort in Psalm 23: "The Lord is my shepherd."

■ TODAY'S SAINT: Jane Frémiot became the mother of six. Widowed by a shooting accident, she took Francis de Sales as her spiritual director and founded the Visitation nuns at Annecy in Savoy. The lectionary's proper of saints suggests readings about the virtuous life and the spiritual family of Christ, but the readings of the weekday are recommended.

■ CHILE CELEBRATES a memorial of the Jesuit priest Blessed Alberto Hurtado Cruchaga (+ 1952) today. He provided housing for the poor, the needy and travelers.

THU 19 #422 (LMC #193–227)   green
Weekday

Optional Memorial of John Eudes (+ 1680), presbyter, religious founder, educator / white ▪ The lectionary skips over a chapter of Matthew's gospel to today's parable, which sums up much of the preceding material: Jesus meets the same resistance from religious authority that the host of the wedding banquet meets from friends.

The promise of a new covenant appears in Ezekiel, as it did in Jeremiah in the passage we heard two weeks ago today. God promises to wash away the peoples' impurities with clean water, foreshadowing the work of baptism. That promise forms the refrain to today's psalm, which prays for a clean heart.

Prayers for today's religious authorities can be found in the Mass for a council or synod (#5).

■ TODAY'S SAINT: John Eudes is regarded as a founder of the Sisters of the Good Shepherd as well as the Priests of Jesus and Mary. He traveled throughout France, evangelizing and catechizing. His day is an obligatory memorial in Venezuela. The lectionary's proper of saints suggests readings about the love of Christ and the wisdom God shares with the simple, but the readings of the weekday are recommended.

■ TODAY MEXICO HONORS Blessed Pedro de Zúñiga, a Dominican, and Blessed Luis Flores (+ 1622), from the order of hermits of Saint Augustine, priests and martyrs. They were martyred at Nagasaki together with 13 Japanese sailor companions.

#423 (LMC #193–227)   white
Bernard (+ 1153), presbyter, monastic, doctor of the church
F R I 20 MEMORIAL

Jesus' conflict with local leadership reaches a climax in the dispute over the greatest of commandments. It gives him the opportunity to summarize his teaching by citing the great commandment of love, a commandment not much in evidence in this series of disputes.

Another prophecy of comfort comes through Ezekiel today. In a vision of a valley of dry bones, God commands the spirit to enter the bones and bring them to life. Israel's bones, languishing in exile without spirit, will have God's spirit within them. The psalm is post-exilic. It remembers how God redeemed Israel through the desert, in anticipation of another rescue.

■ TODAY'S SAINT: Bernard joined the abbey of Citeaux and then Clairvaux, where he served as abbot. An effective preacher and a wise and holy man, he authored hymns we still sing. "O Sacred Head Surrounded" is attributed to him.

The sacramentary has presidential prayers for today. You may use the preface for virgins and religious (P 68). The lectionary's proper of saints suggests readings about wisdom and unity with Christ, but the readings of the weekday are recommended.

#424 (LMC #193–227)   white
Pius X (+ 1914), pope
S A T 21 MEMORIAL

The twenty-third chapter of Matthew is laced with Jesus' criticisms of the Pharisees. We use the word *pharisaical* in English to mean "hypocritical." In today's gospel we learn why.

Today's reading is the last from Ezekiel and closes out this summer's lengthy lectionary series from the history of Israel's exile and prophets. In the prophecy, Ezekiel beholds a majestic vision, the glory of God entering into the temple.

■ TODAY'S SAINT: With the motto, "To renew all things in Christ," Pope Pius X urged children to share communion at a younger age than the customary 12. He also urged adults to share communion frequently, a practice they were reluctant to observe.

In addition to the presidential prayers under August 21, you may use the preface for pastors (P 67). The lectionary's proper of saints suggests readings about evangelization and pastoral leadership, but the readings of the weekday are recommended.

#123 (LMC #118)   green
Twenty-first Sunday in Ordinary Time
22

ORIENTATION

After last Sunday's celebration of the Assumption, normally a holy day in the United States when it falls on a weekday, we return to Ordinary Time. There will be no further interruptions from now until Advent.

LECTIONARY

The people wonder about eternal salvation, and Jesus implies they should be wondering about it. It is not clear to them who will be saved and who will not. There will be some surprises in the kingdom of God. Some of those who think they know the master will find the door locked, but many others will come from the east, west, north and south to dine at the heavenly table.

The vision that concludes the gospel was foreshadowed in today's first reading. Isaiah sees many nations coming to bring an offering to God at Jerusalem. The salvation God offers is beyond what anyone can imagine. The responsory is the shortest psalm in the psalter, but it has the largest theme: All nations—not just Israel—are called to glorify God.

Excerpts from the letter to the Hebrews continue today with an exhortation to spiritual discipline. The trials we undergo will later bring the peaceful fruit of righteousness.

SACRAMENTARY

The eighth preface for Sundays in Ordinary Time (P 36) praises God for gathering children into one church to be a chosen people, the body of Christ, the dwelling-place of the Spirit. Prayer over the people #8 praises our creator and ruler.

OTHER IDEAS

More students will be returning to school this weekend. Remember them, their teachers and families in prayer.

#425 (LMC #193–227)   green
Weekday
M O N 23

Optional Memorial of Rose of Lima (+ 1617)/white ■ "Frauds!" Jesus calls the scribes and Pharisees, not burying his opinion. This is only the first part of seven woes he casts upon their heads, stretched over three lectionary days. Jesus cannot tolerate hypocrisy in general, but especially among religious leaders.

Leaving the Old Testament behind for the first time since June

7, the Ordinary Time first reading today turns to Paul's second letter to the Thessalonians. In a few days we begin hearing from 1 Corinthians. The lectionary pairs these letters into a unit this year. First Thessalonians and 2 Corinthians appear in the cycle of readings next summer. This allows us to hear both letters to the Thessalonians with a fresh ear. Both of these letters claim authorship by Paul, Silvanus and Timothy. Second Thessalonians is addressed to a community expecting the imminent return of Jesus, wondering about the future of their enemies. The letter opens today with an expression of gratitude to God for the reader's perseverance in faith in the face of persecution and trial. A psalm of praise follows.

Remembering the importance of praying for sincere church leadership, consider the sacramentary's Mass for ministers (#8).

■ TODAY'S SAINT: The Peruvian Isabel de Oliva was nicknamed "Rose" because of her beauty. She observed personal asceticism while exercising charity for the sick and elderly. A Dominican Tertiary and a mystic, she was the first canonized saint of the Americas. She is recognized as patron of Latin America with a feast today in Colombia and Costa Rica. The lectionary's proper of saints suggests readings about virginity and poverty, but the readings of the weekday are recommended.

T U E **24** #629 (LMC #452–455) red
Bartholomew, apostle
FEAST

Little is known of Bartholomew. His name appears in all the lists of the Twelve in the synoptics and in Acts, but his name never appears in John. His name frequently follows Philip's in the lists, so some have made the dubious assumption that Nathanael, whom Philip brings to Jesus in today's episode from John, is the same person as Bartholomew. Tradition says he preached the gospel in India and was skinned alive. In the *Last Judgment* fresco on the Sistine Chapel wall, Michelangelo painted his self-portrait on the face of Bartholomew's skinned hide.

The first reading from Revelation is a generic text about the role of the apostles, and the psalm's allusion to people speaking of God's might and making it known seems to foreshadow the apostolic role.

Sing the Glory to God today. Note that the lectionary and sacramentary texts are proper for Bartholomew. The second preface for apostles alludes to today's first reading (P 65). Eucharistic Prayer I includes this apostle's name. There is a solemn blessing for apostles (#17).

W E D **25** #427 (LMC #193–227) green
Weekday

Optional Memorial of Louis IX of France (+ 1270), married man, king / white ▪ *Optional Memorial of Joseph Calasanz (+ 1648), presbyter and religious founder / white* ▪ The crucifixion of Jesus becomes more comprehensible when we hear how he made enemies among the religious leaders. Today we hear the conclusion of his creed against scribes and Pharisees, calling them whitewashed tombs— pretty to look at, but filled inside with filth.

The Thessalonians have been terrified by false religious allegations. Paul, Silvanus and Timothy urge them to hold fast to the traditions they have handed on. Yesterday's psalm of praise continues today with verses about the coming of God's judgment.

■ TODAY'S SAINTS: Louis IX of France fathered 11 children, led the second crusade and built Sainte Chapelle in Paris as a reliquary for the crown of thorns. A city in Missouri is named for him. The lectionary's proper of saints suggests readings about generosity to the poor and love of neighbor, but the readings of the weekday are recommended.

Joseph Calasanz founded the Piarists, the Clerics Regular of Religious Schools. If your parish operates a school that makes room for the poor, Joseph is your patron. He established such a school in Trastevere, a neighborhood just south of the Vatican, across the Tiber from the heart of Rome. The lectionary's proper of saints suggests readings about love and the simple spirituality of childhood, but the readings of the weekday are recommended.

T H U **26** #428 (LMC #193–227) green
Weekday

The gospel draws us toward the end of Matthew's story. Jesus warns the disciples in a parable to stay awake, for they know not the day when God is coming.

The brief series of readings from 2 Thessalonians concludes today with Paul's exhortation to the faithful to work for what they eat. This simple request to engage in secular activities for the sake of the community is enriched with religious purpose. The psalmist blesses those who eat the fruit of their own handiwork.

Prayers for productive land can be found in the sacramentary (#26).

■ COLOMBIA CELEBRATES TODAY the memorial of Teresa of Jesus (+ 1897), founder of the Little Sisters of the Abandoned Aged.

Blessed Junípero Serra, remembered on the first of July in the United States, has an optional memorial today in Mexico.

F R I
27
#429 (LMC #193–227/365)
white
Monica (+ 387), married woman
MEMORIAL

Our semi-continuous reading of Matthew's gospel excludes the parts that we hear during the seasons of the year. So it begins by skipping the stories of Jesus' infancy and ends before the passion. Today and tomorrow the weekday lectionary gives us its final passages from Matthew's story. Today we hear the parable of the ten bridesmaids, a reminder to be on the alert at all times with moral behavior and attentive prayer.

Paul contests the philosophical wisdom of Corinth with the wisdom of the cross. This paradoxical symbol reveals God's wisdom, deeper than that professed by humans. The psalmist praises the uprightness of God's word.

■ TODAY'S SAINT: Monica the African is noteworthy for her devotion and prayer, but her famous son, Augustine, brought her eternal attention. She nearly had Augustine baptized as an infant when the child turned ill, but she waited instead. This delay caused Augustine to believe God wanted him to experience deeper conversion later in life. By the prayers of Monica, Augustine accepted baptism. Monica died in Ostia, Italy. A freeway in California bears her name.

The opening prayer for today's Mass can be found in the proper of saints. You may take the other presidential prayers from the common of holy women (for example, #12). The second preface for holy men and women (P 70) could be used. An optional gospel for this day appears in the lectionary (#632), the story of Jesus raising to life the son of the widow of Naim. The story relates to that of Monica, who prayed for the salvation of her son. Augustine himself noted the connection,

as the lectionary's rubric informs us. The optional first reading praises a holy wife. As always, however, the readings of the weekday are recommended.

S A T
28
#430 (LMC #193–227)   white
Augustine (+ 430), bishop, doctor of the church
MEMORIAL

Our readings from Matthew conclude today with the parable of the talents. It bases God's judgment on the use and development of our gifts. The semi-continuous readings of the gospel omit those sections that pertain to seasons of the year, so we end this series not with the passion and resurrection, but with one of Jesus' last parables before his arrest.

It sounds like Paul is insulting the Corinthians, telling them that not many are wise, influential or wellborn. But he does so to show that God has still thought enough of them to choose them for the divine purpose. The psalmist sings of the blessed nation that God has chosen.

Alternate readings appear in the lectionary for Augustine (#633), highlighting his role as a teacher of faith and a lover of God.

■ TODAY'S SAINT: No theologian influenced the direction of the church in the West as much as Augustine the African did. His conversion from a sinful life as a Manichean to a religious life of commitment to Christ produces a story of immense importance. As writer and preacher, he put his stamp on every aspect of Christian liturgical, moral and intellectual life. A speaker of immeasurable talent, he served as bishop of Hippo in northern Africa for over thirty years.

You may use the preface for pastors (P 67) with the presidential prayers for August 28. These prayers are inspired by quotes from Augustine.

☀ 29
#126 (LMC #121)   green
Twenty-second Sunday in Ordinary Time

ORIENTATION

The brief series of readings from Hebrews ends today on summer's last full weekend. Many schools are back in session and many groups will be convening this week. Include in the general intercessions some of the special needs surfacing in your community as work resumes in many areas.

LECTIONARY

Jesus gives instructions pertaining to meals. More than offering proper etiquette about where to sit and whom to invite, he teaches about relationships in the reign of God. Guests should practice humility, and hosts should invite those who cannot return the favor.

The book of Sirach, known for its practical and parental advice, advises the reader to practice humility. All this humility fits with an attribute of God, who provides for the poor in their need.

The letter to the Hebrews closes its excerpts today with a glorious vision of the heavenly Jerusalem. By coming into God's presence in prayer, we draw near to God, the judge of all and to the spirits of the just made perfect.

SACRAMENTARY

The sixth preface for Sundays in Ordinary Time (P 34) mentions the promise of the paschal feast of heaven. Prayer over the people #21 prays for purity in mind and body.

OTHER IDEAS

For Grandparents' Day you may include a blessing of the elderly from the *Book of Blessings* (ch. 1, XII), but remember that some people become grandparents at a younger age!

Intercessions for schools can be adapted from the *Book of Blessings,* ch. 5.

MON 30 — #431 (LMC #193–227)   green
Weekday

The gospels for weekdays in Ordinary Time offer a semi-continuous reading of the three synoptic gospels in what scholars believe are the chronological order of their composition. Mark opens the series each year after the Christmas season. Matthew governs the summer, and Luke takes over for the final third of the year. This week we begin hearing the passages from Luke. As with Matthew, Luke's infancy account is omitted, as is his version of the passion. Luke, the evangelist of this year's Ordinary Time Sundays, includes themes like prayer, the Holy Spirit, the deference due to the poor, and the role of women in the community. In today's opening passage, Jesus reveals himself as the one who fulfills the prophecy of Isaiah in the hearing of his contemporaries.

Understandably, the first Christians had concerns about those who died before Jesus' return. Paul addresses these in the first reading, which is followed by a psalm of God's judgment.

The sacramentary includes prayers for the spread of the gospel (#14).

■ ROSE OF LIMA, remembered on the universal calendar on August 23, is honored with a solemnity today in Peru and the Dominican Republic as the patron of Latin America. Today is a holy day of obligation in Peru. This celebration is a feast in Argentina, Bolivia, Chile, Ecuador, Mexico, Panama, Paraguay and Puerto Rico. It is a memorial in Honduras, Nicaragua, El Salvador, Uruguay and Venezuela.

TUE 31 — #432 (LMC #193–227)   green
Weekday

As Luke begins his portrait of Jesus, we hear the Savior's powerful teaching and witness his ability to expel demons. The evangelist establishes the dynamic traits of his protagonist from the beginning of the story.

Paul says the spirit scrutinizes deep things, whether of God or of people. Because the Corinthians have been given God's spirit, they are able to enter deeply into the heart of God. According to the psalmist, God's faithful ones give praise for the works and attributes of their maker.

Prayers for the Holy Spirit (#7) might be appropriate today.

September

WED 1 — #433 (LMC #193–227)   green
Weekday

Jesus cures Simon's mother-in-law and expels a host of demons who call him the Son of God. He begins his career as an itinerant preacher.

Paul tries to lift up the Corinthians beyond the human level of social divisions into the spiritual level. He sees local leaders not as competitors but as coworkers with God in the service of the gospel. The psalm says God, who fashioned everyone's heart, knows each one's works.

The sacramentary includes a Mass for promoting harmony (#42).

THU 2 — #434 (LMC #193–227)   green
Weekday

Jesus borrows Peter's boat to preach to a crowd, then thanks Peter by pointing out a catch of fish. Peter makes excuses for not following Jesus, but he leaves everything and follows.

Paul returns to the theme of worldly wisdom and reminds the Corinthians that they should not boast in wisdom or anything else, because God has given them a share in everything present and future. The psalmist says everything on the earth belongs to God.

The sacramentary has texts for the spread of the gospel (#14A). The alternative opening prayer asks for the Spirit to sow the truth in people's hearts so that all may be born again to new life and communion.

■ MEXICO REMEMBERS Blessed Bartolomé Gutiérrez (+ 1632), priest and martyr, today with an optional memorial. Together with five companions he was tortured and martyred during the persecution of Christians in Nagasaki.

FRI 3 — #435 (LMC #193–227)   white
Gregory the Great (+ 604), pope, monastic, doctor of the church
MEMORIAL

Early on in Luke's story, Jesus already meets controversy with scribes and Pharisees. Today they object that his disciples do not fast. He uses images of a new coat and new wine to proclaim a new age.

Paul is not bothered by human judgment, nor does he fear the disparaging remarks of his enemies. God will judge and make all things right. God will save the just, the psalmist says, and be their refuge in time of distress.

■ TODAY'S SAINT: Gregory the Great came from a noted Roman family but humbly entered monastic life. Still, at election time, the people and clergy of Rome unanimously chose him to be their pope. His treatises have earned him the rank of one of the four great fathers of the Latin church. To him has been attributed some of the chants of the early church, and a large repertoire of chant is still called "Gregorian" in his honor.

Presidential prayers are under September 3. You may use the preface for pastors (P 67). Sing some chant today in Gregory's honor. The lectionary's proper of saints suggests using readings about preaching and the rewards of discipleship, but the readings of the weekday are recommended.

SAT 4 #436 (LMC #193–227)   green
Weekday

Optional Memorial of the Blessed Virgin Mary/white ▪ Jesus faces another controversy with the Pharisees as they challenge the disciples' behavior on the Sabbath. Jesus asserts his superiority over the Sabbath.

Paul contrasts his treatment as an apostle with the Corinthians' treatment as sages. In ironic tones he points to his own debasement in society and challenges the Corinthians to see where weakness and strength really lie. Those who call upon God will not be disappointed, the psalmist says. God will destroy the wicked.

The first eucharistic prayer for Masses of reconciliation says now is the time of grace and reconciliation.

Consider the texts for "Mary, Image and Mother of the Church I" (P 25), in the *Collection of Masses of the Blessed Virgin Mary*.

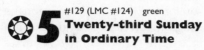

☀ 5 #129 (LMC #124)   green
Twenty-third Sunday in Ordinary Time

ORIENTATION

Noteworthy this weekend is the second reading. It comes from Philemon, the shortest book in the Bible. This is the only day in the Sunday cycle that we hear an excerpt from it.

This Labor Day weekend may include prayers for workers, travelers and those affiliated with schools.

LECTIONARY

By alluding to the crowds traveling with Jesus, Luke briefly reminds us that Jesus is on his journey to Jerusalem. He tells them about the cost of discipleship, the cross. They should include it in their plans, as a builder includes materials in plans for construction.

The book of Wisdom reminds us that wisdom is something we lack. It is hard to know what God is thinking or why things unfold the way they do. Still we trust in God's benevolent intent. The psalm asks God to help us gain wisdom of heart.

On one of his travels, Paul apparently made friends with a believer named Philemon. After leaving the area, Paul was arrested. About that time Philemon's slave Onesimus escaped and located Paul, asking him to help obtain his freedom. Onesimus also became a believer. Paul writes a letter to Philemon, an autograph copy of what will eventually become a book of the Bible. He hands it through the bars of jail into the safekeeping of a runaway

slave. We can only hope that the request was granted. This unusual letter is the shortest book of the Bible and makes its only Sunday appearance today.

SACRAMENTARY

The fourth eucharistic prayer says Jesus proclaimed release to captives. The fourth solemn blessing for Ordinary Time (#13) prays for consolation and freedom from anxiety.

OTHER IDEAS

As the season subtly shifts, you may introduce some changes in the environment if you like—a different tone of green vesture, different plants, even a different musical setting of eucharistic prayer acclamations.

This Labor Day weekend may have an assembly including some visitors and missing some regulars. Invite people to greet those around them. Look for the annual Labor Day Statement from the bishops' conference as a source for the homily and bulletin inserts: www.usccb.org/sdwp/national/index.htm. At www.nicwj.org/pages/materials.LIP01.html you will be able to download interfaith resources for worship, while at www.nicwj.org/pages/materials.LIPcath.html you will find some background resources for specifically Catholic preparation.

MON 6 #437/907–911 (LMC #193–227)   green
Weekday

Optional Proper Mass for Labor Day/white ▪ The week opens with another Sabbath controversy from Luke's gospel. Jesus cures a man with a withered hand to prove what is lawful.

Paul has heard of a case of a man who is now living with his father's wife. Paul criticizes not only the moral behavior of the individual in question, but also the Corinthian's complacency with the situation. The community is responsible for the moral behavior of its members.

On Labor Day you have the choice of observing the ordinary weekday or a votive Mass. The lectionary offers a selection of texts "For the Blessing of Human Labor," and it would be fitting to choose from these today. Choose from the Genesis accounts of creation if you like. Paul's exhortation to the Thessalonians that they work for their food is also good. Both psalm options sing of human labor. The first choice for the gospel helps people put work into its perspective.

The sacramentary includes prayers for the blessing of human labor (#25).

TUE 7
#438 (LMC #193–227)   green
Weekday

Luke's is sometimes called the gospel of prayer because he describes Jesus praying on several occasions. Today his prayer precedes the calling of the Twelve.

The Corinthians faced internal conflicts as much as Matthew's community did. Paul gives advice very similar to what we heard from Jesus this past Sunday. When there is a dispute in the church, bring it first to the church. A psalm of praise follows.

The second eucharistic prayer for reconciliation would be appropriate today.

WED 8
#636 (LMC #447-451)   white
Birth of Mary
FEAST

No one knows for sure when Mary was born, but today has been chosen for the feast because it marks the anniversary of the dedication of a church building to Mary's mother, traditionally known as Saint Anne.

There is no biblical reference to Mary's birth. The lectionary instead gives us Matthew's account of the birth of Jesus. You may include the genealogy (if the assembly is patient) because it places Mary in the long history of the ancestors of Jesus from Abraham to Joseph.

You have a choice for the first reading. The passage from Micah includes a prophecy about Bethlehem, used to interpret the significance of that city in the story of Jesus' birth. The passage from Romans speaks of those whom God predestined to share the image of the Son. Mary, preserved from the original sin from the moment of her conception according to the Catholic tradition, fulfills this description of those God predestined for glory. The exceptionally brief responsorial psalm for the day sings only one verse of scripture. Its theme resonates with that of Mary's *Magnificat*.

Penitential rite option C-iii calls Jesus "Son of God and Son of Mary." Presidential prayers can be found in the proper of saints. If you use the first preface of the Blessed Virgin (P 56), insert the words "the birth" in the third line.

■ TODAY IS THE PATRONAL FEAST OF CUBA, Our Lady of Charity of El Cobre. Tradition holds that conquistador Alonso de Ojeda wrecked on Cuba in 1508 and vowed to present a statue of Mary to the first village he reached. After his rescue, he gave the statue to the town of El Cobre, a site of pilgrimage today.

THU 9
#440 (LMC #193–227)   white
Peter Claver (+ 1654), presbyter, religious, missionary
MEMORIAL

Jesus encourages love for enemies, a striking change from past law and a demonstration of the great challenge that his followers face. He favors more than just getting along. He seeks real demonstrations of care for others.

Some Corinthians believed it was acceptable to eat food offered to idols because they did not believe in the idols. Paul agrees, but suggests they not do this because it may be difficult for others to understand. The psalm invites God to scrutinize our motives.

■ TODAY'S SAINT: Every Episcopal conference may establish some optional memorials as obligatory ones on the local calendar. That is the case with Peter Claver, a Jesuit missionary to the New World who worked for the salvation and freedom of slaves. Colombia and Venezuela also have established this date as an obligatory memorial.

The opening prayer is under September 9. Other prayers may come from the common of pastors, notably those for missionaries. You may use the preface for virgins and religious (P 68).

FRI 10
#441 (LMC #193–227)   green
Weekday

Disciples who want to lead others will have to scrutinize their own behavior first. Jesus says to take the log out of your own eye before removing a splinter from someone else's.

Paul feels absolutely obliged to preach the gospel and disciplines himself for the task. His self-sacrifice for the gospel is like an athlete's preparation for the race. The responsory sings of the psalmist's one desire, to dwell in the courts of God.

The sacramentary includes prayers for promoting harmony (#42).

SAT 11 #442 (LMC #193–227)   green
Weekday

Optional Memorial of the Blessed Virgin Mary/white ▪ Jesus wants results. You can tell good persons by the results they achieve. He disparages those who call him Lord but do not put into practice what he teaches.

In some of the earliest teaching on the eucharist, Paul reminds the Corinthians that the cup and bread they share are a participation in the body and blood of Christ. The Christian meal differs from that of idolators. Paul cautions the Corinthians to partake only of holy food and drink.

On this date in 2001 hijacked planes crashed into the World Trade Center, the Pentagon and in a Pennsylvania field. Thousands lost their lives in a grave assault by terrorists. Pray for peace.

▪ TODAY IS A SOLEMNITY in Venezuela, where the people celebrate their patronal feast of Our Lady of Coromoto. Tradition holds that Mary appeared to an Indian chief of the Cospes, a tribe considering conversion to Christianity. While he vacillated, she appeared to him repeatedly. Finally the chief lost his temper and witnesses saw him attempt to strangle the virgin. She disappeared, leaving him a statue of herself, now venerated in the parish church at Guanare, near Coromoto.

12 #132 (LMC #127)   green
Twenty-fourth Sunday in Ordinary Time

ORIENTATION

One of the most beloved stories in the Bible is in today's gospel. The story of the Prodigal Son inspires a reassuring spirit of repentance in the heart of the believer.

LECTIONARY

Luke is the only evangelist who recorded Jesus' story of the Prodigal Son. How blessed we are that he did! The parable is part of a longer chapter that explores the mystery of sin and forgiveness. The longer form of the gospel this weekend will include the parable of the lost sheep, heard earlier this summer on the solemnity of the Sacred Heart of Jesus.

Today's responsory actually fits the theme of the gospel. It is a psalm of repentance. To make the point, the lectionary assigns this psalm a refrain drawn from the gospel. Even though we sing it before hearing the gospel, it will prepare us for its message of mercy.

Through the intercession of Moses, God relents from wiping out the people who had worshiped the molten calf. Moses reminds God of the divine covenant, and God shows immeasurable mercy.

Today begins a series of readings from the first letter to Timothy. It is one of the so-called "pastoral epistles" because it treats some topics about church governance. The church community it describes seems to be fairly well organized into hierarchies, causing many scholars to believe that an anonymous writer composed this letter some time after the death of Paul. The heart of today's message is right in the middle of the text: "Christ Jesus came into the world to save sinners."

SACRAMENTARY

The first eucharistic prayer for Masses of reconciliation might be a good choice today. "Time and time again we broke your covenant," it says. Prayer over the people #6 praises God who cares for people "even when they stray."

OTHER IDEAS

With themes of repentance in the gospel, you might remind people about the opportunities for the sacrament of reconciliation this week. You could also hold a prayer service on the theme of repentance or a communal celebration of reconciliation.

If you have new liturgical ministers or new staff to commission, you may wish to do so this weekend. See the *Book of Blessings* (ch. 60–65).

MON 13 #443 (LMC #193–227)   white
John Chrysostom (+ 407), bishop, monastic, doctor of the church
MEMORIAL

When Jesus finishes his "sermon on the plain" in Luke's gospel, he returns to his ministry of healing. A centurion approaches seeking the cure of his servant, and Jesus assists the Gentile.

We hear today one of the most important passages from 1 Corinthians, the earliest recorded account of the Last Supper. It comes to us because Paul had to correct misbehavior at the supper and eucharist. The psalmist realizes that God wants a sincere believer, not empty ritual offerings.

Presidential prayers for the day are under September 13. You may use the preface for pastors (P 68). The lectionary's proper of saints suggests readings about building up the church and evangelization, but the readings of the weekday are recommended.

■ TODAY'S SAINT: John led a life of solitude and asceticism before pursuing priesthood. He was named bishop of Constantinople, but suffered at the hands of powerful enemies and spent many years in painful exile. His eloquent preaching, however, earned him the nickname Chrysostom, "Golden-mouth."

T U E **14** #638 (LMC #370) red
The Exaltation of the Holy Cross
FEAST

ORIENTATION

This day celebrates the dedication of the church of the Holy Sepulcher in Jerusalem. It houses the sites of Calvary, the empty tomb, and the discovery of the alleged wood of the cross. This basilica, still an unfortunate bevy of intra-Christian conflict, remains nonetheless one of the most important shrines in the world.

LECTIONARY

The first reading is essential for understanding the gospel. Serpents attack the Israelites wandering in the desert. Moses makes a bronze serpent and mounts it on a pole. All who look upon it are healed. This talisman became a symbol of the cross of Christ, which offers salvation to all those in need. The psalm remembers the struggles surrounding that event in the desert.

In the gospel, then, Jesus compares himself to the lifting up of the bronze serpent. His mission is to save those who suffer the torments of evil. Just as the bronze serpent resembled the source of evil, so Jesus on the cross resembles a source of suffering. But it is an illusion. The cross offers salvation to all who gaze upon it in faith.

The second reading is the classic text from Philippians, singing of the debasement and exaltation of Jesus. This passage likely existed before Paul wrote the letter as a hymn text sung by the faithful. It was incorporated into the letter, preserved for eternity, and now summarizes well the incarnation and ministry of Jesus. Part of this text is much used throughout the Holy Week liturgies, because it captures the theme of the self-emptying of Jesus for the sake of our salvation.

The *Lectionary for Masses with Children* changes the psalm today to 88, a passage that includes this verse: "Ever since I was a child, I have been sick and close to death."

SACRAMENTARY

Sing the Glory to God. The presidential prayers are under September 14. The day has its own preface (P 46), but that of the passion (P 17) may also be used. A solemn blessing is recommended,
but see also the one for the passion (#5).

The sacramentary's first appendix includes a priest's prayer to our redeemer as a thanksgiving after any Mass. The same section includes a prayer to Jesus Christ crucified.

OTHER IDEAS

You may wish to decorate the crucifix in the church in some way today. Draw attention to it as the source of glory. Make the sign of the cross at the beginning of the Mass slowly and deliberately.

W E D **15** #445, 639 (LMC #193–227) white
Our Lady of Sorrows
MEMORIAL

You may use the weekday readings if you wish. Jesus associates his ministry with that of John the Baptist and chides those who reject the message that both of them brought.

One of the most popular passages in the Bible, Paul's hymn to love, is an eloquent paean to this sublime human emotion. The psalmist says God loves justice and right.

You may also use the readings from the memorial of Our Lady of Sorrows. The idea for the feast comes from the two alternative gospels allowed for the day: Mary at the foot of the cross, and Mary hearing the prophecy that a sword of sorrow shall pierce her heart.

More tears and sorrow appear in the first reading. This time it is Christ who offered mournful prayers that God would spare him from death. The psalm is a desperate prayer for rescue.

This is one of the few dates on the liturgical calendar that has retained its sequence. The sequence is a hymn that may be used after the responsorial psalm and before the gospel. The sequences on Easter and Pentecost are obligatory. Today's and the one for Corpus Christi are optional. The sequence for Our Lady of Sorrows, *Stabat mater*, was made popular in the devotion of the Stations of the Cross. You can find the chant in the *Liber cantualis*.

Presidential prayers are in the proper of saints. The second preface for the Blessed Virgin Mary (P 57) may sound too gleeful given the tone of today's feast. Consider the first preface (P 56) instead.

See the *Collection of Masses of the Blessed Virgin Mary* for a selection of solemn blessings at the end of the order of Mass. The one for Lent refers to Jesus' "sorrowful mother."

The sacramentary's first appendix includes a priest's prayer before Mass to the Virgin Mary. It acknowledges that she stood by her Son "as he hung dying on the cross."

#446 (LMC #193–227)   red

THU 16 Cornelius (+ 253), pope, martyr; and Cyprian (+ 258), bishop, martyr
MEMORIAL

Jesus gives a powerful lesson on forgiveness while dining at the home of Simon the Pharisee. A woman known to be a sinner approaches him with kindness, and he proclaims the forgiveness of her sin. Tradition unfairly associates this woman with Mary Magdalene.

Our readings from 1 Corinthians will conclude with passages from the book's final chapter, in which Paul takes up various questions about the resurrection. Today we hear Paul affirm that eyewitnesses saw the risen Jesus. A psalm of thanksgiving associated with Easter follows this reading.

■ TODAY'S SAINTS: Today's saints had a serious disagreement about the proper procedures for readmitting those who had fallen from the faith. Still, their more

serious enemies were outside the church. Novatius claimed to be pope as soon as Cornelius was elected. Cyprian suffered under the persecution of Decius. Both accepted martyrdom for the faith.

Presidential prayers can be found at September 16. The preface for martyrs (P 66) is appropriate. Both saints are mentioned in Eucharistic Prayer I. The lectionary's proper of saints suggests readings about martyrdom and opposition, but the readings of the weekday are recommended.

■ THE BLOWING OF THE RAM'S HORN ushers in the Jewish celebration of Rosh Hashanah. The new year of 5765 is celebrated today and tomorrow.

#447 (LMC #193–227)   green

FRI 17 Weekday

Optional Memorial of Robert Bellarmine (+ 1621), bishop, religious, doctor of the church/white ■ Jesus returns to his preaching ministry, accompanied by the Twelve and a group of women, whose names are noted.

If Christ is not raised, Paul says, faith is in vain. His letter concludes with stirring faith in the resurrection. In the spirit of resurrection, we pray with the psalmist, "On waking, I shall be content in your presence."

Preface V for weekdays in Ordinary Time (P 41) says, "With living faith we proclaim [Jesus'] resurrection."

■ TODAY'S SAINT: Robert Bellarmine, an Italian Jesuit and cardinal, wrote vigorously in defense of the Catholic church in the years following the Reformation. A teacher, scholar and canonist, he found himself part of the Galileo controversy. The lectionary's proper of saints suggests readings about wisdom and teaching, but the readings of the weekday are recommended.

#448 (LMC #193–227)   green

SAT 18 Weekday

Optional Memorial of the Blessed Virgin Mary/white ■ In Luke's version of the parable of the sower, Jesus tells the parable, explains why he uses the form, and then interprets the meaning of his saying. Some will accept the word of God. Others will not.

Paul answers a practical question about how the dead are raised. He compares death and life to the sowing of seed. What is sown corruptible is raised incorruptible. Paul believes in the resurrection of Jesus, but also that we the believers will share in that resurrection. Paul's affirmation of faith concludes this series of New Testament letters.

The first preface for Christian death (P 77) says, "When the body of our earthly dwelling lies in death we gain an everlasting dwelling place in heaven."

From the *Collection of Masses of the Blessed Virgin Mary* see "Mary and the Resurrection of the Lord" (#15).

■ IN PERU, TODAY is the feast of Saint John Macías (+ 1645), who left Spain for the Americas, lived in austerity and served the poor, following the example of his friend Martin de Porres. Bolivia honors him today with an obligatory memorial.

#135 (LMC #130)   green

☀ 19 Twenty-fifth Sunday in Ordinary Time

ORIENTATION

Today's second reading suggests we pray for our civil leaders. You may wish to include them specifically in the general intercessions.

LECTIONARY

Luke gives another sobering reminder that he sides with the poor rather than the wealthy. The shorter version of the gospel collects sayings of Jesus that pertain to God, wealth and responsibility. The longer version of the gospel includes the difficult parable of the rich man's servant who is praised for cheating his employer. The poor are clever in finding ways out of their destitution. Jesus praises the cleverness, not the dishonesty.

In the first reading Amos complains about the unjust practices of the rich who cheat the poor. Together these passages cry out for justice and affirm God's love for those who have less. The psalm takes up the same theme: God lifts up the poor.

The second reading offers suggestions for prayer. Kings and those in authority are specifically listed among those for whom we should make supplication. When they are blessed, all society lives a tranquil life. The letter also suggests a posture for prayer: lifting up hands—holy hands; to be exact: hands free of misdeeds.

SACRAMENTARY

The fourth version of the eucharistic prayer for Masses for various needs and occasions says Jesus "was moved with compassion for the poor and the powerless." Prayer over the people #24 blesses those who trust God, asking that they may be kept from all harm.

OTHER IDEAS

Today is Catechetical Sunday. We remember the service of our catechists. You may include a blessing for them (*Book of Blessings*, ch. 4, I). Be sure to include all sorts of catechists: those who provide religious education for children, formation for sacraments for children and adults, and athletic values on the playing field.

#449 (LMC #193–227)   red
MON 20 Andrew Kim Taegŏn (+ 1846), presbyter, martyr; Paul Chong Hasang (+ 1839), catechist, martyr; and their companions, martyrs (+ 1839–1867)
MEMORIAL

Jesus makes several statements to the crowds today in a compact speech of aphorisms drawn together by Luke. He speaks of different properties of light: helping those in the dark and exposing what is hidden.

We return to the Old Testament for our first readings for the next few weeks. The books excerpted all come from the Wisdom literature: Proverbs, Ecclesiastes and Job. The book of Proverbs is too rich to take in a single hearing, so we proclaim just a few passages from it this week. Today's advice concerns treatment of one's neighbor. The psalm paints a picture of the just person.

■ TODAY'S SAINTS: Andrew Kim of Taegŏn and Paul Chong of Hasang are among 103 Korean martyrs of all ages whose sanctity is recognized collectively on this day. Ninety-two were lay people, the single largest group of laity in the history of the church to be canonized. The martyrs are included in the general calendar so all the world may recognize the universality of their faith and witness.

Prayers for the day are under September 20. A preface for martyrs is at P 66. The suggested scripture readings in the proper of saints—about the death of the just and martyrdom—are optional as they would be for any nonbiblical memorial. The readings of the weekday are recommended.

#643 (LMC #452–454, 376)   red
TUE 21 Matthew, apostle, evangelist
FEAST

Tradition has linked Matthew the tax collector, whose call is reported in today's gospel, with the author of the gospel. Scholars believe the actual author came a little later and find it doubtful that he was an eyewitness to the events of Jesus' life. Nonetheless, the Matthew of the gospel today is an example of forgiveness and evangelization. The first reading is a generic passage about apostles in the service of the early church. The psalm contains the theme of God's message resounding to the ends of the earth.

Sing the Glory to God today. Prayers for Matthew are at September 21. The second preface for apostles (P 65) speaks of the living gospel for all to hear. There is a solemn blessing for apostles (#17).

#451 (LMC #193–227)   green
WED 22 Weekday

Jesus instructs the Twelve and sends them out to overcome demons and cure the sick. They proclaim the good news and move on from those places that will not receive them.

Our excerpts from Proverbs end today with a repudiation of falsehood, poverty and riches. More verses from Psalm 119 follow, every one of them praising some aspect of God's law.

The fifth weekday preface for Ordinary Time (P 41) unites us with the apostles in proclaiming the resurrection.

THU 23

#452 (LMC #193–227)   green

Pio of Pietrelcina (+ 1968), presbyter, confessor, mystic/white
MEMORIAL

Herod, who had been attracted to the words of John, has a similar curiosity about the words of Jesus. He asks the question that underlies the gospel: Who is this man?

The book of Ecclesiastes is placed under the name "Qoheleth," probably meaning "preacher." It is a collection of wise sayings, sometimes erroneously attributed to King Solomon. Written four or five hundred years before the birth of Jesus, the book is filled with practical advice using down-to-earth examples. Today's passage reveals one of its themes: There is nothing new under the sun. The psalmist says of God that a thousand years are as yesterday come and gone.

The first preface for weekdays of Ordinary Time (P 37) proclaims the essence of Jesus' ministry.

■ MEXICO REMEMBERS Blessed Cristóbal (+ 1527), Antonio y Juan (+ 1529) today. These children accepted the Christian faith and encouraged others to believe. They suffered brutal martyrdoms.

When John Paul II canonized Padre Pio in 2002, he placed the new saint's feast on the universal calendar as an obligatory memorial. This Capuchin friar from Italy, an immensely popular saint, was well known as a spiritual guide. He suffered the stigmata for 50 years and worked many cures.

FRI 24

#453 (LMC #193–227)   green

Weekday

Yesterday's passage had Herod wondering who Jesus is. Today Jesus takes the same question to the disciples: Who do people say he is? Peter comes up with the reply, the Messiah of God. And

Jesus tells them of his upcoming sufferings.

Another popular passage from the Bible, today's excerpt from Ecclesiastes proclaims there is a time for everything. In the spirit of Qoheleth's somewhat bleak outlook on life, the psalmist says we are like a breath, our days like a passing shadow.

Prayers for the dying can be found at #33.

■ OUR LADY OF MERCIES is patron of the Dominican people, who celebrate today with a holy day of obligation. The devotion is associated with the Mercedarians and was added to the universal calendar in 1696 and removed in 1969, but it is still celebrated today in the Dominican Republic as a solemnity and in Argentina, Guatemala and Venezuela as a memorial. See the *Collection of Masses of the Blessed Virgin Mary* (#39).

SAT 25

#454 (LMC #193–227)   green

Weekday

Optional Memorial of the Blessed Virgin Mary / white ■ Jesus articulates the teaching on the passion to his incredulous disciples. They fail to grasp his meaning.

We conclude our brief series from the book of Ecclesiastes with a moving poetic description of old age: eyes like the darkened sun, limbs that tremble, backs stooped, teeth idle and few, ears faint, hair like blooming almond trees—before the cord is snapped and the bowl of life is broken. We return to Psalm 90, inviting God to teach us to number our days aright.

The sacramentary has prayers for a happy death (#46).

See the prayers for "Mary, Gate of Heaven," in the *Collection of Masses of the Blessed Virgin Mary* (#46).

■ TODAY IS YOM KIPPUR, the Jewish Day of Atonement, marked by a day-long fast.

☀26

#138 (LMC #133)   green

Twenty-sixth Sunday in Ordinary Time

ORIENTATION

This weekend concludes the series of second readings from the first letter of Timothy.

In Chile, the last Sunday of September is the solemnity of Our Lady of Mount Carmel, Mother and Queen of Chile. See July 16.

LECTIONARY

Yet again, the theme of wealth enters the gospel text. Jesus contrasts a rich man with a poor man named Lazarus. The rich man is greedy and does not share with the poor. When they die, it is the poor Lazarus who is comforted. The rich man is sometimes called Dives (pronounced DYE-veez) because that is the spelling of "rich man" in Latin.

Amos steps up again this week to supplement the message of the gospel. God expresses dissatisfaction with the complacent in Zion, who lie on beds of ivory, eating lambs and playing music while society deteriorates around them. The psalm praises God who sustains the fatherless and the widow, who secures justice for the oppressed and food for the hungry.

The first letter to Timothy concludes today with an exhortation for the reader to pursue virtues by keeping the commandment until Jesus appears. All honor and eternal power belong to him.

SACRAMENTARY

The fourth version of the eucharistic prayer for various needs and occasions says, "Open our eyes to the needs of all; inspire us with words and deeds to comfort those who labor and are burdened." The third solemn blessing for Ordinary Time (#12) prays that God will show the members of the assembly how to walk in charity and peace.

OTHER IDEAS

Alert your social justice committee about the hard-hitting passages in the readings for both this and last weekend. What actions on behalf of the poor can your parish take? What are the economic issues right in your own community?

#455 (LMC #193–227)   white

MON 27 Vincent de Paul (+ 1660), presbyter, religious founder
MEMORIAL

Jesus takes hold of a little child to give the disciples an example of leadership. The least is the greatest. The full impact of his example comes in the light of Saturday's prophecy on his upcoming passion. Jesus then expresses tolerance for some outside his group who use the power of his name. These two stories—one about humble leadership, the other about tolerance—bring to a close the first half of Luke's gospel. Tomorrow's passage starts a new section.

For the first reading we open the book of Job, the story of a man associated with the virtue of patience, but also a study in the meaning of innocent human suffering. It was probably written in conjunction with the Babylonian exile, after 586 BCE. In the opening chapter, which we hear today, Job, known for his faithfulness,

becomes a testing ground for loyalty between God and Satan. The psalm is a prayer asking God for justice.

■ TODAY'S SAINT: Vincent de Paul founded the Congregation of the Missions, serving the poor and staffing seminaries. With Saint Louise de Marillac he also founded the Daughters of Charity. In the office of readings today, we hear him say not to feel bad if you have to put down your prayer book to serve the poor.

Prayers for Saint Vincent are at September 27. You may use the preface for virgins and religious (P 68). The lectionary's proper of saints suggests readings about strength in weakness and service to the church, but the readings of the weekday are recommended.

#456 (LMC #193–227)   green

TUE 28 Weekday

Optional Memorial of Wenceslaus (+ 929),   martyr / red ▪ Optional Memorial of Lawrence Ruiz, married man, martyr, and his companions, martyrs (+ 1633–1637) / red ▪ Luke 9:51 is a pivotal verse in the gospel. Jesus turns his face toward Jerusalem, and with him the entire story moves from a description of his ministry to the preparation for the cross. Although we continue hearing about Jesus' sayings and miracles in this second half of the gospel, Luke reminds us several times that Jesus is heading toward Jerusalem, the ominous yet awesome place of the story's fulfillment.

Job, who endured the punishments meted out to him in yesterday's reading, now curses the day he was born. This, one of the bleakest readings in the lectionary, is followed by an equally sorrowful psalm of abandonment.

The second version of the eucharistic prayer for various needs and occasions says, "You never abandon the creatures formed by

your wisdom, but remain with us and work for our good even now."

■ TODAY'S SAINTS: Wenceslaus, better known for a Christmas carol than a fall festival, served as duke of Bohemia, but his efforts to spread the faith were ended when his brother Boleslaus assassinated him for opposing his military atrocities. The lectionary's proper of saints suggests readings about opposition and martyrdom, but the readings of the weekday are recommended.

Lawrence Ruiz, a married man, was a Dominican tertiary who served the church on mission in Nagasaki. He and 15 companions were martyred by decree of the local ruler, and he became the first canonized Filipino. The opening prayer for this optional memorial is in the 1994 *Sacramentary Supplement.*

#647 (LMC #381)   white

WED 29 Michael, Gabriel and Raphael, archangels
FEAST

We celebrate the feast of three angels mentioned in the Bible by name. But the lectionary today includes stories about only one of them, Michael. This feast day originally belonged to him alone, and vestiges remain. Michael appears in the alternate choices for the first reading today. He takes a dominant role in the vision from the book of Daniel and reappears in the conflict with the dragon in Revelation.

In the gospel, Jesus promises Nathanael that he will see the angels of God ascending and descending on the Son of Man. The vision seems to recall Jacob's ladder. In the psalm, we sing praises of God in the sight of the angels.

Prayers for the feast are in the proper of saints. Sing the Glory to God today and use the preface for the angels (P 60).

#458 (LMC #193–227) white

THU 30 Jerome (+ 420), presbyter, doctor of the church
MEMORIAL

Jesus sends out 72 disciples in pairs to continue his ministry. They proclaim the kernel of his message: The reign of God is at hand.

Even in the midst of his despair, Job states that his vindicator lives, and that in the end his case will receive justice before God and the earth. Christian hymn texts like "I Know That My Redeemer Lives" are based on this passage, seen as a prophecy for the coming of Christ who will bring final, fair judgment. The psalmist sings, "I believe that I shall see the good things of the Lord in the land of the living."

■ TODAY'S SAINT: Jerome served God as an ascetic monk and is frequently depicted as a cardinal. He translated the Bible from Hebrew and Greek into Latin, making it more understandable to people. He is one of the four great doctors of the Latin church. "Ignorance of scripture is ignorance of Christ," he said. He died in Bethlehem.

Presidential prayers can be found at September 30. You may use the preface for pastors (P 67). There are alternate readings in the lectionary for Jerome's day, passages that praise the scriptures he loved, although the readings of the weekday are recommended.

■ THE JEWISH FEAST OF SUKKOTH begins today. This harvest festival, or Feast of Tabernacles, lasts until October 6 this year.

October

#459 (LMC #193–227) white

FRI 1 Thérèse of the Child Jesus (+ 1897), religious, doctor of the church
MEMORIAL

Jesus prophesies ill for those who hear and reject his message. His disciples will be icons of his presence: When people hear them, they hear Jesus. When people reject them, they reject Jesus and the One who sent him.

After the introduction to the book of Job in which the sorrows of Job are detailed, a discussion breaks out between Job and his friends, trying to make sense of it all. Today the voice of God breaks through that discussion and basically affirms what Job has suspected. God's wisdom lies beyond human understanding. With the psalmist, and in the spirit of Job, we admit that God has probed us and knows us.

■ TODAY'S SAINT: At a very young age Thérèse joined a Carmelite monastery in her native Normandy and made a strong impression on the community. Her autobiography, written under obedience, reveals the simplicity and profundity of her faith. Only 24 when she died, she was named a doctor of the church at the end of the twentieth century.

Alternate readings for today's saint can be found in the lectionary. The first reading contains a metaphor for the maternal role of Jerusalem, and the gospel praises those who are like little children. Beware, though, that this same gospel reappears for tomorrow's memorial.

Prayers for the Mass are in the proper of saints. You may use the preface for virgins and religious (P 68).

#460, 650 (LMC #193–227, 384) white

SAT 2 The Guardian Angels
MEMORIAL

The lectionary has readings for this day, but only the gospel is proper. Matthew says of children that their angels constantly behold God's face. This text has been used to justify the belief in guardian angels.

Angels appear in the optional first reading and psalm for October 2, but you may also turn to the weekday for those texts today. There, Job makes his final response to God, admitting his ignorance before God's wisdom. The story comes to a deliriously happy ending. Verses from psalm 119 sing of God's wise decrees.

■ TODAY'S MEMORIAL has been on the calendar since 1670 as a way of proclaiming God's protection for those who are helpless. The preface for angels (P 60) is used with the presidential prayers for October 2.

#141 (LMC #136) green

☀ 3 Twenty-seventh Sunday in Ordinary Time

ORIENTATION

Our long march through Ordinary Time advances. Today's second readings shift subtly to the second letter to Timothy. The dawn of October will bring new shades to trees and flora—some of which may add new luster to your worship space.

LECTIONARY

Today's gospel pairs a saying of Jesus with a short parable. At first he calls the apostles to have faith the size of a mustard seed—that is enough. In the parable he speaks of the responsibilities of servants. His hearers must have understood the expectations of underlings. Jesus expects his disciples to do more than the minimum, more than what is obligatory.

Paul's letter to the Romans includes a classic exegesis on the text that serves for today's first reading, "the just shall live by faith." The issue became enormously divisive between Catholics and Lutherans, but in recent years tremendous progress has been made to unify the theology of these churches. The reason we hear from Habakkuk today is that the prophet's stress on faith fits well with the opening of today's gospel. Several weeks ago we heard a similar passage from Habakkuk on a weekday. These are the only two times the lectionary offers excerpts from that prophet.

The first reading opens with Israel's cry of exasperation that God has not listened. The psalm contains God's cry of exasperation that Israel does not hear.

Together with the letter to Titus, the two letters to Timothy make up the "pastoral epistles" of the New Testament. These letters give us a snapshot of the needs and organization of the late-first-century church. Timothy has received a gift of the Spirit through the imposition of hands. Now he is asked to stir it into flame. This passage provides some of the background for our practice of imposing hands during the ordination rite.

SACRAMENTARY

The fourth preface for Sundays in Ordinary Time (P 32) proclaims the kernel of our faith: the birth, suffering, death, resurrection and return of Jesus Christ. Prayer over the people #9 prays for those who believe in God, that they might spread the gift of love with others everywhere.

OTHER IDEAS

This can be a busy time of year for parishes. If you have lots of announcements, you can just give headlines and keep the details in the printed bulletin, in a voice mailbox and on the parish website.

If you are planning a blessing of animals for Saint Francis tomorrow, announce the arrangements today.

#4610 (LMC #193–227)   white

M O N 4
Francis of Assisi (+ 1226), religious founder
MEMORIAL

Luke is probably the most literary writer of the New Testament. Today's parable of the Good Samaritan is a good example of why this is true. The story reflects not just Jesus' skill as a storyteller but Luke's as a writer. The powerful message of this parable has brought the expression "good samaritan" into the English language.

All first readings from now till Advent are drawn from the New Testament. We begin the series today with Paul's letter to the Galatians. The churches in this group had received the gospel from Paul but were hearing alternate forms. Paul's letter reassures them that his word is authentic. In doing so, he wrote perhaps the earliest document in defense of Gentile Christianity. In the opening verses that we hear today, Paul

tells them there is no other gospel as they may be led to believe. We sing in responsory a psalm of thanksgiving for God's covenant.

■ TODAY'S SAINT: Francis pursued a life of voluntary poverty. He formed a religious community with other like-minded men, which became the Order of Friars Minor. His simple approach to life and his love for God's creation have made him a charismatic figure to every generation. Canonized just two years after his death, he has made Assisi a popular place of pilgrimage. Sing music inspired by his writing: the "Canticle of Creation," "All Creatures of Our God and King" or "Lord, Make Me an Instrument of Your Peace."

In the optional first reading in the lectionary, Paul says he bears the brand marks of Jesus on his body. It is unclear if Paul is referring to a physical share in the wounds of Christ, but the reading is suggested because the story of Francis reports that this saint did receive the stigmata. The optional gospel refers to the simplicity that Francis loved. The readings of the weekday, however, are recommended.

The preface for virgins and religious (P 68) could accompany the presidential prayers for October 4. Some communities have a blessing of animals or of fields and flocks today (*Book of Blessings*, ch. 25–26, or *Catholic Household Blessings and Prayers*, pp. 174–77). If celebrating this day with children, see LTP's *School Year, Church Year*.

#462 (LMC #193–227)   green

T U E 5
Weekday

Although Martha is busy with hospitality, Jesus tells her that Mary listening at his feet has chosen the better part. A passage that still rankles many a devoted

Martha, it has often been used to compare the active and contemplative spiritual life. Nevertheless, when he comes again, Jesus will have some explaining to do with a lot of hard-working homemakers.

Today's first reading is a precious autobiographical account of Paul's preaching career. It is followed by a psalm that prays for God's guidance.

The sacramentary includes prayers for the spread of the gospel (#14B).

W E D 6 #463 (LMC #193–227) green
Weekday

Optional Memorial of Blessed Marie Rose Durocher (+ 1849), virgin, founder, educator / white ▪ *Optional Memorial of Bruno (+ 1101), priest / white* ▪ Luke's version of the Lord's Prayer is briefer than Matthew's, and many scholars believe it is more original. Its simple directness and its divine source have made it one of the most well known prayers in the world.

Paul continues his autobiographical account in Galatians, explaining the evangelical roles he and Peter divided. Paul explains his confrontation with Peter, who was guilty in Paul's mind of hypocrisy. The shortest psalm has the broadest theme. It follows this story of the two great apostles with a verse about commissioning from the end of Mark's gospel.

The preface for Peter and Paul (P 63) relies on today's first reading.

▪ TODAY'S SAINTS: A native of Quebec and the youngest of ten children, Marie Rose Durocher founded the Congregation of the Sisters of the Most Holy Names of Jesus and Mary for the purpose of bringing Catholic education to Canada. Her sisters are at work even outside Canada in countries like the United States, Lesotho, Peru, Brazil and Haiti.

Bruno directed a school at Reims and became chancellor of the diocese there. But he sought the solitary life of prayer and founded the monastery of La Chartreuse, from which the monks are called Carthusians. The monks live an austere life in a remote setting visible not from the main road but only from the peaks of nearby mountains. They gained fame for their secret recipes for a variety of strong but tasty after-dinner liqueurs. The lectionary's proper of saints suggests readings about the spiritual life and discipleship, but the weekday readings are preferred.

T H U 7 #464 (LMC #193–227) white
Our Lady of the Rosary
MEMORIAL

Following yesterday's revelation of the Lord's Prayer, Jesus encourages the disciples to pray frequently, and to ask God persistently for their needs.

The Galatians have confused the role of law with that of the spirit, and Paul believes they have lost their minds! He reminds them that God's Spirit has come to them because of their faith. The responsory comes from Luke's gospel. The *Benedictus* forms a bridge between God's fidelity in the covenant and the revelation of Jesus Christ in the flesh.

▪ TODAY'S MEMORIAL: Today was dedicated to Our Lady of the Rosary after Christians won the Battle of Lepanto over Muslim forces on this date in 1570, the same year the Council of Trent's Roman Missal was finally published. The victory at Lepanto was attributed to Mary's intercession, after people prayed the rosary. Although this history is disturbing, the rosary continues to offer comfort to those who make it a part of their daily prayer.

The second Marian preface (P 57) goes well with today's presidential prayers, which are found in the proper of saints. The lectionary's proper of saints suggests readings about Mary, but the weekday readings are preferred.

The *Collection of Masses of the Blessed Virgin Mary* includes a set of solemn blessings, found at the end of the order of Mass. The second option under Ordinary Time makes a good choice today.

F R I 8 #465 (LMC #193–227) green
Weekday

Jesus meets opposition on his way to Jerusalem, this time in the form of demonic possession and a disbelieving crowd.

Paul says the children of Abraham are those who believe. The inheritance does not depend on mere obedience to the law. We sing a psalm about the covenant.

"All your actions show your wisdom and love," says Eucharistic Prayer IV, before it details the revelation of the new covenant.

S A T 9 #466 (LMC #193–227) green
Weekday

Optional Memorial of Denis (+ 258), bishop, martyr; and his companions, martyrs / red ▪ *Optional Memorial of John Leonardi (+ 1609), presbyter, religious founder / white* ▪ *Optional Memorial of the Blessed Virgin Mary / white* ▪ The spirit of opposition hovers behind today's gospel, where Jesus implies some distance between his family's approval and his ministry. Someone blesses his mother, but Jesus blesses those who hear and keep God's word.

Although the law guided life in the past, Christ brought our justification. Now, Paul says, all are equal: Jew and Greek, slave and free, male and female. The psalmist sings of God's eternal covenant.

The sacramentary's prayer for the universal church (#1C) asks it to be "for all the world a sign of your unity and holiness."

■ TODAY'S SAINTS: Denis is honored as the first bishop of Paris. He was beheaded with several companions at the instigation of pagan priests. According to legend, Denis was decapitated on the site of Sacre Coeur on Montmartre in Paris, then picked up his head and walked two miles, where he died and was buried. The church of St. Denis, built on the site of his grave, is the first Gothic church in history, enclosing the world's oldest rose window of stained glass. France's royalty was buried there. Denis is the patron saint of those with headaches. The lectionary's proper of saints suggests readings about suffering and evangelization, but the readings of the weekday are recommended.

As a priest, John Leonardi took on youth ministry and founded the Congregation of Clerics Regular of the Mother of God to provide better education. He is considered a founder of the Society for the Propagation of the Faith. The lectionary's proper of saints suggests readings about preaching and obedience to Christ, but the weekday readings are preferred.

■ LUIS BELTRÁN (+ 1581) is remembered in Colombia and Venezuela today with a memorial, and with an optional memorial in Bolivia. A Spanish Dominican priest who preached the fear of God, Beltrán traveled to Spanish America and baptized enormous numbers of natives, especially in Colombia, where he is a patron saint.

If you are celebrating the memorial of Mary today, consider "Mary, Pillar of Faith," from the *Collection of Masses of the Blessed Virgin Mary* (#35), which uses the gospel of the day.

#144 (LMC #139)   green
Twenty-eighth Sunday in Ordinary Time

ORIENTATION

In some parts of the country, autumn leaves are reaching their peak color. As we become aware of the cycle of seasons again, Luke reminds us that Jesus continues his journey to Jerusalem.

LECTIONARY

No other story captures the humanity of gratitude as Luke's account of Jesus healing the ten lepers. Only one bothers to say thanks, and Jesus seems disturbed by the statistic. The Samaritan, expected to be the bad guy, is the good guy after all.

The first reading tells the story of another healing, this one of Naaman the Syrian. As the lepers are healed in the gospel, so Naaman is healed in the second book of Kings. He offers praise to God and a gift to Elisha the prophet.

The psalm goes another direction. Instead of offering us a simple song of thanksgiving, like Psalm 138, the lectionary proffers Psalm 98 with its refrain about God revealing salvation to the nations. The first reading records the healing of a Gentile, Naaman, and the gospel records the healing of a Samaritan. Hence, the psalm shows God's mercy to all the nations, not just to the inhabitants of Israel.

The writer of the second letter to Timothy says he is in chains, but that there is no chaining the word of God. He sings a confident hymn of praise: If we have died with Christ, we shall live with him.

Lucien Deiss used these verses for his popular hymn, "Keep in Mind."

SACRAMENTARY

The first preface for Sundays in Ordinary Time (P 29) says Christ has "called us to the glory that has made us a chosen race, a royal priesthood, a holy nation, a people set apart." Prayer over the people #19 prays that God will enrich people with grace.

OTHER IDEAS

Some parishes find autumn a good season for conducting a special campaign for funds. This weekend's readings will challenge the faithful to consider their gifts to the church. How will they return thanks to God for all they have received?

#467 (LMC #193–227)   green
M O N 11 Weekday

Thanksgiving Day, Canada/white ■ In the face of opposition, Jesus reminds the crowds about Jonah and the queen of the south. The Ninevites reformed their lives at Jonah's preaching, and the queen traveled a great distance to listen to Solomon. But this generation does not listen and does not reform. Jesus is referring to the part of the story concerning the effectiveness of Jonah's preaching, not to the prophet's three days in the belly of the great fish.

Paul strengthens his case about the Gentile inheritance of the gospel by comparing Christians to descendants of Abraham's freeborn wife. The psalm praises God who looks upon the lowly.

The first eucharistic prayer for reconciliation says God invites us to serve the human family by opening our hearts to the fullness of the Holy Spirit.

This is the liturgical day for observing the memory of Blessed John XXIII, the beloved, humble pope who catapulted the church into the modern age by opening the Second Vatican Council. You have the option of celebrating a Mass from the common of pastors.

■ MARY SOLEDAD (+ 1887) of Spain founded the Handmaids of Mary Serving the Sick, a community that expanded to Latin America. She is remembered today with an optional memorial in Guatemala.

T U E 12 #468 (LMC #193–227)   green
Weekday

Even when Jesus responds favorably to a dinner invitation, he cannot avoid opposition. The Pharisee who hosts him complains that he did not perform the proper ablutions. For Jesus, his omission gave a prophetic sign that allowed him to preach.

In commanding Gentile men not to be circumcised, Paul reminds them that faith, not circumcision, gains access to the covenant with Christ. Curiously, a psalm in praise of God's law follows this passage.

■ TODAY IS THE PATRONAL FEAST OF SPAIN, Our Lady of the Pillar. According to a twelfth-century legend, the apostle James had a vision of Mary carrying the infant Christ and of angels carrying a pillar. Mary asked for a church to be built on the site. A shrine honors the story at Zaragoza. This is an optional memorial in Argentina and Guatemala.

W E D 13 #469 (LMC #193–227)   green
Weekday

The ill feelings between Jesus and his enemies break out into harsh words. Jesus criticizes the Pharisees and the lawyers as well for their hypocrisy.

Concluding the series of readings from Galatians, we hear Paul contrast the results of the flesh with the fruit of the spirit. Not only does the spirit offer a different freedom than that of the law, it also offers richer fruits. The first psalm, which describes the two ways of justice and wickedness, answers the reading.

The sacramentary's communion prayer for promoting harmony (#42) says, "May we experience the peace we preach to others."

T H U 14 #470 (LMC #193–227)   green
Weekday

Optional Memorial of Callistus I (+ 222), pope, martyr / red ▪ Jesus continues his bleak assessment of hypocritical lawyers. His speech causes his enemies to set traps for him.

The letter to the Ephesians acquired that name after the earliest extant manuscripts. The first versions show no designated recipient, indicating the letter was intended for a general audience, not the specific needs of one ecclesial community. Because its formal style differs from the classic letters of Paul, some scholars believe it was written by a disciple of Paul about 80 or 90. The hymn that opens the letter praises God who from the beginning planned salvation in Christ and the formation of the church. In reply, we sing a general psalm of praise.

The third preface for weekdays in Ordinary Time (P 39) says, "Through your beloved Son you created our human family. Through him you restored us to your likeness."

■ TODAY'S SAINT: Callistus extended forgiveness toward those who had lapsed from their faith but wanted to return. He started Ember Day fasts and opened the first Christian cemetery in Rome. The lectionary's proper of saints

suggests readings about leadership and the rewards of discipleship, but the weekday readings are preferred.

F R I 15 #471 (LMC #193–227)   white
Teresa of Jesus (+ 1582), religious, doctor of the church
MEMORIAL

The crowd following Jesus had reached soccer game and rock concert status. Thousands were walking over one another. Luke strings together a series of aphorisms about avoiding hypocrisy, secrecy and groundless fears.

The letter to the Ephesians says we were chosen by Christ to exist for the praise of the glory of God. In Christ, we were sealed with the promise of the Holy Spirit. Our baptism makes us one with Christ in the Spirit. The psalm answers this theme: "Blessed are the people the Lord has chosen to be his own."

■ TODAY'S SAINT: Born in Avila, Spain, Teresa entered a Carmelite convent and became the author of many spiritual writings that remain very popular. Giovanni Lorenzo Bernini captured her rapturous ecstasies in a remarkable stone sculpture in Rome. Presidential prayers for Saint Teresa are under October 15. You may use the preface for virgins and religious (P 68). The lectionary's proper of saints suggests readings about mystical prayer and union with Christ, but the weekday readings are preferred.

■ FOLLOWERS OF ISLAM begin Ramadan about this time, when this month's crescent moon first appears. Muslims fast for a month from sunrise to sunset.

SAT 16 — #472 (LMC #193–227) green — Weekday

Optional Memorial of Hedwig (+ 1243), married woman, monastic/white • Optional Memorial of Margaret Mary Alacoque (+ 1690), religious/white • Optional Memorial of the Blessed Virgin Mary/white • Jesus warns the disciples that they, too, will face opposition, but he promises the Holy Spirit will teach what they need to know.

The author of Ephesians prays that the readers may see the hope to which they are called, a vision of Christ reigning as head of the church, filling the universe in all its parts. Psalm 8 is chosen because it is frequently interpreted as a prophecy about Christ, the Son whom God gave dominion over creation.

The fifth preface for Sundays in Ordinary Time (P 33) quotes Psalm 8.

■ TODAY'S SAINTS: Hedwig, duchess of Silesia, was a wife and mother of seven children. She donated her fortune to the church and the poor, and retired to a Cistercian convent after her husband's death. The lectionary's proper of saints suggests readings about the virtuous life and the spiritual family of Christ, but the weekday readings are preferred.

Margaret Mary Alacoque of France promoted first Friday devotions in honor of the Sacred Heart, due to her mystical visions as a Visitandine sister. She bore many trials of rejection and contempt with patient love. The lectionary's proper of saints suggests readings about the love of Christ and God's sharing of wisdom with the simple, but the weekday readings are preferred.

See the texts for "Our Lady of the Cenacle" in the *Collection of Masses of the Blessed Virgin Mary* (#17).

■ ON THIS DAY IN 1978, Karol Wojtyla, cardinal of Kraków, Poland, was elected the youngest pope in over a century and the first non-Italian bishop of Rome in 450 years.

☀ 17 — #147 (LMC #142) green — Twenty-ninth Sunday in Ordinary Time

ORIENTATION

Take a look at the alleluia verses for Sundays in Ordinary Time (*Lectionary for Mass,* 163). Any of them may be used on any Sunday in Ordinary Time, but three of them are reserved for the last Sundays of Ordinary Time. These Sundays are not specified, but if you judge that the period of Ordinary Time is reaching its climax, you may switch to those verses.

LECTIONARY

Luke returns to another of his favorite themes, prayer. He tells of a widow who persistently asks for justice from a judge. Jesus says God will be even more attentive in securing the rights of people.

Another favorite passage about prayer serves as today's first reading. The Israelites were winning the battle against Amalek as long as Moses prayed with his hands raised up. When he grew tired, they had him sit on a rock while Aaron and Hur supported his hands. Posture makes a difference when we pray. The psalm expresses our dependence upon God our protector.

Timothy must remain faithful to the sacred scriptures. "All scripture is inspired by God," today's second reading asserts, and is useful for all manner of things. Timothy must proclaim the word whether convenient or inconvenient. And so must we.

SACRAMENTARY

The gospel proclaims that God will secure the rights of the just, and the fourth version of the eucharistic prayer for various needs and occasions says God cares for us as a parent cares for children. The first solemn blessing for Ordinary Time (#10) is the blessing of Aaron, who appears in today's first reading.

OTHER IDEAS

Today is Mission Sunday, a traditional Roman Catholic observance. Choose a hymn to draw attention to the day and include intercessions for the mission of the church. The Mass texts for the spread of the gospel (#14) may be used today.

MON 18 — #661 (LMC #452–454, 396) red — Luke, evangelist — FEAST

The third gospel and the Acts of the Apostles are attributed to Luke, a companion of Paul. In some sections of Acts, the author writes in the first person plural, putting himself into the story. He is called a physician in the New Testament, an occupation associated with artists in the Middle Ages. A late tradition proposed that Luke was also a painter and that he actually created some works of religious art. His combined work takes up nearly a third of the New Testament, and the style of writing is acclaimed for its excellence.

The first reading identifies Luke as a companion of Paul. The psalm is one used for apostles and evangelists because it says the works of creation proclaim God's glory. The gospel, taken from Luke, tells of the appointment of 72 disciples, among whom tradition numbers this saint.

Sing the Glory to God. The second preface for apostles is recommended (P 65) because of its reference to "the living gospel." But the fourth version of the eucharistic prayer for various needs and occasions, "Jesus, the Compassion of God," refers to stories of Luke's gospel. Take the presidential prayers from Luke's feast. You may use the solemn blessing for apostles (#17).

#474 (LMC #193–227)   red
Isaac Jogues and John de Brébeuf, presbyters, religious, missionaries, martyrs; and their companions, martyrs (+ 1642–1649)

TUE 19
MEMORIAL

In another saying about the brevity of life and the importance of vigilant readiness, Jesus tells the disciples to be like those awaiting the master's return from a wedding. Be prepared at all times.

The Gentile recipients of the letter to the Ephesians had no part of the Hebrew covenant, but now in Christ they are brought right into the heart of the new covenant. Christ has reconciled the Jewish and Gentile communities into one body. The psalmist sings of the peace that only God can give.

■ TODAY'S SAINTS: The Jesuit and oblate missionaries we remember today came from France to evangelize North America. They suffered torture and martyrdom for their efforts, and they are honored today as secondary patrons of Canada. Their numbers include Isaac Jogues, John de Brébeuf, Anthony Daniel, Gabriel Lalemant, Charles Garnier, Noel Chabanel, René Goupil and Jean de la Lande.

The opening prayer for these martyrs' day may be augmented with other prayers for missionaries and the preface of martyrs (P 66). Although it's an optional memorial on the universal church calendar, today is an obligatory memorial in the United States. The lectionary's proper of saints suggests readings about martyrdom and evangelization, but the weekday readings are preferred.

In most countries, this is also the optional memorial of Saint Paul of the Cross, but in the United States his day has been transferred to October 20.

WED 20   #475 (LMC #193–227)   green
Weekday

Optional Memorial of Paul of the Cross (+ 1775), presbyter, religious founder/white ▪ We hear another saying about being prepared. People do not know when the thief is coming, nor when the master will return. Jesus proposes that all must be ready for the return of the Son of Man.

Paul says it simply and openly: Gentiles are now co-heirs with Jews, members of the same body and sharers of the same promise. The canticle from Isaiah sings of drawing water joyfully for a saving fountain. It foreshadows the joyful salvation in Christ made possible through the waters of baptism.

The first version of the eucharistic prayer for various needs and occasions says, "You have brought together in a single Church people of every nation, culture, and tongue."

■ TODAY'S SAINT: In the United States we celebrate the optional memorial of Paul of the Cross a day later than almost everyone else in the world. Paul's day (October 19) coincides with that of Isaac Jogues, John de Brebeuf and their companions, martyrs of North America. Consequently, we have permanently displaced Paul of the Cross, not off the calendar, but to the next day.

Paul led an austere life and preached to the poor. He founded the Discalced Clerks of the Most Holy Cross and Passion of Our Lord Jesus Christ, more popularly known as the Passionists. The lectionary's proper of saints suggests readings about the spiritual life and the cross, but the weekday readings are preferred.

THU 21   #476 (LMC #193–227)   green
Weekday

Although we like to think of Jesus in his role as peacemaker, he says today that he has come not for peace but for division. His message will cause people to join his cause or reject it. Even families will be divided. Divided families must have troubled the early church community for whom Luke wrote the gospel.

Because the Gentile converts have union and status in Christ, the author of the letter prays that they may respond appropriately, with charity at the root and foundation of their lives, having experienced the unsurpassable love of Christ. The psalmist sings of God's kindness filling the earth.

The first preface for weekdays (P 37) says God has renewed all things in Christ and has given us all a share in his riches.

■ IN BOLIVIA, today is the optional memorial of Miguel Febres Cordero (+ 1910). See February 9.

O · C · T · O · B · E · R

FRI 22 #477 (LMC #193–227) green
Weekday

People can make the simplest of weather predictions, Jesus says, but they cannot interpret the present age. As a sign of living in urgent times, people should settle with their accusers without going to court. In Jesus' view, there is no time for long cases.

Paul appeals to the Ephesians' sense of unity. They should act with the Christian virtues and preserve the unity that is theirs in the Spirit. The psalmist also lists the qualities of a just person.

Prayers for the progress of peoples (#21) will help the community build on the grace God gives us.

Twenty-six years ago today John Paul II became the bishop of Rome.

SAT 23 #478 (LMC #193–227) green
Weekday

Optional Memorial of John of Capistrano (+ 1456), presbyter, religious, missionary/white ▪ Optional Memorial of the Blessed Virgin Mary/white ▪ Jesus calls on his listeners to reform their lives by recalling disasters that befell their comrades. The care of the soul should at least resemble the care given a barren fig tree. Jesus does not wish judgment but conversion.

Christ ascended so that he might fill people with his gifts. The letter to the Ephesians lists the ministries alive in the early church and urges the community to find its strength through their union and exercise.

The Mass for the ministers of the church (#8) asks God to keep the church's ministers faithful.

▪ TODAY'S SAINT: John was born in Capistrano and educated in Perugia. He joined the Franciscans and became a student of Bernadine of Siena, who encouraged John's love for the name of

Jesus. Renowned for his preaching, he led a crusade against invading Turks and has become the patron of military chaplains. One of the California missions is named for him. The lectionary's proper of saints suggests readings about reconciliation and discipleship, but the weekday readings are preferred.

If you opt for the optional memorial of the Blessed Virgin, consider "Mary, Mother and Teacher in the Spirit," from the *Collection of Masses of the Blessed Virgin Mary,* which makes a reference to our baptismal promises.

☀24 #150 (LMC #145) green
Thirtieth Sunday in Ordinary Time

ORIENTATION

We hear the last passage from excerpts from the pastoral epistles today. It may be a good time to pray for the leaders of our church.

LECTIONARY

Luke returns to his theme of prayer as Jesus reveals the parable of the Pharisee and the tax collector. Both enter the temple to pray, but only one pleases God with the right attitude. Prayer and charity have their effect when they come from a sincere heart.

The prayer of the lowly pierces the clouds, says Sirach. Those who serve God get their petitions heard. This passage perfectly prepares us to hear the point of the gospel. The Catholic church depends largely upon printed texts

for our prayers, but the presider needs to inhabit them with true devotion to bring them to life.

Psalm 34 is used frequently in the lectionary. It appears today because of the verses that proclaim God's defense of the just, the poor and the brokenhearted. Each line of this psalm is an independent statement. In Hebrew, each line begins with a new letter of the alphabet, a clever compositional device, even at the expense of a logical flow of thought.

Today closes the series of readings from the letters to Timothy. Many Christians wish its opening verses will be applied to them one day: "I have competed well; I have finished the race; I have kept the faith." God will save us from every evil threat and bring us safely home. The letter concludes with a note of confidence.

SACRAMENTARY

The third preface for Sundays in Ordinary Time (P 31) captures the sense of prayer from today's gospel. It humbly acknowledges that humanity refused God's friendship, while Jesus restored it. The fourth solemn blessing for Ordinary Time (#13) prays for the gifts of faith, hope and love.

OTHER IDEAS

If the date of your church dedication is unknown, you may celebrate it this Sunday (or October 25) with the common Mass for the dedication of the church. Both the sacramentary and the lectionary texts may be used in place of those assigned for the Ordinary Time Sunday. See *General Norms for the Liturgical Year and Calendar* (the note to #52c), and consult your diocesan offices for local regulations. It is important to celebrate this anniversary each

MON 25 #479 (LMC #228–231)   green
Weekday

Today's gospel unfortunately does not appear in the Sunday cycle of readings. It is a marvelous miracle story. By laying a hand on her, Jesus cures a woman stooped by 18 years of illness. She praises God. The chief of the synagogue is indignant that Jesus healed on the Sabbath and blames the congregation! Jesus is baffled by the tactlessness of his opponents, and the crowd rejoices at the marvels he does.

The letter to the Ephesians gives its exhortation to the readers. Be kind and forgiving, imitators of God. Root out immorality and impurity. In baptism, they have become light in the Lord; they should live as children of light. Because this reading contrasts good and bad behavior, Psalm 1 makes a perfect fit for it. The refrain, however, comes right from Ephesians, an exhortation to behave like God.

Eucharistic Prayer IV says God lives in unapproachable light and leads us all to the joyful vision of light.

This is one of the dates on which you may celebrate the anniversary of the dedication of your church if the date is unknown. Use the sacramentary and lectionary texts for the common of the dedication of a church, sing or recite the Glory to God and the creed.

The *Lectionary for Masses with Children* has a special section devoted to the weeks at the end of the liturgical year. If you like, you could start using them in Masses with children. The regular lectionary has a common psalm (#174, option 22) and verses to the gospel acclamations (#173 and #509) that may be used for the last weeks of the year.

TUE 26 #480 (LMC #228–231)   green
Weekday

Luke gives us a break from all the stories about opposition to Jesus, and we hear instead two short parables about the reign of God. Jesus compares it to seed and to yeast.

Today's first reading compares the relationship of Christ and the church to husband and wife. In an attempt to show how the church seeks to do the will of Christ, Paul uses a symbol that has instigated heated controversy about topics ranging from the role of women to the permanence of marriage. The psalm closes its eyes to the controversy and sings of the blessing of parents and children.

The sacramentary includes prayers for the family (#43).

WED 27 #481 (LMC #228–231)   green
Weekday

Today's gospel opens with the reminder that Jesus is making his way toward Jerusalem. Throughout the second half of Luke's gospel, Jesus is on a physical and spiritual journey toward the city of his death. Luke has planted reminders in the text so we do not lose our way with Jesus, heading toward the cross. A discussion about salvation arises. Jesus suggests that even the Gentiles will find a place at God's feast.

Today concludes the semi-continuous reading of Ephesians for this year. After reflecting on the symbol of husband and wife, Paul gives instructions now to children, parents, slaves and masters. These relationships inspire a psalm about God's works giving their thanks and God's words being faithful.

The preface for Eucharistic Prayer II says Christ fulfilled God's will and won a holy people.

THU 28 #666 (LMC #452–455)   red
Simon and Jude, apostles
FEAST

Simon and Jude were among the Twelve, but this Simon is the Zealot or the Cananaean, not Simon Peter; and Jude (short for Judas) is known as Thaddaeus in Matthew and Mark, and is not the same as Judas the betrayer.

The gospel for today is Luke's listing of the Twelve, which mentions both saints we honor today. The first reading comes from Ephesians, but not in sequence with what we've heard the last few weeks. In fact, we heard this text at Mass a week ago Tuesday. It tells the Gentile Christians they are no longer strangers but members of the household of God, built upon the foundation of the apostles—which is why it appears for this feast. The psalm today is frequently used for apostles because it says the works of God let their voice resound through all their earth, and the message carries to the end of the world. The psalm seems to prophesy the work of apostles.

The presidential prayers come from October 28. Sing the Glory to God. You may use either preface for the apostles, but the second (P 65) relies on today's first reading. Both apostles are mentioned in Eucharistic Prayer I.

■ TODAY IS THE PATRONAL FEAST OF PERU, the Lord of Miracles (El Señor de los Milagros).

F R I **29** #483 (LMC #228–231)   green
Weekday

Today's gospel is omitted from the Sunday cycle of readings. It tells the story of Jesus curing a man who has dropsy. The cure takes place on the Sabbath in the house of a leading Pharisee in the presence of all the religious leaders. They remain silent while he cures the diseased man and lectures them about the law of love.

Today begins a series of readings from Paul and Timothy's letter to the Philippians. In the opening verses, we can sense the warmth between the apostles and this community. Paul prays that their love may increase ever more. A general psalm of praise follows, with an optional refrain of "Alleluia."

The mission of Jesus to the poor, the prisoner and the sorrowful is one of the themes of Eucharistic Prayer IV.

■ In Peru, yesterday's feast of the apostles Simon and Jude is transferred to this date.

S A T **30** #484 (LMC #228–231)   green
Weekday

Optional Memorial of the Blessed Virgin Mary/white ▪ It has been a while since we've heard today's gospel on a Saturday because other feasts suppressed it in the past two years. Jesus dines with a leading Pharisee on a Sabbath and causes controversy. He advises guests to be humble, for those who humble themselves will be exalted.

Paul accepts his fate, whether life or death, knowing that Christ will be proclaimed and the faith will spread. But he yearns to see his friends in Philippi again. We sing a great psalm of yearning, "My soul is thirsting for the living God."

Paul's faith is echoed in the fifth preface for Weekdays in Ordinary Time (P 41): "With love we celebrate his death. With living faith we proclaim his resurrection. With unwavering hope we await his return in glory."

If you wish to celebrate the optional memorial, see "Mary, Fountain of Salvation," in the *Collection of Masses of the Blessed Virgin* (#31).

■ In Guatemala, today is the solemnity for celebrating the dedication of individual churches throughout the Republic.

☀ 31 #153 (LMC #147)   green
Thirty-first Sunday in Ordinary Time

ORIENTATION

Daylight saving time ends for many communities this weekend. The gathering of darkness, Halloween, All Saints and All Souls conspire to turn our attention toward the end of another liturgical year. In that spirit, our second readings will come from one of the earliest books included in the New Testament, Paul's second letter to the Thessalonians. Among other themes, it is preoccupied with the return of Jesus at the end of time.

Bolivia celebrates All Saints today (see November 1).

LECTIONARY

Coming ever closer to Jerusalem, Jesus enters Jericho where he meets Zacchaeus, a tax collector, a rich man—and a short man. Zacchaeus is so overcome by his encounter with Jesus that he amends his ways and wins praise from Jesus, who promises salvation.

The book of Wisdom praises God who overlooks the sins of people. This is ultimately the theme of the gospel: God's willingness to forgive the offender. A generic psalm of praise follows, acknowledging that God is slow to anger and filled with great kindness.

In the second letter to the Thessalonians Paul assures his readers that he prays for them always that God will make them worthy of their calling. Apparently someone has convinced a few of the faithful in Thessalonica that that the day of the Lord has come. Paul wants to set the record straight, while encouraging their patient endurance in the virtues of the gospel.

SACRAMENTARY

One of the eucharistic prayers for Masses of reconciliation might make a good choice today, given the theme of the first reading and gospel. Prayer over the people #14 asks that we may rejoice in redemption and win its reward.

OTHER IDEAS

Remind people of tomorrow's solemnity of All Saints, but this year the obligation does not apply because the celebration falls on a Monday.

The last Sunday of October is Reformation Sunday, the anniversary of the beginning of the Protestant Reformation by Martin Luther, an opportunity for us to affirm the common mission of Christians to reform our lives by the gospel and to celebrate the unity of our baptism.

■ Halloween is the eve of All Saints. See *Take Me Home* for ideas. LTP's *School Year, Church Year* makes several recommendations, as does *Preparing Liturgy for Children and Children for Liturgy.*

November

M O N 1

#667 (LMC #402)   white

All Saints
SOLEMNITY

ORIENTATION

Today we recognize all the saints of heaven in a universal celebration. The feast serves as a catch-all for saints we do not celebrate throughout the year, but it also celebrates the triumphant church of the resurrection. The saints, in a way, are God's harvest. God has reaped the fruits of good sowing and gathered the mature faithful into the eternal storehouse.

November opens a season of the year when our thoughts turn toward the fear of death, the hope of eternal life, the gratitude we feel for God's gifts, and the charity we owe to others. In the northern hemisphere, trees turn barren and the chill of late fall settles in to stay.

All Saints Day is a holy day of obligation in the United States (except in the diocese of Honolulu), but the obligation does not apply today because it falls on a Monday. Today is also a holy day in Chile, Honduras, Peru and Puerto Rico, but not the other Latin American countries. Bolivia transfers the observance to the nearest Sunday.

LECTIONARY

The gospel for All Saints Day is the account of the beatitudes from Matthew. When Jesus opened the Sermon on the Mount, he proclaimed the reign of God for those who were virtuous in poverty, spirituality and persecution. The beatitudes are a job description for sainthood.

In the second reading, John proclaims that we are God's children now, and what we shall later be has not yet come to light. But John proclaims the hope of an eternal reward, which we celebrate today as it shines in the saints.

John's vision in Revelation sees an immense crowd of holy ones gathered before the throne and the lamb. Dressed in white are the martyrs who have survived the period of trial and washed their robes in the blood of the Lamb. One reason we wear white baptismal garments and white albs and drape caskets with a white pall is to stand among the blessed who worship at God's eternal throne. The psalm describes the sinless who long to see God's face.

SACRAMENTARY

The prayers for the day are under November 1. They include a solemn blessing. The preface is proper to the day (P 71) and the first eucharistic prayer will name a number of saints we rarely talk about. The recommended communion antiphon is based on the gospel.

Beginning today, you may want to favor Penitential Rite C-ii or texts like it. Its spirit will move us through this season and on into Advent.

OTHER IDEAS

For the environment, use a harvest motif. See *To Crown the Year* (p. 192–97). Set up a parish Book of the Dead, like the one published by Liturgy Training Publications. Record the names of all who have died in the past year, and arrange the book near the font and the lighted Easter candle. If your parish has a cemetery, you might decorate the entranceway and set out special prayers to encourage visits to the graves of loved ones and strangers.

For prayer at home, see *Catholic Household Blessings and Prayers* (178–83) for prayers for this month and a visit to a cemetery. LTP's *Sourcebook about Death* (1989) has 30 sections for day-by-day reading that families may find useful this month.

T U E 2

#1011–1016 (668) (LMC #531–535)
white, violet, or black

All the Faithful Departed (All Souls)
COMMEMORATION

ORIENTATION

We remember the deceased among the faithful who await their entrance to eternal glory. These two days together honor the dead. Yesterday's celebration remembered the saints whose excellent lives make them sure models of redemption. Today we pray for the rest, those who need forgiveness for their sins, who yearn to see the face of God.

LECTIONARY

Readings are taken from the commons for the Masses for the dead. You are completely free to choose the passages you wish. The text from 2 Maccabees, for example, says it is good to pray for the dead for the forgiveness of their sins. That passage is one of the scriptural foundations for the Catholic traditional belief in purgatory and to justify prayer for the dead as we do today.

If you are using the *Lectionary for Masses with Children* today, you have fewer selections. Try to coordinate the parish Mass readings with these.

SACRAMENTARY

Priests are allowed to celebrate three Masses today, but they need not.

Any of the sacramentary's texts for the All Souls Day Masses may be used. Any preface of Christian Death (P 77–81) may accompany these prayers. The Glory to God is not included in this Mass. The creed is also omitted. A solemn blessing is recommended.

■ SAMPLE FORMULAS FOR THE GENERAL INTERCESSIONS appear in the sacramentary's first appendix. See #11 for those suggested for Masses for the dead.

OTHER IDEAS

Sing music from the parish's funeral repertoire. Does the community know a setting of *"In paradisum"*? The chants from the funeral Mass are among the most beautiful and best remembered of the church's Latin music.

The *Book of Blessings* has an order for visiting a cemetery on All Souls Day (ch. 57). You could arrange a visit to the cemetery after one of the Masses. End Mass

with the prayer after communion and then process in cortege to the cemetery. Display the parish Book of the Dead near the font.

WED 3 #487 (LMC #228–231) green
Weekday

Optional Memorial of Martin de Porres (+ 1639), religious/white ■ In sayings and parables, Jesus stresses the importance of complete conversion and the willingness to accept the pain of the cross. He also explains the virtue of thinking ahead.

In his absence, Paul asks the Philippians to live innocent lives without grumbling and arguing. They should shine like stars in the midst of a twisted generation. With the psalmist we sing that God is our light and salvation.

Eucharistic Prayer IV says, "You live in unapproachable light."

■ TODAY'S SAINT: Martin was born in Peru of a Spanish father and a Black mother freed from slavery. As a teenager he apprenticed in medicine. As a Dominican, his gift for healing was exceeded only by his charity in sharing it with the poor. Because of his power as an intercessor in the Hispanic culture, Martin's image appears on many an *altarcito*. Today is a solemnity in Peru and an obligatory memorial in Bolivia, Colombia, Costa Rica, Panama and Venezuela. The lectionary's proper of saints suggests readings about contemplating holy things and loving one's neighbor, but the weekday readings are preferred.

In Argentina, today is the memorial of Mary, Mother and Mediatrix of Grace. The Servites promoted this devotion with Mass texts that appear in the *Collection of Masses of the Blessed Virgin Mary* (#30).

THU 4 #488 (LMC #228–231) white
Charles Borromeo (+ 1584), bishop
MEMORIAL

The fifteenth chapter of Luke contains Jesus' beautiful teaching on forgiveness and reconciliation. He speaks of God's love for the lost sheep and the lost coin, comparing God's care to that of shepherd and woman.

Paul reflects on his Jewish heritage, but has reappraised everything in the light of his knowledge of Christ. His life in Christ has established a new covenant. The psalm invites the descendants of Abraham to recall God's deeds and to rejoice in them.

The first eucharistic prayer for reconciliation says, "When we were lost and could not find the way to you, you loved us more than ever."

■ TODAY'S SAINT: "Humility" was the motto for Charles Borromeo, a bishop of Milan whose pastoral mind made him extremely influential in applying the teachings of the church after the Council of Trent. He held numerous provincial councils and diocesan synods. Karol Wojtyla, the future Pope John Paul II, was named for this saint. The lectionary's proper of saints suggests readings about the gifts in the Body of Christ and pastoral leadership, but the weekday readings are preferred.

The preface for pastors (P 67) may accompany the presidential prayers for this saint.

FRI 5 #489 (LMC #228–231) green
Weekday

Probably because the story appears so frequently elsewhere in the lectionary, the weekday readings skip the story of the prodigal son and move to another parable. Jesus praises a devious employee who cheats his master in order to win support from others in the community. The parable praises the industriousness of the oppressed.

The Philippians are suffering from persecution, and Paul urges their steadfast commitment to the faith. He reminds them that their citizenship is in heaven. A psalm of Jerusalem follows this reading, inviting us to think of the new Jerusalem, our heavenly home.

The sacramentary includes prayers for a happy death (#46).

SAT 6

#490 (LMC #228–231)   green
Weekday

Optional Memorial of the Blessed Virgin Mary/white ▪ Jesus counsels finding friends because the goods of this world fail. Love God, he says, pricking the conscience of the Pharisees; do not love money.

We conclude Paul's letter to the Philippians today. He exhorts them to a better way of life. Paul is grateful for their support, but he has learned how to live in abundance and in need because God gives him strength.

In the first version of the eucharistic prayer for various needs and occasions, you may pray for the local church by name.

If you celebrate the memorial of Mary today, consider "Mary, Image and Mother of the Church II" (#26), from the *Collection of Masses of the Blessed Virgin Mary.*

7

#156 (LMC #151)   green
Thirty-second Sunday in Ordinary Time

ORIENTATION

Finally, Jesus has reached Jerusalem, and the gospels prepare us for the end of his life. We have entered the final weeks of Ordinary Time and the final weeks of the three-year cycle of readings, a time that already prepares us for the season of Advent.

In Costa Rica, today marks the solemnity of the dedication of all individual churches except cathedrals.

LECTIONARY

Jesus enters into controversy with the Sadducees over the question of the resurrection. They deny it. He lives it. He tries to explain that resurrected life is unlike anything they know. The longer version of this reading includes the preposterous question the Sadducees cook up. The shorter version just gives Jesus' answer.

Even before the coming of Christ a belief in resurrection was beginning to take shape. It can be seen in the struggle of the Maccabees in an important text that serves as today's first reading. Near death at the hand of torturers, the fourth brother speaks of "the hope God gives of being raised up." The psalm expresses the cry of the just person who has been mistreated. With confidence in the resurrection, we sing with the psalmist, "Lord, when your glory appears, my joy will be full."

In the second reading, Paul praises God who will give the Thessalonians hope and encouragement. He also asks for their prayers, while relying on God's faithfulness. As they all await the coming of Christ, they need patient endurance.

SACRAMENTARY

The hope of resurrection shines through the fourth preface for Sundays in Ordinary Time (P 32). See the solemn blessing for the Easter season (7) for a text affirming the same belief.

OTHER IDEAS

If the choir is practicing Advent music, you could test some of it this week. Begin to simplify the environment before Christ the King, so that feast will stand out before the new church year begins.

MON 8

#491 (LMC #228–231)   green
Weekday

In a series of short sayings, Jesus criticizes scandals, promotes forgiveness and encourages faith.

This week we hear from four different epistles having one thing in common: brevity. The letter to Titus is one of the pastoral epistles attributed to Paul. Titus oversees the community at Crete. The letter is filled with practical advice about church administration and reflects a late development in the post-apostolic church. In the opening verses today we hear what is expected of candidates for the presbyterate and the proper behavior expected of bishops. Both types of ministers should lead a just life, the kind of life extolled in today's responsory.

The sacramentary includes a Mass for ministers of the church (#8).

▪ IN URUGUAY the Virgin of the Thirty-three is celebrated with a solemnity today in all churches except cathedrals. See this coming Saturday.

#701–706 (671) (LMC #442–446)
white

TUE 9 Dedication of the Lateran Basilica in Rome (324)
FEAST

ORIENTATION

All churches are invited to celebrate the anniversary of their dedication on the liturgical calendar. Your parish church and your cathedral church should have their days. The cathedral church of Rome and hence of the entire Roman church has its dedication day today. We celebrate it as a feast throughout the Catholic world.

The church is dedicated to John the Baptist and John the Evangelist. It sits on the hill that bears the name of its former owners, the Lateran family. When Constantine won the battle of the Milvian Bridge north of Rome in the fourth century, he made Christianity an acceptable religion in the empire and eventually accepted baptism. The first church to take advantage of the permission for Christianity to go public was the one set up on property given by the Laterans. The original building has undergone many renovations, but it still bears its basic floor plans for the church and the baptistry. The Lateran is the mother church of Rome, and hence of the entire world. It is the cathedral church of Rome, and one of the four major basilicas in the city.

Scriptures may be taken anywhere from the common of the dedication of a church. The passage from 1 Corinthians, for example, places the emphasis not just on the building but on the people it represents.

If you are using the *Lectionary for Masses with Children* today, you have fewer selections. Try to coordinate the parish Mass readings with these.

Texts come from the Anniversary of Dedication, outside the dedicated church (unless you celebrate this day at Saint John Lateran in Rome!). The preface is proper (P 53).

Sing the Glory to God. The solemn blessing for the dedication of a church (#19) implies that you are in the church recalling its anniversary. It could be used if you adapt one phrase: "to recall the dedication of the Lateran church."

See also Appendix VIII in the sacramentary for the prayers for the dedication of a church.

Today is truly a celebration of cathedrals. Let people know something about the cathedral of your diocese. Encourage them to visit, or organize a parish pilgrimage there to help people claim it as the mother church.

#493 (LMC #228–231)   white
WED 10 Leo the Great (+ 461), pope, doctor of the church
MEMORIAL

The first line of today's gospel reminds us that Jesus is on his journey to Jerusalem. This is the third reference to the journey that Luke has mentioned, all the while keeping the reader's view searching for the looming cross.

This brief series of readings from Titus concludes today. Titus is to remind people to obey government officials, take honest employment and avoid quarrels. The author's remembrance of the appearance of Jesus as Savior has

made this passage among those that may be proclaimed on Christmas Day. Because Titus serves in the leadership role as a shepherd, we sing the twenty-third psalm.

You may use the preface for pastors (P 67) with the presidential prayers for Leo the Great. The lectionary's proper of saints suggests readings about God's wisdom and the Petrine service, but the weekday readings are preferred.

■ TODAY'S SAINT: Leo was the first pope claiming to be Peter's heir, exercising authority over not just Rome, but over other bishops as well. The Eastern church was less disposed to accept his claims. He reigned during the time of the Council of Chalcedon. He confronted Attila the Hun and diverted his invasion—according to the legend—with the help of Peter and Paul, who appeared in the sky. Algardi captured the incident in a bas-relief that presides above the tomb of Leo inside St. Peter's in Vatican City.

#494 (LMC #228–231)   white
THU 11 Martin of Tours (+ 397), bishop, monastic
MEMORIAL

Jesus returns to his theme, the reign of God. He says you cannot tell when it is coming, but you must be ready for it at all times.

The shortest book in the Bible is the little letter from Paul to Philemon. Paul, in prison, put this letter into the hands of the runaway slave Onesimus and told him to go back to his master, Philemon. In the letter, Paul asks the master to release the slave. The psalm blesses those who secure justice for the opposed.

■ TODAY'S SAINT: Martin of Tours was still a catechumen when he severed his garment and gave half to a shivering beggar. Later, in a dream, he saw Christ with the beggar's face. He founded the first monastery in the West and became bishop of Tours. He was the first non-martyr to have a day on the calendar, and the *Liturgy of the Hours* honors him with a special set of antiphons, as well as the psalms and canticles from Sunday morning prayer of week one. That distinction is generally reserved for feast days. He appears in the litany of the saints just before Benedict, who wrote the influential rule of monastic life.

You may use the preface of pastors (P 67) with the prayers for Martin's day. The lectionary includes an optional gospel for today, a choice inspired by Martin's care for the poor. Service to the lowly appears also in the optional first reading. The weekday readings are recommended, however.

■ VETERANS' DAY IN THE UNITED STATES AND REMEMBRANCE DAY IN CANADA coincide with the anniversary of the end of World War I. You might invite veterans who are present for the liturgy today to receive the blessing and gratitude of the community for their service.

#495 (LMC #228–231)   red
F R I 12 Josaphat (+ 1623), bishop, religious, martyr
MEMORIAL

Jesus predicts that in the days before the coming of the Son of Man, people will be living sinful lives and only the just will be redeemed. It will resemble the situation of Noah's day.

The second letter of John is addressed to a "Lady" and her children, probably a reference to a church community. John advises the church to observe the commandment of love, even in the midst of deceitful people. Verses from Psalm 119 extolling the law of God follow.

The second eucharistic prayer for reconciliation says Jesus died so that we might turn again to God "and find our way to one another."

■ TODAY'S SAINT: Josaphat worked for the union of churches East and West. His own people nominated him as archbishop, but he suffered martyrdom at the hands of those who opposed his efforts. Like Leo the Great, whom we commemorated earlier this week, Josaphat is buried in St. Peter's Basilica in Vatican City.

The preface for martyrs (P 66) may accompany the presidential prayers for his day. The lectionary's proper of saints suggests readings about building up the church and union with Christ, but the weekday readings are preferred.

#496 (LMC #228–231)   white
S A T 13 Frances Xavier Cabrini (+ 1917), religious founder, missionary
MEMORIAL

Jesus tells a parable of the benefits that come from persistent prayer. He has asked for complete commitment and vigilant readiness from his disciples. Now he offers help through prayer.

The third letter of John is addressed to Gaius. It deals with the hospitality expected among churches. In today's passage John praises the church for the love it has shown to others. The psalm blesses those who fear God and delight in the commands.

■ TODAY'S SAINT: Mother Cabrini founded the Missionary Sisters of the Sacred Heart, left her native Italy and worked for immigrants in the New World, where she attained citizenship. After serving the needy and providing hope to the desperate, she was the first United States citizen to be canonized.

Today's memorial is obligatory in the United States. The opening prayer can be found at November 13. Others may come from the common of virgins. You may pray the preface for virgins and religious (P 68).

■ LEANDER (+ c. 600), the learned and conciliatory bishop of Seville, is remembered with an optional memorial today in Guatemala.

On the Saturday preceding the second Sunday of November, Uruguay celebrates its patronal feast, Our Lady of the Thirty-three (Nuestra Señora de los Treinta y Tres Orientales). The title refers to Mary's protection of 33 insurrectionists, led by Juan Antonio Lavalleja, in 1825. They all prayed for her help in the city of Florida in the church of Our Lady of Luján, and then signed Uruguay's Declaration of Independence from Brazil in the parish office.

#159 (LMC #154)   green
✸ 14 Thirty-third Sunday in Ordinary Time

ORIENTATION

The last Sundays of the year independently form a miniature season. The end of the liturgical year leads us into deeper reflection on the end of all time.

Today concludes the series of readings from 2 Thessalonians and brings the ministry of Jesus to a climax in Luke's gospel.

LECTIONARY

Jesus speaks ominously about the destruction of the Jerusalem temple. He knows the building will be destroyed, and that his life will end in its shadow. The end of time will bring violence and confusion, but believers have the confidence that they can secure their lives by perseverance in faith.

The prophet Malachi predicts the coming day of the Lord, a day coming like fire that will destroy the enemy and preserve the righteous. They will experience the rising of the sun of justice with its healing rays. The responsorial psalm anticipates that God will come to rule the earth with justice.

Even though Paul and the Thessalonians expected the imminent return of Jesus, Paul admonished them to be faithful to their daily work. If you do not work, you do not eat. Anticipation of the coming of Christ might have contributed to some laziness in the community, and Paul would not stand for it. It befits neither the community nor the gospel.

SACRAMENTARY

Eucharistic Prayer IV comes with its own irreplaceable preface. If you are planning to use the seasonal prefaces with other eucharistic prayers on Sundays for the next two months, you might use prayer IV today. The fifth solemn blessing for Ordinary Time (#14) asks that the faithful may walk in God's ways, "always knowing what is right and good."

OTHER IDEAS

Keep the parish Book of the Dead visible this week, as a reminder to pray for those who have died in the past year and of the mortality we face in the scriptures of this month.

The Muslim fast of Ramadan comes to its end about this time. Islam concludes its holy month with the celebration of Id al-Fit'r.

M O N 15 #497 (LMC #228–231)   green
Weekday

Optional Memorial of Albert the Great (+ 1280), bishop, religious, doctor of the church/white ▪ Luke

tells the story of the blind beggar on the road to Jericho. Jesus hears his plea for help and grants him vision. As Jesus moves closer to Jerusalem, all the disciples will need the eyes of faith.

The last two weeks of this church year take the first reading from the last book of the Bible, Revelation. The book tells of a revelation to the seer John, in which he sees present events and a future world in highly symbolic language. In the vision, John sees the conflict between Christians and the Roman Empire. In today's opening vision an angel tells John to send a prophetic letter to each of seven churches "in Asia." The message to Ephesus affirms them for turning from impostor prophets and challenges them not to be discouraged. We sing a psalm of the blessedness of those who follow not the wicked but walk in God's law. Throughout this period, the refrain is almost always taken not from within the psalm but from the book of Revelation.

The second weekday preface for Ordinary Time (P 38) speaks of God's judgment and mercy.

■ TODAY'S SAINT: A Dominican, Albert was the teacher of Thomas Aquinas. He was a student of Greek philosophy, natural sciences, Jewish and Arabic studies, and so he serves as a model of blending the intellectual with the spiritual life. The lectionary's proper of saints suggests readings about wisdom and instruction, but the weekday readings are preferred.

T U E 16 #498 (LMC #228–231)   green
Weekday

Optional Memorial of Margaret of Scotland (+ 1093), married woman/white ▪ *Optional Memorial of Gertrude the Great (+ 1301), monastic, mystic/white* ▪ Too short to see over the crowd,

Zacchaeus climbed a tree to see Jesus. When Jesus invites himself over to the tax collector's home, Zacchaeus professes his conversion from sin.

From Revelation we hear two more letters to churches. Sardis hears of its misdeeds and the promise of salvation for the few who have remained faithful. Laodicea hears that it is too lukewarm in its commitment. Both are called to repent. The psalm praises those who do justice.

The first eucharistic prayer for reconciliation admits, "we broke your covenant."

■ TODAY'S SAINTS: A wife and mother of eight, Margaret was queen of Scotland and devout in serving the poor. The lectionary's proper of saints suggests readings about sharing with the hungry and obedience to Christ, but the weekday readings are preferred.

Gertrude was a Saxon Benedictine mystic who wrote on many themes, including the Sacred Heart. Her prayer reflected on the humanity of Jesus in his passion, the eucharist and Mary. The lectionary's proper of saints suggests readings about union with Christ, but the weekday readings are preferred.

W E D 17 #499 (LMC #228–231)   white
Elizabeth of Hungary (+ 1231), married woman, religious
MEMORIAL

Today's gospel opens and closes with references to Jerusalem. For several weeks we have walked with Jesus on his journey to that city, throughout the second half of Luke's gospel. The story today opens by saying he is near Jerusalem and closes saying he is about to enter. The parable in the middle tells a story of judgment based on responsible usage of the gifts God entrusts to us.

John sees someone seated on a throne, and four living creatures singing praise. The creatures resemble those from the book of Ezekiel and have come to represent the evangelists in Christian iconography. We join with the psalmist and those gathered around the throne to sing praise to God.

The opening prayer for Mass comes from the proper of saints. You may choose the other prayers from those for the common of saints who worked for the underprivileged. The preface for virgins and religious (P 68) may be used. The lectionary's proper of saints suggests readings about service to others, but the weekday readings are preferred.

■ TODAY'S SAINT: Born into Hungarian royalty, Elizabeth eschewed the trappings of the wealthy and lived a simple, austere life. She married and bore three children. After her husband died, she made arrangements for the care of the children and entered a Franciscan community. Notable for her charity toward the sick, she died at the age of 24. Although Elizabeth's life certainly deserves praise, it points out the lack of saints' days honoring married women who raised families.

■ IN PARAGUAY, today is the feast of Roque González of the Holy Cross, Juan del Castillo and Alonso Rodríguez, Jesuit priests and martyrs (+ 1628). All worked on the "reductions" in Paraguay, where natives were housed, acculturated and instructed in the faith. An apostate led a revolt against the priests, and they were tomahawked to death. Although there were earlier martyrs in the Americas, these were the first to be beatified. They are remembered in Argentina and Bolivia today with a memorial.

THU 18 #500 (LMC #228–231) green
Weekday

Optional Memorial of the Dedication of the Basilicas of the Apostles Peter (324) and Paul (390) in Rome/white ▪ *Optional Memorial of Rose Philippine Duchesne (+ 1852), religious, missionary, educator/white* ▪ Seeing the city of Jerusalem now, Jesus weeps over it because the people have lost their way and enemies threaten to bring war. *Jerusalem* means "city of peace." It still promises God's peace even in the midst of its international struggles.

John's vision continues as he beholds a lamb who is slain but standing up. The lamb has come to represent Jesus Christ in Christian iconography. As the living creatures and elders sing a song of praise to the Lamb, so do we join with the psalmist in singing praise.

Among the Masses for various needs and occasions is one in time of war or civil disturbance (#23).

■ TODAY'S MEMORIALS: The basilicas of Peter and Paul are built over the tombs of the two great apostles. Together with St. Mary Major and St. John Lateran they constitute the four major basilicas of Rome. All the dedication days are optional, except for St. John Lateran, which we observed as a feast earlier this month. Optional readings for the dedications are in the lectionary, stories of Paul and Peter, and a psalm of praise.

Rose Philippine Duchesne was born in Grenoble, France, and died in St. Charles, Missouri. A member of the Religious of the Sacred Heart, she founded a house in the United States and opened the first free school west of the Mississippi. Among Native Americans she was called "the woman who prays always." The opening prayer for this optional

memorial is in the 1994 *Sacramentary Supplement*.

FRI 19 #501 (LMC #228–231) green
Weekday

Entering Jerusalem, Jesus makes his way to the temple where he throws out the traders. His prophetic action announces a sea change in the religious center.

John receives another scroll from the angel, which he eats. The sweetness in his mouth and the sourness in his stomach indicate the difficult message he must prophesy. Still, the psalmist insists that the words of God's promise are sweet.

The sacramentary includes prayers for oppressors (#45).

■ TODAY IS THE PATRONAL FEAST OF PUERTO RICO, the Blessed Virgin Mary, Mother of Divine Providence, which is celebrated as a solemnity on the local calendar. The devotion began with the Barnabites, and its Mass was celebrated on the Saturday before the third Sunday of November. See the *Collection of Masses of the Blessed Virgin Mary* (#40).

Argentina transfers the memorial of Elizabeth of Hungary from November 17 to this date.

SAT 20 #502 (LMC #228–231) green
Weekday

Optional Memorial of the Blessed Virgin Mary/white ▪ As his death draws closer, Jesus meets a group of Sadducees who do not believe in the resurrection. They pose an absurd question to him, permitting him to proclaim the living God. Some scribes give him support.

John sees two witnesses, possibly Moses and Elijah, eschatological prophets. John envisions that an enemy attacks and kills them, but they are restored by God's breath of life. The vision may indicate God's ultimate victory over those who try to stifle the divine prophetic word. The psalmist praises God who trains hands for battle.

The fifth preface for weekdays in Ordinary Time (P 41) proclaims the resurrection and the anticipated return of Jesus in glory.

If you celebrate the optional memorial of Mary, see "Mary, Cause of Our Joy," in the *Collection of Masses of the Blessed Virgin Mary* (#34) for one possibility today.

#162 (LMC #157)   white

Christ the King
21 Thirty-fourth or Last Sunday in Ordinary Time
SOLEMNITY

ORIENTATION

Today is the last Sunday of Ordinary Time. As the church year comes to its end, our thoughts turn to the end of all time. The faithful Christian reflects not with fear but with confident hope that Christ will come again as the supreme ruler over all.

LECTIONARY

The last Sunday in Ordinary Time turns again to Luke for its text. Normally, we expect the Sundays in Ordinary Time to tell the story of Jesus' ministry, but not of his death. This year is an exception. We dip once more into Luke's gospel, into the semi-continuous pattern of our readings, to lift up

one last image of Jesus as king. To many, it will be a surprising choice: Jesus on the cross. There he reigns as king, and the one who recognizes this is the poor sinner crucified next to him, who says, "Jesus, remember me when you come into your kingdom." His reference to the kingdom affirms his faith in Christ the King, yet his familiarity with this divine being next to him prompts him to be one of a very few people in any gospel who calls Jesus not rabbi, not teacher, not Lord—but by his name: Jesus.

For the second reading, we turn to the letter to the Colossians. Here we find another reference to the kingdom of Christ. God delivered us from the power of darkness and transferred us to the kingdom of the beloved Son. It is that kingdom we long to inhabit.

The first reading tells of the anointing of David as king of Israel. David is the prototype for the kingship of Jesus. His glorious reign became a symbol of the type of reign for which Israel longed, and which Jesus brought to fruition.

The psalm is a processional song for pilgrims going to Jerusalem. In some ways, it does not fit the first reading, which takes place in Hebron. It links better with the gospel, where Jesus dies in Jerusalem. How poignant the words sound if we imagine Jesus singing them on his way to Calvary: "I rejoice because they said to me, 'We will go up to the house of the Lord.'" More significantly, perhaps, this psalm is the same one that began the three-year cycle of readings on the First Sunday of Advent in Year A. The lectionary gives us a fantastic parenthesis around its contents in this way. The psalm that starts the cycle also concludes the cycle. It is the psalm we sing on our journey to the heavenly Jerusalem. And we

will sing it again next Sunday, as we start the cycle anew.

SACRAMENTARY

The prayers for the day are in the part of the book marked "Solemnities of the Lord during Ordinary Time." Christ the King follows the Sacred Heart. Look it up before Mass. It will be hard to find otherwise.

The preface for the day is at P 51. The first solemn blessing for Ordinary Time prays that God will look upon the faithful with kindness (#10), but see also the solemn blessing for beginning a new year (#3) and for the Passion of the Lord (#5).

The entrance antiphon for the celebration comes from Revelation and has inspired hymns like "Crown Him with Many Crowns," "All Hail the Power of Jesus' Name" and "To Jesus Christ Our Sovereign King." *By Flowing Waters* (296–301) has a complete suite of processional antiphons and psalms. The majestic Canticle of David (I Chronicles 29:10–18) is sung during the communion procession.

OTHER IDEAS

You might end the Sundays of Ordinary Time with evening prayer tonight. Sing again a hymn to Christ the King and ring bells during the *Magnificat* or at the close of the celebration.

As a kind of "Ember Day" observance, the church of the United States recommends setting aside the next three days for deeds of charity, penance and economic justice. See *Catholic Household Blessings and Prayers,* 188–89 for ideas.

Choirs may enjoy learning "Christus vincit" from the *Liber cantualis.*

MON 22 #503 (LMC #228–331) red
Cecilia, martyr (+ 3rd c.)
MEMORIAL

Still at the temple, Jesus sees a woman put in two copper coins and is moved by her complete generosity. He praises those who give everything to God, as he himself is about to do.

John sees a large crowd gathered around the Lamb on Mount Zion, singing praise. This group stands in opposition to those who support the forces of evil. The just will ascend God's mountain, the psalm reminds us.

■ TODAY'S SAINT: Cecilia, an early Roman martyr, is patron of church musicians. There is little reliable information about her life and less about her musicianship, but her complete dedication to Christ even to death will resonate with the dedication felt by many church musicians. Cecilia and the other virgin martyrs are compared in the liturgy to the parable of the bridesmaids who bear their lamps in expectation of the groom. Use the preface for martyrs (P 66). Cecilia is mentioned in Eucharistic Prayer I. You may use other prayers for martyrs to go with the opening prayer for her day, a text which tells virtually nothing of her life because so little can be said. However, since today's memorial is well loved by many musicians, much can be said about the value of music and the other arts in human life and in the life of the church. The lectionary's proper of saints suggests readings about virginity and preparedness for death, but the weekday readings are preferred.

TUE 23 #504 (LMC #228–231) green
Weekday

Optional Memorial of Clement I, pope, martyr (+ c. 100) / red ▪ Optional Memorial of Columban, monastic, missionary (+ 615) / white ▪ Optional Memorial of Blessed Miguel Agustín Pro, presbyter, religious, martyr (+ 1927) / red ▪ Although people admire the construction of the temple, Jesus announces that it will all be destroyed. He predicts a dire future of warfare, earthquake and famine.

One like a Son of Man appears holding a sickle in hand, and another angel also appears with a sickle. Together they reap a harvest at the end of time, gathering the enemies of God like wheat and grapes, the second hurling God's enemies into the winepress of wrath. This image inspired "Mine Eyes Have Seen the Glory" and the title of a novel, *The Grapes of Wrath.*

The prayers of Christ the King replaced those for the Thirty-fourth Week in Ordinary Time this past Sunday. You can find the presidential prayers for this week right after those for the thirty-third week. See also the sacramentary's prayers for after the harvest (#27).

■ TODAY'S SAINTS: Clement served as the bishop of Rome and authored a letter to the Corinthians. He died under the persecution of Trajan. A church dedicated to his name may stand over the place of his home in Rome. He is mentioned in the Roman Canon. The lectionary's proper of saints suggests readings about the Petrine leadership.

Columban the monk came from Ireland and served as missionary to France. His penitential book promoted the individual confession of sins for forgiveness. Exiled for criticizing an immoral court, he died at Bobbio in Italy. The lectionary's proper of saints suggests readings about evangelization and discipleship, but the weekday readings are preferred.

The devout Jesuit Miguel Pro was accused and executed as a conspirator against Mexico's revolutionary government. The widely circulated photograph of him kneeling before his executioners became a twentieth-century icon of courage. His last words proclaimed Christ the king over all civil authority: *"¡Viva el Christo Rey!"* The opening prayer for this optional memorial is in the 1994 *Sacramentary Supplement.* His optional memorial is also observed in Mexico.

WED 24 #505 (LMC #228–231) red
Andrew Dung-Lac (+ 1839), presbyter, martyr; and his companions, martyrs
MEMORIAL

Jesus warns his disciples that they will be persecuted for their loyalty to him. He promises to give them wisdom that will befuddle their adversaries and to preserve them from harm.

Today's reading from Revelation announces the coming of seven plagues, but then pauses for another hymn of praise to the Lamb. A psalm with similar purpose follows the reading.

The presidential prayers for Andrew Dung-Lac and companions are in the Sacramentary Supplement of 1994. Use the preface of martyrs (P 66) today.

■ TODAY'S SAINTS: The Catholic church in Vietnam suffered a series of brutal persecutions between 1745 and 1862. Andrew Dung changed his name to Dung-Lac to avoid recognition but still suffered martyrdom together with another Vietnamese priest, Peter Thi, on December 21, 1839. The emperor who authorized that particular persecution, Minh Mang, believed that Christian missionaries were inciting revolts against him. In 1988, 117 martyrs from several different persecutions were canonized. Ninety-six of them were

Vietnamese, 59 were lay people, one of the largest groups of laity to be canonized in history. Only one was a woman, Agnes De (+ 1841). We remember the entire group of martyrs today.

THU 25 Weekday
#506 or #943–947 (LMC #228–331) green

Thanksgiving Day, U.S.A./white • Optional Memorial of Catherine of Alexandria (+ c. 310?), virgin, martyr/red

ORIENTATION

Throughout the United States citizens set this day aside as a day of thankful prayer. Our church gathers for its eucharist, a celebration with a name that means "thanksgiving."

LECTIONARY

You have a wide selection of readings to choose from. You may even use those assigned for the weekday, but they are not appropriate to the spirit of the day. (Those readings treat the upcoming desolation of Jerusalem and the fall of Babylon.)

Readings may come from the Masses in thanksgiving or from the appendix to the lectionary. Jesus' cure of the ten lepers, for example, strikes home with many of us who often forget to say thanks.

SACRAMENTARY

The prayers for Thanksgiving Day appear after those for November 30. The well-intentioned patriotism of the recommended preface (P 84) manages to denounce Europe ("the desert") and justify aggression ("destiny"). The previous preface may make a better choice. Or use the fourth version of the eucharistic prayer for

various needs and occasions, "Jesus, the Compassion of God," with its own preface.

The *Book of Blessings* (ch. 58) uses as a greeting, "May the Lord, who fills you with his bounty, be with you always."

OTHER IDEAS

Encourage the assembly to bring food for the hungry today. Stock the parish food pantry or give the groceries to a neighborhood food bank.

An order of blessing Thanksgiving food is in the *Book of Blessings* (ch. 58). The *Book of Common Prayer* has a litany of thanksgiving (836–387).

Hymns may include "Come, Ye Thankful People, Come," "We Plow the Fields," "We Gather Together" and "For the Beauty of the Earth." "Father, We Thank Thee" comes from the *Didache* prayer for the eucharist. Frank Schoen's responsorial psalm for Thanksgiving is "May God Have Pity on Us" (GIA).

A table prayer for use at home is in *Catholic Household Blessings and Prayers* (pp. 200–1).

■ TODAY'S SAINT: There is nothing certain known of Catherine of Alexandria. Even the Roman martyrology makes no attempt at dating her death. Legend has it that she lived at the time of Maxentius and converted many people to Christianity, all of whom the emperor slaughtered. Catherine was placed on a spiked wheel, goes the story, which broke, so he had her beheaded. A monastery that claims to be on the site of Mount Sinai also claims to have her body. Hers was one of the voices that Joan of Arc said she heard. This memorial was added to the universal calendar in the third edition of the Roman Missal.

FRI 26 Weekday
#507 (LMC #228–231) green

In the parable of the fig tree, Jesus expects his disciples to be able to read the signs that God is near. His words, the words of life we have heard all year, will never pass away.

In John's triumphant vision an angel hurls the dragon into the abyss. The One seated upon the throne appears to judge the dead according to their conduct. New heavens and a new earth are born, and a new Jerusalem comes down from God. The psalmist sings of the blessedness of those who dwell in God's house.

The sacramentary's prayers for a happy death (#46) might bring the year to a resolute close.

SAT 27 Weekday
#508 (LMC #228–231) green

Optional Memorial of the Blessed Virgin Mary/white • We close the series of gospels from Luke and the entire liturgical year with Jesus' admonition to be on the watch and pray constantly to stand secure before the Son of Man.

The book of Revelation, often regarded for its fearsome violence, ends on a dreamy note. The angel reveals a river of life-giving water, trees of life, and nothing accursed. Night is ended, for the Lord God gives light. The best news is saved for the end: Christ is coming soon. A psalm associated with the Christmas season follows, together with a direct appeal to Christ, using an ancient language: "Marana tha! Come, Lord Jesus!"

If you will not be using Eucharistic Prayer IV during Advent due to its unchanging preface, you might give it one last turn today.

If you celebrate the optional memorial of Mary today, consider "Mary, Gate of Heaven" (#46), from the *Collection of Masses of the Blessed Virgin Mary*.

Wisdom's Order

Proverbs 8:22–31

When the LORD established the heavens, wisdom was there.

THE disorder of our lives keeps us from peace. We race from one event to the next. Emergencies keep us from getting done the work we had planned to do. Our homes need a little more straightening. Our children need a little more attention.

It can be hard to appreciate the order of the world around us—the rhythm of the sun as it gently runs its course, the miracle of plants as they open with new life, the comfort of the wind as it cools and refreshes. The cycle of life and death, although it brings chaos to individual lives, is well ordered, and the world passes from generation to generation.

That order is the wisdom of God. The wisdom of God speaks in the book of Proverbs: "When the Lord established the heavens, I was there." God's wisdom predates creation. God's wisdom assisted in creation. Creation works because of God's wisdom. God's wisdom continues to work around the world and within us.

The disorder of our lives may keep us from sensing the wisdom of God, but wisdom is there. God created us in wisdom, ordered our bodies and gave us health, implanted within us a desire to know our creator, and nurtures us in our hunger for charity. Even when we are busy, even when we are unaware, God's wisdom is at work, keeping the pace of our hectic lives.

Written by Paul Turner. © 2003 Archdiocese of Chicago, Liturgy Training Publications; 1-800-933-1800; www.ltp.org.

Offering Our Prayers

Genesis 14:18–20

Melchizedek brought out bread and wine.

GATHERED at the eucharist we bring our prayers to God. We each have our own needs. Friends are sick. Neighbors are losing their home. Kids need work. The goldfish died. We bring these prayers to church because they remind us of our need and they raise our hopes in the power of God.

We have those hopes because God has rescued us time and time again. Our relationship with God has produced fruitfulness, satisfied our longings and brought us peace. Because of God's faithfulness, we give thanks, offer sacrifice and once again present our needs.

Melchizedek is a mysterious figure from the book of Genesis who prays as we do. King of Jerusalem, priest of God Most High, he blesses Abram, whose armies have just won a victory. Melchizedek brought out bread and wine, and Abram offered him a tenth of his possessions.

The entire scene foreshadows our celebration of the eucharist. God has rescued us from death. Jesus reigns as our king and priest. The community offers bread and wine. We each offer a tenth of what we own. When we worship at Mass, we imitate the pattern of our ancestors' worship. Every generation has the same needs. We present them to the same God, who works the same wonders in our midst.

Written by Paul Turner. © 2003 Archdiocese of Chicago, Liturgy Training Publications; 1-800-933-1800; www.ltp.org.

JUNE 18, 2004
The Sacred Heart of Jesus

God's Love Outpoured
Ezekiel 34:11–16
I myself will pasture my sheep, and I myself will give them rest.

WHEN the prophet Ezekiel describes a good shepherd, he tells of one who loves the flock. The good shepherd is not the one who has the largest flock and not the one who earns the most income because of the flock. The good shepherd gathers sheep that are scattered, leads them from other fields back to their own, finds good pastures for feeding and resting, and takes care of the injured and the sick. The good shepherd treats those sheep with respect.

Ezekiel compares God to that shepherd. God has shepherded Israel. God has brought the chosen people back from foreign lands and given them the rich pasture of their homeland for food and resting. God has bound up their

hurts and cured their illnesses. God did this not for any kind of profit. God did it out of love.

God's love for us is like the love of Ezekiel's "good shepherd" for the sheep. It is not motivated by profit or self-interest. It is just there, meeting our every need, binding up every injury. It is the love pouring out from the sacred heart of Jesus, who loved us so much that he sacrificed his life for our salvation.

JUNE 20, 2004
Twelfth Sunday in Ordinary Time

Zechariah 12:10–11, 13:1
They will look on the one whom they have pierced.

WE can put up with suffering if it has some purpose. If sacrifice gives us gratification later on, we can take it. If doing without helps someone we love to have a little more, we can do it. If pain now will lighten the pain of someone else later, we can handle it.

Suffering without purpose is harder to sustain. When suffering produces no earthly good, it is hard to understand. When someone inflicts suffering on us out of vengeance or hatred, it is hard to forgive. Some suffering is more difficult than other suffering.

Zechariah promised the people that God would pour out a spirit of grace, and that the inhabitants of Jerusalem would have a fountain

to purify them from sin. But all this would come at a price—the price of suffering.

The gospels see in this passage a prophecy about Christ, pierced on the cross with the soldier's lance, mourned as the firstborn, only-begotten Son of God.

The loss of Jesus on the cross is a suffering that would have been hard to bear—if it had no purpose. But it has lightened the loss of nations.

Owning Christ
1 Kings 19:16b, 19–21
Elisha left and followed Elijah as his attendant.

MOST people save stuff. We are pack rats. We save clothes that haven't fit for years. We save computer files we may never look at again. When we run out of closets at home, we rent additional space to store things.

Once in a while we have a garage sale to thin down our possessions. But we rarely hear of anyone getting rid of everything in order to start over again.

When Elisha agreed to follow Elijah as his attendant, he left his livelihood as a farmer. He broke up the yoke he steered for plowing and used it to fuel a fire. He slaughtered his oxen and used the fire to boil their flesh. He served the flesh to his people to eat. Elisha left nothing behind.

To be a follower of Christ, we must be prepared to travel light. Our possessions may distract us from keeping Christ as the center of our being. We may also be distracted by too many interests, too many commitments, too much food or too much play. When Elisha decided to follow Elijah, he broke up, burned up and cooked up everything he owned. When we decide to follow Christ, we will leave some things behind.

It won't feel right at first. It is hard to let go of the things of our past. We are pack rats. But the future is glorious if Christ is all we own.

Written by Paul Turner. © 2003 Archdiocese of Chicago, Liturgy Training Publications; 1-800-933-1800; www.ltp.org.

The City of Gladness
Isaiah 66:10–14c
Behold, I will spread prosperity over Jerusalem like a river.

THERE is little comfort in Jerusalem. Our generation has witnessed great tragedies in the Holy Land. People live in terror. Holy sites have been destroyed. Suicide bombers have killed innocents.

Efforts for peace rise and fall as the nations of the world seek a way for Jerusalem to find its peace. The city is important to many of the world's believers. It deserves to be a place of peace, an example of righteousness, a beacon of justice for anyone who longs for these virtues.

When Isaiah first spoke his prophecy about Jerusalem, the city lay in ruins, ravaged by invaders, its citizens carried off into exile. He heard the voice of God promise a better future for the city: "I will spread prosperity over Jerusalem like a river. In Jerusalem you shall find your comfort."

Those words still resonate deep within the hearts of all who hear them. We yearn to believe that God will bless Jerusalem with the peace and security promised so long ago.

When the day finally arrives, when all the world finds its comfort in Jerusalem, there will be great rejoicing. Until that day, we join in the mission of Christ by bringing comfort wherever we can to the nervous, the suffering, the lonely, the poor and the sorrowing—all those who need what the body of Christ was designed to offer: love.

Written by Paul Turner. © 2003 Archdiocese of Chicago, Liturgy Training Publications; 1-800-933-1800; www.ltp.org.

JULY 11, 2004
Fifteenth Sunday in Ordinary Time

Deuteronomy 30:10–14
God's word is very near to you, that you may observe it.

THE most difficult decisions to make are the ones in which we cannot tell right from wrong. We feel drawn by one solution, but we are not sure why. Are our motives pure? Is the reason we find one option attractive a reason that is ignoble? Or are we truly choosing what is good for ourselves, for those we love and for those we do not know.

Sometimes a decision is hard to make because both options seem bad. We do not want to choose because we will feel sad once we make the choice. But not choosing also brings its frustration and sorrow.

When the answer is not clear outside us, we turn inside us. We pray. We ask God for a sign.

We look for some clear direction. Sometimes God is silent. Sometimes God speaks.

Moses told his people that the task is not as hard as they might think. God's command is not up in the sky. You don't have to look for someone to go up there and bring it back. God's command is not across the sea. You don't have to find someone to cross over and get it. No, God's command is something very near, "already in your mouths and in your hearts; you have only to carry it out."

If we live our lives in the spirit of the gospel, we know what the answers to our dilemmas should be. We only have to carry them out.

Written by Paul Turner. © 2003 Archdiocese of Chicago, Liturgy Training Publications; 1-800-933-1800; www.ltp.org.

JULY 18, 2004
Sixteenth Sunday in Ordinary Time

Biblical Fast Food
Genesis 18:1–10a
Let me bring you a little food, that you may refresh yourselves.

OUR idea of fast food is driving to a local chain, pulling up to the giant menu board with the scratchy speaker system, yelling out the order, driving to the window and paying. Within minutes, you have your food and you speed away. It's fast.

In the book of Genesis, there is a different account of fast food service. Some mysterious visitors come to see Abraham and Sarah. Abraham realizes that there is something divine about their presence. He immediately offers hospitality: a bath, a rest and a meal. They agree. But Sarah has to come with some food, fast.

She bakes rolls from fine flour. A servant slaughters and prepares a juicy steer. The curds

and milk are easier, but the basic ingredients of a hamburger, bread and meat, have to be prepared from scratch on the spot—not fast food by our standards but pretty impressive for its day.

As a result of his hospitality, Abraham receives from God the gift he has waited for all his life: a son, Isaac, whom he will love.

When strangers or friends drop by, we have the opportunity to offer hospitality. Sometimes we are so busy that our primary hope is they will leave as soon as possible. But there is another solution. We can offer hospitality. The blessing we receive may be the one we have desired all life long.

Written by Paul Turner. © 2003 Archdiocese of Chicago, Liturgy Training Publications; 1-800-933-1800; www.ltp.org.

JULY 25, 2004
Seventeenth Sunday in Ordinary Time

Haggling with God
Genesis 18:20–32
Let not my Lord grow angry if I speak.

IF our best friend does us a favor, we want to return it. Sometimes we can get someone to do us a favor if we promise some kindness in return. We might have to negotiate. We might have to give up more than we thought. But we can barter and sustain the friendship.

One of the most delightful passages in the Old Testament is the negotiation between God and Abraham. Both have entered a covenant as friends, although they are not at all equals. Still, Abraham negotiates with God about the number of righteous people who might be found in Sodom and Gomorrah. Abraham speaks humbly of himself in the presence of God's majesty, yet he boldly asks for a better and better deal.

The passage is delightful until we realize what they are negotiating over: the destruction of Sodom and Gomorrah. God has condemned the city for its misdeeds, but Abraham pleads on behalf of the innocent. This quaint conversation concerns the serious business of saving human lives.

In our friendship with God, we often negotiate in a similar way. "Let my mother live, O God, and I will always treat her with respect." "Let me not get into trouble for my sin, O God, and I will always keep my room clean." "Let me get out of debt, O God, and I will give ten percent of all I own to the church." We barter. The conversation delights God's ears. God loves the people of the covenant.

AUGUST 1, 2004
Eighteenth Sunday in Ordinary Time

Wasted Work
Ecclesiastes 1:2; 2:21–23
What profit comes to us from all our toil?

NOBODY likes to waste time. If someone hasn't done the job and it costs us time and effort, we get angry. If a company promised to deliver by a certain date and it misses the deadline, we are furious. If somebody does the job wrong, and we have to redo it, we hate it. We hate to waste time.

But some of the hard work we do is also wasted. Work may feel valuable because it fills our time. It feels worthwhile if we do it faithfully. But not everything we do has value. Some of it keeps us from doing more important things. Workaholics spend less time with family. People concerned with their own lives may volunteer less for others. Our work and our lives are important, but sometimes not as important as we think.

Qoheleth says everything is vanity; everything is worthless. We spend our lives gaining wisdom, knowledge and skill, but at death we give all our property to someone who has not worked for it. We work all day long. We spend our days in sorrow and grief, and our nights without rest. The writer's bleak descriptions keep us humble about our work. We may not be as important as we thought.

Perhaps God gets frustrated with us, too. Why do we waste our time? The time we spend with God is never wasted at all.

AUGUST 8, 2004
Nineteenth Sunday in Ordinary Time

Making Ready
Wisdom 18:6–9
God's people awaited the salvation of the just.

WHAT if tomorrow was "the day"? What if tomorrow someone in your family died? What if someone were to offer you a new job? What if an old friend resurfaced? What if you learned you were free of cancer? What if you heard this was going to happen tomorrow? What would you do today?

Our ancestors knew in advance the night of Passover. They knew that their enemies would be destroyed and the just would be saved. On Passover night, they knew that freedom would follow the next day. They knew all along that God would rescue them one day, and now they prepared with courage—for tomorrow.

We do not always know on what day God will shower new blessings upon us. We do not know how God will act. But we have learned through the testimony of our ancestors and through our own experience that God will do just that: God will destroy the enemy and rescue the just.

While we wait, we spend our days reflecting on God's good deeds. We develop our friendship with God. We train ourselves in the courage that comes from a strong faith. If tomorrow becomes the day of our deliverance, we shall be prepared.

Written by Paul Turner. © 2003 Archdiocese of Chicago, Liturgy Training Publications; 1-800-933-1800; www.ltp.org.

AUGUST 15, 2004
The Assumption of the Blessed Virgin Mary

The First Disciple
Revelation 11:19a; 12:1–6a, 10ab
A great sign appeared in the sky, a woman clothed with the sun.

THERE is no story in the Bible about Mary's assumption into heaven. But it is the logical conclusion to her life. The assumption of Mary is an assumption, but a good one.

From the moment Mary spoke, "Let it be" when the Holy Spirit overshadowed her and she conceived the Savior of the world, she revealed herself to be the one chosen by God. She was the vessel of our salvation, the model of discipleship, and the first to enjoy the fruits of redemption through her assumption into heaven.

There is an image in the book of Revelation that is often applied to Mary. It depicts a woman clothed with the sun, standing on the moon, and wearing a crown of 12 stars. This dynamic image of a woman reigning over the universe has become an icon of Mary as queen of heaven and earth. Artistic representations of Mary often depict her dressed as the woman in Revelation. They signify the belief that the scriptures symbolically verify Mary's place in heaven.

Today's celebration is meant to give all Christians hope. Throughout our lives we strive to keep Mary as our model, ever ready to accept whatever may happen as long as it is God's will. If we pattern our life on hers, her new life will become the pattern for ours.

Written by Paul Turner. © 2003 Archdiocese of Chicago, Liturgy Training Publications; 1-800-933-1800; www.ltp.org.

AUGUST 22, 2004
Twenty-first Sunday in Ordinary Time

Inviting All People
Isaiah 66:18–21

You shall bring all your brothers and sisters from all the nations.

THE greatest music ever written appeals to people of every culture. People who do not speak a common language can all enjoy the same music. If the music is well written, it will touch the spirit of any person.

The same can be said of architecture, sculpture and painting. People of all cultures connect with the same treasures. This is also true of many sports like soccer and athletic achievements like running a marathon.

It is also true of the gospel. The message of Jesus Christ appeals to believers all over the world because it proclaims the news that all can be saved.

In the prophecy of Isaiah, God promises to gather together people of every language. Representatives from Israel will go to foreign nations and distant coastlands. Foreigners will hear about God and will come back to Jerusalem to make an offering there. New leaders would be raised up from these foreigners. It is a bold vision proclaiming the universality of God's intent.

In both the Old and the New Testament, it slowly became evident that God intended to invite all people of all nations into a holy relationship.

How do you help God's work? Do you know the names of people at church? Do you invite your neighbors and friends? Do you introduce yourself to newcomers? Anyone can understand the Christian message, but first it must be heard.

AUGUST 29, 2004
Twenty-second Sunday in Ordinary Time

The Gift of Humility
Sirach 3:17–18, 20, 28–29

Humble yourself and you will find favor with God.

WE learn humility in different ways. Sometimes we try to attain what is beyond our reach. We try to accomplish something we desire to attain. We fail. We humbly learn our limitations.

Sometimes we boast about our accomplishments. We have achieved much and we tell others the truth. But we lose the esteem of our friends when we do. Boasting might be honest, but humility brings rewards.

Still, some people erroneously believe that humility is weak and pride is strong. Some public figures—entertainers, politicians and professional athletes, for example—boast in the midst of combat. They want attention. They disdain the competition. Their success depends on their self-certitude.

Their fall is all the more sharp. In the end, even the most talented share the same mortality as everyone else. We are all humans. We shall all taste death. In the sight of God, humility is the only honest stance we can take.

The book of Sirach urges us to conduct our affairs with humility. We will be loved by others and favored by God. We will recognize that in spite of our gifts, there is One who is greater: the giver of these gifts. When we acknowledge the might of God, humility becomes a way of life.

SEPTEMBER 5, 2004

Twenty-third Sunday in Ordinary Time

Knowledge beyond Us
Wisdom 9:13–18b
Who can conceive what the Lord intends?

As painful as it is sometimes to know the truth, not knowing is worse. If someone we love is rushed to the hospital, the greatest agony comes from not knowing what is wrong. Is it serious? How extensive are the injuries? Are they life-threatening? Will they cause further suffering? Not knowing the answers is very painful.

Once we know, even if it is bad news, the situation is easier to accept. We can start to make adjustments, to deal with the truth. But when truth is unknown, chaos reigns. It terrifies us.

There are things we do not know. You can be the smartest kid in your class, the expert in your field, the parent who knows the habits of your children better than they do, but there are still things you do not know.

Only with difficulty, the book of Wisdom says, do we understand the things of this world. "But when things are in heaven, who can search them out?" As hard as it is to understand the things of earth, it is impossible to grasp the mystery of God.

The closer we come to God, the more awesome is the mystery. The more we understand about God, the more we realize we do not know. Some people quit their relationship with God in despair of ever learning the truth. Others go into that mysterious relationship, deeper and deeper.

SEPTEMBER 12, 2004

Twenty-fourth Sunday in Ordinary Time

Forgiving Big Mistakes
Exodus 32:7–11, 13–14
The Lord relented in the punishment he had threatened to inflict on the people.

IF we say something stupid or do something inappropriate in the presence of people we love, we hope they will forgive us.

When we are with those we love, we relax. We speak more easily the thoughts of our heart, and we do more readily the impulsive deeds that bring relationships to life. Sometimes we act with the spontaneity that love enjoys, but with the inappropriateness that love does not tolerate. We say something insulting. We do something crude. We give in to the temptation to love someone else.

The best relationships tolerate mistakes. If someone loves us completely and wholly for who we are, that person will accept us, mistakes and all. Our misdeeds are a part of us; to love someone is to love the person that commits errors of judgment.

Moses reminds God of this. While Moses was on the mountain receiving the law from God, the people grew tired of waiting down below. They removed their jewelry and threw it into a fire. Out came something resembling a golden calf. So they worshiped it. They worshiped something that was not God. In the spontaneity of the moment, at a time when religious fervor ran high, the people made a terrible mistake.

Moses reminds God of the covenant promised to all the descendants of Abraham, Isaac and Israel. And God relents. God does not punish the people for their sin.

No matter how stupid our mistakes, God will forgive us.

SEPTEMBER 19, 2004
Twenty-fifth Sunday in Ordinary Time

Holy Day Burden
Amos 8:4–7
Hear this, you who trample upon the needy!

To some people, religious holidays are a pain in the neck. Holy days interrupt the flow of business. They keep employees from work. The market's demands remain the same, but the rhythm of work is interrupted. If you run a business, holy days get in the way.

To some people, religious values are a pain in the neck. If our goal in life is to make money, we don't want to hear about giving to the poor. We cannot keep money if we give it away. We will treat employees fairly only if it helps improve the bottom line. We will use human beings for fun or advancement, but not with respect for their lives and persons.

At the time of Amos the prophet, the corrupt business world treated religion with impatience.

"When will the Sabbath be over," people wondered on that holy day, "that we may display our wheat?" Business leaders took advantage of the poor and cheated customers. They had no use for religion. They desired only profit.

We fall into the same sin when work takes precedence over prayer, and when profit trumps charity. Religion is designed to ease our pain, not to cause it. It strives to lighten the burden of all so that all can rejoice together in the love of God.

Written by Paul Turner. © 2003 Archdiocese of Chicago, Liturgy Training Publications; 1-800-933-1800; www.ltp.org.

SEPTEMBER 26, 2004
Twenty-sixth Sunday in Ordinary Time

Rich and Poor
Amos 6:1a, 4–7
Woe to the complacent in Zion!

The gap between rich and poor is uncomfortably large. If you can read, you already have advantages over many other people in the world. If you worship in a church building and have printed copies of bulletins and worship aids, you have resources far beyond those of many others.

Most people are unaware of their privileges. They do not live in the squalor of poverty. They forget about it, except in photographs and letters of appeal. They see the gap between themselves and those who are richer, but they ignore the gap between themselves and the poor.

The prophet Amos had no patience with the rich. They lived a comfortable life. They lay on beds of ivory. They ate meat. They played music.

They drank wine by the bowlful. They anointed themselves with the best oils and perfumes. They had it all and used it all. They showed little concern for the poor.

Amos could envision another society, a society in which the rich shared. Those with more resources have more responsibility to help those who have less.

The rich who thought they had it all lost it all in the exile. When Jerusalem was taken into captivity, invaders took interest in the booty of the rich. The poor had nothing. They had nothing to lose. But the rich lost it all.

Our possessions hold us captive to our desires, to our fears and to ourselves. Freedom is in giving, not in possessing.

Written by Paul Turner. © 2003 Archdiocese of Chicago, Liturgy Training Publications; 1-800-933-1800; www.ltp.org.

OCTOBER 3, 2004
Twenty-seventh Sunday in Ordinary Time

God's Own Time
Habakkuk 1:2–3; 2:2–4
The vision presses on to fulfillment.

GOD is good, but God is slow. We trust in God's plan. We believe that virtue will be rewarded and evil will be punished. But we get tired of waiting for it to happen.

The prophet Habakkuk says God has given a vision that we can easily read. But the vision may not be fulfilled soon. It works in its own time. Still, it will press on to its fulfillment, and it will not disappoint those who hope in it. "If it delays," the prophet says, "wait for it. It will surely come." But it can take a while.

Faith is what happens while we wait on a slow God. We believe because we have experienced God's love and mercy throughout our lives. We rely on the one who alone can fulfill our desires. We trust that God wants goodness as much as we do. But the waiting is still hard.

"How long, O Lord? I cry for help but you do not listen!" says Habakkuk. Actually, God does listen. God longs to hear our prayers. God wants righteousness even more than we do. God will deliver, but the vision has its own time. God asks only one thing of us: patience born from faith.

OCTOBER 10, 2004
Twenty-eighth Sunday in Ordinary Time

The Kindness of Strangers
2 Kings 5:14–17
Naaman returned to Elisha and acknowledged the Lord.

WE expect our family and friends to help us. We expect church and society to help us. But we don't expect help from strangers, from people of other nations and especially not from enemies.

The help we receive from God always delights us. But when it comes through an unexpected source, it brings special delight.

Naaman was a leper who sought a cure. He sought help from Elisha the prophet. But Naaman was a Syrian, not among the children of Israel. Elisha had little or nothing to do with Syrians. But God inspired Elisha to help Naaman. Elisha ignored the nationality and focused on the illness. At his command, Naaman washed in the Jordan River seven times. He came out healed. Naaman decided he would no longer worship any other god in Syria. He would worship only Israel's God.

The help we give strangers proclaims the gospel. In acting charitably toward others we bring Christ to them, even to those who have not yet met Christ.

When we receive the kindness of strangers, we learn how Christ is at work in the world in places we did not imagine. The miracle of charity proclaims the universality of God's work.

OCTOBER 17, 2004
Twenty-ninth Sunday in Ordinary Time

Raising Hands in Prayer
Exodus 17:8–13
As long as Moses kept his hands raised up, Israel had the better of the fight.

WHEN people find it hard to pray, they seek ways to improve. Sometimes a simple change can bring great benefits to our prayer.

Most people derive benefit from prayer if they get into the right routine. For example, the celebration of the eucharist always follows the same outline. The predictability of the structure allows people to enter into the prayer. Some young people express frustration about the repetitive nature of the Mass, and that is understandable. But it takes time with repetition to let the mystery of the Mass sink into one's spirit. Once it does, repetition provides a framework out of which people can pray.

Prayer at home can be improved through routine as well. Many people find it helpful to pick a certain time of day when they will go to pray. Others find a certain place they can use—whether it is a room or a particular chair. The selection of time and place provides the structure in which prayer can happen.

Posture can also help prayer. Some people kneel. Others sit. Early Christians stood for prayer and lifted their hands aloft. The priest still uses this posture when he prays at Mass.

It is similar to the posture taken by Moses when Amalek waged war against Israel. As long as Moses' hands were outstretched, Israel had the better of the fight.

If we are fighting at prayer, a minor adjustment in place, time or posture might help.

OCTOBER 24, 2004
Thirtieth Sunday in Ordinary Time

Life's Prayer
Sirach 35:12–14, 16–18
The prayer of the lowly pierces the clouds.

IF our prayer is not as satisfying as we wish, there may be a problem. Some people think God is the problem—that God does not listen to us when we pray. Some people think the prayer is the problem—that the prayer is too boring or out of touch.

But sometimes the problem is neither with God nor with our prayer. The problem is with the other things we do. Prayer does not exist in a vacuum. It works best when it is coupled with a life of charity and service.

The book of Sirach says God hears the cry of the oppressed. Those who suffer injustice will have their prayer heard. It is not just because they are victims. It is because they live justly. You would think that those who live justly should

be rewarded for it. It does not always work that way. Sometimes the just suffer unfairly. God has mercy on them and listens to their prayer, Sirach says, not just because of the oppressor, but because of their righteousness. "The one who serves God willingly is heard."

If our prayer seems unsatisfying, the problem might be not in the way we pray, but in the way we live. If we live justly and do charity for others, our prayer will be heard. We may still suffer oppression, but God will hear the prayer of the innocent. It pierces the clouds.

OCTOBER 31, 2004
Thirty-first Sunday in Ordinary Time

Gentle Mercy
Wisdom 11:22—12:2
You have mercy on all because you love all things that are.

A single grain of sand or a single drop of morning dew looks quite small. And it is. When God looks upon each of us, we look quite small. And we are.

We feel especially small when we become aware of our sins. We acknowledge with some embarrassment the evil we have done, the people we have hurt, the lies we have told and the cover-up we have made. The awareness of our sin fills us with remorse and diminishes our stature. If our sin becomes public, we want to hide, to go home and to make ourselves as small as we possibly can.

We do all this as if we could hide from God, but we cannot. God notices the tiniest grain of sand and the single drop of morning dew. And God notices us. God notices the tiniest things we do—for good or for ill.

When we sin, when we feel small, we need not hide from God. We can appear before God quite openly and acknowledge the wrong we have done. God will forgive. God sees the intimacy of our lives and loves it.

As the book of Wisdom says, "You have mercy on all, because you can do all things; and you overlook people's sins that they may repent."

NOVEMBER 1, 2004
All Saints

Unnoticed Holy Ones
Revelation 7:2–4, 9–14
I had a vision of a great multitude.

A lot of the good you do goes unnoticed. You care for family. You donate to charity. You pray for the needy. Perhaps you perform civic services that few people ever see. You might even do some things in secret precisely to avoid the attention that a reward would bring. Your satisfaction is often its own reward.

You believe that God sees, and that is enough.

You are not alone. The good that many people do can never be fully rewarded. Society owes a debt of gratitude to everyday heroes who improve life for the masses by performing the simplest of deeds for the sake of giving care.

Imagine that multitude of good people gathered together. Imagine them before the throne of the Lamb, worshiping God. Imagine them wearing as reward the uniform of heaven—white garments washed in the blood of the Lamb.

That is the vision that John sees in the book of Revelation. The throng of the blessed gathers to give praise, only to be counted among those who survived the trials of life and persevered in their faith.

On All Saints Day we remember that numberless host. They inspire us to continue the good we do, even if no one notices.

NOVEMBER 2, 2004
All Souls

Too Good to Be True?
Isaiah 25:6–9
The Lord will destroy death forever.

THE promises of politicians are too good to be true. Before any election, but especially a presidential election, we learn about the platform, we hear the dreams, we are swept up in the speeches—and it all seems too good to be true.

The promises of advertisers are too good to be true. They promise true love, lasting youth, envious friends, happiness, the support of celebrities, and products that will solve life's problems. But the ads are too good to be true.

God's promises also sound too good to be true. Through the mouth of Isaiah, God promises marvelous things to Jerusalem. God promises to destroy "the veil that veils all peoples" and "the web that is woven over all the nations."

God promises to destroy and wipe away the tears from all faces, not just a few.

It sounds too good to be true.

On All Souls' Day we gather to reflect on God's magnificent promise. It began as a promise of relationship. It developed into a relationship of love. It ended as a love swallowed in death, but then death ended, and life began anew. The promise God made to Abraham reached fulfillment beyond anyone's wildest dreams in the resurrection of Jesus Christ.

When we suffer the loss of someone we love, our despair seems endless. We need good news. We need promises. God has promised eternity. This promise is not too good to be true, but it is true.

NOVEMBER 7, 2004
Thirty-second Sunday in Ordinary Time

A Cause Worth Dying For
2 Maccabees 7:1–2, 9–14
The king of the world will raise up to live again forever.

THEY called the World War II generation "the greatest generation" because they were willing to sacrifice everything for the cause of their country. Subsequent generations became more pampered. They were more accustomed to receive rather than sacrifice. The World War II generation was ready to die for what they believed in. Later generations, some argue, do not get up off the couch for anything.

Heroism comes from strong belief. If you believe in something strong enough, you will sacrifice your life for it. You might give up your life for your spouse or your child. But would you be ready to give it up for your country or for your faith?

The second book of Maccabees tells an extraordinary tale of a family who died rather than eat pork. Pork! They realized that to do so would betray the faith of their ancestors. They were ready to be tortured and killed in order to encourage others to keep the faith they had received.

In their distress, they held out hope in a resurrection in which all that was wrong would be made right again. They held this belief even before the coming of Christ, who would reveal the nature of the resurrection to his believers.

As Christians we hold faith in the greatest gift of all, eternal life. Are you willing to lose your life for this cause? Would you give up your life to inspire others and to gain an everlasting reward?

NOVEMBER 14, 2002
Thirty-third Sunday in Ordinary Time

God's Fire
Malachi 3:19–20a
The sun of justice will shine on you.

FIRE burns, purifies, cooks and cleanses. It can work wondrous good. It can also cause unspeakable ill. Fire is powerful, just as God is powerful.

The prophet Malachi envisions the coming of destructive fire. The prevalence of evil is widespread. It was then and is now. Its potential for wreaking havoc is extensive. Malachi believes, as we believe, that God is more powerful than evil, that God is good, and that God will not tolerate the evil of the world. We believe that in time God will set things right. Evil will be punished. We long for that day.

Malachi sees that day as a day of fire: "The day is coming, blazing like an oven, when all the proud and all evildoers will be stubble." The fire will rage over those who do wrong. They will not endure. God's wrath will be stronger than their desire to do ill. God will have power over them, even when our human frailty does not.

There will also be fire for the good. "For you who fear my name," God says through Malachi, "there will arise the sun of justice with its healing rays." The fiery sun will rise in the east and shine with healing upon those who do good.

God comes like fire. God does not change. But those who do evil are like stubble. Those who do good shall be healed.

Written by Paul Turner. © 2003 Archdiocese of Chicago, Liturgy Training Publications; 1-800-933-1800; www.ltp.org.

NOVEMBER 21, 2004
Our Lord Jesus Christ the King

Camelot Restored
2 Samuel 5:1–3
You shall shepherd my people Israel.

CHRIST is our king. If you live in a country with a king this sounds like treason. If you live in a country without a king it sounds like mutiny. No matter where you live, it sounds like faith.

The image of a king comes primarily from the stories of David, the ideal king of Israel. David ruled many years and his kingship became a kind of Camelot, a perfect period in which the nation flourished and God seemed pleased.

David was flawed, of course. He sinned. He ignored God's word. But God still loved him, and David remained an extraordinary example of leadership.

David began his reign as the successor to Saul. The elders of the people came to David in Hebron and made an agreement with him that he should be their king. They chose David because he had a good war record. He "led the Israelites out and brought them back." He also had a relationship with God, and God appointed him to leadership: "You shall shepherd my people Israel and shall be commander of Israel." Because of his exploits and his faith David ruled.

David prefigured the reign of Jesus. Jesus exercised his kingship by his wondrous deeds, spellbinding preaching and intimate prayer with the Father. There is no king but Jesus, who lived out all that David aspired to be, but without sin.

As we acclaim Christ our King we do so, knowing he is our model of leadership, prayer and power.

Written by Paul Turner. © 2003 Archdiocese of Chicago, Liturgy Training Publications; 1-800-933-1800; www.ltp.org.

RESOURCES

■ WHAT FOLLOWS ARE LISTS OF TITLES that communities have found useful in preparing the liturgy. Your favorites may be missing, but the list is a start. Each community needs to keep up to date with the vast world of liturgical literature. Many parishes have found it helpful to elect or appoint someone to serve as "librarian" who maintains published resources, orders new materials, gets on mailing lists, and devises a proposed budget for each project.

Here is a list of abbreviations of publishers. A more complete list of publishers with addresses follows on page 263.

CB: Catholic Book Publishing Co.

CCCB: Canadian Conference of Catholic Bishops

ICEL: International Committee for English in the Liturgy

LP: The Liturgical Press

LTP: Liturgy Training Publications

USCCB: United States Conference of Catholic Bishops

WLP: World Library Publications

LITURGY DOCUMENTS, COMMENTARIES AND HISTORY OF LITURGICAL REFORM

The Code of Canon Law (1983, Canon Law Society of America) contains a significant amount of legislation pertaining to the liturgy.

Documents of Christian Worship: Descriptive and Interpretive Sources (1992, White, James F., Westminster John Knox). This thorough compilation is traced from the beginning (scripture, fathers, councils) and across the traditions (Jewish, Catholic, Orthodox, Anglican, Reformed), and grouped by "area": space, time, sacraments, word, etc. It is a look within but beyond Roman Catholicism toward where we have come from and what we have in common, as well as where we differ.

Documents on the Liturgy, 1963–1979: Conciliar, Papal and Curial Texts (1982, LP). A fine translation and compilation of everything official. The massive index makes this a gold mine of information.

The Liturgy Documents: A Parish Resource, Volume I (LTP). The most recent translations of Roman liturgical documents, along with documents of the United States bishops. An introduction by a liturgical scholar is provided for each document. (Expected late–2004.)

The Liturgy Documents: A Parish Resource, Volume 2 (1999, LTP). A companion to the first volume.

Bugnini, Annibale. *The Reform of the Liturgy (1948–1975)* (1992, LP). The man who worked on the reform of Holy Week under Pius XII went on to be one of the principal, practical architects of the massive reform that followed Vatican II. Rite by rite, meeting by meeting, Archbishop Bugnini takes us through the high points and low points, collaboration and intrigue that attended this tumultuous time of which we are the heirs.

Fenwick, John, and Bryan Spinks. *Worship in Transition: The Liturgical Movement in the Twentieth Century* (1995, Continuum). This is meant to give a sense of historical context to those engaged in the liturgical enterprise at the end of the twentieth century. Written by two Anglicans from England, this concise and comprehensive volume gives us a sense of the liturgical movement beyond Roman Catholicism and outside the United States. A particularly helpful chapter is entitled "Snapshots of the Movement in North America."

Hughes, Kathleen, RSCJ, ed. *How Firm a Foundation, Volume I: Voices of the Early Liturgical Movement* (1990, LTP). A history of the decades of wisdom, humor, patience and frustration before Vatican II.

Tuzik, Robert L. *How Firm a Foundation, Volume II: Leaders of the Liturgical Movement* (1990, LTP). A book about the lives and work of more than forty pioneers and recent leaders from the last three generations.

GENERAL LITURGY RESOURCES

Finn, Peter, and James Schellman, eds. *Shaping English Liturgy* (1990, Pastoral Press). An investigation of the challenges and processes by which ICEL is crafting a contemporary vernacular liturgy for the church. Especially timely in light of present debate on and future publication of ICEL's revised sacramentary.

Huck, Gabe, ed. *A Liturgy Sourcebook* (1994, LTP). This volume contains favorite texts of artists, pastors, scholars, musicians and educators, all about liturgy.

Irwin, Kevin W. *Context and Text: Method in Liturgical Theology* (1994, LP). The author begins with a historical overview of the relationship between liturgy and theology. His thesis: context is text—text shapes context. All those seriously engaged in liturgical planning and ministry will value the subsequent chapters translating theory into practical and pastoral considerations. Especially helpful are Irwin's observations about liturgical texts (euchology) and the liturgical arts.

Jones, Cheslyn, Geoffrey Wainwright, Edward Yarnold, and Paul Bradshaw. *The Study of Liturgy,* Revised Edition (1992, Oxford). An encyclopedic presentation of issues in liturgy, Catholic and Protestant. Extensive illustrations and bibliography. Good background on various elements of calendar, eucharist, vesture, etc.

Leonard, John K., and Nathan D. Mitchell. *The Postures of the Assembly during the Eucharistic Prayer* (1994, LTP). A scholarly, yet practical discussion, in light of the ongoing debate that is sure to continue in the United States beyond the revised sacramentary's publication. Chapter titles bespeak the breadth of presentation:

The Anthropology of Posture and Gesture, The Sociological and Religious Significance of Standing and Kneeling, Ritual Posture in the Context of Meals and the Meal Ministry of Jesus, Posture during the Eucharistic Prayer.

Mazar, Peter. *To Crown the Year: Decorating the Church through the Seasons* (1995, LTP). This resource will help those responsible for church decorations to make a wide variety of seasonal choices. Included are "pep talks" to get a team in the right spirit for thinking about the seasons.

Ryan, Thomas G. *The Sacristy Manual* (1993, LTP). The finest (and nearly only) book on the market that covers the history and use and appointing of the many materials and settings required by the liturgical rites. Those who prepare the liturgy will find the book's many checklists handy.

Schmemann, Alexander. *Introduction to Theology* (1966, 1986, St. Vladimir's Seminary Press). This is an Orthodox theologian's masterful attempt, many years back now, to do what Irwin does more extensively, from the Roman Catholic and contemporary perspective, in *Context and Text*. A classic introduction to the art of theologizing liturgically and looking at liturgy from a theological perspective.

White, James. *Roman Catholic Worship: Trent to Today* (1995, Paulist Press). Like the authors of the preceding volume, White feels that before plunging into the task at hand, liturgical planners and ministers need to know at least something of the movement with which they stand in continuity. This book provides that orientation from the Catholic experience.

THE LITURGY OF THE HOURS AND COMMENTARIES

The Liturgy of the Hours (1975, 4 volumes, CB; 2 volumes, Daughters of Saint Paul). A treasure for all Catholics.

Christian Prayer (1977, CB) is a one-volume excerpt from the full collection.

Shorter Christian Prayer (1987, CB, LP) is a simplified, pocket-sized edition to help introduce the assembly to this form of liturgical prayer.

Supplement with new memorials to be observed in the United States (1987, CB).

Campbell, Stanislaus. *From Breviary to Liturgy of the Hours: The Structural Reform of the Roman Office,* 1964–1971 (1995, LP). For anyone helping to revive and plan the parish celebration of the Hours.

Cones, Bryan. *Daily Prayer 2004* (2003, LTP). A one-volume, handy companion to daily prayer through the calendar year that focuses on scripture reading.

Storey, William G. *An Everyday Book of Hours* (2001, LTP). A four-week cycle of morning and evening prayer using the classic patterns of prayer. *A Seasonal Book of Hours* (2001, LTP) complements *An Everyday Book* with material for feasts and seasons.

Zimmerman, Joyce Ann. *Morning and Evening: A Parish Celebration* (1996, LTP). This work gives a clear explanation of the Liturgy of the Hours and offers practical ideas for its implementation in parishes.

RITUAL BOOKS FOR MASS

The Roman Missal has been published in several parts, mostly to distinguish the various ministries. These volumes form the core of any parish's liturgical library.

Sacramentary (1985, CB, LP). Although a two-volume revision of the sacramentary has been prepared, with revised translations from the Latin, this good work has been in limbo the past decade.

Eucharistic Prayer for Masses for Various Needs and Occasions (1996, CB, LP)
   Four thematic variations:
- Form I or A: The Church on the Way to Unity
- Form II or B: God Guides the Church on the Way of Salvation
- Form III or C: Jesus, Way to the Father
- Form IV or D: Jesus, the Compassion of God

Sacramentary Supplement (1994, CB, LP)
- Propers for saints added to calendar since 1985 sacramentary
- Proclamation of the Birth of Christ
- Proclamation of the Date of Easter on Epiphany
- Reception of Holy Oils

Collection of Masses of the Blessed Virgin Mary (1992, CB, LP)
- Volume I: Sacramentary (only volume needed in most communities)
- Volume II: Lectionary (needed only at Marian shrines)

Lectionary for Mass for Use in the Dioceses of the United States of America: Volume 1: Sundays, Solemnities, Feasts of the Lord and the Saints, Second Typical Edition (1998, CB, LP, LTP). *Volume 2* (2002): Weekdays of Year 1 and the sanctoral cycle with commons. *Volume 3* (2002): Weekdays of Year 2 and the sanctoral cycle with commons. *Volume 4* (2002): Ritual and votive Masses and Masses for special needs and occasions.

The Sunday volume is available in separate editions for Years A, B and C, as well as a one-volume study edition for all years. The Canadian Revision (1992, CCCB) uses the NRSV translation.

Lectionary for Masses with Children, Contemporary English Version (1993, various publishers).

Book of the Gospels (2000, LP, CB; 2001, LTP, WLP).

Revised Common Lectionary (from the Consultation on Common Texts) (1992, Abingdon Press). The Protestant adaptation of the Roman three-year lectionary.

ON THE EUCHARIST AND SUNDAY MASS

Baker, J. Robert, and Barbara Budde. *A Eucharist Sourcebook* (1999, LTP). An anthology that explores what eucharist means. Topics include hungering, gathering, remembering, healing and offering.

Griffiths, Alan, trans. *We Give You Thanks and Praise.*

Huck, Gabe, ed. *Preaching about the Mass* (1992, LTP). Includes sample homilies and reflection questions with reproducible bulletin inserts.

Mazza, Enrico. *The Origins of the Eucharistic Prayer* (1995, LP) and *The Eucharistic Prayers of the Roman Rite* (1986, LP). Both volumes are treasures for those who choose, those who proclaim, and those who affirm in assembly, the great eucharistic prayer. The first volume brings us through the history and multi-faceted developments of eucharistic praying; the second examines the prayers now in use (including the early version of our newest eucharistic prayer: for special needs and occasions).

Philippart, David. *Saving Signs, Wondrous Words* (1996, LTP). The words and actions we use when we pray as an assembly are probed in short essays.

SCRIPTURES OF YEAR C

The New Jerome Biblical Commentary (1990, Prentice Hall). This should be in every Catholic library. This year see especially the chapters on Mark by Daniel J. Harrington, SJ, and on John by Pheme Perkins.

Blain, Susan A., ed. *Imagining the Word: An Arts and Lectionary Resource* (several volumes) (1995, Cleveland: United Church Press). Rich illustrations in all styles and for all periods. Suitable for placement at the entrance of the worship space as a contemporary icon.

Bonneau, Norman. *The Sunday Lectionary: Ritual Word, Paschal Shape* (1998, Collegeville: LP).

Brown, Raymond E. *An Introduction to the New Testament* (1997, Doubleday).

Craddock, Fred B. *Luke* (1990, Louisville: John Knox Press).

Danker, Frederick W. *Luke* (1987, Philadelphia: Fortress Press).

Deeley, Mary Katherine, Michael Cameron, and Kathy Hendricks. *At Home with the Word 2004* (2003, LTP). Families, parish staffs and individuals can use this book to prepare themselves to hear the scriptures Sunday after Sunday and to act on them week by week.

Dornish, Loretta. *A Woman Reads the Gospel of Luke* (1996, Collegeville: LP).

Johnson, Luke Timothy. *The Gospel of Luke* Sacra Pagina (1991, Collegeville: LP).

LaVerdierre, Eugene. *Dining in the Kingdom of God: The Origins of the Eucharist According to Luke* (1994, Chicago: LTP).

Powell, Mark Allan. *Fortress Introduction to the Gospels* (1998, Minneapolis: Fortress).

Tiede, David L. *Luke* Augsburg Commentary on the New Testament (1988, Minneapolis: Augsburg).

West, Fritz. *Scripture and Memory: The Ecumenical Hermeneutic of the Three-Year Lectionaries* (1997, Collegeville: LP).

Wold, Wayne L. *Tune My Heart to Sing: Devotions for Choirs Based on the Revised Common*

Lectionary (1997, Minneapolis: Augsburg Fortress). Brief reflections for all three cycles in one volume. Each entry is coordinated with the gospel of the Sunday and refers to a hymn text appropriate to that gospel.

INTERCESSIONS AND OTHER LITURGICAL TEXTS

Borg, Robert, ed. *Together We Pray* (1994, LP). These intercessions are based on the biblical texts for Sundays and solemnities, and follow liturgical norms.

Cormier, Jay. *Lord, Hear Our Prayer* (1995, LP). This collection of texts for general intercessions on Sundays and major feasts for all three cycles, as well as for Masses, reflecting themes and language of the lectionary readings.

Griffiths, Alan, trans. *We Give You Thanks and Praise: The Ambrosian Eucharistic Prefaces* (2000, Sheed & Ward).

Scagnelli, Peter. *Prayers for Sundays and Seasons: Year C* (1997, LTP). This useful pastoral resource contains scripture-related collect prayers, most translated from European sacramentaries. Also included are lectionary references for the Roman and Revised Common Lectionary (used by the other Christian churches), suggested texts for general intercessions based on the readings, introductions to the Lord's Prayer, invitations to holy communion, and dismissal texts. This book is a companion to *Sourcebook for Sundays and Seasons*.

PRIESTLESS SUNDAYS

United States version: *Sunday Celebrations in the Absence of a Priest* (1994, CB, LTP). Canadian version: *Sunday Celebrations of Word and Hours* (1995, CCCB). Extensive pastoral notes face difficult questions raised by this rite and present carefully crafted rites for celebration. The Canadian version contains more extensive and creative resources than the U.S. edition.

Dallen, James. *The Dilemma of Priestless Sundays* (1994, LTP). Before we charge naively into any resolution of the "priest shortage," Dallen asks us to reflect carefully on its impact on Catholic identity and mission, and to consider alternatives.

RITUAL BOOKS FOR SACRAMENTS OTHER THAN EUCHARIST

The Roman Ritual, published in one volume before Vatican II, has since been published in several volumes, one for each sacrament or rite. The increased number of options and adaptations made this necessary. Every parish, every presider and every planning group needs a full set of the current editions at hand—with the possible exception of the *Rite of Religious Profession.* For the celebration of the rites, beautifully bound editions of these books are to be used. These reflect the dignity of the assembly and its worship. Paperback editions are published for study and preparation only.

Rite of Christian Initiation of Adults (1988, LTP, LP, USCCB, CB). This includes the Rite for the Reception of Baptized Christians, formerly published in a separate booklet. Study editions are available, as well as Spanish volumes.

Book of the Elect (1999, CB) is an enrollment book for the RCIA.

Rite of Baptism for Children (1970, CB, LP). The Canadian bishops published a handsome edition of this book with separate rites "within Mass" and "outside Mass" and with slight revision of ICEL text for inclusive language. Copyright restrictions prohibit bulk sales in the United States, but individual copies can be obtained from the Canadian Catholic Conference.

Rite of Marriage (1970, CB, LP, Ave Maria Press). The Canadian edition, published by the Canadian Catholic Conference, includes suggested texts for the Rite of Reception at the entrance, table and anniversary blessings, and other texts that make it the best volume currently available.

The Vatican issued a new edition in 1990. ICEL and the U.S. Bishops' Conference are working on the U.S. translation and adaptation. Presumably this will be the next section of the ritual to be published.

Order of Christian Funerals (1989 CB, LP, LTP). A study edition of the entire rite and ritual editions of the vigil and rite of committal are also available from LTP. The Canadian edition (1990, CCCB) includes a fine re-ordering of the "Vigil and related rites and prayers," placing them in chronological order. It also contains important appendices: prayers for the end of the day, after vigil and visitation, norms for cremation and ritual directives for a funeral liturgy in the presence of ashes. There is also a laminated card with a practical adaptation entitled "Shorter Rite of Committal for Use in Inclement Weather."

Vigils and Related Prayers (1989, LTP), excerpts from the complete rite.

Rites of Committal (1989, LTP), excerpts from the complete rite.

Book of the Names of the Dead (1991, LTP), in which Christian communities may record and remember the names of their dead; especially for use during November.

Cremation Rite Appendix (1997, LTP). Cremation rite and the U.S. Bishops' statement on cremation.

Rite of Penance (1975, CB, LP). Published in both "sanctuary size" for penance services and "confessional size" for individual penance.

Pastoral Care of the Sick: Rites of Anointing and Viaticum (1983, LTP [Spanish and English], CB, LP). Published in "sanctuary" and "pocket" sizes.

A Ritual for Laypersons: Rites for Holy Communion and Pastoral Care of the Sick and Dying (1993, LP). Rites that may be led by a layperson in the absence of a priest or deacon.

Communion of the Sick (1984, LP). The official texts for bringing the eucharist to the sick.

Holy Communion and Worship of the Eucharist outside Mass (1976, CB).

Order for the Solemn Exposition of the Holy Eucharist (1993, LP):

- for exposition over one or several days
- liturgy of the hours during the period of exposition
- eucharistic services of prayer and praise during exposition
- closing celebration (two forms: with Mass, outside Mass)
- scripture readings, litanies, music resources

Rite of Religious Profession (1988, LTP).

ON THE SACRAMENTS

Fink, Peter, SJ, ed. *The New Dictionary of Sacramental Worship* (1990, Michael Glazier). A vast theological and pastoral resource, whose entries run the whole gamut from theological to practical liturgical, including the pastoral dimension and the insights of the social sciences.

ON BAPTISM/CHRISTIAN INITIATION

Baker, J. Robert, Larry J. Nyberg, and Victoria M., eds. *A Baptism Sourcebook* (1993, LTP). Prose, poetry, scripture and liturgical and patristic texts that help to unfold the mystery of baptism.

Fitzgerald, Tim. *Infant Baptism: A Parish Celebration* (1994, LTP) encourages baptism to be understood as the action of the entire community.

Jackson, Pamela. *Journeybread for the Shadowlands* (1993, LP). Unusual and useful reflections on readings for the various rites of the RCIA throughout the year.

Johnson, Maxwell E. *The Rites of Christian Initiation: Their Evolution and Interpretation* (1999, LP). This study surveys the development and theology of those rites from their New Testament origins to their current shape in the Roman Catholic, Episcopal and Lutheran churches.

Morris, Thomas H. *The RCIA: Transforming the Church: A Resource for Pastoral Implementation* (1997, Paulist). A revised and updated edition of the standard primer for implementing and perfecting the rites of initiation for adult believers in the Catholic church.

Nelson, Gertrud Mueller. *Child of God* (1997, LTP). A "baby book" that commemorates days from birth to age 6 with places to record memories and sacraments.

Ramshaw, Gail. *Words around the Font* (1995, LTP). Reflections on 13 words about the font, arranged in the order of the catechumenate.

Tufano, Victoria M. *Celebrating the Rites of Adult Initiation: Pastoral Reflections* (1992, LTP). Essays about the scrutinies, the Rite of Acceptance, taking a new name and more.

Turner, Paul. *The Hallelujah Highway: A History of the Catechumenate* (2000, LTP). Stories of people and documents that played a role in developing and recording the rites.

Turner, Paul. *Your Child's Baptism* (1999, LTP). What parents should know in preparation for infant baptism.

_____. *The Catechumenate Answer Book* (2000, Resource Publications). Answers the 101 most-asked questions.

ON MARRIAGE

Baker, J. Robert, Kevin Charles Gibley, and Joni Reiff Gibley, eds. *A Marriage Sourcebook* (1994, LTP). Scripture, prayer, poetry, fiction, song and humor expressing the joys and sorrows, deaths and resurrections of the mystery of marriage.

Covino, Paul. *Celebrating Marriage: Preparing the Wedding Liturgy: A Workbook for the Engaged Couple* (1994, Pastoral Press). This workbook walks the engaged couple through each step of the wedding liturgy and offers practical and proven suggestions.

Fleming, Austin. *Parish Weddings* (1987, LTP). A guide for good liturgy at weddings.

_____. *Prayerbook for Engaged Couples* (1990, LTP). An invitation for couples to pray the scriptures that will be heard at their wedding.

Kunde-Anderson, Mary Beth, and David Anderson. *Handbook for Church Music for Weddings* (1992, LTP). A guide for planning wedding music.

Nelson, Gertrud Mueller, and Christopher Witt. *Sacred Threshold: Rituals and Readings for a Wedding of the Spirit* (1998, Doubleday). This book is written for the bride and groom who are searching for more meaningful, gracious and sacred wedding traditions.

Turner, Paul. *The Catholic Wedding Answer Book* (2001, Resource Publications). Answers the 101 most-asked questions.

ON THE SACRAMENT OF RECONCILIATION

Dallen, James, and Joseph Favazza. *Removing the Barriers: The Practice of Reconciliation* (1991, LTP). A call to rethink the way the church reconciles while expanding our ideas about our mission as church.

Hughes, Kathleen, RSCJ, and Joseph A. Favazza, eds. *A Reconciliation Sourcebook* (1997, LTP). The parable of the Prodigal Son is the framework for the texts about division, alienation, penance, mercy and celebration.

Kennedy, Robert, ed. *Reconciling Embrace: Foundations for the Future of Sacramental Reconciliation* (1998, LTP). Seven major presentations from the 1995 symposium on reconciliation sponsored by the North American Forum on the Catechumenate.

ON FUNERALS

Sloyan, Virginia, RSCJ, ed. *A Sourcebook about Christian Death* (1990, LTP). Topics include the communion of saints, prayer for the dead, images of heaven, rest, pilgrimage, reckoning and resurrection. For November or for the period of mourning after death.

Smith, Margaret. *Facing Death Together: Parish Funerals* (1998, LTP). This is a guide for celebrating the order of Christian funerals in a context of pastoral care.

BLESSINGS

Book of Blessings (1989, CB, LP). This book contains numerous blessings and prayers, including several rites once published separately: the orders for crowning an image of the Blessed Virgin Mary, for the commissioning of extraordinary lay ministers of the eucharist, for the installation of a pastor.

Catholic Household Blessings and Prayers (1988, USCC). This is the first attempt by the U.S. bishops since *A Manual of Prayers*, issued by the Baltimore Council of 1888, to provide a standard domestic prayer book for the whole country.

Shorter Book of Blessings (1990, CB, LP) is an abridged form of the *Book of Blessings*. It contains most of the blessings that take place outside of Mass. Study editions are also available.

PONTIFICAL

The Roman Pontifical includes those rites normally celebrated by a bishop. The *Blessing of Oil and Consecration of Chrism* has been included in the sacramentary. The rites for confirmation and for the dedication of a church are published separately and should be in every liturgical library.

Roman Pontifical, Part I (1978, ICEL) contains the now outdated rites of initiation, confirmation, the institution of readers and acolytes, the various ordination rites, and several blessings of persons (blessing of an abbot/abbess and consecration to a life of virginity).

Confirmation (1973, USCC). Excerpted from fuller pontifical. The Canadian version (1973, CCCB) incorporates helpful notes from the *Ceremonial of Bishops*.

Dedication of a Church and an Altar (1989, USCC). An important resource for parishes undergoing renovation or construction; useful for parishes as they prepare for each year's anniversary.

Ceremonial of Bishops (1989, LP). While not a liturgical book of texts, it is an official compilation of rubrics, with liturgical and historical orientation to feasts, seasons and services, and of emendations made since the various ritual books were published. The notes are useful for charting liturgical celebrations in any parish.

HISTORY AND OBSERVANCE OF THE LITURGICAL YEAR

Adam, Adolph. *The Liturgical Year: Its History and Its Meaning After the Reform of the Liturgy* (1981, LP). Contains some "received wisdom" that has been superseded by recent scholarship. One of the best studies available.

Baldovin, John. *Worship: City, Church and Renewal* (1991, Pastoral Press). See chapters on feasting the saints and on a calendar for a just community—all founded on careful scholarship of our ancient Christian heritage.

Carroll, Thomas, and Thomas Halton. *Liturgical Practice in the Fathers* (1988, LP). Carefully chosen quotations and commentary on the various seasons and feasts as they developed in the first centuries.

Days of the Lord: The Liturgical Year, 7 volumes (1990–1994, LP). This is an in-depth commentary on the riches of the liturgical year and companion to the sacramentary, lectionary and *Liturgy of the Hours.* This series comprehends the totality of the liturgical year, its structure and meaning. It is a sort of updated Church's Year of Grace.

Guéranger, Abbot. *The Liturgical Year.* The most-available English edition was published by Newman Press (Westminster, MD) in 1948 and 1949 (15 volumes). Though written through the entire second half of the nineteenth century, readers might search this out in libraries for its plethora of details and for its witness to the liturgical renewal leading to Vatican II.

Hynes, Mary Ellen. *Companion to the Calendar* (1993, LTP) is a daily and seasonal guide to saints and mysteries that make up the Christian calendar, with additional notes on the calendars of Jews and Muslims and the national days of the United States and Canada. It is designed for homes, schools and parishes.

Martimort, A. G., et al. *The Church at Prayer,* 4 volumes, but especially volume 4: "The Liturgy and Time," (1986, LP; one-volume edition, 1993). See especially the essays by Pierre Jounel on Sunday and the year.

Metford, J. C. J. *The Christian Year* (1991, Crossroad). A masterful summary, with many nuggets of fascinating detail, organized season by season.

Nelson, Gertrud Mueller. *To Dance with God: Family Ritual and Community Celebration* (1986, Paulist Press). A helpful collection of essays on celebration and suggestions for family rituals for each season.

Nocent, Adrian. *The Liturgical Year,* 4 volumes (1977, LP). One of the architects of Vatican II's reform takes us Sunday-by-Sunday and season-by-season through the church's liturgy and lectionary with excellent commentaries.

Parsch, Pius. *The Church's Year of Grace,* 5 volumes (1957 and various editions, LP). While commenting on the old calendar, these volumes still offer enormous assistance to readers, especially when looking for guidance to the previous generation's approach to seasons and saints.

The Saint Andrew Bible Missal (1982, Hirten). Contains insightful introductions to the liturgical seasons and to the readings, as well as attention to Christian initiation.

Stuhlman, Byron David. *Redeeming the Time: A Historical and Theological Study of the Church's Rule of Prayer and the Regular Services of the Church* (1992, Church Hymnal Corporation). Taking inspiration from Schmemann's "liturgy of time," but approaching things differently, Stuhlman, writing from an Episcopalian perspective, articulates the theological connections between the various cycles and the rites proper to them.

Talley, Thomas J. *The Origins of the Liturgical Year* (LP, 1986). Challenges much of the "received wisdom" about the development of the liturgical year. Groundbreaking insights into the development of the calendar and the role of the word of God in the lectionary in shaping the framework of our worship. Difficult going, but greatly rewarding for the serious reader.

Turner, Paul. *What Am I Doing for Lent this Year?* and *What Am I Doing for Triduum this Year?* (both also available in Spanish, LTP,

2001). Short booklets used to accompany a person's keeping of Lent and in the celebration of the Triduum.

Walsh, Mary Caswell. *The Art of Tradition: A Christian Guide to Building a Family* (2000, LTP). This book will help to explore the practical wisdom of the ages and apply it to everyday life.

Weiser, Francis X. *Handbook of Christian Feasts and Customs* (various editions, including 1963, Paulist Press). Contains abridged materials from his earlier volumes: *The Christmas Book, The Easter Book* and *The Holy Day Book*. All are invaluable for their references to once-popular traditions.

CALENDAR

Roman Calendar. When the current (1969) calendar was implemented in the dioceses of the United States, several dates proper to this country were added. That list continues to grow. The calendar and the *General Norms for the Liturgical Year and the Calendar* are reprinted at the front of the sacramentary.

Liturgy Documentary Series, #6: Norms Governing Liturgical Calendars (1984, USCCB). The General Norms and the calendar are accompanied by the commentary released by the Vatican in the early 1970s and updated to 1984 by the principles for particular calendars and by clarifications issued by the Vatican.

Dioceses are mandated to issue annual calendars, with local feasts and norms. Many publishers issue annual calendars and *ordos,* some with regional editions.

Roman Martyrology. This is a particular kind of calendar, cataloguing all the saints according to their date of observance. This includes not only the scores that are on the current universal (Roman) calendar, but also the thousands of others who might be part of national, diocesan or religious community calendars. A new edition that takes the revisions of the calendar into account is in the works.

As the Roman martyrology is prepared for issuance, local churches and orders are encouraged to prepare local martyrologies to supplement the universal listing.

THE LORD'S DAY

Pope John Paul II. *Guide to Keeping Sunday Holy* (the apostolic letter *"Dies Domini"*) (1998, LTP).

Porter, Harry Boone. *The Day of Light: The Biblical and Liturgical Meaning of Sunday* (1987, Pastoral Press). A new edition of a classic examination of the primacy of the Lord's Day.

ADVENT AND CHRISTMAS

Advent and Christmastime Table Prayer (1998, LTP). These stand-up cards contain a variety of seasonal prayers for before and after meals.

Alexander, J. Neil. *Waiting for the Coming: The Liturgical Meaning of Advent, Christmas, Epiphany* (1993, Pastoral Press). Combines scriptural insights of Raymond Brown (*Birth of the Messiah*), liturgical research of Thomas Talley (*Origins of the Liturgical Year*), with his own pastoral experience and insights.

Erspamer, Steve, SM, *Fling Wide the Doors: An Advent and Christmastime Calendar* (1992, LTP). This three-dimensional calendar comes with a booklet of prayers for each day from November 30 to January 6.

Irwin, Kevin. *Advent & Christmas: A Guide to the Eucharist and Hours* (1986, LP). Volume one of a guide to liturgical texts in the seasons.

Mazar, Peter. *Keeping Advent and Christmastime* (1996, LTP). This seasonal pocket booklet helps prayer and scripture reading throughout the day.

_____. *Winter: Celebrating the Season in a Christian Home* (1996, LTP). This delightful book helps families celebrate winter in all its shifting moods from Advent through Christmas and carnival.

Mazar, Peter, and Gabe Huck. *Amazing Days: All the Days of Christmas* (1998, LTP).

O'Gorman, Thomas, ed. *An Advent Sourcebook* (1988, LTP). A wonderful collection of texts for reflection throughout this season.

Simcoe, Mary Ann, ed. *A Christmas Sourcebook* (1984, LTP). This delightful collection of historical texts will offer many moments of reflection throughout this holy season.

Welcome, Yule! 2003–2004 (2003, LTP). These Sunday handouts unify the observance of Advent and Christmas and link prayer at church to prayer in the household.

Wild Goose Worship Group, *Cloth for the Cradle: Worship Resources and Readings for Advent, Christmas, and Epiphany* (2000, GIA). This book's main purpose is to allow the adult world to rediscover the stories of Christ's birth, speaking from and to adult experience.

LENT, THE PASCHAL TRIDUUM AND EASTER

Alexander, J. Neil. *Time and Community* (1990, Pastoral Press). Serious essays on such topics as the lenten lectionary in the fourth century and the origins of Candlemas.

Baker, J. Robert, Evelyn Kaehler, and Peter Mazar, eds. *A Lent Sourcebook: The Forty Days,* two volumes (1990, LTP). An outstanding collection of texts for each day of Lent, suitable for meditation and inspiration.

DePaola, Tomie. *The Garden of the Good Shepherd: A Sticker Calendar to Count the Fifty Days of Easter* (2001, LTP). Counts the 50 days from Easter Sunday to Pentecost with images drawn from scripture.

Halmo, Joan, and J. Frank Henderson, eds. *A Triduum Sourcebook,* three volumes (1996, LTP). These volumes are an excellent anthology for the holiest of days.

Huck, Gabe, Gail Ramshaw, and Gordon Lathrop, eds. *An Easter Sourcebook: The Fifty Days* (1988, LTP). This is an outstanding collection of historical texts suitable for reflection and inspiration every day of the season.

_____. *An Introduction to Lent and Eastertime* (1988, LTP). This popular pamphlet will help your community understand the meaning of these holy seasons and to observe them with devotion.

_____. *The Three Days: Parish Prayer in the Paschal Triduum* (1992, LTP). This book offers wonderful advice to parishes on how to get the most out of the Triduum. Suggestions range from scheduling liturgies to cutting baptismal garments.

_____. *Three Days to Save* (1991, LTP). This inexpensive flyer can be slipped into your bulletin on Palm Sunday to explain the Triduum to the assembly and to encourage their participation.

_____. *Los Tres Días para Guardar* (1991, LTP). This is the Spanish translation of *Three Days to Save.*

Irwin, Kevin. *Easter, A Guide to the Eucharist and Hours* (1991, LP). Along with Advent/Christmas and Lenten volumes, this forms a trilogy of exhaustive guides to every day, to every liturgical text.

_____. *Lent: A Guide to the Eucharist and Hours* (1985, LP).

Jarrett, Judy. *Forty Days and Forty Nights: A Lenten Ark Moving toward Easter* (1995, LTP). An Advent-type calendar for Lent.

Mazar, Peter. *Keeping Lent, Triduum and Eastertime* (1996, LTP). This popular booklet contains prayers and reflections for everyone to enrich their celebration of these holy days.

_____. *We Watch and Pray during the Paschal Triduum* (1996, LTP). This pamphlet contains an order for prayer and scripture reading for different times throughout the Triduum.

Nussbaum, Melissa Musick. *Bible Stories for the 40 Days* (1997, LTP). Children will enjoy reading these stories (or having them read to them) and studying the illustrations by Judy Jarrett. Each day of Lent comes with its own story from the Bible.

Paschal Mission (2003, LTP). Give away this set of inexpensive flyers to the assembly week by week throughout the quarter of the year that is Lent, the Paschal Triduum and Eastertime. They contain blessings and reflections to sanctify these holy seasons at home.

Schmemann, Alexander. *Great Lent: Journey to Pascha* (1974, St. Vladimir's Seminary Press, 1974). A classic, with universally applicable meditations on fasting, discipline, celebration and Lent as pilgrimage.

Stevenson, Kenneth. *Jerusalem Revisited: The Liturgical Meaning of Holy Week* (1988, Pastoral Press). Incorporates the latest liturgical scholarship regarding the evolution of this core of the liturgical year.

Table Prayer for Lent and Eastertime (1988, LTP). Provide multiple copies of this card for all the tables throughout your community. They contain a variety of prayers for before and after meals.

Wild Goose Worship Group, *Stages on the Way: Worship Resources for Lent, Holy Week & Easter*

(2000, GIA). An inventive "book of bits" from the Iona Community in Scotland, containing litanies, meditations, monologues, poems and actions for the 90 days.

SAINTS

McGrath, Michael O'Neill. *Patrons and Protectors: Volume 1: Occupations* (2001, LTP), *Volume 2: More Occupations* (2002), *Volume 3: In Times of Need* (2002). Volumes 1 and 2 in this series present images of the saints as patrons of particular occupations with fresh, contemporary interpretations. Volume 3 recalls those saints we turn to in times of need.

Reynolds, Stephen, compiler. *For All the Saints: Prayers and Readings for Saints' Days* (1994, Anglican Book Centre). Produced by the Anglican Church of Canada, most of the Roman Calendar Saints are represented in close to 800 pages.

Thurston, Herbert J., SJ, and Donald Attwater. *Butler's Lives of the Saints,* 4 volumes (1956, Christian Classics). The most complete publication on the saints in English, reprinted from a 1956 edition. While the changes in the Roman calendar have shifted several observances, this is invaluable for researching additions to the litany of the saints and for discovering the dates of saints not appearing in the current Roman calendar.

Walsh, Michael. *Butler's Lives of the Saints: Concise Edition* (1991, Harper Collins). This has about a seventh of the material found in the full edition, but all recent canonizations and calendar shifts are listed in the complete index of saints.

JEWISH AND CHRISTIAN CONCERNS

Bishops' Committee on the Liturgy, United States Conference of Catholic Bishops, *God's Mercy Endures Forever: Guidelines on the Presentation of Jews and Judaism in Catholic Preaching* (1988, USCCB). Includes specific notes on the various liturgical seasons.

Eskenazi, Tamara, Daniel Harrington, and William Shea. *The Sabbath in Jewish and Christian Traditions* (1991, Crossroad).

Fisher, Eugene. *The Jewish Roots of Christian Liturgy* (1990, Paulist Press). The chapters on the Sabbath and Sunday show their similarities and differences. The bishops' document, *God's Mercy Endures Forever,* is reprinted as an appendix.

Jegen, Carol F., BVM, and Rabbi Byron L. Sherwin. *Thank God: Prayers of Jews and Christians Together* (1989, LTP). Prayers and brief orders of service to be used at home, in small groups or in interfaith services.

Pawlikowski, John, and James A. Wilde. *When Catholics Speak about Jews* (1987, LTP). Notes for homilists, catechists and intercession writers, arranged by the liturgical year.

MUSIC RESOURCES

■ HYMNALS

By Flowing Waters: Chant for the Liturgy (1999, LP). The first complete edition in English of the Simple Gradual, one of the church's official songbooks.

Cantate Domino (1980, Oxford). The European ecumenical hymnal (the first edition was produced in the 1920s). An invaluable resource.

Catholic Book of Worship, III (1994, Canadian Conference of Catholic Bishops). The Canadian national Catholic hymnal.

The Catholic Liturgy Book (1975, Baltimore: Helicon Press, Inc.). A fine, early attempt at a service book, well edited.

The Collegeville Hymnal (1990, LP). Contains new seasonal psalm settings and contributions by many Benedictine authors and composers.

The Hymnal 1982 (1985, Church Publishing). The Episcopal hymnal. There's more chant in this volume than in any Catholic hymnal.

Hymnal for Catholic Students (1988, GIA and LTP). A basic book for grade-school students in parochial schools and religious education programs. Children can learn this repertoire and then carry it with them throughout their lives. The leaders' manual of this book, *Preparing Liturgy for Children and Children for Liturgy,* is fundamental reading for anyone interested in public worship.

Hymnal for the Hours (1989, GIA). A gold mine of hymnody.

ICEL Resource Collection (1981, GIA). Hymns in the public domain and settings of service music for the rites by contemporary composers.

Lead Me, Guide Me, A Hymnal for African American Parishes (1987, GIA).

Lutheran Book of Worship (1978, Augsburg).

Peoples Mass Book (1984, WLP). A basic collection with lots of Lucien Deiss.

Songs of Zion (1982, Abingdon). Music from the Black gospel and spiritual traditions.

We Celebrate: Worship Resource (published every three years, WLP). Hymnal and missal form a complementary pair; the missal includes weekly liturgical catechesis.

With One Voice: A Lutheran Resource for Worship (1985, Augsburg). While much of this material will be familiar to Roman Catholics, there are some fine new texts and tunes in this collection.

Worship, Third Edition (1986, GIA). Well-rounded American Catholic service book and hymnal.

■ MUSICAL RESOURCES FOR LITURGY OF THE HOURS

The publications listed here provide settings for the Liturgy of the Hours. (Titles listed in the hymnals section may also offer orders of service, prayer texts and musical settings of invitatories, office hymns, psalms, intercessions and canticles.)

Christian Prayer, organ accompaniment. Various composers (1978, ICEL).

Haas, David. *Light and Peace: Morning Praise and Evensong* (1986, GIA).

Haugen, Marty. *Holden Evening Prayer* (1990, GIA). This setting of vespers follows the traditional form while using contemporary and inclusive language.

Hughes, Howard. *Nightsong: Music for Evening Prayer* (1989, WLP).

Hymnal for the Hours (1989, GIA).

Joncas, Michael. *O Joyful Light* (1985, North American Liturgy Resources).

Melloh, John Allyn, SM, and William G. Storey, eds., with original music by David Clarke Isele, Howard Hughes, SM, and Michael Joncas. *Praise God in Song: Ecumenical Daily Prayer* (1979, GIA).

_____. *Praise God in Song: Ecumenical Night Prayer* (1982, GIA).

Worship, Third Edition: Liturgy of the Hours Leaders' Edition (1989, GIA).

■ PSALM RESOURCES

These collections of responsorial psalmody are available as individual publications. Many contain reprintable refrains.

Alstott, Owen. *Respond and Acclaim* (1991, Oregon Catholic Press).

Cosley, Thomas M. *Six Psalms for Sundays and Seasons* (1995, WLP). Simple refrains and psalm tones make these very effective.

Garcia, Manuel F. *Salmos* (1984, OCP).

The Gelineau Gradual (1977, GIA). Responsorial psalms for the lectionary for Mass for the Sundays and principal feasts of the liturgical year.

The Gelineau Gradual, Volume II (1979, GIA). Responsorial Psalms from the lectionary for Mass for the rites of the church.

Grail / Gelineau Psalms (1972, GIA). It has 150 Psalms and 18 Canticles.

The Grail Psalms: Inclusive Language Version (text only) (1993, GIA).

Haas, David, and Jeanne Cotter. *Psalms for the Church Year,* Volume III (1989, GIA).

Hansen, Jim. *Psalms for Sundays and Seasons* (1984, Chancel). Twelve psalms for soloist, choir and congregation.

Haugen, Marty, and David Haas. *Psalms for the Church Year* (1983, GIA).

_____. *Psalms for the Church Year,* Volume II (1988, GIA).

Hopson, Hal H. *Eighteen Psalms for the Church Year* (1990, Hope).

_____. *Ten Psalms* (1986, Hope).

ICEL Lectionary Music, various composers (1982, GIA). Psalms and alleluia and gospel acclamations for the liturgy of the word.

Isele, David Clark. *Psalms for the Church Year* (1979, GIA).

Kreutz, Robert. *Psalms and Selected Canticles* (1983, OCP).

Psalms for All Seasons: From the ICEL Liturgical Psalter Project, various composers (1987, NPM).

Psalms for the Cantor, Volumes I–VII. Various composers (1985–1987, WLP).

Psalms and Ritual Music: Music for the Liturgy of the Word (1999, WLP). A fine collection of responsorial psalmody that offers simple, effective musical settings that do not intrude on the meaning of the text and keep the spirit of the psalm together with that of the liturgy of the word.

Somerville, Stephen. *Psalms for Singing* (1976, WLP).

Warner, Steven. *Psaltery* (1990, GIA).

Willcock, Christopher, SJ. *Psalms for Feasts and Seasons: Reformed, Anglican, Lutheran & Wesleyan Rites* (1999, LP).

■ MISCELLANEOUS MUSIC RESOURCES

Dalles, John A. *Swift Currents and Still Waters* (2000, GIA). This collection of new hymn texts can be sung to familiar tunes.

Ford, Paul F. *By Flowing Waters: Chant for the Liturgy: A Collection of Unaccompanied Song for Assemblies, Cantors and Choirs* (1999, LP).

Hommerding, Alan J., and Diana Kodner. *A Music Sourcebook* (1997, LTP). A rich anthology containing the texts of hymns, the thoughts of mystics and the words of musicians throughout the ages that sing the praises of music.

Hopson, Hal H. *The Creative Use of the Organ in Worship* (2000, Hope). This volume is part of a series of arrangements of hymns for choirs and instruments.

Petrunak, Stephan, and Kathleen Felong. *Beyond Strumming: A Liturgical Guitar Method Series* (2000, GIA). This useful series helps the liturgical musician play more effectively. It comes with a CD.

Richer, Linda S., and Anita Stoltzful Breckbill, eds. *Chatter with the Angels* (2000, GIA). This delightful collection puts classical hymns and fun songs into the hands and onto the lips of children.

Service Music for the Mass, Volumes 1–5. Various composers (1988–1989, WLP).

Stuempfle, Jr., Herman G. *Awake Our Hearts to Praise! Hymns, Songs and Carols* (1998, WLP). This resource collects hymns popular with young Catholics. The entire community could build its repertoire with some of these selections.

PERIODICALS

Assembly (Notre Dame Center for Pastoral Liturgy, available from LTP). Five times a year.

Each issue explores the tradition, meaning and practice of some aspect of the liturgical event in order to help the community and its ministers enter more deeply into the spirit of the liturgy.

The Bible Today (LP). Provides insights, evaluations and reflections on the word of God that can be readily understood and applied to serve those in ministry.

Catechumenate: A Journal of Christian Initiation (LTP). This bi-monthly publication presents articles on a variety of topics to enhance your understanding and celebration of the rites of initiation.

Celebration: An Ecumenical Worship Resource (NCR). Published monthly, it consists of a magazine section and two resource units: one on scripture and one on ritual.

Chicago Studies (LTP). Published three times a year, it is edited by priests of the archdiocese of Chicago and faculty members of St. Mary of the Lake Seminary for the continuing theological development of priests and other religious educators.

Environment & Art Letter: A Forum on Architecture and Arts for the Parish (LTP). Published bi–monthly, this full-color newsletter explores issues concerning the environment for worship, both permanent and seasonal.

Liturgical Ministry (LP). Quarterly. A new publication, each issue focuses on a single topic, aiming to bridge the academic and pastoral approaches to liturgical ministry.

Liturgy (The Liturgical Conference). Quarterly. The Journal of the Liturgical Conference, an ecumenical organization. Each issue explores a single aspect of liturgy, usually taking in many disciplines and many church traditions. Back issues are available and are excellent resources.

Ministry and Liturgy (Resource Publications). This liturgical magazine includes a planning guide for seasons, as well as features, bulletin inserts, etc.

National Bulletin on the Liturgy (Canadian Catholic Conference). Published four times a year with helpful background on many liturgical topics, each issue exploring one topic in detail, often with extensive bibliographies. Many of the "thematic" back issues of this fine journal are still available.

Newsletter of the Bishops' Committee on the Liturgy (USCC). Timely information on liturgical developments and regulations in the United States. Published ten times a year.

Pastoral Music (NPM). Published six times a year. Often contains several major articles on a single theme together with reviews and announcements. Centers on music but touches on all areas of liturgy.

Rite (LTP). Published six times a year, this magazine features articles on the seasons and sacraments, regular columns on music, environment and art, questions and answers.

Worship (LP). Published six times a year. Scholarly journal which, since 1926, has been the primary support of liturgical renewal throughout the English-speaking world.

VIDEOGRAPHY

Lift Up Your Hearts: The Eucharistic Prayer (1993, LTP) (30 min.). Because liturgical texts function in the context of public worship, this videocassette provides an opportunity to "see" the words of the liturgical texts enacted in their "lived setting" of communal worship.

Liturgies of the Triduum: Holy Thursday, Good Friday, Easter Vigil (2000, LTP). These three videos explore what we do on each day of the Triduum and help to discover what these days can and should be in each parish. Approximately 30 minutes each, they are available individually or as a set.

Our Catholic Wedding (2001, LTP). This video helps anyone to better understand how to prepare a wedding liturgy that is a celebration for the entire community.

Proclaiming the Word: Formation for Readers of the Liturgy (1994, LTP). Comprises two 20-minute sections, this video includes expert demonstrations and thoughtful commentary by readers. A Spanish version, *Proclamadores de la palabra,* filmed and recorded in Spanish (not a voiceover) is also available.

Say Amen! To What You Are: The Communion Rite (1994, LTP) (30 min.). The texts of the communion rite (from the Lord's Prayer through the prayer after communion) are "seen" in their natural setting in this inspirational video. The need to wed ritual gesture and movement to the formal text is illustrated by these powerful images of an inner city worship community.

Video Guide for Ministers of Communion (1997, LTP). This video explores the spiritual dimensions and meaning of this ministry as well as the practical aspects of holy communion at Mass.

We Will Go Up with Joy: The Entrance Rite (1996, LTP) (30 min.). The entrance rite of the Sunday eucharist happens within the context of a living community and comes at the end of a lot of other "entrances" into the orbit of the word and sacrament.

The Word of the Lord (1996, LTP) (30 min.). What elements are woven together into a strong and effective celebration of the liturgy of the word? Some are obvious: good proclamation. Some are preparatory: prayer over the text, communal study of that text in some scriptural, liturgical and practical (proclamatory) detail. Some celebrative: the context of community, silence, song, attentive and focused listening within which the text is proclaimed.

SOFTWARE

Clip Art for Parish Life (1998, LTP). A collection of images with art by Suzanne Novak depicting events and topics for every month and season. Includes a book and CD-ROM.

Clip Art for Sundays and Solemnities (2003, LTP). Artist Julie Lonneman provides an image for each Sunday of the three years of the lectionary cycle, plus images for all the solemnities of the year.

Clip Notes for Church Bulletins, Volume I (2000, LTP). Seventy-five articles, each with an illustration for use in bulletins, handouts and flyers. *Volume II* (2002) includes another 75 articles with illustrations. *Volume III* (2002), with 65 articles with illustrations, highlights Black Catholic ancestors and heroes, Advent, Christmas, fasting and the OCF, among other topics of interest to parish life. Each volume includes a book and CD-ROM.

Liturgy Plus ABC, Version 3.2 (2000, Resource Publications).

LitPlan 2002 (2002, OCP). Liturgy planning software. Includes song suggestions, dismissals and readings.

Religious Clip Art for the Liturgical Year (1997, LTP). Contains all of Steve Erspamer's images from LTP's three clip art books (years A, B and C) in CD-ROM format for Windows and Macintosh.

Schedule Maker for Ministers and Volunteers (2000, LTP). Create, view and print liturgical ministry schedules for lectors, eucharistic ministers, altar servers, ushers, greeters, cantors, etc., and also print minister lists and labels.

WEBSITES

The URLs given below were accurate at the time of *Sourcebook*'s going to press. Because of the evolving nature of this resource, always work with your web browser to do a net search using the keyword *liturgy* (or other appropriate words). Even sites that do not at first appear relevant may provide links to helpful sites.

Publishers' websites are listed beginning on page 255, along with their snail-mail addresses and telephone numbers.

Order of Saint Benedict: http://www.osb.org/ liturgy (a particularly rich site for reference links).

Notre Dame Center for Pastoral Liturgy: http:// www.nd.edu/~ndcpl/

North American Forum on the Catechumenate: http://www.naforum.org

Liturgical Studies: http://www.music.princeton. edu/chant_html/liturg.html

The Catholic Calendar Page, with scripture readings for the day, saints and other useful information: www.easterbrooks.com/personal/ calendar/

Online study Bible with 16 different translations, searchable by words and phrases: http:// bible.crosswalk.com

Catholic Internet Directory with links to many resources: http://catholic.net/RCC/Indices/index.html

Internet lists related to topics in religion: http://www.alapadre.net (more than 2,500 links of Catholic interest)

Times of Masses throughout the United States: www.masstimes.org (not only Mass times but information about reconciliation, devotions, handicapped accessibility, non-English services, etc.

PUBLISHERS

Abingdon Press
201 Eighth Avenue S
Nashville TN 37202
800-251-3320; fax: 800-836-7802
e-mail: info@abingdon.org

Anglican Book Centre Publishing
600 Jarvis Street
Toronto, Ontario M4Y 2J6, Canada
416-924-1332
fax: 416-924-2760
e-mail: abcpublishing@national.anglican.ca
www.abcpublishing.com

Ave Maria Press
PO Box 428
Notre Dame IN 46556-0428
800-282-1865 x 1; fax: 800-282-5681
e-mail: avemariapress.1@nd.edu
www.avemariapress.com

Augsburg Fortress Publishers
426 S. Fifth Street
PO Box 1209
Minneapolis MN 55440-1209
800-328-4648; fax: 800-772-7766
e-mail: info@augsburgfortress.org
www.augsburgfortress.org

Canadian Conference of Catholic Bishops
2500 Don Reid Drive
Ottawa, Ontario K1H 2J2, Canada
800-769-1147; fax: 613-241-5090
e-mail: publi@cccb.ca
www.cccb.ca

Canon Law Society of America
431 Caldwell Hall
Catholic University of America
Washington DC 20064-0002
202-269-3491; fax: 202-319-5719
e-mail: clsa@tidalwave.net
www.clsa.org

Catholic Book Publishing Company
77 W. End Road
Totowa NJ 07512
973-890-1844; fax: 800-890-1844
e-mail: cbpcl@bellatlantic.net
http://.catholicbkpub.com

Chancel Music
(See Oregon Catholic Press)

Christian Classics, Inc.
(See Thomas More Publishing)

Church Publishing Incorporated
(formerly Church Hymnal Corporation)
445 Fifth Avenue
New York NY 10016
800-242-1918; fax: 212-779-3392
e-mail: churchpublishing@cpg.org
www.churchpublishing.org

Cokesbury
PO Box 801
Nashville TN 37202
800-672-1789; fax: 800-445-8189
e-mail: cokes_sew@cokesbury.com
www.cokesbury.org

The Continuum International Publishing Group
370 Lexington Avenue
New York NY 10017-6503
800-561-7704; fax: 703-661-1501
e-mail: info@continuum-books.com
www.continuum-books.com

The Crossroad Publishing Company
481 Eighth Avenue, Suite 1550
New York NY 10001
212-888-1801; fax: 212-868-2171

Doubleday Religious Publishing
Division of Random House
1540 Broadway
New York NY 10036
800-223-5780; fax: 212-302-7985
e-mail: customerservice@randomhouse.com
www.randomhouse.com

Evangel Publishing House
PO Box 189
Nappanee IN 46550-0189
800-253-9315; fax: 219-773-5934
e-mail: sales@evangelpublishing.com
www.evangelpublishing.com

Farrar, Straus & Giroux, Inc.
FSB Associates
19 Union Square West
New York NY 10003
212-206-5326; fax: 212-206-5340
e-mail: sales@fsgee.com
www.fsbassociates.com

Fortress Press
(See Augsburg Fortress Publishers)

GIA Publications, Inc.
7404 S. Mason Avenue
Chicago IL 60638
800-442-1358; fax: 708-496-3828
e-mail: custserv@giamusic.com
www.giamusic.com

Michael Glazier, Inc.
(See The Liturgical Press)

HarperCollins Publishers
10 East 53rd Street
New York NY 10022
800-242-7737; fax: 800-822-4090
e-mail: orders@harpercollins.com
www.harpercollins.com

Hendrickson Publishers
PO Box 3473
Peabody MA 01961-3473
800-358-3111; fax: 978-531-8146
e-mail: orders@hendrickson.com
www.hendrickson.com

William J. Hirten Company
6100 17th Avenue
Brooklyn NY 11204
718-256-4801

Hope Publishing Company
389 S. Main Place
Carol Stream IL 60188
800-323-1049; fax: 630-665-2550
e-mail: hope@hopepublishing.com
www.hopepublishing.com

ICEL (International Committee on English
in the Liturgy)
1522 K Street NW, Suite 1000
Washington DC 20005-1202
202-347-0800; fax: 202-347-1839

The Liturgical Conference
415 Michigan Avenue NE
Washington DC 20017-1518
202-832-6520
e-mail: litconf@sol.com
www.litconf.org

The Liturgical Press
St. John's Abbey
PO Box 7500
Collegeville MN 56321-7500
800-858-5450; fax: 800-445-5897
e-mail: sales@litpress.org
www.litpress.org

Liturgy Training Publications
1800 N. Hermitage Avenue
Chicago IL 60622-1101
773-486-8970, 800-933-1800
fax: 800-933-7094
e-mail: orders@ltp.org
www.ltp.org

NPM (National Association of Pastoral Musicians)
225 Sheridan Street NW
Washington DC 20011-1492
202-723-5800; fax: 202-723-2262
e-mail: npmsing@npm.org
www.npm.org

NCR (National Catholic Reporter Publishing Company)
115 E. Armour Boulevard
Kansas City MO 64111-1203
816-968-2266
e-mail: patmarrin@aol.com
www.ncrpub.com

New Dawn Press
(See Oregon Catholic Press)

North American Liturgy Resources
(See Oregon Catholic Press)

Notre Dame Center for Pastoral Liturgy
PO Box 81
Notre Dame IN 46556-0081
219-631-5435; fax: 219-631-6968
www.nd.edu/~ndcpl

OCP Publications, Inc.
(Oregon Catholic Press Publications)
5536 N.E. Hassalo
Portland OR 97213
800-548-8749; fax: 503-843-8181
e-mail: retail@ocp.org
www.ocp.org

Oxford University Press
198 Madison Avenue
New York NY 10016-4314
800-451-7556; fax: 212-726-6446
www.oup-usa.org

The Pastoral Press
(See Oregon Catholic Press)

Pauline Books & Media
Daughters of St. Paul
50 St. Paul's Avenue
Boston MA 02130
800-876-4463; fax: 617-524-8035
e-mail: orderentry@pauline.org
www.pauline.org

Paulist Press
997 Macarthur Boulevard
Mahwah NJ 07430
800-218-1903; fax: 800-836-3161
e-mail: info@paulistpress.com
www.paulistpress.com

Prentice-Hall
Division of Schuster, Inc.
The Simon & Schuster Building
1230 Avenue of the Americas
New York NY 10020
800-282-0693; fax: 800-835-5327
www.vig-prenhall.com

Pueblo Publishing Company
(See The Liturgical Press)

Resource Publications, Inc.
160 E. Virginia Street, #290
San Jose CA 95112-5876
800-273-7782; fax: 408-287-8748
e-mail: orders@rpinet.com
www.rpinet.com

St. Vladimir's Seminary Press
575 Scarsdale Road
Crestwood NY 10707-1699
914-961-8313; fax: 914-961-4507
e-mail: svspress@svots.edu
www.svots.edu

Sheed & Ward
7373 S. Lovers Lane Road
Franklin WI 53132
800-booklog; fax: 419-281-6883
e-mail: sheed@execpc.com
www.bookmasters.com/sheed

Society of Biblical Literature
825 Houston Mill Road, Suite 350
Atlanta GA 30329
877-725-3334; fax: 802-864-7626
e-mail: sblexec@sbl-site.org
www.sbl-site.org

Thomas More Publishing
An RCL Company
200 E. Bethany Drive
Allen TX 75002
800-527-5030; fax: 800-688-8356
e-mail: rcl@rclweb.com
www.rclweb.com

USCCB (United States Conference of Catholic Bishops)
3211 Fourth Street NE
Washington DC 20017-1194
800-235-8722; fax: 202-541-3089
www.usccb.org

Westminster John Knox Press
Presbyterian Publishing Corporation
100 Witherspoon Street
Louisville KY 40202-1396
800-227-2872; fax: 502-569-5113
www.ppcpub.org

World Library Publications
A division of J. S. Paluch
3825 N. Willow Road
PO Box 2703
Schiller Park IL 60176-0703
800-566-6150; fax: 888-957-3291
e-mail: wlpcs@jspaluch.com
www.wlpmusic.com

A Guide to Concelebration

WHEN AND WHY

Several priests present at the same place and time may be able to concelebrate the eucharist on limited occasions, under certain conditions.

There are only three occasions when liturgical law requires the concelebration of the eucharist by at least some of the priests that are present: the ordination of a bishop or of presbyters; the blessing of an abbot; and the annual Chrism Mass (GIRM, 199). Concelebration is recommended on certain other occasions, unless the good of the people of God requires or suggests otherwise: the Holy Thursday evening Mass of the Lord's Supper; Mass during councils, synods, and meetings of bishops; the conventual Mass, and the principal Mass in churches; and Mass at any kind of meeting of priests (#199). In addition, concelebration is held in high esteem at certain other times: at Mass with the diocesan bishop, and at celebrations of patron saints (203).

Unless the law or a grant from the local ordinary permits otherwise, a priest may either celebrate or concelebrate the eucharist only once per day (canon 905 §1). Liturgical law permits a priest to celebrate or concelebrate more than once on the same day in the following cases:

- on Holy Thursday, priests may celebrate or concelebrate the Chrism Mass and the Evening Mass of the Lord's Supper;

- on Christmas Day, priests may celebrate or concelebrate three Masses;

- on All Souls' Day, priests may celebrate or concelebrate three Masses;

- a priest who has celebrated or concelebrated the Mass of the Easter Vigil may celebrate or concelebrate Mass during the day on Easter Sunday;

- a priest who concelebrates with the bishop at a synod or pastoral visitation, or concelebrates during a Mass at a meeting of priests, may celebrate (not *con*celebrate) Mass again for the benefit of the people (GIRM, 204).

By grant of the faculty from the local ordinary, for a just cause a priest may celebrate (not *con*celebrate) twice a day, and if pastoral need requires it, three times on Sundays and holy days of obligation (canon 905 §2). It is important to note that this faculty is only to preside at the eucharist, not to concelebrate. Priests should therefore be aware that their presence at a Mass does not automatically mean that they may concelebrate that Mass. If they have already celebrated or concelebrated once that day, and none of the cases listed above apply, they may not licitly concelebrate another Mass that day.

The rite of concelebration is intended to express more clearly the unity of the priesthood in the person of Christ, of the sacrifice, and of the action of the whole people of God (GIRM, 199) than do multiple, simultaneous, or sequential Masses celebrated individually. In this way, concelebration is understood as an appropriate expression of the mystery of the church, "the sacrament of unity" (#92). This is most evident when the principal celebrant is the diocesan bishop. The gathering of vested presbyters around the bishop is not done to add external solemnity to the occasion, but to express this mystery in a clearer light (92).

Given the goals of the rite of concelebration, the decision whether to use it is most appropriately based on whether the unity of the church will be more clearly manifested. Concelebration is never encouraged if the welfare of the Christian faithful urges against it (canon 902), and the number of concelebrants may be limited if the dignity of the rite requires it (Rite of Concelebration, 3). The position of the concelebrants should never obscure the fact that only one bishop or priest is presiding over the whole celebration; nor should concelebrants impede the full view of the other members of the assembly (NCCB, Guidelines for the Concelebration of the Eucharist, 12). It is for the diocesan bishop to regulate the discipline for concelebration in the churches of the diocese (GIRM, 202).

HOW

In general, a concelebrant follows the basic norms for celebrating Mass, but with adaptations (GIRM, 205). Seats for concelebrants should be arranged before Mass begins. These belong in the sanctuary or elsewhere in the church, but near the altar (#294, 310). Concelebrants should also have access to texts, and sufficient chalices should be prepared so they may all share communion under both forms (207).

Concelebrants vest in a suitable place. They wear the customary vestments for Mass, but for a good reason they may omit the chasuble and wear only the stole over the alb. The principal celebrant wears a chasuble (209).

In the procession to the altar the concelebrants walk just ahead of the principal celebrant (210). They make a profound bow to the altar, kiss it, and then go to their seats. If incense is used, the principal celebrant alone incenses the cross and altar (211).

If there is no deacon, concelebrants carry out their duties. If other ministers are absent (readers or servers, for example), some members of the faithful perform their duties. Concelebrants fulfill these ministries only if necessary (208).

Throughout the liturgy of the word the concelebrants assume the posture of the principal celebrant and assembly. If there is no deacon, a concelebrant may proclaim the gospel. He asks for and receives the blessing only when a bishop presides. When a priest with no deacon presides, a concelebrant proclaims the gospel without first seeking and obtaining the blessing (212).

The principal celebrant usually delivers the homily, but a concelebrant may do so instead (66, 213).

The principal celebrant prepares the altar and gifts while the concelebrants remain in their places (214).

After the prayer over the offerings, concelebrants approach the altar and stand around it where they will not interfere with the rites or block the view of the faithful. A deacon may assist at the altar with the book and the chalice, but otherwise he remains slightly behind the concelebrating priests (215).

During the eucharistic prayer, all in the church join their hearts and minds to the words they hear. Concelebrants will recite or sing some of the texts aloud. In general, they make gestures only when they are also speaking (217). Concelebrants speak in a very low voice, so that the principal celebrant may be clearly heard above the rest. Nevertheless, it is praiseworthy for concelebrants to sing their parts together (218).

In all the eucharistic prayers the preface is sung or said by the principal celebrant alone (216). The concluding doxology may also be sung by him alone, or together with the concelebrants (236). In general, the concelebrants keep their hands joined unless directed otherwise.

In the Eucharistic Prayer for Masses for Various Needs and Occasions and the Eucharistic Prayer for Masses of Reconciliation the divisions occur as follows:

Eucharistic Prayer for Masses for Various Needs and Occasions I: The Church on the Way to Unity

Preface dialogue:
principal celebrant, making gestures

Preface:
principal celebrant, hands extended

Holy:
all

You are truly blessed, O God of holiness:
principal celebrant, hands extended

Great and merciful Father:
concelebrants, hands extended toward offerings; the principal celebrant makes the sign of the cross

On the eve of his passion and death:
all concelebrants, hands joined; the principal celebrant makes the other gestures

Take this:
all concelebrants, right hand may be extended toward the bread; the principal celebrant makes the other gestures; as the principal celebrant raises the consecrated bread, the concelebrants look toward it, then make a profound bow

When supper was ended:
all concelebrants, hands joined; the principal celebrant makes the other gestures

Take this:
all concelebrants, right hand may be extended toward the chalice; the principal celebrant makes the other gestures; as the principal celebrant raises the chalice, the concelebrants look toward it, then make a profound bow

And so, Father most holy:
all concelebrants, hands extended

Renew by the light of the gospel:
a concelebrant, who extends his hands

Be mindful of our brothers and sisters:
a concelebrant, who extends his hands

When our pilgrimage on earth is complete:
a concelebrant, who extends his hands

Through him, with him, in him:
principal celebrant or all concelebrants; principal celebrant alone lifts chalice and paten, unless assisted by a deacon

Eucharistic Prayer for Masses for Various Needs and Occasions II: God Guides the Church on the Way of Salvation

Preface dialogue:
principal celebrant, making gestures

Preface:
principal celebrant, hands extended

Holy:
all

You are truly blessed, O God of holiness:
principal celebrant, hands extended

Great and merciful Father:
concelebrants, hands extended toward offerings; the principal celebrant makes the sign of the cross

On the eve of his passion and death:
all concelebrants, hands joined; the principal celebrant makes the other gestures

Take this:
all concelebrants, right hand may be extended toward the bread; the principal celebrant makes the other gestures; as the principal celebrant raises the consecrated bread, the concelebrants look toward it, then make a profound bow

When supper was ended:
all concelebrants, hands joined; the principal celebrant makes the other gestures

Take this:
all concelebrants, right hand may be extended toward the chalice; the principal celebrant makes the other gestures; as the principal celebrant raises the chalice, the concelebrants look toward it, then make a profound bow

And so, Father most holy:
all concelebrants, hands extended

Strengthen in unity:
a concelebrant, who extends his hands

Be mindful of our brothers and sisters:
a concelebrant, who extends his hands

When our pilgrimage on earth is complete:
a concelebrant, who extends his hands

Through him, with him, in him:
principal celebrant or all concelebrants; principal celebrant alone lifts chalice and paten, unless assisted by a deacon

Eucharistic Prayer for Masses for Various Needs and Occasions III: Jesus, Way to the Father

Preface dialogue:
principal celebrant, making gestures

Preface:
principal celebrant, hands extended

Holy:
all

You are truly blessed, O God of holiness:
principal celebrant, hands extended

Great and merciful Father:
concelebrants, hands extended toward offerings; the principal celebrant makes the sign of the cross

On the eve of his passion and death:
all concelebrants, hands joined; the principal celebrant makes the other gestures

Take this:
all concelebrants, right hand may be extended toward the bread; the principal celebrant makes the other gestures; as the principal celebrant raises the consecrated bread, the concelebrants look toward it, then make a profound bow

When supper was ended:
all concelebrants, hands joined; the principal celebrant makes the other gestures

Take this:
all concelebrants, right hand may be extended toward the chalice; the principal celebrant makes the other gestures; as the principal celebrant raises the chalice, the concelebrants look toward it, then make a profound bow

And so, Father most holy:
all concelebrants, hands extended

Almighty Father:
a concelebrant, who extends his hands

Keep your church alert in faith:
a concelebrant, who extends his hands

Be mindful of our brothers and sisters:
a concelebrant, who extends his hands

When our pilgrimage on earth is complete:
a concelebrant, who extends his hands

Through him, with him, in him:
principal celebrant or all concelebrants; principal celebrant alone lifts chalice and paten, unless assisted by a deacon

Eucharistic Prayer for Masses for Various Needs and Occasions IV: Jesus, the Compassion of God

Preface dialogue:
principal celebrant, making gestures

Preface:
principal celebrant, hands extended

Holy:
all

You are truly blessed, O God of holiness:
principal celebrant, hands extended

Great and merciful Father:
concelebrants, hands extended toward offerings; the principal celebrant makes the sign of the cross

On the eve of his passion and death:
all concelebrants, hands joined; the principal celebrant makes the other gestures

Take this:
all concelebrants, right hand may be extended toward the bread; the principal celebrant makes the other gestures; as the principal celebrant raises the consecrated bread, the concelebrants look toward it, then make a profound bow

When supper was ended:
all concelebrants, hands joined; the principal celebrant makes the other gestures

Take this:
all concelebrants, right hand may be extended toward the chalice; the principal celebrant makes the other gestures; as the principal celebrant raises the chalice, the concelebrants look toward it, then make a profound bow

And so, Father most holy:
all concelebrants, hands extended

Lord, perfect your church in faith and love:
a concelebrant, who extends his hands

Open our eyes to the needs of all:
a concelebrant, who extends his hands

Let your church be a living witness:
a concelebrant, who extends his hands

Be mindful of our brothers and sisters:
a concelebrant, who extends his hands

When our pilgrimage on earth is complete:
a concelebrant, who extends his hands

Through him, with him, in him:
principal celebrant or all concelebrants; principal celebrant alone lifts chalice and paten, unless assisted by a deacon

Eucharistic Prayer for Masses of Reconciliation I:

Preface dialogue:
principal celebrant, making gestures

Preface:
principal celebrant, hands extended

Holy:
all

Father, from the beginning of time:
principal celebrant, hands extended

Look with kindness on your people:
concelebrants, hands extended toward offerings; the principal celebrant makes the sign of the cross

When we were lost:
all concelebrants, hands joined; the principal celebrant makes the other gestures

Take this:
all concelebrants, right hand may be extended toward the bread; the principal celebrant makes the other gestures; as the principal celebrant raises the consecrated bread, the concelebrants look toward it, then make a profound bow

At the end of the meal:
all concelebrants, hands joined; the principal celebrant makes the other gestures

Take this:
all concelebrants, right hand may be extended toward the chalice; the principal celebrant makes the other gestures; as the principal celebrant raises the chalice, the concelebrants look toward it, then make a profound bow

We do this in memory of Jesus Christ:
all concelebrants, hands extended

Keep us all in communion of mind and heart:
a concelebrant, who extends his hands

Then, freed from every shadow of death:
a concelebrant, who extends his hands

Through him, with him, in him:
principal celebrant or all concelebrants; principal celebrant alone lifts chalice and paten, unless assisted by a deacon

Eucharistic Prayer for Masses of Reconciliation II:

Preface dialogue:
principal celebrant, making gestures

Preface:
principal celebrant, hands extended

Holy:
all

God of power and might:
principal celebrant, hands extended

Therefore we celebrate the reconciliation:
concelebrants, hands extended toward offerings; the principal celebrant makes the sign of the cross

While he was at supper:
all concelebrants, hands joined; the principal celebrant makes the other gestures

Take this:
all concelebrants, right hand may be extended toward the bread; the principal celebrant makes the other gestures; as the principal celebrant raises the consecrated bread, the concelebrants look toward it, then make a profound bow

At the end of the meal:
all concelebrants, hands joined; the principal celebrant makes the other gestures

Take this:
all concelebrants, right hand may be extended toward the chalice; the principal celebrant makes the other gestures; as the principal celebrant raises the chalice, the concelebrants look toward it, then make a profound bow

Lord our God, your Son has entrusted to us:
all concelebrants, hands extended

May this Spirit keep us always in communion:
a concelebrant, who extends his hands

You have gathered us here:
a concelebrant, who extends his hands

Through him, with him, in him:
principal celebrant or all concelebrants; principal celebrant alone lifts chalice and paten, unless assisted by a deacon

During the communion rite, the concelebrants continue their ministry. As they pray the words of the Lord's Prayer, they extend their hands together with the principal celebrant, joining their hands for the embolism and acclamation (GIRM, 237–38). Concelebrants exchange the sign of peace with the principal celebrant before the deacon does. They also exchange peace with one another (#239). They may assist in breaking the bread for the entire assembly (83, 240). They do not join the principal celebrant saying the private prayers addressed to Jesus (241).

Concelebrants are permitted communion under both kinds (283), following one of the three procedures found on the next page.

After communion, if some of the precious blood remains, one or more concelebrants may help the deacon consume it (247, 249).

Concelebrants remain at their seats until the end of Mass, letting the principal celebrant do the rest (250).

After the dismissal, concelebrants make a profound bow to the altar. The principal celebrant and deacon kiss the altar in the usual way (251).

Communion Procedures for Concelebrants
(OPTION 1)

Concelebrants will observe the following procedure for communion:

1. All recite the "Lord, I am not worthy."
2. The principal celebrant receives communion under both forms at the altar.
3. Each concelebrant approaches the altar, genuflects, and then consumes the body of Christ at the middle of the altar.
4. Each concelebrant then moves to the side of the altar, where he consumes the blood of Christ.
5. Each concelebrant returns to his place.

Communion Procedures for Concelebrants
(OPTION 2)

Concelebrants will observe the following procedure for communion:

1. The principal celebrant says the private prayers to Jesus.
2. He genuflects and steps back a bit.
3. Concelebrants approach the middle of the altar, genuflect, and pick up the body of Christ, holding it in their right hand, their left hand underneath. They return to their places.
4. The principal celebrant says, "This is the Lamb of God." All respond, "Lord, I am not worthy."
5. Concelebrants recite privately, "May the body of Christ bring me to everlasting life." They consume the body of Christ.
6. The principal celebrant receives the blood of Christ.
7. Concelebrants approach the altar one by one or two by two. They genuflect, consume the blood of Christ at the altar, wipe the chalice rim, and return to their seats.

Communion Procedures for Concelebrants
(OPTION 3)

Concelebrants will observe the following procedure for communion:

1. The principal celebrant says the private prayers to Jesus.
2. Concelebrants pick up the body of Christ from a paten passed either by one concelebrant or from each one to the next.
3. The principal celebrant says, "This is the Lamb of God." All respond, "Lord, I am not worthy."
4. Concelebrants recite privately, "May the body of Christ bring me to everlasting life." They consume the body of Christ.
5. The principal celebrant receives the blood of Christ.
6. Concelebrants consume the blood of Christ from a chalice passed either by the deacon or a concelebrant, or each one passes the chalice to the next.